The Guide to the American Revolutionary War
In New York

The Guide to the American Revolutionary War In New York

Battles, Raids, and Skirmishes

Norman Desmarais

Busca, Inc.
Ithaca, New York

Busca, Inc.
P.O. Box 854
Ithaca, NY 14851
Ph: 607-546-4247
Fax: 607-546-4248
E-mail: info@buscainc.com
www.buscainc.com

BUSCA = SEARCH

Copyright © 2010 by Norman Desmarais
All rights reserved. No part of this book may be reproduced or transmitted in any form or by any means, electronic or mechanical, including photocopying, recording, or by any information storage or retrieval system, without permission in writing from the copyright owner.

First Edition

Printed in the United States of America

ISBN: 978-1-934934-02-9

Publisher's Cataloging-In-Publication Data
(Prepared by The Donohue Group, Inc.)

Desmarais, Norman.
   The guide to the American Revolutionary War in New York : battles, raids, and skirmishes / Norman Desmarais. -- 1st ed.

   p. : ill., maps ; cm. -- (Battlegrounds of freedom ; [3])

   Includes bibliographical references and index.
   ISBN: 978-1-934934-02-9

   1. United States--History--Revolution, 1775-1783--Campaigns--New York (State) 2. United States--History--Revolution, 1775-1783--Battlefields--New York (State) 3. New York (State)--History, Military--18th century. I. Title. II. Series: Battlegrounds of freedom.

E230.5.N4 D47 2010
973.3/3

All state maps Copyright © 2010 DeLorme (www.delorme.com) Street Atlas USA®.
Reprinted with permission.

Photography: author unless otherwise noted

Composition: P.S. We Type ♦ Set ♦ Edit

The author has made every effort to ensure the accuracy of the information in this book. Neither the publisher nor the author is responsible for typographical mistakes, other errors, or information that has become outdated since the book went to press.

This volume is part of the BATTLEGROUNDS OF FREEDOM series.

To the men and women of our armed forces who go in harm's way to preserve the freedoms our ancestors have secured for us.

Contents

List of Illustrations ix

Acknowledgments xi

Foreword by Mark Hurwitz xiii

Preface...xv
    Strategic Objectives xvi; Nomenclature xvii; Conventions and Parts of This Book xix

Introduction.. 1

1. Upstate New York... 3
    Ticonderoga/Fort Ticonderoga 5; Below Ticonderoga/Sabbath Day Point 13; Mount Independence 13; Fort Ticonderoga and Fort Independence 15; Crown Point 15; Wind Mill Point 17; Isle La Motte, Lake Champlain 17; Valcour Island 17; Split Rock 20; Utica/Fort Stanwix/Schuyler/Moses Kill 21; Whitehall 24; Fort Anne/Fort Edward 26; Fort Edward 27; Schuylerville/Stillwater/Saratoga/Bemis Heights 30; Oriskany 35; Schenectady 36; Vrooman's 37; Cambridge/Sancoick's (or Van Schaick's) Mill 38; North Hoosick/Battle of Bennington 39; Lake George/Fort George, Lake George/Near Lake George 41; Diamond Island 42; Kingston/Esopus 43; Kingston/Slapshine Island, Hudson River 44; Upstate New York 44; Tribes Hill (Sackintago) 44; Manheim 45; Ephrata 45; Cobleskill 45; Otsego County/Near Cherry Valley 47; Springfield (July 18, 1778) 47; Cherry Valley (Nov. 11, 1778) 47; Herkimer/German Flats 48; Shell's Bush/Andrustown (Andrew's Town)/Near head of Unadilla River/Little Falls (Ellis's (Ellice's) mill) 48; Schoharie/Gallupville 51; Cochecton, Sullivan Co. 54; Johnstown/Warrensbush 54; Onondagas 57; Ogdensburg/Oswegatchie 57; Port Jervis/Minisink 59; Elmira/Chemung/Battle of Newtown 60; Havana/Catherine's Town/Appletown/Kindaia 62; Geneva/Cayuga Lake, raid/Canandaigua/Kanadesaga 63; Geneseo 63; Fort Plain/Canajoharie (Fort Rensselaer)/Mohawk Valley 64; Harpersfield/Sacandaga Blockhouse 65; Fonda/Caughnawaga 66; Near Delaware River 66; Greenville/Basic Creek 67; Currytown 67; New Dorlach/Sharon Springs Swamp 67; Wawarsing 68; Middleburg/Fort Defiance or Middle Fort 69; Ballston/Fort Plank 70; Stone Arabia/Fort Keyser 71; Saint Johnsville/Fort Klock, Klock's Field (Fox's Mills)/Kanassoraga 72; Jerseyfield/West Canada Creek 73

2. Downstate/Hudson River Valley.. 74
    Hudson River 74; Hudson River off Tarrytown 76; Haverstraw/Near Fishkill/Hopewell 79; Fort Montgomery and Fort Clinton/Fort Montgomery 80; White Plains 82; Highlands/Ossining/Singsing 87; Nyack/Tappan Meadows 87; New Hempstead/Kakiat 87; Phillipsburg and Greenburg/Near Dobbs Ferry/Phillipsburg/Teller's Point, Hudson River/Phillips Heights/Tappan 88; Pelham Manor/Pell's Point/New Rochelle 92; Eastchester (East Chester)/Near East Chester/Split Rock/Ward's House/Westchester County/Eastchester Bay 94; Peekskill/Cortlandt, Westchester County/Van Cortlandtville/Peekskill 100; Verplanck's Point 103; Tarrytown 104; Near Poughkeepsie/Hudson River Highlands 105; New Windsor

106; Storm King/Butter Hill 106; Port Chester/Sawpits/Byram River/Sherrard's Bridge 106; Mamaroneck, Westchester County/Pine Hills 107; Rye, King Street/Rye Woods/Rye Neck 109; Stony Point and Verplanck's Point 110; Croton/Near Croton 112; West Point 113; Mount Pleasant/Youngs's House/Four Corners, Westchester Co. 118; Crompond 120; Poundridge 121; Bedford 122; Morrisania/New Rochelle/Eastchester 123; Croton River/Pines Bridge 126; Mount Kisco/North Castle/Sawmill River 127; Armonk/Mile Square 129; Harrison, Westchester Co. 129; Suffern 130

3. Eastern Long Island 131
Plum Island, Fisher's Island, Gardiner's Island/Fisher's Island 131; Setauket 131; Near Brookhaven 135; Huntington Bay 135; Huntington 137; Off Wading River 137; Oyster Bay 138; South Oyster Bay/Jefferd's Neck 139; Sag Harbor 139; Smith's Point/Coram/Fort St. George 140; Hempstead Harbor 143; Terry Point 143; Southold 143; Smithtown 144; Lloyd's Neck 145; South Bay 148; Long Island Sound 148; Oak Neck 148; Fire Island 149; Fort Salonga/Fort Slongo/Treadwell's Neck (Threadwell's)/Tredwell's or Treadwell's Farm 149; Cow Neck 151; Cow Bay 153; Hog Neck 154; Eastern end of Long Island 154; Islip 154; Hog Island 154; Mosquito Cove 155; Canoe-Place 155; Long Island 155; Gull Islands 155; Blue Point 156; Hempstead 156; Great Neck 156; Stony Brook 157; Mattituck 157

4. Western Long Island 158
Gravesend Bay 158; New York Harbor/Coney Island/Off Coney Island 158; Flatbush 158; Battle of Long Island (aka Battle of Brooklyn Heights)/Valley Grove/Bushwick/Brooklyn Heights/Long Island/Jamaica 160; Throg's Neck/City Island 168; Governor's or Nutten Island/East River 169; Whitestone Bay/Whitestone 171; Gowanus 172; Canarsie 172

5. Manhattan and Staten Island 173
New York 174; Bedloe's (Bedlow's) Island 176; Roosevelt Island/Blackwell's Island 176; Hunt's Point 177; Wards Island/Buchanan's Island/Montresor's (Randall's) Island 177; Horn's (Hoorn's) Hook 178; Kip's Bay 179; Manhattanville/Harlem Cove/Harlem Plains/Harlem Heights 180; Kingsbridge or King's Bridge/Fort Independence/West Farms/Valentine's Hill, Mount Vernon/Indian Field and Bridge/Mile Square Road, Westchester Co./Near Mount Vernon 183; Bronx/Westchester/Delancey's Mills 192; Mount Washington (Washington Heights)/Fort Washington 193; Fort George 196; Fort Cock Hill (Cock's or Cox Hill or New Battery) 196; Spuyten Duyvil Creek 196; Williams's Bridge 196; Staten Island 198

Notes 214
Glossary 240
Index 244

Please see the Busca website **www.buscainc.com** for more Resources on the volumes by Norman Desmarais including complete chronological and alphabetical lists of battles, raids, and skirmishes; a complete Bibliography for all sources used and cited in the creation of these volumes; and photos.

List of Illustrations

Maps

Upstate New York 4
Downstate New York and the Hudson River Valley 75
Eastern Long Island 132
New York City and Surroundings 159

Photos

NY-1. Earth bastion 6
NY-2. Stone bastion, Fort Ticonderoga 6
NY-3A,B. Shells and artillery shots 7
NY-4 Mortar shell 8
NY-5. Blunderbuss or musquetoon 8
NY-6. Mortar 10
NY-7. Bateau 14
NY-8. British grenadiers (Highlanders) 15
NY-9. Whaleboat with swivel gun 16
NY-10. Gunboat Philadelphia 18
NY-11. Jane McCrea's grave 28
NY-12. Saratoga Victory Monument 31
NY-13. Old Stone Fort, Schoharie 53
NY-14. Johnson Hall, the last home of Sir William Johnson 55
NY-15. Fort Johnstown 57
NY-16. An 18-pound cannon showing the trunnion, the round support
    resting on the gun carriage 58
NY-17. Blockhouse with loopholes for muskets and cannon in the upper structure . 70
NY-18. Pinnace on board the HMS *Victory* 76
NY-19. Chevaux-de-frise for water defense 77
NY-20. Links of the great chain across the Hudson River, U.S. Military Academy,
    West Point 81
NY-21. Pettiauger Mercury (replica) 82
NY-22. Grave of at least five Hessian privates in a mortar pit 95
NY-23. St. Paul's Episcopal Church, Eastchester 96
NY-24. Stony Point Battlefield State Historic Site 111
NY-25. Bend in the Hudson River at West Point 114
NY-26. Site of Major John André's imprisonment 117
NY-27. Hussar, duc de Lauzun's Legion 121
NY-28. Caroline Church, Setauket 133
NY-29. Burying Hill, Huntington Bay 136
NY-30. Manor of St. George 140
NY-31. Smith Tavern, Smithtown 144

NY-32. Replica of the Badge of Military Merit 151
NY-33. Man-of-war (HMS *Victory*) 161
NY-34. German grenadiers 163
NY-35A. Reenactors deploying in open order 166
NY-35B. Reenactors deployed in closed order 166
NY-36. Fort Lee in New Jersey 173
NY-37. Fascines and gabions 185

Acknowledgments

I would like to express my gratitude to Jack Montgomery, acquisitions librarian at the University of Western Kentucky, Bowling Green, for igniting the spark to write this book, for his encouragement through the project, and for introducing me to Connie Mills, the Kentucky Library Coordinator at the Kentucky Library and Museum who provided valuable assistance in locating primary sources for the Kentucky chapter. Michael Cooper, my publisher fanned the flame, nurtured the idea, and brought it to fruition.

I also wish to thank Providence College, my employer, for providing research and faculty development funds as well as time to pursue research. That research began with one sabbatical and extended beyond another. The staffs at the Phillips Memorial Library of Providence College and the other academic libraries in Rhode Island were very helpful in obtaining and providing much material. Amy Goggin, interlibrary loan librarian at Providence College, deserves special mention for her diligent efforts to obtain many obscure items which normally don't circulate such as microforms.

Edward Ayres, Historian for the Jamestown-Yorktown Foundation, based at the Yorktown Victory Center in Yorktown, Virginia provided valuable assistance in locating Revolutionary War era maps. Michael Cobb, curator of the Hampton History Museum in Hampton, Virginia, graciously guided me through his museum collection—both the public display and the storage area and helped me locate sites in southern Virginia. Peggy Haile-McPhillips, City Historian at the Norfolk (Virginia) Public Library, helped greatly in identifying and locating places in the Norfolk area that had changed names and had long ago disappeared.

David Loiterstein, Marketing Manager at Readex, also deserves my gratitude. He arranged for me to review the Early American Imprints Series I: Evans, 1639–1800 and the Early American Newspapers Series I, 1690–1876 and Series II, 1758–1900. The review periods coincided with important stages in my research. This undoubtedly made for better, more thorough, reviews; and it provided me with access to a wealth of primary sources that opened new avenues of research.

The members of the Brigade of the American Revolution (B.A.R.), the Continental Line, and the British Brigade generously give of themselves to help re-create the era of the American War for Independence. Some of these people work at musea or at historical sites. Some are members of their town historical societies or even historians for their city or town. Many are amateur historians who know a great deal about the Revolutionary War in their area. They provided enormous insight into events and the location of sites. Special thanks go to Bob Winowitch and David Clemens who guided me around Long Island to ensure that I visited all the relevant sites there. They also provided historical material and referred me to important sources for further information.

Other B.A.R. members, including Reinhard Batcher III, Todd Braisted, Todd Harburn, Thomas F. Kehr, Lawrence McDonald, Alan Morrison, Thaddeus J. Weaver, and Vivian Leigh Stevens read portions of the manuscript, suggested corrections and/or identified sources of additional information.

Many of the photographs were taken at various re-enactments. Without the efforts of the members of the B.A.R., these photos would not have been possible. Marshall Sloat,

Scott Dermond, Daniel O'Connell, Todd Harburn, Paul Bazin, and Deborah Mulligan deserve credit for providing additional photographs.

There's a certain serendipity to research. During the 225th anniversary re-enactment of the march to Yorktown, Virginia, as the troops crossed the Hudson River in whale boats, I overheard B.A.R. member Daniel Hess talking about an engagement in which one of his ancestors had fought. I had been trying to locate documentation for that event; so I asked him about it after disembarking. He later sent me a copy of his ancestor's pension application which not only described the event which I had been trying to document but also identified two other events unknown to me.

DeLorme's Map 'n' Go software was very valuable in creating and annotating all the maps. GPS devices are useful for locating known places with addresses. They are not so useful for getting to a general location such as a particular hill or field. Maps are more useful for this purpose; but it takes a specially trained eye to identify changes in terrain that may cover earthworks or fortifications. Marshall Sloat has such an eye and I am grateful to him for accompanying me on some research trips, both as a companion and navigator. He helped me locate landmarks, monuments, and other physical features that would elude the common person. He also helped document the visits with photographs.

I wish to extend special thanks to my wife, Barbara, for her patience and support during the long periods of research and writing. She also accompanied me on many research trips and read maps and gave me directions as we drove to sites. She visited more forts and battlefields than she cares to remember.

Mark Hurwitz proofread the entire text and provided valuable feedback and suggestions. He also wrote the foreword. June Fritchman kindly offered some help with corrections and revisions of prior manuscripts in this series.

FOREWORD

by
Mark Hurwitz
Commander
Brigade of the American Revolution

To paraphrase Historian Geoffrey C. Ward, "the American War for Independence was fought from the walls of Quebec to the swamps of Florida, from Boston, to the Mississippi River." Now, if a shot was fired in anger, Norman Desmarais has documented it in this landmark study and guide, *The Guide to the American Revolutionary War*. It is a worthy successor to his *Battlegrounds of Freedom* (2005).

This comprehensive guide to the famous and unknown sites is ground breaking. Beyond Lexington, Concord, Trenton, Brandywine, Saratoga, Monmouth, & Yorktown, Norman has fretted out the smaller actions and skirmishes which make up the eight year conflict, 1775–1783. Amazingly, Norman has found sites where settlers were scalped on the frontier to ships exchanging cannon fire on the high seas.

Norman Desmarais's passion for history comes as no surprise to me. After corresponding with Mr. Desmarais on an earlier multimedia CD-ROM project (*The American Revolution*. — American Journey: History in Your Hands series. — Woodbridge, CT: Primary Source Media, 1996), I finally got to meet him in November, 1995, when he attended a Brigade of the American Revolution (B.A.R.) event at Fort Lee Historic Park, Fort Lee, NJ. At that time, I had the opportunity to introduce him to Carl Becker, Commander of the 2nd Rhode Island Regiment, from his native state. Carl recruited him on the spot, and Norman, the academic historian, began his career as a re-enactor.

Becoming a "living historian" allows one to have laboratory to work in, wearing the uniforms, feeling the sweat, handling the weapons, experiencing the linear tactics, hearing the field music, smelling the smoke, which gives real perspective to the study of this period of history. This experience even goes beyond the "Staff Rides" of historic battlefields that the U.S. Army conducts with its officers.

The B.A.R. and the 2nd R.I. Regiment gave Norman the opportunity to visit many of the historic battle sites and get to see them "from the inside" and with the eye of a common soldier. This travel fueled his love for research and launched his encyclopedic study of Revolutionary War battle sites covering all of North America.

As a re-enactor, I have been studying the American War of Independence for nearly 35 years. Reading Desmarais's manuscript, I made discoveries both near and far.

- Being brought up and currently residing in my hometown of Springfield, NJ, I knew of the famous Battle of Springfield, June 23rd, 1780. Norman's research uncovered the following precursor, among many other actions there: "The militia killed and wounded 8 or 10 Waldeckers near Springfield on Sunday morning, January 19, 1777. They captured the rest of the party, 39 or 40, including 2 officers without suffering any casualties." (The Pennsylvania Evening Post, January 23, 1777)
- Meanwhile he found, west of the Mississippi: "St. Louis, Missouri—A small marker at 4th & Walnut Streets in downtown St. Louis which commemorates

the action that occurred on May 26, 1780." Desmarais's detailed entry then illuminates this unique action.
- Then at the end of the War for Independence, Savage Point, GA (Savage Point is located at a bend in the Ogeechee River at Richmond Hill State Park.): "Gen. Wayne suffered 5 men and horses killed and 8 wounded. He captured a British standard, 127 horses, and a number of packs." (The Pennsylvania Packet or the General Advertiser. 11:924 (August 15, 1782) p. 3)

I hope that readers can use this guide to find for themselves that history truly "happened here" as they travel the breadth of America and Canada.

Preface

The Guide to the American Revolutionary War in New York: Battles, Raids, and Skirmishes is the second volume of a projected multi-volume geographic history of the American War for Independence. The idea for the project came at a re-enactment of a 225th anniversary event when I overheard some of my fellow interpreters commenting about the several events on the calendar that summer that they knew nothing about. There had been no guidebooks published about the Revolutionary War since the nation's bicentennial in 1975. Moreover, those guidebooks and most of the history textbooks only cover the major, better known battles such as Lexington and Concord, Bunker Hill, Trenton and Princeton, Saratoga, Camden, Guilford Courthouse, and Yorktown.

Battlegrounds of Freedom: A Historical Guide to the Battlefields of the War of American Independence[1] served the purpose of an overview. It covered all the major battles and several of the minor ones, along with the winter encampments at Morristown and Valley Forge. It also included a chapter on re-enacting to make it distinctive from other guidebooks. The success of that volume encouraged me to continue the project.

This continuation of the *Battlegrounds of Freedom* series covers the battles and, much more specifically, the raids and skirmishes of the Revolutionary War, many of which do not get covered even in the most detailed history books. The series intends to provide comprehensive, if not exhaustive, coverage of the military engagements of the American War for Independence. It also aims to serve as a guide to the sites and the military engagements. It does not intend to cover specifically naval battles; but it does include naval actions in which one of the parties was land-based. British ships fired frequently on shore installations, ship-building industries, towns, houses, or troops on land. Such actions usually provoked a hostile response, even if a weak one. These minor clashes also illustrate the dangers faced by coastal residents and by troops moving within sight of enemy ships. Actions on inland lakes or bays are considered along with land actions as are attacks on enemy watering parties or other landing parties.

The work also covers engagements between French or Spanish troops and Crown forces as well as raids by Native Americans instigated or led either by British officers and agents or by Congressional forces. It does not attempt to cover raids on the cabins of western settlers that would have occurred regardless of the war, even though the residents retaliated.

Francis B. Heitman's *Historical Register of Officers of the Continental Army during the War of the Revolution, April 1775 to December 1783*[2] provides an alphabetical list of 420 engagements. This list seems to have been adopted as the U.S. Army's official list of battles and actions. Howard Henry Peckham's *The Toll of Independence: Engagements & Battle Casualties of the American Revolution*[3] expands this list to 1,330 military engagements and 220 naval engagements. He gives a brief description of the actions arranged chronologically, but his concern is primarily to tally the casualties. My research started with Peckham's work for the list of engagements, as his is comparatively the most extensive.

The multiple *Guide to the American Revolutionary War* volumes more than double the number of engagements (more than 3,000) found in Peckham. They correct some of the entries and provide documentary references. The lack of primary source materials makes some actions very difficult to discover and document. The problem is most evident in "neutral territory," such as Elizabethtown, New Jersey, and Staten Island, New York, where conflict pretty much became part of everyday life. Sometimes, military actions occurred in several places during the same expedition or as part of a multi-pronged effort. Rather than repeat a narrative in several different places, we refer the reader to the main or a related account through *See* and *See also* references. However, each volume of the series is intended to be self-contained as much as possible with respect to the others.

Mark Mayo Boatner's *Encyclopedia of the American Revolution*[4] and his *Landmarks of the American Revolution: A Guide to Locating and Knowing What Happened at the Sites of Independence*[5] have long been considered the Bible for Revolutionary War aficionados and re-enactors. These works appeared in a new edition in 2007.[6] This is an excellent source to begin research on the Revolutionary War together with *The Encyclopedia of the American Revolutionary War: A Political, Social, and Military History*.[7]

Each volume in the *Battlegrounds of Freedom* series covers its respective states affected by the war and each location where an engagement occurred. It follows a hybrid geographical/chronological approach to accommodate various audiences: readers interested in American history, re-enactors, tourists, and visitors. The states are arranged from north to south and east to west. Within each state, the engagements appear chronologically. Locations with multiple engagements also appear chronologically so readers can follow the text as a historical sequence or "story" of a site before proceeding to the next one. For example, the treatment of Fort Ticonderoga (Ticonderoga, New York) discusses the events of July 8, 1758 before proceeding to those of May 10, 1775; July 1–6, 1777; July, 1775; July 24 to August 11, 1779; and September 13, 1779. Cross references have been added as necessary.

The text identifies the location of the sites as best as can be determined, provides the historical background to understand what happened there, indicates what the visitor can expect to see there, and identifies any interpretive aids. It is not meant to replace the guides produced for specific sites and available at visitor centers. These guides usually provide more details about the features of a particular site. Also, monographs devoted to specific engagements or campaigns will be more detailed than what we can present here.

Strategic Objectives

The presence of large numbers of troops in an area gave residents cause for concern. The soldiers were always short of food and constantly searching for provisions. It took a lot of food to feed an army. While troops were allotted daily rations, they rarely received their full allocation.

A soldier's typical weekly ration would consist of:
- 7 pounds of beef or 4 pounds of pork
- 7 pounds of bread or flour sufficient to bake it
- 3 pints of peas or beans
- ½ pound of rice
- ¼ pound of butter[8]

This would translate to the following weekly rations for an army of 1,000 men:
- 3½ tons of beef or 2 tons of pork
- 3½ tons of bread or flour sufficient to bake it
- 94 bushels of peas or beans
- 1¾ tons of rice
- 250 pounds of butter

The threat of a foraging expedition caused residents to hide their cattle and the expedition usually elicited an attack from the enemy. As one side tried to obtain food and supplies, the other tried to prevent them from doing so or to re-capture the stolen goods along with the enemy's baggage and supplies. While most of these actions were militarily insignificant, they often had the effect of reducing both forces. Crown forces were harder to replace because they usually had to come from overseas.

Military objectives not only included the capture of enemy forts, strongholds, and armies but also the control of important crossroads, rivers, and ferries. The rivers were the 18th-century highways and made travel and transportation much quicker than the unpaved roads. Controlling these strategic points either facilitated or blocked troop movements and supply lines.

Nomenclature

The two sides in the American War for Independence are generally referred to as the British and the Americans. However, this is a gross oversimplification. While it is a convenient way to refer to both sides, it is often inaccurate, particularly when discussing engagements in the South where most of the actions were between militia units or armed mobs with very few, if any, regular soldiers. For example, Major Patrick Ferguson was the only British soldier at the Battle of Kings Mountain (South Carolina). Many actions in the South seem to have been occasions for people to settle grudges with their neighbors in feuds that resemble that between the Hatfields and the McCoys. In a sense, the war in the South was very much a civil war. In other areas, it took on the nature of a world war.

Moreover, the provincials were British citizens—at least until they declared their independence on July 4, 1776. Prior to that date, the provincials believed their grievances were with Parliament and not the King. Most of the citizens did not favor independence but rather hoped for redress of their grievances and the re-establishment of relations with Parliament. However, when King George III sided with Parliament and declared the colonies in rebellion on August 23, 1775, the provincials realized that their hopes were dashed. After the news reached the colonies on October 31, 1775, they began to see independence as their only recourse.

The Declaration of Independence made a definite break between England and her American colonies; but it took a while for those ideas to become widely accepted. In fact, it took 18 months after the outbreak of the war to enunciate that objective; and it took eight years to win the war that secured the independence of the United States of America. Even though England officially recognized the new country with the signing of the Treaty of Paris in 1783, it often continued to act as though it still controlled the colonies. This was one of the factors that led to the War of 1812.

While the provincials called themselves Americans, to refer only to those who favored independence as Americans is too broad, as they were less than a majority of the population. Although all the provincials were British citizens until the signing of Declaration of Independence and their effective independence at the end of the war, to refer to them as Americans confuses a political position with hegemony. That would be comparable to referring to Republicans or Democrats as Americans, implying that the other party is not American. Similarly, to refer to them as Patriots implies that those who remained loyal to the King were less patriotic when they fought to maintain life as they knew it.

Consequently, we refer to the supporters of independence as Rebels, Whigs, or Congressional troops. We also distinguish between the local militias and the regular soldiers of the Continental Army ("Continentals") as narratives allow further distinction. We also refer to Allied forces to designate joint efforts by Congressional forces and their foreign allies, primarily French and Spanish.

Similarly, the "British" armies were more complex than just English troops. They certainly consisted of Irish, Scot, and Welsh troops. We sometimes refer to them by regiment, e.g. 71st Highlanders, Black Watch, Royal Welch Fusiliers, when individual regiments are prominent in an engagement. They are also referred to generically as Regulars or Redcoats. (Some derogatory references call them lobsterbacks or bloodybacks because of the flesh wounds from whipping—a common form of punishment at the time.)

While British troops are often called Redcoats, not all wore red coats. The artillerymen wore dark blue coats. While some of the dragoons wore red, others such as Tarleton's Legion, wore green coats. There are instances where the two sides confused each other because of the similarity of the coats. For example, Major General Henry "Light-Horse Harry" Lee (1756–1818) and his legion tried to surprise Lieutenant Colonel Banastre Tarleton (1744–1833) on the morning of February 25, 1781. The front of Lee's Legion encountered two mounted Loyalists who mistook them for Tarleton's Legion. The Loyalists were taken to General Lee who took advantage of their mistake by posing as Tarleton. He learned that Colonel John Pyle had recruited about 400 Loyalists and that they were on their way to join Tarleton. Lee and his men continued the ruse, surrounded the Loyalists, and captured them all, depriving General Charles Cornwallis of badly needed troops at Yorktown.

Loyalist troops were issued both red and green uniforms with a wide variety of facings. Those who wore the green coats were sometimes referred to as Green Coats or simply as the Greens. Some authors refer to the Loyalists as Tories, a term which has taken on derogatory significance.

Moreover, King George III, who was of German origin, arranged to reinforce his armies with large numbers of German troops. They wore coats of various shades of blue, as well as green with red facings. Many of these soldiers came from the provinces of Hesse Hanau and Hesse Kassel and became known as Hessians. Other regiments were known by their provinces of origin (e.g., Braunschweiger or Brunswick and Waldeck) or by the name of their commander (von Lossberg, von Donop, etc.).

We use the terms Crown forces, King's troops, Royal Navy to refer to these combined forces or the regiment name, commanding officer, or group designation (e.g. Hessians, Loyalists) to be more specific.

People of color fought on both sides. We use the currently politically correct terminology of African Americans, even though not all of them came from Africa, and Native Americans as the generic terms. We also use the specific tribal name, if known: Iroquois, Mohawk, Oneida, Cherokee, etc. Mulattoes referred to people of mixed race. Quotations retain the terminology used by the original writer.

The Native American tribes tended to support the Crown because they realized that the settlers coveted their land and presented a greater threat than the British Army. Great Britain had fewer troops in the West (west of the Appalachians) than in the East (along the East Coast and east of the Appalachians), so it needed their support. More than 1,200 Delawares, Shawnees, and Mingoes lived in the Ohio valley. North of them, 300 Wyandots, Hurons, and 600 Ottawas and thousands of Chippewas inhabited southern Michigan and the shores of Lake Erie. Several hundred Potawatomis extended toward the southern end of Lake Michigan. The area north and east of Fort Pitt was occupied by the Senecas, and several hundred Miamis lived along the Maumeee and upper Wabash rivers. The Weas, Piankeshaws, Kickapoos, and other tribes settled on the Wabash and west toward the Mississippi, while an unknown number of Foxes, Sauks, and Mascoutens lived beyond the Great Lakes.

The Native American tribes were unreliable and not great assets as combatants. Sometimes, they were even a liability. For example, the murder of Jane McCrea by her Native American escorts during the Saratoga campaign brought new recruits to the Congressional forces and deterred Loyalists from actively supporting the Crown troops. British commanders often found it impossible to determine whether the Native Americans would fight and for how long. When they did fight, they usually did so in small groups and for limited periods. They were also often divided by rivalries among themselves, easily frightened by any show of strength, and usually unwilling to leave their families for long campaigns. Without the support of the Native Americans, however, Crown forces had no hope of controlling the West. The Crown forces provided the tribes with gifts every year to insure their continued support. These gifts included a large supply of ammunition and clothing as well as gifts for the chief warriors.[9]

Nobody knows how many provincials remained loyal to King George III during the American War for Independence. Many history books credit John Adams with estimating that one-third of the population favored the Revolution, one-third were against it, and another third leaned to whichever side happened to control the area. The quotation reads:

> I should say that full one-third were averse to the revolution. These, retaining that overweening fondness, in which they had been educated, for the English, could not cordially like the French; indeed, they most heartily detested them. An opposite third conceived a hatred of the English, and gave themselves up to an enthusiastic gratitude to France. The middle third, composed principally of the yeomanry, the soundest part of the nation, and always averse to war, were rather lukewarm both to England and France.[10]

On another occasion, Mr. Adams noted that the colonies had been nearly "unanimous" in their opposition to the Stamp Act in 1765 but, by 1775, the British had "seduced and deluded nearly one third of the people of the colonies."[11]

In the first quotation, Ray Raphael[12] notes that Adams was writing about the political sentiments of Americans toward the conflict between England and France in 1797; but the two quotations somehow blended together in popular historiography to refer to the American War for Independence. So Adams has become the definitive contemporary source on the political allegiance of the period.

Conventions and Parts of This Book

Cognizant that one may begin a tour anywhere, the first occurrence of a person's name in a section identifies him or her as completely as possible with the full form of the name with birth and death dates, if known. Some readers will probably find this awkward or cumbersome as they read several sections. We hope that those who consult a specific section will find this helpful.

Most chapters begin with a map of the sites in that state to facilitate orientation, and additional maps face the beginning of their respective sections. Some chapters with many actions are subdivided north to south and east to west, and these divisions are reflected with references to their respective maps. These maps have pointers to engagement locations and are printed on regular paper like the photos.

Engagements are then listed chronologically within their subdivisions along with the corresponding map. Locations with multiple engagements group those events in chronological order under the same heading to provide a historical sequence or "story" of a site before proceeding to the next one. Cross references have been added as necessary.

Each site begins with the name of the city or town (or the most commonly known name of the engagement), and the name (and alternate names) of the battle or action. The location names are followed by the dates, in parentheses, of significant actions discussed in the text. Specially formatted text identifies the location of the site, indicates what the visitor can expect to see, and identifies any interpretive aids. Historical background to understand what happened at a site follows. In any case, this book does not mean to replace more-detailed tourist guides for specific sites that are available at visitor centers.

Events are marked with a bullet character (★) for easy identification and to dispel confusion.

Travelers should take care to map their route for most efficient travel as many sites are not along main roads. Sometimes, one must backtrack to visit a place thoroughly. Travelers should also be aware that some locations in a particular state may be farther than other locations in a neighboring state. Consulting maps allows the visitor to proceed from one location to another with the least amount of backtracking. It also offers options for side trips as desired. Consult the maps and the appendices at the publisher's web site (**www.buscainc.com**) to see how battle sites are grouped and keyed to major cities or locations.

One of the appendices gives a chronological list of battles, actions, and skirmishes. History books often present events in purely chronological order. However, that is not a good approach for a guidebook to follow, as events can occur simultaneously great distances apart. For example, the powder alarm in Williamsburg, Virginia occurred on the same day as the battles of Lexington and Concord in Massachusetts. The web site also features a comprehensive state-by-state alphabetical list of locations where actions (battles, raids, or skirmishes) took place.

Other books take a thematic approach, covering campaigns or specific themes like the war on the frontier. This technique, while more focused, often ignores information relevant to a site that properly belongs to another theme. For example, a theme covering Major General John Burgoyne's (1722–1792) campaign of 1777 may not cover the capture of Fort Ticonderoga in 1775 or its role in the Seven Years War (also known as the French and Indian War).

The many photographs, with descriptive captions and keyed to the text, are important for identifying details of historic buildings, monuments, battlefields, and equipment. Many of the photos are of battle and event re-enactments. All photos, except otherwise identified, are by the author. Full-color photos of some of the images in this and other volumes are on the publisher's web site (**www.buscainc.com**).

Another feature that modern readers and visitors will find useful are URLs for web sites of various parks and tourist organizations. These URLs are correlated with various battle sites and sometimes events. Visitors may want to consult these web sites ahead of time for important, updated information on special events, hours, fees, etc. These URLs were active and accurate at the time this book went to press.

The Glossary provides definitions for some 18th-century military and historical terms. There are also scholarly reference Notes for sources used in this book and an

Index. The full Bibliography of the sources consulted for the *Battlegrounds of Freedom* series is on the publisher's web site (**www.buscainc.com**).

Most of the sites described in this book are reconstructions or restorations. Many buildings were damaged during the War for Independence or fell into disrepair over the years. They were refurbished, for the most part, for the nation's bicentennial in 1975–1976. Battlefield fortifications were sometimes destroyed after a battle so they could not be re-used by the enemy at a later time. For example, the hornworks and siege trenches at Yorktown, Virginia were destroyed after the surrender of General Charles Cornwallis so the Crown forces could not re-use them for a subsequent assault. They were, however, rebuilt and used again during the War of Rebellion (Civil War). There are many houses and structures still standing that demonstrate what life was like in the 18th century. Only those related to the battles are covered.

Many of the sites have been obliterated by urban development and have nothing to see or visit. Houses and other construction have supplanted them. One battlefield is covered by a shopping mall; another has been submerged under a man-made lake; others were destroyed by high-rise apartment or office buildings. Many are remembered only with a roadside marker. Some don't even have that.

Many sites have little importance to the outcome of the war. Some actions were mere skirmishes or raids lasting only a few minutes. For example, some actions consisted of a single volley. After one of the forces fired, it fled. Yet, some important events, such as the capture of Fort Kaskaskia by George Rogers Clark in Illinois and the capture of Fort Ticonderoga by Benedict Arnold, Ethan Allen, and the Green Mountain Boys were effected without firing a single shot. The battle at Black Mingo Creek, South Carolina lasted only 15 minutes. Other engagements, particularly those involving Lieutenant Colonel Francis Marion, known as the Swamp Fox, were fought in the swamps of South Carolina and are hard to find.

Some sites remain undeveloped and virtually ignored. This is not necessarily bad. While erosion, neglect, and plant or tree growth slowly undermine earthworks, they do significantly less damage than the rapid deterioration resulting from bikers and walkers.

One cannot easily cover all the sites of the American War for Independence. However, one can visit all the sites and events that affected the outcome of the war. One can also visit enough locally significant spots to get an understanding of what the war was like for the people of that region. This book tries to cover the extant battle sites and hopes to serve as a companion on the voyage of discovery.

Norman Desmarais
normd@providence.edu

Introduction

New York City was the main British headquarters during the French and Indian (Seven Years) War (1756–1763) but northern New York was the major theater of fighting. Soldiers and sailors were very familiar to New Yorkers who benefited from their money. However, by the time of the American War for Independence, New Yorkers did not like the British troops, the authority of royal judges, or the taxes passed by the British Parliament.

The Provincial Assembly passed a resolution against the Sugar Act. The Stamp Act Congress met in New York City in August 1765. The city's Stamp Act uprising at the end of October made the act unenforceable. The stamp distributor resigned when Long Islanders apprehended him. A crowd almost assaulted Fort George where the stamps were being kept. After the British officer ordered the fort's guns trained on the city, the crowd sacked his house.

Meanwhile, settlers in newly created Gloucester and Cumberland counties (now Vermont) were struggling to set the boundaries along the frontier. A British map, drawn about 1775 but published only in 1779, indicated that New York claimed much of New England west of the Connecticut River. The map also depicted the Iroquois country of the Six Nations the same way as it presented New England east of the river—as white space not belonging to New York. New Hampshire had made many land grants in the same region. Most of these grants went to people from Connecticut who began making their claims when the French withdrew from Canada in 1763. Some land speculators, like Ethan Allen (1738–1790) and his brothers, also made some claims but not to the extent of the great New York families.

After Parliament punished Boston, Massachusetts with the Coercive (Intolerable) Acts, New York City refused to let the first tea ship dock at Sandy Hook in April 1774. When a second vessel arrived with a cargo of East India Company tea, a party of Whigs boarded the vessel and dumped the cargo. However, unlike at Boston, the perpetrators made no attempt to negotiate or to disguise themselves, nor did they suffer any direct punishment.

New York was deeply involved in the American War for Independence for the entire period from 1775 until 1783. These operations ranged from militia skirmishes between Whigs and Loyalists to full-fledged campaigns by large armies. They included raids and frontier warfare. The Hudson River was a crucially strategic objective. It provided a water route to Canada for the rapid movement of troops and for shipping and commerce. The British saw its control as a way of dividing the colonies. General George Washington (1732–1799) explained to Major General Israel Putnam (1718–1790), in 1777, that "the possession of [the Hudson] is indispensably essential to preserve the Communication between the Eastern, Middle, and Southern States."

The Hudson Highlands, a series of granite hills extending 10 miles east to west and situated 40 miles north of New York City and 90 miles south of Albany, offered the best defensive artillery positions against British warships. General Washington had several forts constructed in the Highlands, including Forts Montgomery, Clinton, and Constitution and the five forts and seven redoubts that fortified West Point. These fortifications were complemented by a great chain stretched across the Hudson to impede the passage of British vessels (see **Forts Montgomery** and **Clinton** below).

New York contributed a total of 21,647 men to the war effort—3,866 militiamen and 17,781 in the Continental Army. Nobody knows how many New Yorkers remained loyal to the King; but more than 30,000 people left the state during and after the war.

> The New York State Museum on Madison Avenue in Albany (phone: 518-474-5877), across from the State Capitol Building, manages the state's historic markers program and publishes the *Historical Area Markers in New York State*. Visitors can obtain this publication and others by calling 518-402-5344 or via email at nysmpub@mail.nysed.gov. These publications include *The Hudson Valley in the American Revolution* and *Landmarks of the Revolution in New York State: A Guide to the Historic Sites Open to the Public* by David C. Thurheimer. *The Mohawk Valley and the American Revolution* is available at **www.fortklock.com/mvinrevolution.htm**. A section on the www.fortklock.com site contains information on American War of Independence landmarks in the Mohawk and Schoharie Valleys. The **www.nysparks.state.ny.us** site offers detailed descriptions and locations of landmarks by clicking on the Historic Preservation button.

1
UPSTATE NEW YORK

See the map of Upstate New York.

General William Howe (1732–1786) proposed to make the Hudson River his main campaign objective for 1776 by landing at New York. He also wanted to capture ports in South Carolina. He would secure a base of operations in New York and position his forces to push north to clear the riverway of Whigs. The overwhelming dominance of the Royal Navy on the waterways would assure him control of the river. General Howe wanted to concentrate the entire British force in America in New York, but the British government had diverted part of it to Canada in early 1776 to repel a Rebel invasion. This diversion of forces laid the groundwork for the divided command structure that plagued British operations throughout the war.

On the Continental side, General George Washington's (1732–1799) problem was to guess accurately where the Crown forces would attack and to make preparations to meet them. He foresaw correctly that New York would be the focus of their assault. He deemed it necessary to build new fortifications along the Hudson River and to fortify New York City and Long Island.

Overall British strategy for 1776 planned for two attacks on the Hudson–St. Lawrence line in the northern colonies. Yet, the British also proposed to mount a separate attack in the South. The objective of this southern attack was to enlist the help of Loyalists, seize some of the major southern cities, and control the southern colonies. General Henry Clinton (1730–1795) left Boston en route to North Carolina on Saturday, January 20, 1776, with a force of 1,500 troops to secure the South, while Howe remained in New York to begin the campaign for the Hudson Valley.

With their command of New York and of the sea, the British could move north up the Hudson to Lakes George and Champlain and to Canada, or south to the Delaware and Chesapeake Bays, to Virginia and the Carolinas. They could also support the many Loyalists they believed lived in Albany and along the Mohawk Valley. Moreover, they could encourage the people of the New Hampshire Grants in their dispute with the Continental Congress over boundary claims and administration. (The New Hampshire Grants, now the state of Vermont, were so-called because most of the land had been settled by people from New England under grants of land made by the governor of New Hampshire. The residents were particularly uneasy because they were nearest the enemy.) Even though Ethan Allen (1738–1790) and his Green Mountain Boys came home heroes after capturing Fort Ticonderoga, Major General John Burgoyne (1722–1792) considered the area ripe for British recruitment as long as the disputes over land grants remained unresolved.

If the British controlled the water route along the Hudson River and Lakes George and Champlain, they would separate the Rebels from both the Iroquois League of Six Nations—the Mohawks, the Oneidas, the Onondagas, the Cayugas, the Senecas, and the Tuscaroras—and the Native Americans of the Western Confederation. General Burgoyne did not yet have a command. He could only advise; so he suggested that the British might enlist some of the 160,000 Native Americans to carry arms to the black slaves of the south. Otherwise, the British could prevent them from joining the Rebels.

4 THE GUIDE TO THE AMERICAN REVOLUTIONARY WAR IN NEW YORK

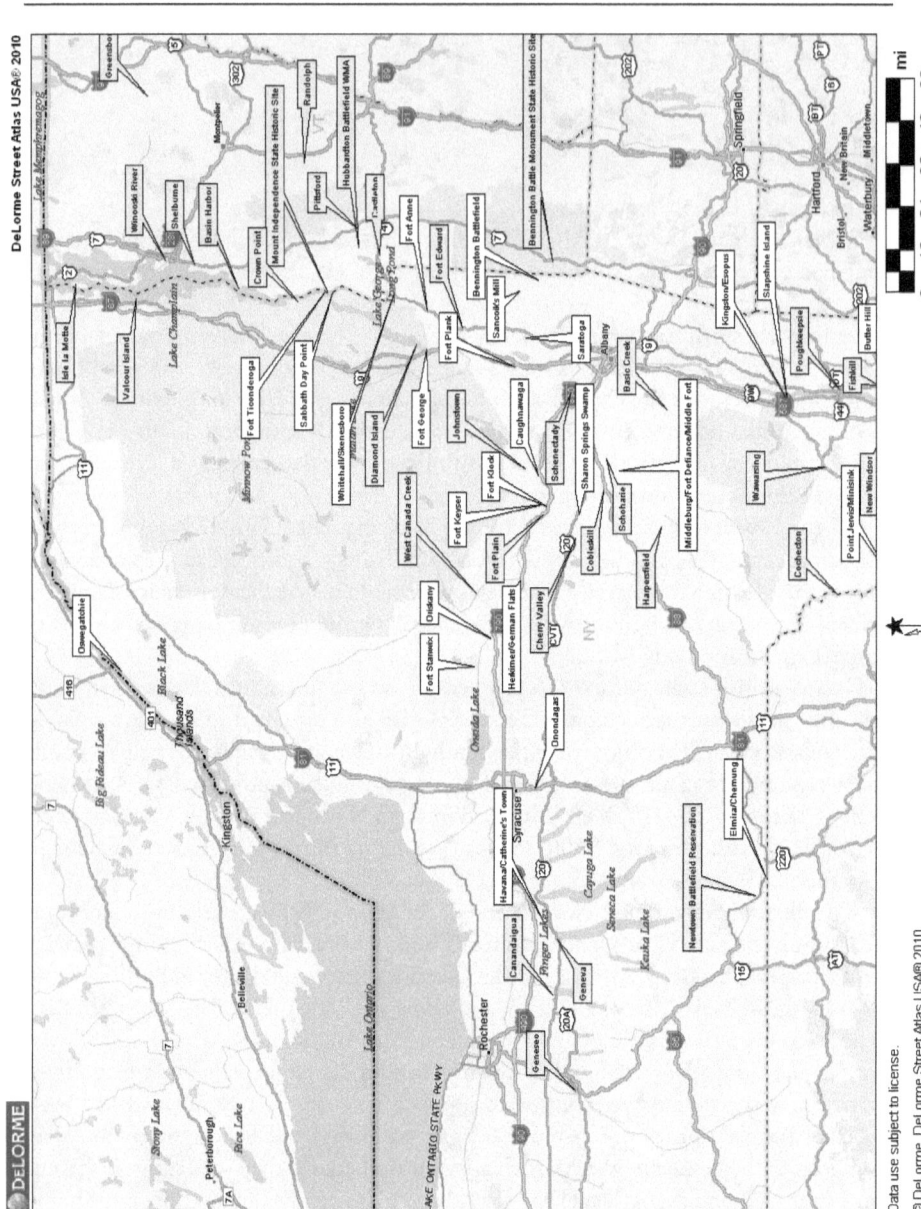

Upstate New York: Map for The Guide to the American Revolutionary War in New York © 2010 DeLorme (www.delorme.com) Street Atlas USA®

In 1777, General Burgoyne concluded that the strategic key to military success was British control of the interior water route between New York and the St. Lawrence River. His "Thoughts for Conducting the War from the Side of Canada" called for his army, Lieutenant Colonel Barry St. Leger's (1737–1789) army, and General William Howe's army to divide New England, the heart of the rebellion, from the colonies farther south. Burgoyne thought that this division of the rebellion would go a long way toward ending it. The plan, however, required close coordination between the three armies, and this, as it turned out, was its fatal flaw.

Burgoyne set out from Canada in June 1777, expecting to reach Albany by fall. His force was divided into two parts: General Sir Guy Carleton (1724–1808) would remain in Canada to defend that province and provide logistic support to the two columns moving south. The first and largest part—7,200 British and Hessian Regulars and 650 Loyalists, Canadians, and Native Americans, under his personal command—was to take the route down Lake Champlain to Ticonderoga and thence via Lake George to the Hudson. The second column—700 Regulars and 1,000 Loyalists and Native American braves under Lieutenant Colonel Barry St. Leger—was to move via Lake Ontario to Oswego and thence down the Mohawk Valley to join Burgoyne at Albany.

General Sir Guy Carleton (1724–1808) gave Burgoyne the task, required by the government, of issuing a proclamation offering a pardon to any Whig who deserted and went home. Burgoyne's proclamation (June 23, 1777) called on the Loyalists to join him, offered protection to those who sided with the King, and threatened to turn the Native Americans loose on the Whigs. He made this announcement using language that caused laughter and ridicule both in the colonies and in the House of Commons in London. A few days later, he told his Native American allies they must make war in a civilized manner. They were not to scalp or torture the wounded and prisoners, and they must not harm old men, women, and children.

Ticonderoga

Fort Ticonderoga (July 8, 1758; May 10, 1775; June 17, 1777; June 26, 1777; July 1–6, 1777; Nov. 8, 1777)

> Fort Ticonderoga (**www.fort-ticonderoga.org/**) is on NY 74, 1 mile northeast of the town of Ticonderoga.
>
> William Ferris Pell purchased the site of Fort Ticonderoga in 1820. The fort remained in his family until Stephen Pell decided to restore it in 1908–10 years before the creation of any national park and 20 years before the reconstruction of Williamsburg, Virginia. The reconstruction restored most of the stone walls and two interior barracks. The four-sided fort faces south on its long axis. Each of its four corners has a bastion (see Photo NY-1, NY-2) shaped like an arrowhead to protect the side walls. The north and west walls also have freestanding triangular bastions called demilunes in front of them for added protection, as they face land approaches where attackers could place heavy artillery to knock holes through the walls. The apex of the demilunes points outward, forming angled walls to deflect cannonballs and shells (see Photo NY-3, NY-4) to the side. Wooden bridges connect the demilunes to the fort proper. If enemy forces captured the demilunes, the bridges could be raised. Some of the bastions housed dungeons, storehouses, and other quarters. Ramps lead from the parade to the ramparts for impressive views of the surrounding area. Many cannons line the bastions of the fort.

Photo NY-1. Earth bastion, Fort George, Castine, Maine

Photo NY-2. Stone bastion, Fort Ticonderoga

> The South Barracks houses a museum which fills the three floors. Pell's private collection became the basis of the museum's collection. It includes Ethan Allen's blunderbuss (see Photo NY-5), General Schuyler's personal flag made of wool with a ring of circular white linen stars, and a hollow silver bullet that concealed a secret message from British General Clinton to Burgoyne telling him of the capture of the Hudson

Upstate New York 7

Photo NY-3A, B. Shells and artillery shots

River forts. (The soldier who carried the message tried to swallow the bullet when he was captured and was hanged as a spy.) There are musket balls with the teeth marks of the men who chewed on them during surgery or punishment (hence the term "bite the bullet"), and a rum horn made by Paul Revere. Some of the rooms are set up to depict the original quarters, a soldier's canteen, and the officer of the day's quarters.

Photo NY-4. Mortar shell

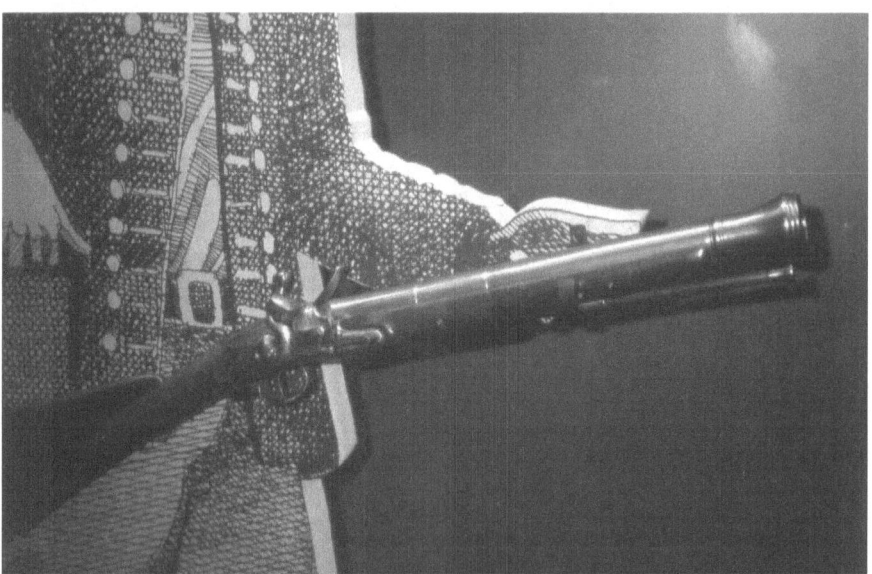

Photo NY-5. Blunderbuss or musquetoon

> Mount Defiance (835 feet), where British general William Phillips (1731–1781) placed four 12-pound cannons that forced the evacuation of Fort Ticonderoga, is off Route NY 22/74, 1 mile southeast of town. A paved road goes to the top.
>
> Fort Mount Hope, 2 miles northwest of Fort Ticonderoga, is privately owned. Mount Independence is in Vermont, across Lake Champlain from the fort (see Photo NY-2).

> The location of Fort Ticonderoga controls a two-mile portage from Lake Champlain to Lake George and consequently the entire route between Canada and New York. The Native Americans called the place "between the waters." The French began building the first fort here in October 1755, and called it Carillon because the builders thought the water from Lake George sounded like a "chime of bells" as it fell over the rocks into Lake Champlain.

★ Fort Ticonderoga originally consisted of squared-off timbers laid horizontally and backed by embankments; but the wood eventually rotted and was replaced by stone. As the fort's outer entrenchment was nearing completion, the British attacked it on July 8, 1758 with 15,000 men—the largest British Army yet fielded in North America. Louis Joseph Marquis de Montcalm de Saint-Véran (1712–1759) did not wait for the attack. He ordered wooden fortifications built in the woods three-quarters of a mile west of the fort. Unlike stone which shatters and acts like shrapnel when struck by artillery, wood was better able to withstand artillery fire and could be easily repaired. The British lost 2,000 men killed and wounded in an unsuccessful attempt to penetrate the defenses. The defenders lost only 300 out of 3,500.

General Jeffrey Amherst, Baron Amherst (1717–1797) returned the following summer to find the fort's garrison drastically reduced. After a four-day siege, the French blew up their powder and evacuated the fort. Amherst had the damage repaired and renamed the fort Ticonderoga. The British occupied Fort Ticonderoga for the next 16 years, but it no longer had any military importance with the French removed from eastern North America, so it was only guarded by a few men and fell into disrepair.

1775–1776

★ Early in May 1775, the Massachusetts Committee of Safety authorized Captain Benedict Arnold (1741–1801) to recruit a company of 400 men to capture Fort Ticonderoga. About the same time, the Connecticut assembly made a similar offer to Lieutenant Colonel Ethan Allen (1738–1790) and his Green Mountain Boys. When Arnold learned of this, he rode to Castleton, Vermont, to confront Allen, but the Green Mountain Boys refused to serve under anybody but Allen. So Arnold and Allen agreed to share the command.

Allen, Arnold, and 83 men boarded the only boats available, a couple of scows, at Hand's Cove on the east shore of Lake Champlain near Shoreham, Vermont. By the time they landed, it was too light for the boats to return for the remainder of the assault party which totaled two to three hundred men. With less than one-third of his total strength, Allen decided to attack the fort about 3:30 AM on Friday, May 10, 1775. They caught the garrison by surprise and both the commanding officer and the second-in-command asleep in bed.

Allen and Arnold climbed the wooden outside stairs leading to the top floor, with swords drawn and demanded the fort's surrender. Allen shouted something like "Come out, you damn old rat!" He later embellished the statement in his memoirs, published in 1779, where he recorded he called for the surrender "In the name of the Great Jehovah and the Continental Congress." The second-in-command described Benedict Arnold as requesting surrender in a "genteel manner." He described Ethan Allen as highly agitated, brandishing a sword, and demanding the keys of the fort.

The fort's position was not as critical as the cannon and ammunition stored there. Many of the guns were in such bad condition that they were useless, but there were at least 78 useful ones. They ranged from 4-pounders to 24-pounders (18th-century artillery is classified by the weight of the shot fired) and included six mortars (see Photo NY-6), three howitzers, thousands of cannonballs of various sizes, nine tons of musket balls, more than 30,000 flints, and a large quantity of miscellaneous supplies, all of which Allen, Arnold, and the raiding party captured at Ticonderoga and Crown Point (about 12 miles further north), which they seized the next day. The captives were marched to a prison in Hartford, Connecticut.

Photo NY-6. Mortar

General George Washington (1732–1799) sent Colonel Henry Knox (1750–1806), later to be his chief of artillery, to Fort Ticonderoga to remove the artillery he needed so badly. Knox arrived on Tuesday, December 5, 1775 and began the task of loading 43 cannons and 16 mortars—119,000 pounds of artillery—for the journey to Boston. He also took 2,300 pounds of lead and a supply of flints. The train of 42 heavy sledges pulled by 80 yoke of oxen traveled 300 miles, despite the poor or nonexistent roads in icebound western New England. They arrived at Framingham (20 miles from Cambridge, Massachusetts) by Thursday, January 25, 1776. The guns were eventually installed on Dorchester Heights, overlooking Boston, in March, and contributed greatly to convincing the British to evacuate the city.

1777

Continental defenses in the north were very weak in 1777. There were only about 2,500 soldiers at Ticonderoga, with 450 occupying old Fort Stanwix in the Mohawk Valley. Dissension was rife among the troops. New Englanders refused to support Major General Philip Schuyler (1733–1804), the aristocratic New Yorker who commanded the Northern Army. They openly intrigued to replace him with their own favorite, Major General Horatio Gates (1728–1806).

★ Before the Crown forces returned in 1777, a band of Native Americans captured and killed three soldiers near Fort Ticonderoga on Tuesday, June 17, 1777. The militiamen, in turn, killed three Native Americans.[1]

★ John Whiting (1765–1777) and John Batty were returning from Lake George landing on Thursday, June 26 when a number of Native Americans fired at them. They shot 12-year old John Whiting through the head and then stabbed him in the throat, breast and belly before scalping him. John Batty was shot twice in the thigh, once in the small of his back, and once in the breast. He was then scalped but feigned dead to avoid being killed. When the Native Americans departed, he got up and called for help and was carried into the fort. He was still alive a week later when the fort was abandoned and he was supposedly left behind.[2]

Major General John Burgoyne (1722–1792) marched from Canada to Albany. His first task was to retake the old British position at Fort Ticonderoga controlling Lake Champlain. Burgoyne's army landed north of the fort on both sides of the lake on Tuesday, July 1. The Germans landed on the east, the British on the west.

In his preparations, Burgoyne evidently forgot the lesson the British had learned in the French and Indian War: that troops had to be prepared to travel light in the wilderness and fight like Native Americans. He carried 138 pieces of artillery and a heavy load of officers' personal baggage. Numerous ladies of high and low rank accompanied the expedition. When he started down the lakes, Burgoyne did not have enough horses and wagons to transport his artillery and baggage once he had to leave the water and move overland.

★ A party of Canadians, Native Americans and some British regulars skulkingly advanced toward the fort on Wednesday afternoon, July 2. A smart engagement ensued between them and the picket guard. "The Indians were uncommonly furious and blood thirsty." The skirmish lasted a considerable time before the pickets returned to the fort. The garrison fired 8 or 10 rounds of grape shot and soon dispersed them; but they lost Lieutenant Thomas Wheeler (d. 1777) of Newark, New Jersey, and four privates killed and 12 wounded, including one who was ordered to be shot for attempting to desert. The dead were buried that same night. The Crown's loss could not be determined; but they lost at least one regular taken prisoner and two Hessians deserters.[3]

Major General Arthur St. Clair (1737–1818) was in command at Ticonderoga. His orders required that he defend the fort itself, Mount Independence (previously known as Rattlesnake Hill) across the lake, and Mount Hope, 2 miles to the northwest of the fort. He neglected to occupy Sugar Loaf (Mount Defiance), a mile to the southwest. This was the highest point in the area and dominated both the fort and Mount Independence, but St. Clair considered it inaccessible and did not have enough men to defend the mountain. Major General William Phillips (1731–1781), Burgoyne's second in command and an artilleryman, directed his engineers and artillery to begin work on Friday, July 4. He reportedly told his men: "Where a goat can go, a man can go, and where a man can go, he can drag a gun." He then led his men up the mountain. He had four 12-pounders in position by noon of July 6. The cannons did not threaten the fort but could destroy the floating bridge and boats needed for evacuation.

★ The Crown forces deployed about 60 boats and vessels in a line across Lake Champlain about 1 PM on Saturday, July 5. General St. Clair prepared for a general attack and ordered his men to their posts; but the boats dispersed soon after sunset, some to one shore and some to the other. St. Clair recognized his danger and evacuated Ticonderoga that night, leaving behind cannon and valuable supplies.

General Burgoyne pursued the retreating Continentals to Skenesboro, New York (now Whitehall), arriving on the afternoon of July 6 in time to capture two ships. The Continentals burned the rest as they evacuated the area. Brigadier General Simon Fraser (1737–1777) and Major General Baron Friedrich von Riedesel (1738–1800) pursued the main body and surprised and defeated the rear guard near Hubbardton, Vermont the next day. General St. Clair managed to escape with the rest of his men and rejoined the army at Fort Edward, New York.

As the British pursued the Continentals after the fall of Fort Ticonderoga, they left their wounded in bark huts under the charge of Sergeant Roger Lamb (1756–1830) who tore up his shirt to make bandages, as there were no supplies to dress their wounds. Burgoyne left several hundred men behind to garrison Fort Ticonderoga after capturing it. He hoped that General Sir Guy Carleton (1724–1808) would send reinforcements for this purpose, but Carleton told him his orders from London forbade him doing so.

Burgoyne could choose one of two routes to reach Fort Edward on the Hudson. He could continue overland via Fort Anne, a distance of 23 miles through a wilderness of tall trees and deep ravines with poor or nonexistent roads; or he could return to Fort Ticonderoga, go up Lake George and across country to a point on the Hudson north of Fort Edward. This route also had its difficulties because the falls and rapids between Lake Champlain and Lake George would require a portage of about 3 miles. The poor road between Lake George and the Hudson would reduce the distance to only 10 miles.

Burgoyne did not want to appear to be retreating by going back to Ticonderoga to take the second and easier route. He decided to continue overland through the forest to the Hudson, but he sent his boats, his artillery, and other heavy equipment by the first route. The overland line of advance was already a nightmare, running along wilderness trails, through marshes, and across wide ravines and creeks that had been swollen by abnormally heavy rains.

Major General Philip Schuyler (1733–1804) adopted the tactic of making it even worse by destroying bridges, cutting trees in Burgoyne's path, and digging trenches to let the waters of swamps onto drier ground. The Whigs encouraged local residents to drive off their horses and cattle and to burn their crops to prevent the Crown forces from getting them. The Crown forces averaged about a mile a day, arriving at Fort Edward on Tuesday, July 29, three weeks later. By that time, Burgoyne was desperately short of horses, wagons, and oxen. Yet Schuyler, with an unstable force of 4,500 men discouraged by continual retreats, was in no position to give battle.

General George Washington (1732–1799) did what he could to strengthen the Northern Army. He first dispatched Major General Benedict Arnold (1741–1801), his most aggressive field commander, and Major General Benjamin Lincoln (1733–1810), a Massachusetts man noted for his influence with the New England militiamen. On Saturday, August 16, he detached Colonel Daniel Morgan (1736–1802) with 500 riflemen from the main army in Pennsylvania and ordered them along with 750 men from Colonel Rufus Putnam's (1738–1824) force in the New York highlands to join Schuyler. The riflemen were intended to furnish an antidote for Burgoyne's Native Americans who, despite his efforts to restrain them, were terrorizing the countryside.

After Burgoyne surrendered at Saratoga (see below), the Continentals once again took control of Fort Ticonderoga which served as the rallying point for raiding parties through the end of the war. The fort was never garrisoned again after the war and fell into disrepair, serving as a quarry for building material.[4]

★ The British abandoned Fort Ticonderoga on Saturday November 8, 1777 after demolishing all the fortifications and bridges and burning all the houses and destroying all the stores, cannon, and everything they couldn't bring with them.[5]

Below Ticonderoga
Sabbath Day Point (Mar. 22, 1777)

> This event occurred about 5 miles north of Sabbath Day Point on the west side of Lake Champlain, south of Ticonderoga.

★ About 18 Cocknewago Native Americans led by Captain McKoy or McCoy, a British officer, captured a Mr. Adams and two others as they were going to Sabbath Day Point with 13 horses about 3 PM on Saturday, March 22, 1777. Soon afterward, Captain Jeduthan Baldwin (1732–1788) came along with about 25 men. They travelled on the ice from Ticonderoga to Fort George to join their corps. The Cocknewagos concealed themselves in the woods until about 3 AM. Captain Baldwin and his men stopped at Sabbath Day Point where they made a fire and lay down to sleep. The Cocknewagos attacked them, tomahawked four of them, fired a ball (not mortal) through the upper part of Captain John Henry's (1753–1793) breast and captured 20 of the men. Mr. Adams knew Captain McCoy well and pleaded that he was only an inhabitant and did not belong to the army. He was released. As soon as the account reached Ticonderoga, Captain Benjamin Whitcomb (d. 1828) was sent with 40 men to attack the enemy on their way to Canada. He killed several Cocknewagos and wounded several more.[6]

Mount Independence (Sept. 7, 1776; July 5, 1777)

> Mount Independence is a high hill (formerly known as Rattlesnake Hill) on the eastern shore of Lake Champlain in Orwell opposite Fort Ticonderoga. The hill slopes to the water of the lake. The Mount Independence State Historic Site (in Orwell 6 miles west of the junction of VT 22A and VT 73) traces the history of the site of the military fortifications.

★ Congressional forces had fortified Mount Independence in 1776 by erecting a star fort on its flat top. It contained extensive barracks and was strongly entrenched to its base and well supplied with heavy artillery. Another battery midway up the mountain covered the lower works. The Congressional forces joined Ticonderoga and Mount Independence with a strong bridge over the inlet. Twenty-two sunken piers supported the bridge at equal distances and had floats between them fastened together with chains and rivets and bound to the sunken piers. A boom of very large timber, fastened together by riveted bolts and double chains made of iron 1½ inches square, was erected on the Lake Champlain side of the bridge.

A company of Redcoats skirmished with the militia near their breastworks at Mount Independence on Saturday, September 7, 1776. The attackers lost three killed and six wounded.[7]

★ The bridge prevented any attack by water from the north; but Sugar Loaf Hill (Mount Defiance), to the south, overlooked and commanded both the works at Ticonderoga and on Mount Independence. The militia could not fortify this place due to insufficient forces. When the British Army left Crown Point, New York on Tuesday, July 1, 1777, they advanced on both sides of Lake Champlain with the fleet in the center until the army had enclosed the militia on the land side. When the right wing approached on July 2, 1777, the Congressional troops burned their works on the side of Lake George and withdrew. British Major General William Phillips (1731–1781) secured Mount Hope which commanded the enemy's line and cut off all communication with Lake George.

The British Army completed works to invest Fort Ticonderoga by July 5th and made a road to the top of Sugar Loaf Hill for the construction of a battery there. The Congressional forces held a council of war and decided to evacuate Ticonderoga and Mount Independence immediately. They loaded their baggage, provisions, and stores in 200 bateaux (see Photos NY-7) and sent them up the south river to Skenesborough (now Whitehall, New York) while the army took the Castletown road to reach Skenesborough by land. The British discovered the retreat at dawn on Sunday, July 6, 1777 and prepared to pursue by removing the obstructions in the water which had taken a year to build. They completed the task by 9 AM and a brigade of gunboats gave chase to the division retreating by water. The gunboats overtook the enemy near the Falls of Skenesborough, engaged and captured some of their largest galleys. The Congressional troops set the others on fire together with a considerable number of bateaux.

Photo NY-7. Bateau

Major General John Burgoyne's (1732–1792) main force approached the Falls in gunboats and the frigates *Royal George* and *Inflexible*. The cannon at the works at Skenesborough saluted them and General Burgoyne decided to return and land his army at South Bay, where some of the Congressional bateaux had taken refuge. The Congressional forces evacuated their stockade fort and other works after setting them on fire along with the mills and storehouses.

Meanwhile, Brigadier General Simon Fraser (1729–1777) led the advanced corps of grenadiers (see Photo NY-8) and light infantry in pursuit of the Congressional division that had taken the route to Hubbardton. He overtook them at 5 AM on Sunday, July 6 and engaged in the battle of Hubbardton the next day.[8]

Photo NY-8. British grenadiers (Highlanders)

Fort Ticonderoga and Fort Independence (Sept. 16, 1777)

Fort Independence was on the east side of Lake Champlain opposite Fort Ticonderoga.

★ A large body of Congressional troops surprised Fort Ticonderoga and Fort Independence on Tuesday, September 16, 1777. They captured part of four companies of the 53rd Regiment that were stationed at the Carrying Place and Sugar Loaf Hill (Mount Defiance). They also destroyed some wagons and boats before being beaten off by the garrisons from the forts. They withdrew entirely when reinforcements from Crown Point arrived.[9]

Crown Point (May 9, 12, 1775; Oct. 14, 1776; June 17, 18, 1777)

Crown Point is about 11 miles north of Fort Ticonderoga.

★ Lieutenant Colonel Ethan Allen (1738–1790), Colonel John Easton, and Captain John M. Brown (1745–1838) and their troops joined Captains Edward Mott, Noah Phelps (1740–1809) and 16 men on Monday, May 8, 1775. The party of 150 men captured Brigadier Major Philip Skene (1725–1780) and his party. The following day, at dawn, they surprised and took Fort Ticonderoga. Allen sent a detachment under Lieutenant Colonel Seth Warner (1743–1784) to Crown Point two days later. The garrison destroyed part of the works there before evacuating. When Warner's party arrived, they found nine enlisted men and ten women and children. They occupied that fort on Friday, May 12.[10]

Colonel Benedict Arnold (1741–1801) reported to the Massachusetts Committee of Safety from Crown Point that he had 150 men and that Colonel Ethan Allen's men had "in general gone home." Arnold planned to hold the fort at Crown Point until wagons and draught animals arrived to enable him to remove the cannon. He mounted "carriage guns" and swivels (see Photo NY-9) on his sloop and his schooner in case the British tried to recapture the fort on Lake Champlain.

Arnold and Allen decided to send a force to fortify Point au Fer. Allen wanted to conquer all Canada. He wrote to the New York Congress "that, with 1500 men and a proper train of artillery, I will take Montreal . . . it would be no insuperable difficulty to take Québeck."[11] However, the Continental Congress had received news of the capture

Photo NY-9. Whaleboat with swivel gun

of Fort Ticonderoga on Thursday, May 18, 1775 and decided to abandon the fort and remove all the guns and stores to the south end of Lake George. Arnold and Allen took inventory of the guns to return them when harmony was restored between Great Britain and the colonies.

Arnold, having no intention of giving up the ground he captured, wrote to the Continental Congress and to the Massachusetts Provincial Congress on May 29. He stated his surprise and alarm at the proposal which would leave "our very extensive frontiers open to the ravages of the enemy." He wrote to the Provincial Congress of New York the same day, stating how many men and supplies he would need to hold the two forts on Lake Champlain.

New England and northern New York also wanted the forts held as they feared that General Sir Guy Carleton (1724–1808), in Canada, would incite the Six Nations (Native Americans) to join an expedition to retake the two forts. The New Yorkers and New Englanders persuaded the Continental Congress to change its mind and to garrison both forts Ticonderoga and Crown Point, the strongest positions on the lake. Congress resolved, on May 31st, to request Connecticut to send strong reinforcements to Crown Point and "Ticonderogo" and New York to furnish supplies. Connecticut had already dispatched 400 men to the forts with 500 pounds of its "pittance of powder" and sent 1,000 more under Colonel Benjamin Hinman (1720–1810). Massachusetts sent a committee to determine the needs of the forts. The committee also told Arnold that he would be second in command under Hinman.[12]

Meanwhile, General George Washington (1732–1799) sent Major General Horatio Gates (1728–1806) and Major General Philip Schuyler (1733–1804) to Crown Point where they arrived on Wednesday, July 5, 1775. They held a council of war which determined that Crown Point was untenable. They decided to send the sick to Fort George and to retire to Ticonderoga.[13]

★ After the battle of Valcour Island, the survivors of Benedict Arnold's battered forces sought refuge at Crown Point before traveling overland to Fort Ticonderoga. The British re-occupied Crown Point on Monday, October 14, 1776. They held it only until

November 3rd as it was too late in the season to continue their advance, and General Sir Guy Carleton (1724–1808) decided not to attack Fort Ticonderoga. When Major General John Burgoyne (1732–1792) began his march from Canada to Albany in June 1777, he occupied it again but the fort was abandoned after his defeat four months later.[14]

★ A band of Native Americans killed two Rangers and wounded three others about halfway between Fort Ticonderoga and Crown Point on Tuesday, June 17, 1777. They captured three militiamen, killed four others and wounded three more between the French lines (constructed in 1758) and the bridge the following day.[15]

Wind Mill Point (mid-Sept. 1776)

Wind Mill Point is on Lake Champlain in the town of Alburg. It is across from Rousses Point and about 2 miles south of the Canadian border.

★ A party of sailors went ashore and were attacked by a number of Native Americans at Wind Mill Point, about 90 miles from Crown Point in mid-September 1776. The Native Americans killed three men and wounded five. When they came near the lake shore, several cannon were fired at them which dispersed them.[16]

Isle La Motte, Lake Champlain (Sept. 20, 1776)

Isle La Motte is an island in Lake Champlain north of Crown Point and just south of the Canadian border.

★ The schooner *Liberty* was cruising off Isle La Motte in Lake Champlain on Friday, September 20, 1776 when a Frenchman came down and signaled to be taken on board. The captain suspected him and approached the shore cautiously with his boat stern in, swivel guns pointed and match lit. The Frenchman waded about 15 feet from the shore. When he found he could decoy the boat no closer, he made a signal, whereupon 300 to 400 Native Americans, Canadians and Regulars emerged and fired on the boat, wounding three crewmen. The *Liberty* returned fire with the swivels and small arms. She also fired several broadsides of grape shot. Several men fell and the rest dispersed. As the *Liberty* proceeded to guard the return boats and bring down the medicine, the crew discovered about 200 or 300 Native Americans on the western shore and a large number of light birch canoes which the Native Americans could use to pass the larger vessels in the night and secure the canoes in the bushes during the daytime. Several Native Americans and Canadians lined the shore to observe the *Liberty*'s movements.

A party went ashore that evening and saw a man on the top of a house looking at them. They pushed forward through a swamp, found fresh tracks, and saw wigwams and fires. They pursued the Native Americans for some distance and took a fine horse and saddle which belonged to some Regular officer. However, the darkness of the night prevented them from overtaking the Native Americans.[17]

Valcour Island (Oct. 11–13, 1776)

Valcour Island is about 6 miles south of Plattsburgh, about 900 yards off the west shore of Lake Champlain.
 The Clinton County Historical Museum (**www.clintoncountyhistorical.org/museum.html**) has a diorama that depicts the engagement. When it moved to

smaller quarters (Cumberland Avenue and Sailly Avenue, Plattsburgh) in the summer of 2004, it loaned the diorama to an exhibit in the old high school on Front Street in Keeseville, New York.

The Smithsonian Institution's National Museum of American History in Washington, D.C. houses the gunboat *Philadelphia* (see Photo NY-10) which was one of the five 2-masted galleys and eight gunboats constructed for Benedict Arnold's fleet for the Battle of Valcour Island. The *Philadelphia*, commanded by Captain Benjamin Rue, was outfitted with a 12-pound cannon, two 9-pounders, and swivel guns. It was sunk by a 24-pound shot through the bow. It lay at the bottom of Lake Champlain with the top of the white pine mast barely 10 feet below the surface of Valcour Bay until 1935 when it was dredged up and restored. The original timbers still show evidence of holes from the musket and cannon fire. The National Museum of American History also displays many items of iron, wood, and pewter from the *Philadelphia* along with reproductions of 18th-century shipboard items.

Photo NY-10. Gunboat Philadelphia, now at the Smithsonian Institution in Washington, DC

★ During the autumn of 1776, while General William Howe (1732–1786) was routing General George Washington (1732–1799) around New York City, other British forces under Sir Guy Carleton (1724–1808) attempted to take advantage of a previous British achievement, the repulsion of an American attack on Canada the previous year. Carleton rather leisurely built a flotilla of boats to carry British forces from Canada down Lake Champlain and Lake George, intending to reduce the fort at Ticonderoga before winter set in. Brigadier General Benedict Arnold (1741–1801) countered by having 150 soldiers and craftsmen build a much weaker flotilla of 16 vessels in the summer of 1776.

The comparatively shallow water of the lake required specially designed ships, most of which consisted of small craft propelled by oars and by small sails on short, stumpy masts. The British fleet consisted of the *Inflexible*, a three-masted sloop; two schooners, the *Maria* and the *Carleton*; the *Loyal Convert*; a large gundalow (open boat about 53 feet long, 15 feet wide and almost 4 feet deep in the center), and about 20 gunboats, each with one gun. They also had four longboats armed with field cannon; 24 bateaux (see Photo NY-7) which carried provisions; and a 422-ton sailing scow, the *Thunderer*. The *Thunderer* was 92 feet long and more than 33 feet wide and carried 300 men, howitzers, and 24-pound and 6-pound guns. However, Arnold disposed his fleet in such a way as to make it impossible for the *Thunderer* to take part in the battle.

Arnold's fleet consisted of the schooners *Liberty* and *Royal Savage* and the sloop *Enterprise*. He also had another schooner built called the *Revenge*, as well as the cutter *Lee*, four galleys: the *Washington, Congress, Trumbull,* and *Gates*, (about 72 feet long, 20 feet wide and 6 feet deep); and eight flat-bottomed gundalows. These ships which comprised the colonial navy carried from 45 to 80 men each and were armed with everything from 2-pounders and smaller swivel guns to 18-pounders.

Arnold's boats waited behind Valcour Island between the island and the west shore of Lake Champlain. They were arranged in a line with their broadside guns facing south. Carleton sailed south with his flotilla on Friday, October 11, 1776 searching for Arnold's boats. He came around the north of Valcour Island and bypassed Arnold by 2 miles without realizing it. When he realized his mistake, he had to turn around and sail into a strong north wind.

While Arnold's line position gave him maximum advantage against a superior enemy force, he made the mistake of sending the *Royal Savage* toward the enemy with orders to return to the line of battle when spotted. Four of the fastest boats, *Royal Savage, Congress, Trumbull,* and *Washington,* would inflict whatever damage they could. When he saw the size of the enemy fleet, Arnold signaled all his ships back to the line of battle, but most of the crew were amateur sailors at best. The *Royal Savage* ran aground in shallow water near the southwest tip of Valcour Island (a marker on U.S. 9 is directly opposite the spot).

The *Carleton* approached the *Royal Savage* to fire on her, but she experienced the same trouble with the adverse wind. She dropped anchor and prepared to fire. Most of the British gunboats lined up with the *Carleton* across the channel and a general engagement followed at about 12:30. The *Carleton* was severely damaged and her skipper seriously wounded. Two smaller boats had to tow the *Carleton* out of the action.

The *Royal Savage* continued firing until the *Thunderer* sent a landing party of Native Americans and Regulars to drive off the gunners. Later, a crew from the *Maria* burned the *Royal Savage* which exploded when the flames reached the magazine. The battle continued until the *Inflexible* managed to bring her guns into effective range. She fired five broadsides and put most of Arnold's guns out of action. The engagement lasted until darkness set in.

Believing he had Arnold trapped, Sir Guy Carleton held his position and prepared to destroy the enemy fleet the next day. But Arnold took advantage of a fog cover and a good northeast wind at his back to sail his boats in single file between the British line and the shore to escape out into the lake. He left the burned-out hulk of the *Royal Savage* behind and the gundalow *Philadelphia* which sank about an hour after the battle ended.

The wind turned during the night and blew from the south. Arnold was only 8 miles from Carleton's ships by daybreak and both fleets had to row into the wind. The wind turned again on October 13, allowing the British to close the gap. They began raking Arnold's boats with broadsides about 11 AM, forcing the galley *Washington* to surrender and the cutter *Lee* to run aground. Arnold's flagship, the *Congress*, and four gundalows continued to resist, moving south as fast as they could.

Carleton recognized Arnold on board the *Congress* and concentrated his attention on him, but Arnold turned into the wind and rowed across the lake to the Vermont shore to escape. He beached the rest of his fleet in Buttonmold Bay (near Panton, Vermont) and marched 10 miles to Crown Point with 200 men. The *Trumbull, Enterprise, Revenge,* and *Liberty* arrived at Crown Point before him. Arnold burned the fort there and withdrew to Fort Ticonderoga.

Arnold lost the naval battle along with 11 of his boats and more than a hundred men killed, wounded, and captured. But he delayed Carleton's advance down the Hudson Valley by more than six months—long enough that the British commander reached Ticonderoga too late in the year to undertake a siege. Carleton returned his army to winter quarters at St. John's, Canada, leaving the British with no advance base from which to launch the following year's campaign. This limited victory did little to dispel the gloom that fell on the Congressional forces after General George Washington's (1732–1799) defeats in New York.

The British, aware that Continental enlistments expired at the end of the year, had high hopes that the Continental Army would simply fade away and the rebellion collapse. Howe halted General Charles Cornwallis's (1738–1805) pursuit of Washington and sent General Henry Clinton (1730–1795) with a detachment of troops under naval escort to seize Newport, Rhode Island. Clinton occupied Rhode Island without resistance and used Newport as a base to harass American shipping. Howe then dispersed his troops in winter quarters, establishing a line of posts in New Jersey at Perth Amboy, New Brunswick, Princeton, Trenton, and Bordentown, and retired himself to New York. Howe had gained the object of the 1776 campaign, a strong foothold, and possibly, as he thought at the time, a great deal more.[18]

Split Rock (Oct. 13, 1776)

Split Rock is at the southwestern end of Lake Champlain about 30 miles north of Ticonderoga.

★ The British overtook Brigadier General Benedict Arnold's (1741–1801) battered squadron just south of Split Rock in Lake Champlain on Sunday, October 13, 1776 as it was fleeing south after the battle of Valcour Island. They captured the galley *Washington*. The galley *Congress* and three gondolas (*Boston, New Haven* and *Spitfire*) were beached at Ferris Bay (now Arnold's Bay, Vermont). The vessels were burned to prevent their capture.[19]

Utica
Fort Stanwix/Schuyler (June 25, 1777; July 3, 1777; July 27, 1777; Aug. 2–22, 24, 1777; June 11, 1778; July 27, 1780; Oct. 8, 1780; Mar. 2, 1781; Apr. 1781; before Aug. 1, 1781)
Moses Kill (Aug. 2, 1777)

> Fort Stanwix, later called Fort Schuyler, was situated on rising ground at the upper end of the Mohawk River, about 300 yards from its source, and about half a mile from the source of Wood Creek which runs into Lake Oneida. The fort was leveled by 1830. However, it was later reconstructed to its 1777 appearance, before the nation's Bicentennial.
> Fort Stanwix National Monument (**www.nps.gov/fost/**) is off Route NY 26 in downtown Rome, New York.

★ The British built Fort Stanwix in 1758 after the outbreak of the French and Indian War to replace three smaller forts that protected the Oneida Carry, a short stretch of level ground between the Mohawk River and Wood Creek. This short portage was the only obstacle for canoe travelers to go from the Great Lakes to the Atlantic Ocean. The fort, named for its builder Brigadier General John Stanwix (1690–1765), never saw action in the French and Indian War, so the British neglected and abandoned it when they won Canada in 1763.

Congressional troops under Colonel Elias Dayton (1737–1807) repaired and restored the fort in June 1776 at the outbreak of the American War for Independence. For a while it was called Fort Schuyler in honor of Major General Philip Schuyler (1733–1804), a leading and powerful figure in this part of the state.

Colonel Peter Gansevoort's (1749–1812) garrison at Fort Stanwix lost two soldiers on a hunting party on Wednesday, June 25, 1777. Native Americans attacked them and killed one and severely wounded the other. [20]

★ A party of 16 men, under Ensign John Spoor (1750–1834), were cutting sod at the Wood Creek Landing, about a mile from the fort, on Thursday, July 3, 1777, when a band of Native Americans fired on them. A party of men went from the fort to help them, but arrived a little too late. One of the men lay on the road scalped and half dead. Another was shot through both arms. A third man was found dead about 2 miles further with a tomahawk sticking in his head and scalped. The relief party returned to the fort toward evening and brought in the wounded and the dead men. Four men and the ensign were taken prisoners.[21]

★ The garrison was alarmed with the firing of four guns at 3 PM on Sunday, July 27, 1777. A party of men immediately went to the edge of the woods, about 500 yards from Fort Stanwix, where the guns were fired. They found the bodies of three girls who were picking raspberries. Two of them had been tomahawked and scalped. One was dead and the other died about half an hour after she was brought home. The third girl had two balls through her shoulder but managed to escape. The four Native Americans who attacked them had disappeared.[22]

★ Although Major General Philip Schuyler (1733–1804) had received reinforcements on July 12th and 29th that brought his troops to nearly 2,900 Continental soldiers and more than 1,600 militiamen present and fit for duty, he knew they could not hold dilapidated Fort Stanwix. He left a small rear guard under Colonel Peter Gansevoort to take care of it until the enemy came. General Schuyler withdrew down the Hudson, first about 5 miles to Moses Creek, then to Saratoga where he arrived on Sunday, August 3, 1777.[23]

★ By July 1777, the fort was garrisoned with 750 troops when Major General John Burgoyne (1722–1792) made it a prime objective in his New York campaign. He sent Lieutenant Colonel Barry St. Leger (1737–1789) with 700 Regulars and 1,000 Loyalists and Native Americans as a diversion to move via Lake Ontario to Oswego, and then march down the Mohawk Valley to join Burgoyne outside of Albany. Joseph Brant (1742–1807), Mohawk Chief Thayendanagea, led another 900 Native American braves to augment St. Leger's force. Most of the Native warriors came from the Mohawk tribe, the most powerful tribe in the Iroquois League whose Six Nations included the Mohawks, Onondagas, Cayugas, Senecas, Oneidas, and Tuscaroras. They marched against Fort Stanwix on July 26 to clear the western approach to Albany and to serve as a diversion to draw troops away from Albany. They traveled about 10 miles a day through the wilderness with some light pieces of artillery. Meanwhile, Burgoyne led the main army of 7,200 British and Hessian Regulars along with 650 Loyalists, Canadians and Native Americans down Lake Champlain to Fort Ticonderoga and then via Lake George to the Hudson.

St. Leger arrived at Fort Stanwix on Sunday, August 3—the same day that Burgoyne learned that General William Howe (1732–1786) was not headed north but south to Philadelphia. He besieged the garrison until August 8, 1777. The garrison consisted of only 750 men commanded by Colonel Peter Gansevoort (1749–1812). St. Leger demanded Gansevoort's surrender, threatening to massacre the defenders and the settlers along the Mohawk. Fearing massacre by the Native Americans, Gansevoort's men were determined to hold out to the bitter end. He "rejected with disdain" St. Leger's demand for surrender.

St. Leger, lacking adequate artillery, decided against a frontal assault, so he and his 1,700 men surrounded the fort and settled into a siege. They fired at the fort with light cannon, small mortars (see Photo NY-6) and small arms. The fort returned fire which continued sporadically until August 22nd. During this time, the Crown forces approach to within 150 paces of the fort. They came no nearer because of the musket fire. They withdrew after killing three and wounding nine. Both sides had a few deserters.

On Monday, August 4, Brigadier General Nicholas Herkimer's (1728–1777) Tryon County militia set out to relieve the fort. However, they were ambushed two days later in a wooded ravine near Oriskany about a mile or two from Fort Stanwix. The militia, under the direction of a mortally wounded Herkimer, scattered in the woods and fought a bloody afternoon's battle in a summer thunderstorm. Both sides suffered heavy losses, and though the militiamen were unable to relieve Fort Stanwix, the casualties they inflicted on St. Leger's Native Americans and Loyalists discouraged the Native Americans, who had already become restless during the static siege operation. Moreover, a sortie from the fort pillaged the camps. The departure of the Native Americans forced the British and Loyalists to abandon the siege.

See also **Oriskany.**

When Schuyler learned of the plight of the Stanwix garrison, he detached Major General Benedict Arnold (1741–1801) with 950 Continentals to relieve them, despite his own weak position before Burgoyne. Arnold left from Fort Dayton (the present day village of Herkimer), 30 miles to the south, and took advantage of the dissatisfaction of St. Leger's Native Americans. Employing a Dutchman, his clothes shot full of holes, and a friendly Oneida as his messengers, he spread the rumor that the Continentals were approaching "as numerous as the leaves on the trees." The Native Americans, who had special respect for any insane person, departed in haste, scalping many of their Loyalist allies as they went. With half his force gone, St. Leger was forced to abandon the siege and retreat to Oswego.[24]

★ Colonel Gansevoort began a heavy cannonade (see Photo NY-3, NY-4) at 11 AM on Friday, August 22, 1777 which the enemy returned with "a number of shells and cannon." Seven deserters arrived about 3 PM and informed him that Gen. St. Leger had learned that Major General John Burgoyne's (1732–1792) army had been defeated and that Major General Benedict Arnold (1741–1801) was nearby with a reinforcement of 3,000 men and 10 cannon for the garrison. Colonel St. Leger retreated quickly with all his troops, leaving considerable baggage and their tents standing. Colonel Gansevoort sent out a party of about 60 men to confirm the intelligence. They returned a short while later and verified the reports.[25]

★ Colonel Gansevoort sent out two wagons with 50 men. They killed two Native Americans, took four prisoners and loaded the wagons. Parties were sent out on Saturday, August 23rd. They brought in three prisoners, six mortars, a 3-pound fieldpiece carriage with all its apparatus, a quantity of baggage, ammunition, camp equipment, and a great number of other articles left by the retreating troops: 23 bateaux (see Photo NY-7); 19 wagons without wheels; two traveling and lumber carriages; 242 3- and 6-pound round shot, 87 of which had fixed flannel cartridges; 27 oil and two hair cloths; eight coil and 300 fathoms of rope; 128 shells; 27 boxes of damaged cartridges; 30 copper hoops; 11 sets of men's harness; eight boxes of musket balls; 2160 musket cartridges; two tanned hides; five deer skins; five camp stools; six mattresses; six pairs of sheets; 18 bed cases; 10 knapsacks; one case of soap; four yards of thread; four brass candlesticks; 14 pewter plates; 250 pounds of iron; 128 pounds of sterling; 106 spades; 100 picks; 80 axes; one set of blacksmith's tools; two casks of nails; two whip saws; three cross cut saws; two hand saws; two barrels of tar; one barrel of pitch; 100 tent poles; 54 tents; five bell tents; one brass and 24 camp kettles; 40 canteens; four frying pans; 56 blankets; 40 coats; 36 blanket coats; 34 pairs of breeches; two pairs of white breeches; 20 white and 49 speckled shirts; 54 pairs of stockings; 20 handkerchiefs; and many smaller articles. They also took several milk cows and horses and 30 or 40 casks of flour.

Several scouts returned the following day with a German prisoner who reported that the Native Americans attacked the scattered Regulars and Loyalists about 10 miles from the fort. The prisoner said he took the soldiers' arms and stabbed them with their own bayonets. He and nine other Germans had fled to the woods in fear; but he was the only one to survive.[26]

★ Major General Arnold made a forced march of 22 miles through a thick wood and arrived at Fort Schuyler at 5 PM on August 24, 1777, expecting to harass the retreating enemy. Colonel Gansevoort had already sent out a small party that captured four Regulars and a considerable quantity of baggage and a number of prisoners and deserters. Most of the Regulars had already boarded their boats at Oneida Lake and got out of range of the pursuers. General Arnold sent out a party of friendly Oneidas that evening and ordered 500 men to go as far as Oneida Lake early the following morning.[27]

★ Some British-allied Native Americans ambushed a timber cutting party at Fort Schuyler on Thursday, June 11, 1778. They killed one and wounded another.[28]

★ About 800 British, Germans, Loyalists and Native Americans approached Fort Schuyler on Thursday, July 27, 1780 after burning the Oneida village of Kanowalohale. The residents sought refuge at Fort Schuyler. When Joseph Brant (1742–1807), Mohawk Chief Thayendanagea paraded his men in front of the fort, Lieutenant Colonel John Graham had the garrison fire its cannon at them. This drove the attackers away.[29]

★ Colonel William Malcom or Malcolm (1745–1791) was on his way to Fort Schuyler with relief troops about Sunday, October 8, 1780 when they encountered some enemy Native Americans. The troops charged and routed them, killing two.[30]

★ The Schoharie Valley had enjoyed comparative peace for about two months when Joseph Brant (1742–1807), Mohawk Chief Thayendanagea went on the warpath again in January 1781. The Governor of Canada, General Sir Frederick Haldimand (1718–1791), had sent an expedition to destroy the Oneida villages in 1780 as punishment for supporting the Congressional forces. The Oneidas fled to the white settlements near Schenectady for shelter and food. Brant visited German Flats in small parties and continued their destruction.

★ A band of 110 of Brant's Mohawks and 30 Rangers executed a surprise attack on the woodcutters from Colonel Philip Van Cortlandt's (1749–1831) 2nd New York Continentals and a covering party of a corporal and 16 men about 10 AM on Saturday, March 2, 1781 as they were bringing provisions to Fort Stanwix. The attackers cut them off, killed and scalped one of them and captured the rest. A similar party was captured in April. Fort Stanwix was abandoned in May after being partly damaged by floods and destroyed in a fire. The garrison moved to Fort Dayton and Fort Plain.[31]

★ Colonel Marinus Willett (1740–1830) and about 250 New York militiamen fell in with about 300 Native Americans and Loyalists above Fort Stanwix before Wednesday, August 1, 1781. A three-hour skirmish ensued. The Native Americans and Loyalists withdrew, leaving 90 killed and wounded.[32]

Whitehall (July 6, 1777; ca. Mar. 22, 1780)

> What is now Whitehall, New York, was Skenesborough, Vermont, in the 18th century. Major Philip Skene (1725–1780) owned 60,000 acres at the southern tip of Lake Champlain. The source of Wood Creek runs into Lake Oneida

See also **Skenesborough** and **Mount Independence.**

★ Major General William Phillips (1731–1781), Major General John Burgoyne's (1732–1792) second in command and an artilleryman, directed his men to position four 12-pounders on Mount Defiance, a mile to the southwest of Fort Ticonderoga. The guns were in place by noon of Sunday, July 6, 1777, making the fort untenable. Major General Arthur St. Clair (1737–1818) ordered the fort evacuated. He retreated with the main body by way of Castleton, Vermont.

Soon after daylight on Sunday, July 6, 1777, Brigadier General Simon Fraser (1729–1777) sent news to General Burgoyne that the Rebels were retiring and that he was advancing with his pickets. Fraser occupied Fort Ticonderoga and raised the British colors. He then set out to pursue the 2,000 Rebels by land while Burgoyne would pursue by water.

One column fled down Lake Champlain in 220 bateaux (see Photo NY-7), covered by five armed galleys. Commodore Skeffington Lutwidge's (1737–1814) officers and seamen made a passage through the great bridge within half an hour. The great bridge consisted of 22 "sunken piers of large timber, at nearly equal distances; the space between were made of separate floats, each about fifty feet long and twelve feet wide, strongly fastened together by chains and rivets, and also fastened to the sunken piers. Before this bridge was a boom, made of very large pieces of timber, fastened together by riveted bolts and double chains, made of iron an inch and a half square."[33]

The gunboats moved forward and immediately cut the boom and one of the intermediate floats, permitting the frigates to pass. General Burgoyne arrived at South Bay, within 3 miles of Skenesborough about 3 PM with the *Royal George* and *Inflexible* and the best sailing gunboats. The Whigs were posted in a stockaded fort, with their armed galleys in the falls below.

General Burgoyne immediately disembarked 850 troops from the 9th, 20th, and 21st Regiments who ascended the mountains intending to get behind the fort and cut off the retreat, but the Whigs fled so fast that this maneuver was ineffectual. The gunboats and frigates proceeded to Skenesborough Falls, where the armed vessels were posted, and attacked immediately. Two vessels soon struck their colors. The other three were blown up. The Whigs had previously prepared combustible materials to set fire to the fort, mills, storehouses and bateaux in case of attack. Most of the officers' baggage was burned, sunk or captured. The detachment left behind to set the fires then retired to join the main body which fled when Burgoyne's troops were ascending the mountain. Burgoyne captured 30 prisoners, including two wounded officers, a great quantity of provisions and some arms. The number of casualties is not known.[34]

The British troops landed at Skenesborough the next day. Although General Burgoyne captured Skenesborough, he failed to trap the defenders who retreated toward Albany. Lieutenant Colonel John Hill and the 9th Regiment pursued the Whigs along 12 miles of rugged wilderness road to Fort Anne and camped a mile from the fort. They skirmished with Colonel Pierse Long's (1739–1789) rear guard of 220 men under Captain James Gray (1749–1822). Colonel Hill killed two, wounded three and captured several boats full of invalids, camp followers and other baggage as they tried to escape up Wood Creek. He lost three men killed.

Early on July 8, a Whig who claimed to be a deserter arrived in Lieutenant Colonel Hill's camp to report that the 1,000 troops at Fort Anne were demoralized, fearing an attack. Hill had only 190 officers and men and did not think it prudent to attack. Nor could he retreat safely; so he held his position and called for reinforcements.

The "deserter" escaped to Fort Anne and reported how weak the British detachment was. Colonel Henry B. van Rensselaer had arrived at the fort with 400 New York militiamen and set out at 10:30 AM with Colonel Long to annihilate Lieutenant Colonel Hill camped in a narrow, heavily wooded area between Wood Creek and a steep, 500-foot ridge. Hill and his men fought their attackers for two hours as they tried to reach the top of the ridge. Attacked from all sides and their ammunition running low, the British heard a Native American war whoop from the north, alerting them that General Burgoyne was arriving from Skenesborough with reinforcements. The Congressional troops, who also were low on ammunition, broke off the engagement, burned Fort Anne, and retreated to Fort Edward. The "reinforcements" turned out to be Captain Money who advanced alone when his Native Americans refused to follow him. The British captured at least 128 pieces of artillery from the northern posts and the armed vessels at Skenesborough. They also captured a considerable amount of flour, biscuit, pork, and beef. Major General Arthur St. Clair (1737–1818) joined Major General Philip Schuyler (1733–1804) at Fort Edward on July 12, bringing the Congressional forces there to about 4,400 men, including militiamen.[35]

★ Colonel Philip Skene (1725–1780) and a party of 100 Native Americans and three Loyalists set out in pursuit of a party of Native Americans who had burned Colonel Skene's house and murdered a soldier in March 1780. They attacked some militiamen and civilians, killed two and captured 10 around Sunday, March 22, 1780.[36]

Fort Anne (July 6, 8, 1777; July 23, 1777; Oct. 10, 1780)
Fort Edward (Oct. 10, 1780)

> Fort Anne was a small stockade, 7 miles south of the head of South Bay, 20 miles east-northeast from Fort George, and 14 miles from Fort Edward. It was located at modern Fort Ann, on U.S. 4 about midway between Fort Edward and Whitehall (formerly Skenesboro). A marker to the east of U.S. 4 and just south of the bridge identifies the "Oldest House" which was part of the site of the stockaded fort. A well that served the fort is diagonally across the highway and 100 feet west on Charles Street. A reconstructed blockhouse just north of the Oldest House is a replica of what is presumed to be the British fort of 1757.

The day after the garrison of Fort Ticonderoga was evacuated (July 6, 1777), Fort Anne was reinforced with 100 men under the command of Lieutenant Colonel Henry B. van Rensselaer on Tuesday, July 8, 1777. They drove in 90 head of fat cattle. A few men went in search of a bateau shortly after they arrived. About 15 minutes later, Captain Samuel Montgomery (1732–1808) and a party of about 150 attacked the people who sought refuge at the fort. They consisted of a party of light armed foreigners (some Canadians and Native Americans) and Colonel van Rensselaer's Claverack militia. The Crown forces gave way after a few minutes and were pursued for 2 miles. The attackers withdrew to Skenesborough where the militiamen surrounded a large scouting party.

The militiamen requested volunteers to turn out with them. Half the militia was ordered up on the first alarm and the other half later. They engaged the Crown forces in a smart skirmish and captured Captain Montgomery, wounded in the leg, a lieutenant, ensign, doctor and some privates. Philip van Rensselaer, the Lieutenant Colonel's brother, was wounded in the thigh.[37]

★ General John Nixon (1725–1815) set off for Fort Edward with his brigade of about 1,000 on Wednesday, July 9, 1777 to obstruct the passages and intercept the enemy's scouts. They captured five, three of them masquerading as Native Americans, between Fort Anne and Skenesborough on Wednesday, July 23, 1777. When they were washed, they were identified as Loyalists from Fort Edward.[38]

See also **Whitehall** and **Mount Independence.**

★ A picket guard of a party on the Fort Anne Road was attacked by a band of British troops and Native Americans about noon on Wednesday, July 23, 1777. The attackers killed and scalped one man and killed and wounded 12 others, five mortally before being driven off.[39]

★ On Monday, August 4, 1777, three Hessian deserters reported that they lost 72 men killed at Fort Anne, including two majors, three Native Americans and a great many wounded. They also reported that a dispute arose between the Brunswickers and the British a short time before because their ration of rum was detained. The Brunswickers killed 82 British in the fray. They thought that 2,000 men might have been able to withstand 10,000 Crown troops because of the advantageous passes of Ticonderoga and Mount Independence and they were surprised to find the forts evacuated. They also reported capturing 200 Congressional troops asleep in a barn on the retreat.[40]

★ Major Christopher Carleton (1749–1787) and a body of 778 British, Loyalist, and Native American troops appeared before Fort Anne on Tuesday morning October 3, 1780 and demanded the fort to surrender. Captain Seth Sherwood (1720–1781 or 1747–1820) refused but was compelled to surrender it a week later.[41]

Captain Sherwood garrisoned Fort Anne with two lieutenants and 75 men. His scouts informed him of the enemy's approach on Monday, October 9th. He immediately communicated that information to Colonel Henry Beekman Livingston (1750–1831), who commanded at Fort Edward; but Colonel Livingston did not forward it to his superiors.

Two gentlemen who occasionally rode out, and narrowly escaped capture that day, informed Colonel Livingston about noon on Tuesday, the 10th, that the enemy had captured Fort Anne and were quickly moving toward Kingsbury, burning and destroying everything before them. Colonel Livingston dispatched expresses from Fort Edward but did not send any to Fort George, even though the communication route was open until 3 PM. The Crown forces surrounded Colonel Livingston and took him and between 50 and 75 men prisoners. The militia had marched to Half-Moon to come to his assistance when they learned of the surrender and were ordered to return. An express was sent to Fort Edward on Wednesday the 11th, as the garrison had been without provisions for two days. The express discovered a party of Native Americans near Bloody Pond, about 1.5 miles from the fort, and returned.[42]

Fort Edward (July 27, 1777)

Fort Edward (www.revolutionaryday.com/usroute4/ftedward/default.htm) is on the portage trail between the Hudson River and Lake Champlain on Route U.S. 4.

A small pyramid on the west side of Route U.S. 4 marks the site of the house Jane McCrea was visiting when she was captured. The house (modern street number 219) is opposite the high school. Jane McCrea was originally buried off U.S. 4, 2 miles south of Fort Edward; but her remains were later moved to the Union Cemetery on Broadway (see Photo NY-11).

A marker on the west side (right) of Route U.S. 4 south marks the approximate location of the northeast bastion (see Photo NY-1, NY-2) of Fort Edward. Following U.S. 4 and proceeding straight on Montgomery Street when U.S. 4 turns to the left, one comes to Old Fort Street. Turning right onto Old Fort Street, one can see a marker on the right (north) identifying the low ground as part of the old moat. A few hundred feet further down the road toward the river, a marker identifies the site of the barracks and other parts of the fort opposite Rogers Island.

Rogers Island Visitors Center (11 Rogers Island Drive, Fort Edward, New York) includes historical displays, videos and archaeological artifacts that detail Fort Edward's earliest known Native American inhabitants through the War for American Independence. The location was one of the largest British forts in the colonies during the Seven Years War and the main base camp for Rogers Rangers, 1757–1759. It was strategically located on the military trail during the War for American Independence.[43]

The Old Fort House Museum (29 Broadway, U.S. Route 4 website: www.ftedward.com/History/OldFort/oldFort.htm), located just to the west of U.S. 4 and 0.1 mile beyond its junction with Route NY 197, is a regional museum which has a scale model of old Fort Edward. Constructed in 1772 as a private residence for Patrick Smyth, the Old Fort House is one of the oldest frame structures in upstate New York. It served as headquarters for both British and Continental generals in the American War for Independence. General George Washington and his party dined here on two different occasions in July 1783. The museum includes five additional buildings.

Photo NY-11. Jane McCrea's grave marker

★ Major General John Burgoyne (1722–1792), in a psychological ploy to terrorize the Whigs, issued a proclamation on Monday, June 23, 1777, that called on the Loyalists to join him, offered protection to those who sided with the King, and threatened to turn the Native Americans loose on the Whigs. A few days later, however, he told his Native American allies they must conduct the war in a civilized manner. They were not to scalp or torture the wounded and prisoners, nor were they to harm old men, women or children. Burgoyne's announcement, though meant to be threatening, used stilted language that provoked only laughter and ridicule in the colonies and even in the House of Commons in London.

Moving south, Burgoyne's next logical objective after the capture of Fort Ticonderoga was Fort Edward on the Hudson River. Burgoyne could choose one of two routes to reach Fort Edward. He could travel overland via Fort Anne, a distance of 23 miles over poor or nonexistent roads through a wilderness of tall trees, deep ravines, marshes, and creeks swollen by abnormally heavy rains. Or he could travel up Lake George and cross the country to a point on the Hudson north of Fort Edward. This latter route had its own difficulties, for the falls and rapids between Lake Champlain and Lake George would require a portage (carrying gear overland) of about 3 miles. Yet taking the poor road between Lake George and the Hudson would reduce his total march to only 10 miles.

Burgoyne proceeded through the forest with his troops but sent his boats, artillery and other heavy equipment by the easier roundabout route. Major General Philip Schuyler (1733–1804) made his trek even more difficult by destroying bridges, cutting trees across the path and digging trenches to let the waters of swamps onto usually dry ground. To further hinder the British troops, the Whigs encouraged local residents to drive off their horses and cattle and burn their crops. Such obstacles reduced the British advance to a snail's pace, an average of one mile a day. The British persisted, however, and arrived at Fort Edward on Monday, July 29, 1777. Burgoyne was desperately short of horses, wagons, and oxen, yet Schuyler, with an unstable force of only 4,500 men who had been discouraged by continual retreats, was in no position to give battle.

Burgoyne's army passed through Fort Edward on July 30. The Continentals abandoned and burned the fort before leaving for Stillwater, about 30 miles north of Albany. Burgoyne needed more baggage animals to continue his slow march, so he decided to take Major General Baron Friedrich von Riedesel's (1738–1800) advice and raid a magazine established by the New England militia at Bennington. They had reports that the magazine contained large supplies of food and ammunition and had at least 100 horses.

The worst single incident for the British-Native American alliance happened away from the field of battle. A 23-year-old white woman named Jane "Jenny" McCrea (1754–1777), the daughter of a Presbyterian minister, was being escorted through the woods by a Native American war party to meet her fiancé, Lieutenant David Jones (1736–1820), a Loyalist officer serving with the British. Somewhere along the way, she was killed on Sunday, July 27, 1777 by her "protectors" in a quarrel over their reward money. When the news spread across the New York frontier, it caused both terror and anger among the people. Wyandot Panther was accused of the crime but went unpunished because Burgoyne felt he could not afford to offend his Native American allies. The incident occurred at a time when the Native Americans raided the farms and settlements of eastern New York and western Vermont, stiffening the Whigs' resolve to resist Burgoyne and thus contributed to his defeat.

After the McCrea incident, British commanders encouraged the Native Americans to return to small-scale raids on frontier farms and settlements. The British hoped that this strategy would damage civilian morale, disrupt food production and force the Continentals to transfer troops from the major eastern battlefields to garrison duty in the West.[44]

Schuylerville
Stillwater
Saratoga (July 29, 30, 1777; Aug. 2–5, 1777; Sept. 19, 1777; Oct. 7, 1777; Sept. 23, 25, 1781)
Bemis Heights (Sept. 13, 15, 25, 27, 28, 1777)

> Schuylerville, known as Saratoga in 1777, was originally a Native American camping ground. French refugees settled here by 1688 and named it Saratoga. It was renamed Schuylerville in 1831 to honor Major General Philip Schuyler. Stillwater was also part of Saratoga.
>
> Saratoga National Historical Park (**www.nps.gov/sara/index.htm**) is 8 miles south of Schuylerville on Route U.S. 4. It covers 2,800 acres and embraces partially wooded country along the west side of the Hudson River. Bemis Heights is a few miles south of Saratoga. Fort Miller was on the Hudson River south of Fort Edward.
>
> A visitor center on Fraser Hill, the highest point in the park, affords a view of the battlefield and the surrounding area. A 9.5-mile scenic driving tour has 10 stops, including the key British redoubts and scenes of action. A unique monument depicts a granite boot, epaulets, and an inscription documenting Benedict Arnold's heroics but does not mention his name.
>
> The Saratoga Victory Monument (**www.victoryatsaratoga.com/visitors.htm**) is 8 miles from the battlefield on Burgoyne Street (Route NY 338) west of Route U.S. 4. It commemorates Major General John Burgoyne's (1722–1792) surrender. The monument was started during the Battle of Saratoga Centennial in 1877 and finished six years later. Its 184 iron stairs lead to the top of the 154-foot, 6-inch monument which overlooks the battlefield sites. Niches around the monument contain life-size bronze statues of Philip Schuyler facing his home to the east; Daniel Morgan, commander of his celebrated riflemen, facing west; and Horatio Gates looking to the north. The fourth niche remains empty, commemorating the leadership of Benedict Arnold who later turned traitor (see Photo NY-12).
>
> The Field of Grounded Arms is on Ferry Street (Route NY 29), one block east of Route U.S. 4. The site is noted only by a small marker.

★ After the Crown forces arrived at Fort George with 27 boats and a large sailboat on Monday, July 28, 1777, they killed one of Colonel John Nixon's (1727–1815) sentries and two men at Fort Miller on the 29th. They crossed the river to the west side on the 30th and attacked the rear of the Continental Army under Brigadier General John Glover (1732–1797), killed one soldier, mortally wounded a lieutenant and wounded four privates. The Crown forces lost an estimated 10 men killed.

★ On Friday, August 1, Crown forces were seen in several places. Lurking Native Americans killed three men, scalping two of them in sight of the camp on the East side of the Hudson. On the 3rd, they killed five more men, wounded seven, scalped another and took two officers and six soldiers prisoners. The Continentals retreated at 6 PM with all their baggage and supplies. They burned nine large bridges and took two Loyalists prisoners. General Glover's brigade arrived at Stillwater at 10 AM on Monday, August 4, a very rainy day, after burning four large bridges on the road. He lost 27 men killed and 30 captured in the previous four days.[45]

Photo NY-12. Saratoga Victory Monument

★ A Continental scout captured five British soldiers at Saratoga on Saturday, September 13, 1777. Another scouting party was driven back by British-allied Native Americans near Bemis Heights on Monday, September 15, 1777. Yet another scouting party clashed with a British outpost at Bemis Heights on the morning of Thursday, September 25, 1777. They took one prisoner and killed eight pickets. The following day, the Continentals captured 16 prisoners in several parties. One of the prisoners deserted on Saturday morning and another prisoner was brought to camp.[46]

Major General John Burgoyne (1722–1792) submitted a plan to the British ministry called "Thoughts for Conducting the War from the Side of Canada" on February 28, 1777. This plan which became the basis for British military strategy in 1777 aimed to cut the American colonies along the Hudson River by moving on Albany. However, Burgoyne suffered defeats at Bennington and Fort Stanwix on the way to Albany. He lost a large percentage of his troops; most of his Native Americans became disheartened and left. He dared not send another detachment in search of supplies fearing it would meet a similar fate as at Bennington. So he had to get everything he needed from Canada which meant a month's delay. Every day that he waited in position, the Congressional forces grew stronger.

Congress deferred to New England sentiment on August 19 and replaced Major General Philip Schuyler (1733–1804) with Major General Horatio Gates (1728–1806). Gates was more the beneficiary than the cause of the improved situation, but his appointment helped morale and encouraged the New England militiamen. General George Washington's (1732–1799) emissary, Major General Benjamin Lincoln (1733–1810), also did his part.

In the first week of September, Major General Benedict Arnold (1741–1801) returned from a successful expedition against General Barry St. Leger (1737–1789) at Fort Stanwix. Colonel Daniel Morgan (1736–1802) arrived with riflemen from Washington's army. General Gates understood Burgoyne's plight perfectly and adapted his tactics to take full advantage of it. He advanced his forces 4 miles northward on Friday, September 12 and took up a position surveyed and prepared by the Polish engineer, Colonel Thaddeus Kosciusko (1746–1817), on Bemis Heights, a few miles south of Saratoga. Gates placed three brigades—about 3000 men—and most of his artillery on the right. He placed his center brigade under Brigadier General Ebenezer Learned (1728–1801) a little to the west near Mr. Nielson's farmhouse.

Freeman's Farm

★ By early September 1777, Burgoyne knew he could expect help from neither General William Howe (1732–1786) nor Lieutenant Colonel Barry St. Leger (1737–1789). Disillusioned about the Loyalists, he wrote Colonial Secretary Sir George Germain (1716–1785):

> The great bulk of the country is undoubtedly with Congress in principle and zeal, and their measures are executed with a secrecy and dispatch that are not to be equalled. Wherever the King's forces point, militia in the amount of three or four thousand assemble in twenty-four hours; they bring with them their subsistence, etc., and the alarm over, they return to their farms.[47]

Nevertheless, gambler that he was, General Burgoyne began crossing to the west bank of the Hudson at Saratoga (now Schuylerville) on his southward march. He crossed on a bridge of boats September 13 and 14, signaling his intention to get to Albany or lose his army. While his supply problem daily became worse, his Native Americans, with a natural instinct for sensing approaching disaster, drifted off into the forests, leaving him with little means of gaining intelligence of the enemy dispositions.

On Saturday morning, September 19, 1777, General Burgoyne engaged the Continentals in the Battle of Freeman's Farm. He advanced toward their position about 10 AM with an army reduced to 6,000 men. (He had left Canada with 10,000). He planned to use 4,200 to attack and 1,800 to act as a reserve and guard his boats and supplies. He divided the 4,200 men into three columns. Brigadier General Simon Fraser (1729–1777) commanded the strongest column of about 2,000 men on the right or the west end of the line. His objective was to take the unfortified high ground overlooking the Continental defenses from the west. Brigadier General James Hamilton (ca. 1710–1783) commanded the center column of 1,100 men. Major General Baron Friedrich von Riedesel (1738–1800) led the left column of about 1,100 men near the Hudson River.

General Gates waited for the Crown forces to attack. His scouts could see the enemy moving through the trees and kept reporting to Gates for three hours, from 10 AM until 1 PM. General Fraser's troops had to march a considerable distance to get into position, so the other two columns waited in place until about 1 PM when Fraser would fire three guns as a signal for the army to advance. The battle swayed back and forth over the farm for more than three hours.

Arnold persuaded Gates to let him move forward to counter the attack of the Crown forces and to send Colonel Morgan's riflemen into a wooded ravine south of Freeman's Farm. Morgan used a turkey call to rally his men. Together, they took a heavy toll of officers and men. When the British advanced against Arnold, they soon found themselves in serious trouble. They charged and Arnold moved forward. Arnold asked Gates for some reinforcements, saying he could defeat the enemy easily. Gates refused and ordered Arnold back to the lines. Arnold ignored the orders. Baron von Riedesel arrived, driving off Arnold's forces.

The Crown forces held the field at the end of the day, but they lost about 600 men—twice as many as the Continental casualties—many of them officers. One regiment lost over three-quarters of its men. The morale of the men was broken, and they knew that Major General Horatio Gates still blocked their intended route.

After the Battle of Freeman's Farm, Burgoyne planned to resume the attack the next day but changed his mind when he heard that General Henry Clinton (1730–1795) left New York to relieve him. Clinton, in fact, stormed Forts Clinton and Montgomery on the Hudson on October 6, but, exercising that innate cautious characteristic of all his actions, Clinton refused to gamble for high stakes. He simply sent an advance guard on to Kingston while he returned to New York, leaving Burgoyne to his fate.

The lines in Saratoga remained stable for three weeks. Burgoyne built an extensive system of field fortifications extending over 2 miles. His ranks, however, were being depleted by desertion and disease. There was not enough food for both horses and soldiers.[48]

★ A few men were beyond the out sentries at Saratoga digging potatoes on Saturday, September 27, 1777, when they were captured by the Crown forces. A detachment of Congressional troops tried to surprise an advanced British post that day but one of them was killed and three wounded. The following day, they captured two scalps and 11 prisoners and deserters.[49]

Bemis Heights

★ Burgoyne's situation was critical by now. He had no hope of assistance and his supplies were dwindling daily. Food was running out; the meadows were grazed bare by the animals; and every day more men slipped into the forest, deserting the lost cause. He strengthened his position by constructing redoubts, digging trenches, and chopping down trees to provide a field of fire in front of his position. Burgoyne had to decide whether to advance or retreat. Gates strengthened his entrenchments and awaited the attack he was sure Burgoyne would have to make. He occupied and fortified the high ground which was Burgoyne's objective since September 19. Military reinforcements increased Gates's forces to around 10,000 by October 7.

With little intelligence of Continental strength or dispositions, Burgoyne sent out a "reconnaissance in force" with 1,500 men and eight cannon on Tuesday, October 7 to attack the Continental left flank and feel out their positions. On learning that the British were approaching Gates sent out a contingent including Morgan's riflemen to meet them, and a second battle developed, usually known as Bemis Heights or the second battle of Saratoga.

Burgoyne's troops marched about three-quarters of a mile southwesterly and deployed in a clearing on the Barber farm. Most of the Crown forces' front faced an open field, but both flanks rested in woods, exposed to surprise attack.

The Continentals attacked in three columns under Colonel Daniel Morgan, General Ebenezer Learned, and Brigadier General Enoch Poor (1736–1780) at about 3 PM. General Poor attacked the east flank first, as he had a shorter distance to go. Colonel Morgan engaged the west flank, breaking the line repeatedly. The Crown forces rallied but were driven back. Both flanks came under tremendous pressure from all sides and could not rally, so they retreated into the fortifications on the Freeman farm.

General Benedict Arnold, who had been relieved of command after a quarrel with Gates, rode onto the field and led Learned's brigade against the German troops holding the Crown's center. Under tremendous pressure from all sides, the Germans joined a general withdrawal into the fortifications on the Freeman farm.

When Arnold saw General Fraser riding back and forth on his horse encouraging his men, he recognized this officer's importance to the Crown forces. He asked Morgan to have his riflemen shoot him. Morgan selected Timothy Murphy (1751–1818), who mortally wounded Fraser on the third shot.

Believing victory close at hand, Arnold led one column in a series of attacks on the Balcarres redoubt. After failing repeatedly to take this position, Arnold wheeled his horse and dashed through the crossfire of both armies toward the Breymann redoubt. He arrived just as the Continental troops began to assault the fortification, so he joined in the attack, overwhelming the German soldiers defending the work. He was shot in the left leg after entering the redoubt and suffered a fractured thigh on the same leg wounded at Québec. Had the shot been fatal, he would have died one of America's greatest heroes. Lieutenant Colonel Heinrich Christoph von Breymann (d. 1777) was also mortally wounded defending the Breymann redoubt which the Germans lost and could not regain.

Burgoyne suffered about 600 casualties to the Continentals' 150. With his position open to attack from the right rear, he had only one choice: to retreat that night if he could, leaving the sick and wounded behind. He withdrew to a position in the vicinity of Saratoga. Militia soon worked around to his rear and cut his supply lines. His position hopeless, Burgoyne finally capitulated on October 17 at Saratoga. The total prisoner count was nearly 6,000, and great quantities of military stores fell into Continental hands.

The victory at Saratoga brought the Continentals out well ahead in the campaign of 1777 despite the loss of Philadelphia. What had been at stake soon became obvious. Morale of the Continental troops improved considerably at a time when General George Washington's (1732–1799) army was being pushed around New York, and it convinced the King of France to support the Continental cause.[50]

Surrender, Schuylerville

Ten days after the Battle of Bemis Heights, with his army of 5,700 surrounded by an army that grew to 20,000 men, Major General John Burgoyne (1722–1792) finally capitulated on Friday, October 17, 1777, at Saratoga. Instead of a surrender, he suggested a «convention» in which the Continentals would let the British return to England if they promised not to fight again in the war. Major General Horatio Gates (1728–1806) accepted, but Congress later cancelled this agreement and sent Burgoyne's soldiers to prison camps in Virginia until the end of the war. These prisoners are sometimes referred to as the «convention army.»

The surrender of an entire British army with all its equipment had a tremendous psychological impact on the Continental cause. What had been at stake soon became obvious, however. On Friday, February 6, 1778, France signed a treaty pledging full military support to the American states, tantamount to a declaration of war against England.

When news of Burgoyne's surrender reached London, Lord Chatham addressed the House of Lords:

> No man thinks more highly than I of the virtue and valour of British troops; I know they can achieve anything except impossibilities; and the conquest of English America is an impossibility. you cannot, I venture to say it, *you cannot conquer*

America.... What is your present situation there? We do not know the worst, but we know that in three campaigns we have done nothing, and suffered much.... Conquest is impossible: you may swell every expense and every effort still more extravagantly; pile and accumulate every assistance you can buy or borrow; traffic and barter with every little pitiful German prince that sells his subjects to the shambles of a foreign power; your efforts are forever vain and impotent; doubly so from this mercenary aid on which you rely; for it irritates to an incurable resentment the minds of your enemies. To overrun them with the mercenary sons of rapine and plunder; devoting them and their possessions to the rapacity of hireling cruelty! If I were an American, as I am an Englishman, while a foreign troop was landed in my country, I never would lay down my arms, never–never–never![51]

★ A detachment of almost 250 men from Sir John Johnson's (1742–1830) corps arrived at St. John's from Montréal around the end of August 1781. They were probably joined by some other troops and Native Americans. The commander at St. John's sent a party toward Saratoga to take a prisoner or two to gain intelligence.

Brigadier General John Stark (1728–1822) had written to Major General William Heath (1737–1814) three times in September 1781 requesting ammunition and supplies for his troops at Saratoga as he anticipated an attack from Canada. He was down to 10 rounds per man and could not get any from Albany. He also requested some horses to procure forage so he could maintain a line of communication with the frontiers. When one of his men tried to pass a dispatch from Canada on the road near Saratoga on Sunday evening, September 23, 1781, he was shot through the arm.

Captain Samuel Dunham (1723–1789) and two other militiamen captured a scouting party of five on Tuesday morning, September 25, 1781. The scouts had been sent out from St. John's, Canada and were in the Saratoga area. They gave no information about the remainder of the party.[52]

Oriskany (Aug. 6, 1777)

Oriskany Battlefield (nysparks.state.ny.us/cgi-bin/cgiwrap/nysparks/historic .cgi?p+20) is 6 miles east of Oriskany, New York on Route NY 69, and is marked by a large 84-foot granite-limestone obelisk. This is the same 84-foot granite shaft mentioned below. It occupies the highest point of ground and lists the names of the militiamen killed at Oriskany. This is where the Whigs rallied after breaking out of the ambush.
 A small granite marker to the right of the battle monument and down the slope marks the spot where Brigadier General Nicholas Herkimer is believed to have directed the defense.

★ Brigadier General Nicholas Herkimer (1728–1777) assembled a militia force of 800 men and boys—all males in the Mohawk Valley between 16 and 60 years of age—and set out from Fort Dayton, now the town of Herkimer, on Monday morning, August 4, 1777 to relieve Fort Stanwix and oppose Lieutenant Colonel Barry St. Leger (1737–1789). He followed a military supply road and camped about 10 miles from Stanwix on the night of August 5.

He sent a message to Colonel Peter Gansevoort (1749–1812), the fort's commander, to fire three cannon when he received the letter and to conduct a diversionary attack on the British siege line. Herkimer had still not heard any cannon two days later. He was inclined to halt his advance, but his regimental commanders pressed him to continue the assault, impugning his loyalty and bravery.

Unaware that his position had been revealed to St. Leger the night before by Molly Brant [Koñwatsiátsiaiéñni or Mary (Molly) Brant (ca.1736–1796)] who was Joseph Brant (1742–1807) Mohawk Chief Thayendanagea's sister and Sir William Johnson's (1715–1774) (a British general and Superintendent of Indian Affairs) mistress and mother of several of his children, Herkimer's mile-long column descended into a gully at Oriskany 6 miles below the fort. Most of the advance force of 600 men were deep into the ravine when about 400 of Brant's Native Americans and some Loyalists opened fire on them from both sides of the road where it dipped down into the ravine and crossed a creek and marshy area. They killed or wounded more than a dozen officers, including Herkimer, in the initial volley. Herkimer's rear guard of 200 had fled down the road.

Herkimer, shot in the thigh, demanded to be propped against a beech tree to direct the operation. He ordered his men to form a circle against the snipers. They managed to keep the line intact for about three-quarters of an hour when a heavy rainstorm broke, wetting everyone's priming pan and delaying the battle about an hour. The same storm delayed the start of Gansevoort's diversionary attack on the enemy camp.

Herkimer took advantage of this relief to order his men to fight in pairs. The Native Americans would wait for a militiaman to fire, then rush in to tomahawk him before he could reload. By fighting in pairs, one man loaded his musket while the other protected him from a tomahawk charge.

When the storm subsided, some of the militiamen broke away and managed to reach higher ground and formed a new line of defense. Brant received reinforcements from the siege lines at Fort Stanwix. They turned their coats inside out in an attempt to trick the militiamen into thinking they were friends (hence the term "turncoat"), but one of the men recognized his Loyalist neighbor. The stiff resistance began to dispirit the Native Americans who were now engaged in protracted hand-to-hand combat. They began to desert, forcing the Loyalists to withdraw.

Although the exact number of casualties at Oriskany has never been determined with certainty, both sides suffered heavy losses in the six-hour battle. It was one of the bloodiest engagements of the war, with one of the highest ratios of casualties suffered to the number of men involved. The militia lost more than 160 killed and 50 wounded; several men were taken prisoner and the rest returned to Fort Dayton. Nicholas Herkimer died 11 days later after an amputation.

The militiamen never managed to relieve Fort Stanwix, but they inflicted such heavy casualties on St. Leger's Native Americans and Loyalists that the Native Americans, who had already become restless during the static siege operation, became discouraged and left. A sortie from the fort pillaged the camps and gave the Native Americans further reason to leave. The departure of the Native Americans forced St. Leger to abandon the siege.[53]

Schenectady (Aug. 11, 1777)

> Jeduthan Baldwin (1732–1788) places this action 6 miles below Fort Stanwix whereas the modern city of Schenectady is about 85 miles southeast of Fort Stanwix and 20 miles northwest of Albany.

★ Major Abraham Switz's (1730–1840) New York militia captured a dozen Loyalists at Schenectady on Monday, August 11, 1777. A survivor of the battle fought 6 miles below Fort Stanwix reported that General Harriman was wounded and had 14 field officers killed and wounded. The Crown forces lost 50 Native Americans killed and left 100 others on the field. General Harriman recovered the field and buried the dead.[54]

Vrooman's (Aug. 13, 1777; Nov. 1, 1781)
"Battle at the Flockey"

> Two small streams run into the Schoharie River directly opposite each other about 0.5 miles above the bridge which crosses the river south of Middleburg. The one on the west side, coming from the northwest, was called the Line Kill (Creek) and was the northern boundary of the first Vrooman Patent which included the part of the town of Fulton called Vrooman's Land.[55]

Captain John McDonald, of Colonel Guy Johnson's (ca. 1740–1788) Royal Greens, Ensign Adam Crysler (1732–1793), and about 100 Loyalists and 25 Native Americans entered the Schoharie Valley on August 10, 1777. Colonel John Harper, Jr. (1743–1811) rode to Albany to get help. He was followed by two Native Americans who fled when he fired his pistols at them. He reached Albany on Tuesday, August 12.

The Loyalists and Native Americans proceeded along the river toward Middleburg on Wednesday, August 13. They camped overnight at the north end of Vrooman's Land, about 4 miles north of Adam Crysler's house. Their presence had been discovered, however. By the time they approached Middleburg the following day, they learned that Colonel Harper and a band of 28 cavalrymen were on their way from Albany.

The Loyalists and Native Americans withdrew toward the Flockey (high ground near a swamp) in front of the Crysler house. They set an ambush there in the pouring rain. When the cavalry arrived, Adam Crysler's men fired a volley that hit nine of the light horsemen. Lieutenant David Wirt (d. 1777) and Private Rose (d. 1777) (who died three days later) were killed and another private was slightly wounded. The militiamen returned fire and the cavalry charged, causing panic among the Loyalists and Native Americans who fled up the river. They were pursued only a short distance because it was nearly dark and the ground was unfavorable for cavalry. Both the men and the horses were tired from their long ride from Albany and there was great danger from ambush.

The Loyalists and Native Americans then retreated toward the British fort at Oswego on Lake Ontario. Adam became ill four days later and was left at the Native American camp called the "Butternuts." He recuperated and began recruiting Native Americans again at the end of November and soon had 100 braves to take with him to Fort Niagara.[56]

★ Joseph Brant (1742–1807), Mohawk Chief Thayendanagea and Captain Adam Crysler (1732–1793) led a party of Native Americans and Loyalists to Vrooman's Land, near the residence of Colonel Peter Vrooman (1763–1838, a little distance from the Upper Schoharie fort, early Thursday morning, November 1, 1781. Isaac Vrooman (1722–1781), Peter's father, had moved his family some time before and had visited his son to get Peter's help to move his family back to his old residence in Schoharie. A few days before his father's arrival, Peter, thinking that it was so late in the season that the enemy would not re-appear, had moved from a hut at the fort to a dwelling, a few hundred yards away, which he intended to be his winter quarters.

Isaac Vrooman was on his way to his son's quarters around dawn when the leader of the Loyalists and a Native American warrior beside him both fired at Isaac. Peter heard the two shots and ran toward the fort. He was only a short distance from his house when he was discovered and fired upon. Several Native Americans pursued him, but he reached the fort safely.

When she heard the gunfire, Peter's wife ran upstairs and saw, from a chamber window, a Native American scalping her father-in-law who was on his hands and knees, screaming. The warrior then killed his victim with a war club, cut his throat, and added another notch on the club with the bloody knife. He then placed the knife on the body of the murdered man and left him.

When some of the Loyalists and Native Americans entered Vrooman's house for plunder, Mrs. Vrooman went below. As she knew several of the warriors, she spoke to them in their own language, and they spared her life. The warriors then headed up the river, plundering whatever they could find. A party of 15 or 20 men was soon sent from the fort to pursue the raiders. They proceeded quickly along the eastern shore of the Schoharie until they reached "Bouck's Island" where the enemy, hidden on the river bank above Panther Mountain fired on them. The militiamen returned fire and retreated. Derrick (Richard) Haggidorn (d. 1781) was mortally wounded. As he fell, he called to his companions not to leave him to the enemy. Two of his friends brought him to the fort where he died the next day.[57]

Cambridge
Sancoick's (or Van Schaick's) Mill (Aug. 14, 1777)

> Sancoick's (San Coick's, Saint Coick's or Van Schaick's) Mill was on the Owl Kill in Cambridge just north of the Hoosick River about 11 miles west-northwest of Bennington, Vermont in what is now Cambridge, New York.

★ Lieutenant Colonel Friedrich Baum (d. 1777) arrived at Sancoick's (or Van Schaick's) Mill on Owl Kill at 8 AM on Thursday August 14, 1777 with 30 Hessians and 50 Native Americans. He was on his way to raid Bennington. About 50 of Brigadier General John Stark's (1728–1822) militia had abandoned the mill before Baum's arrival but fired at the Hessians from the bushes. Colonel Baum, in a letter written on the head of a barrel after his arrival at the mill, reported to Major General John Burgoyne (1732–1792) that the Rebels wounded one of his Native Americans each night. They also broke down the bridge, delaying his march by more than an hour.

Baum captured five prisoners who told him that 1,500 to 1,800 men were at Bennington but were ordered to leave when the Hessians approached. Baum also found "about 78 barrels of very fine flour, 1000 bushels of wheat, 20 barrels of salt, and about 1000l. [livres] worth of pearl and pot ash." He ordered 30 provincials and an officer to guard the provisions and the pass of the bridge while he advanced to be in position to attack Stark's militia early the following morning.[58]

When General Stark learned that the Hessians were advancing on Bennington, he detached Colonel William Gregg (1730–1815) with 200 men to stop them. He then set out with his brigade and a few Vermont militia on the 14th to oppose them and to cover Gregg's retreat. Outnumbered, Gregg was forced to retreat and was about 4 miles from the town with the enemy less than 0.5 miles behind him when General Stark arrived. When the Hessians saw Stark coming with reinforcements, they halted "on a very advantageous piece of ground."

Stark's little army lined up on a hill facing the enemy camp but could not draw them into an engagement; so Stark marched his troops back about a mile and camped. He sent out a few men to skirmish with the Hessians. They killed 30 Hessians and two Native American chiefs.[59]

North Hoosick
Battle of Bennington (Aug. 16, 1777)

> During the War for American Independence, part of Vermont was claimed by New York. The Battle of Bennington was actually fought in and near Hoosick Falls, New York.
>
> The Bennington Battle Monument (**www.dhca.state.vt.us/HistoricSites/html/bennington.html**) is in Bennington Vermont, 0.5 miles west of the junction of VT 9 and U.S. 7, then north to the end of Monument Avenue to 15 Monument Circle. The Bennington Battle Monument was the tallest battle monument in the world when completed in 1891. At 306 feet, it is still the tallest structure in Vermont. It offers a good view of three states from the upper lookout chamber which is reached by elevator. A diorama and exhibit illustrate the battle and the monument.
>
> In New York state, the Bennington Battlefield State Historic Site (**nysparks.state.ny.us/cgi-bin/cgiwrap/nysparks/historic.cgi?p+1**) is located 3 miles east of Hoosick Falls on Rte. NY 67. An interpretive sign explains the course of the battle and a hilltop picnic area overlooks the battlefield.

★ Major General John Burgoyne (1722–1792) marched his army south from Canada in early July, 1777, intending to split the colonies, to capture Albany, and to join the British forces in New York City. His expedition was proceeding swiftly and with better results than anticipated by the end of July, but it soon bogged down.

Burgoyne's army passed through Fort Edward on July 30. The Whigs abandoned and burned the fort before leaving for Stillwater, New York, about 30 miles north of Albany. It became apparent that the expected Loyalist support would be minimal and that the 185-mile supply route from Canada was too long. Burgoyne needed more baggage animals to continue his slow march, so he decided to take Major General Baron Friedrich von Riedesel's (1738–1800) advice and raid a magazine established by the New England militia at Bennington. They had reports that the magazine contained large supplies of food and ammunition and had at least 100 horses.

Burgoyne sent Lieutenant Colonel Friedrich Baum (d. 1777), commander of the Brunswick dragoons, to Bennington on Monday, August 11, 1777 with about 800 men. The force was composed of 374 dismounted Hessian dragoons, grenadiers, and light infantry; about 300 Canadians and American Loyalists; 80 Native Americans; and a company of about 50 of Brigadier General Simon Fraser's (1729–1777) marksmen. Burgoyne expected that Baum would find large supplies of food, forage, and horses guarded by only a few militia. He also thought Bennington was full of Loyalists who would help him, so he didn't send a larger detachment. Baum even insisted on taking a German band that destroyed any attempt at surprise.

A large portion of Baum's soldiers were dragoons who carried heavy packs (knapsacks and blankets) with their arms and accoutrements, 60 rounds of ammunition, haversacks of provisions, hatchets, a portion of the equipment for their tents, an enormous sword, and a large canteen capable of holding about a gallon. They wore long skirted coats and heavy leather gauntlets reaching almost to their elbows. They also wore heavy leather boots and found the 40-mile trek slow going.

The Native Americans ran ahead, plundering and burning any homesteads they could find along the way. They slaughtered cattle along the way to keep the cowbells rather than round them up for food for the army. News that the Native Americans were on the warpath caused the inhabitants to drive their horses and cattle away, making Colonel Baum's task more difficult.

Brigadier General John Stark (1728–1822), of New Hampshire, organized and equipped a brigade of 1,500 men by the first week of August. He marched them to Bennington to defend the frontier. Stark met Baum about 9 AM on August 14 at Sancoick's Mill about 5 miles from Bennington, but the two forces did not conduct battle then. Nor did they do battle on the 15th, even though both sides received reinforcements, because it rained. The Americans now numbered 2,000 militia and a few Native Americans.

Baum sent word to Burgoyne for reinforcements and entrenched on high ground between the Walloomsac River and Little White Creek.

On Saturday, August 16, the sun came out around noon, and both sides prepared for battle. Several men had scouted the enemy force, so the Congressional troops knew their strength and dispositions. Baum had scattered his forces about the hillside. Therefore General Stark sent a column of 200 New Hampshire men to the north flank while another column of 300 Vermont rangers and Bennington militia marched around to the south. An additional 300 men attacked the nearest position east of the Walloomsac River. When the flanking columns began their attack about 3:00 PM, Stark would make the main assault toward the center with 1,200 men.

When Baum, who spoke no English, saw small groups of armed men approaching, he thought they were Loyalists from the area coming to help him or to seek safety. The Congressional flanking columns took advantage of this error and disguised themselves as small groups of farmers to get into position. They said they were Loyalists and offered to join him and to swear the customary oath of allegiance. Brigadier Major Philip Skene (1725–1780) assured Baum that the men were sincere and that he could add them to his force. After having them sworn in, Baum gave them slips of white paper to wear in their hats to identify them as friendly forces so the Native Americans would not harm them. A German officer wrote about the deception:

> How Colonel Baum became so completely duped as to place reliance on these men, I know not. But . . . he was somehow or other persuaded to believe [that they wished] to offer their services to the leader of the King's troops. . . . I cannot pretend to describe the state of excitation and alarm into which our little band was now thrown. With the solitary exception of our leader, there was not a man among us who appeared otherwise than satisfied that those to whom he had listened were traitors. . . . [But] he remained convinced of their fidelity.

When a large group of militia blocked the road, the "new allies" took up positions around Colonel Baum and in his rear. But when the firing started, they began shooting German officers in the back. The Native Americans were caught between two lines of fire and ran off into the forest, followed by the Canadians and the Loyalists after firing one volley. Colonel Baum had only his German and British troops and a few others left. They were running low on ammunition when a wagon containing their reserve supply caught fire and exploded. As the Congressional troops moved in, the Hessians drew their great swords to defend themselves. The attackers had no bayonets to counter this move and were at a disadvantage until Baum received a mortal wound in the abdomen about 5 PM. The Hessians then surrendered.

Lieutenant Colonel Heinrich Christoph von Breymann (d. 1777), sent to support Baum, took 16 hours to march 24 miles through the forest in the pouring rain. When he and his company arrived at Sancoick's Mill about 4:30, they heard no firing and assumed

Baum was still holding out. Flank patrols on the hill drove off the small militia bands that tried to impede their progress.

Breymann forced Stark back as Colonel Seth Warner (1743–1784) arrived with reinforcements that gave the Congressional troops enough strength to repel the German attacks and assault the enemy on both flanks. Heavy firing continued until about sunset when Colonel Breymann, almost out of ammunition, ordered a retreat. The Hessians retreated with as many wounded as they could carry. The Whigs immediately pursued them, changing the retreat into a rout. The German drums beat the signal for a parley, but the Whigs did not understand it and kept firing until dark. Breymann, wounded in the leg and with five bullet holes in his clothes, commanded the rear guard action that permitted two-thirds of his command to escape after dark. Stark ordered his men not to pursue the enemy after dark when they might shoot at each other.

Colonel Baum died without ever knowing that there were never any horses in Bennington. He was buried on the road to Bennington.

Stark reported his casualties as 14 killed and 40 wounded. The Crown forces' casualties amounted to 207 men killed, an unknown number of wounded, and more than 600 captured. The Crown forces also lost 12 drums, 250 broadswords, four ammunition wagons, several hundred muskets, a few rifles, and four brass cannon captured by General James Wolfe (1727–1759) at Québec in 1759. This defeat at Bennington deprived Burgoyne of approximately 1,000 troops at the Battle of Saratoga.[60]

Lake George (Sept. 18, 1777)
Fort George, Lake George (Sept. 2, 1779; Oct. 11, 1780; Nov. 21, 1780)
Near Lake George (Nov. 2, 1781)

> A very narrow gorge at the southwest end of Lake Champlain extends about a mile westward to connect with Lake George. Fort George was 0.5 miles southeast of Fort William Henry, on U.S. 9 on the western shore of Lake George in Lake George Battleground Park. (This should not be confused with the Fort George on Manhattan Island.) It served as a base for three colonial armies and as an army hospital. Fort Hunter was at the confluence of the Mohawk River and Schoharie Creek on the site of an old Mohawk village called Tienonderoga or Icanderoga. It was enclosed by a palisade with blockhouses at each of the four angles.

★ A scouting party of Vermont militiamen was attacked by Crown forces at Lake George on Thursday, September 18, 1777. The scouts lost one killed and about five captured.[61]

★ Colonel Seth Warner (1743–1784), commander of the garrison at Fort George, was on horseback leading his men along the old military road that connected Fort George with Fort Edward, 15 miles to the south on Thursday, September 2, 1779. (Some accounts say he was returning to Fort George from a visit to Fort Edward.) They were caught in an ambush as they were passing Bloody Pond. Warner was shot twice in his left arm and his horse was struck eight times. Two of his officers were killed and several men were also shot. His scouts pursued the 40–50 Native Americans into the woods and up the side of a hill, dispersing them. The men returned to dress Warner's wounds and to collect the rest of the wounded. They returned to Fort George where they arrived about 10 AM. Warner then sent Captain John Chipman (1765–1850) and a detachment to bring in the dead.[62]

★ Alarmed by an account that the enemy had taken Fort Ann, the militia marched to Half Moon and were ordered to return, as the enemy had re-crossed Lake George. They came down South Bay and demanded the surrender of Fort Ann which immediately complied. They then marched to Fort George on Tuesday, October 11, 1780. Fort George was garrisoned by 80 of Colonel Seth Warner's (1743–1784) regiment who were all out on a scouting party, except 14 who were "mostly cut to pieces."[63]

★ Captain John Chipman commanded between 60 and 70 of Colonel Seth Warner's (1743–1784) men at Fort George on Tuesday, November 21, 1780. The rest of the regiment was out scouting around Lake George. Captain Chipman sent an express to Fort Edward for supplies, as the garrison had gone two days without food. About 4 miles from Fort George, an enemy party of about 30 or 40 British regulars, Native Americans and Loyalists fired on the express who escaped to report to Captain Chipman, giving him the first information he received that there were less than 30 or 40 enemy in the vicinity of Lake George.

Captain Chipman, anxious to avenge the losses which the regiment had sustained during the season, immediately dispatched Captain Thomas Sill (1747–1780) and 50 men to pursue the enemy. Unfortunately, Captain Sill took a route different from his orders. He passed the enemy on their approach and returned to fall upon their rear a short distance from the fort, effectively preventing his return to the fort. His alternatives were to attack a body of at least 30 to 1 or to march off through the woods. They chose to fight. They attacked the enemy front which gave way. Sill and his men advanced with fixed bayonets but soon found themselves completely surrounded by a large body of Crown forces. They fought fiercely until the captain, his ensign and 16 noncommissioned officers and privates were killed. A lieutenant and another ensign were wounded and taken prisoners with the rest of the detachment, except for Ensign Grant and about 15 privates who fought their way through the enemy lines and escaped. The Crown forces invested the fort and demanded its surrender. Captain Chipman, greatly outnumbered and unable to defend the post with so few men capitulated.[64]

★ Lieutenant Colonel Barry St. Leger (1737–1789) with about 2,500 Crown troops and another 600 under the command of Major John Ross proceeded through Lake Champlain to Lake George on Friday, November 2, 1781. They went by Oswego and the Oneida Lake to the Oneida Creek where they left their boats under a small guard before heading to Cherry Valley and Schoharie. They attacked Warrensbush, burned about 20 houses, crossed the Mohawk River near Fort Hunter, and proceeded to Johnstown, where Colonel Marinus Willett (1740–1830) attacked them with about 500 men and drove them from the ground. The next morning Willett pursued them for several days until he ran out of provisions and returned to camp about 20 miles north of Lake Oneida. His men had only two pounds of horse flesh per man and a march before them of at least 10 days to get to any place where they could expect relief. The Crown forces lost an estimated 150 prisoners, killed and deserters.[65]

As the weather was beginning to be severely cold and large bodies of Continental troops were gathering in the area, Colonel St. Leger withdrew about December 2, 1781. Due to very adverse winds, however, they got no farther than Chimney Point on the 8th.

Diamond Island (Sept. 24, 1777)

Diamond Island is in Lake George 25 miles south of Ticonderoga and about 3.5 miles from the lake's southern shore.

★ After the Crown forces abandoned Skenesborough, Colonel Benjamin Ruggles Woodbridge (1739–1819) occupied it without opposition and was supposed to move south through Fort Anne to Fort Edward. British Brigadier General Henry Watson Powell still held Ticonderoga and its outposts with the 53rd Regiment and some Canadians. He also commanded Mount Independence with the Prince Frederick Regiment of Brunswickers. However, he posted his 900 troops carelessly, with inadequate security detachments.

Major General Benjamin Lincoln (1733–1810) sent three 500-man detachments to disrupt the Crown forces' supply lines. He sent Colonel John Brown (d. 1781) to attack Ticonderoga from the west. He spent two days near Fort Ticonderoga undetected before attacking at dawn on Thursday, September 18, 1777. The Continentals rushed the Lake George landing (at the outlet from that lake into Lake Champlain) and overwhelmed the sergeant's guard on Mount Defiance to get control of everything on the west shore of the lake, except the French stone fort and the Grenadier's Battery at the tip of the peninsula. Brown also freed over 100 prisoners and captured 300 of the enemy.

Colonel Samuel Johnson (1713–1796), as a diversion, attacked Mount Independence but he arrived too late to surprise the Prince Frederick Regiment. He kept a continuous fire on the Germans and went to support Brown later in the day. Powell refused to surrender Ticonderoga whose main defenses were too strong for Brown to assault without heavy artillery. The Continentals cannonaded the fort for four days and then withdrew.

Johnson went back to Lincoln's camp; and Brown sailed up Lake George with 420 men, in captured British boats, in an attempt to surprise two companies of the British 47th, under Captain Thomas Aubrey (d. 1814) on Diamond Island, 25 miles south of Ticonderoga at dawn on Tuesday, September 23, 1777. Adverse winds delayed the attack until about 9 AM on the 24th. A paroled Loyalist warned Captain Aubrey of the attack. When Brown arrived, he began a short bombardment; but his artillery was no match for the enemy guns, so he withdrew. He landed on the eastern shore where he burned his boats and rejoined General Lincoln.[66]

Kingston

Esopus (Oct. 13, 16, 17, 18, 22, 23, 1777)

> Esopus, now Kingston, is on the west bank of the Hudson River, 16 miles north of Poughkeepsie. It was the third town in the state for size, elegance and wealth. It was the capital of New York during the American War for Independence. The landing site of the Crown forces on October 16, 1777 was at what is now Kingston Point Park at Delaware Avenue.

★ New York militiamen captured a small schooner in the North River, near Rhynebeck, on Monday, October 13, 1777. The vessel had run aground with a valuable cargo. The people took advantage and boarded her with canoes. They captured Nicholas James and George Hopkins, two of the New York pilots, on board.[67]

★ As the British vessels proceeded up the Hudson River past Esopus, they came under fire from troops behind a breastwork on shore. The British army landed a number of men at Esopus on Thursday, October 16, 1777. The soldiers marched up to the defenseless town (the present-day upper town), about 2 miles from the river, and immediately set it on fire. The flames spread quickly and soon reduced the town to ashes, sparing only one house. They burned 326 houses, almost all with barns filled with flour and all kinds of grains, much valuable furniture and other possessions which the soldiers didn't want to take with them. They burned 12,000 barrels of flour and took four pieces of artillery from the town and 10 more on the river. They blew up a large quantity of powder and 1,150 stands of arms.

While some of the inhabitants (mostly of Dutch descent) saved some of their moveable property, others lost almost everything. The troops took little time to plunder, as they heard that Governor George Clinton (1739–1812) was nearby with 1500 men. However, he was not close enough to save the town. Major General John Vaughn's (1738?–1795) troops burned several vessels and houses at Kingston Landing then hurried to board their vessels. The expedition lasted three hours. Major General Israel Putnam (1718–1790) and about 5,000 men watched General Vaughn's movements and fired at the British ships as they came down the Hudson. They did little damage to the vessels but wounded five or six men.[68]

★ The next day, the Crown troops burned several houses at Rhynebeck Flats and proceeded as far as Mr. Robert Livingston's Manor, 45 miles south of Albany, where they burned five more, including that of Judge Robert R. Livingston, Sr. (1718–1775) on the 18th. They burned two more houses on the east side, a sloop and a barn as well as two houses and their dependencies on the west side on the 18th. On Thursday, the 23rd, they burned a sloop on the stocks and destroyed a large quantity of powder and a large number of firearms and many valuable supplies.[69]

Kingston
Slapshine Island, Hudson River (Oct. 18, 19, 1777)

> Slapshine (Sleepshine) Island is a small island at the mouth of Esopus Creek, now Rondout Creek, just south of Kingston.

★ HM Galley *Dependence* and HM Armed Vessel *Diligent* landed a detachment of the army at Slapshine Island at noon on Saturday, October 18, 1777 to destroy some stores. The *Dependence* fired three 24-pound shots to cover their landing. The troops re-embarked at 1 PM. The *Dependence* then sent her boats manned and armed to destroy some stores at Colonel Robert Livingston's Manor at 4 PM.[70]

★ While the sailmakers of the HM Galley *Dependence* were mending their sails off Slapshine Island on Sunday, October 19, 1777. Lieutenant James Clark sent his boats ashore, manned and armed to burn two Whig vessels early that afternoon. He fired five 4-pounders with round and grape shot to cover the boats while they destroyed the vessels. The boats returned at 6 PM after completing their mission.[71]

Upstate New York (Nov. 19, 1777)

★ When the 1st Connecticut Regiment paraded in upstate New York on Wednesday, November 19, 1777, it came under fire from the British who killed one and wounded two.[72]

Tribes Hill (Sackintago) (Mar. 1778)

> Tribes Hill (Sackintago) is in the Mohawk Valley. It is just north of I-90 at Auriesville and about 6 miles east of Caughnawaga.

★ The Caughnawaga Mohawks attacked Sackintago on the Mohawk River, 18 miles above Johnstown. on Wednesday, June 3, 1778. They captured John Putman (1711–?);

Charles Morris (1753–?); Herman Salsberry (1739–?), Godfrey Shew (1721–?), Stephen Shew (1761–1841)), Jacob Shew (1763–1853), John Reese (1745–1825), David Harles (1763–?), John Marenis (1765–?) on their farms, and six others.[73]

Manheim (Mar. 29, 1778; Apr. 3, 1778)

> Manheim is north of the Mohawk River and about 2 miles west of East Canada Creek along NY-167 and about 3.5 miles east of Little Falls.

Mr. Caselman led a party of 50 Loyalists and Native Americans in an attack on the town of Manheim, or Snyders Bush, on Sunday, March 29, 1778. Eight men were taken prisoner, but the women and a man, ill in bed, were left unmolested. One mill was burned but no private houses were destroyed. They took more captives near Salisbury on their way north.[74]

★ Joseph Brant (1742–1807), Mohawk Chief Thayendanagea led a band of Native Americans and Loyalist volunteers in an attack on the town of Manheim on Friday, April 3, 1778. They took about a dozen men prisoners.[75]

Ephrata (April 31, 1778)

> Ephrata is at the intersection of NY-10 and NY-67 about 4.5 miles north of Fort Keyser and 6.5 miles from Fort Plain.

★ About four weeks after the attack on Manheim, Joseph Brant (1742–1807), Mohawk Chief Thayendanagea and his band of Native Americans and Loyalist volunteers returned to the area and attacked Ephrata about Thursday, April 31, 1778. Governor George Clinton (1739–1812) called upon the militia to defend the town and asked General George Washington (1732–1799) for Continental troops to garrison the important posts.[76]

Cobleskill (May 28, 30, 1778; June 1, 1778; May 1779; Sept. 1, 1781)

> Cobleskill, also known as Cobus Kill in the 18th century, is about 9 miles west of Schoharie at the junction of SR 7 and SR 145.

★ Colonel Guy Johnson (ca. 1740–1788) sent Chief Joseph Brant (1742–1807), Mohawk Chief Thayendanagea through the back country to assemble the Native Americans. He drew the Mohawks from their settlement which was partly destroyed by the Whigs and advanced against the troops at Schoharie and Cobleskill in May 1778. With only 100 Native Americans, he drew out more than 300 men to follow him and ambushed them and cut them off. They took 294 scalps and destroyed about 150 houses and barns.[77]

★ Captain William Patrick (1741–1778) and a small company of volunteers arrived at the residence of Captain John M. Brown (1745–1838) on Tuesday, May 26, 1778 and remained there until the 28th, when they moved to Sergeant Lawrence Lawyer's (1758–1848) house. That day, Lieutenant Jacob Borst (1748–1823), his brother Joseph (1749–1812), and another man were scouting a few miles up the creek when two Schoharie Native Americans sprang from a hiding place along the bank of the creek and approached them. They exchanged greetings and the Schoharies began to reprove the brothers for being in the woods to shoot Native Americans. Joseph responded that they intended no harm to those who were friendly. The Schoharies attempted to disarm the scouts but Lieutenant Borst grabbed one of them and struggled with him. The other Schoharie demanded that the lieutenant surrender himself. Instead of surrendering, Lieutenant Borst shot him. The other Schoharie freed himself and fled. Lieutenant Borst ran for his brother's musket and fired it at the fleeing Schoharie; but it was not loaded so the man escaped.[78]

★ A large party of about 350 Loyalists and Native Americans returned to raid Cobleskill on Saturday, May 30. Captain Dirck Miller was sent from the Schoharie fort with part of a company to reconnoitre on Monday morning, June 1, 1778. They arrived at Lawrence Lawyer's house. Several of his men volunteered to remain with Captain Patrick while Captain Miller returned to the fort. After his departure, a force of between 30 and 40 Regulars and 15 Loyalist militia volunteers under Captain Brown arrived and attacked the detachment at the residence of George Warner (1757–1844), the southernmost one in the settlement.

Shortly after the arrival of Captain Miller's scouts at Warner's, a band of 15 to 20 Schoharies and Senecas appeared a short distance from the house. All the scouts marched after them. The Schoharies and Senecas kept up a running fight, increasing in numbers as they were pursued about a mile. The scouts halted with the militiamen on the right toward the creek. A sharp engagement followed in which both parties fought under the cover of trees. Captain Patrick lost several men and he was shot in the thigh. Two of his soldiers tried to take him off the field, were surrounded, and shot. One of Captain Patrick's lieutenants was supposedly spared by giving a masonic sign to Joseph Brant Service (d. 1778).

The families in the settlement heard the firing and sought safety in the forest or by fleeing to Schoharie, 10 miles away. When Captain Patrick fell, Captain Brown ordered a retreat. Eleven or 12 militiamen returned to Schoharie. Three of Patrick's men and two of Brown's returned to Warner's house and fired on the Native Americans, giving the rest of their party time to escape. The Schoharies and Senecas set the house on fire, burning three of its occupants. The others were killed trying to escape. One was shot and the other supposedly taken alive and tortured to death. His body was found cut open and his intestines fastened round a tree several feet away. The Crown forces then plundered and burned all the dwellings in Cobleskill as far down as the churches, except for an old log house. Captain Patrick lost 22 men killed and five or six wounded.[79]

★ A band of between 300 and 400 Loyalists and Native Americans took several families away from Sacanda near Johnstown. They escaped to Canada as the militia mustered. Fourteen people butchered beyond recognition were buried at Cobleskill on Sunday, June 14, 1778.[80]

★ Colonel Goose Van Schaick (1736–1789) and a force of 558 soldiers set out on an expedition to destroy Onondaga in mid-April 1779. Many of the Native Americans in the Mohawk Valley fled Van Schaick's advancing army and sought refuge in Seneca. Many others actively joined the war against the Whigs. They executed retaliatory raids and did as much damage as they could to Cobleskill in the Schoharie valley in May 1779. The inhabitants fled the town. The Onondagas isolated and killed seven soldiers in a running battle. They then plundered the town and burned it. Although they mutilated the fallen soldiers, they did not harm any civilians.[81]

★ A party of Loyalists captured Peter Utman at Cobleskill on Saturday, September 1, 1781. He spent two years in Canada as a captive.[82]

Otsego County
Near Cherry Valley (June 2, 1778; Aug. 1778)

> Cherry Valley is in Otsego County, 54 miles west of Albany.

★ Walter Butler (c. 1752–1781), a despised Mohawk Valley Loyalist, instigated some Native Americans in the Cherry Valley area to acts of hostility against the outback settlements in late May and early June 1778. They cut off 20 families in Cherry Valley and captured Captains James Bedlock, Robert Durkee (Durgee) (1733–1778), and Samuel Ranson (1737–1778) on Tuesday, June 2, 1778. They stripped Captain Bedlock, tied him to a tree and stuck him full of sharp pine knot splinters. They then piled a heap of pine knots around him and set them on fire. They put Durkee and Ranson into the fire and held them down with pitch forks.[83]

★ Captain William Boland's (1742–1800) company of New York militiamen captured some Loyalists and cattle at Cherry Valley in August 1778.[84]

Springfield (July 18, 1778)

> Springfield is on Rte. U.S. 20 about 6 miles northwest of Cherry Valley.

★ A band of Loyalists and Native Americans skirted Otsego Lake where there were no scouts. They attacked Springfield by surprise about 10 or 11 AM on Saturday, July 18, 1778 and burned the settlement. As soon as he received intelligence, Lieutenant Colonel Jacob Ford, Jr. (1744–1837) sent two reconnoitering parties and fired an alarm. He later learned that the settlement was ablaze. As he had so few troops (about 80 men), he did not think it proper to send larger parties than the reconnoitering parties he had already sent so as not to expose himself to a surprise attack. He posted his few troops in the best manner possible to defend their post to the death.

Colonel Ford sent a scout of about 30 men toward evening. They returned later that night and reported that they had gone to the settlement and found it in ashes. As the scouts could not find any evidence of the enemy, they determined that the settlement had been destroyed by a scouting party that came to alarm the people. Colonel Ford requested reinforcements of 400–500 troops, both militia and Continental troops, to defend the Mohawk River Valley.[85]

Cherry Valley (Nov. 11, 1778)

> Settled in 1740, Cherry Valley was an important stagecoach stop on the Cherry Valley Turnpike, now U.S. 20.
> A large stone monument in the village cemetery commemorates the victims of the massacre of 1778. The Cherry Valley Museum (**www.cherryvalleymuseum.org/**) at 49 Main Street maintains the local history and the stone memorial in the village cemetery.

★ Walter Butler (ca.1752–1781) and Joseph Brant (1742–1807) Mohawk Chief Thayendanagea joined forces against the strategic but poorly defended settlement of Cherry Valley on Wednesday, November 11, 1778. Snow had already fallen and weather conditions seemed too severe for campaigning, so the residents were not prepared for an attack by 700 Native Americans and Loyalist rangers.

The raiders had already completed a march of 150 miles when they arrived in the vicinity of Cherry Valley. They attacked the village on the morning of November 11, a foggy, rainy Wednesday, killing or capturing most of the officers. They ransacked the village and settlement of 40 homes spread out in an imperfect semicircle over about 6 miles. They killed 15 militiamen and about 30 of the 300 residents in a four-hour period. They captured the rest of the residents but released them the next day, except for two women and seven children whom they kept as hostages to trade for the release of the relatives of Loyalist officers being held prisoner in Albany. The only buildings still standing when the raiders left were the fort, the church, and one or two homes.[86]

Herkimer

German Flats (June 18, 1778; Aug. 1, 1778; Sept. 16, 17, 1778; May 9, 1779; Feb. 1780; June 7, 1780; May 8, 1781; ca. July 10, 1781; Aug. 6, 1781; Oct. 30, 1781; July 15, 1782)

Shell's Bush (Aug. 6, 1781)

Andrustown (Andrew's Town) (July 18, 1778)

Near head of Unadilla River (Sept. 16, 1778; Oct. 8, 1778)

Little Falls (Ellis's (Ellice's) mill) (June 22, 1782)

> German Flats is between Little Falls and Herkimer. The Dutch Reformed Church in Little Falls was enlarged to serve as Fort Herkimer during the Seven Years War. Fort Dayton, on the north side of the Mohawk River at Herkimer (not to be confused with Fort Herkimer Church or the Herkimer house), protected the inhabitants of German Flats, named for the 10-mile stretch of Palatine villages on both sides of the river. Fort Herkimer was located on the south side of the river.
>
> The Fort Herkimer Church, located on Route NY 5S west of Little Falls, served as a base of military supplies for Fort Herkimer which stood about 400 yards west of the church. There are markers at both sites. The church also has a marker commemorating Lieutenant Adam F. Helmer. The site of Fort Herkimer is now a park with a bike path and picnic tables. It was the second stone house of Johan Jost Herchheimer, and where General Nicholas Herkimer spent his childhood and where he came to rest after the battle of Oriskany.
>
> The Herkimer house at 200 Route NY169, Little Falls, 3 miles east of Little Falls and just off the New York Thruway exit 29A is Johan Jost Herchheimer's last house. General Nicholas Herkimer is buried in the family cemetery near the house.
>
> The site of the May 8, 1781 ambush was in a deep ravine 3 miles north of present day Herkimer on the east side of the West Canada Creek. A mound of earth marks the spot. Andrustown was a settlement of seven families, 6 miles southeast of German Flats probably where Route NY 167 and Route NY 168 meet today. The Unadilla River begins about 7 miles south of Herkimer. Shell's Bush was 5 miles north of Herkimer village. Ellis's (Ellice's) Mill was on the Mohawk River at what is now Mill Street and Canal Place.[87]

★ A band of about 500 Native Americans and 20 Loyalists raided German Flats on Thursday, June 18, 1778. They burned all the buildings on both sides of the river for 5 miles: 63 houses, 57 barns, three grist mills, and one saw mill. They also captured 229 cows and oxen, exclusive of the public cattle, 235 horses, and 269 sheep. They killed

Frederick H. Harder (d. 1778) and one of William Duggeret's (Dygert?) slaves. Teddy McGinnie's lunatic son was burned in Adam Staring's (1714–1795) house and Peter Bellinger (1726–1813) wounded. Only the church and Fort Herkimer, on the south side, were spared.

There were about 50 rangers in the fort. When the enemy appeared on a hill overlooking the fort about 275 yards away, they fired over the pickets into the fort with small arms, killing one man and wounding another. The rangers returned fire but to no effect.[88]

★ Native Americans under Joseph Brant (1742–1807), Mohawk Chief Thayendanagea, plundered and burned Andrustown on Saturday, July 18, 1778. They killed an unknown number of people and captured others. This event alarmed the people in the neighboring area. They then kept scouts on the alert for further attacks.[89]

★ Joseph Brant (1742–1807), Mohawk Chief Thayendanagea and Captain William Caldwell (1763–1849) led a mixed force of 450 Loyalists and Mohawks on a raid on the German Flats area on Tuesday, August 1, 1778.

★ A party of militiamen plundered the Loyalist settlements of Unadilla and Butternuts on Wednesday, September 16, 1778. They took 10 prisoners and freed William Dygert (1723–1802 or 1750–1818 or 1753–1791), a prisoner of the Loyalists at Unadilla.[90]

★ Joseph Brant (1742–1807), Mohawk Chief Thayendanagea was at Unadilla, a Native American town about 50 miles southwest of German Flats in late August 1778. He and Captain William Caldwell (1763–1849) commanded a band of 300 Loyalists and 150 Native Americans, mostly Oneidas and Tuscaroras. They decided to attack German Flats early in September. The inhabitants anticipated an attack and sent four scouts toward Unadilla. Brant's Native Americans spotted them and killed three of them. The fourth, Adam F. Helmer (1754–1830), escaped to alarm the town.

Helmer's warning gave the residents time to gather their most valuable portable possessions and get safely inside either Fort Herkimer or Fort Dayton or the stone church. Brant and Caldwell arrived at German Flats during the stormy night of September 12. They waited until 6 AM on Thursday, September 17th to attack the forts. Colonel Peter Bellinger's (1726–1813) militia resisted and lost two killed, one wounded and five captured. By noon, the attackers had set fire to both sides of the river, burning 63 houses, 57 barns, three gristmills and one sawmill. They gathered over 700 head of livestock (cattle, horses, sheep) and returned to Unadilla without any casualties. The 719 inhabitants (including 387 children) were alive but homeless.[91]

★ The inhabitants retaliated by attacking Unadilla in early October, 1778. Lieutenant Colonel William Butler (ca. 1745–1789) left Schoharie with his 4th Pennsylvania Continental regiment, a detachment of Colonel Daniel Morgan's (1736–1802) riflemen, and a small corps of Rangers. They arrived at Unadilla on Thursday, October 8 to find the town deserted, "the enemy having that day left it in the greatest confusion, leaving behind a large quantity of corn, their dogs, some cattle and a great part of their household furniture." Butler's troops "fared sumptuously, having poultry and vegetables in great abundance." They then burned "ten good frame houses, with a quantity of corn," then "set fire to all the town . . . burned all the houses" except one. They also burned "a saw-mill and grist mill, the latter the only one in the country." After exacting their revenge, they marched back to Schoharie.[92]

★ The attack on German Flats brought retaliation against Unadilla. That attack provoked another reprisal against Cherry Valley on Wednesday, November 11, 1778. Major General John Sullivan's (1740–1795) expedition against the Native American tribes intended to put an end to the attacks.

★ A party of 12 Native Americans from Oswegoche killed three people, scalped two women, and captured one prisoner from German Flats about Sunday, May 9, 1779.[93]
★ A small band of Loyalists and Native Americans did some damage at German Flats in February 1780.[94]
★ Militiamen from Fort Herkimer drove off a party of Native American raiders at German Flats on Friday, June 7, 1780.[95]
★ Lieutenant Solomon Woodworth (1743–1781) led a scouting party of 46 militiamen and six Oneidas from Fort Dayton up the West Canada Creek near Herkimer on Tuesday, May 8, 1781 to look for signs of the enemy. They found tracks and followed them. Loyalist Lieutenant John Clement learned that his war party of 74 Onondagas and Cayugas was being followed and set an ambush.

When Woodworth spotted one of the Onondagas, he and his men pursued the Onondaga into the ambush. The first volley left 10 of Woodworth's men dead or dying. When the skirmish was over, 22 militiamen were dead, including Lieutenant Woodworth. Nine were captured and taken to Canada. The rest of the militiamen and the Oneidas escaped and returned to Fort Dayton. Lieutenant Clement had only two men wounded.[96]

★ Soon after the burning of Currytown, one of Colonel Jacob Klock's sons, who had joined the Loyalists in Canada, led a party of Native Americans and Loyalists against German Flats on Tuesday, July 10, 1781. They encamped one night in the vicinity; but one of his men learned that a family of his relatives was among the intended victims. He deserted and warned the settlers who mustered 25 men led by Lieutenant Jacob Sammons (1752–1834). They went in search of the attackers who retreated when they learned that the settlers were aware of their presence. Jacob Sammons and his men overtook the Loyalists and Native Americans and routed them in a skirmish which ensued. The Loyalists lost a Native American who was wounded, captured and later killed by the deserter who now joined in the pursuit of his former comrades. Three of the wounded who escaped died on their way to Canada. The Loyalists also lost their provisions and some of their arms.

★ Donald McDonald (1712–?), a Scottish refugee from Johnstown, attacked Shell's Bush, 5 miles north of Herkimer village, with 60 Native Americans and Loyalists on Monday, August 6, 1781. After most of the inhabitants of the settlement had fled to Fort Dayton, Mr. Shell decided to defend his stockaded house with two or three of his sons. The attackers tried to burn it and then to force its door. As Mrs. Shell loaded the muskets, her husband and sons held off the attackers for several hours, killing 11 and wounding six. They finally gave up and withdrew.

Captain William Caldwell (1763–1849) of Butler's Rangers made a similar incursion from Niagara later that summer. Colonel Albert Pawling (1750–1837) and a force of state troops and militiamen repelled him and his 400 Native Americans and Loyalists and inflicted considerable losses.[97]

★ Major John Ross, head of the Royal Greens 2nd battalion, assumed command of a Crown forces expedition to the Mohawk Valley when Sir John Johnson (1742–1830) was granted leave to sail to England on family business. His force of 734 men, including 234 Loyalists, 112 Regulars, 12 jaegers, 167 of Butler's Rangers, and 209 Native Americans prepared to return to Canada after raiding the Schoharie Valley. As the Congressional forces knew by which route he had come, he decided to head toward Carleton Island. He could not locate the path until October 29, 1781 due to the snowfall and poor visibility.

The Native Americans from Canada told Ross they intended to go home rather than to Carleton Island and left the next day. They almost encountered Colonel Marinus Willett's (1740–1830) advance force which had been sent out from Fort Dayton to scout for Ross's party. Willett's force numbered about 500 men after 100 Tryon County militiamen joined him. Ross headed west to Garoga Creek and reached West Canada Creek, near the present town of Ohio, about 2 PM on Tuesday, October 30th. Willett's forces marched up the creek's east bank and arrived just as Ross's men were crossing to the west bank. An Oneida sniper, across the creek, spotted Captain Walter Butler (c.1752–1781) and his Rangers covering Ross's rear. The sniper shot Butler through the head and crossed the creek to finish him off and to scalp him. Willett returned to Fort Dayton as he was short of provisions.[98]

See also **Warrensbush.**

★ A large party of 300 Crown troops, comprising about 100 Regulars (believed to be Sir John Johnson's (1742–1830) corps) and 200 Native Americans and Loyalists, surprised a sergeant's guard at Ellis's mill (owned by Alexander Ellice (d.1808)), near Little Falls about daylight on Saturday, June 22, 1782. The guard consisted of the sergeant and six men from Captain McGregor's Company of Continental troops. When the attackers arrived, only a few shots were fired, and Daniel Petri (b. 1715–1722; d.1782) was the only man killed.

The occupants attempted to escape as best they could. Two of the millers, F. Cox and Gershom Skinner, hid in the raceway, under the waterwheel and escaped death and captivity. Two others, Christian Edick (1766–1814)and Frederick Getman (1736–1792/93), jumped into the raceway above the mill and tried to conceal themselves there. When the attackers burned the mill, the last operating grist mill in the Little Falls area, the flames disclosed their hiding place and they were taken prisoners along with 10 people who had brought corn to the mill and were waiting for their flour. Two of the soldiers escaped and five were taken prisoners. The burning of Ellis's mill forced the farmers to cart their grain 22 miles to the next mill. This event is sometimes referred to as Petri's or Petrie's Mill. John Joost Petri (1686–1770) and other Palatines were granted the patent for the lands on the north side of the river, from the upper to the lower end of the falls, in 1725. The patent for the lands on the south side of the river, known as the Fall-Hill patent, was granted to Johan Jost Herchheimer, Herchkeemer or Herkimer (1722–1775), General Nicholas Herkimer's (1728–1777) father, and another person in 1752. Mr. Ellice held the title to two of the four lots on the north side of the river.[98a]

★ A large force of Iroquois and Loyalists struck German Flats again the following month on Monday, July 15, 1782. This time, they burned all but seven of the 60 houses. All the residents remained safe inside the forts. They left five barns standing and carried off or slaughtered all the cattle.[99]

Schoharie (Aug. 1778; early Aug. 1780; Oct. 17 or 19, 1780)
Gallupville (July 26, 1782)

> The Schoharie Valley, about 30 miles west of Albany, was a granary area producing about 80,000 bushels per harvest for the Continental Army. This made the valley an attractive objective for Loyalist and Native American raiders. The Charlotte River is one of the upper tributaries of the Susquehanna, flowing from the mountains south of Schoharie. The inhabitants of the valley formed a committee of safety in 1775,

organized five companies of minutemen, and eventually built three forts to protect the valley.

The Old Stone Fort on Fort Road east of North Main Street in Schoharie, near the intersection of NY 30 and NY 443, was originally built as a church in 1772. It was enclosed by a stockade and two blockhouses in 1778 and called Lower Fort. Blockhouses at the southwest and northeast corners of the stockade mounted small cannon. Sharpshooters manned the church's square tower which once was topped by a belfry and spire (removed in 1830). The roof cornice at the rear of the church has a hole supposedly made by a small cannonball fired by the attackers in 1780 (see Photo NY-13).

The Old Stone Fort Museum Complex contains exhibits of the Schoharie County Historical Society that include electrified maps. An audio-visual program interprets Revolutionary War activities of the region. Other buildings comprise a 1740 Palatine house, an 18th-century Dutch barn, an 1850 law office, an 1860 schoolhouse, and a historical and genealogy library. David Williams (1754–1831), one of the three men who captured Major John André (1751–1780) at Tarrytown, is buried in front of the church. A tall pillar marks the grave.[100]

A highway marker on NY 30 at Watsonville about 4 miles southwest of Middleburg identifies the site of the house where Timothy Murphy (1751–1818) lived for several years and where he died in 1818 at the age of 67. A marker for the Upper Fort appears on the left side of NY 30 about a quarter of a mile south of the marker for Murphy's house.

The stone Becker house still stands on Murphy Road in Gallupville, east of Schoharie. To get there, take Route NY 30 (North Main Street) north from Schoharie. Turn right (east) on NY 443 and proceed about 2.5 miles to Shutter Corners. Turn right on Debriko Road and proceed about 300 yards to Murphy Road which is just across the Fox Creek bridge. There's a marker on Murphy Road, on the right when traveling west. There are also markers on the house itself.

★ Captain Edward Long (1739–1792) was ordered to the Charlotte River valley in August 1778, to arrest a noted Loyalist named Joseph Brant Service (d. 1778) and bring him to the fort. Service's house was a rendezvous and supply depot for Loyalist and Native American scouts. As Captain Long advanced to destroy the house, he intercepted a company of Loyalists near Catskill. They had enlisted for the king's service and were on their way to join Sir John Johnson (1742–1830) at Niagara. When their leader, a Captain Smith (d. 1778), emerged from a thicket, at the head of his men, he was killed by two shots fired simultaneously. His followers fled in every direction. The party had intended to lodge with Service that night, but his house was surrounded by Captain Long's troops. Timothy Murphy (1751–1818) and David Elerson rushed in and captured Service. As they were leaving the house to take their prisoner to Schoharie, Service seized an axe by the door and swung it at Murphy's head. Murphy quickly stepped to the side to avoid the blow and Service fell dead from Elerson's rifle.

★ A party of Loyalists burned the principal part of Canajoharie and 12 or 13 houses in Schoharie in early August 1780 (probably Thursday, August 10). Few lives were lost, as the inhabitants had abandoned their houses.[101]

★ Sir John Johnson (1742–1830) and Joseph Brant (1742–1807), Mohawk Chief Thayendanagea, joined forces at Unadilla late in September 1780, and ravaged the valley. The 800–1,500 raiders advanced from the southwest in the night of Sunday,

Photo NY-13. Old Stone Fort, Schoharie. A cannonball is still lodged in the soffit above the sign.

October 15. They bypassed the Upper Fort (in the vicinity of Toepath Mountain) and approached the Middle Fort (in modern Middleburg) early in the morning. They besieged the Lower Fort and began firing on it on October 17.

Major Melancthon Lloyd Woolsey (1758–1819), the commander, was ready to consider terms of surrender when Timothy Murphy (1751–1818), famous for his marksmanship which killed Brigadier General Simon Fraser (1729–1777) at Bemis Heights, fired on the enemy's "flag" each time Major Woolsey tried to receive Sir John's terms of surrender. When the officers of the garrison tried to arrest Murphy, his fellow soldiers rallied around him to prevent the arrest and called Woolsey a coward for wanting to surrender. When Woolsey ordered a white flag to be raised, Murphy threatened to shoot anyone who tried to obey the order. The raiders, unaware of what was happening inside the fort, withdrew because they could not batter the fort. They proceeded down the valley, burning the houses, barns, and crops of the Whigs and killing or taking their domestic animals.

★ Sir John Johnson (1742–1830); Lieutenant Colonel William Butler (ca. 1745–1789); and Joseph Brant (1742–1807), Mohawk Chief Thayendanagea; and about 485 men, including two or three Senecas, with a brass grasshopper, a 3-pounder and a 4-pound cohorn, descended on Schoharie on Thursday, October 19, 1780. They destroyed the town and burned the homes of the supporters of the Congressional forces and ruined their farmlands along with the grain, forage, etc. They then proceeded up the Mohawk River, destroying towns as far up as Stone Arabia.[102]

See also **Middleburg.**

★ Captain Adam Crysler (1732–1793) and William Crysler (1746–?) led a small band of about 22 Native Americans and Loyalists to the Schoharie Valley in July of 1782 to burn property and capture as many prisoners as possible. They intended to capture George Warner, Sr. (1720–?) at his log cabin near Cobleskill but he was not at home when they arrived. They took his son, George Jr., prisoner instead.

Adam captured two more prisoners Friday morning, July 26, 1782 before attacking the home of Jacob Zimmer of Wright, near Foxes Creek. Jacob Zimmer, Jr. (d. 1782) and a Hessian employee were killed in the skirmish. Jacob Jr.'s brother, Peter Zimmer, was taken prisoner and the house and barn set afire. Mrs. Zimmer was allowed to remain at home. She managed to put out the fire at the house after Adam's party left.

The Cryslers proceeded two farms down Foxes Creek toward Schoharie when they came to Major Joseph Becker's (d. 1806) stone house. Major Becker was at home with his wife and some others at the time. They put up a good defense. One of the marksmen, John Huff, put a bullet through the brim of Adam's hat. The raiders tried to enter the house for several hours. They tried to set the house on fire several times but the inhabitants extinguished the flames each time. The Cryslers abandoned their effort to conquer Major Becker as darkness approached.[103]

Cochecton, Sullivan Co. (Aug. 10, 1778)

> Cochecton is about 17 miles north of Minisink, on the Delaware River which separates New York and Pennsylvania.

★ Captain Tyler led a militia detachment to attack a party of Native Americans and Loyalists at Cochecton, Sullivan Co. on Monday, August 10, 1778. He lost three men killed, two wounded, and three captured.[104]

Johnstown (Apr. 11, 1779; May 22, 1780; Aug. 22, 1781; Oct. 25, 1781)
Warrensbush (Oct. 24, 1781)

> Sir William Johnson (1715–1774), a British general and Superintendent of Indian Affairs during the mid-1700s, founded the town which is named after him. Johnstown has several historic sites, including the Johnstown Battlefield (**www.carogalake .com/Activities/historic_sites/johnstown.htm**). Sir William Johnson erected the

Fulton County Court House (North William and East Main Street **www.courts.state.ny.us/history/elecbook/fulton/pg1.htm**) in 1774. It is the only colonial courthouse still standing in New York and still remains in use. The belfry houses a large iron bar that was bent into a triangle and used as a bell to announce the sessions of court. It was also rung in honor of the Declaration of Independence.

Johnson Hall State Historic Site (Hall Avenue, west of Route NY 29; **www.thenortherncampaign.org/johnsonsite.htm**), a white clapboard Georgian house (see Photo NY-14) built in 1763, was the last home of Sir William Johnson.

St. John's Episcopal Church (North Market Street) was built by Sir William Johnson in 1772. He was buried under the chancel two years later. The church burned in 1836 and was rebuilt in a slightly different location in 1840. Johnson's grave was "lost" and discovered later that year. His body, identified by the lead ball in his hip—a souvenir from his victory at Lake George—was re-interred in the rear of the church and is marked by four simple cornerstones.

Warrensbush is equidistant from Fort Hunter, Schoharie, and Schenectady. Johnstown is about 25 miles northwest of Schenectady and 30 miles east of Herkimer. Colonel John Johnson's house or fort was a base for the Whigs during the Battle of Johnstown, Thursday, October 25, 1781.

Photo NY-14. Johnson Hall, the last home of Sir William Johnson. Note the two stone blockhouses behind the house. Compare with the wooden blockhouse in Photo NY-17.

★ On Sunday April 11, 1779, 12 Native Americans and two Loyalists captured four prisoners near Sir William Johnson's old house. One of them escaped and reported that they intended to take two more inhabitants to gain intelligence. They reportedly killed two people who tried to escape.[105]

May 22, 1780 see **Caughnawauga.**

★ Major John Ross and Walter Butler (ca.1752–1781) headed to Johnstown from Canada by way of Sacondaga in August 1781. They marched with 607 men: 477 British and Provincial troops and 130 Native Americans. They camped on a hill a little north of Johnson Hall, located in the center of Johnstown, about a mile from the court house.

Colonel Marinus Willett (1740–1830) and 300 levies departed from Fort Plain to meet them. Colonel Willett planned to attack their camp on Wednesday, August 22, 1781. He sent Colonel Harper and 100 men to circle through the woods and attack the enemy's rear while he attacked the front. Major Ross met Colonel Willett with all his troops a short distance above Johnson Hall. Colonel Willett's men retreated after the first volley. Colonel Willett tried unsuccessfully to rally them at Johnson Hall. He managed to stop them at the village where 200 militiamen had just arrived to join him.

Colonel Harper's detachment attacked the rear of the Crown forces. When they opened fire, Colonel Willett's forces renewed the attack and drove the enemy from their position. Colonel Willett lost 13 men and killed 17 British and Native Americans.

Major Ross's Crown troops retreated up the north side of the Mohawk, 20 or 30 miles north of Fort Schuyler, after the battle. They marched all night. Colonel Willett pursued them in the morning but never overtook them. Maj. Ross's troops suffered much from hunger in the uncultivated, desolate area. Walter Butler was killed during the retreat when a small party of Oneidas pursued him. When he arrived at West Canada Creek (about 15 miles north of Herkimer), he swam his horse across the creek and turned around to defy the Oneidas on the other side.

One of the Oneidas fired his weapon and wounded Butler who fell to the ground. The Oneida threw down his weapon and his blanket, dove into the creek and swam to the opposite bank. Butler pleaded in vain for mercy; but the Oneida planted the tomahawk firmly into his skull, shouting in broken English: "Sherry Valley! Remember Sherry Valley!" He then scalped Butler who expired before the rest of the Oneidas had crossed the creek.[106]

See also **Herkimer, German Flats** and **West Canada Creek.**

★ Colonel John Johnson's son, Walter, led a force of 1,000 men consisting of four companies of the Royal Greens (Loyalists), Butler's Rangers, and 200 Native Americans. They marched from Oswego to attack the village of Warrensbush, where Schoharie Kill empties into the Mohawk, on Wednesday, October 24, 1781. They arrived undetected and struck the village "as suddenly as though they had sprung from the earth," killing four people, destroying property and burning houses. They destroyed 22 houses, 28 barns, one grist mill, 5,411 bushels of grain and peas, 109 tons of hay, 172 head of cattle, and 33 horses. With Colonel Marinus Willett (1740–1830) in close pursuit, the Crown forces hurried home. They crossed the Mohawk River at 1 AM and headed to Johnstown where the Battle of Johnstown was fought later that day.[107]

★ Militia Colonel Marinus Willett (1740–1830) led a force of 416 men against a Loyalist and Native American raiding party of 1,000 near Johnson Hall on Thursday, October 25, 1781. They attacked from the southeast but were repelled by the larger force under Major John Ross. Fighting into the woods in the rainy twilight, Willett believed he had the advantage, but the enemy captured his one gun and stripped its ammunition cart before he could retake it. Willett's right flank collapsed in panic, but he managed to rally many of his troops and continue fighting until dusk. The Loyalists and Native Americans withdrew to a nearby hill.

Willett and his men retreated and fled to Fort Johnstown (the old jail located on Montgomery and South Perry streets) (see Photo NY-15). Willett reported finding the bodies of seven enemies and three of his own men on the field. He estimated that each side suffered 30–40 wounded and he captured 30 prisoners.

The Battle of Johnstown took place six days after Lord Cornwallis had laid down his arms in Yorktown, Virginia.[108]

Photo NY-15. Fort Johnstown

Onondagas (Apr. 19, 1779)

> Onondagas was about 5 miles south of Syracuse.

General Henry Clinton's (1730–1795) troops were still in winter quarters in New York when General George Washington (1732–1799) began to plan to have part of his army punish the Native Americans who had destroyed the Wyoming and Cherry Valleys the previous year. He assigned New Jersey troops for this duty; but they refused to march until the state legislature made provisions for the support of their families. When the state legislature provided money to pay the officers and men, order was restored; but the expedition to Wyoming Valley was postponed to concentrate on the Southern campaign.

Nevertheless, Colonel Goose Van Schaick, Lieutenant-Colonel Marinus Willett (1740–1830), and Major Cochran made a surprise attack on the towns of the Onondagas on Monday, April 19, 1779. They destroyed the whole settlement without losing a man.[109]

Ogdensburg
Oswegatchie (Apr. 25, 1779; May 21, 26, 1779)

> Fort La Présentation, today's Odgensburg, is along the Oswegatchie River 130 miles northwest of Fort Schuyler and near the St. Lawrence River. The square fort had tower-shaped bastions (see Photo NY-1, NY-2) in the four angles. It was surrounded by a wide moat and an entrenchment with palisades. A parapet constructed of two thicknesses of timber could withstand small artillery fire. It had seven small guns and 11 4- and 6-pounders and was garrisoned by 30 men. The bay between the peninsula and the mainland was not very wide, so the fort commanded all watercraft in the Oswegatchie.

Colonel Goose Van Schaick (1736–1789), commander of the 1st battalion of New York Continental troops, sent Lieutenant Thomas McClennan and 34 men, including a sergeant, a corporal, and about 30 Native Americans, to Oswegatchie (Ogdensburg) on Sunday, April 25, 1779. They attempted to take the fort which was garrisoned by Captain Davis, of the 31st Regiment, a subaltern and 40 men, with four pieces of cannon; but the enemy were on their guard. McClennan tried to draw them out of the fort; but they were cautious and only sent out a few Native Americans. McClennan's men killed two of them and the others retreated into the fort. McClennan returned with six prisoners, four British and two Native Americans.[110]

★ Very early on Friday, May 21, 1779, Colonel Van Schaick's troops proceeded to cross Salt Lake at an arm which was 200 yards over and five feet deep. They forded it, carrying their pouches hung to their fixed bayonets, and advanced to the Onondago Creek, where they took an Onondago warrior prisoner. As they could not ford the creek, the troops crossed it on a log. Once across, they tried to surround the settlements. However, the settlements extended 8 miles with some scattered habitations behind the castles. The troops entered the first settlement totally undiscovered; but some of the advanced parties were soon discovered and the alarm went out to all the settlements. Different parties were ordered to take different routes to surround as many of the settlements as possible; but the Onondagos quickly fled to the woods, not taking anything with them.

The troops killed 12 Onondagos and took 33 of them and one white man prisoners. They burned all the settlements, consisting of about 50 houses, along with a large quantity of corn and beans. They killed a number of fine horses and every other kind of stock. They took about 100 guns, including some rifles, and destroyed everything they could not carry, including a considerable quantity of ammunition. They also broke the trunnions (see Photo NY-16) off one swivel (see Photo NY-9) taken at the council-house.

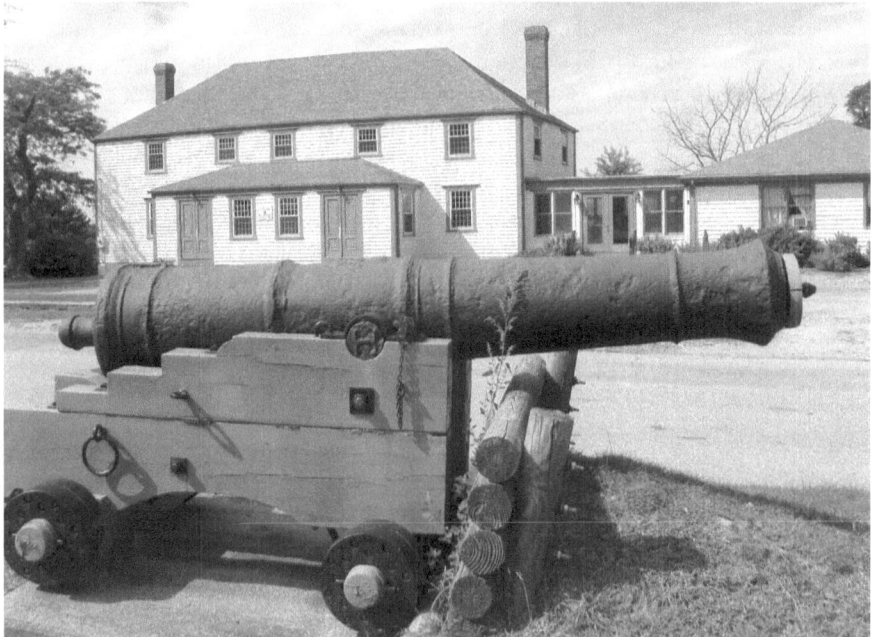

Photo NY-16. An 18-pound cannon showing the trunnion, the round support resting on the gun carriage. The Quaker Meeting House on Quaker Hill in Portsmouth, Rhode Island is in the background.

The troops re-crossed the creek and forded the arm of the lake to return. A small party of Onondagos fired upon them from the opposite side of the creek, but they were soon beaten back by the riflemen who killed one of them. The troops marched to the landing on the 22nd, embarked and rowed to Seven Mile Island. They returned safely to Fort Schuyler, having covered 180 miles in five and one-half days.[111]

★ Colonel Van Schaick captured more than 20 Native Americans, including two or three sachems, at the Onandago Castle on Wednesday, May 26, 1779 and brought them to Albany.[112]

Port Jervis

Minisink (June 22, 1779; July 19–22, 1779; Apr. 14, 1780; Apr. 20, 1780; Sept. 28, 1781)

> Minisink is now called Port Jervis. There were three Native American villages using the name Minisink in the area, including Minisink Ford on the Delaware River. The battlefield is located in the vicinity of the junction of NY 97 and County Road 168. Minisink Ford is on the Delaware River northwest of Port Jervis and opposite Lackawaxen, Pennsylvania.
> The place of the massacre came to be known as Hospital Rock. It is reached by a short path 100 yards west of the battle monument erected in 1830 that lists the names of some 45 casualties. Sentinel Rock, a large boulder about 100 yards to the southwest, is where Joseph Brant stormed through the militia defenses. There are many historical markers along NY 97 commemorating the events.

★ As a body of troops proceeded up the Susquehannah River on their way to Chemung in June 1779, they were dogged by a few Native American scouts. When they reached Minisink, four male inhabitants were killed and scalped on Tuesday, June 22, 1779. The troops remained at Minisink for two weeks waiting for their supplies and some reinforcements to arrive before they could continue their expedition.[113]

★ Joseph Brant (1742–1807) Mohawk Chief Thayendanagea and a party of 60 Native Americans and 27 Loyalists burned and looted Minisink on Monday night, July 19, 1779. They were more intent on looting and destruction, taking only three prisoners and four scalps. Lieutenant Colonel (Dr.) Benjamin Tusten (1743–1779) and about 150 local militiamen pursued Brant for 17 miles the following day before camping for the night.

The militia was about a mile away from Brant at about 9 AM on July 22 and tried to catch him crossing a ford in the Delaware River. When the woods and high ground hid the two forces from each other, Brant circled around to the American rear and set up an ambush along the retreat route.

The militiamen were surprised and disappointed not to find the enemy around the ford. They began to return home when they ran into the ambush. Brant cut off a third of the militia while the rest took a position on the high ground and held it for several hours. As dusk fell and the defenders ran low on ammunition, Brant identified a weak point in the defense and attacked.

Organized resistance collapsed and the defenders were massacred. The casualties included Lieutenant Colonel Benjamin Tusten, a physician, and the 17 wounded he was tending. Several men were also shot trying to swim across the Delaware. There were only 30 survivors from the initial party.[114]

★ After destroying Harpersfield on Sunday, April 2, 1780, Joseph Brant (1742–1807), Mohawk Chief Thayendanagea intended to attack Upper Fort (near Schoharie), but

Lieutenant Alexander Harper (1744–1798), overheard him making plans. Harper deceived Brant by telling him that 300 Continental troops had arrived there three days earlier. Disappointed, Brant and his force of 43 Mohawks and seven Loyalists took their 19 prisoners and attacked Minisink on Friday, April 14, 1780.[115]

★ A party of Native Americans were observed at Minisink on Monday, April 17, 1780. The following Thursday, some New Jersey militiamen crossed the Delaware and engaged them in a very severe conflict. The militiamen killed the commanding officer, a white man from Somerset county, and routed the Native Americans. They lost Captain Dirck Westbrook (1751–1780), a lieutenant, and one private killed. They captured six blankets, two watch coats, several packs, and a quantity of provisions.[116]

★ Sergeant Joseph Garlinghouse (d. 1781) was teaching a couple of recruits stationed at Minisink the manual of exercise Friday morning, September 28, 1781. Standing before them as fugilman, he ordered them to take aim and fire. One of their muskets was loaded and went off at half cock. The entire charge entered Sergeant Garlinghouse's breast, killing him instantly.[117]

Elmira
Chemung (Aug. 13, 15, 1779)
Battle of Newtown (Aug. 29, 1779)

> Newtown Battlefield is on Route U.S. 17, 3 miles east of Elmira. The Battle of Newtown is also known as the Battle of Chemung (**www.mizar5.com/cvlh/camp.htm**).
>
> Newtown Battlefield Reservation (**www.mizar5.com/cvlh/home.htm**) memorializes General John Sullivan's victory with a 60-foot-tall stone obelisk that was erected in 1912. The 300-acre park atop 600-foot high Sullivan Hill lies 1,000 feet east of the Chemung and offers a marvelous view of the Chemung Valley, but it has little relationship to the battle which was fought along the ridge below it and near the river. The battle area is largely undeveloped and is privately owned. Some historical markers along U.S. 17 and on the Wellsburg turnoff identify sites and actions associated with the fight.
>
> Chemung is about 7 miles southeast of the Newtown Battlefield Reservation near the Pennsylvania state line. It was a probable place of rendezvous for the enemy.

★ General Henry Clinton's (1730–1795) inaction allowed General George Washington (1732–1799) to attempt to deal with British-inspired Native American attacks in 1779. Although Major General John Burgoyne's (1722–1792) defeat ended the threat of invasion from Canada, the British continued to incite the Native Americans all along the frontier to bloody raids on American settlements. From Fort Niagara and Detroit, they sent out their bands, usually led by Loyalists, to pillage, scalp and burn in the Mohawk Valley of New York, the Wyoming Valley of Pennsylvania, and the new settlements in Kentucky.

Washington detached Major General John Sullivan (1740–1795) with a force of 4,000 seasoned Continentals to deal with the Iroquois in Pennsylvania and New York. Washington wanted a punitive expedition that would end the problems with the Native Americans. He ordered "the total destruction and devastation of their settlements" and the taking of prisoners, including women and children who would be kept as hostages to insure future cooperation from the Iroquois.

Sullivan organized his troops in Easton, Pennsylvania, on May 7 but waited six weeks before setting out for western New York on June 18. His army, at Wyoming at the end of July 1779, consisted of Brigadier General William Maxwell's (1733–1796) Brigade (Ogden's, Dayton's, Shrive's, and Spencer's Regiments), Brigadier General Enoch Poor's (1736–1780) Brigade (Cilley's, Reed's, Scammel's, and Cortlandt's Regiments), and Brigadier General Edward Hand's (1744–1802) Brigade (the German Regiment, Hubley's Regiment, Short's Corps, and Spalding's Company). The army moved from Wyoming at 1 PM on Saturday, July 31, 1779. General Hand's Brigade preceded the column by a mile to act as light troops. General Maxwell's and Poor's brigades followed with about 1200 pack horses and about 500 head of cattle behind them. They had one regiment for the rear guard and 200 men as a flank guard on the right and 60 men on the left by the river. Colonel Thomas Proctor's (1739–1806) artillery regiment went by water with about 120 boats with provisions and stores. A captain and 60 men marched on the opposite side of the river to prevent ambuscades.

They set out at 9 PM on Thursday, August 12th, and marched through the night to surprise the Native American town of Chemung, about 15 miles from Tioga. When they arrived at dawn on Friday, they found the town of about 40 houses, built chiefly with split and hewn timber, deserted. General Sullivan ordered the "Town to be Illuminated" about sundown. Maxwell's brigade burned more than 30 buildings and cut down and destroyed about 40 acres of corn while Poor's brigade covered the flank. A party of Native Americans and Loyalists on a high bluff across the river fired at them and killed one New Jersey soldier and wounded five.

General Hand pursued the road up the river. About 20 Native Americans fired on him from behind some bushes about 2 miles along the road. They killed six privates and two officers and fled. Four privates were wounded, mostly from friendly fire. Hand pursued them for several miles, but Sullivan called him back to assist in the destruction of the crops. The troops returned to Tioga by nightfall, having marched more than 40 miles in 24 hours.

★ Early Sunday afternoon, August 15, a "discharge of guns" and "immediately afterwards the Indian scalp whoop" startled Sullivan's camp. The Native Americans had fired upon a corporal and four men of the 3rd New Jersey Regiment who had been sent to collect cattle from a grazing herd. They killed and scalped the young herd driver and wounded one soldier. Some of Hand's New Jersey troops went in pursuit and spotted the Native Americans "retreating along the mountains" but could not capture them.

The Battle of Chemung, also known as the Battle of Newtown, was fought two weeks later on August 29.[118]

★ General Sullivan made no effort to hide his movements, so his prey soon learned of his advance. The force of some 800 Iroquois, under Joseph Brant (1742–1807) Mohawk Chief Thayendanagea, 250 Loyalists, and 15 men of the British 8th Regiment, were determined to destroy Sullivan's army before it gained momentum. They decided on a surprise attack over the objections of Walter Butler (ca. 1752–1781), a despised Mohawk Valley Loyalist. They fortified the mountain pass along the Chemung River, just south of Elmira, with a camouflaged log breastwork and waited as Sullivan approached early on Sunday, August 29, 1779.

The advancing column included three companies of Colonel Daniel Morgan's (1736–1802) Virginia riflemen in the lead. They spotted the trap and Sullivan directed Brigadier General Enoch Poor (1736–1780) to lead the main assault on the hill on the enemy's left. As Poor advanced, the artillery fired on the breastwork.

Nathan Davis recorded this account of the battle of Newtown:
> When our front had advanced within a short distance of them, they commenced a fire from behind every tree, and at the same time gave a war whoop. Not all the infernals of the Prince of Darkness, could they have been let loose from the bottomless pit, would have borne any comparison to these demons of the forest.
>
> We were expressly ordered not to fire, until we had obtained permission from our officers, but to form a line of battle as soon as possible and march forward. This we did in good order, and at the same time the Indians kept up an incessant fire upon us from behind trees; firing and retreating back to another tree, loading and firing again, still keeping up the war whoop. They continued this mode of warfare till we had driven them halfway up the hill, when we were ordered to charge bayonets and rush on. No sooner said than done. We then, in our turn, gave our war whoop, in the American style, which completely silenced the unearthly voice of their stentorian throats. We drove them, at once, to the opposite side of the hill, when we were ordered to halt, as the Indians were out of sight and hearing.
>
> How many we killed I never could exactly ascertain, but some were killed, and one scalped to my knowledge, and much blood was seen on their track. We also took two prisoners, one Negro and one white man, said to be a Tory. The white man was found painted black, lying on his face, and pretending to be dead. As no blood was seen near him, after a proper discipline he was soon brought to his feelings. He was then stripped and washed, and found to be white. A rope was then tied round his neck, and he was led in front of the troops, whilst every one gave him his sentence, 'You shall be hung tomorrow.' This, however, was not put into execution.[119]

The defenders retreated under Sullivan's artillery. Other Continentals had taken the enemy's right. The Native Americans, outnumbered five to one and facing encirclement, began to flee. Most retreated over the mountains with much difficulty. Those who remained fought bravely. Sullivan lost three men killed and 39 wounded. The Native Americans lost approximately 12 men killed.

Sullivan did not pursue but kept marching for the next six weeks without encountering much resistance. He destroyed 40 Native American settlements and many fields and orchards, returning to Easton on Friday, October 15 with a few prisoners. His men had been as brutal as their foes, scalping the wounded and mutilating the dead. Sullivan failed to crush the Six Nations, and their warriors renewed their raids in 1780 and 1781 with unprecedented ferocity.[120]

Havana
Catherine's Town (Sept. 2, 1779)
Appletown (Sept. 4, 1779)
Kindaia (Sept. 5, 1779)

> Catherine's Town, now Havana, consisted of about 30 houses 3 miles from the head of Seneca Lake.

See also **Chemung** and **Cayuga Lake.**

★ Major General John Sullivan's (1740–1795) army arrived at Catherine's Town on Thursday, September 2, 1779 and destroyed it the next day. They then marched to the lake and proceeded 9 miles along its east bank. They marched another 12 miles down the lake and burned "a small village" (Appletown) and "several fine fields of corn" on Saturday, the 4th and Kindaia's 30 "neatly built & finished" houses made a fine bonfire on the 5th.[121]

Geneva
Cayuga Lake, raid (Sept. 7–15, 1779)
Canandaigua (Sept. 1779)
Kanadesaga (Oct. 22, 1780)

> Kanadesaga (Seneca Castle), considered as the capital of the Senecas, consisted of 80 houses on the east side of Seneca Lake about 1.5 miles northwest of Geneva and about 40 miles southeast of Rochester.

★ Major General John Sullivan's (1740–1795) expedition returned to the Cayuga Lake region in September 1779 to destroy what it had overlooked before. The soldiers began their march at 7 AM on Tuesday, September 7, 1779 and proceeded 8 miles to the end of the lake where they expected to be attacked as they forded the outlet of the Lake. General Sullivan sent out several scouts to reconnoitre the adjacent wood before crossing. His men then proceeded to a small settlement where the village of Geneva is now located. They destroyed it and continued on to a large town called Kanadesaga (now called Seneca Castle). It consisted of about 40 houses very irregularly situated. The ruins of a stockade fort and blockhouse were in the center and there were a considerable number of apple trees and other fruit trees.

During the following week, the soldiers burned about 40 Native American towns around the lake, including Gagsshongwa (now Cashong), Schoyere, the Cayuga settlement called Skaigus or large falls (now Seneca Falls), Canandaigua ("a very pretty town," "very Compact & Neatly built" with 30 houses), Honeoye, Kanagha, and Conesus. One town had about 100 "exceedingly large and well built" houses with 200 acres of "excellent corn, [and] a number of orchards, one of which had in it 1500 fruit trees." They captured a squaw "so old as not to be able to be brought off" and a Native American boy "decrepid to such a degree that he could not walk." They left one house standing for the squaw and the boy to stay in; but some soldiers fastened the door on the outside and burned the house, killing the old squaw and the crippled boy.

The army arrived at a Native American town at the Genesee River and Flats on Tuesday, September 14th. This was the largest town with more than 100 houses on an excellent piece of land in a large bend of the river. The inhabitants "left this town in a great hurry and confusion as they left large quantities of corn husk'd and some in heaps not husk'd, and many other signs of confusion." The whole army was turned out at 6 AM the following morning to destroy the corn in and about the town. By 2 PM, they had destroyed about 20,000 bushels of corn and the houses by making large fires with parts of houses and other wood, and then piling the corn on the fire. The army then returned to Easton along the same route it had advanced. They arrived at Easton on October 15th.[122]

★ Captain Walter Vrooman (1750–1785) and a detachment of 60 militiamen from Brigadier General Robert Van Rensselaer's (1740–1802) force were attacked and surrounded by Sir John Johnson's (1742–1830) invaders at Kanadesaga on Sunday, October 22, 1780. Vrooman lost four men killed and 56 captured.

Geneseo (Sept. 13, 1779)

> Genesee, now Geneseo, is about 30 miles south of Rochester. It was an old town of 128 houses, "mostly very large and elegant," according to Major General John Sullivan (1740–1795).

★ Lieutenant Thomas Boyd (d. 1779), one of Colonel Daniel Morgan's (1736–1802) riflemen, was sent out with a small party to reconnoiter Genesee on Monday, September 13, 1779. They were ambushed and 22 men were killed. Boyd and his sergeant were captured and taken to Little Beard's town where they were tortured and decapitated. Major General John Sullivan's (1740–1795) entire army later destroyed the surrounding fields of corn and "every kind of vegetable that can be conceived."[123]

Fort Plain (late autumn 1779; Mar. 1780; Aug. 2, 1780; Sept. 7, 1781)
Canajoharie (Fort Rensselaer) (Aug. 2, 1780)
Mohawk Valley (Mar. 1780; Aug. 2, 1780)

> Fort Plain, Fort Clyde, and Fort Plank defended the Canajoharie settlements. Fort Plain, the most important fort, was on the east bank of Canajoharie Creek, or Oquaga Creek, about 0.5 miles from where the creek empties into the Mohawk River. It was never called Fort Plain but given the name when a new fort was erected in the summer of 1780. Its official name was Fort Rensselaer. It was an irregular quadrangle of earth and logs around a three-story blockhouse of heavy hewn timbers. The walls of the upper stories had openings for muskets and the lower ones for three or four cannon. The bastions (see Photo NY-1, NY-2) at the four corners of the fort had smaller blockhouses. It was probably located on Moyer Street.
> Fort Clyde was at Freysbush (in the present township of Minden), about 2 miles southwest of Fort Plain. It was a blockhouse in the center of a strong rectangle of palisades. It had a 6-pounder signal gun.
> Fort Plank, often confused with Fort Plain (Fort Rensselaer), was 2 miles northwest of Fort Plain. It consisted of the house of Frederick Plank enclosed in a square of palisades with blockhouses at the angles. It was a refuge for neighboring families during times of Native American attacks. Three smaller fortifications, which were simply stockades surrounding houses, were also near these forts.

★ George Cuck, a Loyalist, entered the Mohawk Valley late in the autumn of 1779, intending to claim a large bounty for the scalps of Captain Jacob Gardinier (1727–1808) and Lieutenant Abraham D. Quackenboss (1730–1812). Abraham Covenhoven, a former Whig neighbor, spotted Cuck sitting on a rail fence one day and fired at him. The ball entered the rail upon which Cuck sat and he escaped.

★ James Cromwell, went out to see one of John Van Zuyler's three daughters in the town of Glen one evening in March 1780. She was boiling sap to make maple sugar and became very confiding and communicative, probably thinking that Cromwell would soon propose to her. She told Cromwell that Cuck was at their house and that he would hide under the floor when anyone visited the house.

Cromwell went to Captain Jacob Gardinier's house in Kultonville around midnight to tell him what he had heard. Captain Gardinier immediately sent for Lieutenant Quackenboss and ordered him to select a dozen men to meet at Gardinier's house as soon as possible. When Gardinier explained the situation to Quackenboss, Quackenboss claimed ill health and declined to go. He sent his lieutenant instead, cautioning him that Cuck was a terror in the valley and certainly armed.

The well armed party set out on a bright moon-lit night. They halted a quarter of a mile from Van Zuyler's house and the lieutenant lit a fire. The men gathered around the burning stump and were told the purpose of their expedition and planned their attack.

They decided to separate and approach the house from different directions so as not to excite suspicion. When they saw a light in the house, they advanced. A large watch dog began barking as they approached the house. The men forced the door open, frightening the Van Zuyler family. John Van Zuyler asked them what they wanted. He told them that Cuck was not in the house.

As the men began to search the house, one of them moved a large chest from the wall on one side of the room, revealing Cuck who jumped out and fired his pistol. As he leapt into a little cellar hole made for his escape, one of the men fired at him, shooting him in the back of the head. The ball exited through the opposite eye. As he fell on one knee, another man fired, striking Cuck in the chest. He fell to the floor and another man placed the muzzle of his gun near his head and blew out his brains. The party later found that Cuck had two loaded guns in the house and a brace of well charged pistols, only one of which he had taken into his hiding place. The men took Van Zuyler prisoner and brought him to the jail at Johnstown and, a short while later, to Albany.[124]

★ Joseph Brant (1742–1807), Mohawk Chief Thayendanagea advanced on Fort Plain on Wednesday, August 2, 1780 with about 500 Mohawks and Loyalists. Most of the settlers had fled to Fort Plain for protection. Brant avoided the fort and burned the church, 53 houses, many barns and a gristmill. He killed 16 people and captured 50 or 60 more. He and his men then killed or drove away 300 cattle and horses and burned the ripe grain fields, destroying the entire settlement in a single day.

After destroying Fort Plain and the Canajoharie settlements, Joseph Brant proceeded to the Schoharie Valley which he attacked on October 17, 1780.

★ A considerable enemy force appeared at Fort Herkimer on September 7, 1781. Colonel Marinus Willett (1740–1830), at Fort Plain, mustered the militia and sent out a scouting party that determined that the numbers had been exaggerated. A party of 30 men and two officers who were sent to reconnoiter fell into an ambuscade. Lieutenant Solomon Woodworth (1743–1781) was killed in the second volley. Only 15 of his party escaped. Lieutenant Woodworth's body and those of 10 of his men were found. The others were unaccounted for.[125]

Harpersfield (Apr. 2, 1780)
Sacandaga Blockhouse (Apr. 7, 1780)

> Harpersfield is about 20 miles east of Oneonta and south of Schoharie. Sacandaga was an exposed settlement, 20 miles south of Cherry Valley and 15 miles southwest. of the Lower Fort of Schoharie Valley. The Sacandaga Blockhouse was located about 20 miles north of the Mohawk River in old Mayfield Patent, just off Van Den Burgh Road near the point of the same name, and close to the southwestern edge of Sacandaga Lake. A marker commemorates the site.

★ Colonel Peter Vrooman (1763–1838) sent Lieut. Alexander Harper (1744–1798) and a scout of 14 men from the Schoharie forts to the vicinity of Harpersfield on Sunday, April 2, 1780, to observe certain suspected persons living near the headwaters of the Delaware River. A heavy snow fell about the time they arrived at their destination and they began to make maple sugar. Joseph Brant (1742–1807), Mohawk Chief Thayendanagea, and a small force of 43 Mohawks and seven Loyalists surprised the party so much that they did not fire a gun. The Mohawks shot two of the men and captured 18 others who surrendered. They killed and scalped one of the men who was sick in bed that day.

Brant recognized Harper as a former schoolmate and expressed his regret that he had to kill him. He asked Harper if there were any troops at Schoharie. Harper deceived Brant by telling him that 300 Continental troops had arrived there three days earlier. Disappointed, Brant had the 11 prisoners secured in a hog pen with several Loyalists guarding them during the night. The raiders destroyed Sacandaga and headed toward Minisink which they attacked on April 14.[126]

Fonda
Caughnawaga (May 22, 1780; Oct. 18, 1780)

A small blockhouse, called Fort Caughnawaga was built at Sand Flats just west of today's Fonda. The name Caughnawaga was applied to several localities: 1. the Indian castle at Sand Flats, 2. the early white pioneer's settlement in what is now the eastern portion of Fonda, 3. the early Indian village of Ossernenon, on the south bank of the Mohawk, on the site of Auriesville Shrine, and 4. the Christianized Iroquois settlement (Caughnawaga Mohawks who left their nation after Jesuit missionary proselytism in the 17th century) 9 miles from Montreal. The site discussed here is #2, the early white pioneer's settlement in what is now the eastern portion of Fonda.

★ Sir John Johnson (1742–1830) sailed up Lake Champlain to Crown Point with 400 of his Royal Greens, Butler's Rangers and 200 Native Americans in May 1780. He then marched to the Sacandaga River, arriving at the Johnstown settlements in the night of Monday, May 21, 1780 entirely undiscovered. He divided his force, sending half of it westward up the Mohawk to the Dutch village of Caughnawaga to burn "the houses and barns of the inhabitants, putting to death every male capable of bearing arms."

Sir John occupied Johnstown with the other half, and then marched to the mouth of the Cayadutta. They burned houses and killed or captured the inhabitants. He then joined the rest of his force at Caughnawaga and proceeded up the Mohawk valley for several miles. They burned every house not owned by a Loyalist, slaughtered the cattle and sheep and carried off the horses. They killed several people and captured many prisoners.

When they returned to Johnstown, they burned all the houses there. Governor George Clinton (1739–1812) assembled the available militiamen and tried to intercept Johnson at Ticonderoga; but Johnson and his men boarded their boats at Crown Point and escaped to St. Johns with 40 prisoners. Hostilities ceased until August when the Native Americans and Loyalists wrought revenge on Canajoharie.

★ On Wednesday, October 18, 1780, Sir John Johnson (1742–1830) burned Caughnawaga. Colonel Frederick Fisher (Visscher) (1741–1809) and his two brothers defended themselves and their house. Colonel Fisher fled the house when his two brothers were killed. The Native Americans pursued and overtook him. They tomahawked and scalped him and left him for dead. A friend found Colonel Fisher's body the next day and carried him to his house. Colonel Fisher recovered and lived long after the war.[127]

Near Delaware River (June 15, 1780)
★ Lieutenant Ephraim Vroman (1738–1811) and a militia unit pursued some Native Americans who had a white captive. Vroman caught up with them near the upper Delaware River on Thursday, June 15, 1780. He lost one man captured.

Greenville
Basic Creek (June 16, 1780)

> Basic Creek is about 4 miles west of Greenville and about 22 miles southwest of Albany.

★ The Albany Guards attacked some enemy Native Americans at Basic Creek on Friday, June 16, 1780 and killed six of them.[128]

Currytown (July 9, 1781; Oct. 24, 1781)

> Currytown was a small settlement about 11 miles southeast of Fort Plain.

★ A strong party of between 200 and 350 Loyalists and Native Americans under John Doxtader advanced on Currytown Monday afternoon, July 9, 1781. Most of the inhabitants were in the fields when the attack came. They ran into the woods or to Fort Lewis, a fortified house. The raiders burned a dozen houses, sparing only the fort and a dwelling occupied by a Loyalist family. They killed or captured a small number of the people.[129]

★ Major John Ross and Walter Butler (c.1752–1781) led another expedition of about 1,000 British Regulars, Loyalists and Native Americans to the Mohawk Valley settlements in October 1781. They were not discovered until they appeared at Currytown on Monday, October 24, 1781. They quickly proceeded to Warrensbush and the vicinity of Fort Hunter, killing or capturing anybody they met. They destroyed the dwellings near Fort Hunter and plundered the people on the south side of the river before any militiamen could muster to oppose them.

See also **Warrensbush.**

New Dorlach
Sharon Springs Swamp (July 10, 1781)

> A historical marker on the right side of Route NY 20 toward Sharon Springs a short distance beyond a sign for "Sharon Center" identifies the site of a fight early in the morning of Tuesday, July 10, 1781. Outnumbered 3 to 1, Colonel Marinus Willett (1740–1830) and 150 militiamen defeated a force of 300 to 450 Loyalists and Native Americans. Although there is nothing to indicate the direction from which Willett approached, we do know that John Doxtader moved his men from low, swampy ground to high. So we can assume that Doxtader camped on the hill beyond the orchard, that Willett approached him in the vicinity of Route NY 20, formed his crescent here, and lured Doxtader down off the hill and into the trap. The battle ground is about 2 miles east of Sharon Springs.[130]

★ General George Clinton (1739–1812) asked Colonel Marinus Willett (1740–1830), who commanded the 5th New York Continental Regiment in 1781, to take command of the militia and state troops to be raised for the summer campaign. Willett accepted and established headquarters at Fort Rensselaer (Canajoharie). He mustered about 380 men from what remained of the companies engaged in the previous year's campaign and divided them among German Flats, Schoharie, and other settlements.

A few days after assuming command, Colonel Willett sent Captain John Gross (1749–1823) and a detachment of 35 men to New Dorlach, about 11 miles southeast of Canajoharie, to investigate suspected Loyalist activities in that area. Willett and his

Continentals saw smoke rising from the direction of Currytown shortly after Captain Gross departed. Captain Gross came upon John Doxtader's trail and later upon his camp. He immediately sent a dispatch to Colonel Willett at Fort Plain while he went to Bowman's Creek to await orders. Willett sent a messenger to Captain Gross, ordering him to investigate immediately. At the same time, he dispatched Captain Robert McKean (d. 1781) and 16 men to the settlement with orders to collect as many men as possible on the way. The party reached Currytown shortly after Doxtader's men had left but in time to help save some buildings.

Meanwhile, Willett gathered some men and set out in pursuit of Doxtader's force of about 500 men, mostly Native Americans. He joined Gross and McKean that evening, intending to surprise the enemy's camp at night. Doxtader had selected a strong position for his camp, a place which later came to be called Sharon Springs Swamp. However, Willett's guide lost his way in the dense forest. When Willett approached the camp around 6 AM, the Native Americans and Loyalists, having been warned of their danger, were already prepared for battle. A small detachment was ordered forward to engage Willett's men.

Outnumbered two to one, Willett formed his men into a crescent under cover of a dense growth of trees and underbrush and sent Lieutenant Jacob Sammons (1752–1834) and 10 men to fire one volley and retreat. This drew the Native Americans from their position. They pursued Sammons back to the main force. When they got inside the crescent, Willett's concealed force of 100 men opened fire and continued for an hour and a half. Heavy fire from Willett's men on three sides drove them back. Captain McKean's small reserve force struck at their right flank at the same time, catching Doxtader's men completely by surprise, breaking their formation and sending them behind trees for refuge.

Willett ordered a bayonet charge that put the Crown troops in full flight, leaving their camp and booty behind. They left 40 dead on the field. Willett had five killed and nine wounded or missing, including Robert McKean of the Rangers, who was mortally wounded and died the next day on the return march to Fort Rensselaer, and his son Samuel who was shot through both cheeks when a musket ball passed through his mouth.[131]

★ Colonel Willett gave Lieutenant Colonel Volkert Veeder's (1736–1807 or 1740–1813) militia, which arrived a short while later, the task of burying the dead while he hurried to return to Fort Plain. While burying the dead, the militiamen discovered seven Currytown prisoners on the ground, killed and scalped when the Native Americans retreated. The victims included 11-year-old Jacob Dievendorff (1770–?) and a little girl named Mary Miller (d. 1781). Mary died on the way to Fort Plain; but Jacob recovered, as did his brother, Frederick, who had a similar experience at Currytown the day before.[132]

Wawarsing (Aug. 22, 1781) (This event is sometimes dated Aug. 12–13, 1781.)

> Wawarsing is on U.S. 209 about 14 miles west of New Paltz.

★ A party of about 400 Loyalists and Native Americans under Captain William Caldwell (1763–1849) entered the settlement of Wawarsing early Wednesday morning, August 22, 1781. A sentinel at the gate of a picket fort where a sergeant's guard was kept (the only soldiers in that area) hailed them when they first arrived. When they did not answer, the sentinel fired and ran into the fort to alarm the garrison. The Loyalists and Native Americans kept up a constant fire upon the fort for some time but without effect. They eventually retired after losing three killed and two wounded.

The firing at the fort alarmed the inhabitants, all of whom escaped, except for John Kittle (d. 1781) who was killed in the road as he ran to get help. The raiders burned and plundered the village, destroying 13 elegant dwelling-houses with all the out-buildings and furniture, 14 large barns filled with wheat, barracks, stables, and stacks of hay and grain before they withdrew around mid-morning. They also drove off between 60 and 70 mostly very fine horses, a great number of cattle, sheep, and hogs. Colonel Albert Pawling (1750–1837) learned of the raid and immediately collected about 200 New York levies and militiamen. They pursued the raiders about 40 miles the following morning "to be revenged on the villains" but could not overtake them. It appeared that they fled in confusion, as they left a considerable quantity of their plunder behind them in many places.[133]

Middleburg

Fort Defiance or Middle Fort (Oct. 15, 1780)

Middleburg is 5 miles south of Schoharie on NY 30. A marker on the right shortly after the sign for Middleburg identifies the site of the home of Captain George Rechtmyer who commanded the Middle Fort, also called Fort Defiance, in 1780. The approximate site of the fort is a short distance further on the left side of the road, also identified by a marker. A short distance beyond the marker, across from the Dutch Reformed Church, Middle Fort Road goes east and turns to parallel Route NY 30 which it joins a little further north. Two private roads run east (right) off Middle Fort Road. The fort was located about one-quarter mile east of here, close to a stream. It was a stone house enclosed by a stockade like the Lower Fort.

Jephthah Simms's *Schoharie County and the Border Wars of New York* (p. 271) says that the fort enclosed "an area of ground larger than that picketed at the Lower Fort with blockhouses at the northeast and southwest where cannon were mounted. The principal entrance was on the south side [to the right as you face the site]. On each side of the gate were arranged the soldiers' barracks. Pickets as at the fort below were about a foot through and rose some 10 feet from the ground with loopholes (see Photo NY-17) with which to fire on invaders. A brass nine-pound cannon was mounted on the southwest blockhouse and an identical one was mounted on the diagonal corner each of which, as the blockhouses projected, commanded two sides of the enclosure while along the eastern and western sides were arranged huts for citizens similar to those at the Lower Fort."

NY 30 south turns right over a bridge (marked 145 N) crossing the Schoharie Creek and turns left almost immediately onto NY 30 south. A marker for the site of the home of Timothy Murphy, who shot Brigadier General Simon Fraser (1729–1777) at the battle of Saratoga and defended the Lower Fort at Schoharie, is a short distance beyond the sign for Watson's Corners on the left beyond Middleburg. Less than a quarter of a mile beyond the marker for Murphy's home, on the left, is another marker for the Upper Fort.

The Upper Fort was located 500 feet off the road where the home of John Feake had been fortified with a large stockade enclosing four blockhouses, various dwelling houses, and earthworks. Simms (p. 271) described the Upper Fort similarly to the other two: "One side of this enclosure was picketed in; on its other side the breastwork was thrown over timbers and earth some eight or ten feet high and

Photo NY-17. Blockhouse with loopholes for muskets and cannon in the upper structure. Compare with the stone blockhouse in Photo NY-14.

> sufficiently thick to admit of drawing a wagon within its top with short pickets set in the outside timbers of the breastwork. A ditch surrounded the part thus constructed. Military barracks and small log huts were erected within the enclosure to accommodate the soldiers and the citizens. Blockhouses and sentry boxes were built in the northwest and southeast corners each mounting a small cannon and the guard inside. From its construction, this fort was probably better made in the name of fort than either of the others though some have stated that a moat partially surrounded the Middle Fort."

★ When the Continentals arrived within 2 miles of the Stone House (Middle Fort) on Sunday, October 15, 1780, they learned that the enemy were retreating up the valley. The mounted troops moved quickly and overtook them at the Flockeys. As they approached, they found the Loyalists and Native Americans prepared to give them a warm reception. Both sides exchanged a few shots when the cavalry sounded the trumpet and dashed among the Native Americans and Loyalists who panicked and fled up the river. The Continentals pursued them only a short distance because the ground was not favorable for cavalry and because it was nearly dark. The cavalry lieutenant was killed and two privates wounded, one mortally, in this encounter. Native American and Loyalist losses are unknown. The cavalry returned to the Stone House and encamped for the night.[134]

Ballston
Fort Plank (Oct.16, 1780)

Fort Plank was at Ballston which is about 11 miles north of Schenectady.

★ Major John Munroe and a detachment of between 150 and 200 British Regulars, Loyalists and Native Americans attacked Colonel Brown and about 37 men stationed at Fort Plank at Ballston on Monday, October 16, 1780. A guide had told Major Munroe that there were 150 men in the fort and 100 more were expected to arrive soon. He avoided the fort but attacked the residence of its commander, Lieutenant Colonel James Gordon (1739–1810) at 1 AM. Munroe's troops killed one, wounded another and captured 22, including Colonel Gordon and his entire family. Instead of joining Sir John Johnson (1742–1830) at Saratoga, Major Munroe turned back to rejoin General Sir Guy Carleton (1724–1808) at Crown Point on October 23rd. He lost two killed, three wounded and two deserted and two Native Americans killed and one wounded on the expedition.[135]

Stone Arabia (Oct. 19, 1780; Oct. 26, 1781)
Fort Keyser (Oct. 19, 1780)

> Fort Keyser was 1 mile south of today's Stone Arabia, in the area then known as Stoneraby, and consisted primarily of the farm house of Johannes Keyser (Kayser, Keisar) (1722–?). It was a stone structure about 20 feet by 40 feet with loopholes (see Photo NY-17) in the upper part of the first story for muskets. It was abandoned when Fort Paris was built 0.5 miles north in the spring of 1777. Markers on NY 10, 2 miles north of Palatine Bridge, identify the scene of the battle. The site of the fort is about one-quarter mile east of the junction of NY 10 and County Road 43 (Dillenbeck Rd.). The building was torn down in the 1840s and the materials used to construct another farm house.
>
> Fort Paris was located about three quarters of a mile east of NY 10, about midway between Hickory Hill Rd. (County Road 33) and Stone Arabia Rd. (County Road 34) in Stone Arabia. It was built on land owned by Isaac Paris and consisted of the farm and outbuildings, a trading post, and a barracks for at least 100 men. It was surrounded by a palisade with a blockhouse on the western side.

★ Colonel John Brown (d. 1781) held Fort Paris in the village of Stone Arabia with only 130 militiamen when Brigadier General Robert Van Rensselaer (1740–1802) ordered him to attack Sir John Johnson's (1742–1830) Loyalist forces. Van Rensselaer, who had mustered a force of militiamen and marched to Caughnawaga, promised to attack their rear. Colonel Brown engaged Johnson's force near Fort Keyser, an old ruined earthwork, on Thursday, October 19, 1780. Outnumbered almost 10 to 1, Brown's men fought until one third of them had been killed. When Brown got killed, the rest of his men abandoned the fight. Van Rensselaer never arrived to support them. Johnson destroyed Stone Arabia and sent out small bands to pillage and burn the country for miles around.

Brown advanced west along the general route of today's NY 10 when they marched into the ambush. Brown and about 30 of his men were killed and their bodies buried in a common grave near Fort Paris and the Trinity Lutheran Church. Johnson burned Stone Arabia before being cornered at Klock's Field during the afternoon of the same day.[136]

★ The day after the Battle of Johnstown, Friday morning, October 26, 1781, Colonel Marinus Willett (1740–1830) pursued Sir John Johnson's forces to Stone Arabia where he sent a detachment in a failed attempt to destroy the enemy's boats on Oneida Lake.

Colonel Willett learned, at German Flats, that Johnson and his men had taken a northerly course. He took 400 of his best men and 60 Oneidas, marched all day in a driving snowstorm and encamped in a wood in the Royal Grant. He sent Lieutenant Jacob Sammons and some Oneidas to reconnoiter. They found the enemy's camp but decided they should not attack at night. Small guerrilla parties continued to lurk around the frontier settlements during the remainder of the summer and early autumn of 1781, but Colonel Willett's scouts prevented them from doing much damage.[137]

Saint Johnsville
Fort Klock, Klock's Field (Fox's Mills) (Oct. 21, 1780)
Kanassoraga (Oct. 23, 1780)

> Fort Klock was a 1½-story L-shaped stone house with limestone walls 2 feet thick with loopholes (see Photo NY-17). The fort, built by Johannes Klock (1710–1801) in 1750, was on a hill of solid rock. It should not be confused with the home of Johann George Klock (1714–1789), Johannes's brother, also called Fort Klock and about three quarters of a mile to the northwest. Fort Klock stands on NY 5, on the north bank of the Mohawk, east of St. Johnsville and west of the Palatine Church. It was 38 feet wide and 24 feet deep with a log wall encircling the house during the war. It is one of the few surviving fur trading posts in the Mohawk Valley. The battle known as Klock's field occurred just to the east of Fort Klock.

★ After the destruction of Stone Arabia, Sir John Johnson (1742–1830) mustered his men in the evening of Thursday, October 19, 1780 and marched to Klock's Field on the north side of the Mohawk River. His force consisted of 750 picked men from the 10th and 24th British regiments, Hessian jaegers, Sir John's regiment, Butler's Rangers, and Brandt's corps of Mohawks. They had two brass mortars for 4.75 inch shells and one brass 3-pounder. They concealed the mortar along their route.

Brigadier General Robert Van Rensselaer (1740–1802) followed him along the south side with 1,500 militiamen, including a number of Oneidas; but he was delayed searching for a ford. Governor George Clinton (1739–1812) sent Van Rensselaer an invitation to dine with him at Fort Plain, some distance away. Van Rensselaer accepted and his officers became angry at his departure at this time. The Oneida chief Louis Atayataroughta denounced him as a coward and a Loyalist.

In Van Rensselaer's absence, the men drove the baggage wagons into the river in a line to serve as a sort of bridge to allow the troops to cross in single file. Johnson formed his men for battle. He placed the British Regulars, the provincial troops, and the rangers behind a hastily constructed breastwork. The Hessian jaegers and Joseph Brant's (1742–1807), Mohawk Chief Thayendanagea Mohawks were posted on the left, hidden in the shrub oaks.

When Van Rensselaer returned from the dinner, he deployed his force in a line. Colonel Lewis DuBois (1744–?) commanded the right, Lieutenant Colonel Abraham C. Cuyler (1742–1810) the left, and Captain Robert McKean (d. 1781) and the Oneidas were on the right. Colonel Morgan Lewis (1754–1844) took the advance. The whole line advanced upon Johnson's force. DuBois's wing charged Brant's Mohawks with such force that they broke and fled. Sir John supposedly fled with them, leaving the 3-pounder and all the ammunition. Colonel Brown (d. 1780) was killed in the skirmishing that morning.

The rest of Johnson's troops held their ground in the fury; but the flight of Brant's Mohawks greatly weakened Johnson's force and encouraged Van Rensselaer's men who assaulted the feeble breastwork and pursued the fleeing Mohawks. They recovered nearly all the prisoners and all the African Americans, cattle, and other plunder and captured about 40 prisoners, including Sir John's servant and baggage. Instead of pushing for a decisive victory, Van Rensselaer withdrew his troops 3 miles to a place suitable for a bivouac.

The following morning, Oneida chief Louis Atayataroughta and his warriors along with Captain McKean and his volunteers left Van Rensselaer's command and pursued Johnson's retreating men. Van Rensselaer's main force proceeded to German Flats. Van Rensselaer promised to support McKean and chief Louis in their pursuit of Johnson. The advance party reached Johnson's camp the next day. The fires were still burning. Louis distrusted the general and refused to go any farther until assured of the promised support. A messenger arrived later announcing that Van Rensselaer abandoned the pursuit and had already left.

General Van Rensselaer's militia pursued Johnson's force up the Mohawk River so closely that they were prevented from devastating the country. They pursued to within about 15 miles of Fort Herkimer. Their provisions entirely exhausted and many of the men having gone nearly two days without food, they were obliged to return as they had no prospect of supplies arriving. Johnson escaped to Oswego and then to Canada.[138]

Jerseyfield (Oct. 30, 1781)
West Canada Creek (mid-Mar. 1778; Oct. 30, 1781)

West Canada Creek is about 13 miles northeast of Utica. Fairfield is located at the top of a hill 8 miles north of Herkimer and 3 miles east of West Canada Creek.

★ A band of Loyalists and Native Americans appeared at Fairfield on snowshoes in mid-March 1778. They killed and scalped a boy, took a dozen men prisoners and burned the houses before departing to the northeast. They headed toward Salisbury and captured one or two more prisoners near that settlement, but they don't seem to have killed or taken any women prisoners.[139]

★ Colonel Marinus Willett (1740–1830) caught up with Walter Johnson's force of Loyalists and Native Americans at Jerseyfield on Canada Creek on Tuesday, October 30, 1781. The two forces engaged in a fight across the creek. After an Oneida shot Walter Butler (c.1752–1781), the Native Americans fled. The rest of Major John Ross's men followed and Willett pursued them until they were entirely routed and dispersed in the forest. Willett and his troops returned to Fort Dayton in triumph. They lost only one man. Ross's and Butler's losses were never known. This expedition ended the hostilities along the New York border.[140]

2
DOWNSTATE/HUDSON RIVER VALLEY

See the map of Downstate New York and the Hudson River Valley.

Hudson River (July 12, 15, 27, 1776; Aug. 3, 1776; Aug. 16, 1776; Aug. 18, 1776; Sept. 16, 1776; Nov. 5, 8, 1776; Feb. 8, 9, 1777; July 28, 1777; Oct. 4, 1777; Oct. 27, 1778; July 21, 1780)

> The Hudson River was called the North River in the 18th century. Tappan Zee (Tappan Sea or Tappan Bay) is the widest stretch of the river north of Manhattan.

★ The HMS *Rose*, HMS *Phoenix*, schooner *Tryal* and two tenders weighed anchor at 2:30 Friday afternoon, July 12, 1776, left the Watering Place and headed up the Hudson River. Captain Samuel Richards (1753–1840) noted in his diary that the mission of the vessels "appeared to be to reconnauter, to find the position and strength of our works." A Rebel battery at Red Hook, in what is now Brooklyn, began a heavy firing on Captain Hyde Parker's (1739–1807) HMS *Phoenix* and Captain Sir James Wallace's (1731–1803) HMS *Rose* about 3:45 PM, as the ships headed to Paulus Hook near Governor's Island. The ships returned fire about 4:05 when they were between the Red Hook and Governor's Island batteries. The Rebels kept firing from six batteries for a distance of about 11 miles. The ships maintained fire the whole way until they passed the batteries about 5:30.

Several shots fell on the encampment of Colonel William Shepard's (1737–1817) regiment. One killed a cow. Another entered the embrasure of a small redoubt on the side of the encampment, passed through the legs of two soldiers, and struck the banquette on the opposite side of the redoubt without doing any damage. Five artillerists were killed and three wounded because of neglect in swabbing the cannon.

The *Phoenix* received two shots in the hull, one in the bowsprit, and several through the topsails. Her netting was shot away which resulted in the loss of three cots, one seaman and two marines wounded. The *Rose* had her starboard fore shroud, tackle pendant, fore lift, fore topsail clewlines, spritsail and main topsail braces shot away, one 18-pound shot in the head of her fore mast, one through the pinnace (see Photo NY-18), several through the sails and some in the hull. The vessels passed the last battery at 5:30 and anchored at Topsand Bay off Tarrytown.[141]

★ The HMS *Asia* and two other warships headed up the North River, on Sunday, July 15, 1776 when they came under heavy fire from a battery at Paulus Hook. They came back down river about dawn the next morning, moving much faster than when they went up but were nearly all destroyed by four fire ships that sailed in among them. A gale of wind that sprung up at that time prevented their total destruction.

★ Meanwhile, about 11 AM on the 15th, the British, under cover of a tremendous fire from eight or ten ships of war, landed a number of men near Mr. Stuyvesant's house in the bowery, about 2 miles from the city. A few hours later, they took possession of the city of New York.[142]

★ Three hundred New England militiamen left Peekskill and returned home on Saturday, July 27, 1776. New levies from Westchester and Dutchess counties were expected that evening to replace them. However, as the militiamen left the eastern shore of the

Downstate/Hudson River Valley 75

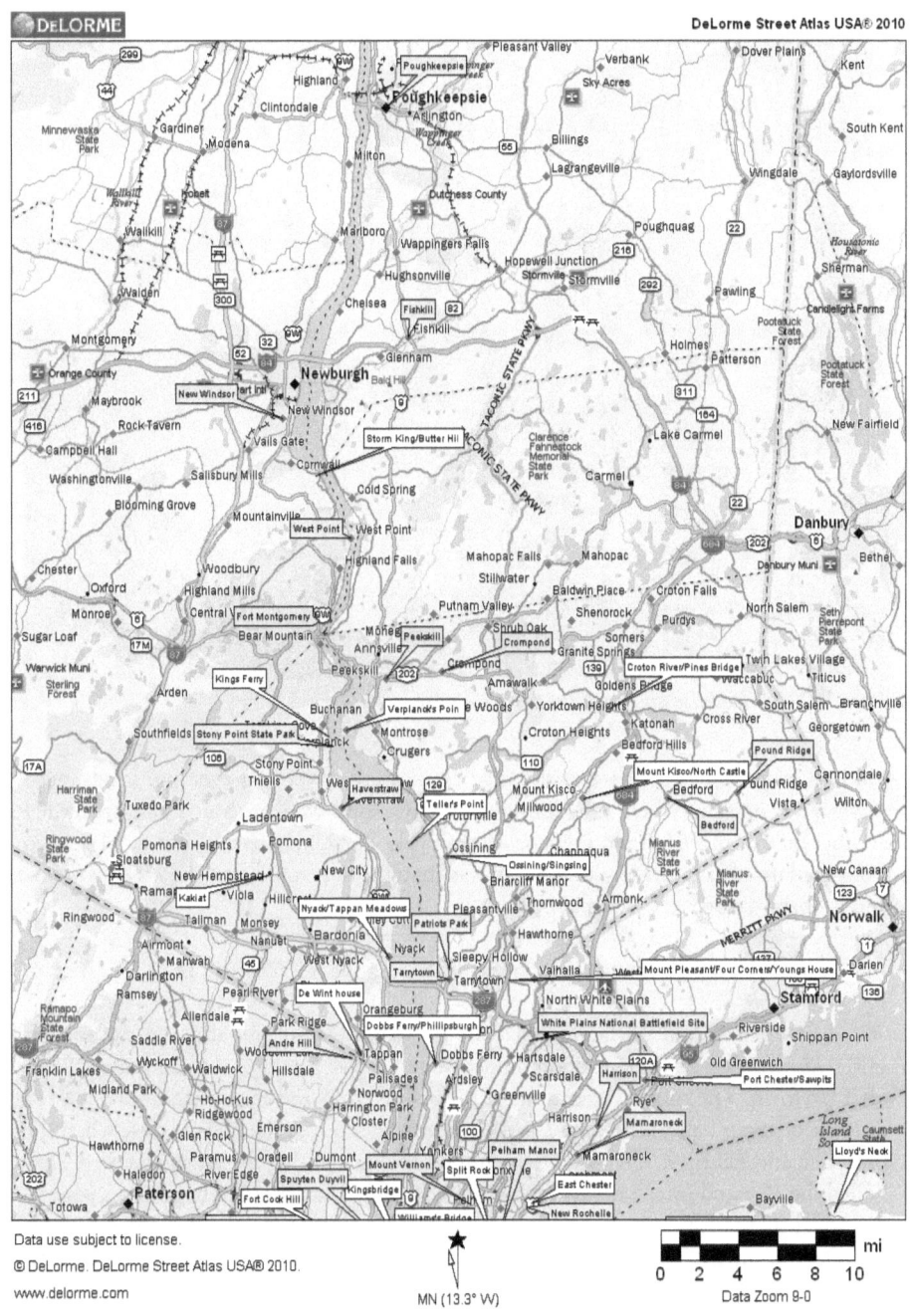

Downstate New York and the Hudson River Valley: Map for The Guide to the American Revolutionary War in New York
© 2010 DeLorme (www.delorme.com) Street Atlas USA®

Photo NY-18. Pinnace on board the HMS Victory

Hudson River unguarded, a British barge came up the river that evening. It advanced to within 6 miles of where the Continental Navy ships were anchored and proceeded another mile or more farther. Her crew took a yoke of oxen, a steer, a cow and 10 sheep from the farm of a Mr. Baily. Mr. Baily was thought to be on board the HMS *Phoenix* and probably served as their guide.[143]

Hudson River off Tarrytown (Aug. 3, 1776; Aug. 16, 1776; Aug. 18, 1776; Oct. 4, 1777)

★ Six row galleys and 12 launches led by the *Lady Washington* attacked the frigates HMS *Phoenix* and *Rose* about noon on Saturday, August 3, 1776, in the Hudson River off Tarrytown. The galleys began a smart fire about 12:45 and continued until 3 PM at a distance of about half a mile. The *Lady Washington* got out of the line of battle when she first fired and fell back. The *Spitfire* then took the lead during the engagement. A shot hulled the *Rose* and forced her to anchor. The *Phoenix* and *Rose* then began a very heavy fire which lasted for an hour and 20 minutes. Both sides maintained a hot fire. Four shots struck the galleys. The smoke increased and enshrouded the vessels to the point that they could no longer be seen. One man aboard a galley was killed, one had his leg shot off, and another was badly wounded and six or eight more slightly wounded. The *Spitfire* received 13 shots in her hull. The *Lady Washington* unfortunately split her gun, and another gondola received considerable damage. "Much disabled," the galleys rowed off to refit. The frigates could not follow them because of the calm winds. The *Rose* had one marine killed and another wounded as well as three seamen. Her starboard quarter gallery was shot away and some of her rigging damaged. She also received several shots in the hull. The Rebels had two killed and 12 wounded.[144]

★ Lieutenant Colonel Benjamin Tupper (1738–1792) and his men tried to assault the five British ships at anchor at Tappan Zee on Friday August 16, 1776 by sending some fire rafts against them. Captain Sir James Wallace (1731–1803) spotted some vessels approaching the HMS *Rose* about 11:30 AM. He thought they were Whig galleys; but two of them were fire ships. The crew of one of the boats boarded the *Rose*'s tender, set her on fire, and prevented her from escaping. The *Rose* managed to get clear of the burning vessel which soon lodged her jib boom over the HMS *Phoenix's* gunwhale and almost set her on fire. Captain Hyde Parker, Jr. (1739–1807) ordered the HMS *Phoenix* to fire on the fire ship, severely damaging her rigging. The fire ship was soon boarded on the starboard bow. The Whigs set fire to the train and left her. The *Rose*'s tender was totally destroyed. The Whigs lost one man missing, the captain of the fire ship. The galleys followed the ships a considerable distance into the bay before Captain Parker ordered the vessels to return down the Hudson River to rejoin the rest of the British fleet.[145]

★ The HMS *Rose*, HMS *Phoenix*, schooner *Tryal* and tender *Shuldham* headed down the Hudson River and passed the chevaux-de-frise (vessels sunk by the Whigs between Jeffery's Hook and Berdetts Mountain to block the channel) (see Photo NY-19) about 5:45 AM on Sunday, August 18, 1776. They were within musket range of a Whig battery on the eastern shore. The Whigs began firing from the high hills on both the eastern and western shores and directed a heavy fire of musketry from a breastwork under the battery. The *Rose* returned fire when she came abreast of New York.

The ships received heavy fire from 11 batteries and returned fire. The *Phoenix* fired several broadsides at some galleys anchored close into the western shore about 6:30 and

Photo NY-19. Chevaux-de-frise for water defense. The iron-tipped spikes were attached to logs and hidden two or three feet below the water's surface at low tide. Ships striking the chevaux-de-frise would have their hulls punctured or damaged.

soon began to fire at the batteries on York Island. During the Whig fire, a young man came from the shore in a canoe and boarded one of the ships. When he left the ship, he was joined by a Captain Jacob Hornneck (d. 1776), an engineer, who swam off with him but drowned by the canoes striking against the *Rose*. The ships anchored off Staten Island with a very large fleet of men-of-war and transports about 7:30. The *Rose* had two men wounded, one from a splinter in the leg. The *Phoenix*'s longboat received a shot which sank her as she passed the batteries. The Whigs lost one man killed and two wounded.[146]

★ The Continentals sent four fireships down the Hudson River at 5:30 AM on Monday, September 16, 1776. They came close to the HMS *Renown*, HMS *Repulse* and HMS *Fowey* but drifted ashore without causing any damage. When the *Renown* came abreast of the Continentals, she fired several broadsides at them.[147]

★ The frigate HMS *Pearl*, Captain Thomas Wilkinson, and two victuallers, the *Joseph* and the *British Queen*, set sail from their anchorage near Jones's house on the North River about 3 PM on Tuesday, November 5, 1776. They came under a very heavy fire from the batteries of Forts Washington and Lee on both sides of the river at 3:30. The forts fired canister, grape, and musket shot. The *Pearl* returned round and grape shot with musketry. The *Pearl* sent all her boats to assist the *Joseph* at 5:30. She received a number of shots in her hull and had most of her rigging cut to pieces. Her sails were badly torn, her mizzen and mizzen topmast shattered and her boat badly damaged. She was taking in five inches of water per hour. The vessels anchored near the mouth of Spuyten Duyvil Creek near Kingsbridge. They came under fire again on November 8 on the return trip.[148]

★ Captain Hyde Parker, Jr. (1739–1807), of the HMS *Phoenix*, discovered some vessels and whaleboats heading up the Hudson River at 4 PM on Tuesday, November 5, 1776. He immediately signaled for the *Tryal*, *Howe*, and *Pembroke* to give chase. He fired two guns at 4:30 and signaled for all the boats to join the chase. One of the cutters returned at 10 PM, having lost one man killed and another wounded. The *Pembroke* and all the boats returned at 8 AM Wednesday morning and anchored down river.[149]

★ Lieutenant James Clark, of the HM Galley *Dependence*, which was formerly the Continental row galley *Independence*, weighed anchor at 7 AM on Saturday February 8, 1777. Together with the sloop *George*, she rowed up the Hudson River. The British discovered five Whig boats crossing the river full of armed men at 9 AM. The *Dependence* fired four 32-pound round and grape shots at them. The boats rowed to the Jersey shore. The *Dependence* sent her boat along with the *George* to destroy them. They returned at 11 AM after completing their task. They had one man wounded.[150]

★ The following day, the *Dependence* drove off a boatload of Whigs who were pursuing a watering party from the *George*.

★ Captain Talbert and a party of men went to the enemy lines at Kingsbridge on Monday, July 28, 1777 to plunder some Loyalists. They brought off about 200 head of cattle. Lieutenant James Clark's HM Galley *Dependence* fired at them.[151]

★ A small detachment of cavalry surprised a party of Crown horsemen along the North River on Tuesday, October 27, 1778. They killed 15 and took 14 prisoners and 20 horses, without suffering any losses in the skirmish.[152]

★ A party of about 1700 men and four pieces of artillery attacked the Loyalist woodcutting post on the west side of the North River Friday morning, July 21, 1780. The attack lasted for more than two hours. The Loyalists repulsed the attack, killing 29 men at the abatis and killing or wounding five officers and 150 men. The approximately 80 Refugees in the post lost four killed and 10 or 12 wounded.[153]

★ Forty-two flat boats with Crown troops on board arrived at Tarrytown at 1 AM on Saturday, October 4, 1777. The HMS *Tartar* signaled for the troops to land at 5 AM and the HM Galley *Dependence* fired four 24-pound round shots to cover their landing. Captain James Montagu (1752–1794), of the HMS *Mercury*, sent his boats ashore with 20 marines at 9 AM. The troops landed with only one casualty.[154]

Haverstraw (July 16, 18, 25, 1776)
Near Fishkill (July 25, 1776; Oct. 13, 1777)
Hopewell (June 25, 1781)

> Haverstraw is on the west bank of the Hudson River south of Stony Point and across from Croton on Hudson.
> Fishkill is on the east side of the Hudson across from Newburgh. Fishkill Village was the largest supply depot for the Continental Army. Fishkill Clove or Wiccopee Pass, on the river 4.5 miles southwest of the village of Fishkill, now the town of Beacon, was fortified with three gun batteries for the duration of the war. Fishkill Landing was opposite Newburgh. The summit of Mount Beacon was used as a signal station during the American War for Independence.
> Hopewell is about 8 miles northeast of Fishkill at the junction of routes NY 376 and 82.

★ The British schooner *Tryal* and her two tenders anchored near the shore at Haverstraw Bay intending to land some men to seize some cattle on Tuesday, July 16, 1776. A number of Rebels assembled and prevented them from accomplishing their mission.[155]

★ Two days later, in the afternoon of the 18th, Captain James Wallace (1731–1803), of the HMS *Rose*, sent a tender into Harverstraw Creek to cut out a sloop that had run ashore. Several armed Rebels fired a number of shots at the tender as she skirted the shore. They would have destroyed her if they had boats. The *Rose* landed 30 men at Haverstraw. They set fire to the house of Loyalist Captain Lilly.[156]

★ Captain Hyde Parker's (1739–1807) HMS *Phoenix* fired two guns at a party of Whigs on shore between Haverstraw and Fishkill on Thursday, July 25, 1776. The Whigs returned fire and slightly wounded one man. They lost one man killed and two wounded.[157]

★ As Lieutenant Thomas Farnham's brig *Diligent* came to off Fishkill Flats at 8 AM on Monday, October 13, 1777, she came under fire from several companies of armed Whigs. She fired several 3-pounders at them as she passed. She had two men wounded. As she headed down river at 1 PM she received several cannon shots from an 18-pounder placed on a height at Newburgh, across the river. She returned fire with several 3-pounders.[158]

★ A number of armed men, believed to be some of Brigadier General Oliver de Lancey's (1718–1785) band, burst open the door of Mr. Garret Storm's (1722–1801) house in Hopewell between 8 and 9 PM on Friday, June 25, 1781. They demanded Mr. Storm's hard cash. The blind old man did not comply with their demands, so the men put a rope around his neck and hanged him. The rope broke and Mr. Storm fell to the floor. One of the men took his knife and cut a gash in Mr. Storm's throat. The rope, still around Mr. Storm's neck, prevented the wound from being mortal.

As the raiders were now in great confusion, an African American slave escaped out of the house and alarmed a guard in the neighborhood. The guard immediately went to Mr. Storm's rescue. The raiders fled, taking with them about 14 pounds hard cash, a silver bowl, some silver spoons and several other articles. One of the guardsmen grappled with one of the raiders. Both fell and the thief escaped. The raiders had four or five horses to carry off their booty. One of the guards grappled one of the raiders. Both fell to the ground. The thief disentangled himself and escaped.[159]

Fort Montgomery and Fort Clinton (Oct. 6, 1777)
Fort Montgomery (Oct. 8, 1777; Oct. 19, 1777; Oct. 16, 1779)

> The Fort Montgomery State Historic Site (**nysparks.state.ny.us/cgi-bin/cgiwrap/ nysparks/historic.cgi?p+41**) is on Route U.S. 9W. The archaeological remains of breastworks and fort structures were excavated and re-dedicated for the 225th anniversary of the battle in 2002. The new Visitor Center has displays of artifacts found during the excavations and shows a video.
> Fort Clinton should not be confused with Fort Arnold which was later renamed Fort Clinton. Fort Arnold is northeast of West Point whereas the one in this battle is south of West Point. It was destroyed in 1777 and no longer existed when Fort Arnold was renamed Fort Clinton in 1780 after Benedict Arnold's (1741–1801) treason. The site of the fort is at Bear Mountain State Park (**nysparks.state.ny.us/cgi-bin/cgiwrap/ nysparks/parks.cgi?p+131**) on Route U.S. 9W, 5 miles south of West Point.

★ Congressional forces began work on Fort Montgomery in 1776, south of West Point and located at another narrow point in the Hudson River. The intent was to build a large work of cannons with a "Grand Battery" of six 32-pounders overlooking a long stretch of the river. When the builders discovered the land on the opposite side of Popolopen Creek was higher and would threaten Fort Montgomery if held by the enemy, they constructed a second fort there and called it Fort Clinton for General George Clinton (1739–1812). These works were completed in 1777. The British attempted to dismantle these defenses after they captured forts Washington and Lee.

As at West Point upriver, Fort Montgomery also had a great chain (see Photo NY-20) at least 2,100 feet long across the Hudson. Specifications for the rafts that supported the chain called for a "Boom of Pine Logs not less than 50 feet long, placed ten feet apart, and framed together by three cross Pieces; that each Raft be placed 15 feet apart and Connected by strong Chains of 1½ inch iron; that the Rafts be anchored with their Butts down the River; that the Butts be armed with Iron."[160]

The boom was supposed to have 40 additional shock-absorbing frames anchored in front of it for further protection. "The points or ends whereof to be shod with Iron so as to answer the double purpose of founding any Ships who may sail up to it, and if that should fail, to Lessen the Shocke of those Vessels when they come to the Boom." The pointed beams were to be about 16 feet long and spaced about 16 feet apart. The boom and frames were never built, so the British broke through the iron chain at Fort Montgomery and sailed past.[161]

Forts Montgomery and Clinton were General Henry Clinton's (1730–1795) objective when he set sail from New York City with 3,000 British, Hessian and Loyalist troops on Monday, October 6, 1777. He landed 2,100 men on the west shore of the Hudson at Stony Point, under the cover of a dense fog. They encountered a scouting party of 30 Continentals sent from Fort Clinton to detect any advance by the Crown forces. Sir Henry beat them back and sent 900 men around 1,305-foot Bear Mountain to attack

Photo NY-20. Links of the great chain across the Hudson River, U.S. Military Academy, West Point

Fort Montgomery. He kept the remaining troops to attack Fort Clinton. In the afternoon, the Crown forces attacked both forts. The 700 defenders fought a bitter defense and refused to surrender. Sir Henry took advantage of the growing dark and the smoky haze of battle to storm both forts which he destroyed after the battle.

The battle delayed the Crown forces from moving north to help Major General John Burgoyne (1722–1792) at Saratoga. General Clinton returned to New York rather than going to Albany. Had this battle not occurred, it is quite possible that Clinton's forces might have changed the outcome of the Battle of Saratoga. Burgoyne surrendered two weeks later. The Crown forces never threatened the Hudson Highlands again.[162]

★ At 6 AM on Wednesday, October 8, 1777, the master carpenter and the armorer of the HMS *Preston* were sent to destroy the chain which stretched across the Hudson River from Fort Montgomery to Anthony's Nose. Captain James Montagu (1752–1794) sent the HMS *Mercury*'s longboats to assist them at 8. The artificers of the HM Galley *Dependence* joined them later. By 11 AM, they had cut the chain.

Part of the troops of the HMS *Mercury* embarked about 1 that afternoon and headed up the river with the HM Brig *Diligent* and the galleys *Dependence*, *Spitfire* and *Crane* and 22 flatboats with troops on board. The troops landed at Fort Constitution without any opposition because the Congressional troops had evacuated it.[163]

★ Two large boats, full of armed men, came to surprise the *Holm* on Sunday, October 19, 1777. Captain Christopher Heely masked the guns and made the vessel appear defenseless until the boats got within range. He then uncovered his guns and fired them with such success that the boats had difficulty reaching the shore.

★ Captain Heely sent his boat's crew on shore a little below Tarrytown on the 24th. They destroyed two pettiaugers (see Photo NY-21) of 10 oars each and a smaller boat.

Photo NY-21. Pettiauger Mercury (replica). Courtesy of Gene Tozzi, Sailing Master, Pettiauger Mercury

Crown troops destroyed the bridge over the Clove, between forts Montgomery and Clinton on Saturday, October 25, 1777. They then boarded transports to New York where they arrived the following evening. Captain Christopher Heely's armed sloop *Holm* was stationed near Pollepel's Island while the British fleet went up the North River to prevent the Congressional forces from sinking a number of chevaux-de-frise (see Photo NY-19) to obstruct their return.[164]

★ British gunboats exchanged fire with militiamen on the Hudson River bank near Fort Montgomery on Saturday, October 16, 1779.[165]

White Plains (Oct. 14, 1776; Oct. 23, 24, 1776; Oct. 27, 28, 1776; Nov. 5, 1776; Sept. 19, 1778; before Oct. 4, 1778; Dec. 25, 1778; May 30, 1779; Mar. 1, 1780; Sept. 30, 1780; July 17, 1781)

> The White Plains National Battlefield Site (www.ohwy.com/ny/w/whplnaba.htm) is in White Plains, New York. White Plains is heavily urbanized. There are three markers to commemorate the battle. One is on Chatterton Hill, two are on Battle Avenue.
>
> The Jacob Purdy House (Spring Street, near the intersection with Rockledge Avenue; whiteplainswatch.com/A55866/wpw.nsf/All/Jacob+Purdy+House) was General Washington's headquarters prior to the battle, October 23–28.
>
> The Elijah Miller House (Virginia Road in North White Plains, at the foot of Miller Hill www.westchestergov.com/history/wash.htm) was Washington's headquarters

> for the battle of White Plains. He stayed here for two weeks after he left the Jacob Purdy House.

★ On Saturday, October 12, 1776, General William Howe (1732–1786) embarked 4000 men in boats at Kip's Bay. He sent them northeast-ward in a thick fog through the channel known as Hell's Gate. They landed at Throg's Neck which was nearly an island, separated from the mainland by a single road that ran through marshes. Howe planned to advance along Throg's Neck over a causeway across swampy ground to attack the Continental Army from their flank and rear. General George Washington (1732–1799) had the causeway demolished and took a strong position at its far end. A small group of Pennsylvania riflemen under the command of Colonel Edward Hand (1744–1802) defended the bridge. Six days later, Howe embarked his men again and proceeded further up the East River to land at Pell's Point, in Washington's rear, where he marched to New Rochelle.

Howe threatened to cut off the Continental Army on Manhattan from the mainland. Washington had already decided to abandon Manhattan and lower New York via Kingsbridge. He fell back to White Plains on October 18, leaving about 6,000 men behind to man two forts, Fort Washington and Fort Lee, on opposite sides of the Hudson. Colonel Robert Magaw (1738–1790) defended Fort Washington with about 2,800 men, and Major General Nathanael Greene (1742–1786) held Fort Lee with about 3,500 men.

★ Crown troops advanced on Brigadier General Alexander McDougall's (1732–1786) brigade at White Plains on Monday, October 14, 1776. Colonel John Haslet's (1737–1777) Delaware regiment reinforced McDougall. The Continentals lost 15 killed and 15 wounded in the skirmish.

★ Connecticut troops had a minor skirmish with Crown forces near White Plains on Wednesday, October 23, 1776. At 5 AM on the 24th, small arms fire was heard from the south as 200 men of Major General Charles Lee's (1731–1782) division skirmished with 250 Hessians. The Continentals killed 10 Hessians and captured two prisoners. The Crown forces continued moving toward White Plains in two columns but with great caution.[166]

★ Washington held a good defensive position on the hills of White Plains. If he had to retreat, he could go north into the Hudson Highlands or west to New Jersey. He had over 25,000 men, but more than half were ill or otherwise unfit for duty. As the British advanced north toward him, Washington drew in as many men as he could afford to defend his camp. He fortified Purdy and Hatfield hills, but re-evaluated his position on Sunday, October 27 and decided to defend Chatterton Hill which sloped 180 feet up from the Bronx River.

General Lord Hugh Percy (1742–1817) marched from New York toward Kingsbridge at 4 AM on Sunday, October 27, 1776. The 22nd Regiment also set out to reinforce him. When the Continentals saw Lord Percy's two columns, they retired from all their advanced posts and withdrew all their troops into the part of their lines nearest to the Morris house. They left only some detached parties in the earthworks.

The Hessian column advanced to a hill about 400 yards away from the right of the Continental works and began a cannonade which had little effect because the Continentals were sheltered by their works and the Hessians only had battalion guns.

Meanwhile, two frigates moved up the North River about 7 AM. They anchored near Burdett's ferry, apparently intending to stop the ferry and to cut off communication between Fort Lee and Fort Washington. About 300 to 400 Continentals appeared in their advanced works. The rest were under cover of the woods and cover near their lines, waiting for an attack. That attack came later in the day, as the Crown forces twice assaulted the Continental positions.

The British column advanced into Harlem Plain and remained in position, exchanging fire with the advanced parties. They prepared to advance on some of the enemy's most advanced works and to penetrate their lines. Noticing that the Continentals received continuous reinforcements from the works behind, to keep at least 3,000 men on the front line, the British abandoned the plan. They thought that if they drove the Continentals from those advanced positions, they could not hold them if the enemy brought any guns into the rear positions which were on higher ground.

Colonel Robert Magaw (1738–1790), commander of Fort Washington, ordered the lines to be manned. When the troops advanced, the frigates HMS *Repulse* and HMS *Pearl* went up the North River in an unsuccessful attempt to dislodge them by firing on their flanks. The barbette battery, on the high hill to the left of the ferry, opened fire on the frigates and continued for some time without doing much damage. When the guns of Fort Washington ceased firing, a gun from Fort Number One on York Island (on the southwest slope of Spuyten Duyvil Hill, just north of the Henry Hudson Monument, at today's West 230th Street and Sycamore Avenue) began to fire at them more successfully. The gun hulled the closest frigate more than 20 times, but only one man was wounded on board the *Repulse*. Firing continued through the day, wounding four or five British. When two 18-pounders opposite the ships began firing, the British hoisted all sails and hurried away. Although rowed by two boats, the forward ship could make no headway. The other one sent two barges to her assistance. After some effort, they dragged her out of range. The frigate was badly damaged and probably had many of her men killed; but the weather was so hazy that it was impossible to see anything distinctly at a distance. The Continentals must also have lost some men.

The Crown forces, by this time, had begun a smart fire on York Island with field pieces and mortars (see Photo NY-6). The Continentals returned fire and killed about a dozen Hessians. There were only a few discharges of small arms. A shell (see Photo NY-3, NY-4) killed one Continental. By the end of the day, Lord Percy's troops remained in the position they occupied in the morning. The Continentals brought two cannon forward in the evening and fired at the British who responded with two guns on their right. They also fired a few shots at the sentries during the night and fired from only one cannon the next day, moving it several times from one place to another.[167]

Two brigades arrived at the hill to reinforce the Massachusetts militia just as the Crown forces were mustering 13,000 troops. These Crown troops across the Bronx River included mounted dragoons who prepared for the main attack on Chatterton Hill, the site of the only real fighting of the battle. General Howe positioned his artillery (near the present-day railroad station) and began bombarding (see Photo NY-4) the Continentals on the hill. The Hessians began to cross the Bronx River at the foot of Chatterton Hill while other forces moved around the hill and into the ridges to the west to put the Continentals in a crossfire. The Crown forces assaulted the hill twice and were driven back both times. The dragoons attacked a Massachusetts militia unit on one flank and forced them to flee. The rest of the Continentals were now vulnerable and were forced to withdraw. The Crown forces took the hill and pushed the defenders off in 50 minutes of heavy fighting. A Continental officer described the scene:

> They advanced in solid columns. . . . The scene was grand and solemn; all the adjacent hills smoked as though on fire, and bellowed and trembled with a perpetual

cannonade and fire of field pieces, howitzers and mortars. The air groaned with streams of cannon and musket-shot. The hills smoked and echoed terribly with the bursting of shells; the fences and walls were knocked down and torn to pieces, and men's legs, arms and bodies, mangled with cannon and grapeshot all around us.[168]

A Connecticut soldier was appalled by mutilation:
> One ball 'first took off the head of Smith, a stout heavy man, and dashed it open, then took Taylor across the bowels. It then struck Sergeant Garrett of our company on the hip [and] took off the point of the hip bone . . . he died the same day. . . . Oh! What a sight it was to see within a distance of six rods those men with their legs and arms and guns and packs all in a heap.[169]

General Washington sent Colonel John Glover (1732–1797) up onto Miller Hill with some artillery. Glover waited until the Crown forces dragged some of their cannon to the top of the lower Travis Hill nearby before opening fire. The Crown forces, caught by surprise, fired four shots and withdrew because they found their position too exposed.

General Howe waited for reinforcements before undertaking a direct, frontal assault which he planned for October 31. However a heavy rainstorm that lasted for more than 20 hours delayed the attack and gave Washington a chance to withdraw to North Castle. Continental casualties totaled about 150 men, including 50 dead. Crown forces casualties amounted to 313. Howe received reinforcements that brought his force to 20,000; but he chose not to pursue Washington. He decided instead to focus on Fort Washington which prevented him from getting supplies overland and forced him to depend on ships traveling the Harlem River and Long Island Sound.[170]

★ The Crown forces departed on Wednesday, October 30, 1776 and withdrew to Dobbs Ferry. The Continentals pursued them for 9 miles and captured two baggage wagons and some prisoners.[171]

★ When British sentinels were withdrawn from their advanced posts at White Plains on Tuesday, November 5, 1776, the Continentals assumed they planned an assault; so the Continental Army was immediately ordered under arms. The Crown troops appeared at 2 PM and formed on Chatterton Hill and on several hills west of it. Several reconnoitering parties were sent out and reported that the enemy were withdrawing. A party of Congressional troops set fire to the courthouse, Dr. Robert Graham's house, and several other private houses between the two armies about midnight. Miles Oakley (1757–1844) found his house robbed and pillaged, his desk split to pieces, his money, books, and papers taken and carried away. Congressional troops then burned his house and barn to the ground. The Commander in Chief wrote in his orders of the 6th: "it is with the utmost astonishment and abhorrence, the General is informed, that some base and cowardly wretches have, last night, set fire to the court-house, and other buildings which the enemy left. The army may rely upon it, that they shall be brought to justice, and meet with the punishment they deserve."[172] Major John Wilson Austin (d. 1816) of Colonel Paul Dudley Sargent's (1745–1827) Massachusetts regiment was court-martialed a week later and dismissed from the army for this infraction.

The Crown forces headed toward Dobbs Ferry. A detachment of Congressional troops was sent out on Wednesday morning to harass their rear; but they could not overtake them.[173]

★ Detachments from Lieutenant Colonels John Graves Simcoe (1752–1806), Andreas Emmerich (1737–1809) and Banastre Tarleton (1744–1833) marched to White Plains at 3 AM Saturday, September 19, 1778. Colonel Tarleton discovered a party of Continental light horsemen and ordered Colonel Emmerich's dragoons, under the command of Lieutenants Hutton and Sylvester Muirson, to reconnoiter their force. They found only a sergeant and six men whom they took prisoners.[174]

★ Colonel Richard Butler (1743–1791) of the Pennsylvania forces fell in with a party of Crown forces near White Plains a few days before Sunday, October 4, 1778. A skirmish ensued and Colonel Butler killed 10 and drove the rest off the field. He captured one officer and 19 men.[175]

★ A party of Crown forces surprised a Continental guard of about 25 men stationed near Mr. Young's house near White Plains on the remarkably cold night of Friday, December 25, 1778. All the troops left their guns in the sloop and were all inside the house, some around the fire, others in bed. They had not even posted a sentry. The Crown forces, who were about equal in number, came to the front of the house, fired at them through the windows and killed one of the soldiers and a Loyalist they held prisoner. The rest of the soldiers escaped through the back door, except for Mr. Young and Mr. Williams who were in bed. Mr. Young put his clothes on; but Mr. Williams only had his shirt and waistcoat on when the two were captured and made prisoners. The Crown forces hurried away with their prisoners, not giving Mr. Williams time to finish dressing.[176]

★ The entire British force, estimated at about 8,000 men, were gathered at White Plains in May 1779. Two sloops loaded with fascines were at anchor in the harbor opposite Whitehall. All the wagons and horses on Staten Island were pressed into service on Friday, May 29, 1779 and sent to New York, Major General John Vaughn (1738?–1795) and Brigadier General Sir William Erskine (1728–1795) at White Plains.[177]

★ Major General Edward Mathew (often misspelled Matthews) (1729–1805) sent a detachment of guards and Loyalist dragoons, under the command of Lieutenant-Colonel Chapel Norton to attack a post at John's house at White Plains, probably on Thursday, March 1, 1780. Although the plan did not succeed as desired, the Whigs posted at the house were dislodged with the loss of about 40 men killed and 97 captured, including a major and five subalterns. The Crown forces lost three killed and 15 wounded.[178]

★ Lieutenant Colonel Banastre Tarleton (1744–1833), of the British Legion, and 300 dragoons and 40 or 50 infantrymen made an attempt to surprise Lieutenant Colonel Henry White's (1740–1787) detachment of about 30 before September 30, 1780. Colonel White had moved his men that night and prevented Colonel Tarleton from bayoneting them. Colonel White's patrols and pickets fired at the British Legionnaires. They withdrew quickly, doing no other damage than knocking in all the windows and doors of the quarters Colonel White left that night.

As Colonel White had some business in the area of Round Hill, he was in a barn with Lieutenant Smith and his guard less than a dozen yards from the road the enemy came up; but they remained undiscovered.

As the Legionnaires withdrew, the dragoons and infantrymen pursued Colonel Tarleton's force as far as White Plains. Colonel White's dragoons charged their rear and captured two prisoners, four horses and wounded several, according to the inhabitants. When all of Tarleton's dragoons began to charge, Colonel White was forced to retreat. When they were pursued, they took a different road from the one where Colonel White had posted 250 infantrymen to salute the British dragoons. Colonel Tarleton "had not time on this last expedition to slaughter a single duck, goose or chicken."[179]

★ A party of about 10 of Colonel James De Lancey's (1747–1804) Loyalists under the command of Lieutenant Jeremiah Vincent (1741–1833), proceeded from Morrisania to Samuel Crawford's (1736–1777), 1750–1828, or 1763–1841) neighborhood, less than

3 miles from White Plains on Tuesday evening, July 17, 1781. There, they fell in with a captain and 30 French hussars who charged the little detachment with their sabers. This forced the Loyalists to leave the road and seek the protection of a fence. Lieutenant Vincent fired and shot the French commander dead. Two of his men also fired and the whole party ran away, leaving their slain captain on the road. A body of French infantrymen immediately advanced briskly. Lieutenant Vincent retreated without any loss.[180]

Highlands (Mar. 24, 1777) see Peekskill
Ossining
Singsing (July 27, 30, 1776)

> Singsing is now known as Ossining.

★ Captain Hyde Parker, Jr.'s (1739–1807) HMS *Phoenix* fired two 18-pounders at a party of Whigs on shore near Singsing about 6 PM on Saturday, July 27, 1776.[181]

★ Hessian detachments went out to seek and defeat Colonel Elisha Sheldon (1740–1805) and Lieutenant Colonel Henry White (1740–1787) Tuesday night, July 30, 1779. Lieutenant Colonel Ludwig Johann Adolph von Wurmb took the mounted jaegers and probably went to Drew Hills at present Carmel in Putnam County. Captain Johann von Ewald (1744–1813) took 100 jaegers between Tarrytown and Singsing to cover his rear. Lieutenant Colonel John Graves Simcoe (1752–1806) and his Queen's Rangers took the route along the Saw Mill Creek and occupied Storm's Bridge. Lieutenant Colonel Andreas Emmerich (1737–1809) took his corps and the Legion almost to White Plains. The four detachments could mutually assist each other, assuring that they could locate and defeat any enemy party in this area.

Lieutenant Colonel Emmerich's dragoons ran into Colonel Sheldon's dragoons at daybreak and were overthrown, losing 10 to 12 men killed and captured. Lieutenant Colonel von Wurmb heard the pistol firing and rushed to help. He defeated Colonel Sheldon, took some 20 men prisoner, and pursued him as far as Singsing.[182]

Nyack
Tappan Meadows (July 29, 1776)

> Tappan Meadows is now Nyack on the west side of the Hudson River opposite Tarrytown.

★ Five boats of British men-of-war tried to land at Tappan Meadows on Monday, July 29, 1776. About 15 local militiamen concealed themselves in a fishing hut on the edge of the meadows. They barricaded the hut and lay there until three of the boats came within musket range. They fired, loaded again, and fired 11 rounds without losing a man. They killed and wounded several of the Crown troops.[183]

New Hempstead
Kakiat (Sept. 28, 1778; Nov. 1778)

> Kakiat (Cakiatt, Kakeate) is now called New Hempstead.

★ The Crown forces were retiring from Herringtown on Monday morning, September 28, 1778, pursued by the Orange County militia. The Regulars outnumbered the militia and soon surrounded them at Kakiat, making it impossible to retreat. Captain Abraham Blauveldt offered to surrender but was fired upon and wounded in the thigh. He was later stabbed in the breast with a bayonet and left for dead. He later reported that he heard "the British officers and soldiers swear that they would give no quarter to militia man."[184]

★ Six New York Loyalists disarmed a guard and captured two officers at Kakiat in November 1778.[185]

Phillipsburg and Greenburg

Near Dobbs Ferry (Oct. 9, 1776; Oct. 25, 1776; May 13, 1777; May 15, 1777; May 23, 1777; May 24, 1777; Sept. 12, 1777; Nov. 17, 1777; Nov. 23, 1777; June 23, 1778; July 19, 1781; Aug. 3, 1781)

Phillipsburg (May 25, 1777; June 3, 14, 16, 17, 18, 1777; July 4 –5, 1777; July 24, 1777; Aug. 30, 1777; June 27, 1778)

Teller's Point, Hudson River (July 9, 1778)

Phillips Heights (Sept. 16, 1778)

Tappan (Sept. 28, 1778)

> Dobbs Ferry is in the modern towns of Phillipsburg and Greenburg. The shoreline has been altered considerably since the 18th century. Teller's Point was on the Hudson River about 10.5 miles north of Dobbs Ferry. It is now Croton Point.
> Tappan is on the west side of the Hudson River, opposite Dobbs Ferry and Phillipsburg.

★ Major General William Heath (1737–1814) ordered Colonel Paul Dudley Sargent (1745–1827) with 500 infantrymen and 40 light-horsemen, Captain Jotham Horton (1749–1795), of Knox's artillery, with two 12-pounders, and Captain Edward Crafts (1746–1806) with a howitzer, to march to Dobbs Ferry on Wednesday, October 9, 1776 to watch the enemy movements along the Hudson River. The British took a schooner loaded with rum, sugar and wine and sank a sloop which had David Bushnell's (1742–1824) submarine *Turtle* on board.[186]

★ The 44-gun ships *Phoenix* and *Roebuck*, the 20-gun frigate *Tartar*, the schooner *Tryal* and three or four small tenders weighed anchor about 7:30 AM and headed up the North River on Wednesday, October 9, 1776. The Continentals at Fort Washington and Fort Constitution (Lee) briskly cannonaded them about 8 AM. The *Phoenix* had two seamen and a boy killed and 12 others wounded in passing the forts. She sustained much damage and received four shots through her hull. The *Roebuck* had two officers and three seamen killed and seven seamen wounded. The *Tartar* was hulled several times. A cannonball struck a mast, cutting a great deal of the rigging and sails. Another went through the mizzenmast and killed a midshipman. The splinters of the masts wounded two other officers.

The ships passed the forts and the chevaux-de-frise (see Photo NY-19) and headed toward about 20 small craft, some galleys, and two large ships ahead of them. Some batteries up the river began firing at the British vessels about 10 o'clock and small arms fire from the woods continued for several miles up the river. The two Rebel ships were run on shore near Phillips's mills (present Yonkers) about 11 AM. The two galleys, *Independence* and *Crane*, were run on shore and captured just above Dobbs Ferry at 12:30 PM.

The crews escaped but did not have enough time to get themselves on shore in the boats before the ships began to fire. They were obliged to swim ashore. Several men landed and plundered a store, stove the casks, and then set the store on fire. The Whigs soon extinguished the fire.[187]

★ A Continental battery near Dobbs Ferry began firing at Captain Cornthwaite Ommanney's HMS *Tartar* at sunrise on Friday, October 25, 1776. The *Tartar* returned fire which continued until 7:30 when she anchored farther north. One shot splintered the head of the capstan and cut some of the rigging.[188]

★ Lieutenant James Clark of the HM Galley *Dependence* spotted a Whig schooner off of Dobbs Ferry at 3 PM Tuesday, May 13, 1777. He chased her and ran her on shore at 4:30 and fired four 24-pound round shots to sink her. As the shots were unsuccessful, he sent a boat to burn her at 6 PM, when he considered it safe to do so.[189]

★ Lieutenant James Clark had the HM Galley *Dependence* fire seven 4-pound round shots at a party of rebels on shore at Dobbs Ferry at 4 AM on Thursday, May 15, 1777.[190]

★ The HM Galley *Dependence* fired two 4-pounders with round shot to bring to a sloop off Dobbs Ferry on Thursday, May 23, 1777. She was a flag of truce from Peekskill on her way to New York, so Lieutenant James Clark sent an officer to ensure that none of the crew landed.[191]

★ The HM Galley *Dependence* fired two 4-pound round shots at two Whig whaleboats that were chasing a pettiauger near Dobbs Ferry on Friday, May 24, 1777. The pettiauger (see Photo NY-21) escaped.[192]

★ Lieutenant James Clark discovered some boats carrying troops across the Hudson at Phillipsburg at 5 AM on Sunday, May 25, 1777. He ordered the HM Galley *Dependence* to weigh anchor and give chase. He caught up with the boats at 6 o'clock, and they rowed toward the eastern shore near Teller's Point. The *Dependence* fired eight round and canister shots from her 22-pounders and 18 4-pound round and grape shots at them. Lieutenant Clark then sent his boats, manned and armed, to destroy the boats at 8 o'clock. They burned 14 boats and returned without any loss.[193]

★ Lieutenant James Clark saw a party of rebels going to burn some Loyalists' houses in Phillipsburg at 6 AM on Tuesday, June 3, 1777. He fired 4-pounders with round shot which dispersed them.[194]

★ When a party of Whigs were robbing Colonel Frederick Phillips's (d. 1785) house in Phillipsburg at 5 AM on Saturday, June 14, 1777, the *Dependence* dispersed them by firing five rounds from her 4-pounders at them. Two days later, a band of Whigs fired on a watering party from the *Dependence* at Phillipsburg. The *Dependence* covered the boats returning with the water by firing 15 4-pound shots at the militiamen.[195]

★ The *Dependence* fired a 24-pounder with round and grape shot at a sloop near Verplanck's Point at 11 AM on Tuesday, June 17, 1777. It turned out she was a flag of truce going from Peekskill to New York. She exchanged fire with Whig boats again on Friday and Saturday, July 4–5, 1777.[196]

★ Lieutenant James Clark saw a body of Congressional troops advancing toward British lines at Phillipsburg at 6 AM on Wednesday, June 18, 1777. He had the HM Galley *Dependence* fire four 4-pounders at them which also alerted the camp.[197]

★ HM Galley *Dependence* fired round and grape shot from two of her 4-pounders at a party of Whigs at Phillipsburg about 6 PM on Thursday, July 24, 1777. The following day, Lieutenant Clark saw four Whig boats at 4 AM and ordered the *Dependence* to fire a 24-pounder with round shot at them at 5 AM. She weighed anchor at 8 AM and gave chase to the boats and fired two 4-pound round shots at them at 8:30, forcing them to run ashore. The *Dependence* pursued them closely until a party of Whigs appeared on the adjacent hills.[198]

★ Lieutenant James Clark had the HM Galley *Dependence* fire five 4-pound rounds at a party of Whigs at Phillipsburg at 10 AM on Saturday, August 30, 1777, to disperse them.[199]

★ Lieutenant Thomas Farnham's HM Brig *Diligent*, accompanied by the HM Galley *Dependence* and the galley *Spitfire*, began to disembark some troops on the western shore of the Hudson, 5 miles north of Phillips Farm, at 4 AM on Friday, September 12, 1777. Several armed Whigs fired from the cliffs. The *Diligent* fired one 3-pound shot in response. The *Dependence* sent a boat ashore with provisions for the troops at 11 AM when a party of Whigs hidden in the woods attacked. The boat fired two 4-pound shots at them and returned at noon.[200]

★ Lieutenant Colonel Andreas Emmerich (1737–1809) led an excursion of Crown troops to the Saw Mill Valley on Monday, November 17, 1777. They completely surprised the Van Tassels, burned their houses, "stripped the women and children of the necessary apparel to cover them from the severity of a cold winter's night," and took two brothers, Peter (1728–1784) and Cornelius Van Tassel (1743–1830), prisoners. The Whigs retaliated by organizing an expedition to Tarrytown which plundered and burned the house of Brigadier General Oliver de Lancey (1718–1785) at Bloomingdale on York Island on Sunday, November 23rd. The party returned to Tarrytown safely.[201]

★ Lieutenant James Clark's HM Galley *Dependence* chased a Whig sloop ashore near Dobbs Ferry at 9 AM on Tuesday, June 23, 1778. She sent a boat, manned and armed, to bring back the sloop. The boat returned with the prize an hour later at which time the *Dependence* fired one 24-pounder and two 4-pound shots at a party of light horsemen on shore. The *Dependence* had one man in the boarding party wounded.[202]

★ A band of Whigs were harassing a wood gathering party from the HM Galley *Dependence* at Phillipsburg on Saturday, June 27, 1778. Lieutenant James Clark had his crew fire two 4-pound shots on the men who fired at his boats.[203]

★ The Hessians were put aboard ship and sailed down the East River toward Rhode Island on Thursday, July 9, 1778. On the way, they were attacked by some Whigs at Teller's Point. HM Galley *Dependence*, Lieutenant Clark, chased some Whig boats ashore at 7 AM, firing four 24-pound rounds at them. Lieutenant Clark sent his boats, manned and armed, after the Whig boats. His crews returned at 10 o'clock, having taken and burned four enemy vessels.[204]

★ When news arrived on Tuesday, September 15, 1778, that General Charles Scott (ca. 1739–1813) and a corps of 3,000 to 4,000 men pushed Colonel Nathaniel Gist's (1733–1796) 500 men (16th Virginia Regiment) to Babcock's Hill (also known as Boar Hill), the Crown forces began to prepare for a surprise attack. Lieutenant Colonels Andreas Emmerich (1737–1809) and John Graves Simcoe (1752–1806) set out with their corps at midnight. They took the route to the right past Mile Square to attack the left flank and rear of the Congressional troops. Major Pruschenk (d. 1806) and 200 jaegers began to go around toward Philipse's Bridge at 1 AM to cut off Gist's retreat route along the Albany road. Captain Carl August von Wreden and 100 jaegers marched over the hills on Richland road at 3 AM to attack the front line at daybreak.

Each unit arrived at its destination at the appointed time; but Lieutenant Colonel Emmerich decided to cut off the enemy's retreat with his own corps. He made the arc too small, allowing the Congressional troops to keep open a small ravine for their retreat.

Instead of capturing the whole party, they only took six officers and about 70 privates. They then burned the camp and baggage.[205]

See also **Mile Square Road.**

★ General Charles Cornwallis (1738–1805) and a column consisting of the Guards, the 1st Battalion of Grenadiers (see Photo NY-8) and the 42nd Regiment marched at 10 PM on Sunday, September 27, 1778. They went by way of Liberty Pole to Tappan where they arrived about sunrise. Two deserters had alerted the 500 militiamen stationed there of their advance so they deserted the town. Major General Charles Grey (1729–1807) led another column consisting of the 2nd Battalion Light Infantry and Grenadiers and two regiments. They marched northward by another road and surprised a cantonment of about 100 light horsemen about an hour before daylight. They bayoneted between 40 and 50 and captured 30 to 40 prisoners.[206]

★ The HM Galley *Dependence* returned to the vicinity of Tarrytown to annoy the French and Continental troops camped in that area to rest prior to resuming their march to Yorktown in the summer of 1781. She was anchored off Tarrytown together with the frigate *Tartar* and the galley *Crane* on Thursday, July 12, 1781. The following morning at 10, the *Dependence* fired eight 24-pound round shots to prevent the Congressional troops from constructing earthworks. The battery cannonaded the ships at 6 PM that evening, forcing them to weigh anchor and row farther up the river. The French, camped along the river 4 miles above Dobbs Ferry, heard the cannonade and mustered, thinking that their camp was under fire. They were later dismissed. The soldiers had barely returned to their tents when they were ordered to send 200 men with six 12-pounders and two howitzers to Tarrytown. The order was countermanded when they were ready to march. Only Major General Robert Howe (1732–1786) marched out with a detachment of his own troops.[207]

★ On Sunday evening, the 15th, two British sloops of war, two tenders and one galley came up the Hudson River to destroy the stores being transported from West Point to the army. Meanwhile, two sloops going down the river, laden with cannon and powder, turned about and headed for Tarrytown as soon as they discovered the enemy. They ran aground and the British, having the advantage of a fair wind and tide, came up the river so fast that the infantry did not have time to arrive to unload or protect the stores. The only troops at Tarrytown were an outpost from the Soissonais Regiment under the command of a sergeant.

Colonel Elisha Sheldon's (1740–1805) dragoons, who were stationed at Dobbs Ferry to guard several barges, set out for Tarrytown, dismounted and helped to unload the stores. The British, anchored off Tarrytown, began a heavy cannonade to cover two gunboats and four barges sent to destroy the vessels. Captain George Hurlbut (d. 1783), of the 2nd Regiment light dragoons, was stationed on board one of the vessels with 12 dragoons armed only with pistols and sabres. He kept his men hidden until the British came alongside. The dragoons fired. The British returned fire and killed one of the dragoons. Surrounded, Capt. Hurlbut ordered his men to jump overboard and swim to shore.

The British boarded and set fire to the vessels, one of which had cloaks and swords for Sheldon's dragoons and another had a number of French bakers and a large quantity of bread, on board. But severe fire from the dragoons and the French guard forced them to retire. Captain Hurlbut and several others jumped in the river and swam to the sloops to extinguish the fire and save the vessels. While in the water, Captain Hurlbut received a musket ball through the thigh.

Major General Robert Howe (1732–1786) arrived with a division of troops and some artillery about daybreak. They opened a battery on the enemy, forcing them to slip their cables and head down the river about 2 miles, where they remained until about noon on Tuesday, July 17. At that time, Gen. Howe opened another battery on them, forcing them to sail up the river. They remained near Teller's Point until Thursday, when they sent their gunboats on shore, to burn the elegant house of Captain Roberts at Haverstraw.

★ The HMS *Savage* and the 18-gun HM sloop *General Monk* (formerly the privateer *George Washington*) headed down the Hudson River about noon on Thursday, July 19, 1781 when they came near Dobbs Ferry, where a battery of two 18-pounders, two French brass 12-pounders, and two 7.5 inch howitzers was located. The ships came under heavy fire from both sides of the river. They returned fire but did little damage. The *Savage*, the largest of the ships sustained the greatest damage, with many shots fired through her. One of the shells (see Photo NY-3 and NY-4) burst on board, throwing the crew into great confusion. Eighteen or 20 men jumped overboard. Three or four of them swam to shore and the rest were presumed drowned. One of the survivors reported that more than 20 balls pierced the ship and that the shells had set her on fire.[208]

★ British and Congressional guard boats met in the Hudson River near Dobbs Ferry about 11 PM on Friday, August 3, 1781. A considerable firing ensued leaving one Continental mortally wounded. British casualties were not known. Four days later, about 2 AM on Tuesday, the 7th, cannon fire at Dobbs Ferry awakened the Continental army when two British gunboats approached the ferry, probably to seize some vessels. When they realized they were spotted, they fired four cannon shots with no effect. The shore battery returned fire with four cannon shots and the boats returned down river.[209]

Pelham Manor (Oct. 18, 1776)
Pell's Point (Oct. 18, 1776)
New Rochelle (Oct. 18, 1776; Jan. 29, 1777; Nov. 27, 28, 1777; July 5, 1779; Aug. 5, 6, 1779 ; Jan. 18, 1780)

> Pelham Manor is 13 miles north of New York City. The Pell family owned the original grant in the Throg's Neck and Pell's Point area. Pelham Manor is named after them. Throg's Neck is the area in the Bronx where the Throg's Neck Bridge (I-295) connects the Bronx with Queens. Pell's Point is 3 miles to the north in Westchester in what is now Pelham Bay Park. It is about halfway between Throg's Neck and modern Pelham Manor.

See also **Throg's Neck.**

★ After the Battle of Harlem Heights (September 16, 1776), General George Washington (1732–1799) worried that General William Howe (1732–1786) would take Kingsbridge and cut off the Continental Army's only escape route at the north end of Manhattan.

General Howe outflanked the Continental fortifications at Fort Washington and Fort Constitution (later called Fort Lee). He sent a strong fleet up the East River from Kip's Bay during the night of Friday, October 11, 1776. The following day, 4,000 Crown troops landed at Throg's Point across the creek from a small but well-placed force of Continental troops who blocked General Howe's advance. With the arrival of Continental reinforcements, Howe's 4,000 troops were stopped for six days.

When General Washington learned of General Howe's plan, he held a council of war on Wednesday night, October 16th, and decided to abandon Harlem and move the army and its supplies across Kingsbridge up to White Plains where he could form another effective defense line. He decided to leave 3,000 men to hold Fort Washington and 2,000 men to hold Fort Constitution on the New Jersey side. He instructed Major General Nathanael Greene (1742–1786) to hold the positions only as long as he thought possible. However, Fort Washington was 15 miles away, isolated in a country entirely held by the enemy, with no possibility of help or supplies except from Fort Constitution across the Hudson. Yet, Congress determined that it should be defended.

The British Grenadiers, Light Infantry and Reserve advanced early Thursday morning, the 17th; but the weather was so bad that they could not proceed. They waited until the following day and advanced toward Eastchester. The Continentals fired at them from behind trees and heaps of stones, killing or wounding 10 Regulars; but they were soon forced to retire. The British soldiers halted until General Howe came up. The Continentals formed themselves in front of the British "behind all the fences and high stone walls." The British advanced a little and halted until noon when the 1st Light Infantry Battalion advanced on their left flank. The Continentals fired at them from behind trees and walls and soon forced them to retire after killing or wounding 12 men and wounding three officers. The British Grenadiers advanced on the right and the Hessian Grenadiers in the center. After some cannonading, they forced the Continentals from the heights, killing a few and taking many prisoners. They took their position on the heights of Pelham Manor between East Chester Creek on their left and New Rochelle on their right. The Crown forces occupied New Rochelle by October 21 and Mamaroneck on the 22nd. General Washington was then at White Plains awaiting Howe's advance.[210]

★ Brigadier General David Wooster's (1711–1777) division was ordered to New Rochelle on Wednesday, January 29, 1777. A severe skirmish took place on the east side of the village between Colonel Stephen Moylan's (1734–1811) Continental light horsemen and Lieutenant Colonel John Graves Simcoe's (1752–1806) Queen's Rangers. Although the Queen's Rangers far outnumbered the Continental dragoons, the Continentals beat them off. The Rangers retreated to Horseneck (Greenwich, Connecticut).[211]

★ Colonel Samuel Webb's (1754–1825) regiment skirmished with Crown troops near New Rochelle on Thursday, November 27, 1777 and suffered two men wounded. The following night, a scouting party went down to West Chester and captured Colonel James De Lancey (1747–1804) and several other Loyalists. James De Lancey, Jr. was sheriff of Westchester County prior to the war and formed a separate unit known as the Westchester Refugees. His unit was not on the regular army payroll and raised money by selling raided cattle to the British army, earning them their nickname, "the Cowboys."[212]

★ Lieutenant Colonel Henry White (1740–1787) and a party of 100 horsemen, assisted by 50 infantrymen of Brigadier General John Glover's (1732–1797) brigade, engaged 300 Crown horsemen and 200 infantrymen at New Rochelle on Monday, July 5, 1779. Colonel White repulsed the enemy several times and retreated with the loss of one killed, one wounded, and one missing. He killed 15 of the enemy and took eight horses with their accoutrements.[213]

★ Having received intelligence that a party of the enemy might be surprised within their lines, a party was sent to attempt to do so. Lieutenant Colonel Henry White (1740–1787) of Colonel Stephen Moylan's (1734–1811) dragoons commanded the party composed of 35 of Moylan's and 10 of Colonel Elisha Sheldon's (1740–1805) light dragoons with 40 infantrymen of Brigadier General John Glover's (1732–1797) brigade and about 50 militiamen. They got within the enemy's lines by midnight on Thursday, August 5, 1779 and proceeded almost 2 miles beyond Delancey's Bridge without being discovered. Although Col. White did not meet with the party he was sent to surprise, he did engage 300 enemy horsemen and 200 infantrymen at New Rochelle.

He had just passed New Rochelle when a strong body of horsemen vigorously attacked his rear about daybreak. Although Col. White's troops put up a good defense, the superior number of enemy forced his cavalry to retire a little to allow the infantry to fire effectively. The sudden attack and the nature of the ground did not provide the opportunity to gain a favorable situation; but Col. White's force sustained the attack firmly and with well-directed fire. They checked the enemy until the cavalry regrouped and resumed their attack while the infantry took a more defensible position. The cavalry was again obliged to retire when the infantry gave the enemy another severe check; but their numbers increased continually; so General Howe ordered the infantry to retire to a wood where they could defend themselves and retreat if necessary. The dragoons retired by the road which led to Horseneck. The Crown forces pursued them for some time and there were frequent encounters between small parties; but the dragoons always had the advantage. The conflict continued until the dragoons arrived about 4 miles from Byram Bridge. The Crown forces withdrew and the dragoons proceeded to Horseneck.

Lieutenant Gull counted 14 men lying on the field in one place and concluded more must have fallen at other places. Only three or four dragoons were slightly wounded while the infantry lost two killed and three or four wounded. They captured four men.

The Continentals lost one killed, one wounded and one missing. They captured eight horses with their accoutrements and killed 15 men. They capture 16 prisoners, two or three African Americans, more than 30 horses, a few arms, some accoutrements and many other things of value.[214]

January 18, 1780 see **Morrisania.**

Eastchester (East Chester) (Oct. 11, 1776; Oct. 18, 1776; Feb. 26, 1779; Oct. 3, 1779)

Near East Chester (Aug. 22, 1777)

Split Rock (Oct. 18, 1776)

Ward's House (Mar. 16, 1777)

Westchester County (Mar. 16, 1777)

Eastchester Bay (Nov. 13, 1781)

> Eastchester was northeast of New Rochelle, along the Boston Post Road (Route U.S. 1). It should not be confused with the modern town of East Chester.
>
> Split Rock, which gives Split Rock Road its name, was so designated for a huge boulder with a crack or split, probably caused by frost and ice. This Native American landmark was on a grassy island between the north and southbound lanes of the New England Throughway (I-95) about where the Hutchinson River Parkway meets it (I-95 exit 14). The large volume of high-speed traffic in this area makes it difficult to find. The boulder may have been removed in highway construction projects since the nation's bicentennial.
>
> St. Paul's Episcopal Church is at 897 South Columbus Avenue (Route NY 22) (on the right, going north) north of its intersection with Route U.S. 1 and about 0.4 miles

past the intersection with E. 233rd St. It is a pre-Revolution fieldstone building with a tower and steeple at one end. It was still under construction at the time of the battle. The original church, erected between 1692 and 1699, stood about 60 yards in front of the present church. Construction of the present church began in 1763 and ended around 1790. Lieutenant General Wilhelm von Knyphausen used the church as a hospital during the battle. Only the exterior walls were completed at that time.

The old church was demolished to provide shelter and firewood to the wounded and dying Hessians in the unfinished new church. A white marble D.A.R. stone close to the back wall of the graveyard behind the church marks the site of a mortar pit where at least five Hessian privates were buried (see Photo NY-22). A plaque on the church identifies at least 13 known Revolutionary War dead who are also buried here, including three members of the Pell family which owned the original grant here and for whom Pelham Manor is named. It notes a number of unknown dead were also buried here.

The bell now in the belfry is a sister to the Liberty Bell in Philadelphia. The two bells were cast about the same time at the same foundry. It was taken down in October 1776, as the Crown forces approached, packed with the church silver, and submerged in a nearby swamp. After the war, it was re-hung.

Photo NY-22. Grave of at least five Hessian privates in a mortar pit

From the church steeple, one can see Eastchester Creek and the Split Rock battleground (Battle of Pell's Point), about a mile to the southeast, now occupied by industrial and suburban sprawl.

The church is also noted for another event. John Peter Zenger (1697–1746) reported in his newspaper on an election held on the village green adjacent to the church in 1735. Zenger was tried for libel and acquitted and the event became a precedent in establishing the principles of freedom of the press and freedom of religion (see Photo NY-23).

Photo NY-23. St. Paul's Episcopal Church, Eastchester, is also noted for its role in the trial of John Peter Zenger, which set a precedent in establishing the principles of freedom of the press and freedom of religion

> A Revolutionary War tavern stood on the other side of Columbus Avenue directly opposite the church. It was the first stagecoach stop along the route to Boston from New York.
> Stephen Ward's (d. 1777) house was on the White Plains Road (Route NY 22) in Eastchester, 9 miles north of Kingsbridge and southeast of Dobbs Ferry.

★ Colonel John Glover's (1732–1797) whole brigade was at Eastchester on Friday, October 11, 1776 when they were ordered to oppose a large body of enemy troops landing at Rodman's Point. Colonel Glover ordered three regiments to cross a causeway, the only passage, to confront them. One regiment with three pieces of artillery occupied a hill overlooking the causeway to secure an avenue of retreat for the others and to prevent an enemy advance. The other three regiments occupied the wood and annoyed the enemy greatly. When the Crown forces attempted to flank him, Colonel Glover ordered a retreat. The Crown forces' artillery kept up a constant fire at the regiment on the hill which returned fire. The distance between the two forces was out of range of the muskets.

Colonel Glover had six or seven men killed and about 18 wounded, while the Crown forces lost about 140 or 150. Reports spread that General William Howe (1732–1786) was wounded in the leg by a cannon shot. Colonel Glover then retreated to Mile Square where he encamped until Friday, the 18th when the remainder of Major General Charles Lee's (1731–1782) division, joined the main body of the army at White Plains 1.5 miles away.[215]

★ General William Howe (1732–1786) withdrew his forces from Throg's Point and moved them to Pell's Point on Eastchester Bay on Friday, October 18, 1776. The Congressional forces began to evacuate Manhattan on the same day. They moved slowly because they lacked horse-drawn wagons to move their supplies. The same day, 120 ships brought Lieutenant General Wilhelm von Knyphausen (1716–1800) and 3,997 Hessians, 670 Waldeckers, a company of jaegers, and about 3,400 British recruits to New York. The Germans were sent immediately to New Rochelle by water to hold that position while General Howe proceeded toward White Plains.

Colonel John Glover (1732–1797) had been posted near the little village of Eastchester (north of New Rochelle) to guard the roads from Pell's Point toward the rear of the Congressional forces. Early in the morning of the 18th, he ascended a hill near the Eastchester village green and saw through his glass that "upwards of two hundred [boats] ... all manned and formed in four grand divisions" were coming ashore in Eastchester Bay, beside the Point.

He commanded about 750 men—his own Marblehead regiment (14th Continental Infantry) and the Massachusetts regiments of Colonel Joseph Reed (1741–1785) (14th Massachusetts), Colonel William Shepard (1737–1817) (4th Massachusetts), and Lieutenant Colonel Loammi Baldwin (1740–1807) (26th Continental Infantry). He also had three guns and decided to do his best to block the enemy advance. The attackers had to use Split Rock Road to reach the Post Road (the Boston Post Road or Route U.S. 1), the only road available. Glover and his men met the attackers about a mile from the Point near the rock which gives Split Rock Road its name.

Glover placed his men along the road behind stone walls. Reed's division took the front end or left of the line, Shepard's next, and then Baldwin's. Glover's regiment was stationed in the rear as a reserve. He sent forward a captain and 40 men to meet the enemy's advance guard. They received fire at a distance of 50 yards without loss and returned fire, striking four men. The two sides exchanged five rounds and Glover lost two killed and several wounded. The advanced party fell back when the Crown forces got "not more than thirty yards distant." "The enemy gave a shout and advanced" about 100 feet from Reed's men who remained undiscovered behind the stone wall. Reed's men then "rose up and gave them the whole charge; the enemy broke and retreated for the main body to come up."

There was no further conflict for an hour and a half until the entire advance unit of 4,000 men and seven guns advanced. When they came within 50 yards, Reed's men fired a volley. The Crown forces replied with musketry and fieldpieces. After firing seven rounds, Reed's regiment retreated past Shepard's battalion. The Crown forces "shouted and pushed on till they came to Shepard, posted behind a fine, double stone-wall." Shepard's men fired 17 rounds by platoons, causing them to retreat several times and preventing Lieutenant General Wilhelm von Knyphausen (1716–1800) from making much progress.

Glover ordered his brigade to cross a creek, and to take a position on a hill to his rear. The two sides exchanged artillery fire until nightfall, "without any damage on our side and but little on theirs," says Glover. After dark, the Congressional forces withdrew about 3 miles and encamped, "after fighting all day without victuals or drink, laying as a picket all night, the heavens over us and the earth under us."

Glover lost eight killed and 13 wounded. Major General William Heath (1737–1814) estimated that total Continental casualties were between 30 and 40 men killed and wounded. Colonel Shepard was wounded in the throat—not mortally, but the ball came close to killing him instantly. Howe reported three killed and 20 wounded; but those figures may only reflect British losses. The Hessians, who bore the brunt of the fighting, made no report of casualties. However, that night and for days afterward, St. Paul's Episcopal Church, about a mile away, was crowded with Hessian wounded.[216]

★ Major General William Heath (1737–1814) commanded the New York troops and Brigadier General David Wooster (1711–1777) commanded those from Connecticut. It was determined that the main body would remain east of the Bronx with lines radiating from the Stephen Ward house toward New Rochelle on the east to "Turkehoe" (a village in the town of Yonkers) on the west, and on the south to the house of Benjamin Drake near the intersection of White Plains Road and Columbus Avenue in Mount Vernon.

The Ward house served as the base for foraging parties. It was garrisoned by a company of about 31 new levies from Dutchess County and a company of Westchester militia of about equal size.

A foraging party consisting of five or six teams went down to Williams's Bridge near Morrisania on Wednesday morning, March 16, 1777 to forage in the vicinity of Morrisania. Captain Samuel Delavan (1752–1785) and a scout of about 120 Westchester militiamen went to cover them.

Major Archibald Campbell (d. 1777) and Captain John Brandon (d. 1781) led a detachment of about 50 Crown troops, consisting of Queen's Rangers and New York companies and 20 Hessian troops and a subaltern, up from Kingsbridge to surprise the Congressional forces. About 40 militia scouts accompanied the foraging teams while the other 80 fought the attackers all day long across the Bronx River until the foraging teams returned and the entire force proceeded to the Ward house in Eastchester that night. Captain Samuel Delavan survived because he was wearing a red coat and passed for a British officer. The militia lost one man killed and 10 taken prisoners in this skirmish.

The Crown troops approached Ward's house from the west side of the road about 9 PM. A sentinel challenged them but the troops rushed to the house and surrounded it. Captain Noah Bouton (1745–?) came to the door and asked for quarter, offering to surrender; but Major Campbell called out "Fire boys! Kill all the d .... d rebels you can." Captain Bouton discharged his musket and shot Major Campbell in the heart. He fell dead at Bouton's feet. All the troops in the house escaped, except six who were killed and 27 taken prisoners and were brought to New York City.

A company of militiamen advanced to the house to find the Crown troops firing into the windows. They posted themselves behind a stone wall and attacked the Regulars. However, the militiamen were greatly outnumbered and outflanked, so they had to retreat. The Crown forces took about 24 head of cattle and four horses which the foragers captured earlier in the day. The Crown forces lost five privates killed on the spot and six wounded, one mortally.

The militiamen withdrew about 2 miles. They returned the next day to bury their dead in a beautiful locust grove west of Ward's house and directly behind the barn. They withdrew as far as North Castle on Friday, the 18th, and to White Plains about a week later. Several hundred militiamen who responded to the call for the foraging expedition soon quit active service. General Wooster considered his men Connecticut state troops and remained near the state boundary to protect it.[217]

★ Major General Israel Putnam (1718–1790) sent Brigadier General James Mitchell Varnum's (1748–1789) brigade and some of Brigadier General Andrew Ward's (1727-1799) Connecticut militiamen to surprise the British advanced post and hospital at the village of Eastchester on Sunday, August 22, 1777. They captured two officers and some privates along with some Loyalists and African Americans and took some of the hospital supplies the Continental Army desperately needed. General Varnum sent out two picket companies, of about 50 men each, toward Westchester and Mile Square about 2 PM as the medical supplies were being gathered.

The Crown forces attacked the company that went to Westchester, killed the captain and several privates. The rest of the company retreated to the main body which returned to its original position, leaving Colonel Israel Angell's (1740–1832) company that went to Mile Square to fend for itself.[218]

★ Governor William Tryon (1729–1788) and about 1400 or 1500 men made an excursion within 4 miles of Stamford, Connecticut. They reached Horseneck without incident, about 9 AM on Friday, February 26, 1779. They were discovered at 9 o'clock the preceding evening but the residents were not alarmed until 10 o'clock when they reached Stamford. Captain Titus Watson (1744–1820) and a small guard of Continental troops, at Eastchester, were obliged to give way, fighting as they retreated. Some of them were wounded and taken prisoners. A light-horseman closely pursued Captain Watson who killed the dragoon and took his horse to escape.

Major General Israel Putnam (1718–1790) happened to be at Stamford but the Continental troops were too scattered to muster in time to oppose the raiders. About 200 militiamen and a few Continental troops gathered and attacked the enemy's rear as they were leaving Horseneck around mid-afternoon. The raiders killed eight or ten and took about 50 prisoners and burned a schooner at anchor in Mianos Creek. They plundered the inhabitants, stripping many families of everything but the clothes they wore. They broke windows and damaged property, not even sparing the house where Governor Tryon had his headquarters. They returned to Rye on Friday evening, leaving behind two wagons loaded with plunder. The next day, they proceeded to Kingsbridge. The militia had not a man killed.[219]

★ First Lieut. Erasmus Gill (1757–1807), of the dragoons, patrolling in East Chester on Sunday, October 3, 1779, "found a superior force in his rear, and no alternative but to surrender or cut his way through them; he chose the latter, and forced his way, when he found a body of infantry still behind the horse; these he also charged, and on his passing them, his horse was wounded and threw him, when he fell into the enemy's hands. Two of the Lieutenant's party, which consisted of 24, were killed, and one taken prisoner; the rest escaped safe to their regiments."[220]

★ Six whaleboats from Brunswick came among the British transports and vessels lying in Gravesend Bay Saturday night November 10, 1781. Several ships which had troops on board hailed them. They answered that they belonged to the men-of-war. They rowed alongside *The Father's Desire*, a victualler and were hailed again. They answered that they were boats belonging to the warships coming to attack. All the men ran below deck and the Congressional troops boarded the vessel. They cut her cable and set sail toward Amboy, New Jersey but they were discovered by the HM Galley *Crane* near Billop's Point about daybreak. The *Crane* fired some shots and set out after them. Unable to escape with the ship, the raiders set her on fire and abandoned her. She was entirely burned with her cargo of 1,000 barrels of provisions and 30 puncheons of rum taken from the ships of war near Sandy Hook.

Captain Daniel Lockwood and 25 Connecticut Continentals and 15 Connecticut militiamen planned to board a sloop of 10 carriage guns at anchor in East Chester Bay on Tuesday morning, November 13, 1781. They took a small sloop of about 30 tons in East Chester Creek and headed to the bay. The sloop hailed them and they answered that "the rebel boats were down and they had pushed out of the creek to anchor under their protection." They then boarded the sloop and cut through her netting. One man entered and was seriously wounded. He was followed by the rest who carried the vessel after a five minute skirmish with bayonets and lances. She had 25 men on board. Meanwhile, part of the detachment attacked the wood fleet and took six vessels that were brought to Stamford. Captain Lockwood's men badly wounded the captain of the sloop and four men and captured about 40 prisoners, including 25 soldiers. Lockwood had nobody killed and only four men wounded.[221]

Peekskill
Cortlandt, Westchester County
Van Cortlandtville (Mar. 23, 1777)
Peekskill (Mar. 23, 1777; Oct. 5, 1777; Oct. 7, 1777; Oct. 9, 1777; Aug. 19, 1779)

> Peekskill is on the eastern side of the Hudson River. Van Cortlandtville is about 2 miles northeast of Peekskill on Oregon Road off Route U.S. 9 and 4 miles east of Bear Mountain. The village grew around the Upper Van Cortlandt Manor House which still stands but has been altered considerably as the Cortlandt Nursing Home. General Washington stayed here frequently.
>
> Despite Van Cortlandtville's meager population, it became, along with Peekskill, a focal point during the American War for Independence. General George Washington (1732–1799) established the headquarters for the Highland Command here for three years and maintained his headquarters in Peekskill off and on for several extended periods. The location became a major assembly area for troops and militia as well as arms and supplies because the area was centrally located for the movement of men and material up and down the Hudson, east into New England or west and south via King's Ferry at nearby Verplanck's Point.
>
> Some accounts locate Soldier's Spring (now destroyed by a widening of the road) on Highland Avenue near the intersection with Phoenix Avenue. Others (Lossing, Bolton and local historian Wygant) locate it on the north slope of Gallows Hill, just over the brow.

★ When General George Washington (1732–1799) withdrew from North Castle (Mount Kisco), in November 1776, he left Major General William Heath (1737–1814) at Peekskill with four brigades, about 3,300 men, to guard the Highlands of the Hudson.

However, the troops had been drawn away for one reason or another until few remained to guard the very large quantity of military stores that had accumulated in the magazines. He wrote to General Heath, at home in Roxbury, Massachusetts for a brief furlough, to send eight Massachusetts battalions to Peekskill to support the Eastern or Middle States to oppose the British if they decided to head up the North (Hudson) River.

One of Washington's greatest fears was that the British would move troops up the river with their fleet, seize control of the Hudson Valley and split the colonies in two. The string of defenses included several forts and the placement of giant chains in the river. Washington's fears were well founded. A fleet of nine or ten British ships appeared in Peekskill Bay around noon on Sunday, March 23, 1777. Some 500 men landed at Lent's Cove.

Brigadier General Alexander McDougall (1732–1786), an inexperienced officer, had succeeded Heath to the command on March 12th. He had only 250 men in the Highland Command. The British tried to trick him by sending an officer they had captured at Fort Washington up the river with a flag. They allowed him to overhear conversations about raids down the river so he would repeat them. He reported that the British were planning a foraging expedition to come up the river as far as Tarrytown. However, General McDougall guessed that Peekskill was the real objective. However, he could not defend the place with so few men. So he hurried to transfer as much of the munitions and stores as he could to Forts Independence and Montgomery. He ordered the burning of supplies and a retreat toward Continental Village to protect the supply depot there.

A British fleet consisting of a frigate, two ships, two brigs, three galleys, four transports and some smaller craft sailed up the Hudson on Saturday, March 22, 1777 and anchored opposite Tarrytown. The next day, they anchored in Peekskill Bay at noon. Soon afterward, eight flatboats carrying about 500 men headed to Lent's Cove to burn a house nearby that was owned by the Lent family. As the Lent family fled up a lane leading from the Post Road just north of Welcher Avenue to Jockeytown, they saw some British soldiers, probably dragoons, over a rise of ground to the west near where Washington Street now runs. One of the Lents supposedly fired and killed one of them.

The invasion of Van Cortlandtville began with a detachment of 200 men who marched as far as Twin Hills, just south of the Van Cortlandt Upper Manor House, where McDougall had posted an advance guard. Meanwhile, the main force headed to Drum Hill with four light field pieces and began shelling Peekskill and the area to the north. McDougall set fire to the barracks, the principal storehouses and a wharf, and began to retreat through Van Cortlandtville toward Continental Village. He sent a message to Lieutenant Colonel Marinus Willett (1740–1830), commander of Fort Independence, to leave a small guard at the fort and join him.

The men were assembling for their usual Sunday parade when the order arrived, unaware that the British had landed. Willett set out immediately to join McDougall with 80 men. They joined forces at Gallows Hill in the late afternoon.

The British had already mounted their artillery on Drum Hill and were cannonading the town. General McDougall disposed his forces to protect Continental Village and posted an advance guard at the Upper Manor House. A detachment of about 200 British advanced to Van Cortlandtville and occupied a hill a little to the south of the Upper Manor House.

About this time, Nathan Brown (d. 1777), a Continental soldier fleeing from the British, paused to drink at a spring located on Highland Avenue near the intersection with Phoenix Avenue. A cannonball fired from a British field piece on Drum Hill struck him and shattered his thigh. A passing wagon picked him up and brought him to Fishkill where he died. Another version of the story (Scharf II, 369–370) says he was killed on the spot and buried in the immediate vicinity. A human skeleton was discovered with a cannonball lying beside it in a sandbank shortly before the Civil War and believed to be that of the soldier.

As night approached, Colonel Willett urged General McDougall to attack before the British could bring up their main body. The general thought it would be unwise to do so. Willett begged for permission to attack, and McDougall consented reluctantly. Willett's detachment reached the enemy's position after sunset, fired one or two volleys then charged with fixed bayonets, overwhelming the enemy with the unexpected assault and driving them back on the main body.

The British withdrew to the village, leaving their baggage and nine men dead on the field. They then withdrew to the shore at night and tried to set fire to some Whig boats by the light of a full moon. The militiamen were aroused and attacked the British, killing four more men. The Regulars boarded their ships and sailed down the river.

The next day, McDougall returned to Peekskill to find several buildings burned in addition to the ones he had burned. Some small craft loaded with provisions were destroyed in the river, and the villagers reported the theft of about 40 sheep and eight or ten head of cattle. Charles Stedman, a British officer, reported:

> Immediately upon landing, the troops advanced to the execution of their design and burnt and destroyed the whole magazine, the barracks, the workshops, storehouses and all the appurtenances of this principal deposit of Military furniture and stores, which the rebels had been forming for a long time with the greatest expense and labor.... Above one hundred and fifty new wagons were committed to the flames, together with a vast collection of intrenching tools, carpenters tools and an immense quantity of beef, pork, flour, rice and biscuit all in casks, and above four hundred hogsheads of rum. Many casks of tallow, boxes of candles, hogsheads of molasses, about a dozen casks of coffee, chests of arms, artillery stores, thirty casks of nails, twenty boxes of grape shot, and a large quantity of bar and slit iron were either conveyed to the ships or entirely destroyed.... In the conflagration, which with such a collection of combustible matters may be easily imagined to have been prodigious, a large quantity of bark for tanning and of leather for shoes and other purposes was consumed.[222]

The skirmish successfully stopped the advance on the Whig storage depot at Continental Village and the British did not get the ammunition and stores which were there. General McDougall was relieved of his command and replaced by General Rufus Putnam (1738–1824). The British did not return to the Hudson Valley in force until the following October, six months later.[223]

★ A party of Whigs on shore at Peekskill were breaking down a bridge on Lent's Creek when HM Galley *Dependence* and *Diligent* fired on them at 3 PM. on Sunday, October 5, 1777. *Dependence* fired four 24-pound round shots at them. She weighed anchor at 3:30 PM and chased five whaleboats which ran to shore as soon as they spotted the *Dependence* chasing them. The *Dependence* pursued them closely and sent her boats, manned and armed, to capture the whaleboats while she fired 14 24-pound round and canister shots to cover the boats. The boats returned at 4:30 PM after capturing three of the whaleboats and destroying three more.[224]

★ Some British ships tried to break the chain across the Hudson, below Peekskill about 6 AM on Tuesday, October 7, 1777. The chain stretched across the Hudson from Fort Montgomery to Anthony's Nose on the eastern bank. Whig fire beat off the ships.[225]

★ Peekskill was raided again on Thursday morning, October 9, 1777, when Major General William Tryon (1729–1788) was detached with Lieutenant Colonel Andreas Emmerich's (1737–1809) chasseurs, 50 jaegers and royal fusiliers and the Trumback regiment with a 3-pounder, to destroy Continental Village. He burned the barracks for 1500 men, several storehouses and loaded wagons. This was the main supply depot for the troops and the only Continental establishment on that part of the Highlands.[226]

★ A galley and one of the enemy's gunboats fired a number of cannon shots at a party of 250 men, under the command of Major General Israel Putnam (1718–1790), who covered 23 wagonloads of forage taken from the vicinity of Peekskill on Thursday, August 19, 1779. The artillery did them no harm.[227]

Verplanck's Point (June 17, 1777; Aug. 6, 1777; Oct. 5, 1777; Apr. 15, 1778; June 1, 1779; July 15–16, 1779)

Verplanck's Point is on the east shore of the Hudson River, opposite Stony Point.

★ The HM Galley *Dependence* fired one 24-pounder with round and grape shot at a sloop near Verplanck's Point at 11 AM on Tuesday, June 17, 1777. The sloop turned out to be a flag of truce from Peekskill headed to New York.[228]

★ Lieutenant James Clark's HM Galley *Dependence* weighed anchor and gave chase to four Whig vessels near Verplanck's Point at 2 PM on Wednesday August 6, 1777. She fired five 24-pound and eight 4-pound round shots at them. The Whigs opened a battery on the *Dependence* at 6 PM and struck her four times, causing her to give up the chase.[229]

★ The HM Galley *Dependence* anchored off Verplanck's Point at 11 AM on Sunday, October 5, 1777 in company with the HMS *Mercury*, brig *Diligent* and galleys *Spitfire* and *Crane*. The flat boats landed some troops on Verplanck's Point at noon without any opposition. The brig *Diligent* and the galleys came to off King's Ferry to cover the landing.

Lieutenant James Clark, of the HM Galley *Dependence*, discovered a party of Whigs breaking down a brig on Lent's Creek at 3 PM and fired four 24-pounders with round shot at them while the *Diligent* fired 14 12-pound shots.[230]

The *Dependence* weighed anchor at 3:30 PM and chased five whaleboats which spotted them at 4 o'clock and headed to shore. The *Dependence* followed them and sent her boats manned and armed to capture them while she fired 14 24-pounders with round and canister shot to cover the boats. The boats returned at 4:30, having captured three boats and destroyed three more. The flat boats landed the remainder of the troops on Stony Point at 5 PM.[231]

★ The *Dependence* was near Verplanck's Point to get water on Wednesday, April 15, 1778 when a party of Whigs tried to prevent the crew from taking the water aboard ship. She exchanged fire with them, firing one 24-pounder and three 4-pound shots.[232]

★ Major William Hull (1753–1825) of Massachusetts was notified, toward the end of May 1779, that Major General John Vaughn (1738?–1795) and a body of Crown troops were marching north from Kingsbridge. Major Hull and his troops marched just ahead of General Vaughn's troops until they joined Brigadier General Alexander McDougall (1732–1786) at Peekskill. Meanwhile, a fleet of "13 ships, 3 Brigs, 4 Topsail Schooners, 6 do Sloops, 3 Gallies, 15 or 20 Smaller Vessels, and a great number of Flat Bottomed and Gun Boats" transported the main body of nearly 5,000 men. A strong detachment landed at Teller's Point (now Croton Point) on the east side of the Hudson on Monday, May 31st. The rest landed a few miles below Stony Point on the west side of the river.

The 40-man garrison at Stony Point saw the large body of troops landing just below them and hurried to destroy everything which could be of any use to the enemy. They then abandoned the fort which the British occupied and immediately mounted cannon for an attack on Fort Lafayette on Verplanck's Point on the opposite shore.[233]

Captain Thomas Armstrong commanded the 70-man garrison at Fort Lafayette which was a more substantial fortification than that at Stony Point. He began a bombardment (see Photo NY-3, NY-4) as soon as the British landed at Stony Point but without much effect. The firing from Stony Point was more effective. It killed an officer and three men and wounded a number of others, making Fort Lafayette untenable. As the garrison tried to leave, General Vaughn blocked their way with a vastly superior force. The Continentals returned to the fort and renewed their fire on Stony Point. General Henry Clinton (1730–1795) sent Major John André (1751–1780) to demand the garrison's surrender. Captain Armstrong was compelled to accept the terms of capitulation on June 1st.[234]

July 15–16, 1779 see **Stony Point.**

Tarrytown (Apr. 28, 1777; Aug. 20, 1777; July 12, 1778; Aug. 30, 1779; July 15, 1781)

> Tarrytown is on the east bank of the Hudson River just north of where I-87 S (I-287 E|New York State Thruway) crosses the river.
> A bronze tablet was supposed to be placed on the west front of the Hudson River Railroad Station and dedicated on July 15, 2008 to commemorate "the action of Tarrytown, which occurred near this spot on July 15, 1781, and also the heroism of Colonel Sheldon and Captain George Hurlbut (d. 1783) of the Second Regiment of Dragoons."

★ Lieutenant James Clark of the HM Galley *Dependence* sent his boats manned and armed to burn two Congressional sloops that were anchored near her off Tarrytown on Monday, April 28, 1777. The *Dependence* fired 15 4- and three 24-pound round shots to cover the boats. The boat crews destroyed both sloops and returned at 9 AM.[234a]

★ Lieutenant James Clark of the HM Galley *Dependence* saw several Whig boats anchored at half mast near Tarrytown on Wednesday, August 20, 1777. He came within gun shot and gave the signal to chase out four of them. He fired nine round 24-pound shots and they took shelter under cover of one of their batteries.[235]

★ Captain Howorth's HMS *Tartar* and Lieutenant James Clark's HM Galley *Dependence* exchanged fire with a Whig battery at Tarrytown at 10 AM on Monday morning, July 12, 1778. The *Dependence* fired eight 24-pound round shots to prevent the troops from doing their work. The Congressional forces opened a battery and cannonaded the *Dependence* at 6 AM Wednesday morning. She weighed anchor and rowed farther up the river to join the *Tartar* and the *Crane* at 8 o'clock.[236]

★ Captain David Hopkins (1753–1824), of Colonel Stephen Moylan's (1734–1811) light dragoons, and a small detachment from Colonel Elisha Sheldon's (1740–1805) light horse left their quarters in North Castle on Monday, August 30, 1779 and headed to the upper cross roads. They determined that Lieutenant Colonel Andreas Emmerich (1737–1809) was advancing by way of White Plains. Emmerich had previously learned of Hopkins's advance and sent Colonel Mansfield Baremore, Bearmore or Barrymore (d. 1780) and a strong body of Colonel James De Lancey's (1747–1804) dragoons with orders to proceed by way of Davis's brook east of the upper cross roads. Hopkins took another route and posted a strong detachment of light dragoons south of the Tarrytown road. He then took the rest of his detachment to meet Emmerich.

When he saw Emmerich advancing with a small body of cavalry, Hopkins retreated, leading him into an ambuscade in Storms's wood. The ambuscade killed 23—the entire corps except for Emmerich and a few dragoons. Hopkins pursued Emmerich for half a mile, exchanging several strokes until Emmerich cleared a stone wall behind which he had concealed his jaegers. The entire company rose and fired simultaneously. Hopkins escaped unharmed but his companion was slightly wounded. Captain Hopkins retreated a short distance with his party when he saw Colonel Baremore approaching with a strong force of dragoons. His retreat route blocked, Captain Hopkins took the Bedford road only to find that Colonel Emmerich had blocked it. Captain Hopkins decided to charge and managed to cut his way through the enemy line with the loss of a few of his prisoners.

A running fight ensued for about 2 miles when Lieutenant Colonel Ludwig Johann Adolph von Wurmb's (d. 1813) jaegers blocked Captain Hopkins's way again. The whole detachment of Crown forces pursued Captain Hopkins in a running battle until they came to the Croton Acqueduct on the road to Singsing. Captain Hopkins presumed that the enemy dragoons were far in advance of the rest of the column, so he turned about and became the pursuer. He captured one or two prisoners at the spring brook which crosses the road in the Beeckman wood and escaped.[237]

★ Continental and French troops exchanged fire with British ships in the Hudson River off Tarrytown on Sunday, July 15, 1781. They suffered one killed and one wounded.[238]

Near Poughkeepsie (Oct. 12, 15, 16, 23, 1777)
Hudson River Highlands (Oct. 12, 1777)

> Poughkeepsie is on the eastern shore of the Hudson River about 10 miles north of Fishkill and Newburgh.

★ Lieutenant James Clark and Lieutenant Thomas Farnham sent the boats of HM Galley *Dependence* and HM Brig *Diligent* on shore within 3 miles of Poughkeepsie at 8 AM on Sunday October 12, 1777. They burned two Whig vessels and several old vessels, Van Burrens Mills, several buildings and some storehouses. The *Dependence* fired two 24-pound and one 4-pound shots to cover the boats as they returned at 10 after completing their task. The ships then withdrew below Wappingers Creek where they sent their boats to destroy vessels in the Creek. The *Dependence* fired 10 4-pound round shots and two round and grape shots to cover the boats as they returned after completing their mission that afternoon.[239]

★ The HM Brig *Diligent*, Lieutenant Thomas Farnham, sailed in convoy with the galleys *Crane* and *Spitfire* and 13 transports on Wednesday, October 15, 1777 when a number of armed Whigs fired at them from the bushes as they passed. The *Diligent* fired several 3-pound shots at them. Her crew captured three Whig sloops attempting to escape from Fishkill and burned them at 4 PM along with two pettiaugers (see Photo NY-21). They burned the house, mills, out-houses, and a sloop at Crum Elbow and two sloops on the east side that evening.[240]

★ The following day, the Crown forces set fire to two brigs and several sloops in Esopus Creek.[241]

★ Several Whigs fired at four British ships from the heights on the east bank of the Hudson between Rhinecliff and Poughkeepsie across from the highlands above Esopus Meadows as they passed Poughkeepsie at noon on Thursday, October 23, 1777. The ships returned fire. HM Brig *Diligent* fired 10 grape shots from her 3-pounders. The Whigs opened a five-gun battery at 1 PM while the transports were passing. The galleys *Dependence, Spitfire* and *Crane* cannonaded the battery during this time. *Dependence* fired 14 round and grape shots from her 24-pounders.[242]

New Windsor (Oct. 13, 1777)

> New Windsor is less than 2 miles south of Newburgh and 7 miles north of West Point.

★ A Whig battery on the Heights of New Windsor fired at Lieutenant James Clark's HM Galley *Dependence* and other ships as they passed at 2:30 PM on Monday, October 13, 1777. The *Dependence* returned fire with three round shots from her 24-pounders and 18 round shots from her 4-pounders as she passed the battery. The *Dependence* suffered damage to her sails and rigging.[243]

Storm King
Butter Hill (Oct. 24, 1777)

> Butter Hill was renamed Storm King after the Revolutionary War. The area is preserved as the Storm King State Park in Cornwall on Hudson.

★ As the transports were heading down river in company with the HMS *Mercury*, the brig *Diligence* and the galleys *Crane, Dependence,* and *Spitfire* around noon on Friday, October 24, 1777, they came under fire from a party of Whigs posted on Butter Hill. Lieutenant James Clark's HM Galley *Dependence* returned fire with 17 round and grape shots from her 4-pounders and two 24-pound shots. The *Diligence* fired 12 3-pound shots.[244]

Port Chester
Sawpits (Jan. 25, 1778; June 8, 17, 1779; June 29, 1779)
Byram River (May 22, 1779; May 10, 1780; June 4, 1780)
Sherrard's Bridge (June 17, 1780)

> The Byram River separates Connecticut from New York. Sawpits or Saw Pits was on the New York side of the river in what is now Port Chester. It became Port Chester in 1837. Sherrard's Bridge, previously known as Sherwood's Bridge, crossed the Byram River at Glenville.

★ Colonel James De Lancey (1747–1804) and a party of Loyalists proceeded 30 miles into enemy territory on Saturday afternoon, May 22, 1779. The infantry occupied a post at Byram Bridge while the horsemen proceeded to Horseneck (Greenwich, Connecticut) where they attacked a post of Congressional troops, killed eight or ten, and took a lieutenant, a commissary, a Mr. Knap, a Presbyterian minister, and 36 Continental and militia troops prisoners and 100 head of cattle. They also took and destroyed a cannon, which the Whigs unsuccessfully tried to defend. The Loyalists attacked them so quickly that they could not fire it more than twice before it was captured. Lieutenant James Kipp's (1751–1785) small detachment took six prisoners at another place and might have captured more had there not been a wood near their post. The Whigs took shelter in the wood where Colonel De Lancey's horsemen could not maneuver. The Loyalists only lost Captain Solomon Fowler (d. 1779) who was killed from a window of the house where the picket guard was posted. The house was immediately burned to the ground.[245]

★ The area along the Byram River in southwestern Connecticut was convenient for the Loyalists to raid as they were in close proximity to the regular army in New York. Some Loyalists ambushed Lieutenant Barber (d. 1778) and another officer near the Sawpits on Sunday, January 25, 1778. The officers were returning to camp from a walk a few miles away. The hidden Loyalists rose and fired on them with buckshot, killing Lieutenant Barber of Groton on the spot.[246]

★ Major Baremore or Bearmore led a force of Loyalists in an attack on Captain David Leavenworth's (1737–1820) militia along the Byram River on Wednesday, June 8, 1779. The attack killed three of Leavenworth's men, wounded five and four were made prisoners. Nine days later, on Thursday, June 17, Captain James Bonnel (d. 1814) and a detachment of 32 Loyalists were foraging for cattle when they surprised the river guard. The guard fired on the enemy for two hours and escaped.

★ Lieutenant Colonel Andreas Emmerich (1737–1809) with about 30 Hessian dragoons and 30 Loyalists under Major Baremore attacked two groups of pickets at Sherard's Bridge on the Byram River on Tuesday, June 29, 1779. They killed five of the pickets, wounded about seven, and captured one officer and 11 men.[247]

★ A party of Lieutenant Colonel Oliver de Lancey, Jr.'s (1749–1822) Loyalists made an excursion to Horseneck (Greenwich, Connecticut) on Friday, May 5, 1780. They captured a captain and five privates. On Wednesday, May 10, 1780, they captured nine privates near Byram River.[248]

★ A party of Loyalists surprised a party of Whigs stationed at Byram River on Sunday, June 4, 1780. They killed three, wounded some, and captured four prisoners and some livestock.[249]

★ A party of Lieutenant Colonel Andreas Emmerich's (1737–1809) dragoons, consisting of a sergeant and 12 privates, under the command of Lieutenant Sylvester Muirson, with Cornet Thomas Merritt, U.E.L. (1759–1842), Cornet in Queen's Rangers (1776–1803), took part of two Whig pickets, at Byram and Sherrard's Bridge, and captured 18 prisoners Thursday, June 17, 1780. The picket guard supposedly heard the sound of the horses' hooves as they approached, and succeeded in making their escape.[250]

Mamaroneck, Westchester County (July 9, 1778; Oct. 22, 1778)
Pine Hills (Dec. 7, 1782)

> Mamaroneck is on the Boston Post Road (Route U.S. 1), about 4 miles northeast of New Rochelle.
> Pine Hills is in Mamaroneck on Long Island Sound.

★ The Crown forces marched to Mamaroneck in two columns on Wednesday, July 8, 1778. The following day, General Henry Clinton (1730–1795) marched the army to Byram's bridge and returned to Mamaroneck on Friday. During this march, three soldiers wandered a short distance from their huts and were captured by the militia.[251]

★ The Crown forces occupied New Rochelle by Wednesday, October 21, 1778. Major Robert Rogers (1732–1795), commanding about 500 Loyalists called "The Queen's American Rangers," entered Mamaroneck on the 22nd and camped near the right wing of the main body. Colonel John Haslet (1737–1777) tried to cut them off with 750 men from his Delaware regiment and reinforcements from some Virginia and Maryland companies. They set out on the road from White Plains late in the night of Tuesday the 22nd and headed to Mamaroneck, about 5 miles away. (Boatner dates this event on October 22, 1776.) They approached Rogers's camp in profound silence to avoid discovery. Knowing how Rogers usually disposed his men, they seized and silenced the lone sentinel and prepared for a surprise attack on the whole camp.

However, Rogers decided to post a stronger guard that day. He posted Captain John Eagles and 60 men between the lone sentinel and the main position. Haslet's men stumbled over Eagles's sleeping troops in the darkness. This alerted the rest of Rogers's force who rushed to the scene. The darkness made it impossible to distinguish friend from foe. A melee ensued, the men fighting each other indiscriminately. Eagles escaped in the confusion with about one third of his men. The rest were captured.

Haslet then proceeded toward the Crown forces' main camp which had already been alerted by Rogers's troops. They were ready to receive Haslet. Both sides exchanged fire. Haslet withdrew and returned to White Plains with 36 prisoners, a pair of colors, 60 muskets, and 60 valuable blankets. He lost three killed and 12 wounded. Rogers's losses remain unknown, except for the prisoners.[252]

★ Major Benjamin Tallmadge's (1754–1835) detachment was posted near Long Island Sound with orders to prevent commerce with the British army. About 600 British troops came down Long Island into Suffolk county and encamped at Huntington, as if for winter quarters. When Major Tallmadge learned that a considerable portion of the British light horse, covered by a body of infantry, had taken up their quarters at Huntington, on the north side of Long Island, he planned to attack their quarters. The attack occurred on Thursday night, December 5, 1782. Meanwhile General George Washington (1732–1799) sent an expedition down the North River to have a large detachment of his army below Fort Washington, while he moved down to Fort Independence and Kingsbridge with the main body. The enemy caught between two fires, would have been forced to yield. With Tallmadge's detachment on Long Island, they would have been attacked on all sides.

Major Tallmadge's detachment consisted of about 700 men: four companies of light infantry, a body of dismounted dragoons who would mount the enemy's captured horses, and a body of Connecticut levies. The different detachments met in the vicinity of Stamford, Connecticut on Thursday evening December 5th and moved on to Shippan Point to board the boats after sunset. Before half of the troops had boarded the boats, a squall of wind and rain mixed with snow moved in from the west. The storm became so violent that the troops disembarked, drew up the boats and turned them over to protect themselves from the pelting storm which continued through the night.

The next morning the rain had ceased, but the Sound was so turbulent that "no boat could have been kept above water for five minutes." The wind lasted through the day and abated a bit by sunset. A few of the boats were put into the water, but the wind rose again and the expedition postponed another day. The troops spent a second night as the first. Major Tallmadge was informed the next day that three boats from Long Island had sought refuge on one of the Norwalk islands a few miles east of him. When the wind and sea calmed somewhat, and Major Tallmadge saw the enemy's boats in the Sound returning to Long Island, he ordered six of his best boats with sails to be manned. He directed Captain Caleb Brewster, an experienced sailor, to pursue the enemy and to capture them if possible.

The boats left shore, but the wind forced three of them to turn back. The enemy saw the boats closing in on them and headed to Long Island under all sails and oars. Before Captain Caleb Brewster had reached the middle of the Sound (about 12 miles wide at this point) he engaged two of the enemy's heaviest boats with great fury. The first volley either killed or wounded every man in one of the enemy boats. Captain Brewster received a ball in his breast, which passed through his body. Although believed to be mortally wounded, he recovered and lived to be nearly 80 years old. He captured the two boats and the third one escaped and alerted the Crown forces that a body of troops were at Shippan Point.

After three nights of stormy weather, Major Tallmadge abandoned the expedition and marched his troops to camp on December 8th. The other enterprise on the North River and below Fort Washington also failed because the day before the troops were to have gone down the river, some British ships anchored above Fort Washington, preventing any boats from passing by them undiscovered. At the time these two expeditions were to have occurred and unknown to the commanders, the preliminary articles of peace had been signed.[253]

Rye, King Street (Oct. 7, 1778)
Rye Woods (Nov. 13, 1778)
Rye Neck (Feb. 27, 1779)

> King Street branched off the Post Road (roughly corresponding to Route U.S. 1) northeast of Rye and proceeded north roughly following the New York/Connecticut boundary.

★ Lieutenant Colonel John Graves Simcoe (1752–1806) and his Queen's Rangers went on a foraging party to Rye on Wednesday, October 7, 1778. They captured "six light dragoons belonging to Seldon's [Colonel Elisha Sheldon (1740–1805)] Regiment," on King Street near Byram River. They also burned a store with a considerable quantity of merchandise.[254]

★ Colonel John Graves Simcoe (1752–1806) and a party of the Queen's Rangers made a surprise raid on the house of Colonel John Thomas, Jr. (1751–1819), at Rye Woods on Friday, November 13, 1778. Colonel Thomas, like his father Judge John Thomas, Sr. (1720–1811), was a very active and fearless Whig and was bitterly hated by the Loyalists. He had not passed the night at home for some time, but now that the British troops were reported to have gone into winter quarters, he thought himself comparatively safe.

The Rangers marched all night, and surrounded the house by daybreak. As they approached the house, someone [local tradition says it was James Brundage (ca. 1731–1778), a son of Gilbert Brundage (1759–1847)] fired a shot from a window, killing a man by Simcoe's side. The house was immediately forced, and the person who fired the shot was killed "while on his knees, begging for his life." Thomas Carpenter (1747–1817), another young man who was also in the house at the time, was stabbed in many places by the soldiers' bayonets while hiding under a bed. Colonel Thomas leaped out a window and came near escaping but was taken by one of the hussars.

The Queen's Rangers proceeded to the American picket, about a mile further, hoping to surprise a party of light horsemen who were stationed at the head of King Street, near Rye-Pond. However, the sound of musket fire had alerted them. They fired their carbines and wounded one of the officers of the Queen's Rangers and retreated. Colonel Thomas was taken to General William Tryon (1729–1788), who was then at Ward's house in East Chester, and "was much pleased at this mischievous partizan's being taken." Colonel Thomas's father was captured in the same way the year before.[255]

★ A small party of a captain and 30 Congressional troops from Horseneck (Greenwich, Connecticut) advanced toward New York on Thursday night, February 27, 1779. They discovered a British force, consisting of several regiments, a body of dragoons, and a detachment of artillery, at New Rochelle advancing toward Rye. The troops were actually on their way to Horseneck to destroy the salt works there. The Congressional troops retired as far as Rye Neck undiscovered; but, as it was growing light, the British spotted them and attacked. The Congressional troops defended themselves as best they could; but, as they were outnumbered, they were soon defeated. Several were killed and the rest scattered.

The Crown forces drove some of the Congressional troops from the post-road into Milton, where "they managed to keep away from their pursuers, crossing the heads of the creeks, and hiding in the swamps; while others made their way to Saw Pit, where they took advantage of an elevated piece of ground, and made some stand." However, the superior numbers of Crown forces compelled them to retire over Byram Bridge. They took up the bridge and managed to reach Horseneck safely.

The Crown forces destroyed the salt works at Horseneck while Major General Israel Putnam (1718–1790), who had observed their approach, went to Stamford to muster a body of militia and other troops. When he returned, the Crown forces retreated and crossed the Byram River before dusk. The militiamen annoyed the Loyalist rear with a "considerable fire." Local tradition says that a party of 150 to 200 militiamen occupied the brow of the hill on the right of the road, east of Byram Bridge. Here, protected by some rocks or boulders, they fired down at the Crown troops as they crossed the bridge and killed several.

General Putnam reported capturing a number of prisoners and two baggage and ammunition wagons. The baggage wagons contained a portion of the plunder. General Putnam restored it to the inhabitants.[256]

Stony Point (June 1, 1779) see Verplanck's Point
Stony Point and Verplanck's Point (July 15–16, 1779)

> The Stony Point Battlefield State Historic Site (**nysparks.state.ny.us/cgi-bin/cgiwrap/nysparks/historic.cgi?p+27**) is in/near Stony Point, New York, 8 miles south of the Bear Mountain bridge off Route U.S. 9W on Park Road.
> Stony Point became a public park in 1902 (see Photo NY-24). There is an elaborate arch over the entrance. A short trail meanders through the remains of the site. The park redesigned the exhibit and renovated the museum/Visitor Center for the 225th anniversary of the battle in 2004.

★ General Henry Clinton (1730–1795) tried to draw General George Washington (1732–1799) into a general engagement in the summer of 1779. He occupied Stony Point on the west side of the Hudson in May and Verplanck's Point on the opposite

Photo NY-24. Stony Point Battlefield State Historic Site. The tent is on the approximate site where Lieutenant Colonel François Louis Teissedre de Fleury, the first to enter the fort, captured the flag.

shore on June 1. This was an important link between the Continental forces in New York and New England. Clinton then began to enlarge the earthen forts at these points by cutting down trees and protecting them with an abatis. He left 625 officers and men under Lieutenant Colonel Henry Johnson (1748–1835) to defend them.

Washington sent Brigadier General "Mad Anthony" Wayne's (1745–1796) brigade of about 1,360 light infantrymen selected from every regiment for their agility, alertness, and daring to retake Stony Point 150 feet above the Hudson River. At first, Wayne was somewhat dismayed by his observations of the position which was practically immune to attack except by a surprise assault. He decided to target specific objectives rather than mount an all-out assault. His men would advance during the night with unloaded muskets to maintain silence. Any man who fired his musket or panicked in the advance would be punished by death.

Major John Stewart (d. 1782) would lead one column of 300 men, advancing on Stony Point from the north through the marshes of the Hudson River. Wayne would lead the second column through the waters of Haverstraw Bay on the south. Each column would be preceded by a "forlorn hope" of 20 men to guide the way for the second group of 150 men who would enter enemy lines first, overcome sentries, and sever the abatis.

Meanwhile, Lieutenant Colonel Hardy Murfree (1752–1809) would lead two companies in a diversionary attack on the fort's front in the center. They were the only troops allowed to load their muskets to draw the Crown forces from their posts with musket fire. The others would rely only on the bayonet. Wayne's brigade began to advance around midnight on Thursday, July 15, 1779. They only had to travel about 1.5 miles to their objective. They traveled along Frank Road which becomes Crickettown Road. Stewart's column followed what is now Wayne Avenue toward the river.

The sound of hundreds of men moving waist-deep in the water alerted a British sentry who sounded the alarm. The Continentals, unable to return fire, hurried to dry ground where they climbed the rocky slope and entered the British earthworks. Colonel Henry Johnson charged down the hill with six companies to counter what he thought was the main attack. Wayne's column arrived from the south and cut him off from the central redoubt at the top of a huge outcropping of rocks.

Colonel Johnson was caught between Wayne's men and Murfree's column, unable to get back. The Continentals were now in the main redoubt, and he was forced to surrender. The Continentals captured the fort at Stony Point in about half an hour with only 15 lives lost, mostly from volunteers in the forlorn hope, and 83 wounded. Casualties might have been higher had the defenders not had to fire downhill in the dark. The British lost 63 killed, 74 wounded, 58 missing, and 472 prisoners, including the wounded. One officer escaped by jumping into the river and swimming out to the HMS *Vulture*, the same ship that would carry Major John André (1751–1780) to his rendezvous with Major General Benedict Arnold (1741–1801) 14 months later and take Arnold to safety after his treason. The British occupying Fort Lafayette on Verplanck's Point probably heard the fighting at Stony Point and wondered who won. When the victors fired their guns at the *Vulture*, they knew.

Wayne offered a $500 prize for the first man into the fort which went to Lieutenant Colonel François Louis Teissedre de Fleury (1749– ca. 1796), a French engineer. Fleury was also awarded a silver medal which became a gold one when finally awarded in 1783—the only medal awarded to a European volunteer during the war. Wayne also received a gold medal. He continued to lead the charge despite suffering a head wound from grape shot. He thought he was seriously wounded and asked his men to carry him to the top of the hill so he could die in the redoubt. Major John Stewart (d. 1782), the leader of the second column, was awarded a silver medal. The action at Stony Point accounted for three of the 11 medals Congress awarded during the war.

General Washington also planned to take Fort Lafayette at Verplanck's Point after receiving word of Wayne's victory at Stony Point. Wayne wrote to him at 2 AM on Friday morning, July 16: "The fort and garrison with Colonel Johnson are ours. Our officers and men behaved like men who are determined to be free." He dispatched the message immediately, but it went astray. By the time the attack force was in position around Fort Lafayette, General Clinton learned of the defeat at Stony Point and sent reinforcements. The Continentals abandoned their plans to take Fort Lafayette.

Washington could not spare enough men to defend the fort. He destroyed and abandoned it two days later. Clinton reoccupied it the following day, July 19, but withdrew in October. The battle at Stony Point had little tactical importance, but it boosted morale.[257]

Croton (Oct. 1, 1779)
Near Croton (Mar. 4, 1782; Apr. 2, 1782)

> Croton is now the town of Croton on Hudson. It is on the eastern shore of the Hudson River, opposite Haverstraw and about 5 miles southeast of Verplanck's Point.

★ The Crown forces set fire to their works on Verplanck's Point and Stony Point about noon on Wednesday, October 1, 1779 and embarked on board their transports. They

Downstate/Hudson River Valley 113

previously put their cannon, baggage, etc. on board and proceeded down the Hudson a little below Croton where they anchored. The Congressional troops immediately took possession of the works. Several loaded shells which were left in the blockhouses exploded after the troops went onto the point.[258]

See also **Verplanck's Point** and **Stony Point.**

★ Lieutenant Isaac Van Wart (1758–1782), cousin of the Isaac Van Wart who was one of Major John André's (1751–1780) three captors, was returning from the attack on the Loyalists at Morrisania when he was killed on the field on Monday, March 4, 1782.[259]

★ Several of Brigadier General Oliver de Lancey's (1718–1785) Loyalists advanced to the west side of the Croton River on Tuesday, April 2, 1782. They drove off a number of cattle, but they were followed and the cattle recovered. One of the thieves was killed on the spot and several were presumed wounded, judging by the blood on the ground.[260]

West Point (Sept. 1780)

> The United States Military Academy (**www.usma.edu/**) is in/near Highland Falls, New York, on the west bank of the Hudson River off scenic Old Storm King Highway (Route NY 218); the academy can also be reached from Route U.S. 9W. A visitors center (Building 2107) just outside Thayer Gate (South Post) is the starting point for tours of the U.S. Military Academy (**www.usma.edu/PublicAffairs/vic.htm**).
>
> The West Point Museum (**www.usma.edu/Museum/**) (Olmsted Hall at Pershing Center, Route U.S. 9W) contains a large collection of military artifacts from antiquity to modern times. It has flags, vehicles, paintings, tanks, uniforms, and weapons, including Revolutionary War uniforms, weapons, and accoutrements. Other galleries feature the history of West Point and the U.S. Military Academy and the story of the founding of the regular army.
>
> The east wall of the Old Cadet Chapel displays marble shields commemorating the Continental brigadier and major generals. The space for Benedict Arnold remains empty.
>
> The cemetery behind the chapel contains the grave of Molly Corbin. Molly Corbin was wounded in the assault of Fort Washington when she took her husband's place at the cannon after he fell severely wounded. She is the first woman to be buried at West Point and hers is one of very few Revolutionary War era graves here.
>
> Polish engineer Colonel Thaddeus Kosciusko (1746–1817) planned most of the defenses at West Point (see Photo NY-25) which consisted of five forts and seven redoubts and a giant iron chain that stretched across the Hudson River. The series of forts included Fort Arnold at the eastern edge (northeast of the parade ground); Sherburne's Redoubt across the river on Constitution Island; Fort Putnam; three redoubts covering the southern approaches, named Webb, Wyllis, and Meigs for their commanders under Colonel Rufus Putnam (1738–1824); four additional redoubts on the hills; and a number of gun batteries along the shoreline facing upriver from what is now Trophy Point and overlooking the channel between the Point and Constitution Island. The location was so well fortified that it never came under military attack during the war.
>
> The Continental Army built Fort Arnold in 1778. It was constructed of earth and logs and housed 700 men, 12 cannon, and 11 mortars (see Photo NY-6). It was renamed Fort Clinton after Benedict Arnold's (1741–1801) defection and after the fall of Fort Clinton south of West Point. Fort Arnold remained in use as an arsenal after

Photo NY-25. Bend in the Hudson River at West Point. Buildings in the foreground are part of the U.S. Military Academy. Sherburne's Redoubt is across the river on Constitution Island.

the war and was closed in 1802 for the creation of the U.S. Military Academy. Only a piece of a parapet remains. A monument on the east front of Fort Clinton honors Colonel Kosciuszko.

Fort Putnam, named for Colonel Rufus Putnam (1738–1824) and his soldiers of the Fifth Massachusetts Regiment who constructed it, was built 400 feet above the water to the west of Fort Arnold to protect against an overland attack from the mountains.

Fort Putnam was first restored as a war monument in 1909 and then again for the Bicentennial in 1975–1976.

Fort Montgomery covered the water approach to West Point from the south. And Fort Constitution stood across the river on the high bluffs of an island in the Hudson.

The Hudson River provided a direct water route to Lake Champlain and to Canada. The British objective was to use the river to split the colonies, so it was important for the Continentals to impede British traffic on the river if they couldn't control it. They established a series of forts on opposite sides of the Hudson at points where the river narrows. Guns from these forts could work together firing on passing vessels. These narrow passages in the river also served as ideal spots to block the river with a chain or other obstacles.

Two great chains (not contemporaneous) stretched across the Hudson River at Trophy Point. Sterling Iron Works (about 25 miles west of West Point) forged the chains. Each link was made of bar iron about two inches square with dimensions about 18 inches long and 12 inches wide. The smallest links weighed between 98 and 109 pounds; the largest ones weighed 130 pounds. The entire 600-yard chain weighed about 186 tons and floated on log rafts to prevent the passage of enemy ships. Each end was attached to a large block, one in a cove near Constitution Island, the other on the West Point side of the river. It was taken in every winter with a windlass to prevent damage from the ice. (See Photo NY-20.)

> Another strategy was to block the channel with scuttled ship hulks placed end to end. Friendly vessels would find their way through a secret passage while enemy vessels would be lured to an apparent channel protected by a line of chevaux-de-frise (see Photo NY-19). This device consisted of "cassoons" created out of caissons sunken with rocks. The cassoons had pointed spears embedded in them. The iron-tipped pikes were hidden two or three feet below the water's surface at low tide. Ships striking the chevaux-de-frise would have their hulls punctured. If a ship managed to get past the chevaux-de-frise, it would encounter the great chain and possibly other obstacles.
>
> At West Point, the Hudson makes two turns that almost form a right angle, forcing vessels sailing in either direction to come about to negotiate each turn. A square-rigged warship, with sails slack and the ship not firmly under control, would be particularly vulnerable attempting to maneuver the turn as it came directly under the gun batteries placed on the heights.
>
> Visitors can view captured weapons from every American war at Trophy Point which also offers a spectacular view of the Hudson Valley and the ruins of Fort Constitution. There is also a display of several links from the great chain that stretched 600 yards across the Hudson to impede British ships.

Benedict Arnold, Traitor

General Henry Clinton (1730–1795) could not take West Point by force, so he had to find another way to gain control. He found that way in 1779 when he began a traitorous correspondence with Major General Benedict Arnold (1741–1801), the hero of the march to Québec and of the battles at Valcour Island, Fort Stanwix, and Saratoga.

In September 1779, Clinton appointed Captain John André (1751–1780) as his chief of intelligence and promoted him to the rank of major in October. André organized spy rings that extended into Vermont, New Hampshire, Rhode Island, Connecticut, New York, New Jersey, Pennsylvania, Maryland, and Delaware. He ignored Massachusetts because there were very few Loyalists there and because the British did not plan any military operations there.

André promised Arnold lucrative rewards which led to his treason. One of Arnold's enemies had said of him earlier "Money is this man's God," and evidently he was correct. Arnold's treachery may have had its roots in the ingratitude of the Continental Congress that did not recognize him for his heroism in previous battles. Maybe it came from his discontent that the Continental cause was being supported by a Catholic kingdom against whose soldiers he had once fought. It may also have come from the jealousy of rivals which resulted in many quarrels and grievances, or through the influence of his second wife, Margaret Shippen (1760–1804 or 1836), a Loyalist.

Shortly after his marriage, he announced that he intended to resign his commission and to obtain land near New York where he would live as a retired country gentleman. He first offered to sell military information to General Clinton a month after his marriage in 1779. The British appointed Arnold a brigadier-general and awarded him £6315 (approximately $894,725) and an annuity of £500 (approximately $70,840) for his wife. His three sons by his first marriage all received commissions, and the two sons of his second marriage later each received pensions of £100 (approximately $14,167) a year.

Arnold also resented the slights Congress had dealt him, and he justified his act by claiming that the Continentals were now fighting for the interests of Catholic France and not their own. He obtained an appointment as commander at West Point after insistently lobbying General George Washington (1732–1799) and then entered into a plot to deliver this key post to the British. Washington discovered the plot on Thursday, September 21, 1780, just in time to foil it, though Arnold himself escaped.

André received Arnold's secret correspondence and returned to New York after meeting with him to finalize a deal to surrender to Clinton the American fortress at West Point and several nearby American strongholds for £20,000 (approximately $2,833,646). Along the way, he visited a British major quartered in Robert Townsend's (ca. 1753–1838) house and aroused the suspicions of Townsend's sister. She overheard the conversation and reported it to her brother. André was caught September 20, 1780, trying to go through the Continental line with a pass Arnold had issued him.

He also had Arnold's report on Fort Putnam: "F.P., stone, wanting great repairs. Wall on the east side broke down, and rebuilding from the foundation. At the west and south side have been a cheveaux-de-frise; on the west side broke in many places. The east side open; two bombproofs and provision magazine in the fort, and a slight wooden barrack."

On the evening of September 21, 1780, Major Benjamin Tallmadge (1754–1835) happened to be in North Castle, a Continental stronghold. Here, he learned that three local militiamen had stopped and searched a man by the name of John Anderson whom they encountered near Tarrytown. They found some suspicious papers in his boots. When the man offered to pay for his freedom, the soldiers became even more suspicious, so they brought him to North Castle and turned him over to Lieutenant Colonel John Jameson (1758–1842) of the Light Dragoons. Jameson wrote a report of the matter and sent it and Anderson, under guard, to General Benedict Arnold who now commanded West Point. He also sent the papers found on Anderson to General Washington who was on his way to West Point from a meeting with General Donatien Marie Joseph de Vimeur Vicomte de Rochambeau (1750–1813) at Wethersfield, Connecticut.

Tallmadge persuaded Jameson to have Anderson brought back to North Castle and insisted that the report continue on to Arnold. Arnold, who had already tried unsuccessfully to learn the identities of Washington's spies, issued orders to Tallmadge:

> If Mr. James Anderson, a person I expect from New York should come to your quarters, I have to request that you will give him an escort of two Horse to bring him on his way to this place, and send an express to me that I may meet him.[261]

Tallmadge must have wondered whether the prisoner John Anderson was the same man Arnold wanted to meet with. Tallmadge recalled his impressions on seeing the prisoner:

> As soon as I saw Anderson, and especially after I saw him walk (as he did almost constantly) across the floor, I became impressed with the belief that he had been bred to arms.[262]

Tallmadge got Anderson to admit, on Sunday afternoon, September 24, that he was "Major John André, Adjutant General to the British Army." Lieutenant Colonel Jameson's report of Anderson's arrest reached Arnold at breakfast the following morning. Had Washington not been delayed, he might have been sharing that meal. When Arnold learned of André's capture on the morning of the 25th, he left quickly for the Hudson River where he boarded the HMS *Vulture* which took him to New York. Jameson's rider, who missed Washington on the road from Hartford, arrived later in the day with André's incriminating papers, making it clear why Arnold left in such a hurry.

Court-Martial of Major John André

Instead of hanging André after a summary hearing, as General William Howe (1732–1786) had done for Nathan Hale (1755–1776), Washington turned the matter over to a 14-member board of general officers which convened at Tappan, New York, on Friday, September 29 (see Photo NY-26). André admitted the facts but insisted that he did not regard himself as a spy. The British and Continentals considered spying something the lowborn were paid to do, so it was difficult for Major André, a British officer and a gentleman, to think of himself as a spy, even if he was caught behind enemy lines in civilian clothes with incriminating information in his shoes.

Photo NY-26. Site of Major John André's imprisonment

The board convicted André and recommended the death penalty. Washington sentenced him to hang at 5 PM on Sunday, October 1. He notified General Clinton of his decision. Clinton protested that Arnold, a Continental general, invited André to meet with him and that André went under a flag of truce. Washington postponed the execution for a day and sent a representative to hear further arguments from a deputation of three British officers at Dobbs Ferry. He finally decided that he would spare André only if Clinton traded Arnold for him. Clinton refused. André wrote to Washington in an attempt to make him change his mind:

> I trust that the request I make of your Excellency at this serious period, and which is to soften my last moments, will not be rejected.
>
> Sympathy towards a soldier will surely induce your Excellency, and a military tribunal, to adapt the mode of my death to the feelings of a man of honour.
>
> Let me hope, Sir, that if aught in my character impresses you with esteem towards me, if aught in my misfortune marks me as the victim of policy and not of resentment, I shall experience the operation of these feelings in your breast by being informed that I am not to die on the gibbet.[263]

André was hanged at noon on October 2, just like Nathan Hale.

Brigadier General Oliver de Lancey (1718–1785) succeeded André as chief of intelligence in October 1780, after André's execution. General Frederick Haldimand

(1718–1791), the British commander in Canada, ran his own intelligence operation in Québec, the Northern Department of the British Secret Service. He also operated in the northern colonies, trying to regain Vermont.

The British had never fully trusted Arnold. He never received a high command and resorted to leading raids along the Connecticut and Virginia coasts. After the American War of Independence, he retired on half pay and lived as a merchant in Canada, the West Indies, and London.

Arnold's treason in September 1780, marked the nadir of the Continental cause. In the closing months of 1780, the Continentals reorganized the army and its administration and somehow put together the ingredients for a final and decisive burst of energy in 1781. Congress persuaded Robert Morris (1734–1806), a wealthy Philadelphia merchant, to accept a post as Superintendent of Finance, and Colonel Timothy Pickering (1745–1829), an able administrator, to replace Nathanael Greene (1742–1786) as Quartermaster General. Greene, as Washington's choice, was then named to succeed Major General Horatio Gates (1728–1806) in command of the Southern Army. Major General Benjamin Lincoln (1733–1810), exchanged after Charleston, was appointed Secretary at War. Morris took over many of the functions previously performed by unwieldy committees. Working closely with Pickering, he abandoned the old paper money entirely and introduced a new policy of supplying the army by private contracts, using his personal credit as eventual guarantee for payment in gold or silver. It was an expedient but, for a time at least, it worked.[264]

Mount Pleasant
Youngs's House (Dec. 25, 1778; July 30, 1779; Feb. 3, 1780)
Four Corners, Westchester Co. (Dec. 25, 1778)

> Youngs's House at the "Four Corners" was an important post and the scene of several bloody skirmishes. The house was on the west side of the old Pines Bridge Road, later known as the Unionville Road, about 700 feet north of the Corners. Now in the town of Mount Pleasant, it was on what is called the County House Road, about 4 miles east of Tarrytown, where it intersects the road to Unionville. The skirmish began on the Unionville road and ended on the Saw Mill River Road about three-quarters of a mile north of the Elmsford Church. The village of the Four Corners was a cluster of about six small, dilapidated houses built around the intersection. A memorial marks the grave of soldiers from both sides killed in the skirmish on February 3, 1780. It is in Eastview on Route NY 100C in Westchester County, in the triangle at the entrance to Grasslands Hospital.

★ Samuel Youngs (1760–1839), son of Joseph Youngs or Young (1722–1789), was cutting wood about a quarter mile from his father's house on Friday, December 25, 1778, when he learned that a party of British were coming. He went home immediately to find them driving the stock from the yard. He then ran toward the house of Sergeant John Dean (1759–1837) to inform him. He soon met Dean along the way. Dean, who was well armed, told Youngs that he would find arms and ammunition at his house and that he would try to get a shot at the raiders.

Samuel Youngs went to Dean's house where Mrs. Dean handed him three muskets and two bunches of cartridges. The raiders were now less than 300 yards away. Youngs hurried to join about 25 militiamen who hid behind a stone wall near the road that the raiders must pass with their plundered livestock. When they came within about 50 yards, the militiamen opened fire.

The main party of Captain Althause's raiders approached the stone wall while the others drove the stock. John Dean and his companions began firing on the party driving the stock and killed a man before the main attack began. The others then opened fire, killing one and wounding three. The militiamen then jumped over the wall to attack the raiders with the bayonet. Captain Althause returned fire, shooting a man through the shoulder and another through the thigh before abandoning his plunder and retreating. John Dean and his companions then joined the main body of militia who engaged the raiders in a running fight of 4 miles. The militiamen killed or captured Althause and all his men, except his guide.

★ Loyalist Major Mansfield Baremore (Bearmore or Barrymore) (d. 1780) attacked the house again on Christmas night and captured Joseph Youngs and about five Continental soldiers, burned one of the barns, and drove off all the cattle. A Loyalist prisoner, hit by a shot fired by his friends who had come to rescue him, was the only person killed.[265]

★ Captain David Hopkins (1753–1824) and a party of light dragoons fell in with a party of Lieutenant Colonel Andreas Emmerich's (1737–1809) jaegers near Youngs's tavern on Friday, July 30, 1779. The dragoons charged vigorously; but the jaegers forced Captain Hopkins to retreat. Captain Hopkins killed six jaegers and wounded several others and captured three prisoners and four horses. However, the jaegers retook several of Captain Hopkins's prisoners. Captain Hopkins had one dragoon and two horses wounded.[266]

★ Lieutenant Colonel Joseph Thompson (1733–1795) of Massachusetts, in command of about 250 Continental troops, had specific orders to keep moving between the Croton River and White Plains, the Hudson River and Bedford and never to stay at one place long enough for the enemy to attack him. He did not follow his orders strictly and stopped at Youngs's House near White Plains for several days in February 1780. The Loyalists in this area informed the Crown forces of his position. Colonel Chapel Norton and about 500 infantrymen and 100 cavalrymen, composed of British, Hessians and Colonel James De Lancey's (1747–1804) Provincial troops, left their camp near the Harlem River between 10 and 11 PM Wednesday evening, February 2, 1780. The cavalry headed north on the Saw Mill River Road from Phillipse's. The infantry, consisting of four flank companies of the 1st and 2nd British regiments of guards, detachments from two Hessian battalions, some mounted jaegers, and mounted Loyalists, followed either in the roads or the fields. They had to abandon their sleighs and field pieces because the snow was so deep. They marched 20 miles and arrived at the Four Corners shortly before 9 AM the following morning.

Stephen Campbell, a scout, spotted the Crown forces about 9 AM and alerted Lieutenant Colonel Thompson that they were coming in large numbers and advised him to take a stronger position a little in his rear. Thompson, convinced that the enemy only consisted of a body of dragoons that he could easily disperse, held his ground. He formed his own force in front of the house and placed the four other companies (Captain Abraham Watson's company of the 3rd Massachusetts, Captain Moses Roberts's company of the 15th Massachusetts, Captain-Lieutenant Michael Farley's (1716–1789) company of the 9th Massachusetts, and Captain James Cooper's of the 14th Massachusetts) on his flanks.

Colonel Norton's Guards first attacked a small advance-guard, consisting of a sergeant and eight men, and captured them. The dragoons then appeared, fired from a distance, and waited for the infantry. A sharp conflict ensued for about 15 minutes when Colonel Norton flanked the Continental left and occupied an orchard behind the house. Surrounded, the Continentals broke. Some fled into the house and others into the woods, pursued by the mounted Loyalists. The grenadiers (see Photo NY-8) of the Guards forced the house, killed or captured all its occupants, and burned Mr. Youngs's house, with five wounded men inside, and the other buildings. The Continentals lost 13 killed, 17 wounded, several of whom died. Lieutenant Colonel Thomson, five officers and 89 privates were taken prisoners. The Crown forces left three men dead on the field and had a captain of the grenadiers wounded in the hip, and a lieutenant of infantry wounded in the thigh. They also lost five men killed and 18 wounded. The Crown forces withdrew before the Continentals could regroup and attack. They took Joseph Youngs prisoner a second time and brought him to Manhattan with the others.[267]

Crompond (June 24, 1779; Mar. 1, 3, 1781; July 3, 1782)

> Crompond is about 3 miles east of Peekskill. The June 24, 1779 engagement happened on the road from Crompond to Pines Bridge, about three quarters of a mile from Crompond.

★ Lieutenant Colonel Banastre Tarleton (1744–1833) was on a mission to seek out and destroy partisan strongholds north of Croton in June 1779. The Continentals used these bases for raids into British-held land in Southern Westchester County. Toward evening on Wednesday, June 23, 1779, a detachment of jaegers and a battalion of light infantry under Lieutenant Colonel Robert Abercromby or Abercrombie (1740–1827) proceeded to Dutch Crompond to surprise an enemy party while a battalion of light infantry and Tarleton's Legion were posted on the heights of Peekskill to cover Abercromby's rear. A local Loyalist sympathizer directed Tarleton to the Crompond Presbyterian Church and Parsonage which had served as a local headquarters for the Continentals. The church was situated on the only road from Peekskill to New England.

Abercromby arrived at the village at daybreak. Captain Johann von Ewald (1744–1813) was detached with 50 jaegers and 50 light infantrymen to surround the place and to cut off the enemy's retreat by seizing a defile formed by a dam. Tarleton's Legion swooped down upon Colonel Samuel Drake's (1730–1794) militia (100 infantry and 50 horse) at breakfast time on Thursday, June 24, 1779. About the time Ewald arrived at his post, he heard small-arms fire begin. A large body of infantry and cavalry approached the jaegers who immediately fired at them. Fifty men of the light infantry were ordered to charge, cutting down a few. Almost 100 men threw down their arms and surrendered.

The Crown forces killed about 5, wounded 11, and captured 34 prisoners. Those not taken prisoner escaped to the woods. The raiders then set the church and parsonage on fire.[268]

★ The advance guard of the Continental Army, consisting of about 200 men, was posted at Crompond, about 20 miles below West Point in the late winter of 1781. Major Lemuel Trescott (1751–1826) commanded the post. Both sides took every opportunity to attack each other's quarters and to kill or capture any soldiers they could. A party of volunteers on horseback gathered for a secret expedition and marched Thursday night, March 1, 1781, with a party to cover their retreat. The party returned the next day with six Loyalist prisoners, three of whom were wounded by the broadsword. One of the volunteers, named Hunt, received a dangerous wound through his shoulder and lungs. With each breath, air escaped from the wound. He was treated and eventually recovered.

★ On Saturday, March 3rd, Dr. James Thacher (1754–1844), who was treating the wounded, learned that six Continentals had taken 30 head of cattle from the Loyalists.

They were overtaken by 40 of De Lancey's corps and all but one were killed and the cattle retaken. He went to the house of a friendly Quaker family that morning to treat a wounded man. As the doctor dressed the man's wounds, the patient told him about four of his companions who had been killed. In another house, he saw four dead bodies "mangled in a most inhuman manner by the refugees, and among them one groaning under five wounds on his head, two of them quite through his skull-bone with a broadsword." This man said his four companions surrendered and "begged for life; but their entreaties were disregarded, and the swords of their cruel foes were plunged into their bodies so long as signs of life remained."[269]

★ A farmer near Crompond returned to his house on Wednesday, July 3, 1782 after mowing his field all day. As he was dining with his wife, a party of Loyalists appeared at his door. He tried to escape by running to the opposite door, but they ordered him to surrender or they would fire at him. He returned and was shot by one of the Loyalists. Thinking the farmer was still alive, the men dragged him out of the house and smashed his skull with the butts of their muskets.[270]

Poundridge (July 2, 1779)

> Poundridge is 20 miles northeast of White Plains.

★ The British offered a reward for the arrest of Major Ebenezer Lockwood (1737–1821) who lived in the village of Poundridge. Colonel Elisha Sheldon (1740–1805) was encamped near Poundridge with 90 2nd Continental Dragoons. Lieutenant Colonel Banastre Tarleton (1744–1833) and a force of about 360 set out after dark on Thursday, July 1, 1779, both to arrest Lockwood and defeat Sheldon. Tarleton's force consisted of 70 of the 17th Light Dragoons; part of his own Legion of foot and horse, all mounted; Lieutenant Colonel John Graves Simcoe's (1752–1806) Queen's Rangers; a detachment of hussars (see Photo NY-27) and some mounted jaegers.

Photo NY-27. Reenactor portraying a hussar in the duc de Lauzun's Legion

A spy discovered Tarleton's approach and alerted Lockwood and Sheldon. Sheldon formed his men a little above the Poundridge church. The ground forced Tarleton to advance in a narrow column with his dragoons at the head. The dragoons drove Sheldon's small force from its position and Tarleton pursued him for 2 miles. Both forces kept up a scattered fire until the neighborhood militia turned out and began to fire on Tarleton's flanks from fences and farm buildings. Tarleton realized his danger, turned around, and retreated, with Sheldon and the militia in pursuit.

Tarleton had left part of his force at Poundridge. They burned the church and several houses, including Lockwood's. In one of the houses, they found Sheldon's colors and some officers' baggage and carried them off. Tarleton escaped with the loss of one man killed and one wounded. Sheldon had 10 men wounded and eight missing. (Captain Christopher Tarleton Fagan, a descendant of Banastre Tarleton, sold Sheldon's captured colors for $14,500,000 to an anonymous bidder at an auction on flag day, June 14, 2006.)[271]

Bedford (July 2, 10, 1779; July 17, 1781)

> Bedford is about midway between North Castle (Mount Kisco) and Pound Ridge and about 15 miles northeast of White Plains.

★ Major Benjamin Tallmadge's (1754–1835) regiment was ordered to a post below Bedford about Thursday, July 1, 1779. Shortly after they arrived there, Lord Francis Rawdon (1754–1826) attacked them in the night of July 2 with nearly all the British light horse and a body of light infantry—about 700 men. The violent conflict was conducted mainly with the broadsword, until the light infantry appeared on Tallmadge's flanks. Colonel Elisha Sheldon (1740–1805) was forced to retreat so quickly that the enemy gained little advantage. Tallmadge lost a fine horse, most of his field baggage, and 20 guineas in cash which were in a valise on the horse. Lieutenant Colonel Banastre Tarleton's (1744–1833) dragoons burned the village on their way to Fairfield, Connecticut and destroyed much valuable property in the immediate vicinity. The Loyalists did most of the damage while the light infantry kept guard. They then retreated by the White Plains road.[272]

★ All the British dragoons set out at 9 PM on Saturday, July 10, 1779 to surprise 400 Continentals thought to be at Bedford. Major General William Heath (1737–1814) determined that the British ships had left for New York; so he moved his troops on July 15th and took a strong position between Ridgefield and Bedford. He also sent out patrols of dragoons and infantry on all the roads.[273]

★ Eight Westchester Loyalists went out on Tuesday night, July 17, 1781, in an attempt to surprise some French officers lodging in a house in front of their camp. On their way, they encountered a patrol of six hussars (see Photo NY-27) of Armand Louis de Gontaut-Biron, Duc de Lauzun's (1747–1793) Legion. An officer and 25 dragoons followed the hussars. The Loyalists hid near the side of the road. The hussars passed without discovering them, but the officers spotted them and were preparing to fire. The Loyalists immediately fired back, shot and killed the officer, rushed out, and fired at the dragoons who rode off as fast as possible.[274]

Morrisania (Aug. 5, 1779; Jan. 18, 1780; Jan. 22, 1781; July 2, 1781; Dec. 23, 1781; Jan. 10, 11, 1782; Mar. 4, 1782; Dec. 23, 1782)
New Rochelle (Jan. 18, 1780)
Eastchester (Jan. 18, 1780)

> Morrisania is on the New York City and Surroundings map while New Rochelle and Eastchester are on the Downstate map. Morrisania was located in what is now the South Bronx. It was on the Crown forces' route of advance to White Plains during the New York campaign and was a key point in the British lines of defense and a frequent camp site for Loyalist troops. Events at Morrisania are sometimes referred to as happening at Delancey's Bridge, Williams's Bridge, Kingsbridge or Eastchester.
> Eastchester is located on the Boston Post Road (Route U.S. 1) northeast of New Rochelle. It should not be confused with the modern town of East Chester.

★ About 100 of Colonel Elisha Sheldon's (1740–1805) light horse and 40 of Brigadier General John Glover's (1732–1797) brigade, proceeded by De Lancey's mill, avoiding the British posts, to attack the quarters of several Loyalists near Morrisania on Thursday, August 5, 1779. They captured 12 or 14 prisoners and were on their way back through Eastchester before the Loyalists alarmed the camp. Lieutenant Colonel John Graves Simcoe (1752–1806) returned to camp at Kingsbridge about midnight to find it in an uproar due to the arrival of a Loyalist who barely escaped capture in the attack. Lieutenant Colonel Simcoe's Queen's Rangers and Lieutenant Colonel Andreas Emmerich's (1737–1809) jaegers set out in pursuit. They caught up with the Congressional troops near New Rochelle and engaged in a running battle through Mamaroneck. Congressional troops posted behind stone walls along the road fired at them obliquely, throwing the dragoons into confusion, killing and wounding a number of them. The Congressional troops had two killed and two wounded in the affair.[275]

★ A detachment of about 80 men from Colonel John Mead's (1725–1790) regiment of levies at Horseneck (Greenwich, Connecticut) under the command of Captain Samuel Keeler, Jr. (1737–1811) and a number of volunteers from Greenwich under the command of Captain Daniel Lockwood marched to Morrisania on Monday, January 17, 1780. They attacked Colonel Isaac Hatfield's picket at about 1 AM, killed three, and drove the rest into the colonel's quarters at a house between Kingsbridge and De Lancey's Mills. The Colonel and his men fired out the windows and down stairs at those who entered the house for about 15 minutes. As it appeared difficult, if even possible, to dislodge them, the attackers set the house on fire by putting a straw bed into a closet. This compelled the occupants to jump out the windows to avoid the flames. The militiamen captured Colonel Hatfield, a captain, a lieutenant, a quartermaster, and 11 privates.

Major Huggerford and 35 dragoons and 28 infantrymen pursued the raiders. The infantrymen took a position upon the heights beyond Eastchester while the dragoons continued the pursuit. They caught up with the rear of the militia between New Rochelle and Mamaroneck. Some of the militiamen were fatigued and loitered on the road, thinking there was no danger. The dragoons overtook them and killed 23 of them and captured 40, some of whom were wounded. Major Huggerford's only weapon was the sabre.[276]

★ Major Oliver Lawrence was detached with a reconnoitering party under Colonel Neigal Gray (d. 1786) on Monday, January 22, 1781. They accidentally met with Lieutenant Colonel James De Lancey (1747–1804). He mistook Major Lawrence for one of his officers and reprimanded him for having the New York militia so close to his rear. Major Lawrence told him his men were in confusion and he couldn't rally them. Colonel De Lancey rode up until he came within several yards of Major Lawrence. One of his men, with G. W. on his cap, rose from behind a stone wall. The colonel, realizing his mistake, wheeled about, put spurs to his horse, and leaped down a craggy precipice.[277]

★ Major Hugh Maxwell (1733–1799) was directed to take a position near Redoubt No. 8 on Fordham Heights which was guarded by about a hundred Regulars. Major Maxwell took two companies commanded by Captains John Dix (1734–1806) and J. Williams to prevent the Regulars from attacking the troops preparing to attack Morrisania and to capture any of the enemy who tried to flee there for security and to destroy a pontoon bridge constructed over Harlem Creek for communication. The cannon in the redoubt covered this bridge.

Captain White took his own company and a small party of militiamen who were ordered to advance to Delancey's bridge, surprise the guard posted there, if possible, and to secure the pass for the troops on the west side of the Bronx, then to attack the enemy at West Farms.

Captain Thomas Pritchard (1752–1795) and his company and Lieutenant Moster's levies were ordered to proceed to Frog's (Throgg's) Neck to surprise the enemy stationed there.

Captain John Dennet and Captain Selah Benton (1740–1832) were posted at Williams's Bridge with their companies to observe enemy movements on the road leading from Kingsbridge and to repulse them if they tried to cross the bridge. They would take up the bridge at sunrise and retire to East Chester to join the troops posted there to cover the retreat of the main force.

Three companies under the command of Captains Christopher P. Fox (1740–1804) or Elisha Fox (1743–1800); Samuel William Williams (1752–1812) and David Dorrance (1750–1822) were to proceed to Morrisania with most of the volunteer horsemen to destroy the enemy's huts. They were to attack at 3:30 AM. All the detachments on the west side of the Bronx were ordered to retire to Delancey's bridge at dawn, after completing their assignments.

The troops marched out in a single column on Sunday morning, January 21, 1781. They headed down the road, passed Young's, went through Mile Square, and arrived nearly opposite Kingsbridge where they took to the fields to avoid enemy patrols along the roads.

When the troops arrived near most of the huts at Morrisania, they deployed as directed. Lieutenant Colonel William Hull's (1753–1825) intelligence reported that a bridge crossed a small creek, but a very heavy rain the night before and the morning of the 21st had swollen the creek and filled it with broken ice that made crossing very difficult. Determined to attempt the crossing, the infantrymen mounted behind the horsemen and about 70 men had crossed in 15 minutes. It was deemed very important to secure this pass because both these men and Major Maxwell's command would have to pass this way to go to Delancey's Bridge.

The 70 infantrymen and the horsemen proceeded to burn the huts while the rest of the troops positioned themselves to secure the pass. However, the enemy heard the noise generated in crossing the creek and immediately fired an alarm. This alerted the Crown forces who prevented the attack from being so much of a surprise as planned. The infantrymen and the horsemen advanced, captured a number of Regulars and destroyed all the huts. They then returned and were joined by Major Maxwell who had destroyed the bridge over Harlem Creek. They then proceeded to Delancey's Bridge where Captain White had captured the guard and took possession of the pass over which the troops retired with little or no loss. A considerable force of Regulars gathered and tried to regain the pass.

When the main body arrived at West Chester, they were joined by Captain Thomas Pritchard (1752–1795) who tried to capture Frog's Neck. As he was passing over the causeway, the guard posted there fired on him, sounding the alarm. He charged the guard, wounded one and captured six. As he proceeded to Captain Simmons's quarters, he encountered a patrol, killed one and captured two. When he arrived, every man had left the house and hid in the woods. Captain Pritchard's troops scoured the Neck and captured a number of prisoners before returning and re-passing the causeway.

Lieutenant Colonel Hull retreated to East Chester as fast as his fatigued troops would allow. But no sooner had they begun to march, the Regulars appeared on his flanks and rear and began a scattering fire. As the Regulars received continuous reinforcements and their fire increased, Hull's retreat was exceedingly slow. When they arrived near East Chester, the main body secured their retreat. The number of Crown casualties was undetermined but assumed to be considerable. Fifty-two of Colonel Oliver de Lancey, Jr.'s. (1749–1822) corps were taken prisoners, between 30 and 40 large huts were destroyed along with a quantity of forage. A large number of horses and cattle were captured. Colonel Hull lost Ensign John Thompson (d. 1781), of the 6th Massachusetts, killed and Captain Dorrance of the 5th Connecticut wounded.[278]

★ Lieutenant Colonel William Hull (1753–1825), of General Samuel Holden Parsons's (1737–1789) Connecticut Brigade attacked the quarters of the 3rd Battalion of Lieutenant Colonel James De Lancey's (1747–1804) Loyalist Brigade, burned barracks and the pontoon bridge over the Harlem River and destroyed a large amount of forage. He captured 52 prisoners, some horses and some cattle but lost 25 casualties in doing so.[279]

★ The following morning, at daybreak, Lieutenant Colonel James De Lancey's Loyalists pursued the raiders as far as Williams's Bridge. Congressional troops defended the far side of the bridge; so the Loyalists retreated.

★ When General George Washington's (1732–1799) spies informed him that General Sir Henry Clinton (1730–1795) had detached a large force from his command for an incursion into New Jersey, Gen. Washington selected the night of Monday, July 2, 1781 for an expedition to capture the forts in the vicinity of Kingsbridge. He requested General Jean Baptiste Donatien de Vimeur Comte de Rochambeau (1725–1807) to join him at the place and time indicated. Washington also expected to cut off a detachment of light troops under the command of Colonel James De Lancey (1747–1804), stationed outside of Kingsbridge, near Morrisania.[280]

See also **Kingsbridge.**

★ Captain Israel Honeywell or Hunnewell (1740–1790) and a party of Westchester county volunteers, covered by a detachment of regular infantry under Major Lemuel Trescott (1751–1826), made an excursion to Morrisania on Thursday night, January 10, 1782. They attacked a guard at De Lancey's bridge a little after sunrise, killed several on the spot, wounded and left several others, captured Captain Gilbert Totten and three men of De Lancey's corps, without any loss. The rest of the guards escaped in the darkness. Captain Honeywell pursued them but did not find them.[281]

★ On Monday morning, March 4, 1782 (General Heath dates this event on March 26th), Major Benjamin Ruggles Woodbridge (1739–1819) of the 2nd Connecticut Regiment and Captain Israel Honeywell or Hunnewell (1740–1790) of the state dragoons proceeded between the British Fort No. 8 and De Lancey's camp and attacked De Lancey's corps at Morrisania by surprise a little after sunrise. They rushed into their camp, killed several on the spot, wounded and left several others, destroyed a number of arms, and captured a subaltern and 20 men and 12 horses. The attackers had two men killed and three or four wounded, one of them mortally. The dragoons left by the Eastchester Road after the alarm guns had been fired. The Crown forces pursued and fell into an ambuscade along the Eastchester Road where Major Woodbridge had stationed the infantry. The infantrymen fired one or two vollies which broke the lines of the pursuers who retired, regrouped, and made another charge. Skirmishing continued for a considerable distance. The Continentals lost two privates killed and their guide mortally wounded and three privates slightly wounded.[282]

★ Captain David Williams (1754–1831), of the New York levies, made an excursion to Morrisania with 25 volunteer horsemen during the night of Monday, December 23, 1782. They captured one captain, one lieutenant, and seven privates without any loss. Captain Thomas Pritchard (1752–1795) and a detachment of infantrymen covered the retreat route. Some of the Congressional troops were cut down near the house where they were staying; others rushed to the steep bank of the frozen river with the Loyalists in close pursuit. Several were slain on the ice. Captain Williams fled to the opposite bank, closely pursued by a British dragoon. As his pursuer approached, Captain Williams reined his horse. Unable to stop, the dragoon passed Captain Williams who rose in his stirrups and gave him a back-handed blow with his sword, bringing him to the ground. He wanted to exchange his prisoner for Captain Richard Sackett (1745–1799) who had been taken earlier in the month.[283]

Croton River (Mar. 12, 1781; May 14, 1781; Oct. 17, 1781; ca. Nov. 1, 1781)
Pines Bridge

> The Croton River runs along Interstate 684 near the Connecticut border. It supplied water power for all the grist mills in the hamlets along its banks. Pines Bridge, named after a man who owned the land there, was one of two bridges across the Croton River in the town of Crompond (now Yorktown, New York). The old bridge was situated west of the present structure and served as a principal line of communication during the American War for Independence.
> Colonel Christopher Greene (1737–1781) and Major Ebenezer Flagg (1747–1781) are buried in the cemetery of the Yorktown Presbyterian Church (routes NY 202 and 132) in Yorktown Heights.

★ A small party of Colonel James De Lancey's (1747–1804) Loyalist troops fell in with eight Continentals near Croton's River on Monday March 12, 1781. They killed two Continentals, including the commanding officer, Samuel Ward, Jr. (d. 1781), and took the other six to the woods. They left their horses behind and escaped.[284]

★ The Crown forces had moved as far north as White Plains in May 1781 while General George Washington (1732–1799) had retreated to northern Westchester. Colonel Christopher Greene (1737–1781) and his Rhode Island Regiment were stationed at the Davenport House to protect the Oblenus Ford over the Croton River. Loyalist Colonel James De Lancey (1747–1804) and 60 dragoons and 200 infantrymen crossed the ford about sunrise on Monday, May 14, 1781 and marched up the valley along Turkey Mountain. They surprised the Rhode Islanders at Pines Bridge.

One party of Loyalists struck at Colonel Greene's camp while another struck at Lieutenant Jeremiah Greenman's (1758–1828) position. They dragged Colonel Greene from his quarters in a large bedroom in the northwest corner of the second story of Richardson Davenport's house and slashed him, Major Ebenezer Flagg (1747–1781), and several soldiers with the sword. Major Flagg had been shot in the head reaching for his pistols at the foot of the bed and was later slashed in the back of the neck as he was thought to be still asleep. Colonel Greene's "right arm was almost cut off in two places, the left in one, a severe cut on the left shoulder, a sword thrust through the abdomen, a bayonet in the right side, and another through the abdomen, several sword cuts on the head and many in different parts of the body."[285]

They lashed Colonel Greene to a horse and took him back toward British lines but, for some unknown reason, cut him from the saddle and left him on the road to die, perhaps because his body hindered their movement or he cried in agony too much. A witness reported: "Between ten and twenty fell, in and around the house, and were afterward interred in one common pit or grave, in the northwest corner of the lot, under an ash tree."[286] A large stone monument marks the spot. General Washington reported that Colonel Greene, Major Flagg, a sergeant and five privates were killed and three officers and a surgeon were taken prisoners (the surgeon and two of the officers were wounded) and 33 privates captured or missing.

The Loyalists took Lieutenant Greenman prisoner along with the guards. Greenman spent the next year in confinement on Long Island. Lieutenant Colonel Jeremiah Olney (1749–1812) took command of the regiment after Colonel Greene's death. General Washington concluded his report to Congress on May 17, 1781 by saying: "The loss of these two officers [Greene and Flagg] is to be regretted, especially the former [Colonel Greene] who has, upon several occasions, distinguished himself." Both officers were given a military funeral and buried in the churchyard of the Yorktown Presbyterian Church. The Rhode Islanders lost 44 killed, wounded and missing.[287]

★ A detachment of Colonel James De Lancey's (1747–1804) Loyalists surprised a party of 19 militiamen along the Croton River on Wednesday, October 17, 1781 and captured them all.[288]

★ Around Thursday, November 1, 1781, Captain Richard Sackett (1745–1799), First Lieutenant William Mosher (1735–1790) and a scouting party of 30 men were about 3 miles east of White Plains when they were attacked by 45 British light dragoons. They captured Captain Sackett while he was breakfasting at a nearby house and made two attacks in which they lost one man and two horses killed and several wounded. The scouts only had one man wounded before the British retired.[289]

Mount Kisco
North Castle (July 1, 1780; Feb. 15, 16, 1781; Mar. 18, 1781; July 3, 1781)
Sawmill River (July 1, 1781)

> North Castle is now Mount Kisco, about 12 miles north of White Plains. Middle Patent was between North Castle and Bedford. The Sawmill River is just west of Mount Kisco.

Colonel Hatfield and about 200 Crown horse and some infantry, came into the neighborhood of Middle Patent on Saturday, July 1, 1780. They collected more than 100 head of horned cattle, some horses, and more than 200 sheep. Captain Richard Sackett (1745–1799) and about 40 New York state levies ambushed them, retook all the sheep and cattle, and wounded several of them. As the Crown forces tried to retreat toward Long Island Sound, where Lieutenant Colonel Bezaleel Beebe (1741–1824) was posted with some Connecticut levies, Colonel Beebe's troops also fired on them. They killed six raiders, wounded several and took some prisoners. Colonel Beebe lost one man shot through the hip.[290]

★ Major Huggerford or Huggerssford and a party of about 250 infantrymen and 90 dragoons of Colonel James De Lancey's (1747–1804) Loyalists went as far as North Castle on Wednesday, February 14, 1781. They burned a total of eight houses and barns, including those of Lieutenant Benjamin Carpenter (1737–1813 or 1750–1827) and Esq. Lynch's two and Mr. Benjamin Clap's. They also plundered the inhabitants of everything they could carry off. They destroyed what they could not take.

★ A party of horsemen came out the following day, to continue the destruction. They took 10 prisoners, including two African Americans.[291]

★ Lieutenant James Kipp (1751–1785) and a party of 24 of Colonel James De Lancey's (1747–1804) Loyalist dragoons attacked a party of Whigs at North Castle on Sunday morning March 18, 1781. They captured 12 privates and a lieutenant and killed three. The others escaped.[292]

★ A party of militiamen ambushed a German patrol under Captain Carl von Rau (d. 1781) at the Sawmill River on Sunday, July 1, 1781. Jaeger Cavalry Captain von Rau was mortally wounded, shot in the breast and in the leg.[293]

★ The French grenadiers and chasseurs camped on a height to the left of the New York road in front of a pond adjoining the North Castle meetinghouse in early July 1781. The rest of the army camped on high ground in back of the pond and the little North Castle River (Kisco River). Their left flank was at the meetinghouse and their right near a wood. They held an excellent position protected by marshes on the left and nearby mountains and woodland. They could advance toward the enemy in three columns or retire in two: one by way of Pines Bridge, which crossed the Croton River 4 miles to the north of the camp, and the other by way of Ridgebury and Bedford, 22 and 5 miles away respectively. Troops advancing to attack them, especially if numerous, would have to march on the roads, unable to make detours without coming up against woods, mountains and many insurmountable obstacles. These natural obstacles made the position easy to defend.

Major General Benjamin Lincoln (1733–1810) led the vanguard of the Continental Army to surprise an enemy post at North Castle on Tuesday, July 3, 1781. They were to reconnoiter the enemy posts on the northern end of Manhattan Island: Forts Knyphausen (Washington), Tryon and George (Laurel Hill), with Fort George the "preliminary object." However, if he deemed it inadvisable to attack them, Lincoln would remain on the mainland above Spuyten Duyvil Creek and cover Armand Louis de Gontaut-Biron, Duc de Lauzun's (1747–1793) operation. Lauzun would advance to Morrisania (on the east bank of the Harlem River) and cut off the enemy corps believed to be quartered in that vicinity. Both of these movements depended on surprise to be successful.[294]

General Lincoln decided not to attack the Manhattan Island forts, as the enemy became aware of his movements and he could not surprise them. Colonel James De

Lancey's (1747–1804) corps had moved farther inland from Morrisania toward Williams's bridge on the Bronx River.

As General Lincoln proceeded along Guard Hill Road with 1,000 men on Tuesday, July 3, 1781, he was himself surprised and would have been cut off had the Duc de Lauzun and his hussars (see Photo NY-27) not been posted in the rear to protect it. Colonel James De Lancey's dragoons did not dare take on the hussars.

Meanwhile, General George Washington (1732–1799) took the rest of his army to White Plains and camped at Phillipsburg, sending word to the French army to march as rapidly as possible to North Castle to form a second line in reserve, 20 miles to the rear, in case the Crown forces advanced in considerable force.

When the French appeared, nearly 3,000 Crown troops marched out in several columns, forcing the French to cross a small stream and form in line of battle behind it. General Lincoln joined up with the French troops but his vanguard fired before they were ordered, alerting the English and enabling them to retire in good order after a brisk fire. General Lincoln had four men killed and 15 wounded; Lauzun's Legion lost none.[295]

Armonk
Mile Square (July 3, 1781)

> Mile Square is now Armonk.

★ A detachment of Continental troops under Colonel Alexander Scammel (1747–1781) and Colonel Jedediah Huntington (1743–1818) was sent to Mile Square on Tuesday, July 3, 1781 to dislodge a party of Crown forces strongly posted behind a stone wall between Williams's and Mile Square. The Crown forces made an obstinate defense that lasted a long time before they were finally evicted. The Continentals had about 23 men killed and wounded. The Crown forces were believed to have greater losses.[296]

Harrison, Westchester Co. (Dec. 2, 1781)

> Harrison is about 2 miles northeast of Mamaroneck on Route NY 127 in Westchester County.

★ A party of 45 of Brigadier General Oliver de Lancey's (1718-1785) dragoons, commanded by Captain Kipp, advanced as far as King Street in Harrison on Sunday, December 2, 1781. Here, Captain Kipp fell in with Captain Richard Sackett (1745–1799), who commanded the New York levies near Harrison Purchase. Sackett had gone a short distance from his men and was captured along with an ensign and a private. The command of the New York levies then devolved on Lieutenant William Mosher (1735–1790), who retreated with his 22 militiamen to a spot near Merritt's tavern. There he "formed his Men in a solid Body, with fixed Bayonets." They were ordered not to fire a shot, but to receive the enemy's charge in silence, until further instructions. They repulsed the first charge.

The Loyalist officer called to Mosher to surrender or he would cut his party to pieces. Mosher refused and the Loyalists made a second charge which was also repulsed. After the third attack, Mosher ordered his men to fire on the retreating troops. They did so, killing one man and wounding eight others, including Captain Kipp. Two of the Loyalist officers had their horses killed under them. Mosher's men escaped to a nearby woods, without having a single man wounded. General George Washington (1732-1799) often spoke of this affair to show how a small party of infantry armed with the bayonet could successfully resist a strong body of cavalry.[297]

Suffern (Mar. 30, 1782)

> Esq. John Suffern lived at "The Point of the Mountains" or "Sidman's Clove" which became Suffern in 1796. It is in southwestern New York near exit 15 of I-87N and I-287W less than a mile from the New Jersey border.

★ Lieutenant James Moody (1744–1809) and his party of Loyalists ambushed the dragoons who accompanied the western mail on Saturday, March 30, 1782 about 4 or 5 miles below Esq. John Suffern's (1741–1836) house. The dragoons rode through the fire and saved the mail, but one was mortally wounded. A country gentleman who rode with them was shot through the arm. He knew one of the Loyalists who was soon after captured in his house. The prisoner revealed the identities of several other Loyalists who were accomplices in the matter. The militia was alarmed and set out in pursuit of Moody.[298]

3
EASTERN LONG ISLAND

See the map of Eastern Long Island.

Plum Island, Fisher's Island, Gardiner's Island (Aug. 11, 1775)
Fisher's Island (Mar. 6, 1777)

> Plum Island, Fisher's Island, and Gardiner's Island are off the north and eastern coasts of Long Island. Plum Island is a small island east of Terry Point. Gardiner's Island is off the east coast of Long Island between Sag Harbor and Montauk. Fisher's Island is in Long Island Sound, off the coast of New London, Connecticut.

★ The residents of Plum Island learned as early as Tuesday, August 8, 1775, that the King's troops planned to plunder Fisher's, Gardiner's, Plum and Block Islands for stock and provisions. The residents had time to have the stock removed and actually took some away. Some differences arose between the proprietors and the committees concerning the expense of removing the stock and supplies. Before they could come to agreement, the enemy ships arrived.

The people immediately sent dispatches to the people of the Connecticut and Long Island shores to alert them. Although they hurried to assemble and to come to the aid of the islanders, they were too late to prevent the enemy from carrying out their plan. The British force of seven transport ships, two brigs, two men of war, one snow of 10 guns, one armed schooner of 17 men, and 200 Regulars took 1,100 sheep, 94 lean cattle (the fat cattle had already been removed), and five cows from Fisher's Island as well as a sloop belonging to New Haven, Connecticut loaded with livestock, and a vessel belonging to New London loaded with salt.

The British then sailed to Gardiner's Island on Friday the 11th. When they landed on the island, 10 Loyalists from Southhold assisted them to seize 1,000 sheep, 30 hogs, 13 geese, three calves, 1,000 pounds of cheese, and seven tons of hay. They also damaged gardens, fences and other property. Only one company of about 40 militiamen went to Gardiner's Island. They arrived in time to see the enemy sail away.

When the plunderers landed on one side of Plum Island, about 100 of Colonel David Wooster's (1710–1777) troops, who had landed on the other side, fired on them. However, Colonel Wooster was informed that the island was nearly surrounded by armed enemy vessels that could cut off his retreat. After they fired a single volley, which had little effect, the militia retired to the mainland. The plunderers seized 14 fat cattle, one wood boat, and a transport brig.[299]

★ A British foraging fleet that sailed from Newport, Rhode Island, on Thursday, March 6, 1777, returned from Fisher's Island with cattle, sheep and hay.[300]

Setauket (Sept. 7, 1776; Nov. 1, 1776; Aug. 22, 1777; Dec. 10, 1777; Nov. 27, 1778; June 20, 1781; June 27, 1781)

> Setauket is on the north shore of Long Island, opposite Bridgeport, Connecticut. The Caroline Church (see Photo NY-28) occupied by the Crown forces is on Route NY 25A (North Country Road) on the east side of the town green in East Setauket.

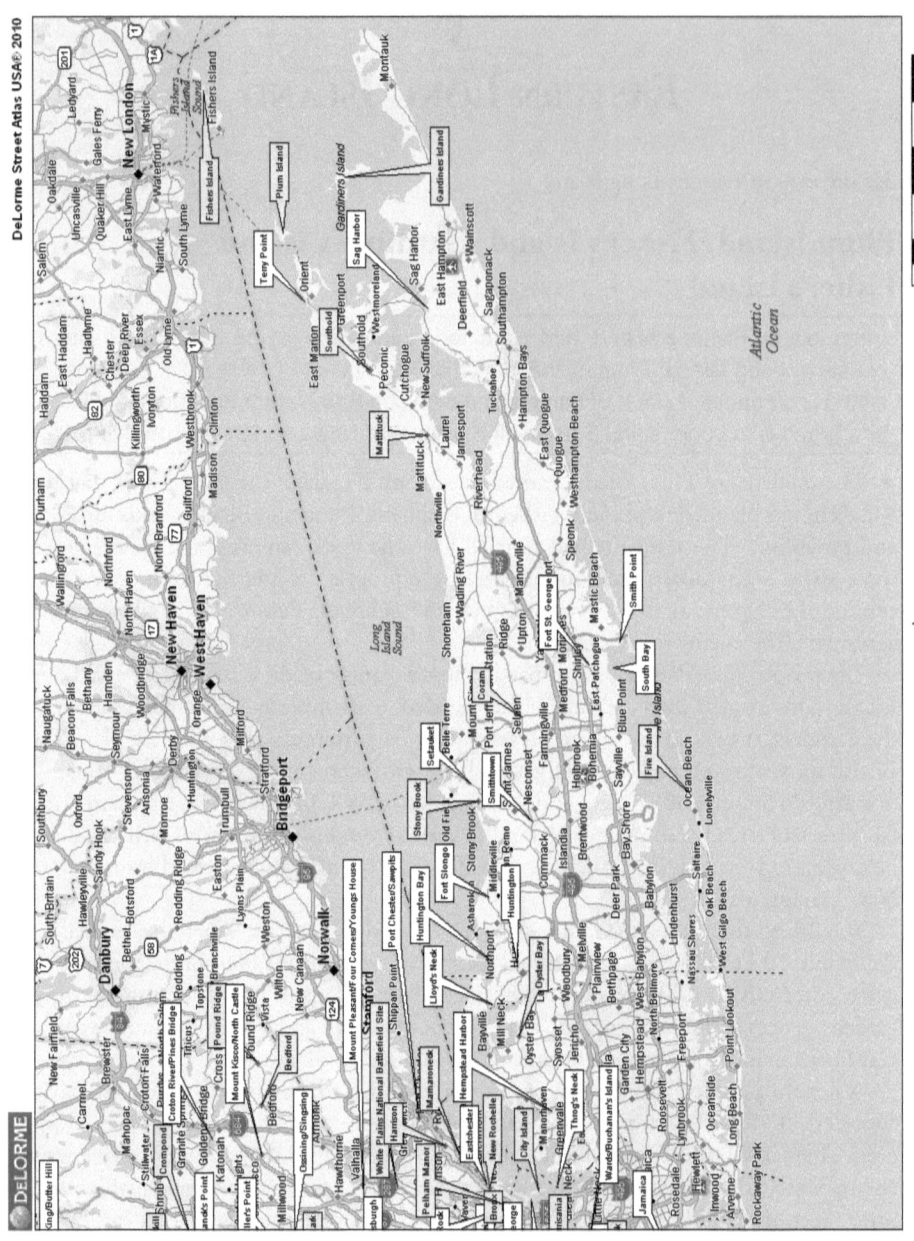

Eastern Long Island: Map for The Guide to the American Revolutionary War in New York © 2010 DeLorme (www.delorme.com) Street Atlas USA®

Photo NY-28. Caroline Church, Setauket

> The Setauket Presbyterian Church is on North Country Road on the south side of the green on Ridgeway Ave.

★ Whigs in 60 whaleboats, accompanied by Captain Robert Niles (1734–1818) and the 10-gun schooner *Spy*, crossed over Long Island Sound during the night of Saturday, September 7, 1776. They arrived at Setauket about 11 PM and divided forces to surround the Loyalist guardhouse and headquarters at the same time. When the militia arrived at the guardhouse, several guards fled to their headquarters where they were captured along with the rest of their men. The militiamen killed 13 Loyalists and captured 40 men, two sloops, and some cattle, while having only one man killed. They returned to New Haven the following day.[301]

★ Between 300 and 400 Rhode Island and Connecticut troops crossed Long Island Sound and landed near Setauket on Friday, November 1, 1776. They intended to capture some Loyalists and engaged a party of new British recruits, commanded by Captain Jacob Smith (1749–1837), of General De Lancey's brigade. The New Englanders killed five or six men and captured Captain Smith and 23 of his company along with "75 excellent muskets." They lost only one man killed and one wounded. About half of the prisoners were African Americans or Native Americans and two were deserters from the Continental Army.[302]

★ General Samuel Holden Parsons (1737–1789) and about 500 men with several pieces of brass cannon embarked in six whaleboats and a single sloop at Black Rock, Connecticut on Friday August 22, 1777. They crossed Long Island Sound and landed at Crane Neck Bend, approximately 3 miles from Setauket, early in the morning. They intended to destroy a Loyalist stockade, a fortified Presbyterian church surrounded by breastworks. The earthen walls 30 feet from the church were six feet high and five feet thick. The six feet high picket logs at the top were set so close together that they allowed just enough space for men to fire muskets at attackers. Four swivel guns (see Photo NY-9) had been placed in the upper windows of the church, making it practically impregnable. The redoubt was garrisoned by 250 men of Delancey's 1st Battalion commanded by Lieutenant Colonel Richard Hewlett (1712–1789). Many of the defenders resided in the nearby town when not on duty.

Despite their precautions, General Parsons and his men were detected and an express rider was sent for reinforcements. When asked to surrender, Colonel Hewlett requested one hour to consider but was granted only 10 minutes. He decided to defend the fort for his Majesty King George III (1738–1820), as long as he had a man alive. A smart fire ensued immediately. The attackers fired their 6-pounder at the church which the Loyalists answered with their swivel guns. The firing continued unsuccessfully for two or three hours. General Parsons learned that reinforcements were on their way and re-embarked his men and returned to Connecticut before British ships could cut off his retreat across Long Island Sound. They destroyed a few military stores but lost about four men killed. Much blood was seen on the ground after they left. Colonel Hewlett had one man killed and two or three wounded.[303]

★ Congressional forces planned a three-pronged assault on Setauket for Wednesday, December 10, 1777. General Samuel Holden Parsons (1737–1789) would cross to Southold where he would destroy timber gathered for the British army barracks in New York City. Colonel Return Jonathan Meigs (1740–1823) would leave Saw Pits (first called Saw Log Swamp and now Port Chester) and cross to Hempstead Harbor, about 12 miles away, and attack a regiment stationed 8 miles east of Jamaica, while Colonel Samuel Blachley Webb (1754–1825) would land at Huntington to support either or both of the other forces as needed.

General Parsons and his men crossed the sound in whaleboats, landed at Hockaback, about 40 miles from the east end of the island, destroyed the timber and took some prisoners. High seas prevented Colonel Meigs from crossing Long Island Sound. The other two divisions left Norwalk, Connecticut, on the evening of the 9th. Colonel Webb left with 73 men aboard the sloop *Schuyler* in company with the schooners *Spy* and *Mifflin*. They crossed Long Island Sound but, at 5:30 AM, were spotted by the frigate HMS *Falcon*, Captain Harry Harmood, on her way from New York to Newport. The *Falcon* gave chase and the *Schuyler*, with six 4-pounders and 12 musketoons (see Photo NY-5), headed to shore at Old Man's harbor off Setauket at 6:30. The *Falcon* anchored near the entrance of the harbor at 8 AM and fired four 6-pound shots at the *Schuyler* which ran aground about 200 yards from the beach and struck her colors. The British captured the *Schuyler*, 12 musketoons and 73 men. The master, Lieutenant John Kerr, and four others escaped.

Parsons's division arrived to find that the fleet had sailed, except for the sloops of war *Swan*, Captain James Ayscough, and *Harlem*, Captain Hart, and four other vessels.

Only one of the vessels had loaded her cargo of timber and boards. Parsons captured the loaded sloop and destroyed all the timber and boards and a large quantity of wood cut for another fleet expected from Newport.

Captain Hart and about 40 men found Captain Ayscough and more than 20 men aboard the *Swan*'s boats within about 20 yards from shore. They refused to surrender and Captain Hart's men gave them "several well-directed shots" that broke Captain Ayscough's thigh, badly wounded two officers, killed about eight and wounded about eight more. The ships immediately weighed anchor and sailed for Newport. General Parsons's division returned safely to the mainland with about 20 prisoners.[304]

★ A party of Connecticut Whigs surprised and captured Colonel Benjamin Floyd at his home at Setauket on Friday, November 27, 1778.[304a]

★ The Associators were returning from an expedition to Connecticut in the brig *Sir H. Clinton,* the sloop *Association* and the brig *Keppel* on Wednesday morning, June 20, 1781, when they discovered seven Whig boats off Setauket. As the Whigs were too close to the shore to be cut off, the Associators landed, hauled their boats into the woods, and then ran off. Loyalist Captain Amos Hubbell (1747–1817) landed with all his force. In two hours, he and his men captured a very fine 12-oared barge or gunboat, called *General Wooster*, with two swivels and a blunderbuss, and six very good whaleboats, most of which were new. The boats contained a quantity of plunder worth £100. The Loyalists tried unsuccessfully to find the Whigs on shore.[305]

★ A party of about 50 New England Whigs under the command of Dan Jackson (1753–1836)(?), of Newark, New Jersey landed at Crane Neck in Setauket in five whaleboats on Wednesday night, June 27, 1781. They went to the house of Captain Nathan Woodhull (1720–1804) early the next morning and plundered it and three neighboring houses. They then took Captain Woodhull and his son with them. However two brigs and a sloop in Long Island Sound discovered the whaleboats and gave chase immediately. The New Englanders were forced to run their boats ashore and escape to the woods, leaving their boats and plunder behind. The goods were returned to their owners, and Captain Woodhull and his son were rescued.[306]

Near Brookhaven (Sept. 29, 1776)

Brookhaven is on the south shore of Long Island, north of South Bay.

★ Captain John Rowe (1751–1810) and a party of men landed at The Old Man's, near Brookhaven, on Sunday, September 29, 1776 to remove Captain Rowe's family from Coram to the mainland. There, Captain Rowe met Richard Miller (d. 1776), a native of East Hampton, who had taken a commission under General William Howe (1732–1786) and was enlisting men for the British Army. As he was riding by Capt. Rowe's door where a sentry was placed, Miller was hailed and ordered to stop. Refusing to do so, Miller rode faster. The guard fired at him after he disregarded several appeals to stop. One of the balls struck Mr. Miller and he died the next morning.[307]

Huntington Bay (Nov. 13, 1776; May 5, 1778)

Huntington Bay is on the north side of Long Island, opposite Stamford, Connecticut. The so-called Arsenal is located on Park Avenue near South Woodhull Road one block east of Route NY 25A (E Main St.). A short distance further east on Route NY 25A (E Main St.) is Fort Hill where Huntington's first cemetery was opened around

> 1700. Loyalist Colonel Benjamin Thompson (1753–1814), later Count Rumford, vandalized the site and built Fort Golgotha at its summit which the Crown forces occupied in 1782.

★ Captain Roger Curtis (1746–1816) sailed the HM Sloop *Senegal* from Huntington Bay to Connecticut on Wednesday, November 13, 1776. He spotted almost 200 armed men boarding a privateer sloop at Norwalk about noon. He pursued the privateer which tacked and ran in the harbor. The *Senegal* tacked and headed for the Neck. When he saw a sloop heading for Fairfield, Connecticut, Captain Curtis gave chase at 3:30 PM. The sloop entered Mill Creek and ran aground. Captain Curtis anchored near the sloop and sent armed boats to burn her. They fired two shots at some Rebels firing at the boats from behind some rocks.[308]

★ Captain Stanhope's HMS *Raven* fired two guns on Tuesday, May 5, 1778, to bring to a Whig sloop from City Island. He heard several guns fired near Oyster Bay about 6 PM, weighed anchor and set sail. He sent all his boats to cut off a schooner which was heading toward shore at Huntington Bay and to tow the ship to port. Later that evening, he learned that the vessel was a row galley which had fired upon the HMS *Halifax* in Oyster Bay.[309]

Colonel Benjamin Thompson, later Count Rumford (1753–1814), in command of a Loyalist regiment of about 500 men called the King's American Dragoons, came to Huntington toward the close of the war after hostilities had ceased but before a peace treaty was concluded. He constructed "Fort Golgotha" by dismantling the First Presbyterian Church and using the beams and planks to build the fort on Burying Hill (see Photo NY-29). He pulled up the tombstones and used them as baking stones and leveled the graves.

Tradition says that Thompson pitched his headquarters tent near the grave of Ebenezer Prime (1723–1779), the minister, so that whenever he went in or out of his

Photo NY-29. Burying Hill, Huntington Bay

tent he could "step on the damned old rebel's head." The soldiers built an earthwork six feet high around the two-acre fort and erected barracks over the graves, and used the tombstones for tables, fireplaces, and ovens. It was said that when bread loaves were taken out of the oven, they had words from the epitaphs imprinted on the bottom crust. The fort was not involved in any military action, as the peace treaty had already been signed by the time of its construction.[310]

Huntington (Aug. 8, 18, 26, 1778; Dec. 5, 1782)

> Huntington is on the north of Long Island and south of Lloyd's Neck.

★ A party of Whigs crossed Long Island Sound from Connecticut on Tuesday night August 17, 1778. They concealed themselves in a wood below Huntington and fired on three light dragoons returning from the east end of the island. They killed one on the spot; the other two escaped unhurt with their horses. A party was immediately dispatched from Huntington to search for the attackers; but they escaped back to Connecticut.

★ Two days later, a lieutenant and a few of the crewmen from a privateer recently wrecked on the east end of Long Island were apprehended and secured.[311]

★ On Saturday, September 26, 1778, several inhabitants of Huntington were brought to the jail in Trenton, New Jersey for piloting the Whigs in their different excursions from Connecticut on Long Island.[312]

★ The June 28, 1779 issue of Gaine's *The New-York Gazette; and the Weekly Mercury* describes some of the dangers British soldiers faced in the Huntington area. If one or two of them went about alone, young Whigs of Huntington who often hid along the roadside in the woods at "Mutton Hollow" would "pick off" the soldiers when they were alone or in small groups and leave their bodies on the side of the road.

Ezekiel Wicks (1725–1803) shot a light dragoon at the foot of the hill near Platt Carll's and left his body there. Another was shot in "Shoemaker Lane" and his body lay in the road for a whole day before it was discovered. Whenever the Whigs had an opportunity to attack their enemies, they took advantage of it.

Some British officers were accustomed to come to the village on horseback from Lloyd's Neck and to return in the night. The young Huntingtonians would sometimes run a rope across the road, tied to stout trees. They would then hide in the woods. When the British officers came galloping in the dark, their horses would run into the rope and toss their riders to the ground. The young men would then rush from their hiding place, capture the officers, and take them to the harbor, where whaleboats waited to take them across Long Island Sound as prisoners.[313]

December 5, 1782 see **Mamaroneck, Westchester County.**

Off Wading River (Dec. 6, 1776)

> The Wading River is on the north side of Long Island near Shoreham and northeast of Coram.

★ Captain George Talbot sent the barge of the HMS *Niger* ashore at the Wading River around noon on Friday, December 6, 1776. The crew burned a small schooner and a boat belonging to the Whigs.[314]

See also **Coram** and **Smith's Point.**

Oyster Bay (May 19, 1777; Mar. 24, 1778; May 27, 1778; June 22, 1778; July 27, 1779; Nov. 15, 1779; Dec. 7, 1779)

> Oyster Bay is on the north side of Long Island, west of Huntington and opposite Stamford, Connecticut. Long Neck Point is near Oyster Bay.

★ The HM Brig *Halifax* anchored off Long Neck Point near Oyster Bay at 10 PM on Saturday May 18, 1777. She sent her boats and a tender manned and armed to Scotch Cove to gather intelligence. The party returned at midnight with two head of cattle. The *Halifax* fired two 4-pound shots at a party of armed Whigs on shore at 4 AM the following morning. She weighed anchor at 8 and returned to Oyster Bay at noon.[315]

★ Forty-three marines and 20 Loyalists from HM Galley *Dependence* and other vessels landed in Stamford harbor at 6. AM on Tuesday, March 24, 1778 and burned a Whig galley. Lieutenant James Clark's *Dependence* fired round and grape shot from four 24-pounders and four 4-pounders to scour the woods before the troops landed. The troops re-embarked at 8 AM and headed for Lloyd's beach where they anchored at noon. They lost one man in the skirmish.[316]

★ The Whig schooner *Wild Cat,* mounting 14 swivels (see Photo NY-9) and a crew of 40 men, came over from Connecticut to Oyster Bay on Wednesday, May 27, 1778. She landed 14 of her crew who shot several sheep. A number of inhabitants appeared in arms to oppose them; so they left.[317]

★ A Whig whaleboat came near Mosquito Cove to carry off a boat on Monday, June 22, 1778. A few men on shore observed their approach and got on board armed and unnoticed. When the whaleboat got close enough, they fired a volley that killed three Whigs. The others left in a great hurry.[318]

★ A party of Whigs led by Jonas Youngs (1745–1803)(?) captured John Townsend, Esq. at his home at Oyster Bay at 2 AM Tuesday morning, July 27, 1779. They then robbed his house of many valuable articles (silver tankard, linen, etc.) and partly demolished it.

At the same time, William Sutton, of Mamaroneck, and a young man named Arnold Fleet (1754–1839), were taken to Stamford and paroled. The men carried their boat over the beach. Their sentinel did not hear the signal, was left behind, and wandered around on Mill Neck until hunger forced him to give up.[319]

★ Two small privateers, of four guns each, commanded by Captain Samuel Lockwood (1737–1807) and Captain Johnson ran into Oyster Bay under British colors on Monday November 15, 1779. A large 8-gun brig protected four wooden vessels there. The captain of the brig asked the privateers where they were from. They answered from New York and were permitted to come alongside the brig unsuspected. The privateers boarded the brig, surprised the 20-man crew and forced them to surrender without firing a gun. The crews of the other vessels also surrendered and were taken toward Norwalk or Stamford, Connecticut. Some armed vessels from Huntington Harbor pursued them. The brig ran onto a reef of rocks near Norwalk harbor and was captured again. The Loyalists got her off and took her away. The other prizes got into port safely.[320]

★ The 70-ton *Lively* was captured in Oyster Bay on Tuesday December 7, 1779 with her cargo of salt.[321]

South Oyster Bay (Nov. 7, 1779)
Jefferd's Neck (Nov. 7, 1779)

> Oyster Bay was the headquarters of Lieutenant Colonel John Graves Simcoe's (1752–1806) Queen's Rangers.

★ Cavalry under Captain Thomas Hawley (1734–1813) raided South Oyster Bay on Sunday, November 7, 1779. British dragoons opposed them and captured six of them.[322]

Sag Harbor (May 23, 1777)

> Sag Harbor was a profitable port for trade with the West Indies in the 1770s; and the shipbuilding industry flourished here. The large wharf was extended to 495 feet to accommodate the larger coastal and West Indies trading vessels. It was extended even more in later years and is now known as Long Wharf. It was the second most important port in the colony after New York City. When the Crown forces occupied Long Island in 1776, many of the three dozen families moved away and the prosperous trade disappeared. By April 1777, the British had accumulated a very large stock of provisions, munitions and forage at Sag Harbor and the town became a prime target for a raid.
> Colonel Return Jonathan Meigs (1740–1823) and his party landed at Long Beach along Noyack–Long Beach Road and proceeded to the fortified house where a British foraging party was staying on Noyack Road near its intersection with Parkway Drive. The customs house is on Garden Street near its intersection with Route NY 114 (Main St). The Meigs Monument on Union Street occupies part of the Sag Harbor Fort site.

★ A British foraging party left New York on Friday, May 23, 1777 in 12 vessels bound for Sag Harbor near the eastern end of Long Island. They traveled under the protection of an armed schooner carrying 40 men and 12 guns and a company of 70 men from Lieutenant Colonel Stephen De Lancey's (d. 1817) Loyalists. Colonel Return Jonathan Meigs learned of this expedition and embarked 170 men in whaleboats (see Photo NY-9) at Sachem's Head near Guilford, Connecticut that evening. They crossed Long Island Sound, which was "full of British cruisers," and landed at Long Beach at Southold at 2 AM. They carried their boats overland to Peconic Bay where they were launched again. They hid the boats in a wooded area about 4 miles from Sag Harbor and proceeded on foot. They completely surprised De Lancey's Provincial Corps, capturing the commanding officer asleep in his bed in the house of Loyalist James Howell (1734–1808). They killed six and captured about 70 at the point of the bayonet.

A 12-gun British schooner in the harbor opened fire on the raiders, but without result. Meigs and his men destroyed all 12 vessels in the harbor, except the schooner. They also burned vast supplies of hay, corn, oats, rum, and other merchandise designated for the army. They took 90 prisoners and returned to Guilford by noon, without a single casualty. They covered a distance of nearly 100 miles in 18 hours. Congress commended Meigs and his men for their exploits and voted Meigs "an elegant sword" on Friday, July 25, 1777.[323] General Samuel Holden Parsons's (1737–1789) letter to Connecticut's governor, Jonathan Trumbull (1710–1785), dated "N. Haven, May 25, '77," reports the action:

[Having] made the proper dispositions for attacking the enemy in 5 different places, proceeded with the greatest order and silence till 20 rods of the enemy, when they rushed with fixed bayonets upon the different barracks, guards, and quarters of the enemy: whilst Capt. Troop, with a party under his command, at the same time took possession of the wharves and vessels lying there. The alarm soon became general, and an incessant fire of grape and round shot was kept up from an armed schooner of 12 guns, which lay within 150 yds. of the wharves, for near an hour; notwithstanding which the party burnt all the vessels at the wharf, killed and captivated all the men belonging to them, destroyed about 100 tons of hay, large quantities of grain, 10 hhds. of rum, and other W. Indian goods, and secured all the soldiers who were there stationed. 90 prisoners . . . not a man killed or wounded on our side. The officers and men behaved with the greatest order and bravery.[324]

Smith's Point (July 1777; Nov. 23, 1780)
Coram (Nov. 21, 1780)
Fort St. George (Nov. 23, 1780)

> The Manor of St. George (see Photo NY-30) is on the south shore of Long Island, near present-day Brookhaven. It is off William Floyd Parkway at Smith's Point near Mastic Beach. It was a triangular fort consisting of three fortifications: the strongly barricaded manor house, another fortified house, and a small fort. Three stockaded walls, 12 feet high, connected the structures to make the fort 96 feet square. The fort was near a little harbor where supplies were loaded to be shipped to Manhattan. William Floyd's estate is nearby.
>
> The site of the burning of the hay is now occupied by a large shopping center. The hay would have been located in what is now the parking lot at the intersection of Route NY 25 (Middle Country Rd.) and Route NY 112.[325]

Photo NY-30. Manor of St. George

★ After the British captured Long Island in 1776, they fortified the Manor of St. George which then became known as Fort St. George. It was a supply base for land and sea forces because of its proximity to the inlet that then existed in the barrier beach opposite Mastic and because the British coveted the wood in its forests.

General Samuel Holden Parsons (1737–1789), with 1,000 men and several pieces of cannon, crossed Long Island Sound from Fairfield, Connecticut to Long Island in July 1777. They laid siege to a small Loyalist fort at Brookhaven garrisoned by Lieutenant Colonel Richard Hewlett (1712–1789) and about 300 men of the 3rd Battalion of De Lancey's Brigade. Parsons occupied some high ground near the fort, mounted his cannon and demanded the garrison to surrender, promising honorable terms. Hewlett replied that he had enough men to defend his small garrison and enough provisions and stores to stand a longer siege than Parsons could successfully carry on. He said his loyal subjects were determined to spend the last drop of their blood in the cause of their Sovereign rather than submit to Rebel banditti commanded by a shoemaker. General Parsons, irritated by this answer, began his cannonade which the fort returned. The cannonade continued about 12 hours before General Parsons, having sustained a considerable loss (about 30 men), withdrew. He embarked his men and returned to Connecticut. Colonel Hewlett only lost one man in the cannonade.[326]

★ Major Benjamin Tallmadge (1754–1835) wrote to General George Washington (1732–1799) from Fairfield, Connecticut on November 7, 1780 to notify him of the fort and a 300 ton stack of hay at Coram only a little off the route to Smith's Point. Four days later, General Washington responded, authorizing him to try to destroy the forage. He also instructed Colonel Elisha Sheldon (1740–1805) to furnish Major Tallmadge with a detachment of dismounted dragoons for this purpose and to capture the Smith house if not too hazardous.

Major Tallmadge and two companies of dismounted dragoons (about 80 men) embarked in eight whaleboats at 4 PM on Monday, November 21, 1780 and rowed from Fairfield across Long Island Sound and landed at Old Man's (Mt. Sinai) Harbor, near Cedar Beach, about 9 o'clock that night. They began to cross Long Island when a southeast wind began to blow, followed by rain, before they had gone 4 or 5 miles. They returned to their boats, concealed in the bushes, and sheltered themselves under the boats during the hard rainstorm. The next night, when the rain stopped, they marched across the island to Mastic where they arrived by 4 AM about 2 miles from the fort. They paused for a short time to refresh themselves.

Major Tallmadge divided his troops into three companies to attack the fort from three directions at dawn. He led the main company which was not discovered until they reached 20 to 40 yards from the fort. The sentinel halted his march, looked attentively at the column, demanded "Who comes there?" and fired. Before the smoke cleared, the sergeant at Tallmadge's side bayoneted the guard. The other two companies, with orders to keep concealed until the enemy fired on the main column, moved forward and soon made a break in the stockade. The rear platoon halted to prevent the prisoners from escaping while Major Tallmadge's column moved directly through the Grand Parade against the main fort, which they took with the bayonet, in less than 10 minutes, without firing a single shot.

The officers of the other two detachments mounted the ramparts on the other side. The men shouted the watchword, "*Washington and glory,*" as the Loyalists fired a volley from the windows of one of the barricaded houses nearby. Major Tallmadge ordered his whole detachment to load and return the fire. They then moved directly to the house as the pioneers cut through the strong barricades with their axes. After taking the fort, they captured most of the men who had fired from the windows and threw them headlong from the second story windows to the ground.

They secured the prisoners and soon discovered that the boats near the fort were getting under way with stores and supplies. The dragoons pointed the fort's guns at them and soon captured the fleeing men. The dragoons began to demolish the enemy's works after sunrise, destroying an immense quantity of stores, of various kinds and burning the boats and their cargoes. The prisoners were pinioned together two by two and made to carry bundles of valuable dry goods across the island on their shoulders.

Having completed their mission of capturing and destroying the fort, the troops began to return to their boats, at 8 AM. At a point at the middle of the island, Major Tallmadge then picked 10 or 12 men for the raid on Coram. They mounted horses captured at the fort and rode off. They turned off the River road at Millville (Yaphank) and rode through the oak forest that covered the middle of the island. They reached Coram in about an hour and a half and quickly routed the small guard. They set the 300 tons of hay (enough to feed 117 horses for a year) on fire and headed to Old Man's (Mt. Sinai) Harbor where they joined up with the main force and the prisoners another hour and a half later. They reached their boats by 4 PM, boarded, and were on their way by sunset, returning to Fairfield around midnight or 1 AM. The expedition had covered about 40 miles on land and 20 on water in a little over 30 hours. Only one man was badly wounded, while the Loyalists lost seven killed and wounded, most of them mortally, and many prisoners, including the commandant, a captain, a lieutenant, a surgeon, 50 privates and a garrison standard.[327]

General Washington was so pleased with the results of the expedition that he sent the following letter of commendation to Major Tallmadge.

Morristown, November 28, 1780

Dear Sir:

Both your letters of the 25th came to my hand this day. I received with much pleasure the report of your successful enterprise upon Fort St. George and the vessel with stores in the Harbour, and was particularly well pleased with the destruction of the Hay which must I should conceive, be severely felt by the Enemy at this time.

I beg of you to accept my thanks for your judicious planning and spirited execution of this business and that you will offer them to officers and men who shared the honors of the Enterprise with you.— The gallant behavior of Mr. Muirson gives him a fair claim to an appointment in the 2nd Regim't. of Dragoons or any other of the state to which he belongs, where there is a vacancy and I have no doubt of his meeting with it accordingly if you will make known his merit with these sentiments in his favor.

You have my free consent to reward your gallant party, with the little booty they were able to bring from the Enemy's works. With much esteem and regard I am

Your Most Obedient Servant

G. Washington

Rivington's Gazette gives one British account:

A party of rebels, about eighty in number, headed, it is said, by a rebel Major Tallmadge, assisted by a certain Heathcot Muirson, Benajah Strong, Thomas Jackson, and Caleb Brewster, officers belonging to the said party, all formerly of Long Island, came across in eight whale boats from somewhere about New Haven on the Connecticut shore, and landed between the Wading River and the Old Man's, and are supposed to have been concealed two or three days on the island by their old friends, the rebels. On Thursday morning, the 23d instant, about fifty of them marched across the island, the remainder being left to guard the boats, and just after daylight arrived at Smith's Point, St. George's Manor, south side Long Island, where they surprised a body of respectable loyal refugees belonging to Rhode Island and the vicinity thereabout, who were establishing a post in order to get a present subsistence for themselves and their distressed families. The sentry, upon observing them, fired, which they returned and mortally wounded him, and rushed into a house. Mr. Isaac Hart, of Newport, in Rhode Island, formerly an eminent merchant and ever a loyal subject, was inhumanly fired upon and bayoneted, wounded in fifteen different parts of his body, and beat with their muskets in the most shocking manner in the very act of imploring quarter, and died of his wounds a few hours after, universally regretted by every true lover of his king and country. Four more refugees were wounded also, but are in a fair way of recovery; a poor woman was also fired upon at another house, and barbarously wounded through both breasts, of which wounds she now lingers a specimen of rebel savageness and degeneracy. The rebels carried off about forty prisoners. On their return, at Coram, they burnt a magazine of hay about one hundred tons, and the same day embarked or the Connecticut shore.[328]

Hempstead Harbor (Oct. 12, 1777)

★ A whaleboat with about 10 men from Byram River went into Hempstead Harbor on Sunday, October 12, 1777. They took a wood boat out into Long Island Sound and were returning for two others that remained in the harbor already loaded. A few militiamen gathered and prevented them from doing so, forcing them to row away in a hurry.[329]

Terry Point (Oct. 19, 1777)

Terry Point is on Long Island northeast of Southold.

★ Congressional and Crown forces skirmished at Terry Point on Sunday, October 19, 1777. Congressional forces lost one killed and one wounded.[330]

Southold (Dec. 12, 1777; Dec. 23, 1777)

Southold is on the northeastern end of Long Island.

★ Lieutenant John Knight (1748–1831), Master of the HM Sloop *Haerlem*, observed a number of Whigs at the Southold Landing firing on the boats of HM Sloop *Swan* at 3 PM on Friday, December 12, 1777. Captain James Ayscough had sent two boats ashore to get water that morning. The Whigs wounded Captain Ayscough, the surgeon, Kenneth McKenzie, William Searl, George Davis, and Joseph Pickford, a marine. They captured marine sergeant Joseph Collingsworth and seamen James Parrot, James Edmonds, and Charles Wakefield. Lieutenant Knight brought the *Haerlem* broadside and fired 16 4-pounders at the Whigs on shore. The *Swan* fired 50 guns. Both the *Haerlem* and the *Swan* then weighed anchor and moved eastward, closer to Shelter Island, at 4 PM to protect two sloops coming down Little Peconic Bay or Great Peconic Bay.[331]

★ A party of men under the command of Captain Samuel Hart, Sr. (1738–1813) marched to Southold on Tuesday December 23, 1777 and came close to capturing Captain James Ayscough and more than 20 men belonging to the HM Sloop *Swan*. They were at a house in Southold, learned of Captain Hart's approach, and hastened to their boats with Captain Hart in close pursuit. Captain Ayscough and his men were fired upon as they boarded their vessel. Most of them were either killed or wounded and seven marines and seamen were made prisoners. Captain Hart's troops remained on the island for several days without accomplishing much of anything before returning to the mainland.[332]

Smithtown (Feb. 25, 1778; Oct. 7, 1780)

> The Smith Tavern (see Photo NY-31), in Smithtown, was originally on Route NY 111. It was moved three times and now occupies the site at 210 Jericho Turnpike (Route NY 25|Middle Country Road).

★ Brigadier Major David Humphreys (1752–1818) and a detachment of 30 volunteers from Colonel Return Jonathan Meigs's (1740–1823) 6th Connecticut Regiment boarded four whaleboats on Wednesday night February 25, 1778 and headed to Smithtown, Long Island to destroy several enemy ships. They were particularly interested in a large ship of 20 guns that was aground near that place; but the ship got off the preceding day. The raiders set fire to, and destroyed a brig of about 200 tons, a large schooner and an armed sloop, all of which were in the king's service. They captured two captains and several seamen together with as many sails, rigging, and furniture as the boats could contain. The party returned to the mainland the next morning without any losses.[333]

★ Lieutenant Matthew Prendergast (1756–1838) and a party of Lieutenant Colonel Abraham C. Cuyler's (1742–1810) Loyalists captured Major Brush, Captain Cornelius Conklin (1727–1791), Captain Jacob Conklin (1741–1813), Captain Rogers, Captain Ketcham (d.1780) and Lieutenant Fieley at Smithtown on Saturday, October 7, 1780. Captain Ketcham was killed trying to escape. Captain P. Luke of the Royal Refugees brought the other prisoners to New York two days later.[334]

Photo NY-31. Smith Tavern, Smithtown

Lloyd's Neck (Apr. 21, 1778; June 24, 1778; June 27, 1778; Sept. 2, 1778; before Sept. 3, 1778; Sept. 5, 1779; before Sept. 14, 1779; Mar. 31, 1781; July 12, 1781)

> Lloyd's Neck seems to have been both a shipping and supply dock and an area to shelter Loyalist refugees where they could work for the British with some sense of security. Loyalist activities here made the Neck a target of numerous Whig raids from Connecticut. Most often the duties performed here involved cutting down the timber and carting it to designated storage areas for the use of Crown troops.
>
> Behind the clubhouse of the Stamford (Connecticut) Yacht Club is a marker commemorating Major Benjamin Tallmadge's (1754–1835) embarkation for the raid at Lloyd's Neck. A private residence in the area of West Neck Rd. and Lloyd Harbor Rd. in the village of Lloyd Harbor in Huntington now occupies the site of Fort Franklin, named for Royal Governor William Franklin (1731–1813), Benjamin's son. The fort was situated on a bluff on the west side of Lloyd's Neck overlooking Long Island Sound and the entrance to Oyster Bay. Fort Golgotha is at the corner of Nassau Road and Main Street in Huntington.

★ On Monday evening, April 20, 1778, two row galleys and an armed vessel crossed from Connecticut to Lloyd's Neck where a party of Loyalists were cutting wood. The militiamen captured 18 Loyalists the next morning and brought them back to Connecticut.[335]

★ A number of well-manned whaleboats crossed from Connecticut to Lloyd's Neck in convoy with the galley *Wild Cat* and a little sloop, formerly the *Raven*'s tender on Wednesday, June 24, 1778. They came to harass his Majesty's woodcutters. The militiamen captured a boat and took it out of the harbor but were pursued and attacked by a number of boats from the ships. The *Wild Cat*, *Raven*'s tender, and the wood boat were taken along with some of the whaleboats. The Loyalists killed two and captured 30 prisoners without any losses.[336]

★ Three or four whaleboats attempted to land at Lloyd's Neck on Saturday, June 27, 1778 to attack the woodcutters. A detachment of De Lancey's brigade manned some boats and cut off the raiders. They also allegedly cut off and secured two armed brigs which were to cover the whaleboats.[337]

★ A privateer sloop from Connecticut captured a sloop with some provisions and a boat loaded with wood at Lloyd's Neck on Wednesday, September 2, 1778.[338]

★ Major Grey, of Colonel Return Jonathan Meigs's (1740–1823) regiment, killed three Connecticut Loyalists and captured 15 others at Lloyd's Neck before September 3, 1778. As a result of all the raids at Lloyd's Neck, General Henry Clinton (1730–1795) ordered the 3rd battalion there in the fall of 1778 to protect the woodcutters.[339]

★ Major Benjamin Tallmadge (1754–1835), son of the Presbyterian minister at Setauket, embarked with 130 men at Shippan Point (now the location of the Stamford Yacht Club off Ocean Drive West in Stamford, Connecticut) at 8 PM and crossed Long Island Sound to raid Lloyd's Neck on Sunday, September 5, 1779. They landed at 10 PM and proceeded in different divisions to surprise 500 Loyalist woodcutters, based at Fort Franklin, a small stockade there. They attacked so suddenly and unexpectedly that they succeeded in capturing almost the whole party. Only a few escaped into the bushes and began firing, alarming the garrison and preventing any attempt to attack the out-posts and guards of the fort. The dragoons destroyed all the boats they could find, as well as the Loyalists' huts, before returning to their boats with their prisoners. They embarked and landed safely in Connecticut before sunrise the next morning, without losing a single man.[340]

★ A party crossed Long Island Sound a few nights before Monday, September 14, 1779. They plundered near Lloyd's Neck and captured 13 prisoners and some plunder. One of the prisoners was a Mr. Glover, the person who headed the party that captured Brigadier General Gold Sellick Silliman (1732–1790) and his son.[341]

★ Captain David Ives and a party of 22 Associated Loyalists boarded an unarmed schooner at City Island and went to Lloyd's Neck in company with two other vessels armed with swivels. They were attacked by four whaleboats full of men from Stamford, Connecticut on Saturday, March 31, 1781. Captain Ives engaged the whaleboats and beat them off only with muskets, even though the Whigs had captured the armed vessels and turned the swivels against Captain Ives's party.

Two Whigs were seen to fall overboard in the midst of the firing. Three others appeared to be disabled and two of the boats which were shot through in several places and spattered with blood later drifted to shore. One of them had a dead man, four muskets, and several coats in it.

Captain Church, who commanded the schooner, was forced to run his schooner on the Long Island shore during the contest. The Whigs landed a party to annoy the Loyalists but were driven off by the militia there. The body of another man was found on the shore the following morning. He was thought to have been killed in this engagement.[342]

★ General George Washington (1732–1799) gave Major Benjamin Tallmadge command of two companies of light infantry (dismounted dragoons) and a body of horse in the summer of 1780. Major Tallmadge moved his troops to New Canaan, or North Stamford, Connecticut to observe the enemy either on the lines or across the Sound on Long Island. General Samuel Holden Parsons (1737–1789) requested his aid to capture Fort Franklin on Lloyd's Neck, opposite Stamford. General Parsons had a very select detachment of about 700 men from the Connecticut line and sent a refugee to gain the needed intelligence and directed him to meet him at a given place at an appointed time.

General Parsons proposed that Major Tallmadge take command of the expedition but Tallmadge, suspicious of the character of Parsons's agent, declined the command but offered to take his detachment under Parsons's orders. This put an end to the expedition. The officers later learned that a large body of the Lloyd's Neck garrison was stationed at the landing place on the night they were to cross.[343]

★ A Congressional fleet consisting of a large sloop of war, five brigs and about five whaleboats, all fully loaded with infantry, left Fairfield, Connecticut and joined a detachment of three French ships from the fleet of Admiral Louis, Comte de Barras (d. ca. 1800) out of Newport, Rhode Island. The ships had a battalion of French infantry on board. The Congressional fleet landed their troops on the unguarded beach on the north shore of Lloyd's Neck, at 8 AM on July 12, 1781. The infantry, with some rangers on the flanks of the column, took a logging road through the woods, guided by Heathcote Muirson (ca. 1755–1781) a veteran of many similar raids on Long Island. Muirson had scouted the enemy works a few days earlier and found that the large, well-fortified redoubt mounted only two long 12-pounders which faced out over Oyster Bay. The Loyalist camp extended from the south side of the fort to the causeway connecting the Neck to the mainland. A large parade ground on the land side of the fort extended half a mile eastward. The fort had an opening with no gate in the southeast corner for wagons to pass through and a picket guard on the eastern end of the Neck overlooking Huntington Bay. However there were no guards along the intervening shoreline.

The fleet returned into Long Island Sound to watch for enemy shipping. One of the French frigates blockaded Huntington Harbor and bombarded (see Photo NY-3, NY-4) the Loyalist fleet in Lloyd Harbor while the large Continental sloop of war went to Oyster Bay to blockade that port and to bombard the fort. The infantry followed the logging road for about a mile before turning into the woods for another mile. They planned a "hit and run" assault against the undefended side of the fort and brought no artillery. When they got to the edge of the woods, they displayed into a line formation on the east side of the parade ground.

The Continental sloop of war sailed within range of the fort and began to cannonade it at 11 AM. The gunners on the west parapet returned fire and were quickly supported by running fire from Captain Thomas's 10-gun brig *Restoration*, a Loyalist privateer anchored just below the fort. Meanwhile, the French 40-gun frigate in Huntington Bay fired a broadside at the Loyalist vessels in the Lloyd Harbor inlet. These included a large, unarmed schooner commanded by Captain Church, the one swivel gun whaleboats *Henry Clinton* and *Association* and one or two small coasters which were being loaded with firewood. A shore battery of two long 12-pounder deck guns, which had been landed from a British warship, unexpectedly returned fire from an earthwork dug the day before on the east end of the Neck, overlooking the mouth of Lloyd Harbor.

All the Loyalist vessels moved as quickly as they could toward the head of Lloyd Harbor to get out of cannon shot. The French ship held her position in Huntington Bay and continued a running fire against the shore battery and the inlet.

About 600 to 700 Loyalists assembled on the parade ground outside the fort while messengers galloped on horseback to call out all available reinforcements from the nearby towns of Huntington and Oyster Bay. Major Benjamin Tallmadge's allied force of about 450 men marched out onto the parade and halted about 400 yards from the fort, in full view of the Loyalists.

Both sides advanced across the parade ground in a line formation until they came within effective musket range of each other. They then halted, less than 150 yards apart, and began to fire at each other in the hot, mid-day sun. When it became evident that the smaller attacking force was not going to route or capture the Loyalist militia, the attackers began to destroy the large number of unprotected huts on the south side of the fort.

While Tallmadge's main force attacked the Loyalist militia to keep them in their position against the outer defenses of the fort, Heathcote Muirson went to the left flank to scout ahead and to guide a French detail to the Loyalist camp. Some of the French troops headed toward the high hill at the south end of the parade with some combustibles. They marched uphill across about 200 yards of open ground covered with tree stumps and low bushes to reach the huts along the main road on the far side of the hill.

The Loyalists perceived this flanking movement by the French as an attempt to place artillery on the hill. This would give them a good field of fire into the fort. The Loyalist gunners hurried to the east parapet of the fort to load and fire the two 12-pounders covering the open ground. A brisk cannonade raked the French position with grape shot. Heathcote Muirson's arm was severed at the shoulder. The French gathered their casualties and retreated east toward the woods where they set up a field hospital on the edge of the parade ground.

The Loyalist artillery dashed any hopes of capturing the fort. The French regrouped and joined the main line which retreated slowly and in good order. The Loyalist militia did not pursue the attackers who consisted mostly of regular army troops. The first Loyalist reinforcements of about 50 mounted men from Oyster Bay and Huntington began to arrive and deployed along the West Neck road to protect the southern approach to the fort. A company of 50 Oyster Bay militiamen joined them, but no other attack occurred. Major Tallmadge's troops disappeared into the woods and headed to the beach to re-embark under the protection of a rear guard. They took evasive courses back to the Connecticut shore and the French returned to Newport, Rhode Island. The Loyalists patroled the battlefield and found "a number of surgeon's instruments, a great quantity of lint, bandages, etc., a bayonet, sword, and a very large quantity of port-fire and other materials for burning our houses; also, some few fragments of coats and shirts; and the grass besmeared with blood."[344]

The Loyalists from Lloyd's Neck attacked Middlesex, Connecticut, two weeks later in retaliation for the raid against Fort Franklin. The whaleboat war across Long Island Sound continued for another two years.[345]

South Bay (May 29, 1778)

> South Bay is on the south side of Long Island east of Patchogue.

★ A party of Whigs landed on Long Island about 4 AM Friday, May 29, 1778 and came to within 2 miles of South Bay. They surprised three sloops while the crews were asleep and carried them off to Connecticut.[346]

Long Island Sound (Aug. 26, 1776; Nov. 29, 1776; Dec. 6, 1776; Dec. 20, 1776; Aug. 10, 1779; May 13, 1781)

> Long Island Sound is the body of water that separates Long Island from Connecticut.

★ Captain George Talbot sent an armed barge from the HMS *Niger* in shore about 3 AM on Monday, August 26, 1776 to pursue a Whig sloop in Long Island Sound near Killing, Long Island. The sloop ran ashore and the Whigs fired at the barge from the shore.[347]

★ Lieutenant William Quarme, of the HM Brig *Halifax*, sent his boats, manned and armed, to Horseneck, at 8 AM on Friday, November 29, 1776. They took four head of cattle before a band of Rebels came down to the shore and fired several shots at the boats. The *Halifax* weighed anchor at 10 AM and headed for Killing.[348]

★ Lieutenant Quarme saw a sloop on the Connecticut shore at 8 AM on Friday, December 6, 1776. He sent his tender to chase it. He dispatched his armed boats at noon to join the tender in the chase. The Rebels fired at the boats from the shore. The boats ran the sloop on shore and returned to the HM Brig *Halifax* at 4 PM which then went to Huntington Bay at the end of the day.[349]

★ HM Brig *Halifax* weighed anchor at 7 AM on Friday, December 20, 1776, and sailed between the Norwalk Islands and the mainland. A party of Rebels came down behind the rocks and fired muskets at her. The *Halifax* fired several shots from her 4-pounders at them.[350]

★ Captain Nathan Post (1748–1803) of the *Revenge* brought the 14-gun privateer sloop *Mosquito* (*Musqueto*) into port at New London, Connecticut on Tuesday morning, August 10, 1779. The vessel was captured on the south side of Long Island.[351]

★ A party of Whigs from Horseneck (Greenwich, Connecticut) in several whaleboats were intercepted around Sunday, May 13, 1781 as they crossed to Long Island. Thirty-nine were captured.[352]

Oak Neck (Sept. 8, 1778)

> Oak Neck is west of Lloyd's Neck.

★ A number of armed Whigs boarded 20 whaleboats at Norwalk, Connecticut and landed at Oak Neck at Huntington, Long Island on Tuesday September 8, 1778. They attacked the house of the widow Chichester where 25 Loyalists were quartered. The Loyalists made some resistance but were soon overpowered. Two of them were killed, one badly wounded and 16 made prisoners. The rest escaped.[353]

Fire Island (Oct. 27, 1778; Aug. 16, 1781)

> Fire Island is a long barrier island off the south coast of Long Island.

★ Two whaleboats, with about 10 men in each, attacked a small schooner with three men, four swivel guns (see Photo NY-9) and a cohorn on Tuesday afternoon, October 27, 1778. The engagement occurred on the south side of Long Island at a place called the Fire Place. The boats approached, intending to board the schooner. When they got within about 20 yards, they received the fire of the cohorn that forced them to sheer off. People on shore observing the action saw most of the oars drop. Both sides fought well. The boats had nine men killed and several wounded and were forced to return to shore.[354]

★ The 14-gun HM sloop of war *Swallow* and the 10-gun *Venus*, a Whig prize taken by the *Swallow* and in company with her, were driven ashore on Fire Island, on the south side of Long Island on Thursday, August 16, 1781 by four Whig privateers. Both vessels were burned. Captain Thomas Wells 3rd (1738–1790) of the *Swallow* had dispatches from Sir George Brydges Rodney (1718–1792) to Admiral Thomas Graves (1725–1802). Everybody got safely ashore on Long Island.

★ A Whig privateer took the HM armed brig *Dispatch* as she headed out to sea to join the British fleet. She was brought to New London, Connecticut.[355]

Fort Salonga
Fort Slongo (Oct. 3, 1781)
Treadwell's Neck (Threadwell's)
Tredwell's or Treadwell's Farm (June 16, 1779)

> Some accounts erroneously date the Fort Slongo event October 10, 1781.
> Fort Slongo was a strong earth and wood post at Treadwell's Neck, high on the bluffs overlooking Long Island Sound between Huntington and Smithtown. It was built by a party of about 150 Loyalist woodcutters. The stockade was surrounded by a ditch and an abatis. It was named in honor of a British officer. Only vague traces of the fort remain on private property in the town of Fort Salonga.

★ Major Jesse Brush (1737–1790) and a party of Whigs went to Tredwell's or Treadwell's Farm on Long Island several days before June 23, 1779, probably on Wednesday, June 16. They captured Justice John Hewlett and Captain Youngs. The Loyalists retaliated by going over to Greenwich, Connecticut and capturing 13 prisoners, 48 cattle and 4 horses. The militia guard captured a whaleboat with three men on board.[356]

★ General George Washington (1732–1799) and the Allied forces were besieging the main British Army at Yorktown, Virginia, in early October 1781. Concerned that the English troops in New York City and Long Island might march south to Yorktown, Washington left a small force to distract them. Major Benjamin Tallmadge (1754–1835), his chief of intelligence, planned an attack on Fort Slongo, now called Fort Salonga. The fort housed a corps of dragoons that patrolled the north shore of Long

Island and stored cordwood for the British in New York City. The raid was partly in retaliation for Major General Benedict Arnold's (1741–1801) expedition against New London and Groton, Connecticut in September 1781 in which more than 70 soldiers were massacred after surrendering.

Major Lemuel Trescott (1751–1826) led a detachment of more than 100 cavalry and infantry from Major General William Heath's (1737–1814) army. They boarded a small fleet of whaleboats at 9 PM on Tuesday, October 2, 1781 and left the Connecticut shore at Norwalk around midnight with oars muffled. They arrived at a beach near Fort Slongo early Wednesday morning, surprised and took the fort. Sergeant Elijah Churchill (1755–1841), of the Second Continental Light Dragoons, who led a raid that captured Fort St. George on the south shore the year before, was chosen to lead the charge.

When the whaleboats landed on the beach at 4 AM, the troops immediately disembarked. Fifty of them scrambled up the bluff to cover the fort from the rear. Sergeant Churchill, aware that his men were outnumbered, prepared to attack from the front with his company. He knew the layout of the stockade and the position of every sentry and depended on surprise.

Sergeant Churchill and 10 men started up the hill early Wednesday morning watching the guard to make sure he didn't sound an alarm. When the sentry stopped pacing and peered down the hill, Churchill dashed toward him. The guard fired, ran into the stockade and tried to lock the gate, but Churchill and his men forced themselves against it and entered the fort.

The British and Loyalists in the fort grabbed their weapons to defend themselves. Some of them scaled the walls and ran into the woods. The attackers killed two, mortally wounded two others and captured two captains, a lieutenant and 18 privates. They destroyed two double fortified iron 4-pounders and took Fort Slongo's colors, one brass 3-pounder, 70 stand of arms, a quantity of ammunition and British goods, and clothing, with only one man wounded. Before they sailed back to Connecticut, the attackers set fire to the blockhouse and the cordwood.[357]

Badge of Military Merit

On Saturday, May 3, 1783, Sergeant Churchill was awarded the Badge of Military Merit (see Photo NY-32), the first ever awarded to an enlisted man in the Continental Army. The design was a purple heart embroidered with the word Merit. It is sometimes referred to as the forerunner of the modern Purple Heart medal. While its design resembles the Purple Heart, it is rather more akin to the Medal of Honor in its importance. Only three such awards are known to have been given. Sgt. Churchill's badge is on exhibit at the National Purple Heart Hall of Honor (374 Temple Hill Road, New Windsor, New York). The Hall of Honor is adjacent to the New Windsor Cantonment, the last Continental Army encampment of the war.

Sergeant William Brown (1759–1808), of the 5th Connecticut Regiment of the Connecticut Line was also awarded the Badge of Military Merit on May 3, 1783 for the attack on Redoubt #10 at Yorktown, Virginia. His badge, discovered in a Deerfield, New Hampshire barn in the 1920s, is now displayed at the American Independence Museum in Exeter, New Hampshire.[358]

Sergeant Daniel Bissell (1754–1824), of the 2nd Connecticut Regiment of the Connecticut Line, received the badge on Tuesday, June 10, 1783 for his work as a spy. He joined the British Army for 13 months and served in the British Infantry Corps under Benedict Arnold (1741–1801). When he returned to the Continental Lines, he was

Photo NY-32. Replica of the Badge of Military Merit. While it appears as the ancestor of the modern Purple Heart, it is more akin to the Medal of Honor.

arrested, court-martialed, and sentenced to death. General George Washington (1732–1799) verified his story and saved him from execution. Sergeant Bissell furnished valuable information along with detailed maps he drew of the enemy's positions. His badge was lost in a house fire in 1813.[359]

Cow Neck (June 24, 1779; June 30, 1779; Aug. 23, 1779; June 30, 1781; Sept. 29, 1782; Oct. 24, 1782; Dec. 2, 1782)

Cow Neck is on the western shore of Hempstead Harbor.

★ A party of about 30 people from Connecticut crossed Long Island Sound in three whaleboats on Thursday night, June 24, 1779. They went to Cow Neck to plunder the house of Mr. Stephen Thorne (1717–1800), a Loyalist. They took many valuable articles. Some of the men also surrounded the house of his son, Mr. Edward Thorne (1747–1820), and ransacked it. Neither of these men were home that evening, preventing them from being taken prisoners.

The Whigs found Captain Lewis McDonald in Mr. Edward Thorne's house. Captain McDonald was banished by the Bedford legislature in Westchester county. The Whigs robbed him of his valuables, broke open his chest and took about 70 livres in gold, silver and York currency. They also took the most valuable part of his clothing but refused to take £400 in Continental currency.[360]

★ Major General Robert Howe (1732–1786) discovered that the enemy were advancing toward him at dawn on Friday, July 30, 1779. He prepared to charge them. It turned out to be Lieutenant Colonel Andreas Emmerich's (1737–1809) corps. Captain

Charles Pope's (1748–1803) infantry led the attack with such vigor that he captured half of Emmerich's corps in a short time. When he discovered a large body of infantry which emerged from behind a stone wall, he was obliged to retreat. The regiment of jaegers pushed him so hard he had to leave all his prisoners, except for three men and four horses, behind. He left one man and three horses and one in the woods as his horse gave out. The Hessians, numbering about 500 intended to cut off his retreat. The Continentals left six men dead on the field and a great number of wounded.[361]

★ A party of about 50 Whigs under Aspinwall Cornell (ca. 1750–ca. 1825) landed in seven whaleboats at Mitchell's Landing on the west side of Cow Neck. They intended to capture Colonel Cornelius Ludlow (1729–1812) and Judge George Duncan Ludlow (1734–1808) to exchange them for Whig prisoners of equal rank. However they failed to capture them, as Colonel Ludlow was at Lloyd's Neck and Judge Ludlow took the precaution of sleeping away from home. Some people said he escaped through the scuttle to the roof and hid behind a chimney. The raiders proceeded to plunder their houses at Hempstead Plains between 12 and 2 on Monday morning, August 23, 1779. They then escaped with their booty. They seized horses and rode them off the road to avoid detection, knocking down fences and riding across lots.[362]

★ Connecticut Governor Jonathan Trumbull (1710–1785) ordered Major Fitch and 40 men to Cow Neck on Saturday night, June 30, 1781. They landed at the foot of Cow Neck and half the party marched 4 miles inland to the house of Justice Daniel Kissam (1739–1812). They intended to capture Justice Kissam and his second born son; but, as they were not home at the time, they took Major John Kissam (1748–1828), of the Queens county militia, prisoner along with his son, his younger brother, Benjamin T. Kissam (1728–1782), his brother-in-law, Dr. Benjamin Tredwell (1735–1830), and a neighbor, Thomas Pearsall (1735–1807). They took their prisoners to Stamford, Connecticut and thence to Wethersfield, where they were kept on parole until exchanged the following October. Major Fitch did not allow his men to go into the room where Mrs. Townsend, an old lady and Justice Kissam's mother, was in bed. They took some plunder and a guard, Alexander Haines, whom they found sleeping under a tree near where they landed.[363]

★ A party of Connecticut Loyalists landed at Cow Neck in a whaleboat on Sunday evening, September 29, 1782. They went to James Hewlett's house to rob him. Hewlett suspected them to be robbers and called for his firelock. They then forced the windows and demanded his money. He said he had none, but his wife asked how much they wanted. They told her they wanted £100. Mr. Hewlett then went down cellar with a light in his hand, followed by the Loyalists. He took a horn from under a hogshead, which contained 190 odd guineas and began to count out the £100 which they had demanded. The Loyalists, seeing the money, told him that because he had made some resistance at first, they would take all he had. Mr. Hewlett gave them another horn which contained about 40 guineas and then gave them a number of dollars. As they left the house, they soon came to the conclusion that if he had so many guineas, he most likely had some other money, probably gold; so they went back and demanded the remainder. Mr. Hewlett gave them another horn containing 32 half joes. The Loyalists also took his plate and clothing all worth about $400.

The Loyalists also planned to rob Mr. Hewlett's brother's house but apparently did not. Some of the inhabitants suspected where they had landed and captured their boat and keeper. The Loyalists soon learned of this and headed to Butler's Creek at Oyster Bay where they seized a boat and escaped to the mainland with the loss of only one of their party, Richard Barrick (1763–1784), who was taken to New York for trial. He remained in jail for three weeks when he broke out and returned to Greenwich, Connecticut. He was re-captured for the same crime and taken back to New-York. He broke out of jail a second time and returned to Greenwich again. Richard Barrick, was hanged at Cambridge, Massachusetts on November 18, 1784 for highway robbery.[364]

★ About 20 Whigs, under the command of Captain Silvanus Martin, Sr. (1727–1782), of Massachusetts, crossed Long Island Sound in two whaleboats, with muffled oars. They landed at Thorne's dock near Cow Neck on Thursday evening, October 24, 1782. They proceeded to James Burr's store in Manhasset Valley. As Burr had been robbed once before, he slept in the store with his musket loaded. As soon as the Whigs demanded admittance, Burr fired. The robbers fired diagonally through the front corners of the store and struck Burr who went to the bedside, told his little brother he was a dead man, and fell to the floor. Unable to force open the door, the robbers ripped off the boards and entered through the side of the store. They loaded themselves with everything valuable.

As they returned, they went around the corner of John Burtis's blacksmith shop. David Jervis, an apprentice boy, fired on them from the second story, one after another. Mr. Burtis loaded the weapons as his wife, Molly, handed him the powder. He wounded several men before Captain Martin arrived, staggering under an enormous load of goods. David fired buckshot in the center of Captain Martin's forehead and his breast was tattooed with shot. Captain Martin threw down his carbine and stumbled up the hill, dropping his load along the way. He fell down dead at the summit.

The firing alarmed the neighbors, who had assembled in great numbers before dawn. Someone was sent to get Major John Kissam (1748–1828). When Major Kissam arrived, he examined Captain Martin's pocket-book and found a list of his crew and a captain's commission from the State of Massachusetts, authorizing him "to *cruise* against the enemies of the United States," but not to go on land.

Captain Martin's clothes, shoes with silver buckles, and watch, together with the guns dropped in the flight, were given to David Jervis who was also presented with a pair of new pistols as a reward for his brave deeds. The Whigs carried off three of their party who were badly wounded. They escaped to their boats.[365]

★ A number of whaleboats from Stamford, Connecticut crossed Long Island Sound on Monday night, December 2, 1782. They landed at the Two Brothers and took five boats from Great Neck and Cow Neck loaded with produce for market. They ransomed some of it and took the rest with them.[366]

Cow Bay (Nov. 27, 1780; Nov. 15, 1780)

★ Captain Elisha Elderkin (1754–1822)(?), commissioned by Governor Jonathan Trumbull (1710–1785) as commander of armed whaleboats, captured a 35-ton British sloop with its cargo in Cow Bay on Monday, November 27, 1780.[367]

★ Captain Johann von Ewald (1744–1813) received news about noon on Wednesday, November 15, 1780 that about 100 Whigs had just landed at Cow Bay. Since this bay belonged to his district, he hurried there followed by the Company of Lieutenant Colonel Ludwig Johann Adolph von Wurmb (d. 1813). The Whigs plundered a few houses and were already returning and were out of rifle range when the Hessians arrived. The Hessians remained in the area until before daybreak the following day because the people there believed the Whigs would return during the night.[368]

Hog Neck (Feb. 1, 1779)

Hog Neck is on the eastern part of Long Island, about 2 miles south of Southold.

★ A brig (the 16-gun *Middleton*) and two sloops (one with 14 guns, the other with 10) were seen heading for Sag Harbor about daybreak on Sunday, February 1, 1779. They came within range of the King's armed vessel *Neptune* lying in the harbor between 8 and 9 AM. The *Neptune* fired three shots across their bow. Their only response was to hoist the Continental colors. They headed toward the Long Island shore until they came within range of the guns on shore which fired a few 12-pound shots at them. They then headed out of the harbor toward the end of Hog Neck. Both sides exchanged long shots for some time until the *Middleton* seemed to be aground or having met with some accident. A 12-pounder was moved down to the end of Long Wharf which was nearly level with the water. This deterred the two sloops from going to the aid of the *Middleton*.

Meanwhile Major Charles Cochrane (1749–1781), of the British Legion, crossed over to Hog Neck with his infantry and their 3-pounder. The *Middleton* struck her colors and launched her five whaleboats. All but three of the crew escaped and the sloops immediately left the bay. The Loyalists had only one casualty, a corporal wounded by grape shot. This is probably the only instance of a vessel of 16 6-pounders and 100 men being taken by a single 3-pounder on shore, even though her broadside fired on the troops the whole time.[369]

Eastern end of Long Island (May 17, 1779; Nov. 20, 1779)

★ Captain Daniel Scovel or Scovil (1718–?), in a privateer brig from the Connecticut River, was captured by a British privateer near the east end of Long Island a few days before May 17, 1779. The two privateers engaged in a severe action that lasted about an hour and a half before Captain Scovel struck his colors. The brig and her crew were taken to New York.[370]

★ A party of about 20 volunteers, commanded by Captain Thomas Hawley (1734–1813), of Stratford, Connecticut, crossed Long Island Sound about Saturday, November 20, 1779. They captured Judge Thomas Jones, one of the judges of the Supreme Court.[371]

Islip (June 18, 1779)

Islip is in Suffolk County on the south side of Long Island.

★ Morris Simmons (d. 1779), a Loyalist from Dutchess County who occupied the farm of a Mr. Strong, was murdered at Islip on Friday, June 18, 1779. The murder was believed to have been committed by three men who first wounded Mr. Simmons in the knee with a pistol and then "beat his brains out with an ax." As he lived alone, his body was not found until the next day.[372]

Hog Island (June 27, 1779)

Hog Island is a small island in Long Island Sound just north of Pelham Bay Park in the Bronx.

★ Two Congressional whaleboats, each with 17 men on board and a brass 2-pounder in the bow and a commission from Governor Jonathan Trumbull (1710–1785) to plunder the inhabitants of Long Island, arrived at Hog Island, on Sunday, June 27, 1779. The Loyalist militiamen were soon alarmed and a party was dispatched in two boats while the others marched along the shore and hid themselves in the brush at the entrance of and along the creek where the Connecticut boats arrived.

No sooner had the whaleboats landed when they spotted the two boats coming into the inlet. They immediately tried to escape; but, finding they were surrounded and fired on from all sides, they surrendered.

A while later, three other men rowed along the shore. Seeing the Loyalists' two boats, they entered the inlet and were also captured by the militiamen. The Loyalists captured 41 prisoners who were brought to New York on Tuesday, June 29.[373]

Mosquito Cove (June 29, 1779)

> Mosquito Cove is on the north of Long Island and north of Hempstead Harbor.

★ A party of Connecticut militiamen landed on Long Island about 1 AM Tuesday, June 29, 1779. They surprised and captured Mr. Abraham Walton, Dr. Brooks and eight other Loyalist inhabitants of Mosquito Cove.[374]

Canoe-Place (Apr. 15, 1781)

> Canoe-Place is on Long Island about 13 miles south of Southold.

★ A party of Loyalists, who lay in ambush, surprised and captured Captain Joseph Pierpoint in an armed whaleboat from New Haven at the Canoe-Place on Sunday, April 15, 1781.

Long Island (Apr. 16, 1781; Aug. 1781; Aug. 5, 1781)

★ A boat left New London, Connecticut on Monday, April 16, 1781 to go to a wreck near Long Island. A party of Loyalists, commanded by a man named Ketcham and piloted by Prosper Brown, in a small row galley with 26 men and thee armed whaleboats with eight men each captured the boat and brought her and her crew to Fisher's Island that night. The prisoners were released the next morning.

★ Captain Adam Hyler (1735–1782) and his companions went 3.5 miles into the country on Long Island and captured Colonel Jerome Lott in August 1781. Lott was noted for his cruelty to Whig prisoners. Captain Hyler and his men also took about £600 in cash and a bag which they expected to contain guineas. As they headed up the Raritan River, they opened bag to divide the contents and found that it contained only half pennies from the church collections. Colonel Lott was forced to ransom his slaves, two of whom had also been taken. He was then released on his parole.[375]

★ Captain Adam Hyler (1735–1782) went from New Brunswick to Long Island in an armed boat on Sunday, August 5, 1781. He marched 3 miles into the country and halted. He captured Captain Jeromus Lot, a lieutenant-colonel of militia, and John Hankins, a captain of a vessel. He then brought his prisoners safely back to New Brunswick.[376]

Gull Islands (Apr. 16, 17, 1781)

> Great Gull Island and Little Gull Island are in Long Island Sound between Plum Island and Fishers Island.

★ A small Loyalist row galley, with 26 men, and three armed whaleboats, with eight men each, commanded by one Ketchum and piloted by Prosper Brown captured a boat from New London, Connecticut at the Gull Islands on Monday April 16, 1781.

★ The following morning, they went to the wreck of the *Culloden* man-of-war near Long Island. They found several small vessels from the mainland. Their crews landed two howitzers and defended themselves for some time. However, when they realized they were not likely to save their ship, they went further down the island where they found a small boat. About this time, they discovered the privateer *Young Cromwell* coming from Newport, Rhode Island. They rowed to her and notified the crew of what had happened. The *Young Cromwell* immediately headed for the wreck. She captured the galley and retook three vessels. The Loyalists hauled their three whaleboats across Long Island at Fort Pond Bay and escaped. They lost one man in the skirmish and took off with a Norwich schooner which they had in their possession, but the *Young Cromwell* pursued them.[377]

Blue Point (before Apr. 22, 1781; Nov. 1, 1781)

> Blue Point is on the southern shore of Long Island on Great South Bay. It is about 7 miles southwest of Fort St. George.

★ A whaleboat and two half-galleys from Philadelphia captured two or three small sloops at Blue Point before April 22, 1781. They were brought to New London, Connecticut.[378]

Captain Elisha Elderkin (1754–1822)(?), of New Haven, with the armed sloop *True Blue* captured the 35-ton schooner *Willing Lass* at Blue Point on Thursday. The *Willing Lass* had a mixed cargo also.[379]

Hempstead (Sept. 6, 1781)

> Hempstead is on the southwest side of Long Island, north of Point Lookout.

★ A frigate drove Captain Elisha Hart's sloop *Restoration*, from Saybrook, Connecticut, aground on a sand bar at Hempstead on the south side of Long Island, about 1.5 miles from land Thursday night, September 6, 1781. The *Restoration* remained there until the next day when two militia companies commanded by a Captain Jones and a Captain Uriah Seaman attacked her. Captain Elisha Hart (1758–1842) captured Captain Jones and eight of his men. The following morning, five captain's companies, three of foot and two of horse, attacked Captain Hart again. They sent a flag demanding him to surrender his vessel and his men. Captain Hart refused to surrender but instead offered to exchange himself and his prisoners for Captain Jones and an equal number of his men and that all his crew be allowed to return home on parole, unmolested. Captain Jones accepted the offer. Captain Hart returned home with his crew the following Wednesday.[380]

Great Neck (before Sept. 21, 1781)

> Great Neck is on the western part of Long Island, opposite Throg's Neck. Port Washington is at the tip of Great Neck.

★ Seven or eight dead bodies of officers and soldiers drifted ashore on Great Neck and three others bodies on the Groton, Connecticut shore prior to September 21, 1781. They were thrown out of Benedict Arnold's (1741–1801) burning fleet. The Crown forces lost 220 men, killed and dead of their wounds, and 70 deserters in their attack on Groton and New London. A total of 61 Crown troops were found buried in Groton.[381]

Stony Brook (Nov. 11, 1781)

Stony Brook is on the north side of Long Island opposite Fairfield, Connecticut and west of Setauket.

★ Major Benjamin Tallmadge (1754–1835) and about 20 Continental soldiers left Fairfield, Connecticut and went to Long Island about Sunday, November 4, 1781 to gather information and destroy some enemy supplies and shipping. They lived for several days on clams dug from the beaches. The enemy were near them on all sides. Shortly after landing, the Continentals marched about 5 miles westward to a place called Craneneck where about 20 or 30 troops were posted, to guard some vessels. The Crown troops learned of their approach and withdrew by water.

Tallmadge and his men waited anxiously for eight days for an opportunity to return to Connecticut. The wind began to abate at 3 AM on Sunday, November 11, 1781 for the first time in eight days. Having learned that the detachment which previously guarded the enemy vessels at Craneneck had returned, Tallmadge set out to attack them before he returned. They arrived a short distance from the enemy by sunrise. Tallmadge, hiding in a thicket, observed their guard on a high hill near the shore. A large schooner, a number of boats, and the remainder of their party were at the foot of the hill. The Continentals had to cross an open field before reaching them, so Tallmadge was apprehensive that they would seek refuge in their boats. He made certain to secure the vessel and ordered his troops to advance quickly without firing on the guard. The enemy immediately got on board their boats. As soon as the Continentals reached the hill, they began a brisk fire on them, which continued until the enemy were out of range. Tallmadge's troops captured one prisoner and saw several killed. They took possession of the vessel they secured, but she was aground. They stripped her completely of all her rigging and set her on fire. They brought the rigging back to Fairfield.[382]

Mattituck (May 15, 1782)

Mattituck is on the northeastern end of Long Island, west of Southold.

★ Major Ayres (d. 1782), with eight men in a whaleboat, made an excursion from Saybrook, Connecticut to Mattituck, Long Island on Wednesday, May 15, 1782. They took two vessels near Wading River and took some goods out of the vessels before going ashore to cook some provisions. As they were cooking under a bank, Captain Nehemiah Marks (1747–1799) and a party of Colonel James De Lancey's (1747–1804) Loyalists suddenly began firing at them. Major Ayres and one or two of his party were killed.[383]

4
WESTERN LONG ISLAND

See the map of New York City and Surroundings.

Gravesend Bay (Apr. 9, 1776; July 2, 1776)

> Gravesend Bay is now known as Jamaica Bay. It is on the southwest end of Long Island.

★ The HMS *Phoenix*, moored in Graves End Bay, fired a 9-pound shot at a party of Congressional troops on shore on Tuesday afternoon, April 9, 1776. She also fired a shot to bring to the sloop *Sukey*. The *Sukey* was headed from Black Point to New York with a cargo of oysters when she was captured.[384]
★ A detachment of Crown troops attempted to land at Long Island, near Gravesend Bay on Tuesday, July 2, 1776. A party of Rebels ambushed them, killed several, and captured four.[385]

July 4, 1776 see **Staten Island.**

New York Harbor/Coney Island (June 8, 1776; Apr. 8, 1781)
Off Coney Island (April 8, 1781)

> Coney Island is at the southwestern tip of Long Island, opposite Richmondtown, Staten Island. It is no longer an island, having been connected to Long Island by landfill.

★ The HMS *Asia* fired three times at two whaleboats full of men as they crossed from Coney Island for Amboy on Saturday noon, June 8, 1776 but without effect.[386]
★ Captain Adam Hyler (1735–1782) and Captain Captain Robert Dickie (1760–1782), each in command of a whaleboat, attacked and captured a sloop from New York off Coney Island on Sunday, April 8, 1781. The crews plundered the vessel and ransomed it for $500 cash.[387]

Flatbush (Aug. 22, 27, 1776; June 14, 1778; June 1781)

> Flatbush is on the western end of Long Island, west of Jamaica and south of Brooklyn. The Nicholas Schenck house was dismantled in 1929 and reconstructed in the Brooklyn Museum of Art.

★ A large body of 8,000 to 9,000 Crown troops landed at Gravesend Bay on Long Island early Thursday morning, August 22, 1776. They "marched across the low, cleared grounds, near the woods at Flat Bush" and came within 3 miles of Continental lines where they halted. Continental riflemen harassed them and scouting parties were sent out. The Continentals on the surrounding heights kept a continual, though irregular, fire on the Crown troops but they were too far away to have any effect. Both sides had some killed and wounded.
★ On Monday, August 26, 1776, a large body of about 4,000 Crown troops troops marched from their main body to their advance posts at Flatbush. That night, the Continentals began to dig entrenchments on the highest hill near Flatbush to command

Western Long Island 159

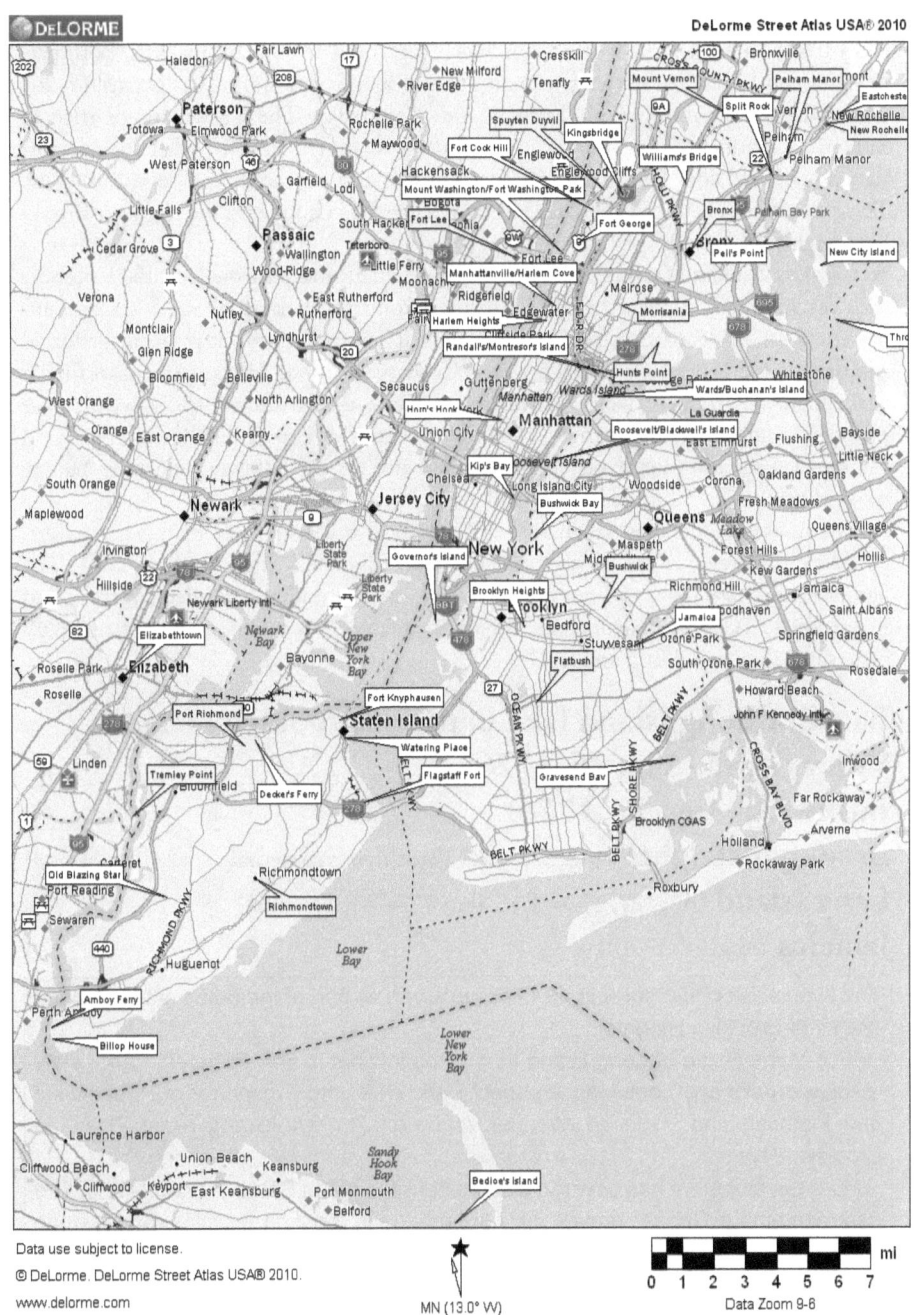

New York City and Surroundings: Map for The Guide to the American Revolutionary War in New York
© *2010 DeLorme (www.delorme.com) Street Atlas USA®*

the town. However, the Crown forces decided to take possession of the hill that night. They began to erect some works from which they fired at the Continentals. Both parties met and began a smart engagement about 4 AM. Severe skirmishes between many detached parties continued all Tuesday and Wednesday. The Crown troops tried to force the Continental lines several times, but were always repulsed with considerable slaughter. Both sides lost many killed, wounded, and captured, and several missing. These skirmishes heralded the Battle of Long Island also known as the Battle of Brooklyn Heights.[388]

★ Captain William Marriner, Lieutenant John Schank and 20 armed militiamen, some with blackened faces, went from Middletown Point to Flatbush about 2 AM on Sunday, June 14, 1778 to capture a few prisoners. They tried to break into mayor David Matthews's (d. 1800) house which was well-secured. An old African American fired a gun which they thought would alarm the people so they withdrew quickly with their prisoners: Major James Moncrieff (1744–1793) and Mr. Theophilus Bache, and David Matthews, Esq. and four slaves. They returned at 6 AM the following morning, having traveled more than 50 miles by land and water.[389]

★ The house of Nicholas Schenck (1732–1810), 3 miles south of Flatbush, was surprised by the crews of two Whig whaleboats one Thursday night in June 1781. The family was eating supper and not prepared to resist. The raiders wounded a man named Bogart (d. 1781) with a bayonet and took his valuables. They then took all the family's plate silver they could find and left.[390]

Battle of Long Island (aka Battle of Brooklyn Heights)
Valley Grove (Aug. 26, 1776)
Bushwick (Aug. 27, 1776)

Brooklyn Heights (Aug. 27, 1776) (Brooklyn is sometimes spelled Brookland)

Long Island (Aug. 27, 1776; Dec. 10, 1777—see **Setauket**)

Jamaica (Aug. 28, 1776)

> The events listed here for August 1776, occurred as part of the Battle of Long Island (Battle of Brooklyn Heights).
> Much of the Battle of Long Island took place in what is now Prospect Park (www.prospectpark.org/) between Prospect Park West and Prospect Park Southwest and Flatbush and Parkside Avenues (subway: 7th Ave./Grand Army Plaza) in Brooklyn, NY.
> Urban development has covered the original sites of the Battle of Long Island. The park contains a Quaker graveyard, gardens, trails, boating facilities, and historic buildings. A semicircular tablet on a boulder near the Grand Army Plaza entrance commemorates the Battle of Long Island.
> The Battle Pass Marker (Flatbush Pass) in Prospect Park (near the back of the zoo) was designed by Frederic Wellington Ruckstull and installed in 1923 at the site of a strategic road during the Battle of Long Island. The granite marker with a bronze eagle also marks the site where General John Sullivan was captured. A boulder at Battle Pass once bore a bronze plaque that noted: "Line of Defense/Aug. 27, 1776/Battle of Long Island/175 Feet South/Site of Valley Grove House/150 Feet North."[391]

The Cortelyou House in Brooklyn (**www.brooklynonline.com/bol/history/stonehouse.html**) was built in 1699 and remained standing until it was demolished in 1897. The reconstruction uses some of the original stones.

The Maryland Monument near Lookout Hill on Third Avenue between 7th and 8th streets marks the burial site of Lord Stirling's Maryland troops who died attacking the Cortelyou house.

Sir William Howe hesitated to attack General George Washington's main army on Brooklyn Heights and began to dig entrenchments for a siege. One of these earthworks was a star fort named Fort Putnam. The fort no longer exists. The site became a park in 1815 and was named for Major General Nathanael Greene. It became Washington Park in 1847 and later renamed Fort Greene Park. Fort Greene Park (**www.fortgreenepark.org/**) is at the intersection of Myrtle and DeKalb avenues and St. Edwards and Cumberland streets in Brooklyn.

Stanford White designed the "Martyrs' Monument" (**www.fortgreenepark.org/pages/prisonship.htm**) in the center of Fort Greene Park which is dedicated to the Continental soldiers who died on British prison ships in Wallabout Bay. Ships like the *Jersey*, originally a 64-gun man-of-war (see Photo NY-33), were virtually floating tombs—crowded, filthy, and full of disease. The deceased were often thrown into shallow graves on the shores of Wallabout Bay. The remains of many were collected early in the 19th century and placed in this monument's crypt, dedicated in 1908 and marked by a 145-foot granite column.

Flatlands was where Flatlands Avenue intersects Kings Highway. A bronze plaque on the lawn of the Flatlands Reformed Church (formerly the Dutch Reformed Church

Photo NY-33. Man-of-war (HMS Victory*)*

> of Flatlands) on Kings Highway, just east of Flatbush Avenue, marks the path of the British advance on the night of August 26, 1776.
> Of the four roads running through the hills toward the Continental positions on Long Island, only the Jamaica–Bedford road was left unguarded. It became the main route of attack by the Crown forces during the Battle of Long Island.

★ General William Howe (1732–1786) had an army of about 32,000 men supported by a powerful fleet of 280 warships and transports off Staten Island under the command of his brother, Admiral Richard Howe (1726–1799). General George Washington (1732–1799) brought most of his army down from Boston in March and April 1776, to oppose him. Congress exerted its utmost efforts to reinforce him by raising Continental regiments in the surrounding states and issuing a general call for the militia. Washington was able to muster a paper strength of roughly 28,500 men, but only about 19,000 were present and fit for duty. The larger part of them were raw recruits, undisciplined and inexperienced in warfare, and militiamen, never to be assuredly relied upon.

Washington decided to defend the territory in the most forward positions and paid the price for his mistake. The geography of the area gave the side possessing naval supremacy an almost insuperable advantage.

The city of New York stood on Manhattan Island, surrounded by the Hudson, Harlem and East Rivers. There was only one connecting link with the mainland, Kingsbridge across the Harlem River at the northern tip of Manhattan. Across the East River on Long Island, Brooklyn Heights stood in a position dominating the southern tip of Manhattan. With the naval forces at their disposal, the Howes could land troops on either Long Island or Manhattan and send warships a considerable distance up either the East or Hudson Rivers.

Washington expected Howe to attack him from the western end of Long Island, so he decided to establish a strong position on Brooklyn Heights opposite the southeastern edge of Manhattan (below the Brooklyn side of today's Brooklyn Bridge). If the British captured Brooklyn Heights, they could aim their artillery at New York City and dominate it just as effectively as the Rebels had done at Dorchester Heights. Washington should have considered the city indefensible and abandoned it to take a position farther upriver. But Congress wanted New York defended. Losing it without a fight would hurt the morale of the colonists.

Washington divided his army between Manhattan and Brooklyn Heights, separating the two parts by a wide stretch of water which the British could control. Dividing the army was dangerous as it could result in gradual destruction, yet failure to occupy Brooklyn Heights would guarantee the loss of New York City. Washington also set up a line of defense along the Heights of Guan, a ridge of hills stretching about 5 miles from Gowanus Bay northeast to the Jamaica Pass.

For all practical purposes, command on Long Island was also divided. Major General Nathanael Greene (1742–1786), to whom Washington first entrusted the command, came down with malaria and was replaced by Major General John Sullivan (1740–1795) on Tuesday, August 20, 1776. Greene had a thorough knowledge of the terrain on Long Island but Sullivan did not. Not completely satisfied with this arrangement, at the last moment, Washington placed Major General Israel Putnam (1718–1790) over Sullivan on the 24th, but Putnam hardly had time to become acquainted with the situation before the British struck.

About 3,500 Continental troops defended the line from Gowanus Bay to the Bedford Pass near where modern Bedford Avenue intersects with Eastern Parkway. They were disposed in fortifications on Brooklyn Heights and in forward positions back of a line of thickly wooded hills that ran across the southern end of the island. Colonel Edward Hand (1744–1802) guarded the Gowanus road with about 550 men. Major General John Sullivan (1740–1795) commanded 1,000 troops with four artillery pieces at the Flatbush Pass over 1.5 miles to their left. Lieutenant Colonel Solomon Wills (1731–1807) guarded the Bedford Pass, a mile to the east, with about 880 men and three guns. Brigadier General Samuel Miles (1740–1805) with about 400 Pennsylvania riflemen from Brigadier General William Alexander's (Earl of Stirling, 1726–1783) brigade patrolled toward the Jamaica Pass, 3 miles northeast of Bedford Pass (approximately at the southern end of today's Cemetery of the Evergreens, just above the intersection of Broadway and Jamaica Avenue). Of the four roads running through the hills toward the Continental positions, only the Jamaica–Bedford road was left unguarded.

With the Continentals entrenched on Brooklyn Heights, General Howe did not want to risk either the heavy loss of life which his army suffered taking Bunker Hill or a possible defeat which would have widespread political consequences. At 8 AM on Thursday, August 22, 1776, General Howe sent a force of 4,000 men under General Henry Clinton (1730–1795) and General Charles Cornwallis (1738–1805) to Denyse Point (now occupied by Fort Hamilton; the Verazano Narrows Bridge connects Brooklyn with Staten Island at this point). The landing boats returned across the Narrows to Staten Island for more troops. These men landed at Gravesend Bay on the southwestern tip of Long Island. By noon, a force of almost 15,000 men, mostly Hessians, (half of Howe's army and twice the size of Washington's army), 40 cannon, and the horses of the dragoons had arrived on Long Island.

Three days later, General Leopold von Heister (1707–1777) landed to the right (southeast) of the previous troops with two brigades of German grenadiers (see Photo NY-34). They traveled 4 miles inland to Flatbush to join General Cornwallis's 10 light infantry battalions and Major General Count Karl Emil Kurt von Donop's (1740–1777) jaegers and grenadiers.

Photo NY-34. German grenadiers

Brigadier General James Grant (1720–1806) led the left wing up the coast. Some Continental scouting parties spotted the British advance about midnight on Monday, August 26 and sounded the alarm. About 3,000 men turned out, mostly Marylanders and Pennsylvanians, to attack them.

General Leopold von Heister (1707–1777) made the second thrust in the center, along the Flatbush Road, with the Hessians and Scots. These two advances were decoys to occupy the Continentals while General William Howe's (1732–1786) main force of about 14,000 troops on the right wing maneuvered behind them. General Howe left his campfires burning to deceive the Continentals. The Crown forces moved north and east, following Kings Highway to the New Lots. They flanked the outer line of defenses and turned west to strike the Continental positions at the Bedford and Battle Passes and on the Gowanus.

Meanwhile, General Henry Clinton's (1730–1795) corps of light infantry advanced during the night to cut any trees that blocked the way. They used saws rather than axes to keep the noise to a minimum. They also arrested any civilians they encountered and held them until after the battle.

General Howe led the main column which set out by 9 PM and extended about 2 miles. Each segment had its own flankers and skirmishing parties to protect against surprise attacks. He had allotted 12 hours to travel 8 miles—5 miles to the Jamaica Pass and 3 more to Bedford Village. The troops found their route unguarded and feared the Congressional forces had been withdrawn and moved to some other point where they might inflict greater casualties.

A British foraging party encountered a party of Colonel Edward Hand's (1744–1802) Pennsylvania Regiment in a watermelon patch near the Red Lion Inn (near Martense Lane, just below where 39th Street meets Fifth Avenue) about 10 PM.

Colonel Samuel John Atlee's (1739–1786) battalion took their post in an orchard and behind a barn and maintained "a very severe fire for a considerable time, till they were nearly surrounding him." They then retreated to the woods. An officer in Colonel Atlee's battalion (which joined forces with Colonel Edward Hand's Pennsylvania Regiment) recorded:

> Yesterday (Monday) about 120 of our men went as a guard to a place on Long Island called Red Lion; about eleven at night the sentries described two men coming up a water-melon patch, upon which our men fired on them. The enemy then retreated, and about one o'clock advanced with 200 or 300 men, and endeavored to surround our guard, but they being watchful, gave them two or three fires, and retreated to alarm the remainder of the battalion, except one lieutenant and about fifteen men who have not been heard of as yet. About four o'clock this morning, the alarm was given by beating to arms, when the remainder of our battalions, went to the place our men retreated from. About a quarter of a mile this side we saw the enemy, when we got into the woods (our battalion being the advanced guard) amidst the incessant fire of their field-pieces loaded with grape-shot, which continued till ten o'clock.[392]

By dawn, this encounter had become a major firefight that stretched across a quarter mile front (from between 38th and 39th Streets from near Second to about Fifth Avenues). General Grant used up his supply of ammunition and needed to request an emergency resupply.

The light infantry reached the bridge without resistance and found the route to the Jamaica Road open. The main column began to arrive at a small settlement around the Rising Sun Tavern about midnight. (The tavern was at the intersection of Broadway and Jamaica Avenue.) They waited in the woods for the rest of the troops to arrive. At 2 AM, they fixed bayonets and surrounded the houses in the settlement to prevent the occupants from sounding the alarm. Generals Howe, Clinton, Charles Cornwallis (1738–1805), and Lord Hugh Percy (1742–1817) broke into the tavern with a party of soldiers and forced the tavern owner to show them the route over the Rockaway Path around the Jamaica Pass or be shot in the head. That location was only lightly guarded.[393]

After the various Crown units had occupied the Bushwick hills, they had their breakfast and continued on to Bedford where they started arriving about 5:30 AM to await the signal guns as they planned to attack in unison at 9 AM. Colonel Stephen Kemble (1740–1829), in General Clinton's column, summarized the action of the next few hours:

> About a mile before we came to Bedford we saw the Rebels on our Left. The Light Infantry [were] ordered to attack them which they did with success and drove them every way; the Grenadiers continued the road to Brooklyn with the general at their head to cut off the Enemy's Retreat from Brookland Heights which was happily executed. [In the center] Lieut.-Gen. de Heister attacked from Flatbush at the same time & [on the British left] Major-Gen. Grant with the Fourth & Sixth Brigade from the Heights of the Narrows [moving up from Fort Hamilton] by which measure the Rebels were cut off from all Retreat and cooped up in the woods to the Right of the road from Brooklyn to Flatlands. Major-Gen. Grant had attacked early in the morning, but the Enemy under Brigadier-General Lord Stirling & Major-Gen. Sullivan being strongly posted in the woods could not proceed far. The action between them and part of the Main body continued until late in the afternoon.

The Continental forces were surrounded by Generals Grant and von Heister advancing from the south and General Clinton cutting off their avenue of retreat on the east and north.[394]

Howe stopped for breakfast before resuming his march west and behind the Continental left. Brigadier General James Grant (1720–1806) had a brief skirmish with the lower end of the Continental right (near modern Greenwood Cemetery) around 7:30 AM. German troops distracted the Continental center at Flatbush. The firing of two British cannon at Bedford (near the present intersection of Nostrand Avenue and Fulton Street) about 9 AM gave the signal for a general assault.

Howe's column smashed the rear of the Continental left, crumpling the entire Continental position. The Germans broke through the center of the Continental line (at what is now called Battle Pass on East Drive in Prospect Park). Stirling's troops were arrayed in open order (see Photo NY-35), their colors flying about 8 AM. Stirling reminded his troops that Brigadier General James Grant (1720–1806), a member of Parliament, boasted in the House of Commons (February 2, 1775) that the Continentals would not fight and that he could march from one end of the American continent to the other with 5,000 men. General Alexander's (Lord Stirling) troops, who numbered about 1,600 after the arrival of reinforcements, stood firm for four hours, enduring artillery fire and light infantry moving to within 150 yards.

General Grant's 5,000 men, reinforced to 7,000 with the arrival of the 42nd Highlanders who had been with Heister, attacked the Continental right flank along Gowanus Bay. Sullivan and some of his men at the Flatbush Pass tried to fight their way to the rear. Sullivan's artillery fired their three guns on Grant's light infantry battalion that blocked the way. When Grant's light infantry battalion received reinforcements from the Guards, they attacked. They took heavy casualties but captured Sullivan's guns and drove his troops back to face the bayonets of von Donop's jaegers. The retreating forces met light infantrymen, dragoons, and jaegers along the way to the fortified camp. These sporadic encounters inflicted most of the Continental casualties.

Photo NY-35A. Reenactors deploying in open order

Photo NY-35B. Reenactors deployed in closed order

The heaviest fighting occurred near Baker's Tavern (near the intersection of Fulton and Flatbush Avenues). This is where Sullivan and most of his troops were captured. Howe and the Germans had routed the Continental left center by about 11 AM.

The Germans, moving along the ridge from the east, attacked the Maryland and Delaware Regiments. Grant's overwhelming numbers, further reinforced by 2,000 marines, attacked and penetrated the Continental lines where they joined to form a V. General Cornwallis and the 71st Regiment (Fraser's Highlanders) blocked the retreat route, forcing the Continentals across Gowanus Creek—80 yards of water, a swift tide, broad salt marshes on both banks—under fire from musket and artillery fire.

General Alexander led a detachment of 250 Marylanders to attempt to force through the escape route at the stone Cortelyou House (west of Fifth Avenue near 3rd and 8th streets). They attacked the house five times to divert British musket fire, allowing their troops to cross Gowanus Creek west of the house, the only possible escape route to Brooklyn. Many drowned as they fled. British reinforcements stopped Alexander's sixth attack, leaving almost all of his 250 Maryland troops dead.[395]

Retreat

General Howe hoped that the British ships sailing up the East River between Brooklyn and Manhattan would cut off the Continental retreat, but a violent storm prevented the ships from sailing and flooded both camps. Had Howe pushed his advantage immediately he could have carried the heights and destroyed half the Continental Army then and there. If the British could capture Brooklyn Heights on Long Island, they could aim their artillery at New York City and dominate it just as effectively as the Rebels had done at Dorchester Heights overlooking Boston. Instead, Howe halted at nightfall and began to dig trenches signaling his intent to take the heights by "regular approaches" in traditional 18th-century fashion.

General Washington managed to evacuate his forces across the East River (around where the Brooklyn Bridge now stands) and retreated into New York on Manhattan Island on Thursday night, August 29. According to one theory, wind and weather stopped the British warships from entering the river to prevent the escape. According to another, the Continentals had placed impediments in the river that effectively barred their entry. The skill, bravery, and perseverance of Colonel John Glover's (1732–1797) Marblehead Regiment of Massachusetts fishermen, who manned the small fishing boats when the tide was too low for the British fleet to move, made the narrow escape possible. They ferried 10,000 or 12,000 troops across the East River in six hours, losing only three stragglers who stopped to plunder, and five cannon which the matrosses could not haul through the hub-deep mud.

As dawn approached on the morning of August 30, a thick fog hid the movements of Washington's men from view. By seven o'clock, all his men and most of his supplies were safely on the other shore of the East River. His men were exhausted and soaked by the constant rain. They only had pickled pork to eat. Their powder was wet; so they couldn't fire, and their muskets were clogged with mud.

The official British report lists casualties of 89 Continental officers and 1,097 others. Continental strength returns of October 8 show a loss of 1,012 men in the campaign for Long Island. The losses of the Crown forces amounted to only 377. The British lost five officers and 56 men killed, 13 officers and 275 men wounded and missing. The Germans had two men killed, three officers and 23 men wounded.

The defeat crushed Continental morale. Many soldiers thought the war was as good as over and left for home. Others remained behind to plunder. Washington and Greene decided to abandon New York. Greene wanted to burn it to the ground first, as two-thirds of it belonged to Loyalists, but Washington decided against this.

Morale of the British and German troops was high. General Howe knew that Washington could not hold New York and that the Crown forces could take it without losing any more men. General Lord Hugh Percy (1742–1817) thought the campaign would end the war. British ships commanded both the East River and the Hudson River on the other side of New York.

After the Battle of Brooklyn Heights, the two armies faced each other on Manhattan Island for over three weeks. They occasionally shouted good-natured insults across the lines and even exchanged gifts. Major General William Heath (1737–1814) recorded that they were so civil to each other, on their posts, that one day, at a part of the creek where it was practicable, a British sentinel asked an American, who was nearly opposite to him, if he could give him a chew of tobacco. The latter, having in his pocket a piece of a thick twisted roll, sent it across the creek to the British sentinel who, after taking off his bite, sent the remainder back.[396]

Throg's Neck (Aug. 28, 1776; Oct. 12, 1776; Apr. 14, 1781; July 3, 1781; July 22, 1781; July 28, 1781)

City Island (Aug. 27, 1776)

> "Throgs" Neck is an abbreviation of Throckmorton's or Throgmorton's Neck from the name of its first English settler. In the 18th century, it was further corrupted to "Frog's" Neck, or Point. Throg's Neck is a point of land in Westchester County opposite Willett's Pont, Long Island. In 1776, it was nearly an island connected with the mainland by a single road that ran through the marshes. A bridge spanned a mill dam built by Colonel Caleb Heathcote (1666–1721), the first Mayor of the Borough of Westchester. The mill stood until February 1875 when it was accidentally burned.
>
> City Orchard is probably "City Island," then called New City Island and now known simply as City Island. It is east of the Bronx, just below Mill's Creek, or New Rochelle Harbor, which is about 1 mile from the village of that name.

★ The HMS *Brune*, HMS *Niger* and the HM Brig *Halifax* anchored a little above Throg's Point early Tuesday morning, August 27, 1776, the same day as the battle of Long Island. General George Washington (1732–1799) sent Colonel Morris Graham's two companies to prevent their landing to plunder or burn. However, several barges full of men had already landed on New City Island before they arrived. Colonel Graham and his men ferried over to the island immediately on their arrival and skirmished with the enemy who captured one man and 14 head of cattle.[397]

★ The following day, about 11 AM, HMS *Brune* chased a sloop heading toward New York from Great Bay. Lieutenant William Quarme, of the HMS *Halifax,* heard musket fire at noon and supposed the Rebels were firing on the *Brune*. He weighed anchor and went to her assistance but the sloop got away. As the Whigs had fired on the boat from a house and bushes on Throg's Point, the *Halifax* fired several shots at the house.[398]

★ The British landed at Frog's point in Westchester County without any opposition at noon on Saturday, October 12, 1776. The Whigs had posted an officer and 30 men there; but when they saw the troops about to land, they fled without firing a shot. General William Howe (1732–1786) advanced 2 miles into the country and encamped on his chosen ground without any opposition.

Captain William Dansey's company (33rd Regiment of Foot) and another company under his command skirmished with 150 or 200 riflemen at a distance of about 200 yards for more than seven hours at "Frogneck" that day. The riflemen took cover behind a house, a mill, and a wall while the Crown forces had only trees. The riflemen opened fire before they were noticed, whereupon Captain Dansey ordered his men to seek shelter behind trees and rocks. He then asked for volunteers to move closer to the Continental riflemen. The Hessian riflemen maintained fire for more than an hour before they withdrew. A "popping fire" continued between the two parties for some time and several riflemen were knocked down. Sporadic firing between the Light Infantry and the Continental riflemen continued across the water for two or three days. Captain Dansey said his men killed an officer and several men but he had nobody wounded.[399]

The Whigs were much alarmed by the troop movement. They mustered and manned all their works as soon as possible. A body of about 6,000 men marched down toward Harlem, expecting an attack in that area. But they were very surprised when they learned the troops had gone further north.[400]

Western Long Island 169

The Whigs fortified the mill and successfully prevented General Howe's troops from crossing. The troops should have been marched to Harlem Point, at Horn's Hook, where boats would take them to City Orchard (probably "City Island," just below Mill's Creek, or New Rochelle Harbor, which is about 1 mile from the village of that name) and then to Mill's Creek and New Rochelle. However, that plan was overruled because Admiral Richard Howe (1726–1799) thought that it would not be safe for ships to anchor there.

General Howe joined Lieutenant General Wilhelm von Knyphausen (1716–1800) at New Rochelle. Knyphausen had landed at Mill's Creek. It took him two weeks to get to White Plains, about 12 miles away where they engaged the Whigs in a major battle on October 28, 1776.[401]

See also **Pelham Manor.**

★ Captain Jabez Fitch, Jr. (1703–1784) and 112 men skirmished with a detachment of Crown forces at Throg's Neck for two hours on Saturday, April 14, 1781. They killed six and wounded one but lost one man killed and three wounded.[402]

See **Pelham Manor.**

★ Three Continental dragoons pursued some mounted Loyalists on Frog's Neck (Throg's Neck) on Sunday, July 22, 1781. With no avenue of escape, one rode his horse into Long Island Sound and swam his horse over the Sound to Whitestone. Another mounted Loyalist swam his horse over Harlem Creek opposite Harlem.[403]

★ A detachment from Brigadier General David Waterbury's (1722–1801) command had a skirmish with a party of Crown forces at Frog's Neck on Tuesday, July 3, 1781.[404]

★ Colonel Elisha Sheldon's (1740–1805) dragoons went to Frog's Neck and Morrisania on Saturday, July 28, 1781. They brought off more than 200 horned cattle; a considerable number of horses, hogs, and sheep believed to be the property of Colonel James De Lancey (1747–1804) which he had plundered from the inhabitants to fatten and sell to the New York butchers.[405]

Governor's or Nutten Island (Apr. 15, 1776; July 12, 1776; Aug. 28, 1776; Aug. 30, 1776; Aug. 31, 1776; Sept. 1, 1776; Sept. 2, 1776; Sept. 3, 1776; Sept. 5, 1776; Sept. 6, 1776; Sept. 13, 1776; Sept. 14, 1776)

East River (Sept. 13, 14, 15, 1776)

> Governor's Island or Nutten Island is about 0.5 miles off Manhattan's Battery, opposite Brooklyn's Red Hook. The East River runs along the east side of Manhattan.

★ One thousand Rebels took possession of Governor's Island on Monday night, April 15, 1776 and began to fortify it. A regiment went over to Red Hook that same evening and began to fortify that place. The island's fortifications were sufficiently completed to accommodate the mounting of 32-pounders and four 18-pounders by May. General George Washington (1732–1799) wrote to Major General Charles Lee (1731–1782) on May 9: "We have done a great deal of work at this place. In a fortnight more I think the City will be in a very respectable posture of defense. . . . Governor's Island has a large and strong work erected and a Regiment encamped there." The defenses covered almost the entire island by August.[406]

While both sides were flexing their military muscles, the Continental Congress, on Thursday, July 4, 1776, proclaimed the Declaration of Independence, adopted two days earlier. The New York Provincial Convention ratified and adopted the Declaration on July 9. General Washington saw to it that it was read to every unit of his army in the New York area. A large congregation of soldiers and citizens, in a burst of joyous patriotic enthusiasm, pulled down the gilded equestrian statue of King George III that had been erected on Bowling Green six years before. Most of its 4,000 pounds of lead was molded into more than 42,000 bullets for the muskets of Connecticut's troops.

★ On July 12, there was a spirited artillery duel between the British men-of-war *Phoenix* and *Rose* and the Continental batteries located at Governor's Island, the Battery, Red Hook, and Paulus Hook.

★ Two months after the proclamation of the Declaration of Independence, the first Continental submarine attempted an underwater attack against an enemy vessel. The *Turtle*, designed and built by David Bushnell (1742–1824) of Connecticut, was built of oak and shaped like a coconut. Standing on end, it was a piggyback time bomb attached to an auger that was to be screwed into the hull of an enemy vessel. Sergeant Ezra Lee, of the Connecticut line, manually operated the submarine to attack the HMS *Asia* anchored in New York Bay. However, Sergeant Lee could not pierce the *Asia*'s copper sheathing and the bomb was set adrift to explode harmlessly.

★ General Washington evacuated his army from Brooklyn Heights to Manhattan under cover of a dense fog after the Battle of Long Island. The Continentals left a strongly fortified garrison upon Nutten Island, less than a mile from Brookland (Brooklyn) when they evacuated Long Island. The garrison of 2,000 men, 40 pieces of heavy artillery, military stores and an abundance of provisions were trapped on the island which was now dominated by Crown forces at Brookland. However, the Royal army made no attempt to capture the garrison and take its defenders prisoners. During the evening of the 28th, a detachment of the Continental Army took a number of boats from New York to Nutten Island and evacuated the troops, artillery, stores, and provisions without any interference from the Royal army, less than a mile away, and the Royal navy in the bay, a little south of the island.[407]

★ The HMS *Roebuck* began firing upon Congressional forces as they retreated from Governor's Island at 3 PM on Friday, August 30, 1776. The cannonade lasted an hour before the *Roebuck* weighed anchor and turned abreast of the island.

★ The following afternoon, the Congressional troops on Governor's Island fired upon the HMS *Roebuck* which returned fire with several broadsides.[408]

★ The HMS *Roebuck* came under fire again from Governor's Island at 11 AM on Sunday, September 1, 1776. She got under way to anchor close to the battery but the admiral ordered her to drop farther down from the battery. Two companies of Hessians were sent to take possession of the Island.[409]

★ The HMS *Rose* anchored between Red Hook and Governor's Island at 9 AM on Monday, September 2, 1776 to cover the landing of troops. The troops landed and took possession of the island before noon. At 10 PM, the *Rose* headed up the East River with a number of flat boats when a battery at Curtis Hook fired on her. She was struck several times by the shot of a 12-pounder on the river's bank. Major John Crane (1744–1805), of the artillery, was wounded in the foot by a cannonball fired from the ship. The Congressional forces had to decide whether to defend the city or to evacuate it and occupy the strong grounds above. They determined to defend the city, as they had already expended a good deal of time, labor, and money to increase the number and the strength of their defenses.

★ The following morning at 9 AM, some troops on York Island fired on the HMS *Rose* which returned fire and shifted her berth. That afternoon, Congressional troops on Blackwell's Island kept a constant fire on her until about 200 British troops from Long Island came over and took possession of Blackwell's Island.[410]

★ Captain Charles Phipps (1753–1786), of the HM Fireship *Strombolo,* went on shore with his lieutenant, gunner, midshipman and 10 men to assist with the fortifications at Governor's Island on Thursday September 5, 1776. The following morning, seven Whig boats tried to land on the island; but British sailors and Hessians beat them off.

★ Seven Congressional boats tried to land on Governor's Island on Friday morning, September 6, 1776 but the crew of the HM Fireship *Strombolo* and some Hessians beat them off. The HMS *Phoenix, Roebuck, Orpheus* and *Carysfort* headed up the East River at 5 PM. They came under fire from batteries on New York. Several other batteries on Long Island and Governor's Island fired on the town, but nobody was injured.[411]

★ The 44-gun frigates HMS *Phoenix* and *Roebuck,* the 30-gun *Orpheus*, and the 40-gun *Carysfort* weighed anchor about 4 PM on Friday, September 13, 1776, and sailed up the East River under a gentle breeze. As they sailed toward Hellgate, the Whigs began to fire their great guns from their batteries in New York. The ships, "in supreme Contempt of the Whigs and their Works, did not fire a Gun." The Royal Artillery returned fire from their batteries on Governor's Island and the eastern shore, and kept up an incessant fire on New York along with the cannon at Governor's Island. The batteries from the city returned fire. A cannonball struck and killed three male spectators. Some of the buildings had a few holes and one shot struck within six feet of General George Washington (1732–1799), as he rode into the fort on horseback. The British had one man killed upon the forecastle of the *Phoenix*. The ships passed by the batteries about 5 PM and anchored off Bushwick Creek about 20 minutes later.[412]

★ Whig batteries fired on four British frigates and two transports in the East River Saturday evening, September 14, 1776 as they sailed to join a man-of-war that had sailed upriver the previous night. The vessels exchanged many shots with the shore batteries and a house, or part of one, in the town was destroyed. On Sunday morning, five more frigates sailed up the East River and anchored off Bushwick Creek near the four that sailed there on the 13th and joined the HMS *Rose.* There were now 10 ships anchored off Bushwick Creek.[413]

★ Meanwhile three ships went up the North (Hudson) River which provoked a tremendous firing from the Whig batteries in New York. The artillery on Governor's Island assisted the ships' cannon, making a few holes in some of the buildings. With few heavy cannon in and around New York, because most of them had been brought to fortify a hill about 4.5 miles south of Kingsbridge, the Whigs fired as well as they could.[414]

Whitestone Bay (Sept. 3, 1776)
Whitestone (Sept. 6, 1776)

Whitestone is on the northwest side of Long Island opposite the Bronx. Whitestone Bay is in the East River on the west side of the Whitestone Bridge (I-678).

★ The HMS *Niger*, at anchor in Whitestone Bay, fired ten 12-pound round shots at a number of armed Whigs on the north shore in the late afternoon of Tuesday, September 3, 1776.[415]

★ The HMS *Niger*, moored off Whitestone, fired three 12-pound and two six-pound shots at some Whigs passing in a boat at 8 AM on Friday, September 6, 1776. Captain George Talbot then sent his boat, manned and armed, in pursuit. They captured the boat but the crew escaped on shore.[416]

Gowanus (Apr. 15, 1781)

> Gowanus is a neighborhood in Brooklyn.

★ Captain Adam Hyler (1735–1782) went to Gowanus, Long Island on Sunday night April 15, 1781 and captured a Hessian major and ensign and their servants. The prisoners were taken into New Jersey.[417]

Canarsie (June 1781)

> Canarsie is near the southwestern shore of Long Island, near Gravesend Bay and east of Flatbush.

★ Captain Adam Hyler (1735–1782) entered a house at Canarsuit, in June 1781, where a sergeant's guard was eating supper. Captain Hyler seized their weapons which were standing in the hall.[418]

5
MANHATTAN AND STATEN ISLAND

See the map of New York City and Surroundings.

★ After the siege of Boston, General George Washington (1732–1799) moved to New York in April 1776, and turned his attention to the defense of the city and the Hudson Valley. The city at that time extended from the southern tip of Manhattan to Wall Street and had a population of approximately 25,000 people. Defending the city seemed an impossible task, however, as Manhattan was almost surrounded by water and Washington had no navy to contest the Royal Navy that could move men and supplies or bombard (see Photo NY-3, NY-4) the island from three sides. Along with the construction of fortifications at New York City and Long Island, Washington thought it imperative to build new fortifications along the Hudson River (see Photo NY-36 of Fort Lee in New Jersey).

His army of 19,000 men began digging fortifications and creating gun positions all around the city, awaiting a British attack. General William Howe (1732–1786) brought an army of 31,600 men to Staten Island in June and July 1776. His brother, Admiral Richard Howe (1726–1799), supported him with a flotilla of 280 ships. Washington felt compelled to spread his army to cover the highly vulnerable area. He stationed 4,000 men on Long Island to hold the high ground of Brooklyn Heights overlooking the East River and New York City. He placed most of the rest on Manhattan, at the northern end of the island at Kingsbridge, and at Fort Washington.

Photo NY-36. Fort Lee in New Jersey

New York (June 12, 1775; Aug. 23, 1775; July 4, 5, 19, 1776; Sept. 4, 5, 1776; Oct. 28, 1776)

> Manhattan was known as York in the 18th century. It was defended by many forts. Fort Number One (on the southwest slope of Spuyten Duyvil Hill, just north of the Henry Hudson Monument, at today's West 230th Street and Sycamore Avenue) was a small square fort protected by an abatis. Fort Number Two (located 200 feet south of 230th Street and 230 feet west of Arlington Avenue on the crest of Spuyten Duyvil Hill) was probably a circular fort with an abatis. Fort Number Three was a square abatised earthwork located on the eastern slope of Spuyten Duyvil Hill on a line with today's Netherland Avenue, between 227th and 231st Streets. The fort was intended to cover the valley and the main road to Phillipsburgh (now Yonkers).
>
> Fort Number Four (located at the south end of the Jerome Park Reservoir, 700 feet east of Sedgwick Avenue) was a square earthwork redoubt with each side about 70 feet in length. It was surrounded by a ditch and palisade and protected the Harlem River front. The Daughters of the American Revolution placed a tablet on an outcropping of rock on Reservoir Avenue, just west of University Avenue, in 1914.
>
> Fort Number Five, a square abatised earthwork located on Kingsbridge Road, was designed to cover the approach to the Farmers or Dyckman Bridge across the Harlem River. The fort's site is on the grounds of the U.S. Veterans Hospital, formerly a Catholic orphan asylum. Fort Number Six, also on the grounds of the U.S. Veterans Hospital, was at Kingsbridge Road and Sedgwick Avenue.
>
> Fort Number Seven was an earthwork at the current intersection of Fordham Road and Sedgwick Avenue. Fort Number Eight (on what is now University Heights in the Fordham section of the Bronx) was a four-pointed star fort built by the British and surrounded by an abatis on the east side of the Harlem River. A boulder on Battery Hill, 80 yards south of New York University's Hall of Chemistry, bears the inscription: "The site of Fort Number Eight, 1776–1783." Fort Number Eight was larger than the other forts in the area and covered the advance of the Hessians and Lord Percy's troops during their attack on Fort Washington. Fort Number Eight was opposite Fort George on Laurel Hill (192nd Street and Audubon Avenue on the west bank of the Harlem River, about 0.5 miles east of Fort Washington).
>
> Fort Number Nine was renamed Fort Prince Charles or the Charles Redoubt after the fall of Fort Washington on November 16, 1776. Citizens Redoubt was on the high ground (Rutgers Hill) at Market and Madison Streets, just east of the Jewish cemetery. Fort Cock Hill (Cock's Hill or Cox Hill) was also known as the New Battery. It was located at the top of Inwood Hill, about where 207th Street is, just south of Spuyten Duyvil Creek.
>
> Fort Amsterdam, on the southern tip of Manhattan in an area known as the Battery, was renamed Fort George (not to be confused with Fort George on Laurel Hill or the one at Lake George or the one on Staten Island). The United States Custom House now occupies the site bounded by Whitehall, State, and Bridge Streets, and Bowling Green. The Grand Battery was located just below Fort George. The Lower Barracks were south of Fort George and Pearl Street in what is now Battery Park. The Upper Barracks were northeast of the Common and east of Broadway, between Warren and Chambers street, about where City Hall now stands.
>
> Other forts defending Manhattan include those at Montresor's Island (now Randall's Island at the mouth of the Harlem River), Governor's Island, Horn's Hook,

the Grenadier's Battery (on the banks of the Hudson River at the intersection of Washington and Harrison Streets), the Jersey Battery (to the left of the Grenadier's Battery along what is now Reade Street, west of Greenwich Street), the Hospital Redoubt (West Broadway and Worth Streets), Fort Independence (west of Giles Place, about 1,000 feet north of the intersection with Sedgwick Avenue), Jones Hill Fort (Corlear's promontory jutting out into the East River), Kingsbridge Redoubt (where the old Post Road crossed Spuyten Duyvil Creek), Lispenard's Redoubt (on Lispenard's Hill and anchoring the western line of defenses), McGowan's Pass Redoubt (on one of two small hills at the northeast corner of Central Park near the intersection of Fifth Avenue and East 107th Street).

Fort Tryon, on the northern end of Manhattan Island, was the northern outpost of Fort Washington (on the east side of the George Washington Bridge). It is now commemorated by Fort Tryon Park. Turtle Bay Depot, a rock-lined cove in the East River at the end of 47th Street was the site of a British magazine and storehouse. Turtle Bay has since been filled in and is now a plaza one block north of the United Nations Building. Waterbury's Battery was at the foot of Catherine Street at the intersection with Cherry Street and is now buried beneath the ramps of the Williamsburg Bridge. The Shipyard Battery was another artillery position nearby. The Whitehall Battery, behind General Washington's headquarters at No. 1 Broadway was a little east of the Grand Battery. The site was once known as the Whitehall Dock and is now South Ferry.[419]

★ A quantity of military stores were taken and carried off from what were called the King's stores at Turtle Bay on Monday morning, June 12, 1775.[420]

★ Captain George Vandeput (d. 1800) had the man-of-war HMS *Asia* (see Photo NY-33) fire on Congressional troops who were moving a cannon from a battery in New York on Wednesday night, August 23, 1775. The Congressional troops suffered three men wounded and they killed one seaman.[421]

★ A Rebel sentinel of the Upper Barracks Guard was wounded by someone in New York city on Thursday, July 4, 1776. (The Upper Barracks was roughly where City Hall is located.) Another sentry was shot the following day and bled to death. A Loyalist was suspected of firing the shot out of a window but the suspect could not be found.[422]

★ A Whig battery firing on the enemy on Friday, July 19, 1776, had an accident that killed four men.

★ Whigs had fired at the HMS *Rose*, Captain James Wallace (1731–1803), from York Island on Wednesday, September 4, 1776. One of the shells fell within eight feet of her side. Other shells fell on her decks, spraying splinters and causing a good deal of damage.[423]

★ A party of Whigs began to fire upon the HMS *Rose* from two batteries of 18- and 24-pounders on York Island at 4 PM on Thursday, September 5, 1776. The *Rose* returned fire but suffered much damage.[424]

★ Some Continental dragoons crossed the Hudson from New Jersey on Tuesday, October 14, 1777. They skirmished with British troops and took some prisoners.[425]

★ A large armed flatboat full of Whigs tried to infiltrate British lines during the night of Monday, October 28, 1776. The HMS *Brune* fired on them with her great guns and small arms. The following morning, the crew of the *Brune* took the boat which was greatly damaged and its bottom covered with 2 inches of blood. More than 60 shots passed through its sides and probably killed more than 50 men.[426]

Bedloe's (Bedlow's) Island (Apr. 3, 1776; June 27, 1776; July 6, 1776; Sept. 6, 1776)

Bedloe's or Bedlow's Island was in Lower New York Bay, off the coast of New Jersey, about 15 miles southeast of South Amboy, New Jersey.

★ Governor William Tryon (1729–1788) was having some earthworks constructed on Bedloe's Island, a small island in New York harbor, about 0.5 miles from Captain George Vandeput's (d. 1800) man-of-war HMS *Asia* (see Photo NY-33). Major General William Heath (1737–1814), determined to drive him off the island, sent Major William De Hart and 200 New Jersey militiamen to dislodge them. The troops embarked on board several boats around midnight and landed on the island a little after 1 AM on Wednesday, April 3, 1776. The workmen were all on board the *Dutchess of Gordon*; but nearly 40 women and children were in a house on the island. The militiamen set fire to all the buildings except the cottage occupied by the women and children, damaged the earthworks, and took the entrenching tools, a large number of white shirts and great coats and a quantity of poultry. Meanwhile the *Asia* fired one 9- and one 18-pounder on the militiamen but did no harm.[427]

★ Captain George Vandeput (d. 1800), of the HMS *Asia*, moored off Bedloe's Island, sent all his boats manned and armed to join those of the *Phoenix* at 10 PM on Wednesday, June 27, 1776. They cut the ship *Lady Gage* from her moorings and towed her away. They also set fire to the *Blue Mountain Valley*, a transport ship captured by the Rebels.[428]

★ Admiral Lord Richard Howe (1726–1799) arrived at Sandy Hook from England with a large fleet on Thursday morning July 6, 1776. About 3 o'clock that afternoon, the 44-gun *Phoenix*, a 28-gun frigate, and three tenders left Staten Island and headed for New York. The army was alarmed. Every man was at his station within a few minutes. As the ships approached Bedloe's Island, they veered toward the Jersey shore to avoid the batteries firing at them from both sides of the river. They headed up the Hudson River, firing several broadsides as they went. Several shots went through some houses in the town.[429]

★ Several muskets were fired at the guard boat of the HMS *Eagle*, moored off Bedloe's Island, on Friday, September 6, 1776 about 1 AM.[430]

Roosevelt Island
Blackwell's Island (Sept. 3, 4, 1776)

Blackwell's Island is now known as Roosevelt Island in the East River, east of Manhattan.

★ Whigs fired a good deal at Captain James Wallace's (1731–1803) HMS *Rose*, at anchor south of Blackwell's Island, on Tuesday and Wednesday, September 3 and 4, 1776. They began about 9 PM, causing the *Rose* to return fire and shift her position. One shot passed through her and another beat off one of her anchors, without doing any further damage. The Whigs fired two artillery pieces at her from a battery opposite Bushwick and wounded two or three men. They kept a constant fire on the *Rose* and fired several shells over the island at her on Wednesday afternoon but without effect. About 200 Regulars came from Long Island and took possession of Blackwell's Island that afternoon but withdrew on Thursday, the 5th. The Whigs soon sent a detachment to retake possession of it.[431]

Hunt's Point (Sept. 4–5, 1776; Oct. 19, 1776)

> Hunt's Point is in the South Bronx on the East River.

★ Lieutenant William Quarme, of the HM Brig *Halifax*, saw several Whigs on Hunt's Point on Wednesday afternoon, September 4, 1776. He weighed anchor, moved toward them and fired several shots at them. The Whigs left at 8 PM with one wounded. The *Halifax* then shifted her berth between Hewlets Island and West Farm Point.[432]

★ General William Howe (1732–1786) embarked at Frog's Point with most of his army Saturday morning, October 19, 1776 and landed at Hunt's Point. He encountered some opposition from about 60 men concealed behind a stone wall. He had three officers wounded and about 30 privates killed and wounded. The fire continued "till the troops were on the point of landing, and then, giving their fire, took to their heels."[433]

★ The Whigs kept firing at passing boats that Saturday morning, October 19, 1776; so Captain George Talbot had the HMS *Niger* fire two 6-pounders at them. He also fired a 12-pound shot at some Whigs attempting to take a boat from Hunt's Point about 4 PM.[434]

Wards Island
Buchanan's Island
Montresor's (Randall's) Island (Sept. 10, 1776; Sept. 23, 1776; Oct. 8, 1776)

> Buchanan's Island is now known as Wards Island. Montresor's (Randall's) Island is at the mouth of the Harlem River.

★ The 1st and 2nd battalions of British light infantry embarked in flatboats at daybreak on Tuesday, September 10, 1776. They landed on Montresor's and Buchanan's Islands, nearly opposite Harlem, with no opposition, except from one man who fired three shots at the boats and wounded two men with the same ball. There were less than 20 Whigs on the islands who escaped as soon as the Redcoats landed. Possession of the islands facilitated the landing of troops on York Island (Manhattan) and protected boats passing through Hellgate or coming down from Flushing or Whitestone.[435]

★ Two British deserters reported that Montresor's Island was lightly defended. Major General William Heath (1737–1814) got General George Washington's (1732–1799) permission to retake it. Lieutenant Colonel Michael Jackson (1734–1801), of the 16th Massachusetts Continental Infantry, led about 200 to 240 Continentals in a surprise attack on the island about dawn on Monday, September 23, 1776. (Some sources date this action as September 24th.) They travelled down the Harlem River in five large boats, a little before daybreak. One of the boats had a detachment of artillery with a light 3-pounder. Two men who had deserted from the frigate *Brune*, stationed nearby, and a man who had been Captain John Montresor's (1736–1799) servant and knew the island perfectly served as their guides.

The deserters informed the Whigs that the British detachment was less than 20 men when it consisted of a captain and 100 men. The guards and pickets on the York Island side were notified not to hail the party as they proceeded down river. Unfortunately, the lower sentinel had not received the instructions and challenged the boats and ordered them to come to the shore. The boats continued on; and the sentinel fired, alerting the British to their approach.

The boats reached the island almost at the intended time, around dawn. The British captain ordered his men to let them land. The three field officers were in the first boat. Upon landing, one of the seconds in command was to spring to the right, while the other was to spring to the left and lead the troops from the other two boats which were to land on each side of the first boat. The field officers and the men from their boat landed; but before they could form their ranks, the British rushed them with fixed bayonets. Some of the 71st Regiment, in their eagerness, disobeyed orders and charged soon after the first boat had reached the shore and the men landed.

The other boats pulled away from the shore and fired on the Highlanders, killing two of them and wounding others. Lieutenant Colonel Jackson received a musket ball in the leg, and Major Henley (d. 1776) was shot through the heart as he was getting into the boat. The Rebels had about two men killed and about four wounded in the boats, as the detachment fired at them less than 20 yards from the shore. They also lost about 28 captured. The firing continued as long as the Whigs were in sight. They rowed off in great confusion. The men in the other boats were arrested, tried by court-martial, and one of the captains cashiered.[436]

★ Three hundred and forty Whigs came down the Harlem River in five flat-bottomed boats with two cannons shortly after 4 AM on Tuesday morning, October 8, 1776. They attacked a British outpost on Montresor's Island where there were about 80 men. HMS *Brune*, at anchor near the island, fired at the boats in the dark. The first shot sank one of the boats full of men. The rest were beaten off the island after a short skirmish. The *Brune* ceased firing because she could not distinguish friend from foe. The raiders lost a major and 27 men wounded. The 71st regiment, which suffered most of the casualties, lost four men killed and six wounded.[437]

Horn's (Hoorn's) Hook (Sept. 1–13, 1776)

> Horn's Hook was a projection of land now partly hidden by the East River Drive and incorporated in Carl Schurz Park located at what is now 92nd Street at East 88th Street on East End Avenue. It was a battery of nine guns, six of them mortars (see Photo NY-6). The site of the fort is occupied by the Gracie Mansion at 88th Street and East End Avenue. Horn's Hook Fort's strategic value was that it was at the entrance to Hellgate, the gateway for British penetration into upper Manhattan by way of the Harlem River.

★ A battery was opened on a point of land on Long Island opposite the east end of Blackwell's Island which cannonaded the Continental fort at Horn's Hook for several days beginning on September 1, 1776 in an attempt to neutralize it. On the 4th, a battery of two 24-pounders, six 12-pounders, and three mortars cannonaded Horn's Hook Fort from the Queens shore and "greatly destroyed it." The inexperienced gunners in the fort inflicted few casualties—only two men killed and one wounded by mortar fire. The cannonade killed two men and wounded four in the fort.

A severe cannonade was heard on Thursday morning, September 12, 1776. It was believed to be from Horn's Hook where the British were trying to dislodge the Congressional forces. They were already in possession of Montresor's and Buchanan's islands. The British lost one sailor, who was killed by a cannonball as he lay sleeping on the grass. An engineer lost an arm; and two or three other slight accidents occurred. The cannonade continued the following day.[438]

Manhattan and Staten Island **179**

Kip's Bay (Sept. 15, 1776)

> The area of the Battle of Kip's Bay extends from 32nd Street to 38th Street in Manhattan, but landfill extends the shoreline, obliterating the small inlet where the Crown forces landed on September 15, 1776. The Kip house was located on 35th Street, about 100 feet east of Second Avenue. The Crown forces came ashore just east of that house.
>
> Nathan Hale (1755–1776) is thought to have been hanged as a spy at 46th Street and First Avenue. The spot is part of the plaza surrounding the United Nations building.

★ General George Washington (1732–1799) had two weeks after the Battle of Long Island on August 27, 1776 and his retreat to Manhattan on August 29–30 to prepare his defenses on Manhattan before General William Howe (1732–1786) struck again, landing a force at Kip's Bay above the city of New York (now about 34th Street) on Sunday, September 15, 1776.

Washington placed 5,000 men in the city and another 5,000 behind earthworks along the East River. He also had 9,000 north of Harlem Heights. They were in a precarious situation. Early on Sunday morning, September 15, 1776, a British naval squadron took a position in the East River about 200 yards from Continental earthworks at Kip's Bay. The squadron consisted of the *Renown* (44 guns), *Phoenix* (44 guns), *Orpheus* (28 guns), *Rose* (20 guns), and another 28-gun ship. The warships began a cannonade just before 11 AM that continued for over an hour.

Meanwhile 84 flatboats moved from Long Island at 10 AM with 4,000 British and Hessian troops. Lord Francis Rawdon (1754–1826) recorded in his diary:

> As we approached [Kip's Bay] we saw the breastworks filled with men and two or three large columns marching down in great parade to support them.
>
> The Hessians, who were not used to this water business and who conceived that it must be exceedingly uncomfortable to be shot at whilst they were quite defenceless and jammed so close together, began to sing hymns immediately. Our men expressed their feelings as strongly, though in a different manner, by damning themselves and the enemy indiscriminately with wonderful fervency.
>
> The ships had not as yet fired a shot but upon a signal from us, they began the most tremendous peal I ever heard. The breastworks were blown to pieces in a few minutes, and those who were to have defended them were happy to escape as quick as possible through the ravines. The columns broke instantly, and betook themselves to the nearest woods for shelter. We pressed to shore, landed, and formed without losing a single man. As we were without artillery, upon an island where the enemy might attack us with five times our number, and as many cannon as he thought proper, it was necessary to attain some post where we might maintain ourselves till we were reinforced, which we knew could not be done quickly. We accordingly attacked and forced a party of the Rebels from the Inchenberg, a very commanding height, taking from them a new brass howitzer, some waggons of ammunition, and the tents of three or four battalions who were encamped on it.[439]

Ambrose Serle (1742–1812), secretary to Admiral Richard Howe (1726–1799) wrote: "So terrible and so incessant a roar of guns few even in the army and navy had ever heard before."[440]

The flatboats began to land about 4,000 men on both sides of Kip's Bay at 1 PM. Raw Connecticut militia posted at this point abandoned their position, broke and ran north "as if the Devil was in them." Washington himself tried unsuccessfully to halt them and to rally them (near where the New York Public Library stands on Fifth Avenue at 42nd

Street). He was reported to have exclaimed as he flung his hat to the ground in despair at the unwillingness of his men to stand their ground: "Good God! Good God! Have I got such troops as these!" or "Are these the men with which I am to defend America?" He even lashed out with his cane at the officers and men of the Connecticut brigade who fled past him in their anxiety to escape the advancing Redcoats.

The Crown forces could have destroyed the retreating column very easily had they chosen to do so. Instead, the first division of 4,000 men secured the beachhead and blocked the Boston Post Road (now Lexington Avenue). Here, they seized and held Murray Hill, then called Inchenberg, a mile northwest of Kip's Bay. (It is an area enclosed by 35th and 38th Streets between Lexington and Fifth Avenues.) The Crown forces waited for the second division of 9,000 men to land before advancing any further.

The Boston Post Road, which ran the length of Manhattan Island, was the only main road. The Crown forces immediately seized and blocked it, cutting off the escape route. The Continentals had to abandon their artillery—more than 70 guns, about half of the artillery in the army—and travel on foot. This allowed them to march faster, as they expected the Crown forces to march quickly across the island to cut their forces in half. Major General Israel Putnam (1718–1790) would have led the retreating Continentals into a trap had he not learned from Major Aaron Burr (1756–1836), one of his aides, of a possible alternate route, the Bloomingdale Road which branched off the Boston Post Road. (It followed the route of today's Broadway up the west side of the island, almost up to the location of Grant's Tomb.)

When the Crown forces began advancing up the Boston Post Road, they marched north in parallel with Putnam's column, separated by little more than the width of Central Park, about a mile. Neither column was aware of the existence of the other. They finally met entirely by accident. The Crown forces advance guard on the Post Road reached the point where it entered the east side of present-day Central Park. Here, it came across Colonel William Smallwood (1732–1792) and the remainder of the Maryland Regiment. A brief skirmish followed, and the Continentals retreated north to join their compatriots in new fortifications on Harlem Heights.[440]

Manhattanville
Harlem Cove (Nov. 16, 1776)
Harlem Plains
Harlem Heights (Sept. 16, 1776; Sept. 18, 1776; Oct. 3, 1776)

> Harlem Cove was an inlet of the Hudson River just below Harlem Heights (West 147th, 153rd and 159th streets). It has long since been filled in to form part of West 125th Street. General George Washington's maps refer to it as the Hollow Way. The Battle of Harlem Heights started here and this part of the battle is sometimes referred to as the Battle of Harlem Plains.
>
> The Battle of Harlem Heights took place about 1.5 miles south of Fort Washington near the present day Grant Memorial and Columbia University, off 120th Street, Manhattan. The site of the battle is covered by urban development. Grant's Tomb occupies the site of the main position of the Crown forces. The heaviest fighting took place in a buckwheat field along 120th Street. The Hollow Way, where the battle started, runs along 125th Street near the location of the 125th Street subway station. The Morris–Jumel Mansion (**www.morrisjumel.org/**) (160th Street and

> Edgecomb Avenue) was General George Washington's headquarters during the battle and was used by the British and Hessians until their evacuation in 1783.
> The Continentals occupied a strong position on Harlem Heights. Fort Lee and Fort Washington, on opposite banks of the Hudson River, protected them from the British fleet as did batteries commanding Harlem Creek. The Crown forces landed on Manhattan at Kip's Bay on Sunday, September 15, 1776 and advanced northward to form a line from Horn's Hook on the East River (at 90th Street) across to the Hudson (97th Street and Broadway). The northern outposts extended from McGowan's Pass (near the northeast corner of Central Park at 106th Street) to the Hudson (near 105th Street).

★ Major General Nathanael Greene (1742–1786) guarded the southern edge of the Harlem Heights plateau with 3,300 men (between Manhattan Avenue and the Hudson overlooking West 125th Street). Major General Israel Putnam (1718–1790) and his 2,500 men were half a mile behind Greene. Major General Joseph Spencer's (1714–1789) 4,200 men were another half a mile behind Putnam.

Lieutenant Colonel Thomas Knowlton (1740–1776) with 150 Connecticut rangers set out before dawn on Monday morning, September 16, 1776, to reconnoiter the enemy position about 2 miles south of the Continental forward position. They encountered the 2nd and 3rd British light infantry battalions and part of the 42nd Highland Regiment ("Black Watch") about daybreak near Jones's farm at Harlem Cove (West 106th Street at Broadway). Knowlton's scouts fired about eight volleys at the light infantry in a half-hour firefight. General Lord Hugh Percy (1742–1817) drove in the Continental pickets who retreated to avoid being flanked after suffering 10 casualties.

The superior Crown forces then pursued Knowlton down a depression known as the Hollow Way (south of West 125th Street). General George Washington (1732–1799) rode forward from his headquarters at the Jumel mansion (near West 161st Street) shortly before 9 AM to observe the skirmish when a British light infantry bugler on the high ground (just north of Grant's Tomb) sounded the hunting call to signal the end of a successful chase.

Washington ordered Lieutenant Colonel Archibald Crary and 150 volunteers from Brigadier General John Nixon's (1727–1815) brigade to counterattack. They advanced across the Hollow Way as Colonel Joseph Reed (1741–1785) led Knowlton's Rangers and three rifle companies—a total of about 230 men—behind the enemy's right flank. Premature musket fire disclosed the flank attack, and the two forces exchanged fire at too great a distance to be effective. Washington sent the rest of Nixon's brigade (about 800) to reinforce Crary.

The Highlanders, realizing the danger, started withdrawing, and the Continentals pursued. The British reformed behind a fence and began a firefight. Lieutenant Colonel Knowlton and Major Andrew Leitch (d. 1776) were mortally wounded within 10 minutes, but the fighting continued. Washington reinforced the attack with parts of two Maryland regiments and some New Englanders, making sure to include the Connecticut militiamen who had run from Kip's Bay so that they might redeem themselves.

The British retired south into a buckwheat field (near 120th Street between Broadway and Riverside Drive). They received reinforcements of fresh light infantry troops and Highlanders and formed a line (running just below 119th Street) to take a stand. They held their ground here and engaged in the heaviest fighting of the battle between noon and 1 PM. When their ammunition ran low, they retreated again (to present-day 106th Street).

Not wanting to bring on a general engagement, Washington ordered his troops to withdraw about 2 PM as large numbers of British reinforcements were arriving. But some Continentals did not receive the orders right away and pursued the enemy (as far as 110th Street) before breaking off the action.

The Continentals lost 30 killed and 100 wounded and missing out of approximately 2,000 men engaged. The Crown forces probably had about the same number engaged and lost 14 dead and 157 wounded.

This small engagement was a tremendous boost to Continental morale. It was the first time the Continental Army won a victory in open warfare and showed that troops from the various colonies could work together in harmony. General Howe made no further advances on the Continental lines in more than a month, but the position on Harlem Heights was basically untenable.[441]

★ A little before noon on Monday, September 16, 1776, a party of Hessian jaegers, British Light Infantry and Highlanders skirmished with a party of riflemen and some other troops on the heights west of Harlem Plain, and south of Morris's house. The Continentals had several officers killed and wounded but turned back the Crown forces. A general action might have ensued but the general officers had different opinions about how to proceed. The council decided to guard against both an attack on Fort Washington and a landing either at Morrisania, Hunt's or Frog's Point which might result in destroying the works on York Island with very little loss to the Crown forces. A floating bridge was laid across Harlem Creek for communication and mutual support of the troops on each side.[442]

★ On Wednesday, September 18, 1776, two days after the battle of Harlem Heights, the British Army was encamped between the Continental Army and New York City. A scouting party of 200 encountered a superior force of Crown troops at Harlem Heights. They inflicted a few casualties and had five men wounded.

Major General William Heath (1737–1814) posted a chain of 450 sentinels about 50 yards from each other from one side of the island to the other. They were on constant alert and ordered not to fire at the British sentinels unless they fired first. The two sides frequently shot at each other. On Wednesday, September 18, a Continental guard who had been exchanging some shots with his British counterpart saw a British officer walking along the bank on the west side of York Island (Manhattan) and decided he was a better target. He shot the officer and wounded him. The officer was carried to a house on the island and another officer soon came down to the creek with a flag of truce and called for the commander of the picket and informed him, that if the Continentals continued to fire, the commanding officer on the island would cannonade Colonel Morris's house where the captain of the guard was quartered. The officer notified General Heath who advised him to inform the British officer, that the sentinels had always been instructed not to fire unless they were fired upon and would continue to do so. The firing ceased for a while.

A new Scot sentinel soon afterward discharged his piece at a nearby guard who immediately returned fire. A British officer then came down and called to the Continental officers to remind them of the agreement. When told that the Scot fired first, the British officer replied, "he shall then pay for it." The sentinel was immediately relieved and there was no more firing between the sentinels. They were so civil to each other that one day, across a narrow part of the creek, the British sentinel asked a Continental who was nearly opposite him if he could give him a chew of tobacco. The Continental took a thick twisted roll out of his pocket and passed it across the creek. The Englishman took off his bite and returned the remainder.[443]

★ A party of about 250 Rangers was sent out Wednesday night, October 2, 1776 to capture an enemy post on Montresor's Island. They proceeded down Harlem Creek and the crew of the front boat landed on signal. The sentinels fell back, but the other boats lagged behind. The British rallied and attacked the landing party. A few managed to get aboard their boat and retreat; but most of them were captured. The major was killed and the operation failed.[444]

See also **Kingsbridge.**

Kingsbridge or King's Bridge (Sept. 25, 1776; Oct. 3, 1776; Jan. 18–25, 1777; Aug. 22, 1777; Nov. 27, 28, 1777; Dec. 7, 1777; Dec. 15, 1777; before Sept. 21, 1778; Nov. 27, 1778; July 3, 21, 22, 1781)
Fort Independence (Jan. 18–25, 1777)
West Farms (Jan. 25, 1777; May 1780)
Valentine's Hill, Mount Vernon (mid-July 1778; Sept. 16, 1778)
Indian Field and Bridge (Aug. 31, 1778)
Mile Square Road, Westchester Co. (Aug. 31, 1778)
Near Mount Vernon (Jan. 1780)

> Kingsbridge was at King's Bridge Avenue and West 230th Street where the old Post Road crossed Spuyten Duyvil Creek separating Manhattan from the Bronx. Broadway now passes about 200 yards southeast of the bridge site. A plaque on St. Stephen's Church on West 230th Street denotes the site. Possession of the site controlled the land approach to New York City.
>
> Fort Independence was an earthen fort in the rough shape of a parallelogram with bastions (see Photo NY-1, NY-2) in the northwest and southwest angles. It was located on the heights between the old Boston and the Albany Post Roads just north of Kingsbridge. It was on the west side of what is now Giles Place, about 1,000 feet north of where it intersects Sedgwick Avenue. Fort Independence Park at the south end of the Jerome Park Reservoir now contains the site of the fort.
>
> West Farms is now Bronx Park in New York City. The Van Cortlandt house is in Van Cortlandt Park just north of Kingsbridge and between Kingsbridge and Williams's Bridge which was once a part of the town of West Chester where a bridge crossed the Bronx River. It is now within New York City limits about where East Gun Hill Road crosses the Bronx River at the northern perimeter of Bronx Park.
>
> Valentine's Hill was 4 miles above Kingsbridge. The Valentine–Varian house (3266 Bainbridge Avenue at East 208th Street) abutting Williamsbridge Park was located across the street from its present location until moved in 1965.
>
> The Van Cortlandt mansion (Van Cortlandt House Museum in Van Cortlandt Park at Broadway and 246th Street) is reputed to be the oldest house in the Bronx. General Washington used the house in 1776 and in 1783, first when his army was being driven toward the Highlands and again on the eve of his triumphal reentry into New York City. Inside the northeastern edge of the adjoining park, at a place called Indian Field, a DAR marker reads: "August 31, 1778. Upon this field Chief Nimham and 17 Stockbridge Indians from Massachusetts, as allies of the Patriots, gave their lives for Liberty."

> Mile Square, in Woodlawn Heights where Mile Square Road meets Mount Vernon Avenue and Kimball Avenue, was a favorite campground for both armies during the American War for Independence because of its sheltered location near the water. British Hussars were quartered here for several summers and Lieutenant Colonel Andreas Emmerich's (1737–1809) light horsemen were also billeted here.

★ The Continentals made a stand behind their redoubts near Kingsbridge on Wednesday, September 25, 1776, as there was nothing behind them to cut off their retreat. Two or three companies of British light infantry pressed them to take cover at their lines. The light infantry suffered some casualties but "would have suffered more but for the Magnanimity &; Heroism of the Grenadiers and Highlanders, who ran (it is said) about two Miles in 15 Minutes to their Relief." As the Continentals were outnumbered, thousands of other troops came out of their works to cut off the light infantrymen. The small party held their ground until their reinforcements arrived. They then retreated while the reinforcements advanced. The grenadiers and Highlanders concealed two field pieces less than 30 yards away and began to fire at the reinforcements in full flank, driving them back to their works in great confusion, leaving many dead behind them. The Crown forces had nine men killed and about 80 wounded.[445]

★ Major General William Heath (1737–1814) approached Fort Independence and demanded its surrender about October 3, 1776. (British authors complained that the Rebels frequently named their forts "Independence." This one was in the Fordham area, directly north of Spuyten Duyvil.) He wasted some gunpowder, and marched away as the British laughed and mocked him.[446]

★ Major General Heath headed to Manhattan with nearly 6,000 Continental troops in mid-January, 1777. His three divisions began to move toward Kingsbridge during the night of Friday, January 17. Major General Benjamin Lincoln's (1733–1810) column took the Albany road from Tarrytown, while Brigadier General David Wooster (1711–1777) and General Samuel Holden Parsons (1737–1789) left New Rochelle and East Chester. General Charles Scott's (ca. 1739–1813) column marched in the center from below White Plains. They joined forces just before sunrise on the 18th. General Lincoln's column occupied the heights above Colonel Philip Van Cortlandt's (1749–1831) property while General Wooster's went to Williams's Bridge; and General Scott's took the back of Valentine's house where the guards were quartered.

As General Heath approached Valentine's house, he ordered Captain Lieutenant David Bryant or Briant to bring a field piece to the advance guard and to cannonade the house immediately if there was any opposition. He then ordered 250 men from the head of the column to incline on the double to the right and to push into the hollow between the house and the fort to cut off the guard at the house if they tried to run toward the fort.

At this moment, a Crown patrol of two light-horsemen sent out at dawn to reconnoiter the vicinity, arrived unexpectedly at the foot of the hill and ran right into the head of Wooster's column. They tried to turn about, but a field piece fired at them before they could do so. The shot knocked one of the scouts from his horse and he was taken prisoner. The other galloped back to the fort to sound the alarm. The outguards and pickets ran to the fort, under fire, some leaving their arms, blankets, tools, and provisions behind. None were killed but one, who could not run so fast as the rest was taken prisoner. The Continentals captured 10 muskets at Valentine's house.

General Lincoln completely surprised the guard near Van Cortlandt's where he captured about 40 muskets, some blankets and supplies. The left and center divisions moved into the hollow, between Valentine's house and the fort. General Heath sent a messenger demanding the commanding officer to surrender the fort. The Hessian commander refused to surrender and ordered the fort's guns to fire at the attackers. General Heath ordered a detachment with two field pieces to move to a hill above Harlem Creek, south of the fort, not far from the New Bridge.

A battalion of Hessians appeared on the side of the hill just within Kingsbridge and back of Hyatt's tavern. General Heath ordered the artillery to cannonade them. The battalion withdrew quickly to get behind the redoubt and hill at the bridge while the cannon in the redoubt cannonaded General Heath's artillerymen.

The Hessian artillery killed one man on the 19th during the changing of the guards at the Negro Fort. General Heath decided to try to cut off the battalion within Kingsbridge, early the next morning, by sending a detachment of 1,000 men over the ice on Spuyten Duyvil Creek. Although the weather was cold, the ice was not very strong. As the weather warmed during the night, the general officers decided, on the 20th, that the venture was too hazardous.

Both sides cannonaded each other on the 20th. General Heath noticed that the Hessians sheltered themselves behind a little hill near the bridge, next to Spuyten Duyvil Creek, during the cannonade. He rode to Tibbett's Hill and a brook near Spuyten Duyvil that afternoon and found that the enemy would have no hiding place if he brought a field piece to that side.

Both sides resumed the cannonade on the 21st. That afternoon, a field piece was hauled up to Tibbett's Hill. The Hessians, cannonaded both in front and in the rear, were thrown into great confusion. Some sought shelter in the redoubt, others under the banks, others lay flat on the ground, and some hid in the cellars.

A pretty smart skirmish ensued on the 22nd and the Continentals began building chandeliers, fascines, and gabions (see Photo NY-37) to lead the Hessians into believing

Photo NY-37. Fascines are the bundles of sticks in the foreground. Gabions are the basket-like objects in the middleground, between the fascines and tents. Together, they are used to strengthen the walls of earthworks or fortifications. Yorktown Victory Center

they were going to make a major attack on the fort. General Heath also sent for a brass 24-pound field piece and a howitzer from North Castle.

Another skirmish took place near the south side of the fort just before dusk on the 23rd. An ensign and a New York militiaman were killed and five wounded. The loss of the enemy is unknown, as it was close under the fort.

The stormy weather on the 24th caused General Lincoln's division to leave their huts in the woods behind Colonel Van Cortlandt's house and to seek shelter in whatever houses they could find. Some went as far as Dobbs Ferry. The rainfall was so great that the Continentals lost a great many cartridges because of defective cartridge boxes and the water ran over Williams's Bridge.

The Hessians made a sally toward De Lancey's Mills (in the former town of West Farms, now Bronx Park in New York City) early in the morning of the 25th. They surprised and routed the guard and wounded several. They then advanced toward Valentine's house about 10 AM, drove the guards and pickets from the Negro Fort and Valentine's house and pushed on, keeping up a brisk fire.

The retreating guards sought shelter in the old redoubt on the north side of the road, to the west of the bridge. The Hessians lined a strong stone wall a few yards away to the southwest. Two militia regiments formed in the road near Williams's. General Heath ordered Captain Bryant to cross the bridge with his field piece. The militia followed to cover the artillery. Captain Bryant unlimbered his horses near the top of the hill to prevent them from being shot. The men took the drag ropes but the hill was so steep that they had to drag the piece almost within pistol range to get it in firing position. A round shot breached the wall, making a hole four or five feet wide. A second shot opened another and sent the Hessians back to the fort in a hurry. Two Congressional troops were killed and a number wounded.

The brass 24-pounder and the howitzer opened fire on the fort on the 27th. On the cannon's third discharge, she sprang her carriage. There were no shells for the howitzer, as there were none at the supply depot at North Castle. The Continentals made every attempt to draw the Hessians out of the fort. They sent a detachment to Morrisania to light many fires that night to deceive the Hessians into thinking that a large force was gathering to cross to York Island, at or near Harlem. They also sent for several large boats to increase the impression. The boats were brought forward on carriages. The British guards on Montresor's Island were so alarmed that they set the buildings on fire and fled to New York. A band of Loyalist and British soldiers came to reinforce the Hessians and forced General Heath to withdraw to Spuyten Duyvil.[447]

★ About 3000 Continentals attacked Kingsbridge on Friday morning, August 22, 1777. Some of the defenders marched out, beat them back, and pursued them 6 miles. They captured a captain, lieutenant, and 12 privates prisoners while losing only three privates.[448]

★ Lieutenant-Colonel John Graves Simcoe (1752–1806) and his Queen's Rangers along with Lieutenant Colonel Andreas Emmerich (1737–1809) and his chasseurs, and a detachment of the second battalion of Brigadier General Oliver de Lancey's (1718–1785) brigade, Lieutenant Colonel Banastre Tarleton (1744–1833) , with the dragoons of the legion, and one troop of Colonel Emmerich's, and the Hessian jaegers, moved from their respective encampments near King's Bridge early Tuesday morning September 16, 1778. They marched undiscovered between two enemy pickets and got 1.5 miles behind a body of 230 Viriginia riflemen, posted in a strong position in front

Manhattan and Staten Island **187**

on Babcock's Heights, under the command of Colonel Mordecai Gist (1743–1792). Lieutenant-Colonel Tarleton marched to Colonel Philip's farm.

Lieutenant-Colonel Emmerich and the detachment of de Lancey's, attacked the Congressional forces about 6 AM. Even though they were discovered as they prepared to attack, they killed three on the spot, wounded several, and took 35 prisoners, including three officers. They charged the Congressional troops so vigorously that many of them forgot their weapons and fled in a hurry. Colonel Gist ran away without his breeches or boots and may have been wounded as he fled.

At the same time, Lieutenant-Colonel Tarleton's dragoons charged a body of Congressional troops posted on Valentine's Hill, near a very thick wood. They took shelter where the dragoons could not maneuver. This prevented the cavalrymen from taking more than a few prisoners. The only loss sustained by the Crown troops in both attacks was one of Emmerich's horses was killed.[449]

★ Major General Israel Putnam (1718–1790) marched toward Kingsbridge on Thursday, November 27, 1778, hoping to draw the Crown forces into battle. He detached Colonel Return Jonathan Meigs (1740–1823) over the Bronx, near the fort, with orders to retreat in such a manner that would draw the enemy toward the main body of Continentals posted about a mile away. Colonel Meigs executed his orders, but the Crown forces cautiously avoided the danger and sent only a small party of rangers who could not be enticed to cross the river. A skirmish ensued which left about three men killed and an equal number wounded.

Several small parties were sent down to alarm the Crown camp the following night. The Crown troops turned out in a severe storm. The raiders captured Colonel James De Lancey, Mr. Ogilvie, a lieutenant in Colonel Beverley Robinson's (1721–1792) regiment and four other prisoners.[450]

★ Major General Philemon Dickinson (1739–1809) intended to make an attack on Staten Island on Thursday, November 27, 1778. Major General Israel Putnam (1718–1790) ordered Brigadier General Samuel Holden Parsons's (1737–1789) Continentals and Brigadier General Jonathan Warner's (1741–1803) Massachusetts militia to march toward Kingsbridge to make a diversion. The force consisted of 300 foot and 100 horsemen with field pieces and mortars.

Lieutenant Colonel Andreas Emmerich's (1737–1809) 17 riflemen, covered by 30 musketeers, repulsed that diversion and drove them over the river back to the main body at Williams's. They killed seven and wounded 26 and lost only one killed and one captured. They did not retreat until the Continentals fired their artillery at them.[451]

★ A party of 400 Whigs from Horseneck (Greenwich, Connecticut) under the command of a colonel and Major David Humphreys (1752–1818) approached Mr. Phillip Van Cortlandt's (1749–1831) house at Kingsbridge on Sunday morning, December 7, 1777. They broke open the house, expecting to surprise Lieutenant Colonel Andreas Emmerich (1737–1809) and his chasseurs, but they were disappointed. They returned home by way of Phillipsburgh.[452]

★ Nine Crown light horsemen were captured by a foraging party near Kingsbridge on Monday, December 15, 1777.[453]

★ Loyalists began to gather at the camp in Kingsbridge in July 1778. By mid-July (before the 18th), Lieutenant Colonel John Graves Simcoe (1752–1806) and Lieutenant Colonel Ludwig Johann Adolph von Wurmb (d. 1813) began to organize a scouting expedition in force and agreed to meet on Valentine's Hill in Mount Vernon, on the other side of the Bronx River. Before von Wurmb reached the hill, Simcoe learned that a body of Continentals occupied nearby Hunt's Hill and planned for an ambuscade. He sent a small body of cavalry to march down the road toward Kingsbridge in full sight of the Congressional troops, while he hid a large body of his infantry in an orchard where the roads fork to Hunt's bridge and Valentine's Hill.

The Continentals crossed the bridge and attacked the dragoons as Simcoe had hoped. However, some of Simcoe's infantry officers climbed on a fence to reconnoiter and were spotted. The Continentals immediately turned their cannon on the hidden troops, forcing them to retreat through the hollow ground out of range, and return to camp. The Continentals sent a party to observe enemy movements. They came under fire after they crossed the Bronx and approached Simcoe's infantry and were driven back.[454]

★ Colonel Mordecai Gist (1743–1792) and a light corps of Continentals were posted near Babcock's house on Valentine's Hill in late August 1778. Colonel Gist sent out frequent patrols but a deserter gave an accurate report of Gist's position to Lieutenant Colonel John Graves Simcoe (1752–1806) Sunday night, August 30, 1778. Simcoe determined to attack Gist the following morning with a detachment of jaegers. Lieutenant Colonel Andreas Emmerich (1737–1809) led the march as he had troops who were well acquainted with the country. The Queen's Rangers followed Emmerich's infantry, marching through the meadows on the side of Valentine's hill, opposite Cortland's Ridge. They were to pass between the Whig sentries to Babcock's house to get behind Gist's encampment and attack immediately. Lieutenant Colonel Banastre Tarleton (1744–1833) and the entire cavalry were ordered to cover the right and arrive at Valentine's Hill by daylight. Captain Carl August von Wreden and a detachment of jaegers had orders to march on Cortland's Ridge and halt opposite Gist's encampment while a larger detachment of jaegers prepared to force Phillip's bridge and then to proceed to the bridge opposite Babcock's house to cut off the enemy's retreat.

Lieutenant Colonel Emmerich's corps observed silence, passed the enemy sentinels, and gained the heights in the rear of the camp without being detected. Major John Ross was detached to occupy Post's house, to maintain communication with Lieutenant Colonel Tarleton on Valentine's Hill, while the remainder of the Rangers moved to the right, toward Gist's camp. Firing soon began, giving the signal to attack Gist's camp. Lieutenant Colonel Emmerich secured the Saw Mill Road while Lieutenant Colonel Simcoe moved rapidly into the road and up the hill to the enemy's camp rather than take the shorter way through the thickets. When he arrived at the camp, he was surprised to find that the jaegers had not forced Phillip's bridge as planned but had crossed and joined Captain von Wreden on Cortland's Ridge. Colonel Gist had escaped through the open passage.

Lieutenant Colonel Tarleton encountered a patrol of cavalry and dispersed it. After occupying Gist's camp, the Queen's Rangers captured a patrol which returned to camp when they heard the firing. The Rangers set fire to Gist's huts and returned to their camp. One of Lieutenant Colonel Tarleton's patrols later reported that an enemy picket was 2 miles to the right of the White Plains. Tarleton requested a detachment to go there. Lieutenant Colonel Simcoe went to the White Plains while Tarleton galloped to the enemy's post, put the picket to flight, and took some prisoners.[455]

★ Colonel Archibald Campbell (1739–1791) advanced to Mile Square with the 71st Regiment and the light troops at the end of August 1778. The Provincial troops consisted of the Queen's Rangers, De Lancey's, Emmerich's, and Legion cavalry under Lieutenant Colonel John Graves Simcoe (1752–1806) and Lieutenant Colonel Banastre

Tarleton (1744–1833). They ambushed a detachment of a little over 50 Continentals and 50 Stockbridge braves under Captain Daniel Williams and Sachem Daniel Nimham (ca. 1710–1778) at Mile Square Road (at Woodlawn Heights where Mile Square Road meets Mount Vernon Avenue and Kimball Avenue) in Westchester County, about 2.5 miles from Colonel Cortland's (in Van Cortlandt Park), about 10 AM on Monday, August 31, 1778.

The dragoons planned to hide in the low ground on the right of the road and in the woods on the left to flank Captain Williams and Chief Nimham as they proceeded down the road. Simcoe, halfway up a tree, saw an enemy flanking party approaching. The Native Americans, lining the fences of Mile Square Road a little below McLean Avenue, began a smart firing, exchanging shots with Lieutenant Colonel Emmerich's troops. Simcoe's Queen's Rangers moved rapidly to gain the heights while Lieutenant Colonel Tarleton advanced with the hussars and the Legion cavalry. Unable to pass the fences in his front, Tarleton circled further on the enemy's right. When Simcoe learned this, he ordered the grenadier (see Photo NY-8) company to take the hill. His men advanced to within 10 yards of the Stockbridge braves without being noticed because the braves were preoccupied with the attack of Emmerich's corps and the Legion. The braves now gave a yell and fired upon the grenadier company, wounding four of them. Lieutenant Colonel Simcoe was wounded in the arm.

The braves had no bayonets nor time to reload their weapons so the Rangers drove them from the fences, killing 37 of them. Tarleton's Legion got among them and pursued them rapidly down Cortland's Ridge. He struck at one of the fugitives, lost his balance, and fell from his horse. The brave he was pursuing had no bayonet and his musket had been discharged. An orderly riding close behind Tarleton, killed the brave giving him a narrow escape, and allowing him to rejoin his battalion and seize the heights. The braves captured a light infantry captain and a few of Tarleton's men but had two of their own taken prisoners. The skirmish killed or severely wounded almost 40 Stockbridge braves, including Chief Nimham and his son, and killed 17 Continentals, wounded about eight and captured 19. The Crown forces lost one man killed and seven wounded, including Colonel Simcoe who was wounded by Chief Nimham just before Simcoe's orderly killed him.

The Queen's Rangers attacked Captain Daniel Williams's (1752–1823) small company north of McLean Avenue. They wounded a few and took eight prisoners. The Crown forces lost two killed in Tarleton's Legion, two of Emmerich's men and four of Simcoe's wounded. The bodies of the 17 Stockbridge braves were buried in a common grave at a place called Indian Field at the northeastern edge of a park adjoining Van Cortlandt Park.[456]

★ A party of Whigs killed 13 jaegers a few miles from Kingsbridge before September 21, 1778.[457]

★ Three militiamen who tried to recover stolen cattle were pursued by a body of enemy troops near Mount Vernon in January 1780. One of them was captured.[458]

★ Captain Thomas Cushing (1725–1788), of the Massachusetts line, and 100 infantrymen advanced on West Farms in May 1780. Their guide, Michael Dyckman, observed that the Crown sentinels did not change their countersign daily, so the Continentals captured a Loyalist from whom they learned the countersign. They then made a surprise attack on the Loyalist camp and either killed or captured more than 40 of them. They wanted to capture Colonel James De Lancey (1747–1804) but he was absent from his quarters. As soon as the attack began, a large party of jaeger dragoons mustered and pursued Captain Cushing who managed to escape. The Hessians pursued the Continentals until they got to the Saw Mill valley.[459]

★ Major General Benjamin Lincoln (1733–1810) commanded two regiments of light infantry and a detachment of artillery in an attempt to re-take the north end of Manhattan Island. The force of 800 came down from Peekskill in boats during the night of Sunday, July 1, 1781. They landed secretly on the New York shore below Fort Knyphausen, formerly Fort Washington. They planned to capture by surprise not only Fort Knyphausen but also Fort Tryon, Fort George on Laurel Hill, the works on Cox Hill at the mouth of Spuyten Duyvil, and those at Kingsbridge. General George Washington (1732–1799) was scheduled to arrive at Valentine's Hill, 4 miles above Kingsbridge, early the next day with the main army.

If circumstances prevented the execution of the main plan, the secondary plan was for the main body to cooperate with Armand Louis de Gontaut-Biron, Duc de Lauzun's (1747–1793) force to proceed to Morrisania to capture, or at least defeat, De Lancey's corps of Loyalists. In this event, Lincoln would land above Spuyten Duyvil and march to the high ground in front of Kingsbridge. There, he would remain concealed until the beginning of Lauzun's attack to prevent De Lancey from turning Lauzun's right as he cut off the Loyalists' escape over the bridge.

Examining the ground from Fort Lee on the New Jersey shore, Lincoln saw it was occupied by a large force that had just returned from foraging in New Jersey and a man-of-war (see Photo NY-33) was anchored in the river between. He abandoned the main plan and went for the second which failed. He landed his troops above Spuyten Duyvil but another foraging party stronger than his own discovered him and attacked.

Lauzun's Legion, Colonel Elisha Sheldon's (1740–1805) dragoons, and a detachment of Connecticut state troops under General David Waterbury (1722–1801) arrived, after a hot and tiring forced march, only to find the intended surprise of De Lancey impossible. Lauzun gave his support to General Lincoln and General Washington hurried down from Valentine's Hill.

The Crown forces escaped by boat; and Washington spent the rest of the day in reconnoitering the ground about Kingsbridge, in the event of a future operation. The next day, he withdrew his army to Dobbs Ferry where the French army joined it on July 6th.[460]

★ Hessian Lieutenant Colonel Andreas Emmerich (1737–1809) and 100 men marched to Phillips's house (Yonkers) in the evening of Monday, July 2, 1781. The next morning, a number of wagons, under an escort of 200 foot and 30 mounted jaegers, were to be sent there for some hay. The Crown forces learned, about 10 PM, that General Washington had been at Singsing that afternoon. They decided to leave the wagons within the lines and send a detachment to recall Colonel Emmerich. The detachment left the camp at Kingsbridge at daybreak. An advance guard of a sergeant and 10 men reconnoitered Fort Independence and its environs.

Meanwhile, General Washington planned an expedition to cut off Colonel James De Lancey (1747–1804) in the vale and Major Pruschenk (d. 1806), commanding the jaeger horse on Cortlandt ridge. The Duc de Lauzun would march to Williams's Bridge at daybreak the following morning. Major General Benjamin Lincoln (1733–1810) would go from Tappan and land below Yonkers and General Washington would occupy Valentine's Hill.

As it was not quite day yet, the Crown scouting parties did not perceive the enemy drawn up in line of battle until they were within 10 yards of them. The Continentals fired at them; they returned fire and fell back to a proper distance. The scouts, under fire, tried to gain the height behind the fort. They succeeded in taking possession of the ruins of a house formerly fortified by Colonel Emmerich. From this location, they tried to attack the Continentals to dislodge them from their advantageous position.

The scouts noticed a battalion with flying colors in the fort. That battalion outnumbered them and attacked furiously with the bayonet. Unable to gain any ground, the scouts fell back, under cannon fire, to Charles's redoubt. The Continentals pressed them so hard that they began to lose ground because of the narrow defiles. The cavalry charged the advancing Continentals and stopped them. The jaegers re-formed and resumed the attack with redoubled vigor, driving the Continentals from the fort and down from the heights as far as Deveaux's house. The jaegers then took possession of the ground.

Lieutenant Colonel Ludwig Johann Adolph von Wurmb (d. 1813) arrived from Kingsbridge with the rest of the jaeger corps and took possession of the rising ground between the bridge and Fort Independence. He reconnoitered the enemy's new position, extending from Mile Square Road over the heights to Williams's bridge. A thick wood in the rear of the Continentals indicated their intention to conceal their real strength. Repeated intelligence told Colonel von Wurmb that 300 French dragoons covered the enemy's left at Williams's Bridge, so he acted carefully, not thinking it advisable to risk another attack.

Lieutenant Colonel Emmerich retreated over Spuyten Duyvil Creek and was cut off by the Continental position. Meanwhile, 200 Regulars had arrived along with Loyalists from Morrisania. It was decided to force the Continentals from their position and to allow Colonel Emmerich an opportunity to advance on Cortlandt's house, still occupied by the Continentals.

The jaegers advanced and took possession of Cortlandt's bridge. The Loyalists and the jaeger advanced parties engaged the Continental advanced posts and drove them to their main body. The Continentals withdrew to the left and retreated toward Williams's Bridge. With the passage now open, Colonel Emmerich was now able to leave Spuyten Duyvil. He informed General Friedrich Wilhelm von Lossburg (b. ca. 1720) that he drew 200 Whigs into his ambuscade at Phillips's house, killed three and took nine that the Continentals were moving in two columns toward Cortlandt's bridge. One of the columns had already been seen on Valentine's Hill. The troops were now ordered to fall back to their former position, leaving 100 jaegers at Fort Independence to observe enemy movements. General Washington reconnoitered Spuyten Duyvil at 3 PM and the troops moved into their lines and to their encampment at 4 PM.

The jaegers lost three men killed; one officer, one sergeant, 26 men wounded; and five missing. The Continentals suffered considerable losses. Reports said they embarked 101 wounded men at Singsing and sent them up the North River and that a great many died of their wounds before reaching Singsing. They also reported one officer and 17 men who were left dead on the field and 17 stand of arms.[461]

★ Loyalist Captain Gilbert Totten was wounded near Kingsbridge on Saturday, July 21, 1781 and two or three stragglers were captured.

★ A large body of Continental and French troops was observed in motion in front of Kingsbridge at daybreak on Sunday, July 22, 1781. They positioned themselves on the heights from Cortland's house to Williams's bridge and placed strong advanced posts in the old forts: Independence, King's Fort and others in that line. The Loyalists from Morrisania were forced to retire within British lines but did not have time to bring their stock, which the Continentals seized and drove off.

The Continentals brought two artillery pieces to fire at a scow at Holland's ferry about 6 AM. The scow was transporting Loyalists from the rear of Redoubt No. 8 on Fordham Heights. The artillery did little damage. General George Washington (1732–1799) marched a large column of about 4,000 men, with some cavalry, and a few field pieces and two or three French battalions toward Morrisania Point soon afterward. He came so near the point with some cavalry, that some cannon shots were fired at him, forcing him to withdraw. This column returned in the afternoon and joined the other troops near Fort Independence where they remained all day without attempting anything further.

The British reinforced Redoubt No. 8 with 20 men and kept the troops stationed near Kingsbridge ready to move if necessary. The French and Continentals killed three or four British and captured eight or ten on the march. The Continentals lost about two men killed, one wounded, and about five captured.

★ A detachment of the Continental Army, encamped near White Plains, captured Fort No. 8, a few miles above Kingsbridge, by surprise one night during the week of August 4 to 10, 1782. The fort was garrisoned by 200 Hessians.[462]

Bronx (Oct. 22, 1776)
Westchester (Jan. 3, 1778)
Delancey's Mills (July 21, 1778; Aug. 5, 1779)

> Delancey's Mills were in Westchester, which is now in the Bronx.

★ General George Washington (1732–1799) began to evacuate his troops from Manhattan on October 18, 1776; but they moved slowly because they lacked horse-drawn wagons to move their supplies. He sent Brigadier General William Alexander's (Earl of Stirling, 1726–1783) brigade northward to seize and hold the desired position at White Plains until the main army arrived. Stirling made the march in about four hours; but the main army took four days to get to Kingsbridge, which crossed the Harlem River. The 13,000 men dragged the artillery by hand along the west bank of the Bronx River and used the few wagons they had to transport their baggage and supplies a day's journey. They dumped their loads at the end of the day and returned for more.

They established entrenched posts at intervals along the heights on the west side of the Bronx River to protect the troops moving along the road farther west and close to the Hudson. Major General Joseph Spencer's (1714–1789) division held that line until the main army reached White Plains.[463]

See also **Mamaroneck.**

★ A party of Colonel Return Jonathan Meigs's (1740–1823) regiment captured about 50 Loyalists near Westchester on Saturday, January 3, 1778. They brought the prisoners to Hartford, Connecticut under a strong guard the following Saturday. Captain Barns, who had recently burned Tarrytown, was one of the prisoners.[464]

★ A captain, two subalterns, and 23 Congressional troops surprised and captured Delancey's Mills in West Chester Monday night, July 20, 1778.[465]

★ After the Continental Army retreated north and established its lines on the Croton River, the British corps of Loyalists was stationed at Morrisania under the command of Colonel James De Lancey (1747–1804). Colonel De Lancey made his headquarters at Colonel William H. Morris's house situated on the high ridge west of the mill brook vale.

About 100 horse of Colonel Elisha Sheldon's (1740–1805) and Colonel Stephen Moylan's (1734–1811) dragoons, along with the militia, and about 40 infantrymen of Brigadier General John Glover's (1732–1797) brigade, passed by Delancey's mills near Morrisania on Thursday, August 5, 1779. They took 12 or 14 prisoners, and some livestock. The Loyalists gathered and a skirmish ensued, in which the Loyalists had a number of men killed and wounded. The Continentals lost two killed and two wounded. The frequency of attacks compelled Colonel De Lancey to shift his quarters closer to the protection of the British guns of Fort No. 8, at Fordham. The dwellings at Morrisania were burned on the same day along with the Westchester court house.[466]

Mount Washington (Washington Heights) (Nov. 8, 1776)
Fort Washington (Nov. 16, 1776)

> Washington Heights was on the east side of the Hudson River in the area where the George Washington Bridge is located. Fort Washington was located here. The Morris–Jumel Mansion (160th Street and Edgecombe Avenue) was General Washington's headquarters from September 14 to October 18, 1776. The British and Hessians also used the building until 1783 when they left the city.
>
> Fort Washington Park (**www.washington-heights.us/history/archives/000427.html**) occupies the site of Fort Washington. Fort Washington Park, also known as Gordon Bennett Park (**www.nps.gov/fowa/**) (Fort Washington Avenue and 183rd Street, Manhattan), is undeveloped. The site of Fort Washington has a marker at a rock outcropping which identifies it as the highest natural point on Manhattan, at 265 feet.
>
> Fort Tryon Park (**www.nyrp.org/theparks_forttryon.htm**) (192nd Street between Broadway and Riverside Drive, Manhattan) marks the site of the northern redoubt of Fort Washington.

★ General George Washington (1732–1799), sensing his inability to meet the British in battle on equal terms, moved away to the north toward the New York highlands. Again he was outmaneuvered. General William Howe (1732–1786) quickly moved to Dobbs Ferry on the Hudson between the Continental Army and the Hudson River forts. On the advice of Major General Nathanael Greene (1742–1786) (now recovered from his bout with malaria), Washington decided to defend the forts. At the same time, he split his army, moving across the Hudson and into New Jersey with 5,000 men and leaving Major General Charles Lee (1731–1782) and Major General William Heath (1737–1814) with about 8,000 men between them to guard the passes through the New York highlands at Peekskill and North Castle.

After the Battle of White Plains, Howe planned to attack Fort Washington, a pentagonal earthwork built on the highest natural point on Manhattan Island 265 feet above the Hudson, which was now isolated. Colonel Robert Magaw (1738–1790), the commanding officer, held a strong position and believed he and his 1,200 men could hold out for at least a month. He received an additional 1,700 reinforcements in the few days preceding the attack. Although a strong position, the fort had no ditch, no casements, no palisade, no barracks, and weak outworks, making it vulnerable to siege or attack. It also lacked water, food, and fuel. Magaw intended to use the Hudson River to his rear as the escape route if necessary. Steep and densely wooded slopes protected his front. Where natural defenses of rocks and deep ravines did not protect the approaches, he built entrenchments and batteries.

★ The Continentals brought two cannons out of Fort Washington and fired on the advance posts of Lieutenant General Wilhelm von Knyphausen's (1716–1800) corps on Friday, November 8, 1776. General Knyphausen's Hessian Chasseurs annoyed the Whigs greatly. The Whigs also fired on the frigate HMS *Pearl* as she returned to New York.[467]

★ General Howe, now reinforced to 20,000, sent one of his staff to Fort Washington with a drummer and another soldier carrying a white flag on Saturday, November 15, 1776, to formally invite the commander to surrender. He gave the traditional warning that, if Magaw failed to surrender, the Crown forces would kill his entire garrison when they took the fort. Colonel Magaw refused to surrender, saying that mankind had never fought for a better cause.

The Crown forces began the assault at daybreak the next day as the guns of the *Pearl* in the Hudson River and the batteries on the eastern bank of Harlem Creek opened fire at 7 AM and continued firing until about 11 AM. The army attacked on four fronts. Lieutenant General Wilhelm von Knyphausen (1716–1800) advanced from the north, crossing Kingsbridge about noon with 3,000 Germans, Highlanders, light infantry and nine battalions of the line. (Eighteenth-century soldiers fought shoulder to shoulder in lines. Battalions of the line consist of the companies that remain when the companies of grenadiers (see Photo NY-8 and NY-34) and light infantry that protect the flanks are detached.)

The attackers advanced under a heavy fire, scrambling over rocks, dragging cannon up steep, rough roads, clinging to the bushes which sprouted from the crevices. Officers urged their men forward shouting and waving swords.

Brigadier General Edward Mathew (often misspelled Matthews) (1729–1805) and two light infantry battalions (3,000 British soldiers) crossed the Harlem River at noon to attack from the east. They landed in a cove or creek near present day 200th Street. General Sterling's (d. 1780) 42nd Highland Regiment ("Black Watch") crossed the Harlem River below the fort as a feigned attack, but they came under fire from Colonel John Cadwalader's (1742–1786) 3rd Pennsylvania regiment. Magaw reinforced his 150 men with another 100 from the fort.

General Lord Hugh Percy's (1742–1817) column of 2,000 men (one Hessian brigade and nine British battalions), originally intended as a diversion, prepared to lead the main assault against the fort from the south. As Percy's column attacked the fort, a little dog would dart out from behind the breastworks and tear the fuses out of shells with its teeth until one exploded in its face.

Washington, Greene, Brigadier General Hugh Mercer (1725–1777), and Major General Israel Putnam (1718–1790) crossed the Hudson from Fort Lee, New Jersey, to Fort Washington for personal reconnaissance. They determined that they could do nothing to help Magaw and returned to Fort Lee. Washington instructed Magaw to fight until dark and then evacuate the fort.

The Continentals were soon surrounded by cannon and troops with fixed bayonets. Knyphausen demanded Magaw's surrender about one o'clock and gave him two hours to make up his mind. Magaw surrendered about 3 PM. Some of the Germans wanted to make good Howe's threat to kill the entire garrison, but they were ordered to take prisoners instead. The Crown forces captured 2,818 Continental troops and large quantities of valuable munitions, including ammunition and guns. The Continentals also suffered 53 killed. The Crown forces lost 458 men killed and wounded, 72 percent (330) of them Germans and half of the British casualties from the 42nd Highlanders. Hessian casualties numbered 58 killed and 272 wounded. The British suffered 20 killed, 6 missing, and 102 wounded. Howe renamed the fort Fort Knyphausen to honor his German allies. He now commanded all of Manhattan Island and was in a good position to seize Fort Lee across the Hudson in New Jersey.

General Greene hastily evacuated Fort Lee and retreated west to join General Washington at Hackensack on Wednesday, November 20. Washington, with mere remnants of his army, about 3,500 men, was in full retreat across New Jersey with General Charles Cornwallis (1738–1805), detached by Howe, pursuing him rapidly from river to river.

The fall of Fort Washington was another major Continental defeat, and Washington's army was slowly melting away. Militiamen left by whole companies, and desertion among the Continentals was rife. When Washington finally crossed the Delaware into Pennsylvania in early December, he could muster barely 2,000 men. The 8,000 men in the New York highlands also dwindled away. Even more appalling, most enlistments expired with the end of the year 1776, and a new army would have to be raised for the following year.

Yet, neither the unreliability of the militia nor the short period of enlistment fully explained the debacle that had befallen the Continental Army. Washington's generalship was also faulty. Criticism of the Commander in Chief, even among his official family, mounted, centering particularly on his decision to hold Fort Washington. Major General Charles Lee (1731–1782), the ex-British colonel, ordered by Washington to bring his forces down from New York to join him behind the Delaware, delayed, believing that he might himself salvage the Continental cause by making incursions into New Jersey. He wrote Major General Horatio Gates (1728–1806), ". . .*entre nous*, a certain great man is most damnably deficient."

Colonel Moses Rawlings (1745–1809) guarded the northern redoubt of Fort Washington (renamed Fort Tryon after the Crown forces captured it) about three-quarters of a mile north of Fort Washington. This fort on a 250-foot hill protected the northern end of Fort Washington. Rawlings commanded 250 Maryland and Virginia riflemen and three cannon. Margaret Cochran (Molly) Corbin (1751–1800) carried water to the men firing the guns when she saw her husband John fall severely wounded during the bombardment. She caught his rammer staff and took his place at the muzzle. The assault waves continued to advance under the heavy fire. When the Crown forces stormed the fort, Molly lay bleeding beside her gun. One arm was nearly severed and part of a breast mangled by three grape shot. She survived the wagon journey to Philadelphia with other wounded prisoners of war.

Washington issued her a warrant as a noncommissioned officer for her exploits. But, when the commissary at West Point refused to give her the rum portion of her ration because it wasn't customary to give liquor to women, she got angry and began voluminous correspondence to put pressure on him. A higher authority finally ruled: "It appears clearly to me that the order forbidding the issue of Rum to a woman does not apply to Mrs. Corbin." The commandant was directed to issue her the rations and cautioned that "perhaps it would not be prudent to give them to her all in liquor." (The Daughters of the American Revolution verified her records in 1926 and had her remains transferred to the West Point Cemetery, making her the first woman to be buried there.)[468]

Fort George (Nov. 16, 1776)

> Fort George, at the northern end of Laurel Hill in Manhattan, consisted of a pair of fleches during the battle for Fort Washington on November 16, 1776. When the Crown forces took Fort Washington, they built Fort George as part of what they called Fort Knyphausen. Remnants of the fortifications are on the west bank of the Harlem River on a hill now known as Fort George Hill. A Daughters of the American Revolution marker east of Broadway at 192nd Street and Audubon Avenue reads: "In grateful remembrance of the Patriot Volunteers of the Pennsylvania Flying Camp led by Colonel William Baxter (d. 1776) of Bucks County, Pennsylvania, who, with many of his men, fell while defending this height, 16 November 1776, and was buried near this spot." The site is now occupied by George Washington High School.

★ During the attack on Fort Washington, half a mile west, the Royal Highland Regiment (Black Watch) overran the fortifications of Fort George. Colonel William Baxter's (d. 1776) Bucks County Volunteers put up a valiant defense but were greatly outnumbered and abandoned the works.

Fort Cock Hill (Cock's or Cox Hill or New Battery) (Nov. 16, 1776)

> Fort Cock Hill was located at the mouth of Spuyten Duyvil Creek on Cock or Cox Hill. It was located on the summit of Inwood Hill, about in line with today's 207th Street, just south of Spuyten Duyvil Creek, which defines the northern boundary of Manhattan.

★ Fort Cock Hill was an outpost of Fort Washington and came under attack when that fort was assaulted on Saturday, November 16, 1776. The Hessians bypassed the fort in their attack on Fort Washington.
    See also **Kingsbridge.**

Spuyten Duyvil Creek (Aug. 14, 1777; July 13, 1778)

> Spuyten Duyvil Creek separated Manhattan Island from the Bronx.

★ Lieutenant James Clark, of the HM Galley *Dependence,* landed a foraging party of marines at Spuyten Duyvil Creek at 6 AM on Thursday, August 14, 1777. They returned at 9 AM with a number of cattle. He then sent the boats on shore to bring off the marines and fired two 24-pounders and two 4-pounders to cover their retreat. The boats returned at noon, having suffered no casualties. The tender *Mercury* came alongside the *Dependence* at 4 PM to get the cattle.[469]
★ A Whig battery along Spuyten Duyvil Creek, where two armed transports were anchored, cannonaded the frigate HMS *Tartar* and the galleys *Dependence* and *Crane* on Tuesday, July 13, 1778, forcing them to move.[470]

Williams's Bridge (Jan. 21, 1781)

> Williams's Bridge crossed the Bronx River at the northern edge of today's Bronx Park. It roughly corresponds to today's East Gun Hill Road just east of the Bronx River Parkway.

★ General George Washington (1732–1799) directed General Samuel Holden Parsons (1737–1789) to take command of a detachment of four battalions, including the guards upon the lines in January 1781, to protect the defenseless inhabitants between Greenwich and New York and, at the same time, to strike a blow to raise the spirit in the army. General Parsons marched quickly to destroy the barracks and forage of Lieutenant Colonel James De Lancey's (1747–1804) corps of Loyalists at Morrisania and Throg's Neck.

Colonels Moses Hazen (1733–1803), Alexander Scammel (1747–1781), and Peleg Sherman (1747–1811) each led a battalion from the Highlands by Golden's Bridge, through Bedford to Kingstreet, while Lieutenant Colonel William Hull (1753–1825) marched, with a fourth battalion, from the outpost at Pine's Bridge on the Croton River to Youngs. Both columns reached their destinations on Sunday evening, January 21, 1781.

Hull's column, which was to make the attack, pushed on toward Kingsbridge. It passed Fort Independence at 1 AM and halted opposite Fort Washington where a pontoon bridge crossed the Harlem River. Here, Colonel Hull told his men of the object of the expedition. He left Major Hugh Maxwell (1733–1799) to destroy the pontoon bridge and to prevent the Crown forces from crossing. They would have to take a long detour via Kingsbridge. Hull continued to march along the east bank of the Harlem River. He placed guards at Williams's and De Lancey's bridges over the Bronx River and sent a detachment to attack Throg's Neck.

General Parsons's column rested at Kingsbridge for a few hours before continuing to march to East Chester by way of White Plains. There, they could observe the enemy and cover Hull's retreat. They expected to take the enemy by surprise, but a small creek near De Lancey's quarters was so swollen by the recent rains that the troops could only cross by mounting the infantry behind the horsemen. The noise made in crossing alarmed the enemy but they made such a rapid and vigorous assault that their plan succeeded. They destroyed all the barracks and a great quantity of forage gathered for use in New York. They captured 54 prisoners, a number of cattle and about 60 horses and then retreated.

Hull was now 8 miles inside the enemy's lines and Fort Independence was only 4 miles from Eastchester where Parsons was. Half of the British army was in his rear. The noise of the musketry and the light of the burning barracks had aroused the neighboring garrisons. All the posts fired alarm guns and rockets in quick succession.

Hull crossed De Lancey's Bridge under enemy fire, putting the Bronx and the Harlem rivers between his corps and the forts. He marched without much interruption until he reached a stone church and jail where the enemy fired at him from the windows of these buildings. He attacked with the bayonet and released 32 Whig prisoners.

The detachment sent to Throg's Neck successfully completed its mission and joined Hull. The skirmishing was sharp and the firing constant and heavy for the last 2 miles of his retreat. Parsons sent word twice that a large body of Crown troops were advancing from Kingsbridge and that Hull must hurry to prevent both detachments from being cut off. He directed Sherman to oppose this force until Hull could arrive. He also sent Hazen's regiment to relieve Hull. Hazen's regiment hid behind a stone wall and checked the enemy's pursuit with sudden and well-directed fire. The battalions joined forces without further molestation.

General Parsons ordered the retreat in one column by way of New Rochelle. The Crown forces continued a scattered fire and Colonel Scammel covered the retreat with the artillery. Parsons's force of less than 2,000 men was more than 30 miles from any part of the main army or other support. The officers and men were tired from the difficulties of the day and a large part of the British Army was within 5 or 6 miles. General Parsons, having successfully completed his mission, did not deem it prudent either to attack the column advancing from Kingsbridge or to follow up the advantage secured by Hazen's regiment. Nor did he think it safe even to halt for refreshments. He continued his march through a severe snow storm until midnight. He stopped to rest his troops one day at Horseneck (Greenwich, Connecticut) before marching them back to their camp in the Highlands.[471]

Staten Island (before Nov. 20, 1775; Feb. 12, 1776; Apr. 7, 1776; Apr.14, 1776; July 2, 3, 4, 1776; July 23, 24, 1776; Oct. 13, 1776; Oct. 14, 1776; Oct. 15, 1776; Oct. 16, 1776; Mar. 14, 1777; Aug. 8, 1777; Aug. 19, 1777; Aug. 22, 1777; Aug. 23, 1777; Aug. 27, 1777; Sept. 1, 1777; Sept. 10, 1777; Nov. 18–21, 1777; Nov. 27, 1777; Dec. 26, 1777; June 5, 1778; June 10, 1778; June 24, 1778; Nov. 3, 1778; Nov. 28, 1778; Feb. 8, 1779; Mar. 18, 1779; June 23, 1779; June 29, 1779; June 30, 1779; July 9, 1779; Aug. 6, 1779; Aug. 16, 1779; Oct. 15, 1779; Oct. 27, 1779; Jan. 14, 1780; Jan. 18, 1780; Feb. 10, 1780; Feb. 12, 1780; July 1780; Aug. 25, 1780; Sept. 3, 1780; Sept. 19, 1780; Nov. 24, 1780; Jan. 3, 1781; Mar. 26, 1781; Apr. 9, 16, 18, 1781; May 1781; May 8, 1781; May 9, 1781; July 26, 1781; Aug. 23, 1781; Oct. 13, 1781; Nov. 8, 1781; Nov. 10, 1781; Dec. 15, 1781; Jan. 22, 1782; Mar. 15, 1782; Apr. 12, 1782; Apr. 19, 1782; mid-May 1782; May 22, 1782; May 23, 1782; June 21, 1782; July 5, 1782; July 9, 1782; Nov. 3, 1782)

> Staten Island is located at the entrance of New York Harbor, one of the world's greatest natural ports. It became a borough of New York City in 1898. Approximately 1 mile across the Narrows from Brooklyn and 7 miles from Manhattan's Battery, the island served as the launching area for the Crown forces' invasion of Brooklyn. Its proximity to New Jersey made it a very good starting point for many of the raids into that colony as well. The Crown forces erected forts and redoubts on all the strategically important heights and shore points on the island.
>
> Historic Richmond Town, 441 Clarke Avenue, Staten Island, NY (718) 351-1611 (www.historicrichmondtown.org/) is a living history village and museum complex that occupies 25 acres of a 100-acre site. It has about 15 restored buildings, including homes and commercial and civic buildings, as well as a museum elucidating the diversity of the American experience, especially that of Staten Island and its neighboring communities, from the colonial period to the present. Richmond Town was first established as a crossroads settlement among the scattered farms of Staten Island. It was not the first village; but, because of its central location, the Dutch Reformed congregation chose this place for its religious activities. In the 1700s, Richmond Town began to take shape as the government center of Richmond County. During the American War for Independence, British troops were stationed here, sleeping in the homes and barns of Richmond Town's families. Fort Richmond occupied the top of the hill overlooking the restored village of Richmond Town. It consisted of three redoubts covering both sides of the crest of the hill. The garrison was between the redoubts.
>
> Old Blazing Star Post, just off of Arthur Kill Road east of Rossville Avenue, was a fortified inn on the north bank of the mouth of Fresh Kills, west of Richmond Town.

> Decker's Ferry fort was located opposite Bayonne Neck, New Jersey. The site faces the Bayonne–Staten Island ferry landing in the town of Port Richmond on Kill van Kull. The fort's guns also covered the ferry to Bergen Neck. The stone house of a Loyalist named Decker was burned when the Whigs fled Staten Island in the face of General Howe's troops. A week after landing, the British converted the house into a fort. A January 1779 report described it as a "stone house fortified with loopholes [see Photo NY-17] and an abatis."[472]
>
> Flagstaff Fort was on Signal Hill at the Narrows, near the modern town of Rosebank. The site is now occupied by Fort Wadsworth north of the Verrazano-Narrows Bridge.
>
> The Watering Place redoubts were at the modern town of Tompkinsville at the spring at Pavillion Hill. It consisted of three circular, double abatised and picketed redoubts with 200 men in each. The parade was large enough for 2,000 men to march in order of battle.
>
> Fort Knyphausen was an earthen redoubt, located at St. George, overlooking the harbor at the Watering Place. Today, it is known as Fort Hill. Fort George was also located at St. George but it was considered "only an encampment."
>
> The Dutch Church Fort was a fortified stone church at Port Richmond.
>
> The Elizabeth Ferry redoubts consisted of three redoubts armed with one 18-pounder and four 24-pounders.
>
> Amboy Ferry Post was on the southwestern shore of the island. Lieutenant Colonel von Wurmb garrisoned it in 1777 with three companies.
>
> The Conference (Billopp) House (**www.theconferencehouse.org**; 718-984-6046) is at 7455 Hylan Boulevard, Tottenville, on the southwest tip of Staten Island. Christopher Billopp built the two-story stone house before 1688 on his grant of 1,163 acres. Benjamin Franklin (1706–1790), John Adams (1735–1826), and Edward Rutledge (1749–1800) met here with Admiral Lord Richard Howe (1726–1799) on September 11, 1776 in an unsuccessful peace conference. That peace conference gave the house the name Conference House.

★ Captain Robert Harris (1741–1809) had enlisted several recruits for the ministerial army by mid-November 1775 and was at Nassau Ferry, on Long Island before November 20, 1775. Colonel Alexander McDougall (1732–1786) and some friends went over to capture him. They forced several houses along the way in search of him. When they reached Decker's Ferry, they found Harris in an upper room, prepared to defend himself. Two pistols lay on his bed, primed and loaded; but, as he was caught by surprise, he had no opportunity to use them. Harris was taken with two of his men and brought to New York and placed under a strict guard.[473]

★ A man-of-war (see Photo NY-33), transports; and a tender came down from New York to the Watering Place (Tompkinville) about 11 PM on Sunday, February 11, 1776. The ships had 200 marines on board to plunder Staten Island and seize the livestock the next day. New Jersey Governor William Livingston (1723–1790) ordered Captain John Blanchard (1730–1811) and 300 militiamen of the Essex county light-horse to march to prevent the plundering. He sent a party to reconnoiter the south side of the island and to procure all possible intelligence of enemy movements. Captain Blanchard marched to the Sandy Hook lighthouse with his detachments about 3 AM. He learned that the fleet had left Sandy Hook the day before. So he ordered his troops to march back, leaving some to guard the coast in case the departure might prove a feint.[474]

★ The HM Sloop *Savage* and the pilot boat *James* went to the Watering Place on Staten Island under cover of a thick fog about 10 AM on Sunday, April 7, 1776. Each sent a boat ashore to get water. They placed a sentinel on a hill with his musket and colors. Captain Hugh Stevenson or Stephenson (1735–1776) received intelligence and prepared to attack them with three companies. He arrived about 10 AM when the sentinel fired, struck his colors and ran for the shore. The *Savage* received information of Stevenson's approach and fired a signal gun for the boats to return. She began firing to cover the embarkation of her men who were all running to their boats. The sailors left their 27 water casks and tried to escape under a brisk and constant fire from the *Savage*; but Stevenson's riflemen out-ran them, surrounded them, and took many of them prisoners, despite the fire from the ship.

The riflemen secured one of the boats and captured 13 men; but the other boat pushed off with two men in it. One of the riflemen ran after it in the water. Unable to catch it, he fired and killed one of the men who fell overboard. The other lay on his back and rowed to the *James*. The *Savage* kept up a continual fire for several hours, without hurting anybody. The Whigs lay behind the rocks and fired at the ship during the lulls.

A sailor from the *Phoenix* and another from the *Savage* were wounded and two men were killed trying to escape. The riflemen kept up such a hot and incessant fire on the *Savage* that a number of men fell from her tops and bowsprit. One man, presumed to be an officer, was seen to tumble off the quarter-deck into the water. The *Phoenix* cut her cable and withdrew out of range. The eight prisoners and four deserters from the *Phoenix* were taken to headquarters the next evening along with one standard, one musket, 27 iron bound casks, a cable and anchor, a speaking trumpet, great coats, and other captured supplies.[475]

★ Rebel riflemen fired on Captain George Vandeput's HMS *Asia* as she came through the Narrows at 4 PM on Sunday, April 14, 1776. She returned fire with two 18-pounders.[476]

★ After the siege of Boston, the British moved to New York in April 1776. General William Howe (1732–1786) occupied Staten Island with his army of 31,600 men in June and early July 1776. The island became a haven for Loyalists. Four British ships cannonaded Rebels on shore on Tuesday, July 2, 1776. Three other ships fired on the Rebels and made a landing on Wednesday. They wounded one and captured 30. Rebels brought cannon down to Decker's Ferry during the night and fired on the *George* and other schooners at anchor opposite the ferry. They killed one man and wounded four aboard the *George*. The following day, July 4th, two men crossed from Elizabethtown in a canoe and fired on the British encampment on Staten Island. Captain William Dansey's Company went toward Elizabethtown with two 12-pounders that night. They fired at a tender so much that she ran ashore at Staten Island and was taken by the militia. One of Captain Drury's sergeants was killed by accident and the captain of a British ship was taken by one of the Rebel boats.[477]

★ Captain George Vandeput's (d. 1800) HMS *Asia* was off the Watering Place about noon on Thursday, July 4, 1776, and fired several guns at the Rebels on Long Island. The Rebels returned a constant fire of small arms from Long Island as the ships passed. The following day, the Rebels resumed constant firing at the rest of the fleet coming through the Narrows with a 12-pounder which they had on Long Island.[478]

★ On July 9, 1776, inhabitants of Staten Island traveled to Richmond Town, the county seat, to hear Governor William Tryon (1729–1788) speak followed by the

Manhattan and Staten Island **201**

administration of the oaths of allegiance. Recruits were then formed into a Provincial Corps to defend the island.
★ A band of Whigs tried to capture two British sentries on Tuesday, July 23, 1776. One of them was killed in the attempt. A rifleman crossed the river from Elizabeth, New Jersey to Staten Island on Wednesday, July 24, 1776. He got within 15 yards of the outposts and demanded the Regulars to surrender. He was shot in the head and killed on the spot.[479]
★ On Wednesday, July 24, 1776, a four-gun Continental battery fired on two sloops on their way from Staten Island to Sandy Hook. The cannonade did no damage but provoked a reply from the British artillery on Billop's Point "which lasted for an hour." The Continentals had two casualties: a man confined in an upper room of the courthouse and a horse which was killed in High Street near the town pump in Amboy, New Jersey.[480]
★ General Matthias Williamson, Sr. (1716–1807) and men from Colonel Matthias Slough's (1733–1812) battalion conducted a raid on Staten Island on Sunday, October 13, 1776.[481]
★ Captain George Keith Elphinstone, viscount Keith (1746–1823) anchored the HMS *Perseus* at Staten Island to get water at 8 AM on Monday, October 14, 1776. The frigates *Greyhound* and *Orpheus* were already there getting water. That night, a party of Whigs came to the Watering Place and destroyed many of their casks.[482]
★ Brigadier General Hugh Mercer (1725–1777) and a party of Continentals crossed over to Staten Island during the night of Tuesday, October 15, 1776, to attack the enemy at the east and near the Watering Place. Colonel Samuel Griffin (1746–1810) took a detachment consisting of Colonel Alexander Patterson's (1743–1822) battalion and Major Robert Clarke's (d. 1821) riflemen to attack the east end of the town, while the remainder of the force enclosed it in on the other sides. Both divisions reached their positions by daybreak. As they advanced toward Richmond Town, they received information that some companies of British and Hessian troops were stationed at St. Andrew's Church there. Their first goal was to surprise them at dawn. The Crown troops fired a few vollies and retreated in disorder, leaving two of their men mortally wounded. The Continentals captured eight Hessians and nine British, one of them wounded, in addition to the two mortally wounded at Richmond Town. They also captured 45 much-needed muskets and a standard of the British Light Horse. The Continentals lost two men killed in the action. Colonel Griffin was wounded in the heel and Lieutenant Colonel Samuel Smith (1752–1839) was slightly wounded in the arm.[483]
★ A Party of Whigs went down to the Jersey shore and fired at some boats that were taking in forage at New Blazing Star on Staten Island on Friday morning, March 14, 1777. Major Robert Timpany (1709–1811) led 40 Bergen County Volunteers (Loyalists) across the river and drove the Whigs more than 3 miles inland. They seized 10 head of cattle and about 30 sheep without losing a man.[484]
★ A party of Whigs crossed the Kills and landed somewhere on the shore at West New Brighton and headed for Richmond on Friday, August 8, 1777. A party of British met them as they approached the village. A small skirmish ensued and the Whigs retreated slowly until they reached St Andrews Church. The entered the church and fired at the windows until they broke every pane of glass. They then fired through the broken windows until they drove out the British. Reinforcement from the vicinity hurried forward but reached Richmond just after the church had been vacated.

The Whigs retreated by the Fresh Kill, keeping their prisoners (both soldiers and civilians) in their rear. The British refrained from firing so as not to kill their own friends, or at least the noncombatants. After the Whigs had descended the hill and crossed the bridge, they hid in a cornfield where they waited for the British to come into range. They then fired a volley at them, killing the colonel in command. They continued their retreat until they reached the shore of the Sound. They drove their prisoners, about 30 in all, into a large hog-sty, while they seized the boats they needed to make their escape. The British reached the shore while they were crossing, and opened fire on them with their artillery, which they had not yet had the occasion to use, and killed several of them.[485]

★ Colonel Dungan and Major Robert Drummond, of the 3rd Battalion of the New Jersey Volunteers, crossed from Staten Island to New Jersey with about 60 men during the evening of Tuesday, August 18, 1777. The following morning, they marched about 27 miles inland and took 14 prisoners, 62 head of cattle, 9 horses, and more than 20 stand of arms. They destroyed some powder and shot, salt, rum, and other supplies. On their return trip, they marched to Amboy, New Jersey where the cattle, horses, and booty were loaded on the ferry to Staten Island. They left two pickets at Amboy with several sentries to observe enemy activities. Dr. William Barnet (1728–1790) and some Whig light horsemen appeared on the heights near Amboy but kept their distance when they found the Jersey Volunteers so well posted.[486]

★ Colonel Abraham Van Buskirk (1750–1783) was encamped near Decker's Ferry with his regiment of 250 Loyalists in mid-August 1777. Colonel Joseph Barton's regiment of equal number camped near the New Blazing Star Ferry. Colonel Dungan and Lieutenant Colonel Isaac Allen (1741–1806) were camped near Amboy about 2 miles apart, each with about 100 men. The 55th (200 men) and about 100 men of the 27th British regiments and two regiments of Anspachers (450 men each) and one of the Waldeckers (about 400) were encamped near the Watering Place, by their fortifications. There were also two small detachments of new recruits, one at Richmond, the other at Cuckolds Town.

Major General John Sullivan (1740–1795) intended to land on the west and north sides of Staten Island and to entrap the new recruits in their different camps. He decided that he could not force the other troops from their fortifications without cannon and would probably have to fight all the troops in and around New York which would come as reinforcements.

Sullivan's troops were 20 miles away from Staten Island and would be too tired to march that distance and execute a surprise attack. Moreover, their movements toward the island would alarm the residents of the area around Spanktown who would send messengers to the island. Nevertheless, General Sullivan determined to make as sudden and as fierce a march as possible.

He selected about 1,000 men from General William Smallwood's (1732–1792) and General De Boor's brigade and ordered them to march from Hanover to Elizabethtown at 2 PM on Friday, August 22, 1777. They arrived at 10 PM. Colonel Matthias Ogden (1754–1791) joined him with his own and Colonel Elias Dayton's (1737–1807) regiment. Colonel Frederick Frelinghuysen (1753–1804) and 100 militiamen were to march from Elizabethtown in the evening and cross the river opposite a creek called the Fresh Kills. They would then head up the creek to attack at dawn. The other troops were to cross from Haley's Point. General Smallwood's brigade would attack Lieutenant Colonel Abraham Van Buskirk's (1750–1783) camp and General De Boor's brigade would attack

Colonel Barton's regiment. The generals were both instructed to leave one regiment each on the main road to cover their rear and to arrest any fugitives.

General Sullivan managed to collect only six boats to make the crossing. He kept three for his men and sent the other three to Colonel Ogden. General Sullivan's troops crossed before daylight, undiscovered. As they marched, they heard a severe firing from Colonel Ogden's direction. It lasted about two minutes.

General Smallwood proceeded to Decker's Ferry; but his guide deceived him and led him to the wrong side of the enemy. This gave the British an opportunity to escape to their forts, leaving their colors and their tents standing. General Smallwood took the colors and destroyed the tents and the stores and burned about 35 tons of hay. He burned seven vessels laden with dry goods and killed a few men, wounded others as they ran off, and took two prisoners. General Sullivan's troops marched briskly to Colonel Barton's quarters where the Loyalists were prepared for the attack.

General Sullivan's main body halted and formed ranks while Lieutenant Colonel Samuel Smith (1752–1839) and his men went around Colonel Barton's rear to prevent any escape. As the main body moved up to charge, the Crown forces threw down their arms and ran away. Colonel Smith killed many of the fugitives but could not prevent them all from escaping, as the fugitives were well-acquainted with the creeks and marshes and eluded the Continentals. Several fugitives got into the boats moored at the ferry and crossed to the Jersey shore. The Continentals captured "a considerable number of arms, blankets, hats, cloaths, &c Col. Barton and about 40 privates were made prisoners."

General Sullivan's men returned to join General Smallwood. Together, they proceeded toward Colonel Ogden's position. As they heard nothing from that direction, General Sullivan concluded that Colonel Ogden routed the Crown forces and waited for General Sullivan who hastened his march as much as possible and sent a boat to order the boats at Halsey's Point to meet him at the Old Blazing Star Ferry. They arrived at the ferry at noon and found that Colonel Ogden had routed the enemy and taken the commander, three captains, one lieutenant, two ensigns and 80 privates prisoners, a large quantity of stores and a loaded sloop as well as a great number of horses and cattle.

Colonel Ogden's troops re-crossed the river. The boats from Halsey's Point had not arrived with the men's packs and provisions because they saw the sloop captured by Colonel Ogden coming up the sound and took her to be a tender. They ran the boats up the river preventing the messenger from finding them. General Sullivan began crossing the river as soon as possible with his three boats before the enemy collected their forces and attacked his rear with a superior force and cut off any retreat. The rear guard of 100 men, posted on a hill about 100 yards from the ferry, were just pushing the boats away from shore when Brigadier General John Campbell (d. 1806), commander of the king's troops on the island, and General Cortlandt Skinner (1728–1799) arrived with a superior number of British troops and Anspachers to attack their rear. They expected no opposition from such a small party and advanced boldly. However, the Continental officers formed their ranks and "gave the enemy so warm a reception, that they were various times driven back in the greatest confusion." The Crown troops took heavy fire and executed a bayonet charge on the Continental flank and put them to flight.

Realizing the Crown forces were about to surround them, the rear guard retired to a hill about 500 feet to their rear. After a while, they retreated to another about 50 yards farther. They held their ground until they almost ran out of ammunition. Seeing the boats in the river not coming over and, with no other means of getting off the island, about 40 men surrendered themselves prisoners of war. Some of the remainder swam the river and landed safely on the Jersey shore. The others went to Amboy where some troops were sent to take them across.

If the boatmen had done their duty, not a man would have been lost. However, the Crown troops brought a field piece and a howitzer to play upon the water, frightening the boatmen so much that they refused to put ashore on either side of the river. General Sullivan ordered his men to fire upon them to force them over, but the boatmen rowed toward Amboy. The Crown forces picked up some stragglers, including three majors, one captain, three lieutenants, two ensigns, one surgeon, and 127 privates, and either took them prisoners or killed them. General Sullivan captured two lieutenant colonels, three captains, two lieutenants, two ensigns, one surgeon, one sergeant major, four sergeants, two corporals, two musicians, and about 130 privates and 28 Loyalists. He estimated killing and wounding at least 400, destroyed their forts and vessels, and captured their arms, baggage, and a great number of cattle. General Sullivan reported 10 men killed and 15 wounded, two seriously.[487]

★ The Congressional forces remaining in the New York area attacked Staten Island on Saturday, August 23, 1777. The island was heavily garrisoned by Loyalist troops, many of them from Bergen County, New Jersey at the time. They captured about 30 or 40 prisoners, including Colonel Joseph Barton and Lieutenant Jacob Van Buskirk (1760–1834), son of Lieutenant Colonel Abraham Van Buskirk. Some soldiers thought they should be tried for treason but General George Washington (1732–1799) insisted that they be treated as prisoners of war. Even though the British treated their prisoners outrageously, they did not try them for treason.[488]

★ Crown troops captured Uriah Chamberlain, a private in one of the Jersey regiments, during a raid on Staten Island on Wednesday, August 27, 1777. He died in prison the following winter.[489]

★ Major General John Sullivan's (1740–1795) division attacked Staten Island on Monday, September 1, 1777. They drove the Crown forces and took some prisoners but they suffered many losses in their retreat. General Sullivan was later court-martialed for the raid but acquitted. (Although William Adair's diary records this raid on September 1, 1777 and James Sullivan's letter to General Sullivan dated Sept. 3, 1777 notes that he just learned of the attack, both authors are probably referring to the raid of August 22nd.)[490]

★ Three detachments of the British Army, one from New York City, another from Kingsbridge, and one from Staten Island, went into New Jersey on Wednesday, September 10, 1777. They captured several prisoners and a very large drove of oxen, sheep and other cattle. They returned the following Tuesday.[491]

★ Parties of Whigs from Elizabethtown, New Jersey landed on Staten Island on Tuesday, Wednesday, Thursday and Friday November 18–21, 1777 and were beaten off each time.[492]

★ General Philemon Dickinson (1739–1809) embarked at Halstead's Point in New Jersey and landed on Staten Island in three divisions in an attempt to surprise Loyalist General Cortlandt Skinner (1728–1799). They landed early in the morning of Thursday, November 27, 1777 and marched 7 miles to a rendezvous, hoping to get in the rear of the Provincials, surprise Skinner's Corps, and cut them off. They observed the utmost secrecy, not informing the officers of the object until 8 PM the previous evening. Skinner got word of it at 3 AM and retreated.

When Dickinson arrived at the rendezvous, he found General John Campbell (d. 1806) in force with artillery and two war vessels to cover the fortifications. When troop reinforcements and warships approached the island, the militiamen took to their boats in a hurry and returned to the Jersey shore. They were on the island eight hours, killed five or six Loyalists and captured 24 prisoners before retreating. They had 14 men slightly wounded and only three taken prisoners.[493]

★ A raid on Staten Island on Friday, December 26, 1777, resulted in the capture of Loyalist Benjamin Williams.[494]

★ Captain Nathaniel Fitz Randolph (1747–1780) of Woodbridge, New Jersey, led a Whig raiding party to capture Colonel Christopher Billopp (1737–1827) and several members of the Staten Island Loyalist militia who were on patrol on Friday, June 5, 1778. They captured Billopp and took him to a jail in Burlington, New Jersey, where he shared a cell with Colonel John Graves Simcoe (1752–1806). He was chained to the floor and allowed only bread and water. Billopp was later exchanged. He was recaptured about a year later (see June 23, 1779).[495]

★ Congressional forces began a heavy cannonade of Staten Island from their works at Elizabethtown, New Jersey about 1 AM on Wednesday June 10, 1778. Soon afterward, they tried to land upon the island in a number of flat boats. Three boats carrying about 150 troops tried to land between the Blazing Star and Burnt Island about 2 AM. They intended to surprise a post of the Royal Provincials but were discovered, fired upon, and beaten off. At the same time, three other boats carrying about 50 volunteers landed on a point of meadow nearly 2 miles northeast of Burnt Island and 3 to 4 miles from the other party's landing place. They marched about half a mile, undiscovered, to the Bridge Creek before a sentinel on the other side of the creek challenged them. They responded by a volley of well-directed fire on the guardhouse, which threw the Royal Provincials into such a panic that they fled without returning a shot.

Anticipating a general alarm on the island, the raiding party retired to their boats and re-embarked. When they ceased firing, the Royal Provincials probably concluded that the danger was over and returned to their old post.[496]

Rivington's Gazette reported that the Congressional troops returned to the Jersey shore and came back to Staten Island about 4 AM the same morning in 10 boats, each supposedly containing 100 men. They tried to "land at the same place under cover of the fire from their batteries, and a continued Discharge of Small Arms from the Boats; but they were so vigorously opposed by General Skinner's Brigade, that they were obliged to make a final and disgraceful Retreat." The *New Jersey Gazette* (no. 30) reported that instead of 10 boats with 100 men each, there were three boats with about 50 men. They marched half a mile into the interior before being discovered. They fired and the Loyalists ran away. They troops returned to their boats and were fired upon as they approached the Jersey shore.[497]

★ Colonel Christopher Billopp (1737–1827) was captured on Staten Island a second time on Wednesday, June 23, 1779. This time a band of Whigs rowed across the Arthur Kill from Perth Amboy, New Jersey, and raided the Conference House. According to legend, a servant girl placed a candle in the window as a signal that Colonel Billopp was at home. They captured the colonel and took him out of the house through a basement tunnel that led to the shore. The colonel was taken to the Burlington County, New Jersey jail where he was chained to the floor and fed a diet of bread and water by order of Elias Boudinot, Commisary General of Prisoners. His harsh treatment was in retaliation for the suffering of John Lesher (1740–1811) and Captain Nathaniel Fitz Randolph (1747–1780), of Woodbridge, New Jersey, who were imprisoned in a British jail. The colonel was released the day after Christmas in an exchange of prisoners-of-war. When

Colonel Billopp returned home, he confronted the 15-year-old servant girl. The two quarreled on the staircase of the mansion and Billopp pushed her down the stairs to her death. Some accounts say that he stabbed the girl.[498]

★ Captain Randle and 14 men went from Elizabethtown to Staten Island on Wednesday, June 24, 1778 and fired at the Loyalist militiamen on guard. They wounded Mr. Richard Connor, Jr. (1763–1853) in the arm, and one Ashar Tappen in the leg. The Loyalists pursued the raiders who quickly boarded their boat and escaped to the Jersey shore.[499]

★ A party from Elizabethtown landed on Staten Island Tuesday night, November 3, 1778. They captured Mr. Isaac Bonnell (1737–1806), the Barrack Master, who was released on his own parole on November 8.[500]

★ New Jersey militiamen raided Staten Island from Halstead's Point on Saturday, November 28, 1778.[501]

★ Captain Nathaniel Fitz Randolph (1747–1780) raided Staten Island during the night of Monday, February 8, 1779. He returned to Woodbridge where he was captured early the following morning. News arrived the following day that the Crown forces were collecting a number of boats at Billop's Point which has caused the militia in the vicinity of Woodbridge and Brunswick to muster to oppose them.[502]

★ A party of Whigs from Jersey went to Prince's Bay on the south side of Long Island on Thursday morning, March 18, 1779. They intended to take a boat loaded with wood, but a few of the inhabitants assembled on the beach and fired at them before they could do so. They kept up such a brisk fire that the raiders abandoned the boat which happened to be aground. The only known casualty was a Mr. Sleight, an inhabitant of Staten Island, who was wounded in the breast.[503]

★ About 40 Regulars and an equal number of Loyalists went from Staten Island to Rahway and Woodbridge on Tuesday night, June 29, 1779. There, they shot Captain Richard Skinner (1740–1779), of the militia, and captured 15 inhabitants, including Captain Samuel Meeker (1740–1804), of the light horse, and Captain Christopher Marsh (1743–1810). A few militiamen gathered immediately and prevented them from committing any further mischief. Several Crown troops were wounded, including one who was captured and died later in the day.[504]

★ A party of men from Brunswick went to Staten Island on Wednesday night, June 30, 1779. They captured Colonel Cortelyou and Mr. William Smith (1728–1793), who was taken prisoner for high treason the previous summer, but he deserted again when released on bail. They also took a sloop in the Narrows but could not bring her off due to unfavorable wind and tide. They left the sloop after stripping her of several valuable articles.[505]

★ A party of Congressional troops crossed from Jersey to Staten Island early Friday morning, July 9, 1779. They surprised two inhabitants named Doughty and Butler and took them prisoners before the light horse could arrive.[506]

★ A small party of troops stationed at Elizabethtown made an excursion to Staten Island on Friday night, August 6, 1779. They captured two Crown troops without opposition, including Jacob Mercereau (1730–1807), the younger of the two.[507]

★ Some New Jersey militiamen, commanded by two captains, were going from Monmouth County to Elizabethtown in mid-August 1779 when a few "people unknown" fired upon them at Blazing Star Landing. The commanding officer was wounded in the thigh and the rest were routed, several of them having been wounded.[508]

★ Captain John Palfrey's small sloop of war *Neptune* was serving as a guard boat at the Bergen Point ferry in mid-October, 1779. The vessel became unmanageable on Friday morning, October 15. It drifted within range of the Whig guns at the fort at Elizabethtown Point and ran aground. Captain Coogle, the British commander at Decker's ferry (Port Richmond), soon discovered the *Neptune*'s plight. He ordered Captain Cornelius Hatfield or Hetfield, Jr., who commanded 20 men and a small gunboat at that post to recover the sloop.

Job Hatfield or Hetfield (1754–1825) joined him in another well-manned boat. They set off together to rescue the *Neptune*; but before they arrived, a party of about 30 militiamen from the fort at Elizabethtown Point had already boarded her. The militiamen, seeing they were outnumbered, abandoned the sloop and the Hatfield party went on board. The militiamen in the fort trained their cannon on the sloop and opened fire. The Hatfields returned fire. The fire continued with more or less activity for several hours before the tide rose enough to re-float the *Neptune*. Even though several men were killed and wounded and the vessel sustained considerable damage, the *Neptune* managed to escape to her station.[509]

★ Colonel John Graves Simcoe (1752–1806) enlisted the help of a New Jersey Loyalist named Captain Peter Sanford (ca. 1755-1812), who was captain of a troop on Long Island and was supposed to be familiar with the topography of that part of the country, as a guide. He also sent Major Armstrong to South River, where he was to ambush some Continental troops. Colonel Simcoe set out from Richmond at 8 PM on Tuesday, October 26, 1779 and marched to Billop's Point. The boats which should have been at the Point at midnight to ferry the troops across did not arrive until the morning.

Colonel Simcoe planned to reach the place where he understood the Whig boats were collected, burn them, and then return by way of New Brunswick and then to South Amboy where Major Armstrong's ambuscade was to be placed. In the event of any mishap, Major Armstrong was instructed to give credit to anyone who could give the countersign of "Clinton and Montrose."

When the British arrived at Quibbletown, a party of men with knapsacks came out of a tavern. The Rangers prepared to attack them; but Colonel Simcoe, trying to make them think that his men were part of the Continental Army, cried out, "These are not the tories we are in search of!" Most of the men were deceived, except for one who knew Colonel Simcoe by sight. As soon as the party had left, he sent an express to Colonel John Neilson (1745-1833) at New Brunswick. Neilson immediately ordered out his regiment and marched them to the bridge at the Raritan Landing.

The British were then guided by a boy, who thought Captain Sanford was a French officer because he was dressed in red. This boy told them that all the boats except 18 had been sent on to General George Washington's (1732–1799) camp. Colonel Simcoe proceeded to burn those 18 boats, thinking that if he had arrived earlier, he might have captured all of them and taken them down the river.

As people gathered from all directions and alarm guns were heard all over the countryside, Colonel Simcoe's situation got progressively more dangerous. The people who had already assembled fired at them as they passed, wounding several soldiers. Shots were also fired at them from the front. Fearing an ambuscade, Colonel Simcoe tried to lead his troops across some fields. His horse received five musket balls, fell on him and bruised him badly. He fell to the ground unconscious. When he regained consciousness, he found himself a prisoner. One man was killed and several wounded.

The British, in their haste to retreat, did not notice Colonel Simcoe's absence for some time. When they realized it, they halted immediately west of Brunswick and sent Dr. John Ryker and Mr. John Polhemus, his servant, with a flag to request permission to tend to Colonel Simcoe. Captain Peter Voorhees (d. 1779) came forward to meet the flag when Captain Sanford ordered a file of men to fire upon them, killing Captain Voorhees. The Continentals withdrew and the Crown forces returned without obtaining the information they had come to seek. When they reached South River, they rejoined Major Armstrong's force and returned to Staten Island.[510]

Col. Simcoe was transferred from Brunswick to Bordentown on Thursday, October 28, 1779, where he was kept in a tavern owned by Colonel Oakley Hoagland (or Hoogland) of the Jersey Militia. He was brought to the Burlington jail on November 7 and was exchanged for other prisoners on December 31st. The militia killed three Rangers, made six prisoners, and wounded a considerable number in the affair.[511]

★ Brigadier General William Irvine (1741–1804) was instructed, in January 1780, to obtain information "of the enemy's strength, corps, situation, and works" on Staten Island, to ascertain the state of the ice at Halstead's Point and at the Blazing Star Ferry, and to act in concert with Colonel Elias Dayton (1737–1807) in making the necessary preparations for an attack on the island. They procured several hundred sleds or sleighs, ammunition, rations, tools, guns, and spare shoes.

Major General William Alexander (Earl of Stirling, 1726–1783) commanded the expedition that hoped to capture, if possible, the entire enemy force of about 1,200 Crown troops on the island. His corps of between 3,000 and 4,000 men with six field pieces and two howitzers proceeded from the neighborhood of Morristown, New Jersey toward the Watering Place.

They crossed the ice over the Sound in sleighs at de Hart's Point on Friday night, January 14, 1780, and reached Mercereau's dockyard on Staten Island before daybreak. As soon as they crossed the river, General Stirling detached a party under Lieutenant Colonel Marinus Willett (1740–1830) to march toward Decker's Ferry to surprise Lieutenant Colonel Abraham Van Buskirk (1750–1783), commanding the 4th battalion of about 200 Loyalists from Brigadier-General Cortlandt Skinner's (1728–1799) brigade posted there. At the forks of the Blazing Star road, one column proceeded by Douban's Mills, while the other went by the back road toward the Watering Place. The communication between the Island and New York was open, so, as soon as Stirling's forces arrived in front of the earthworks, the Loyalists sent a boat to the city. Several vessels came down to the island that evening.

Van Buskirk had received intelligence of Willett's approach and withdrew toward Ryerson's Ferry on the east side of the island. The Continentals pursued them and, before noon, took a position on the heights, near the redoubts constructed at the north end of the island. This position cut off communication between Van Buskirk's troops and those at Richmond Town. Willett's troops reconnoitered the position, remained overnight and retired about sunrise the next morning, returning to De Hart's Point about 11 AM. They burned Decker's house and eight or nine small vessels frozen in the ice at Decker's Ferry. They captured eight or ten prisoners and received several deserters and took a considerable quantity of blankets and other stores.

A party of British dragoons charged Stirling's rear guard under Major Evan Edwards (1752–1798). The dragoons were repulsed immediately with one man killed. The Major had three men killed and a few men frostbitten. Everyone suffered considerably from the cold, as the snow was three or four feet deep. The British retaliated 10 days later, raiding Elizabethtown and Newark, New Jersey.[512]

★ General George Washington (1732–1799) sent a detachment of 2,500 men under Brigadier General William Alexander (Earl of Stirling, 1726–1783) and Brigadier General James Irvine (1735–1819) across the upper bay early Monday morning, January 17, 1780. They crossed at de Hart's Point and proceeded toward the Watering Place, hoping to strike the enemy force estimated at 1,000 to 1,200 men. However, the Crown forces learned of their movements. As they were well situated and a surprise was out of the question, an assault was deemed inadvisable as Washington would probably have lost more than he could have gained if successful.

Several vessels came from New York to Staten Island that evening. As Washington retreated the following morning, a party of enemy dragoons charged his rear guard under Major Edwards but was immediately repulsed. The Major lost three men killed; but he killed one of the dragoons and took his horse. He took a few prisoners and a few deserters from the enemy. A few of his men were frostbitten, despite efforts to have all those unable to march transported in sleighs.

Immediately after crossing, Washington detached Lieutenant Colonel Marinus Willett (1740–1830) and a party to Decker's house. The corps there had been alarmed and barely escaped. Willett burned the house and eight or nine small vessels and took a considerable quantity of blankets and other stores.[514]

★ Lieutenant Colonel John Graves Simcoe (1752–1806) received intelligence from deserters and other sources that General George Washington (1732–1799) was quartered at a considerable distance from his army in January 1780. Colonel Simcoe thought that it would not be difficult to capture him. He persuaded a man, who had been persecuted by the Whigs, to draw a detailed map of the country. He sent out a trusty person to ascertain some details but gave him no information that might lead him to guess at the plan.

Lieutenant Colonel Simcoe intended to march by very secret ways, made even more so by inclement weather, and to arrive near General Washington's quarters by daybreak. The detachment was to consist of 80 men, taken randomly from the cavalry or infantry with an officer for every six men. The dragoons would tie up their horses in a swamp and storm the quarters. They would carry both muskets and swords to attack General Washington's guard on foot. The party would halt at two cottages in a wood if they should arrive ahead of schedule. Lieutenant Colonel Simcoe's only apprehension was how to bring off General Washington and preserve his life if he should resist.

Captain George Beckwith (1753–1823), Lieutenant General Wilhelm von Knyphausen's (1716–1800) aid-de-camp had a similar idea. He planned to send the hussars of Lieutenant Colonel Simcoe's Queen's Rangers to march with a convoy over the ice to New York. He would gather cavalry at New York, including the hussars. A general movement from Staten Island would be advantageous. Lieutenant Colonel Simcoe received orders "to send a party to surprise the enemy's post at Woodbridge or Rahway, and to give a general alarm."

His party was to cross the ice at 1 AM on Monday, February 10, 1780 and return around 9 or 10. Lieutenant Colonel Simcoe and 200 infantrymen crossed the ice at the appointed time. Major Armstrong occupied the heights at the Old Blazing Star with some infantrymen, the cavalry, and cannon to cover their return. The snow required the troops to march on the beaten road. They found no posts in Woodbridge, New Jersey and continued to the crossroads from Amboy to Elizabethtown where they encountered a patrol and halted. They maintained such profound silence in the middle of the road that night that they deceived the enemy into thinking they were mistaken, as they learned from the conversations they overheard.

Another patrol on horseback came across the flank of the marching column and fired. The Queen's Rangers sounded the bugle-horns, drums, and bagpipe in succession, giving a universal alarm. A chance shot of the sentinels killed a soldier. The party returned toward Woodbridge. The Whigs assembled in their rear and appeared at 8 AM when the party passed Woodbridge Creek. The snow was so deep that the troops had to stay on the road. This helped the Rangers because the companies advanced "alternately in front of the march, occupied such orchards or trees, as were at a small distance from the road, and checked the enemy who pressed upon the rear."

As he approached the Sound, Lieutenant Colonel Simcoe heard the enemy plan to occupy the houses at the ferry and to fire on the Rangers as they crossed back to Staten Island. He ordered Sergeant Wright to gallop over the ice to Major Armstrong with orders to point his cannon at the ferry house. He also detached Captain David Shank (d. 1831) to cross ahead of the troops and to conceal himself behind the ridges of the ice floes to cover the retreat. The party would cross the Sound safely between the angle formed by the fire of Captain Shank's detachment, directly opposite, and of Major Armstrong's cannon, at a greater and more oblique distance.

As the enemy approached, the Rangers suddenly turned about and charged them. The Whigs fled and were pursued until they went over a small hill. The Rangers turned around and were halfway across the ice before the Whigs noticed them. The Whigs quickly occupied the houses while some pursued the Rangers on the ice. Capt Shank's fire from his ambuscade drove them back immediately. Cannon shot struck the houses at the same time, killing some of the occupants.

The party returned to Richmond with the loss of only one man and a few wounded. The Whigs lost considerably more men, many of whom were seen to fall. The heavy rain froze on the surface of the snow, cutting the fetlocks of the horses, making it impossible for Captain Beckwith's plan to succeed. The hussars (see Photo NY-27) soon returned to Staten Island. The ice began to melt on February 22nd, making the Sound impassable.[514]

★ A few inhabitants of Rahway, New Jersey made an excursion to Staten Island on Saturday night, February 12, 1780. They captured a Loyalist militia captain and seven loyal inhabitants.[515]

★ Former New Jersey militia officer David Forman (1733–1812) organized the Association for Retaliation so the Whigs could protect themselves against Loyalist raids, particularly those of Colonel Tye's (ca. 1753–1780) gang who used Staten Island as a base to conduct their raids in Monmouth County in July 1780.[516]

★ Ensign Lewis Fitz Randolph (1756–1822) took a party of men to Staten Island on Friday night, August 25, 1780. They took Justice Lake and five other Loyalists prisoners without any casualties.[517]

★ Ensign Lewis Fitz Randolph led another excursion onto Staten Island on Sunday night, September 3, 1780. They captured Anthony Wright and two other noted Loyalists.[518]

★ Ensign Lewis Fitz Randolph and eight men of the state regiment visited Staten Island from Woodbridge on Tuesday night, September 19, 1780. They surprised a picket of 14 new levies but took only four prisoners. The remainder of the guard fled.[519]

★ A party of about 16 Whigs crossed the water from Elizabethtown to Staten Island about 5 AM on Friday, November 24, 1780 to go foraging. The Hessians, unaware of their number, began firing at them and lit the alarm signals. Some of the foragers were taken prisoners.[520]

★ Captain Adam Hyler (1735–1782) captured the sloop *Susannah* near Prince's Bay on the south side of Staten Island before Wednesday, January 3, 1781.[521]

★ A detachment of eight Jersey militiamen in Elizabethtown went to Staten Island on Monday night, March 26, 1781. They captured a lieutenant and one private of the Loyalist militia. They also took two others; but they could not bring them back because of the small boat and adverse winds.[522]

★ Captain Baker Hendricks (1756–1789) led a party from Elizabethtown to Staten Island on Monday, April 9, 1781. They captured a captain and two others. Captain Hendricks returned on Monday, April 16, 1781 to capture one Loyalist lieutenant and a private and one inhabitant. Two days later, on Wednesday the 18th, he went back to Staten Island and captured 10 prisoners.[523]

★ Captain Adam Hyler (1735–1782) captured a pilot boat and two other boats between Robin's Reef and Yellow Hook with a single whaleboat one Saturday night in May 1781. The pilot boat was plundered then redeemed for $400.[524]

★ Captain Baker Hendricks (1756–1789) with another officer, a sergeant, and 11 privates conducted a raid on Staten Island on Tuesday, May 8, 1781 to capture a patrol of the 1st Battalion New Jersey Volunteers and to plunder the inhabitants. However, finding that Ensign Henry L. Barton's (ca. 1761–?) patrol was already on the alert, they concealed themselves in a wood a short distance from Mr. Salter's house. When the patrol left the neighborhood, they immediately surrounded Salter's house. Although the patrol had proceeded a distance, they turned back, attacked, and soon dispersed Captain Hendricks's party, capturing two men, killing one, and wounding Captain Hendricks. The sergeant became lost and was captured by the militia. The Loyalists had no casualties.[525]

★ Captain Maffet, commander of a Philadelphia whaleboat, captured a sloop out of New York laden with fish off Long Beach on Thursday, July 26, 1781. He also captured three Loyalist boats off Shrewsbury Point that had 30 plundered sheep on board and "23 sheep stealers."[526]

★ Lieutenant Asher Fitz Randolph (1755–1817), of the state regiment stationed at Woodbridge, New Jersey, took a party of 70 men in six whaleboats and landed at Staten Island on Thursday night, August 23, 1781. They proceeded as far as Fort Richmond where more than 200 Loyalists were stationed. A severe firing began about daybreak and continued until 11 AM. Anybody who came out of the fort was either killed or captured. Lieutenant Fitz Randolph captured several prisoners and nine horses and had only three men slightly wounded. Captain John Storer (1750–1816), who commanded one of the whaleboats, was wounded in three different places but not mortally.[527]

★ Captain Adam Hyler or Huyler (1735–1782) and a party of Whigs from Brunswick, New Jersey landed on Staten Island in six boats that same night. They took three inhabitants and nine horses away with them. They had driven nearly 100 head of cattle to the waterside; but the militia gathered and forced them to leave their booty and one of their boats behind. The inhabitants were paroled the next day and got home.[528]

★ Captain Adam Hyler (1735–1782), with one gunboat and two whaleboats, boarded a sloop and two schooners on Saturday, October 13, 1781. All but two crewmen had left the vessels which were anchored under cover of the Sandy Hook lighthouse. Captain

Hyler took the vessels; but the sloop was such a "dull sailer" that he set her on fire about 3 miles from the fort when he was annoyed by a galley anchored near Staten Island. One of the schooners ran aground and was stripped and left. The other, a very fast pilot boat with one 4-pounder, was taken to New Brunswick, New Jersey with the two prisoners.[529]

★ William Hatfield or Hetfield (d. 1781), a resident of Elizabethtown went to Staten Island to sell a small quantity of flour on Thursday, November 8, 1781. As he returned that evening, he encountered Peter Terrat in the Sound. Terrat was "a noted thief, who supports himself and a gang of such miscreants by robbing and plundering." Hatfield surrendered himself to Terrat and his party. Terrat thought Hatfield threw something overboard, drew a pistol and shot him dead.[530]

★ Captain Adam Hyler (1735–1782) and a small party of men went to the Narrows in a gunboat on Saturday night, November 10, 1781. There, they captured a ship, the *Father's Desire*, with 14 or 15 hands and took her away, intending to run her up the Raritan River. However, the ship ran aground near the mouth of the river. She was loaded with rum and pork. As the Loyalists approached in force, Captain Hyler took several hogsheads of rum and the prisoners then set the ship on fire.[531]

★ Captain Adam Hyler (1735–1782), commanding seven or eight stout whaleboats manned with about 100 men, engaged two Loyalist sloops at the Narrows on Saturday, December 15, 1781. The vessels were headed to Shrewsbury, New Jersey. One of them was commanded by Shore Stephens, a noted Loyalist. It had on board £600 in specie and a large quantity of dry goods. The other had similar cargo in addition to sugar and rum. Both vessels were taken to New Brunswick, New Jersey.[532]

★ A party of Whigs from Woodbridge, New Jersey landed near the Old Star on the west side of Staten Island on Tuesday night, January 22, 1782. They went to the house of Jacob Winant (1725–1810) where they captured two of the inhabitants and a little boy and stole two horses. After carrying their plunder over the river, they returned to the island intending more devastation. A party of Colonel Billopp's militiamen and some of Captain Robins's Loyalists spotted them and immediately attacked them, killing one, wounding two, and capturing the whole party and their boat.[533]

★ Captain Robert Quigley (1736–1813), Major William Crane and a party of six townsmen from Elizabethtown captured the sloop *Katy* on Monday night, March 3, 1783. The *Katy*, with 12 double fortified 4-pounders, contained 100 hogsheads of Jamaica rum and some muskets and was lying aground within pistol-shot of the grand battery of New York and alongside of the 24-gun ship *Eagle*. The men also captured the *Eagle*, but had to leave her there, as she lay aground. The captains and crews of both vessels were taken to Elizabethtown, New Jersey in the sloop and put in jail. The *Katy* and her cargo were sold at auction at Elizabethtown, on Monday, March 17.[534]

★ Congressional forces seized a Hessian paymaster and a large sum of money (2,000 guineas) intended for Hessian prisoners in Pennsylvania on Friday, March 15, 1782. The Congressional troops claimed the money was intended for General Charles Cornwallis's (1738–1805) army and blamed the Loyalists for the raid.[535]

★ Captain Adam Hyler (1735–1782) took a 1-gun boat and a barge on an expedition to the Narrows on Friday night, April 12 or 19, 1782. He surprised and captured a British cutter mounting six 18- and ten 9-pound guns. However, the wind was unfavorable for sailing her away; so he landed her crew of about 50, removed such articles as he thought proper, and set her on fire. He also took a sloop which he ransomed for 400 dollars.[536]

★ Captain Adam Hyler (1735–1782) captured four vessels near New York in mid-May 1782. One of them was retaken; but he ran the other three ashore and stripped them.[537]

★ Captain Robert Quigley (1736–1813) and three men boarded a small boat and captured a brig bound for Halifax on Wednesday, May 22, 1782. They were within sight of a 20-gun ship and a fort on Staten Island. They brought their prize to Egg Harbor.[538]

★ Major William Crane received intelligence at Elizabethtown that two whaleboats were bound from New York for a cruise in the Delaware and were ready to cast off. He took 30 Continentals stationed at Elizabethtown and any volunteers who wanted to join him. They crossed to Staten Island on Friday morning, June 21, 1782 to capture the boats. They brought both boats, the *Ladies Delight* and the *Victory*, along with 17 prisoners to the garrison without being detected by an armed vessel in the Kills. The *Ladies Delight*, mounting two 4-pounders and eight swivels (see Photo NY-9), and the *Victory*, with two 4-pounders and four swivels, had interrupted river trade and had their stores and ammunition on board.[539]

★ Captain Adam Hyler (1735–1782) captured two fishing boats near the Narrows on Tuesday night, July 2, 1782. He liberated one of them and took the other which was re-captured the following day by Captain John Storer (1750–1816). He captured it in the Narrows about 8 PM on Friday, July 5 and ransomed it for $100.[540]

★ Captain Adam Hyler (1735–1782), with eight large 24-oared boats, attacked a galley stationed at Prince's Bay on the south side of Staten Island a little before sunset on Tuesday night, July 9, 1782. There was little or no wind that evening. Captain Cashman gave him an 18-pounder which went through the stern of one of the boats and forced Captain Hyler to put ashore on the island. A skirmish ensued and Captain Hyler had to leave one of his boats behind and escape with two others.

John Althouse and 12 men were on board a guard boat at anchor in Prince's Bay, when he saw two whaleboats near the South Amboy shore. He fired a 24-pound shot through Captain Hyler's boat. Captain Robert Dickie (1760–1782) took Captain Hyler's crew aboard his boat and headed for New Brunswick with General Jacob S. Jackson whom they had captured in South Bay. General Jackson was kept prisoner until he was ransomed.[541]

★ John Storer (1750–1816) embarked with two boats at Point Comfort on Sunday evening, November 3, 1782. They proceeded to York Bay by way of the Narrows. After a fruitless search for detached vessels, he headed toward Middletown. On his return, he passed through the British fleet at anchor near the Watering Place. He ran along the Long Island shore and spotted the 50-ton sloop *Chance* anchored under the Flagstaff fort and within half a pistol shot of the 14-gun battery at the Watering Place. He immediately boarded the vessel and captured her without firing a shot. The sloop was auctioned off the following month along with her tackle, apparel, furniture and six cast iron stoves.[542]

NOTES

ABBREVIATION

NDAR: United States. Naval History Division. *Naval Documents of the American Revolution.* William Bell Clark, editor; with a foreword by President John F. Kennedy and an introd. by Ernest McNeill Eller. Washington: Naval History Division, Dept. of the Navy: For sale by the Supt. of Docs., U.S. G.P.O., 1964-

Preface

1. Desmarais, Norman. *Battlegrounds of Freedom: A Historical Guide to the Battlefields of the War of American Independence.* Busca: Ithaca, NY, 2005.

2. Heitman, Francis B. *Historical Register of Officers of the Continental Army during the War of the Revolution, April 1775 to December 1783.* Washington, DC. : The Rare Book Shop Publishing Company, 1914; Baltimore: Genealogical Publishing Company, 1967.

3. Peckham, Howard Henry. *The Toll of Independence: Engagements & Battle Casualties of the American Revolution.* Chicago: University of Chicago Press, 1974.

4. Boatner, Mark Mayo. *Encyclopedia of the American Revolution.* 3d ed., New York: McKay, 1980.

5. Boatner, Mark Mayo. *Landmarks of the American Revolution: A Guide to Locating and Knowing What Happened at the Sites of Independence.* Stackpole Books: Harrisburg, PA, 1973; 2nd ed. Library of Military History. Detroit: Charles Scribner's Sons, 2007.

6. Selesky Harold E., editor in chief. *Encyclopedia of the American Revolution,* 2nd ed. Detroit: Charles Scribner's Sons, 2007.

7. Fremont-Barnes, Gregory, Richard Alan Ryerson, eds. *The Encyclopedia of the American Revolutionary War: A Political, Social, and Military History.* Santa Barbara, CA: ABC-CLIO, 2006.

8. Anderson, Fred. *A People's Army: Massachusetts Soldiers and Society in the Seven Years' War.* Chapel Hill, N.C. 1984. pp. 84–85, 129.

9. Waller, George M. *The American Revolution in the West.* Chicago: Nelson Hall, 1976. pp. 30–31.

10. Adams, Charles F., ed. *The Works of John Adams.* Boston: Charles C. Little and James Brown, 1850. vol. 10 p. 110.

11. Ibid. pp. 192–93.

12. Raphael, Ray. *A People's History of the American Revolution: How Common People Shaped the Fight for Independence.* New York: New Press, 2001. pp. 145, 342.

New York

1. Allen, Thomas. Extracts from a Manuscript Journal. *Continental Journal.* LXIX (Sept. 18, 1777) p.1.

2. Ibid.

3. Ibid.

4. *Encyclopedia of the American Revolution.* Harold E. Selesky, editor in chief.–2nd Ed. Detroit: Charles Scribner's Sons, 2007. II:1151–1156. *The Encyclopedia of the American Revolutionary War: a political, social, and military history.* Gregory Fremont-Barnes, Richard Alan Ryerson, editors. Santa Barbara, CA: ABC-CLIO, 2006. II:439–443. Allen, Thomas. Extracts from a Manuscript Journal. *Continental Journal.* LXIX (Sept. 18, 1777) p.1, 4. French, Allen. *The Taking of Ticonderoga in 1775: The British Story: A Study of Captors and Captives.* Cambridge: Harvard University Press, 1928. Gerlach, Don R. *Proud Patriot: Philip Schuyler and the War of Independence, 1775–1783.* Syracuse, NY: Syracuse University Press, 1987. Hamilton, Edward P. *Fort Ticonderoga: Key to a Continent.* Boston: Little Brown, 1964. Hargrove, Richard J. *General John Burgoyne.* Newark: University of Delaware Press, 1983. Hatch, Robert M. *Thrust for Canada: The American Attempt on Quebec in 1775–1776.* Boston: Houghton Mifflin, 1979. Jellison, Charles. *Ethan Allen: Frontier Rebel.* Syracuse, NY: Syracuse University Press, 1969. Ketchum, Richard M. *Saratoga: turning point of America's Revolutionary War.* New York: Holt, 1997. Martin, James Kirby. *Benedict Arnold: Revolutionary Hero.* New York: New York University Press, 1997. Nelson, Paul David. *Anthony Wayne: Soldier of the Early Republic.* Bloomington: Indiana University Press, 1985. Nelson, Paul David. *General Horatio Gates: A Biography.* Baton Rouge: Louisiana State University Press, 1976. Nelson, Paul David. *General Sir Guy Carleton, Lord Dorchester: Soldier-Statesman of Early British Canada.* Madison, NJ: Fairleigh Dickinson University Press, 2000. Nelson, Paul David. *William Alexander, Lord Stirling.* University of Alabama Press, 1987. Pell, Stephen H. P. *Fort Ticonderoga, a Short History: Compiled from Contemporary Sources.* Fort Ticonderoga, NY: Fort Ticonderoga Museum, 1948. Roberts, Robert B. *New York's Forts in the Revolution.* Rutherford: Fairleigh Dickinson University Press, 1980. Ward, Christopher. *The War of the Revolution.* New York: Macmillan, 1952. 63–72.

5. Colonel Samuel Herrick to the President of the Vermont Council of Safety, Nov. 14, 1777. NDAR 10:481–2.

6. Baldwin Jeduthan. *The Revolutionary Journal Of Col. Baldwin 1775–1778.* Edited With A Memoir And Notes By Thomas Williams Baldwin. Bangor: Printed For The De Burians, 1906. pp.95–96. Extract of a letter from Albany, dated March 29. *The Pennsylvania Evening Post.* III:342 (April 22, 1777) p.223.

7. Peckham, Howard Henry. *The Toll of independence: Engagements & Battle Casualties of the American Revolution.* Chicago: University of Chicago Press, 1974. p.22.

8. Stedman, Charles. *The History of the Origin, Progress and Termination of the American War.* London: printed for the author, 1794. 1:322–330.

9. *Royal Gazette* 150:3 (Jan. 3, 1778) p.3. *The Massachusetts Spy: or, American Oracle of Liberty.* V:222 (May 24, 1775) p.3. *New England Chronicle.* VII:357 (From Thursday, May 25, to Thursday, June 1, 1775) p.3. *Connecticut Journal.* 398 (May 31, 1775) p.3. T*he New-London Gazette (Connecticut Gazette).* XII:603 (June 3, 1775) p.3. *Dunlap's Pennsylvania Packet or, the General Advertiser.* VI:263 (November 5, 1776) p.4. *The Pennsylvania Ledger: or the Virginia, Maryland, Pennsylvania, & New-Jersey Weekly Advertiser.* XCIII p.2. Extract of Another Letter from Ticonderoga, October 22. *The Newport Mercury.* 952 (November 11, 1776) p.3.

10. *The Pennsylvania Evening Post.* I:51 (May 20, 1775) p.205. *The Massachusetts Spy; or, American Oracle of Liberty.* 5:222 (May 24, 1775) p.3.

11. Atherton, William Henry. *Montreal: 1535–1914.* Montréal: S.J. Clarke, 1914. II:72.

12. *Dunlap's Pennsylvania Packet or, the General Advertiser.* VI:263 (Nov. 5, 1776) p.4.

13. Stember, Sol. *The Bicentennial Guide to the American Revolution.* New York: Saturday Review Press, [distributed by] Dutton, 1974; [s.l.]: New York Times and Arno Press, 1969. 1:19–22, 27, 47–48, 51–52. Ward, Christopher. *The War of the Revolution.* New York: Macmillan, 1952. pp.70–71, 384–386.

14. Stember, Sol. *The Bicentennial Guide to the American Revolution.* Saturday Review Press: New York, [distributed by] Dutton, 1974; [s.l.]: New York Times and Arno Press, 1969. 1:20.

15. Baldwin Jeduthan. *The Revolutionary Journal of Col. Jeduthan Baldwin 1775–1778.* Edited with a Memoir and Notes by Thomas Williams Baldwin. Bangor: Printed For The De Burians, 1906. p.106. Peckham, Howard Henry. *The Toll of Independence: Engagements & Battle Casualties of the American Revolution.* Chicago: University of Chicago Press, 1974. p.37.

16. Extract of a letter from Ticonderoga. *Pennsylvania Journal.* Wednesday, September 25, 1776. NDAR 6:993.

17. Brigadier General Benedict Arnold to Major General Horatio Gates. Gates Papers, Box 4, New York Historical Society. NDAR 6:925.

18. *Encyclopedia of the American Revolution.* Harold E. Selesky, editor in chief.–2nd Ed. Detroit: Charles Scribner's Sons, 2007. II:1181–1184. *The Encyclopedia of the American Revolutionary War: a political, social, and military history.* Gregory Fremont-Barnes, Richard Alan Ryerson, editors. Santa Barbara, CA: ABC–CLIO, 2006. IV:1281–1284. Barton, John. "The Battle of Valcour Island." *History Today.* 9 (1959):791–797. Clowes, William Laird. *The Royal Navy: a history from the earliest times to 1900.* 7 vols. London: Chatham, 1996. Fowler, William M., Jr. *Rebels Under Sail: The American Navy during the Revolution.* New York: Scribner, 1976. Gardiner, Robert, ed. *Navies and the American Revolution, 1775–1783.* London: Chatham, 1996. Hubbard, Timothy. "Battle of Valcour Island: Benedict Arnold." *American Heritage.* 17 (1966):87–91. Mahan, A. T. "The Naval Campaign of 1776 on Lake Champlain." *Scribner's Magazine.* 23 (1898):147–160. Martin, James Kirby. "The Battle of Valcour Island." In *Great American Naval Battles.* Edited by Jack Sweetman. Annapolis, MD: Naval Institute Press, 1998. Miller, Nathan. *Sea of Glory: The Continental Navy Fights for Independence.* New York: McKay, 1974. Nelson, James L. Dutton, 1794. Camden, ME: International Marine/McGraw-Hill, c2006. Nelson, Paul David. "Guy Carleton versus Benedict Arnold: The Campaign of 1776 in Canada and on Lake Champlain." *New York History.* 57 (1976):147–160. Ward, Christopher. *The War of the Revolution.* New York: Macmillan, 1952. pp.384–397.

19. *Encyclopedia of the American Revolution.* Harold E. Selesky, editor in chief.–2nd Ed. Detroit: Charles Scribner's Sons, 2007. II:1099–1100. "Beebe's Journal" *Pennsylvania Magazine of History and Biography.* LIX, 353, 354. NDAR 6:1245. Governor Sir Guy Carleton to Captain Charles Douglas, R.N. Guy Carleton Letter Book. Haldimand Papers, Additional Ms. 21699. NDAR 6:1257.

20. Peckham, Howard Henry. *The Toll of Independence: Engagements & Battle Casualties of the American Revolution.* Chicago: University of Chicago Press, 1974. p.36. Sterling. Alan E. *Defenders of Liberty: Fort Stanwix During the American War for Independence.* Utica, New York: Graphics of Utica, 2005. p.5.

21. *The Norwich Packet and the Connecticut, Massachusetts, New-Hampshire, and Rhode-Island Weekly Advertiser.* IV:199 (July 14–July 21, 1777) p 2. Sterling. Alan E. *Defenders of Liberty: Fort Stanwix During the American War for Independence.* Utica, New York: Graphics of Utica, 2005. p.5.

22. Simms, Jeptha R. *History of Schoharie County, and Border Wars of New York.* Albany: Munsell & Tanner, Printers, 1845. p.232.

23. Letter of Gansevoort 22 August 1777 in *Massachusett's Spy.*7:31 (September 4, 1777) p.2.

24. *Encyclopedia of the American Revolution.* Harold E. Selesky, editor in chief.–2nd Ed. Detroit: Charles Scribner's Sons, 2007. II:1019–1021. *The Encyclopedia of the American Revolutionary War: a political, social, and military history.* Gregory Fremont-Barnes, Richard Alan Ryerson, editors. Santa Barbara, CA: ABC–CLIO, 2006. II:436–437. Luzader, John. *Fort Stanwix: Construction and Military History, 1758 to 1777.* Washington, DC: National Park Service, 1976. Nickerson, Hoffman. *The Turning Point of the American Revolution or Burgoyne in America.* Boston: Houghton Mifflin, 1928. Scott, John. *Fort Stanwix and Oriskany.* Rome, NY: Rome Sentinel Company, 1927. Stone, William Leete. *The Campaign of Lieutenant General John Burgoyne and the Expedition of Lieutenant Colonel Barry St. Leger.* New York: Da Capo Press, 1970. Ward, Christopher. *The War of the Revolution.* New York: Macmillan, 1952. p.420. Willett, William M. *A Narrative of the Military Actions of Colonel Marinus Willett.* 1831; New York: New York Times, 1969.

25. Letter of Col. Gansevoort to John Hancock 22d August. *The Massachusetts Spy: or, American Oracle of Liberty.* 7:331 (September 4, 1777) p.2. *The Pennsylvania Evening Post.* 3:399 (September 2, 1777).

26. *Connecticut Journal.* 520 (October 1, 1777) p.1.

27. Letter of Benedict Arnold to Major General Gates. Fort Schuyler, August 24, 1777. *The Boston Gazette and Country Journal* 1202 (September 15, 1777) p.2. *Continental Journal.* 68 (September 11, 1777) p.2. *The Norwich Packet and the Connecticut, Massachusetts, New Hampshire and Rhode Island Weekly Advertiser.* 4:207 (September 8 to September 15, 1777) p.3. *The Pennsylvania Evening Post.* 3:399 November 2, 1777. p.458.

28. Peckham, Howard Henry. *The Toll of Independence: Engagements & Battle Casualties of the American Revolution.* Chicago: University of Chicago Press, 1974. p.51.

29. Peckham, Howard Henry. *The Toll of Independence: Engagements & Battle Casualties of the American Revolution.* Chicago: University of Chicago Press, 1974. p.73. Mintz, Max M. *Seeds of Empire: the American Revolutionary Conquest of the Iroquois.* New York, London: New York University Press, 1999. p.164.

30. Peckham, Howard Henry. *The Toll of Independence: Engagements & Battle Casualties of the American Revolution.* Chicago: University of Chicago Press, 1974. p.76.

31. Journal of Samuel Tallmadge (threerivershms.com/orderlybookjournalST.htm). Stone, William L. *Life of Joseph Brant—Thayendanegea: Including the Indian Wars of the American Revolution.* Buffalo: Phinney & Co., 1851Vol. II Chapter V (threerivershms.com/borderwarsjbch5.htm).

32. *The Providence Gazette and Country Journal.* 18:920 (August 18, 1781) p.3.

33. Dawson, Henry B. *Battles of the United States by Sea and Land.* New York: Johnson, Fry, & Company, 1858. p.233.

34. Ibid. pp.233–234.

35. Boatner, Mark M. *Encyclopedia of the American Revolution.* McKay: New York, 3d ed., 1980 374–375. Stedman, Charles. *The History of the Origin, Progress and Termination of the American War.* London: printed for the author, 1794. vol. 1 pp.322–330. Hughes, Thomas. *A Journal by Thos: Hughes for his Amusement, & Designed Only for his Perusal by the Time He Attains the Age of 50 if He Lives So Long. (1778-1779)* with an introduction by E. A. Benians. Cambridge: At the University Press, 1947. pp.10–11.

36. ftp.rootsweb.com/pub/usgenweb/ny/chautauqua/military/revwar/pensions/adams-levi-jr.txt.

37. *The Independent Chronicle and the Universal Advertiser.* 9:468 (August 14, 1777) p.3.

38. *The Pennsylvania Evening Post.* 3:379 (July 17, 1777) p.378. *The New-York Gazette; and the Weekly Mercury.* 1344 (July 28, 1777) p.2. *The Massachusetts Spy or the American Oracle of Liberty.* 7:325 (July 24, 1777) p.2. *The Pennsylvania Evening Post.* 3:384 (July 29, 1777) p.398. *Continental Journal.* 62 (July 31, 1777) p.2.

39. *Dunlap's Pennsylvania Packet or the General Advertiser.* 6:299 (August 5, 1777) p.3.

40. *The Independent Chronicle and the Universal Advertiser.* 9:468 (August 14, 1777) p.3.

41. Extract of a letter from Albany, dated Oct. 21, 1780. *The New Jersey Gazette.* III:149, p.3. Petersen, James E. *Seth Warner.* Middlebury, Vt.: Dunmore House (P.O. Box 1026), 2001. pp.153–156.

42. *Norwich Packet and the Weekly Advertiser.* 381 (January 23, 1781) p.1. *The New-York Gazette; and the Weekly Mercury.* 1516 (November 6, 1780) p.3.

43. www.thenortherncampaign.org/rogislandsite.htm.

44. *Encyclopedia of the American Revolution.* Harold E. Selesky, editor in chief.–2nd Ed. Detroit: Charles Scribner's Sons, 2007. II:704. *The Encyclopedia of the American Revolutionary War: a political, social, and military history.* Gregory Fremont-Barnes, Richard Alan Ryerson, editors. Santa Barbara, CA: ABC-CLIO, 2006. III:778–780. Elting, John. *The Battles of Saratoga.* Monmouth Beach, NJ: Philip Freneau, 1977. Lossing, Benson John. *The Pictorial Field-Book of the Revolution; or, Illustrations, by Pen And Pencil, of the History, Biography, Scenery, Relics, and Traditions of the War for Independence.* New York, Harper & Brothers [1860]. Ward, Christopher. *The War of the Revolution.* New York: Macmillan, 1952. Wilson, David. *The Life of Jane McCrea.* Albany, NY: [s.n.], 1853.

45. Baldwin Jeduthan. *The Revolutionary Journal of Col. Jeduthan Baldwin 1775–1778.* Edited with a Memoir and Notes by Thomas Williams Baldwin. Bangor: Printed for the De Burians, 1906. p.113. Peckham, Howard Henry. *The Toll of Independence: Engagements & Battle Casualties of the American Revolution.* Chicago: University of Chicago Press, 1974. p.38.

46. Baldwin Jeduthan. *The Revolutionary Journal of Col. Jeduthan Baldwin 1775–1778.* Edited with a Memoir and Notes by Thomas Williams Baldwin. Bangor: Printed for the De Burians, 1906. p.119. Peckham, Howard Henry. *The Toll of Independence: Engagements & Battle Casualties of the American Revolution.* Chicago: University of Chicago Press, 1974. p.40.

47. Gen. Burgoyne's letter to Colonial Secretary Sir George Germain dated «Camp, near Saratoga, Aug. 20, 1777,» in Coburn, Frank Warren. *The Centennial History of the Battle of Bennington: compiled from the most reliable sources, and fully illustrated with original documents and entertaining anecdotes, Col. Seth Warner's identity in the first action completely established.* by Frank W. Coburn, embellished with a portrait of General Stark, a plan of the battle-field, and other engravings. Boston: G.E. Littlefield, 1877. p.19.

48. *Encyclopedia of the American Revolution.* Harold E. Selesky, editor in chief.–2nd Ed. Detroit: Charles Scribner's Sons, 2007. II:1027–1030. Furneaux, Rupert. *Saratoga: The Decisive Battle.* London: Allen and Unwin, 1971. Ketchum, Richard M. *Saratoga: Turning Point of America's Revolutionary War.* New York: Holt, 1997. Nickerson, Hoffman. *The Turning Point of the American Revolution or Burgoyne in America.* Boston: Houghton Mifflin, 1928. Ward, Christopher. *The War of the Revolution.* New York: Macmillan, 1952. pp.504–512.

49. Baldwin Jeduthan. *The Revolutionary Journal of Col. Jeduthan Baldwin 1775–1778.* Edited with a Memoir and notes by Thomas Williams Baldwin. Bangor: Printed for the De Burians, 1906. p.122. Journal of Oliver Boardman of Middletown 1777 in *Collections of the Connecticut Historical Society.* Hartford: the Society, 1899. 7:227. Peckham, Howard

Henry. *The Toll of Independence: Engagements & Battle Casualties of the American Revolution*. Chicago: University of Chicago Press, 1974. p.42.

50. *Encyclopedia of the American Revolution*. Harold E. Selesky, editor in chief.–2nd Ed. Detroit: Charles Scribner's Sons, 2007.II:1030–1033. *The Encyclopedia of the American Revolutionary War: a political, social, and military history*. Gregory Fremont-Barnes, Richard Alan Ryerson, eds. Santa Barbara, CA: ABC-CLIO, 2006. IV:1116–1123. Alden, John Richard. *The American Revolution, 1775–1783*. New York: Harper and Row, 1954. Bird, Harrison. *March to Saratoga: General Burgoyne and the American Campaign, 1777*. New York: Oxford University Press, 1963. Carrington, Henry B. *Battles of the American Revolution 1775–1781, including battle maps and charts of the American Revolution*. New York: Promontory Press, (1974), originally published in 1877 and 1881. Cuneo, John R. *The Battle of Saratoga: The Turn of the Tide*. New York: Macmillan, 1967. Elting, John. *The Battles of Saratoga*. Monmouth Beach, NJ: Philip Freneau, 1977. Furneaux, Rupert. *Saratoga: The Decisive Battle*. London: Allen and Unwin, 1971. Hargrove, Richard J. *General John Burgoyne*. Newark: University of Delaware Press, 1983. Higginbotham, Don. *The War of American Independence: Military Attitudes, Policies, and Practice, 1763–1789*. New York: Macmillan, 1971. Ketchum, Richard M. *Saratoga: Turning Point of America's Revolutionary War*. New York: Holt, 1997. Lunt, James. *John Burgoyne of Saratoga*. New York: Harcourt Brace Jovanovich, 1975. Mintz, Max M. *The Generals of Saratoga: John Burgoyne and Horatio Gates*. New Haven, CT: Yale University Press, 1990. Nickerson, Hoffman. *The Turning Point of the American Revolution or Burgoyne in America*. Boston: Houghton Mifflin, 1928. Scheer, George F. and Hugh F. Rankin. *Rebels and Redcoats*. Cleveland and New York: World Publishing Co., 1957. Upham, George B. "Burgoyne's Great Mistake." *New England Quarterly*. 3 (1990):657–680. Ward, Christopher. *The War of the Revolution*. New York: Macmillan, 1952. pp.521–531. Wood, W. J. *Battles of the Revolutionary War, 1775–1781*. Chapel Hill, NC: Algonquin, 1990.

51. *Encyclopedia of the American Revolution*. Harold E. Selesky, editor in chief.–2nd Ed. Detroit: Charles Scribner's Sons, 2007.II:1033–1035. Nelson, Paul David. *General Horatio Gates: A Biography*. Baton Rouge: Louisiana State University Press, 1976. Nickerson, Hoffman. *The Turning Point of the American Revolution or Burgoyne in America*. Boston: Houghton Mifflin, 1928. Ward, Christopher. *The War of the Revolution*. New York: Macmillan, 1952.

p.52. Letter from John Stark to Major General Heath. September 25, 1781. Peckham, Howard Henry. *The Toll of Independence: Engagements & Battle Casualties of the American Revolution*. Chicago: University of Chicago Press, 1974. p.91. *The Pennsylvania Evening Post, and Public Advertiser*. VII:784 (Oct. 15, 1781) p.172.

53. *Encyclopedia of the American Revolution*. Harold E. Selesky, editor in chief.–2nd Ed. Detroit: Charles Scribner's Sons, 2007. II:860–861. The *Encyclopedia of the American Revolutionary War: a political, social, and military history*. Gregory Fremont-Barnes, Richard Alan Ryerson, eds. Santa Barbara, CA: ABC-CLIO, 2006. III:935–939. Carrington, Henry B. *Battles of the American Revolution 1775–1781, including battle maps and charts of the American Revolution*. New York: Promontory Press, (1974), originally published in 1877 and 1881. Foote, Allan D. *Liberty March: the Battle of Oriskany*. Utica, NY: North Country Books, 1998. Nickerson, Hoffman. *The Turning Point of the American Revolution or Burgoyne in America*. Boston: Houghton Mifflin, 1928. Swiggett, Howard. *War Out of Niagara: Walter Butler and the Tory Rangers*. New York: Columbia University Press, 1933. Ward, Christopher. *The War of the Revolution*. New York: Macmillan, 1952. Wood, W. J. *Battles of the Revolutionary War, 1775–1781*. Chapel Hill, NC: Algonquin, 1990.

54. Peckham, Howard Henry. *The Toll of Independence: Engagements & Battle Casualties of the American Revolution*. Chicago: University of Chicago Press, 1974. p.38. Baldwin Jeduthan. T*he Revolutionary Journal of Col. Jeduthan Baldwin 1775–1778*. Edited with a Memoir and notes by Thomas Williams Baldwin. Bangor: Printed for the De Burians, 1906. p.114.

55. Simms, Jeptha R. *History of Schoharie County, and Border Wars of New York*. Albany: Munsell & Tanner, Printers, 1845. pp.3–4.

56. Chrysler, C. Donald. *The Blue-eyed Indians: the Story of Adam Crysler and his brothers in the Revolutionary war*. Grand Rapids, MI: Chrysler Books, 1999. ch. 2. Greene, Nelson. *History of the Mohawk Valley, gateway to the West, 1614–1925; covering the six counties of Schenectady, Schoharie, Montgomery, Fulton, Herkimer, and Oneida*. Chicago: S.J. Clarke, 1925. ch. 61 www.schenectadyhistory.org/resources/mvgw/history/060.html. www.schohariehistory.net/Library/DaysOfTheFlockey.htm.

57. Simms, Jeptha R. *History of Schoharie County, and Border Wars of New York*. Albany: Munsell & Tanner, Printers, 1845. pp.481–483.

58. Burgoyne, John. *A State of the Expedition from Canada, as Laid Before the House of Commons*, by Lieutenant-General Burgoyne. 2nd ed. London: J. Almon, 1780. Appendix, lxx-lxxi.

59. *The Providence Gazette; And Country Journal*. XIV:714 (September 6, 1777) p.1.

60. Ward, Christopher. *The War of the Revolution*. New York: Macmillan, 1952. pp.417–432. *The Encyclopedia of the American Revolutionary War: a political, social, and military history*. Gregory Fremont-Barnes, Richard Alan Ryerson, editors. Santa Barbara, CA: ABC–CLIO, 2006. I:93–96. *Encyclopedia of the American Revolution*. Harold E. Selesky, editor in chief.–2nd Ed. Detroit: Charles Scribner's Sons, 2007. I:64–69. Burgoyne, John. *A State of the Expedition from Canada*. London: J. Almon, 1780. Ketchum, Richard M. *Saratoga: Turning Point of America's Revolutionary War*. New York: Holt, 1997. Lord, Philip, Jr., comp. *War over Wallomscoick: Land Use and Settlement Pattern on the Bennington Battlefield, 1777*. Albany, NY: University of the State of New York, State Education Dept., 1989. Nickerson, Hoffman. *The Turning Point of the American Revolution or Burgoyne in America*. Boston: Houghton Mifflin, 1928. Riedesel, Friederike Charlotte Luise. *Letters and Memoirs Relating to the War of American Independence, and the Capture of the German Troops at Saratoga*. Translated by William L. Stone. New York: G. and C. Carvill, 1827. Wasmus, J. F. *An Eyewitness Account of the American Revolution and New England Life: the journal of J. F. Wasmus, German Company surgeon, 1776–1783*. Edited by Mary C. Lynn. Translated by Helga Doblin. New York: Greenwood Press, 1990.

61. Peckham, Howard Henry. *The Toll of Independence: Engagements & Battle Casualties of the American Revolution*. Chicago: University of Chicago Press, 1974. p.41.

62. Dean, Leon W. *Green Mountain Boy: The Story of Seth Warner.* New York, Toronto: Farrar & Rinehart, Inc., 1944. pp.223–225. Houghton, George Frederick. *An outline of the Controversy of the New Hampshire Grants with a Sketch of the Life and Services of Colonel Seth Warner: an address delivered before the legislature of the State of Vermont, in Montpelier, October 20, 1848.* Burlington, [Vt.]: Free Press Office Print, 1849. p.20. Chipman, Daniel. *The life of Col. Seth Warner, with an Account of the Controversy Between New York and Vermont, from 1763 to 1775.* Burlington [Vt.], C. Goodrich & Co., 1858, 1848. Petersen, James E. *Seth Warner.* Middlebury, Vt.: Dunmore House (P.O. Box 1026), 2001. pp.153–156.

63. *The New-York Gazette; and the Weekly Mercury.* 1516. (November 6, 1780) p.3. *The Norwich Packet and the Weekly Advertiser.* 369 (October 31, 1780) p.3.

64. Petersen, James E. *Seth Warner.* Middlebury, Vt.: Dunmore House (P.O. Box 1026), 2001. pp.153–156. *Norwich Packet and the Weekly Advertiser.* 381 (Jan. 23, 1781) p.1.

65. Extract of a letter from and officer of rank in the American army. Fishkill, November 26, 1781. *The Pennsylvania Packet or the General Advertiser.* XI:818 (Dec. 11, 1781) p.2. *The Boston Gazette, and the Country Journal.* 1427 (Dec. 31, 1781) p.2.

66. Ward, Christopher. *The War of the Revolution.* New York: Macmillan, 1952. p.523. Arnold, Isaac N. T*he Life of Benedict Arnold.* Chicago, 1880. p.194. Boatner, Mark M. *Encyclopedia of the American Revolution.* McKay: New York, 3d ed., 1980. Jones, Thomas. *History of New York During the Revolutionary War.* Edited by Edward Floyd De Lancey. New York: New York Historical Society, 1879. 1:202–204.

67. *The New York Packet.* (October 30, 1777). NDAR 10:244–245.

68. *The New York Packet.* (October 30, 1777). NDAR 10:244–245. *New York Loyal Gazette.* 141 (November 1, 1777) p.2. Kemble, Stephen. *Journals of Lieut.-Col. Stephen Kemble, 1773–1789; and British Army Orders: Gen. Sir William Howe, 1775–1778; Gen. Sir Henry Clinton, 1778; and Gen. Daniel Jones, 1778.* Prepared by New York Historical Society; Boston: Gregg Press, 1972. p.140.

69. *The New York Packet.* (October 30, 1777). NDAR 10:244–245. *New York Loyal Gazette.* 141 (November 1, 1777) p.2. Kemble, Stephen. *Journals of Lieut.-Col. Stephen Kemble, 1773–1789; and British Army Orders: Gen. Sir William Howe, 1775–1778; Gen. Sir Henry Clinton, 1778; and Gen. Daniel Jones, 1778.* Prepared by New York Historical Society; Boston: Gregg Press, 1972. p.140.

70. Journal of HM Galley *Dependence.* British National Archives, Admiralty 51/4159. NDAR 10:203.

71. Ibid. 10:213.

72. Peckham, Howard Henry. *The Toll of Independence: Engagements & Battle Casualties of the American Revolution.* Chicago: University of Chicago Press, 1974. p.45.

73. *Genealogical Quarterly Magazine and Magazine of New England History.* by Eben Putnam. 3 (April 1902) p.45.

74. Clarke, Thomas W. *The Bloody Mohawk.* New York: The Macmillan company, 1940.

75. Williams, Glenn F. *Year of the Hangman: George Washington's Campaign Against the Iroquois.* Yardley, PA: Westholme, 2005. p.79.

76. Williams, Glenn F. *Year of the Hangman: George Washington's Campaign Against the Iroquois.* Yardley, PA: Westholme, 2005. p.79. Washington, George. *Papers of George Washington.* Dorothy Twohig, ed.–Revolutionary War Series.– Charlottesville and London: University Press of Virginia. 15:78-79.

77. *Royal American Gazette.* XCIX (August 25, 1778) p.3.

78. Clinton, George. *Public Papers of George Clinton, First Governor of New York, 1777–1795,* 1801–1804. Hugh Hastings, ed. New York and Albany: Pub. by the State of New York, 1900. 3:377.

79. Simms, Jeptha R. H*istory of Schoharie County, and Border Wars of New York.* Albany: Munsell & Tanner, Printers, 1845. pp, 274–277. Clinton, George. *Public Papers of George Clinton, First Governor of New York, 1777–1795, 1801–1804.* Hugh Hastings, ed. New York and Albany: Pub. by the State of New York, 1900. 3:377.

80. Extract of a Letter Albany, June 27, 1778. *Pennsylvania Packet.* (July 16, 1778) p.3. *Connecticut Journal.* 558 (June 24, 1778) p.3. *Independent Ledger.* I:3 (June 29, 1778) p.2.

81. Mann, Barbara Alice. *George Washington's War on Native America.* Westport, Conn.: Praeger, 2005. p.36.

82. Thomas Patrick Hughes. *American Ancestry: Giving Name and Descent, in the Male Line, of Americans Whose Ancestors Settled in the United States Previous to the Declaration of Independence, A. D. 1776.* Frank Munsell, 1893. 8:132.

83. *The Independent Ledger, and American Advertiser.* I:2 (June 22, 1778) p 2. *The Norwich Packet.* 253 (August 3, 1778) p 2.

84. Peckham, Howard Henry. *The Toll of Independence: Engagements & Battle Casualties of the American Revolution.* Chicago: University of Chicago Press, 1974. p.53.

85. Jacob Ford to Brigadier General Abraham Ten Broeck in Clinton, George. *Public Papers of George Clinton, First Governor of New York, 1777–1795,* 1801–1804. Hugh Hastings, ed. New York and Albany: Pub. by the State of New York, 1900. 3:555–556.

86. *Encyclopedia of the American Revolution.* Harold E. Selesky, editor in chief.–2nd Ed. Detroit: Charles Scribner's Sons, 2007. I:202–203. *The Encyclopedia of the American Revolutionary War: a political, social, and military history.* Gregory Fremont-Barnes, Richard Alan Ryerson, editors. Santa Barbara, CA: ABC-CLIO, 2006. I:214–215. Goodnough, David. *The Cherry Valley Massacre, November 11, 1778: the Frontier Atrocity That Shocked a Young Nation.* New York: Franklin Watts, 1968. Kelsay, Isabel T. *Joseph Brant, 1743–1807: Man of Two Worlds.* Syracuse, NY: Syracuse University Press, 1984. Swiggett, Howard. *War out of Niagara; Walter Butler and the Tory Rangers.* Port Washington, NY, I. J. Friedman, 1963. Van Every, Dale. *A Company of Heroes: The American Frontier, 1775–1783.* New York: Morrow, 1962. Ward, Christopher. *The War of the Revolution.* New York: Macmillan, 1952.

87. Benton, Nathaniel S. *A History of Herkimer County, Including the Upper Mohawk Valley, from the Earliest Period to the Present Time with a Brief Notice of the Iroquois Indians, the Early German Tribes, the Palatine Immigrations; also Biographical*

Notices of the Most Prominent Public Men of the County, with Important Statistical Information. Albany: J. Munsell, 1856. p.92. www.rootsweb.com/~nyherkim/ancestors/herkimerbiognotes.html.

88. *The Pennsylvania Evening Post.* IV:545 (October 26, 1778) p.396. *Connecticut Courant.* 716 (October 13, 1778) p.3.

89. Lossing, Benson John. *The Pictorial Field-book of the Revolution; or, Illustrations, by Pen and Pencil, of the History, Biography, Scenery, Relics, and Traditions of the War for Independence.* New York, Harper & Brothers [1860], I:255. Boatner, Mark M. *Encyclopedia of the American Revolution.* McKay: New York, 3d ed., 1980. p.22.

90. Graymont, Barbara. *The Iroquois in the American Revolution.* [Syracuse, NY] Syracuse University Press, 1972. www.fortklock.com/Timeline1778.htm.

91. Graymont, Barbara. *The Iroquois in the American Revolution.* [Syracuse, NY] Syracuse University Press, 1972. Kelsay, Isabel Thompson. *Joseph Brant, 1743–1807, Man of Two Worlds.* Syracuse, NY: Syracuse University Press, 1984.

92. Fitzpatrick, John C. ed. *The Writings of George Washington.* Washington, 1931–1934. XIV:3, 18, 75, 94, 168, 314. Ward, Christopher. *The War of the Revolution.* New York: Macmillan, 1952. pp.633–634.

93. Extract of a letter from Tryon County, dated May 17. *The Pennsylvania Packet or the General Advertiser.* (June 8, 1779) p.2.

94. Hanson, Willis Tracy, jr. *A History of Schenectady During the Revolution, to Which is Appended a Contribution to the Individual Records of the Inhabitants of the Schenectady District During that Period.* [Brattleboro, Vt.]: Priv. print. [E. L Hildreth & Co.] 1916. p.95. Beauchamp, William Martin. *A History of the New York Iroquois, Now Commonly Called the Six Nations..* New York: AMS Press, [1976]. p.368.

95. Peckham, Howard Henry. *The Toll of Independence: Engagements & Battle Casualties of the American Revolution.* Chicago: University of Chicago Press, 1974. p.71.

96. Morrison, James. *The Fate of a Scouting Party* (Fulton County rootsweb site). www.fortklock.com/timeline1781.htm. Simms, Jeptha R. *History of Schoharie County, and Border Wars of New York.* Albany: Munsell & Tanner, Printers, 1845. p.469.

97. Ward, Christopher. *The War of the Revolution.* New York: Macmillan, 1952. pp.633–634, 651–652.

98. Colonel Marinus Willett to George Clinton, Nov. 2, 1781 in Clinton, George. *Public Papers of George Clinton, First Governor of New York, 1777–1795, 1801–1804.* Hugh Hastings, ed. New York and Albany: Pub. by the State of New York, 1900. 7:472–475. Colonel Marinus Willett to Maj. Gen. Lord Stirling, November 2, 1781. *The Pennsylvania Gazette.* (November 21, 1781). Greene, Nelson. *History of the Mohawk Valley, Gateway to the West, 1614–1925; Covering the Six Counties of Schenectady, Schoharie, Montgomery, Fulton, Herkimer, and Oneida.* Chicago, S. J. Clarke, 1925 2:1080. Journal of Gilbert Tice. *Ontario Historical Society Papers and Records* 21 (1924) 196–197. Cruikshank, Ernest. "The King's Royal Regiment of New York." *Ontario Historical Society Papers and Records.* Toronto, 1931. p.275. Mintz, Max M. *Seeds of Empire: the American Revolutionary Conquest of the Iroquois.* New York, London: New York University Press, 1999. pp.169–171. *Connecticut Journal.*767 (July 11, 1782) p.3.

98a. *Massachusetts Gazette.* I:10 (July 16, 1782) p.3; Benton, Nathaniel S. (Nathaniel Soley). *A history of Herkimer County, Including the Upper Mohawk Valley, from the Earliest Period to the Present Time; with a Brief Notice of the Iroquois Indians, the early German Tribes, the Palatine Immigrations into the Colony of New York, and Biographical Sketches of the Palatine Families, the Patentees of Burnetsfield in the year 1725; and also Biographical Notices of the Most Prominent Public Men of the County; with Important Statistical Information.* Albany: J. Munsell, 1856. Chapter Five.

99. Two Petitions of the Inhabitants of German Flats to the State Legislature, July 24, 1782 and Feb. 15, 1783. Miscellaneous Papers of Tryon County. New York Historical Society. Ward, Christopher. *The War of the Revolution.* New York: Macmillan, 1952. 2:633. *The other New York: the American Revolution beyond New York City, 1763–1787.* edited by Joseph S. Tiedemann and Eugene R. Fingerhut. Albany: State University of New York Press, c2005. p.191.

100. www.schohariehistory.net/OSF.htm.

101. *The Pennsylvania Packet or the General Advertiser.* (September 12, 1780) p.2.

102. *The New-York Gazette; and the Weekly Mercury.* 1516. (November 6, 1780) p.3. *The Norwich Packet and the Weekly Advertiser.* 369 (October 31, 1780) p.3. *Connecticut Journal.* 679 (November 2, 1780) p.1. Stember, Sol. *The Bicentennial Guide to the American Revolution.* New York: Saturday Review Press, [distributed by] Dutton, 1974; [s.l.]: New York Times and Arno Press, 1969. 1:81–82. *Encyclopedia of the American Revolution.* Harold E. Selesky, editor in chief.–2nd Ed. Detroit: Charles Scribner's Sons, 2007.II:1043. *The Encyclopedia of the American Revolutionary War: a political, social, and military history.* Gregory Fremont-Barnes, Richard Alan Ryerson, editors. Santa Barbara, CA: ABC-CLIO, 2006. IV:1132. Blanco, Richard L., ed. *The War of the Revolution, 1775–1783: an encyclopedia.* New York: Garland Pub., 1993. Earle, Thomas. *Sir John Johnson: Loyalist Baronet.* Toronto: Dundurn Press, 1986. Kelsay, Isabel Thompson. *Joseph Brant, 1743–1807, Man of Two Worlds.* Syracuse, NY: Syracuse University Press, 1984. Mays, Terry M. *Historical Dictionary of the American Revolution.* Scarecrow Press: Lanham, MD, 1999. Stone, William L. *Life of Joseph Brant–Thayendanegea: Including the Indian Wars of the American Revolution.* Buffalo: Phinney & Co., 1851; New York: Kraus, 1969. Ward, Christopher. *The War of the Revolution.* New York: Macmillan, 1952.

103. Chrysler, C. Donald. *The Blue-eyed Indians: The Story of Adam Crysler and his Brothers in the Revolutionary war.* Grand Rapids, MI: Chrysler Books, 1999. ch. 4. www.rootsweb.ancestry.com/~nyschoha/crbook.html.

104. Peckham, Howard Henry. *The Toll of Independence: Engagements & Battle Casualties of the American Revolution.* Chicago: University of Chicago Press, 1974. p.53.

105. Extract of a letter from Albany, April 17, 1779. *The Pennsylvania Evening Post.* 594 (April 30, 1779) p.106. *The New Jersey Gazette.* II:73 (April 28, 1779) p.2.

106. Campbell, William W. *The Border Warfare of New York, During the Revolution or, the Annals of Tryon County.* New York: Baker & Scribner, 1849. pp.173–174.

107. Ward, Christopher. *The War of the Revolution*. New York: Macmillan, 1952. pp.. 651–652. John Ross to Haldimand. Nov. 7, 1781 in Cruikshank, Ernest. "The King's Royal Regiment of New York." *Ontario Historical Society Papers and Records*. Toronto, 1931. pp.271–272. Colonel Marinus Willett to George Clinton, Nov. 7, 1781 in Clinton, George. *Public Papers of George Clinton, First Governor of New York, 1777–1795, 1801–1804*. Hugh Hastings, ed. New York and Albany: Pub. by the State of New York, 1900. 7:488. Greene, Nelson. *History of the Mohawk Valley, Gateway to the West, 1614–1925; Covering the Six Counties of Schenectady, Schoharie, Montgomery, Fulton, Herkimer, and Oneida*. Chicago, S. J. Clarke, 1925 2:1078. Journal of Gilbert Tice Oct. 5–Nov. 12, 1781. Frederick Haldimand Papers. British Library. Add. Mss. 21,767. Mintz, Max M. *Seeds of Empire: the American Revolutionary Conquest of the Iroquois*. New York, London: New York University Press, 1999. p.170. The *Pennsylvania Gazette*. (November 21, 1781).

108. *Encyclopedia of the American Revolution*. Harold E. Selesky, editor in chief.–2nd Ed. Detroit: Charles Scribner's Sons, 2007. I:573. *The Encyclopedia of the American Revolutionary War: a political, social, and military history*. Gregory Fremont-Barnes, Richard Alan Ryerson, editors. Santa Barbara, CA: ABC-CLIO, 2006. II:656. Mays, Terry M. *Historical Dictionary of the American Revolution*. Scarecrow Press: Lanham, MD, 1999. Stone, William L. *Life of Joseph Brant–Thayendanegea: Including the Indian Wars of the American Revolution*. Buffalo: Phinney & Co., 1851; New York: Kraus, 1969. Willett, William M. *A Narrative of the Military Actions of Colonel Marinus Willett*. 1831; New York: New York Times, 1969.

109. *Encyclopedia of the American Revolution*. Harold E. Selesky, editor in chief.–2nd Ed. Detroit: Charles Scribner's Sons, 2007. II:859. Roberts, Robert B. *New York's Forts in the Revolution*. Rutherford: Fairleigh Dickinson University Press, 1980.

110. *The Independent Ledger, and the American Advertiser*. II:54 (June 21, 1779) p.4. *The New Jersey Gazette*. II:76 (May 19, 1779).

111. *The Independent Chronicle and the Universal Advertiser*. XI:559, p.2.

112. *The Independent Chronicle and the Universal Advertiser*. XI:563 (June 3, 1779) p.3.

113. Extract of a letter from a Field Officer at Wyoming, dated June 24. *The Independent Ledger, and the American Advertiser*. II: 58 (July 19, 1779) p.4.

114. *Encyclopedia of the American Revolution*. Harold E. Selesky, editor in chief.–2nd Ed. Detroit: Charles Scribner's Sons, 2007. II:726–727. *The Encyclopedia of the American Revolutionary War: a political, social, and military history*. Gregory Fremont-Barnes, Richard Alan Ryerson, editors. Santa Barbara, CA: ABC-CLIO, 2006. III:788–789. Kelsay, Isabel T. *Joseph Brant, 1743–1807: Man of Two Worlds*. Syracuse, NY: Syracuse University Press, 1984. Mays, Terry M. *Historical Dictionary of the American Revolution*. Scarecrow Press: Lanham, MD, 1999. Stone, William L. *Life of Joseph Brant–Thayendanegea: Including the Indian Wars of the American Revolution*. Buffalo: Phinney & Co., 1851; New York: Kraus, 1969.

115. *Encyclopedia of the American Revolution*. Harold E. Selesky, editor in chief. – 2nd Ed. Detroit: Charles Scribner's Sons, 2007.II:726 dates this event as ca. April 4, 1780 whereas I:493 puts it on April 14.

116. *The American Journal and General Advertiser*. II: 63 (May 24, 1780) p.2.

117. *Connecticut Journal*. 728 (October 11, 1781) p.2. *The Pennsylvania Packet or the General Advertiser* 789 (October 2, 1781) p.3. *The New Jersey Gazette*. 4:197 (October 3, 1781) p.2.

118. Extracts from the manuscript journal of Major James Norris, of New Hampshire, an officer under Sullivan in his expedition against the Indians of Western New York in Jones, Thomas. *History of New York During The Revolutionary War*. Edited by Edward Floyd De Lancey. New York: New York Historical Society, 1879. p.614. Copy of a letter from Major Marshall to his brother, dated Tioga, August 15. *The Independent Chronicle and the Universal Advertiser*. XIII: 577 (Sept. 9, 1779) p.3. Ward, Harry M. *General William Maxwell and the New Jersey Continentals*. Westport, CT; London: Greenwood Press, 1997. p.131.

119. Davis, Nathan. History of the Expedition Against the Five Nations, Commanded by General Sullivan, in 1779. *Historical Magazine*. 3:4 (April 1868) p.200.

120. *Encyclopedia of the American Revolution*. Harold E. Selesky, editor in chief.–2nd Ed. Detroit: Charles Scribner's Sons, 2007. II:819–820. *The Encyclopedia of the American Revolutionary War: a political, social, and military history*. Gregory Fremont-Barnes, Richard Alan Ryerson, editors. Santa Barbara, CA: ABC-CLIO, 2006. III:905–906. Fischer, Joseph R. *A Well-Executed Failure: The Sullivan Campaign Against the Iroquois, July–September 1779*. Columbia: University of South Carolina Press, 1997. *Journals of the Military Expedition of Major General John Sullivan Against the Six Nations of Indians in 1779 with Records of Centennial Celebrations*. by Frederick Cook. Auburn, NY: Knapp, Peck, & Thomson, 1887. Kelsay, Isabel Thompson. *Joseph Brant, 1743–1807, Man of Two Worlds*. Syracuse, NY: Syracuse University Press, 1984. Swiggett, Howard. *War out of Niagara; Walter Butler and the Tory Rangers*. Port Washington, NY: I. J. Friedman, 1963. Ward, Christopher. *The War of the Revolution*. New York: Macmillan, 1952.

121. Extracts from the manuscript journal of Major James Norris, of New Hampshire, an officer under Sullivan in his expedition against the Indians of Western New York in Jones, Thomas. *History of New York During The Revolutionary War*. Edited by Edward Floyd De Lancey. New York: New York Historical Society, 1879. pp.615–617.

122. Extracts from the manuscript journal of Major James Norris, of New Hampshire, an officer under Sullivan in his expedition against the Indians of Western New York in Jones, Thomas. *History of New York During The Revolutionary War*. Edited by Edward Floyd De Lancey. New York: New York Historical Society, 1879. pp.615–617. Sullivan, John. *Journals of the Military Expedition of Maj. Gen. John Sullivan Against the Six Nations of Indians*. Auburn, NY, 1887. p.13. Fisher, Sydney George. *The Struggle for American Independence*. Philadelphia, London, J.B. Lippincott Co., 1908. II:245. Dawson, Henry B. *Battles of the United States*. New York, 1858. I:541. Ward, Christopher. *The War of the Revolution*. New York: Macmillan, 1952. 644–646.

123. Sullivan, John. *Letters and Papers of Major-General John Sullivan*. Concord, NH, 1930–1939. III, 131. Ward, Christopher. *The War of the Revolution*. New York: Macmillan, 1952.

124. Simms, Jeptha R. *History of Schoharie County, and Border Wars of New York*. Albany: Munsell & Tanner, Printers, 1845. pp.322–326.

125. *The Massachusetts Spy: or, American Oracle of Liberty*. 11:542 (September 27, 1781) p.3.

126. Campbell, William W. *The Border Warfare of New York, during the Revolution or, the Annals of Tryon County*. New York: Baker & Scribner, 1849. p.151; Swiggett, Howard. *War out of Niagara; Walter Butler and the Tory Rangers*. Port Washington, NY, I. J. Friedman, 1963. p.212. Boatner, Mark M. *Encyclopedia of the American Revolution*. McKay: New York, 3d ed., 1980. p.492. Simms, Jeptha R. *History of Schoharie County, and Border Wars of New York*. Albany: Munsell & Tanner, Printers, 1845. pp.322–327.

127. Campbell, William W. *The Border Warfare of New York, during the Revolution or, the Annals of Tryon County*. New York: Baker & Scribner, 1849. p.163.

128. Peckham, Howard Henry. *The Toll of Independence: Engagements & Battle Casualties of the American Revolution*. Chicago: University of Chicago Press, 1974. p.71.

129. Beauchamp, William M. «Indian Raids in the Mohawk Valley,» New York Historical Association *Proceedings*, 1915, 204. Boatner, Mark M. *Encyclopedia of the American Revolution*. McKay: New York, 3d ed., 1980. pp.90, 331, 998–99. Clarke, T. Wood. *The Bloody Mohawk*. New York: The Macmillan Company, 1940. pp.290–91. Hugh P. Donlon. *Outlines of History: Montgomery County, State of New York*. Amsterdam, NY, 1851. I:284–95. Colonel James Bruyn to Governor George Clinton, Kingston, July 23, 1781 in Clinton, George. *Public Papers of George Clinton, First Governor of New York, 1777–1795, 1801–1804*. Hugh Hastings, ed. New York and Albany: Pub. by the State of New York, 1900. 7:105.

130. Stember, Sol. *The Bicentennial Guide to the American Revolution*. New York: Saturday Review Press. [distributed by] Dutton, 1974; [s.l.]: New York Times and Arno Press, 1969. 1:76–77.

131. Pension Application of William Van Slyke and Samuel McKean S27161 and S28806, N.Y. www.fortklock.com/vanslyke.htm. www.nps.gov/revwar/revolution_day_by_day/1781_bottom.html. Beauchamp, William M. «Indian Raids in the Mohawk Valley,» New York Historical Association *Proceedings*, 1915. p.204. Boatner, Mark M. *Encyclopedia of the American Revolution*. McKay: New York, 3d ed., 1980. pp.90, 331, 998–99. Clarke, T. Wood. *The Bloody Mohawk*. New York: The Macmillan company, 1940. pp.290–91. Hugh P. Donlon. *Outlines of History: Montgomery County, State of New York*. Amsterdam, NY, 1851. I:284–95. Col. James Bruyn to Governor George Clinton, Kingston, July 23, 1781 in Clinton, George. *Public Papers of George Clinton, First Governor of New York, 1777–1795, 1801–1804*. Hugh Hastings, ed. New York and Albany: Pub. by the State of New York, 1900. 7:105.

132. www.threerivershms.com/beersmoncoch14.htmCHAPTER XIV. Boatner, Mark M. *Encyclopedia of the American Revolution*. McKay: New York, 3d ed., 1980 New Dorlach.

133. *Connecticut Journal*. 728 (October 11, 1781) p.2. *The Pennsylvania Packet or the General Advertiser*. 789 (October 2, 1781) p.3. *The New Jersey Gazette*. 4:197 (October 3, 1781) p.2.

134. Simms, Jeptha R. *History of Schoharie County, and Border Wars of New York*. Albany: Munsell & Tanner, Printers, 1845. pp.247–249.

135. *The Pennsylvania Packet or the General Advertiser*. (November 7, 1780) p.2. *Connecticut Journal*. 682 (November 23, 1780) p.1. *The New-York Gazette; and the Weekly Mercury*. 1516 (November 6, 1780) p, 3. *Virginia Gazette*. November 18,1780 89 p.2. Mintz, Max M. *Seeds of Empire: the American Revolutionary Conquest of the Iroquois*. New York, London: New York University Press, 1999. pp.168–169. John Munro to Sir John Johnson, Oct. 24, 1780 in Cruikshank, Ernest. "The King's Royal Regiment of New York." *Ontario Historical Society Papers and Records*. Toronto, 1931. Clinton, George. Public Papers of George Clinton, First Governor of New York, 1777–1795, 1801–1804. Hugh Hastings, ed. New York and Albany: Pub. by the State of New York, 1900. 6:408, 288–289, 292.

136. Peckham, Howard Henry. *The Toll of Independence: Engagements & Battle Casualties of the American Revolution*. Chicago: University of Chicago Press, 1974. p.76.

137. Ward, Christopher. *The War of the Revolution*. New York: Macmillan, 1952. 651–652. *The New-York Gazette; and the Weekly Mercury*. 1516 (Nov. 6, 1780) p.3.

138. *The Pennsylvania Packet or the General Advertiser*. November 7, 1780. p.2. *Connecticut Journal*. 682 (November 23, 1780) p.1. *The Pennsylvania Evening Post*. VI:704 (November 4, 1780) p.133. *The Providence Gazette; and Country Journal*. XVII:880 (November 8-1780) p.3. Ward, Christopher. *The War of the Revolution*. New York: Macmillan, 1952. pp.649–650.

139. Clarke, T. Wood. *The Bloody Mohawk*. New York: The Macmillan company, 1940. pp.238–239.

140. Ward, Christopher. *The War of the Revolution*. New York: Macmillan, 1952. 651–652. Willett, William M. *A Narrative of the Military Actions of Colonel Marinus Willett*. 1831; New York: New York Times, 1969.

141. Journal of HMS *Phoenix*. British National Archives, Admiralty 51/694; NDAR 5:1037. Journal of HMS *Rose*. British National Archives, Admiralty 51/805; NDAR 5:1037-1038. Smith, William. *Historical Memoirs from 16 March 1763 to 25 July 1778 of William Smith*. edited by William H. W. Sabine, New York Times Original Narratives, New York, 1958; (Eyewitness accounts of the American Revolution). [New York]: New York Times; Arno Press, 1969. II:1. NDAR 5:1039. George Washington to John Hancock. July 12, 1776. Brigadier General Hugh Mercer to George Washington. Amboy. October 16, 1776. Washington, George. *The Papers of George Washington*. Revolutionary War series. Philander D. Chase, editor. Charlottesville: University Press of Virginia, 1985–<2008>. 5:283-285. NDAR 5:1040. Heath, William, *Memoirs of Major-General Heath, Containing Anecdotes, Details of Skirmishes, Battles, and other Military Events, during the American War. Written by Himself*. Boston, 1898. (Edition edited by William Abbott, New York, 1901.) [New York]: New York Times, [1968]. 41, 42. NDAR 5:1041. Richards, Samuel, *Diary of Samuel Richards, Captain of the Connecticut Line, War of Revolution, 1775–1781*. Philadelphia: [Press of the Leeds & Biddle Co.] 1909. pp.31–32. NDAR 5:1041. Clap, Caleb. «Diary of Ensign Caleb Clap, of Colonel Baldwin's Regiment, Massachusetts

Line." *Historical Magazine,* 3d ser. 3 (1874–1875) p.247. Kemble, Stephen, «Kemble's Journals, 1773–89,» New York Historical Society *Collections.* 16 (1883) I:80, 81. NDAR 5:1042.

142. *The Massachusetts Spy: or, American Oracle of Liberty.* VI:283 (October 2, 1776) p 3. *The Pennsylvania Evening Post.* 2:265 (October 1, 1776) p.488.

143. Clinton, George. *Public Papers of George Clinton, First Governor of New York, 1777–1795,* 1801–1804. Hugh Hastings, ed. New York and Albany: Pub. by the State of New York, 1900. I:282–283. NDAR 6:20.

144. Journal of HMS *Rose.* British National Archives, Admiralty 51/805. NDAR 6:38–39. *The Pennsylvania Evening Post.* 2:241 (August 6, 1776) p.389.

145. Journal of HMS *Rose.* British National Archives, Admiralty 51/805. NDAR 6:206. Journal of HMS *Phoenix.* British National Archives, Admiralty 51/694. NDAR 6:206. Heath, William. *Memoirs of Major-General William Heath.* Ed. by William Abbatt. New York: William Abbatt, 1901. pp.39–40. *Pennsylvania Evening Post.* (August 20). Moore, Frank. *Diary of the American Revolution from Newspapers and Original Documents.* New York: Charles Scribner; London: Sampson Low, Son & Co., 1890. 1:292–293.

146. Journal Of HMS *Rose,* Captain James Wallace, British National Archives, Admiralty 51/805. NDAR 6:225. Journal Of HMS *Phoenix,* Captain Hyde Parker, Jr., British National Archives, Admiralty 51/694. NDAR 6:225–226.

Serle, Ambrose. *The American Journal Of Ambrose Serle Secretary To Lord Howe 1776–1778.* edited by Edward H. Tatum, Jr., San Marino, California, 1940; Eyewitness accounts of the American Revolution). [New York] : New York Times; Arno Press, c1969.

147. Journal of HMS *Fowey,* Captain George Montagu. British National Archives, Admiralty 51/375. Journal of HMS *Renown* Captain Francis Banks. British National Archives, Admiralty 51/776. NDAR 6:860.

148. Journal of HMS *Pearl,* Capt. Thomas Wilkinson. British National Archives, Admiralty 51/674. NDAR 7:48. Mackenzie, Frederick. *The Diary of Frederick Mackenzie.* Cambridge, MA: Harvard University Press, 1930. 1:98.

149. Journal of HMS *Phoenix.* British National Archives, Admiralty. 51/694. NDAR 7:64. Journal of HMS *Tartar.* British National Archives, Admiralty. 51/972. NDAR 7:64.

150. Journal of HM Galley *Dependence.* British National Archives, Admiralty 51/4159. NDAR 7:1144–1145.

151. *The Providence Gazette; and Country Journal.* XIV:710 (August 9, 1777) p.3. Peckham, Howard Henry. *The Toll of Independence: Engagements & Battle Casualties of the American Revolution.* Chicago: University of Chicago Press, 1974. p.37. Journal of HM Galley *Dependence.* British National Archives, Admiralty 52/1694.

152. *Documents Relating to the Revolutionary History, State Of New Jersey.* Edited by William S. Stryker. Trenton: The John L. Murphy Publishing Co., 1901. Series 2. vol. 2:463.

153. Robertson, Archibald. *Archibald Robertson: His Diaries and Sketches in America 1762–1780.* Edited With An Introduction By Harry Miller Lydenberg. New York: The New York Public Library, 1930. pp.235–236.

154. Journal of HMS *Dependence.* British National Archives, Admiralty. 51/4159. NDAR 10:38. Journal of HMS *Mercury.* British National Archives, Admiralty. 51/600. NDAR 10:38. Journal of HMS *Preston.* British National Archives, Admiralty. 51/720. NDAR 10:39.

155. Journal of HMS *Phoenix,* Captain Hyde Parker, Jr., British National Archives, Admiralty 51/694. NDAR 5:1102.

156. Journal of HMS Rose. British National Archives, Admiralty 51/805; NDAR 5:1125. *Continental Journal.* 11 (August 8, 1776) p.3.

157. Journal of HMS *Phoenix.* British National Archives, Admiralty 51/694; NDAR 5:1213.

158. Journal of HM Brig *Diligent.* British National Archives, Admiralty 51/4163. NDAR 10:143.

159. *Pennsylvania Evening Post.* VII:752 (July 9, 1781) p.103.

160. Diamant, Lincoln. *Chaining the Hudson: the fight for the river in the American Revolution.* New York, NY: Carol Pub. Group, c1989. p.90.

161. Ibid.

162. *Encyclopedia of the American Revolution.* Harold E. Selesky, editor in chief.–2nd Ed. Detroit: Charles Scribner's Sons, 2007. I:223–226. *The Encyclopedia of the American Revolutionary War: a political, social, and military history.* Gregory Fremont-Barnes, Richard Alan Ryerson, editors. Santa Barbara, CA: ABC-CLIO, 2006. II:417–418, 429–430. Carr, William H. and Richard J. Koke. *Twin Forts on the Popolopen: Forts Clinton and Montgomery.* New York: Bear Mountain Trailside Museums, 1937. Clinton, Henry. *The American Rebellion: Sir Henry Clinton's Narrative of His Campaigns, 1775–1782, with an appendix of original documents.* Edited by William B. Willcox. New Haven: Yale University Press, 1954. Diamant, Lincoln. *Chaining the Hudson: The Fight for the River in the American Revolution.* Secaucus, NJ: Lyle Stuart, 1989. Higginbotham, Don. *The War of American Independence: Military Attitudes, Policies, and Practice, 1763–1789.* New York: Macmillan, 1971. Mackesy, Piers. *The War for America, 1775–1783.* Lincoln: University of Nebraska Press, 1993. Mintz, Max M. *The Generals of Saratoga: John Burgoyne and Horatio Gates.* New Haven, CT: Yale University Press, 1990. Palmer, David R. *The River and the Rock: The History of Fortress West Point, 1775–1783.* New York: Greenwood, 1969. Roberts, Robert B. *New York's Forts in the Revolution.* Rutherford: Fairleigh Dickinson University Press, 1980. Symonds, Craig L. *A Battlefield Atlas of the American Revolution.* Mount Pleasant, SC: Nautical and Aviation Publishing Company of America, 1986. Ward, Christopher. *The War of the Revolution.* New York: Macmillan, 1952.

163. Journal of HMS *Preston.* British National Archives Admiralty 51/720. NDAR 10:68. Journal of HMS *Mercury.* British National Archives Admiralty 51/600. NDAR 10:69. Journal of HM Galley *Dependence.* British National Archives Admiralty 51/4159. NDAR 10:69. Journal of HM Brig *Diligent.* British National Archives Admiralty 51/4163. NDAR 10:69.

164. *New York Loyal Gazette.* 141 (November 1, 1777) p.2.

165. Peckham, Howard Henry. *The Toll of Independence: Engagements & Battle Casualties of the American Revolution.* Chicago: University of Chicago Press, 1974. p.65.

166. Heath, William. *Memoirs Major-General William Heath By Himself.—New Edition, With Illustrations And Notes.—* Edited By William Abbatt. New York: William Abbatt, 1901. pp.67–68.

167. Mackenzie, Frederick. *The Diary of Frederick Mackenzie.* Cambridge, MA: Harvard University Press, 1930. pp.89–91. *The Pennsylvania Evening Post.* 2:278 (October 31, 1776) p.548. Extract of a letter from Fort Lee; *Pennsylvania Journal.* (November 6, 1776) Moore, Frank. *Diary of the American Revolution: from Newspapers and Original Documents.* New York: Charles Scribner; London: Sampson Low, Son & Co., 1890. 1:292–293. *The Pennsylvania Ledger or the Virginia, Maryland, Pennsylvania, & New Jersey Weekly Advertiser.* XCV (November 16, 1776) p.2.

168. Extract of a Letter from a Gentleman in the Army, dated camp near the Mills, about three miles north of White-Plains, November 1, 1776. In Force, Peter. *American Archives: Consisting of a Collection of Authentick Records, State Papers, Debates, and Letters and Other Notices of Publick Affairs, the Whole Forming a Documentary History of the Origin and Progress of the North American Colonies; of the Causes and Accomplishment of the American Revolution; and of the Constitution of Government for the United States, to the Final Ratification thereof.* In six series. [Washington, 1837–1853]. Series 5, *3:474.*

169. Hibbert, Christopher. *Redcoats and Rebels: the American Revolution Through British Eyes.* New York: Norton, 1990. p.129.

170. *Encyclopedia of the American Revolution.* Harold E. Selesky, editor in chief.–2nd Ed. Detroit: Charles Scribner's Sons, 2007.II:1268–1269. *The Encyclopedia of the American Revolutionary War: a political, social, and military history.* Gregory Fremont-Barnes, Richard Alan Ryerson, editors. Santa Barbara, CA: ABC-CLIO, 2006. IV:1353–1355. Anderson, Troyer Steele. *The Command of the Howe Brothers During the American Revolution.* New York: Oxford University Press, 1936. Atwood, R. *The Hessians.* Cambridge: Cambridge University Press, 2002. Billias, George Allen. *General John Glover and his Marblehead Mariners.* New York: Henry Holt, 1960. Carrington, Henry B. *Battles of the American Revolution 1775–1781, including battle maps and charts of the American Revolution.* New York: Promontory Press, (1974), originally published in 1877 and 1881. Gruber, Ira D. *The Howe Brothers and the American Revolution.* New York: Norton, 1972. Johnston, Henry P. *The Campaign of 1776 Around New York and Brooklyn.* [n.d.]; reprint, New York: Da Capo, 1971. Tallmadge, Benjamin. *Memoir of Col. Benjamin Tallmadge.* New York: Thomas Holman, 1858. Ward, Christopher. *The War of the Revolution.* New York: Macmillan, 1952. 260–266. Washington, George. *Papers of George Washington.* Dorothy Twohig, ed.–Revolutionary War Series.–Charlottesville and London: University Press of Virginia.

171. Extract of a letter from a gentleman at North Castle (near White Plains) November 7, 1776. *Freeman's Journal.* 1:27 (11–26–1776) p.3.

172. Washington, George. *The Papers of George Washington.* Revolutionary War series / Philander D. Chase, editor. Charlottesville: University Press of Virginia, 1985–<2008> 7:91.

173. Heath, William. *Memoirs of Major General William Heath.* [New York]: New York Times [1968, c1901] pp.74–75. Force, Peter. *American Archives: Consisting of a Collection of Authentick Records, State Papers, Debates, and Letters and Other Notices of Publick Affairs, the Whole Forming a Documentary History of the Origin and Progress of the North American Colonies; of the Causes and Accomplishment of the American Revolution; and of the Constitution of Government for the United States, to the Final Ratification Thereof. in Six Series.* [Washington, 1837–1853. 5th Series, Vol. III, p.654. (November 9, 1776). Hufeland, Otto. *Westchester County during the American Revolution, 1775–1783.* White Plains: Westchester County Historical Society, 1926; Harrison, New York: Harbor Hill Books, 1974. pp.155–156.

174. *The Royal American Gazette.* CVII (September 22, 1778) p.5. *The Massachusetts Spy: or, American Oracle of Liberty.* VIII:390 (October 22,1778) p.4.

175. Extract of a letter from Head-Quarters, Oct. 4, 1778. *The Pennsylvania Packet or the General Advertiser.* February 4, 1779. p.2.

176. *The New Jersey Gazette.* II:79 (June 9,1779) p.3. *The American Journal And General Advertiser.* I:XV (June 24,1779) p.3.

177. Extract of a letter from Elizabeth-Town, May 30. *The Boston Gazette, and Country Journal.* 1312 (October 18, 1779) p.4.

178. Extract of a letter from Lieut. General Knyphausen to Lord George Germain, dated New York, March 27, 1780. *The New-York Gazette; and the Weekly Mercury.* 1498 (July 3, 1780) p.1.

179. Ibid.

180. *The Pennsylvania Evening Post.* VII:758 (July 27,1781) p.115.

181. Journal of HMS *Phoenix.* British National Archives, Admiralty 51/694. NDAR 5:1240.

182. Ewald, Johann. *Diary of the American War: A Hessian Journal.* Translated and edited by Joseph P. Tustin. New Haven and London: Yale University Press, 1979. pp.172–173.

183. *The New-Hampshire Gazette, and Historical Chronicle.* I:12 (August 8, 1776) p 2.

184. *The Boston Gazette, and Country Journal.* 1267 (December 7, 1776) p.2.

185. Peckham, Howard Henry. *The Toll of Independence: Engagements & Battle Casualties of the American Revolution.* Chicago: University of Chicago Press, 1974. p.55.

186. Heath, William. *Memoirs of Major-General William Heath.* Ed. by William Abbatt. New York: William Abbatt, 1901. pp.60–61. NDAR 6:1184–1185.

187. George Washington To Governor Nicholas Cooke, Washington Papers, Library of Congress. NDAR 6:1238. Lieutenants Jeremiah Putnam And Nathaniel Cleaves To George Washington. *Washington Papers.* NDAR 6:1184. Mackenzie, Frederick. The Diary of Frederick Mackenzie. Cambridge, MA: Harvard University Press, 1930. 1:74–75. Journal of HMS *Phoenix.* British National Archives, Admiralty 51/694. NDAR 6:1178–1180. Master's Log of HMS

Roebuck. British National Archives, Admiralty 51/1965. NDAR 6:1180. Journal of HMS *Tartar* Capt. Cornthwaite Ommanney. British National Archives, Admiralty 51/972. NDAR 6:118. Heath, William. *Memoirs of Major General William Heath.* [New York]: New York Times [1968, c1901] p.60.

188. Journal of HMS *Tartar.* British National Archives, Admiralty 51/972. NDAR 6:1415.

189. Journal of HM Galley *Dependence* British National Archives, Admiralty 51/4159–Captain's Log No. 4159 Part 3 (1777) p.16-17.

190. Ibid. p.17.

191. Ibid.

192. Ibid. p.18.

193. Ibid.

194. Ibid. p.19.

195. Ibid. p.20.

196. Ibid. pp.19, 20.

197. Ibid. p.20.

198. Journal Of HM Galley *Dependence,* Lieutenant James Clark, British National Archives, Admiralty 51/4159. NDAR 9:336.

199. Ibid.

200. Journal of HM Brig *Diligent.* British National Archives, Admiralty 51/4163. NDAR 9:917. Journal of HM Galley *Dependence.* British National Archives, Admiralty 51/4159. NDAR 9:917–918.

201. Letter of Gen. Samuel Parsons to Governor Tryon. November 21, 1777. Letter of Governor Tryon to Gen. Samuel Parsons, November 23, 1777. Bolton, Robert. *The History of the Several Towns, Manors, and Patents of the County of Westchester from its First Settlement to the Present Time.* New York: Chas. F. Roper, 1881. I:355. 500, 501.

202. Journal of HM Galley *Dependence.* British National Archives, Admiralty 51/4159–Captain's Log No. 4159 Part 3 (1777) p.57.

203. Journal of HM Galley *Dependence.* British National Archives, Admiralty 51/4159–Captain's Log No. 4159 Part 3 (1777) p.58.

204. Journal of HM Galley *Dependence.* British National Archives, Admiralty 51/4159–Captain's Log No. 4159 Part 3 (1777). Popp, Stephan. *A Hessian Soldier in the American Revolution: the diary of Stephan Popp.* Translated from original text by Reinhart J. Pope. Private printing, 1953. p.11.

205. Ewald, Johann. *Diary of the American War: A Hessian Journal.* Translated and edited by Joseph P. Tustin. New Haven and London: Yale University Press, 1979. pp.145–149.

206. Peebles, John. *John Peebles' American War: the Diary of a Scottish Grenadier, 1776–1782.* edited by Ira D. Gruber. Mechanicsburg, PA: Stackpole Books, 1998. pp.222–223.

207. Journal of HM Galley *Dependence.* British National Archives, Admiralty 51/4159–Captain's Log No. 4159 Part 3 (1777) p.59. Rice, Howard C, Jr. and Anne S. K. Brown. *The American Campaigns of Rochambeau's Army 1780, 1781, 1782, 1783.* Princeton: Princeton University Press; Providence: Brown University Press, 1972. 1:34–35; 248–251.

208. Rice, Howard C, Jr. and Anne S. K. Brown. *The American Campaigns of Rochambeau's Army 1780, 1781, 1782, 1783.* Princeton: Princeton University Press; Providence: Brown University Press, 1972. 1: 34–35; 248–251. *Connecticut Journal.* 718 (August 2, 1781) p.2. Mackenzie, Frederick. *The Diary of Frederick Mackenzie.* Cambridge, MA: Harvard University Press, 1930. 2:569. Heath, William. *Memoirs of Major-General William Heath.* Ed. by William Abbatt. New York: William Abbatt, 1901. pp.76, 294. Thacher James. *Military Journal of the American Revolution.* Hartford: Hurlbut, Williams & Company, 1862. p.259. Bolton, Robert. *The History of the Several Towns, Manors, and Patents of the County of Westchester from its First Settlement to the Present Time.* New York: Chas. F. Roper, 1881. I:274.

209. Heath, William. *Memoirs of Major-General William Heath.* Ed. by William Abbatt. New York: William Abbatt, 1901. p.273.

210. Robertson, Archibald. *Archibald Robertson, Lieutenant-General Royal Engineers: His Diaries and Sketches in America, 1762–1780.* edited with and introduction by Harry Miller Lydenberg. New York: The New York Public Library, 1930; The New York Public Library and The New York Times & Arno Press, 1971. pp.102–103. Stember, Sol. *The Bicentennial Guide to the American Revolution.* New York: Saturday Review Press, [distributed by] Dutton, 1974; [s.l.]: New York Times and Arno Press, 1969. 1:241–244. Ward, Christopher. *The War of the Revolution.* New York: Macmillan, 1952. pp.261–262.

211. Heath, William. *Memoirs of Major-General William Heath.* Ed. by William Abbatt. New York: William Abbatt, 1901. p.106. Bolton, Robert. *The History of the Several Towns, Manors, and Patents of the County of Westchester from its First Settlement to the Present Time.* New York: Chas. F. Roper, 1881. I:696.

212. Hall, Charles Samuel. *Life and letters of Samuel Holden Parsons: Major General in the Continental Army and Chief Judge of the Northwestern Territory, 1737–1789.* New York: From the archives of James Pugliese, 1968. p.125. Peckham, Howard Henry. *The Toll of Independence: Engagements & Battle Casualties of the American Revolution.* Chicago: University of Chicago Press, 1974. p.45.

213. Extract of a letter from St. Eustatia, dated July 25. *The New Jersey Gazette.* II:86 (August 18, 1779) p.3.

214. *The Pennsylvania Packet or the General Advertiser.* (August 26, 1779) p.2. *The Independent Chronicle and the Universal Advertiser.* XII:576 (September 2, 1779) p.3. *Connecticut Courant.* 840 (February 27, 1781) p.2.

215. Extract of a letter from an officer in the American army, dated North-Castle, near New York, Oct. 19. *The Norwich Packet and the Connecticut, Massachusetts, New-Hampshire, and Rhode Island Weekly Advertiser.* 4:165 (November 18–25, 1776) p.3. *The Independent Chronicle.* IX:428 (October 31, 1776).

216. Heath, William. *Memoirs of Major-General William Heath.* Ed. by William Abbatt. New York: William Abbatt, 1901. pp.64–65. Hufeland, Otto. *Westchester County during the American Revolution, 1775–1783.* White Plains: Westchester County Historical Society, 1926; Harrison, New York: Harbor Hill Books, 1974. pp.118–122. Force, Peter. *American Archives: Consisting of a Collection of Authentick Records, State Papers, Debates, and Letters and other Notices of Publick Affairs, the Whole Forming a Documentary History of the Origin and Progress of the North American Colonies; of the Causes and Accomplishment of the American Revolution; and of the Constitution of Government for the United States, to the Final Ratification thereof. In six Series.* [Washington, 1837–1853. Fifth Series. II:1188–1189. Ward, Christopher. *The War of the Revolution.* New York: Macmillan, 1952. pp.256, 257, 261. *Pennsylvania Journal and Weekly Advertiser.*(October 23, 1776). *Documents Relating to the Revolutionary History, State Of New Jersey.* Edited by William S. Stryker. Trenton: The John L. Murphy Publishing Co., 1901. Series 2. 1:216–217.

217. *The New-York Gazette; and the Weekly Mercury* (March 24, 1777). Hufeland, Otto. *Westchester County during the American Revolution, 1775–1783.* White Plains: Westchester County Historical Society, 1926; Harrison, New York: Harbor Hill Books, 1974. pp.195–199.

218. Cornelius, Elias. *Journal Of Dr. Elias Cornelius, A Revolutionary Surgeon.* Washington, D.C.: C. M. Tompkins and C. T. Sherman, 1903. Hufeland, Otto. *Westchester County during the American Revolution, 1775–1783.* White Plains: Westchester County Historical Society, 1926; Harrison, New York: Harbor Hill Books, 1974. pp.226–227.

219. *The American Journal.* I:1 (March 18, 1779) p.4. See also Greenwich, Connecticut in the previous volume on Canada and New England.

220. Heath, William. *Memoirs of Major-General William Heath.* Ed. by William Abbatt. New York: William Abbatt, 1901. p.201.

221. Mackenzie, Frederick. *The Diary of Frederick Mackenzie.* Cambridge, MA: Harvard University Press, 1930 2:693–694. *The New Jersey Gazette.* IV:207 (December 12, 1781) p.3.

222. Charles Stedman, *The History of the Origin, Progress and Termination of the American War.* (1794). 2:278–279.

223. *The New-York Gazette; and the Weekly Mercury* (March 31, 1777). Patterson, Emma L. *Peekskill in the American Revolution.* Peekskill, New York: The Friendly Town Association, Inc., 1944. pp.39–44. Albertson, J Donald; Varian, Helen. *Historic Van Cortlandtville.* [Van Cortlandtville, NY]: Van Cortlandtville Historical Society, 1976. www.cortlandt. advinc.com/museum/mainpage.htm. Charles Stedman, *The History of the Origin, Progress and Termination of the American War.* (1794). 2:278–279. Smith, William. *Historical Memoirs of William Smith.* Edited by William H. W. Sabine. New York, 1956. 2:97.

224. Journal of HM Galley *Dependence*, Lt. James Clark. British National Archives, Admiralty 51/4159. NDAR 10:42–43.

225. Journal Of HMS *Preston*, Captain Samuel Uppleby. British National Archives, Admiralty 51/720. NDAR 10:68.

226. Letter of General Sir William Howe to Sir Henry Clinton written at Fort Montgomery on October 9th, 1777. supplement to *Gaines' Military Gazette.* 1372 (February 9, 1778). Patterson, Emma L. *Peekskill in the American Revolution.* Peekskill, New York: The Friendly Town Association, Inc., 1944. p.69. Bolton, Robert. *The History of the Several Towns, Manors, and Patents of the County of Westchester from its First Settlement to the Present Time.* New York: Chas. F. Roper, 1881. I:159.

227. Heath, William. *Memoirs Major-General William Heath by Himself.*—New Edition, With Illustrations And Notes.—Edited By William Abbatt. New York: William Abbatt, 1901. p.198.

228. Journal of HM Galley *Dependence* British National Archives, Admiralty 51/4159–Captain's Log No. 4159 Part 3 (1777) p.20.

229. Journal Of HM Galley *Dependence*, Lieutenant James Clark, British National Archives. Admiralty 51/4159. NDAR 9:718–719.

230. Journal Of HM Galley *Dependence*, Lieutenant James Clark, British National Archives. Admiralty 51/4159.

231. Journal of HMS *Mercury.* British National Archives Admiralty 51/600. NDAR 10:42. Journal of HM Galley *Dependence.* British National Archives Admiralty 51/4159. NDAR 10:42. Journal of HM Galley *Mercury.* British National Archives Admiralty 51/4163. NDAR 10:43.

232. Journal of HM Galley *Dependence.* British National Archives, Admiralty 51/4159–Captain's Log No. 4159 Part 3 (1777). Peckham, Howard Henry. *The Toll of Independence: Engagements & Battle Casualties of the American Revolution.* Chicago: University of Chicago Press, 1974. p.49.

233. Washington, George. *The Writings of George Washington*, ed. John C. Fitzpatrick. Washington, D.C., 1963, VI: 269.

234. Letters of Gen. James Pattison. (June 9, 1779) *Coll. N. Y. Hist. Socy.*, 1875. p.73. Hufeland, Otto. *Westchester County during the American Revolution, 1775–1783.* White Plains: Westchester County Historical Society, 1926; Harrison, New York: Harbor Hill Books, 1974. pp.284–89. Kemble, Stephen. *Journals of Lieut.-Col. Stephen Kemble, 1773–1789; and British Army Orders: Gen. Sir William Howe, 1775–1778; Gen. Sir Henry Clinton, 1778; and Gen. Daniel Jones, 1778.* Prepared by New York Historical Society; Boston: Gregg Press, 1972. p.179.

234a. Journal of HM Galley Dependence British National Archives, Admiralty 51/4159–Captain's Log No. 4159 Part 3 (1777) p.15.

235. Journal of HM Galley *Dependence*. British National Archives, Admiralty 51/4159–Captain's Log No. 4159 Part 3 (1777) p.27. Peckham, Howard Henry. *The Toll of Independence: Engagements & Battle Casualties of the American Revolution*. Chicago: University of Chicago Press, 1974. p.38.

236. Baldwin Jeduthan. *The Revolutionary Journal of Col. Jeduthan Baldwin 1775–1778*. Edited with a Memoir and notes by Thomas Williams Baldwin. Bangor: Printed for the De Burians, 1906. p.129. Journal of HM Galley *Dependence*. British National Archives, Admiralty 51/4159–Captain's Log No. 4159 Part 3 (1777).

237. Bolton, Robert. *The History of the Several Towns, Manors, and Patents of the County of Westchester from its First Settlement to the Present Time*. New York: Chas. F. Roper, 1881. I:561–562.

238. Peckham, Howard Henry. *The Toll of Independence: Engagements & Battle Casualties of the American Revolution*. Chicago: University of Chicago Press, 1974. p.88.

239. Journal of HM Galley *Dependence*. British National Archives, Admiralty 51/4159. NDAR 10:128. Journal of HM Brig *Diligent*. British National Archives, Admiralty 51/4163. Library of Congress, Peter Force Collection, Horatio Gates Papers. 2:213–10–101. NDAR 10:128.

240. Journal of HM Brig *Diligent*. British National Archives, Admiralty 51/4163. NDAR 10:172. Journal of HM Galley *Dependence*. British National Archives, Admiralty 51/4159. NDAR 10:172. *New York Loyal Gazette*. 141 (November 1, 1777) p.2.

241. *New York Loyal Gazette*. 141 (November 1, 1777) p.2.

242. Journal of HM Brig *Diligent*. British National Archives, Admiralty 51/4163. NDAR 10:244. Journal Of HM Galley *Dependence*, Lieutenant James Clark, British National Archives, Admiralty 51/4159. NDAR 10:243–244.

243. Journal of HM Galley *Dependence*, Lt. James Clark. British National Archives, Admiralty 51/4159. NDAR 10:143.

244. Journal of HM Galley *Dependence*. British National Archives, Admiralty 51/4159. NDAR 10:250. Journal of HM Brig *Diligence*. British National Archives, Admiralty 51/4163. NDAR 10:259.

245. *Rivington's Gazette*. May 27, 1779. Moore, Frank. *Diary of the American Revolution: from Newspapers and Original Documents*. New York: Charles Scribner; London: Sampson Low, Son & Co., 1890. 2:281–282. Baird, Charles W. *Chronicle of a Border Town: History of Rye, Westchester County, New York, 1660–1870, Including Harrison and the White Plains till 1788*. New York: Anson D. F. Randolph and Co., 1871. p.259.

246. *Connecticut Journal*. 537 (Jan. 28, 1778) p.2.

247. *Revolution in America: Confidential Letters and Journals 1776–1784 of Adjutant General Major Baurmeister of the Hessian Forces*. Translated and annotated by Berhard A. Uhlendorf. New Brunswick, NJ: Rutgers University Press, 1957. pp.288–289. Peckham, Howard Henry. *The Toll of Independence: Engagements & Battle Casualties of the American Revolution*. Chicago: University of Chicago Press, 1974. p.60.

248. Baird, Charles W. *Chronicle of a Border Town: History of Rye, Westchester County, New York, 1660–1870, Including Harrison and the White Plains till 1788*. New York: Anson D. F. Randolph and Co., 1871. p.259.

249. Ibid.

250. Ibid.

251. Simcoe, John Graves. *Simcoe's Military Journal, A History of the Operations of a Partisan Corps Called The Queen's Rangers, commanded by Lieut. Colonel J. G. Simcoe...* New York: Bartlett & Welford, 1844. pp.102, 103.

252. Ward, Christopher. *The War of the Revolution*. New York: Macmillan, 1952. 258–259. *Encyclopedia of the American Revolution*. Harold E. Selesky, editor in chief. – 2nd Ed. Detroit: Charles Scribner's Sons, 2007. II:672-73.

253. Tallmadge, Benjamin. *Memoir Of Col. Benjamin Tallmadge*. New York: Thomas Holman, 1858. pp.47–52.

254. *The New-York Gazette; and The Weekly Mercury*. 1408 (October 12, 1778) p.3. Baird, Charles W. *Chronicle of a Border Town: History of Rye, Westchester County, New York, 1660–1870, Including Harrison and the White Plains till 1788*. New York: Anson D. F. Randolph and Co., 1871. p.256.

255. Simcoe, John Graves. *Simcoe's Military Journal, A History of the Operations of a Partisan Corps Called The Queen's Rangers, Commanded by Lieut. Col. J. G. Simcoe, During the War of the American Revolution New-York*: Bartlett & Welford, 1844; [New York]: New York Times; Arno Press. – Eyewitness Accounts of the American Revolution. [1968]. Baird, Charles W. *Chronicle of a Border Town: History of Rye, Westchester County, New York, 1660–1870, Including Harrison and the White Plains till 1788*. New York: Anson D.F. Randolph and Co., 1871. pp.256–257.

256. *The New-York Gazette; and the Weekly Mercury* (March 3, 1779). Mead, Daniel M. *A History of the Town of Greenwich, Fairfield County, Conn., with Many Important Statistics*. New York: Baker & Godwin, printers, 1857. p.166. Baird, Charles W. *Chronicle of a Border Town: History of Rye, Westchester County, New York, 1660–1870, Including Harrison and the White Plains till 1788*. New York: Anson D. F. Randolph and Co., 1871. pp.258–259.

257. *Encyclopedia of the American Revolution*. Harold E. Selesky, editor in chief.–2nd Ed. Detroit: Charles Scribner's Sons, 2007. II:1116–1120. *The Encyclopedia of the American Revolutionary War: a political, social, and military history*. Gregory Fremont-Barnes, Richard Alan Ryerson, editors. Santa Barbara, CA: ABC-CLIO, 2006. IV:1212–1214. Clinton, Henry. *The American Rebellion: Sir Henry Clinton's Narrative of His Campaigns, 1775–1782, with an appendix of original documents*. Edited by William B. Willcox. New Haven: Yale University Press, 1954. Dawson, Henry B. *The Assault on Stony Point, by General Anthony Wayne, July 16, 1779*. Morrisania, NY: Henry B. Dawson, 1863. Johnston, Henry P. *The Storming of Stony Point on the Hudson, Midnight, July 15, 1779: Its Importance in the Light of Unpublished Documents*. New York: James T. White, 1900. Nelson, Paul David. *Anthony Wayne: Soldier of the Early Republic*. Bloomington: Indiana University Press, 1985. Palmer, David R. *The River and the Rock: The History of Fortress West Point, 1775–1783*. New York: Greenwood, 1969. Skarsky, I. W. *The Revolution's Boldest Venture: The Story of "Mad Anthony" Wayne's Assault on Stony Point*. Port Washington, NY: Kennikat Press, 1965. Stillé, Charles J. *Major-General Anthony Wayne and the Pennsylvania Line in the Continental Army*.

Philadelphia: Lippincott, 1893. Ward, Christopher. *The War of the Revolution.* New York: Macmillan, 1952. Wildes, Harry Emerson. *Anthony Wayne: Trouble Shooter of the American Revolution.* New York: Harcourt, Brace, 1941.

258. Extract of a letter from a general officer at camp, (Highlands) dated October 2, 1779. *Continental Journal.* CXCIV (October 5, 1779) p.3.

259. *The American Historical Register and Monthly Gazette of the Patriotic-Hereditary Societies of the United States of America.* Philadelphia: Historical Register Pub. Co., 1895–1897. 1:276.

260. *Connecticut Courant.* 898 (April 9, 1782) p.2.

261. Lancaster, Bruce. *From Lexington to Liberty: the Story of the American Revolution.* Garden City, NY: Doubleday, 1955. p.395.

262. Tallmadge, Benjamin. *Memoir of Colonel Benjamin Tallmadge.* New York: Thomas Holman, 1858; (Eyewitness accounts of the American Revolution). [New York] New York Times [1968] p.36.

263. André, John. *Major André's Journal: Operations of the British Army under Lieutenant Generals Sir William Howe, and Sir Henry Clinton, June 1777, to November 1778*, edited by Henry Cabot Lodge, Boston, 1902; Tarrytown, NY: William Abbatt, 1930. p.9.

264. *Encyclopedia of the American Revolution.* Harold E. Selesky, editor in chief.–2nd Ed. Detroit: Charles Scribner's Sons, 2007.I:32–37. *The Encyclopedia of the American Revolutionary War: a political, social, and military history.* Gregory Fremont-Barnes, Richard Alan Ryerson, editors. Santa Barbara, CA: ABC-CLIO, 2006. I:52–57; IV:1343–1344. Ambrose, Stephen E. *Duty, Honor, Country: A History of West Point, 1966:* Baltimore, MD: Johns Hopkins University Press, 1999. Boylan, Brian Richard. *Benedict Arnold: The Dark Eagle.* New York: Norton, 1973. Brandt, Clare. *The Man in the Mirror: A Life of Benedict Arnold.* New York: Random House, 1994. Codman, John. *Arnold Expedition to Quebec.* New York: Macmillan, 1901. Crackel, Theodore J. *West Point: A Bicentennial History.* Lawrence: University Press of Kansas, 2002. Flexner, James Thomas. *The Traitor and the Spy: Benedict Arnold and John André.* New York: Harcourt Brace, 1953. Luzader, John. "The Arnold–Gates Controversy." *West Virginia History.* 27 (2) (1966):75–84. Martin, James Kirby. *Benedict Arnold: Revolutionary Hero: An American Warrior Reconsidered.* New York: New York University Press, 1997. Miller, Charles E. Jr., Donald V. Lockey, and Joseph Visconti Jr. *Highland Fortress: The Fortification of West Point During the American Revolution.* West Point: USMA, 1988. Palmer, David R. *The River and the Rock: The History of Fortress West Point, 1775–1783.* New York: Greenwood, 1969. Randall, Willard Sterne. *Benedict Arnold: Patriot and Traitor.* New York: Morrow, 1990. Roberts, Kenneth Lewis. *Arundel.* Rockport, ME: Down East Books, 1995. Roberts, Kenneth Lewis. *March to Quebec: Journals of the Members of Arnold's Expedition.* Rockport, ME: Down East Books, 1945, 1967. Roberts, Kenneth Lewis. *Rabble in Arms.* Rockport, ME: Down East Books, 1996. Royster, Charles. *A Revolutionary People at War: The Continental Army and American Character, 1775–1783.* Chapel Hill: University of North Carolina Press, 1979. Van Doren, Carl. *Secret History of the American Revolution: An Account of the Conspiracies of Benedict Arnold and Numerous Others.* New York: Viking, 1941. Ward, Christopher. *The War of the Revolution.* New York: Macmillan, 1952.

265. Ward, Christopher. *The War of the Revolution.* New York: Macmillan, 1952. p.620. Raymond, Marcius D. *Souvenir of the Revolutionary Soldiers' Monument Dedication, at Tarrytown, NY October 19th, 1894.* [New York: Rogers & Sherwood] 1894. pp.74–5. Bolton, Robert. *The History of the Several Towns, Manors, and Patents of the County of Westchester from its First Settlement to the Present Time.* New York: Chas. F. Roper, 1881. I:252–253.

266. Heath, William. *Memoirs of Major-General William Heath.* Ed. by William Abbatt. New York: William Abbatt, 1901. p.197.

267. Hufeland, Otto. *Westchester County during the American Revolution, 1775–1783.* White Plains: Westchester County Historical Society, 1926; Harrison, New York: Harbor Hill Books, 1974. pp.324–326. Heath, William. *Memoirs of Major-General William Heath.* Ed. by William Abbatt. New York: William Abbatt, 1901. p.230. Ward, Christopher. *The War of the Revolution.* New York: Macmillan, 1952. p.620. Raymond, Marcius D. *Souvenir of the Revolutionary Soldiers' Monument Dedication, at Tarrytown, NY October 19th, 1894.* [New York, Rogers & Sherwood] 1894, 74–5. Bolton, Reginald Pelham. *The Raid on Young's Corners, 1780.* [White Plains]: White Plains Chapter, Daughters of the American Revolution, 1923. Bolton, Robert. *The History of the Several Towns, Manors, and Patents of the County of Westchester from its First Settlement to the Present Time.* New York: Chas. F. Roper, 1881. I:53–561.

268. Ewald, Johann. *Diary of the American War: A Hessian Journal.* Translated and edited by Joseph P. Tustin. New Haven and London: Yale University Press, 1979. p.169. Heath, William. *Memoirs of Major-General William Heath.* Ed. by William Abbatt. New York: William Abbatt, 1901. pp.189–190.

269. Thacher James. *Military Journal of the American Revolution.* Hartford: Hurlbut, Williams & Company, 1862. p.255.

270. Extract of a Letter from Elizabeth-Town, Dated July 9. *The Independent Gazetteer.* 14 (July 13,1782) p.3. *Connecticut Courant.* 914 (July 30, 1782) p.2. *Connecticut Journal.* 770 (August 1, 1782) p.2. *The Massachusetts Spy: or, American Oracle of Liberty* XII: 587 (August 1, 1782) p.3. *The Pennsylvania Packet or the General Advertiser.* XI: 911 (July 16, 1782) p.3. *The New Jersey Gazette.* V: 238 (July 17, 1782) p.4. *The New-York Gazette; and the Weekly Mercury.* 1603 (July 8, 1782) p.3.

271. Ward, Christopher. *The War of the Revolution.* New York: Macmillan, 1952. p.618. Bolton, Robert. *The History of the Several Towns, Manors, and Patents of the County of Westchester from its First Settlement to the Present Time.* New York: Chas. F. Roper, 1881. II:118, 121–124. Heath, William. *Memoirs of Major-General William Heath.* Ed. by William Abbatt. New York: William Abbatt, 1901. p.208.

272. Tallmadge, Benjamin. *Memoir Of Col. Benjamin Tallmadge.* New York: Thomas Holman, 1858. p.32. Bolton, Robert. *The History of the Several Towns, Manors, and Patents of the County of Westchester from its First Settlement to the Present Time.* New York: Chas. F. Roper, 1881. I:71.

273. Robertson, Archibald. *Archibald Robertson: His Diaries And Sketches In America 1762–1780.* Edited With An Introduction By Harry Miller Lydenberg. New York: The New York Public Library, 1930. p.198. Heath, William. *Memoirs of Major-General William Heath.* Ed. by William Abbatt. New York: William Abbatt, 1901. p.270. Bolton,

Robert. *The History of the Several Towns, Manors, and Patents of the County of Westchester from its First Settlement to the Present Time.* New York: Chas. F. Roper, 1881. p.73. Hinitt, Dorothy Humphreys. *The Burning of Bedford July 1779 as Reported in Contemporary Documents and Eyewitness Accounts: A Salute to the Bicentennial 1976.* Dorothy Humphreys Hinitt, Frances Riker Duncombe, Janet Doe, Technical Editor, Arthur I. Bernhard, maps. Bedford, NY: Bedford Historical Society, 1974.

274. Mackenzie, Frederick. *The Diary of Frederick Mackenzie.* Cambridge, MA: Harvard University Press, 1930 2:568. Lossing, Benson John. *The Pictorial Field-book of the Revolution; or, Illustrations, by Pen and Pencil, of the History, Biography, Scenery, Relics, and Traditions of the War for Independence.* New York, Harper & Brothers [1860] Vol. II, Chapter XXIII.

275. Simcoe, John Graves. *Simcoe's Military Journal, A History of the Operations of a Partisan Corps Called The Queen's Rangers, commanded by Lieut. Col. J.G. Simcoe...* New York: Bartlett & Welford, 1844. pp.105–106. Heath, William. *Memoirs of Major-General William Heath.* Ed. by William Abbatt. New York: William Abbatt, 1901. p.197. Hufeland, Otto. *Westchester County during the American Revolution, 1775–1783.* White Plains: Westchester County Historical Society, 1926; Harrison, New York: Harbor Hill Books, 1974. p.308.

276. Heath, William. *Memoirs Major-General William Heath By Himself.*—New Edition, With Illustrations And Notes.—Edited By William Abbatt. New York: William Abbatt, 1901. p.210. *Rivington's Gazette.* (January 22, 1780). Moore, Frank. *Diary of the American Revolution: from Newspapers and Original Documents.* New York: Charles Scribner; London: Sampson Low, Son & Co., 1890 2:252–253.

277. *The Independent Ledger, and the American Advertiser.* 3:141 (February 12, 1781) p.3.

278. *New-Jersey Gazette.* IV:165 (February 21,1781) p.1. Extract of a letter from an officer at Horse neck, dated Jan. 23, 1781. *American Journal and General Advertiser.* II:104 (February 24, 1781) p.1.

279. Thacher, James. *Military Journal of the American Revolution, From the Commencement to the Disbanding of the American Army: Comprising a Detailed Account of the Principal Events and Battles of the Revolution, with Their Exact dates, and a Biographical Sketch of the Most Prominent Generals.* Hartford, CT: Hurlbut, Williams & Company, 1862; The New York Times & Arno Press, 1974. p.245. Bolton, Robert. *The History of the Several Towns, Manors, and Patents of the County of Westchester from its First Settlement to the Present Time.* New York: Chas. F. Roper, 1881. II p.526.

280. Clinton, George. *Public Papers of George Clinton, First Governor of New York, 1777–1795, 1801–1804.* Hugh Hastings, ed. New York and Albany: Pub. by the State of New York, 1900. 7:xi.

281. *Connecticut Journal.* Issue 743 (January 24, 1782) p.2. *Salem Gazette.* 1:16 January 31, 1782. p.2. *Newport Mercury.* 1062 (February 2, 1782) p.1. *Boston Gazette and the Country Journal.*1431 (January 28, 1782) p.2.

282. *The Massachusetts Spy: or, American Oracle of Liberty.* XII: 567 (March 21, 1782) p.3. Heath, William. *Memoirs of Major-General William Heath.* Ed. by William Abbatt. New York: William Abbatt, 1901. p.330. Bolton, Robert. *The History of the Several Towns, Manors, and Patents of the County of Westchester from its First Settlement to the Present Time.* New York: Chas. F. Roper, 1881. II:527.

283. Irving, Washington. *Life of George Washington.* New York: Putnam, 1856–1857. IV:388. Heath, William. *Memoirs of Major-General William Heath.* Ed. by William Abbatt. New York: William Abbatt, 1901. p.325. Hufeland, Otto. *Westchester County During the American Revolution, 1775–1783.* White Plains: Westchester County Historical Society, 1926; Harrison, New York: Harbor Hill Books, 1974. pp.408–409. *The New Jersey Gazette.* 5:210 (January 2, 1782) 3. Bolton, Robert. *The History of the Several Towns, Manors, and Patents of the County of Westchester from its First Settlement to the Present Time.* New York: Chas. F. Roper, 1881. II:19. Clinton, George. *Public Papers of George Clinton, First Governor of New York, 1777–1795, 1801–1804.* Hugh Hastings, ed. New York and Albany: Pub. by the State of New York, 1900. 7:605, 626.

284. *The New-York Gazette; and the Weekly Mercury.* 1535 (March 19, 1781) p.3.

285. Lee, Henry, *Memoirs of the War in the Southern Department of the United States.* New York: University Publishing Co., 1869. p.590.

286. www.crotonheights.org/Historynew.html.

287. www.crotonheights.org/Historynew.html. www.blupete.com/Hist/BiosNS/1800-67/Delancey.htm. Greenman, Jeremiah. *Diary of a Common Soldier in the American Revolution, 1775–1783: an Annotated Edition of the Military Journal of Jeremiah Greenman.* Edited by Robert Bray and Paul Bushnell. DeKalb, IL: Northern Illinois University Press, 1978. p.208. *Rivington's Royal Gazette.* (May 16, 1781). Albee, Allison. *The Nasty Affair at Pines Bridge.* (originally published as *The Defenses at Pines Bridge*) Prepared and edited by Monica Doherty with an introduction by Lincoln Diamant. Silent Sentinel Studio, 2005. Bolton, Reginald Pelham. "The Defense of Croton River in the Revolution." *New-York Historical Society Quarterly.* 8 (July 1924) pp.35–39. Bolton, Robert. *The History of the Several Towns, Manors, and Patents of the County of Westchester from its First Settlement to the Present Time.* New York: Chas. F. Roper, 1881. II:673–686. "The Life of Loyalist Colonel James DeLancey" by George DeLancey Hanger, NSHR#3:2 (1983) p.42. Raymond, Marcius D. Colonel Christopher Greene. *Magazine of History.* September–October 1916. pp.138–149.

288. Mackenzie, Frederick. *The Diary of Frederick Mackenzie.* Cambridge, MA: Harvard University Press, 1930. 2:667.

289. John Saxon Revolutionary War Pension Application, Steuben County, New York. Rev. War Pension Application S# 32507; BLWT # 9054-160-55. ftp.rootsweb.com/pub/usgenweb/ny/steuben/military/revwar/pensions/jsaxon.txt.

290. Extract of a letter from Continental Village, July 2, 1780. *The New Jersey Gazette.* 3:134 (July 19, 1780) p.3. *Independent Ledger and the American Advertiser.* 3:110 (July 17, 1780) p.2. *The Independent Chronicle and the Universal Advertiser.* 12:620 (July 13, 1780) p.3. *Maryland Journal (La Prensa).* VII:358 (July 25, 1780) p.1.

291. *Connecticut Courant.* 840 (February 27, 1781) p.2. *Royal Gazette.* 206 (September 19, 1778) p.3. *The American Journal and General Advertiser.* II:106 (March 3, 1781) p.2.

292. *Royal Gazette.* 467 (March 21, 1781) p.3.

293. Peckham, Howard Henry. *The Toll of Independence: Engagements & Battle Casualties of the American Revolution.* Chicago: University of Chicago Press, 1974. p.87. Krafft, John Charles Philip von. *Journal of Lieutenant John Charles Philip von Krafft.* Collections of the New-York Historical Society for the year 1882. –Eyewitness Accounts of the American Revolution.—New York: The New York Historical Society; New York: The New York Times & Arno Press, 1968. p.142.

294. Washington, George. *The Diaries of George Washington, 1748–1799.* Boston, New York: Houghton Mifflin Company, Kraus Reprint Co., [1925] 1971. II: 231–233.

295. Rice, Howard C, Jr. and Anne S. K. Brown. *The American Campaigns of Rochambeau's Army 1780, 1781, 1782, 1783.* Princeton: Princeton University Press; Providence: Brown University Press, 1972. 1:32, 132, 248–251.

296. *The Massachusetts Spy: or, American Oracle of Liberty.* XI:532 (July 19, 1781) p.3. *The New Jersey Gazette.* IV:188 (August 1, 1781) p.2.

297. Simcoe, John Graves. *Simcoe's Military Journal. A History of the Operations of a Partisan Corps Called The Queen's Rangers, Commanded by Lieut. Col. J. G. Simcoe, During the War of the American Revolution.* New-York: Bartlett & Welford, 1844; [New York]: New York Times; Arno Press. – Eyewitness Accounts of the American Revolution. [1968]. *The New Jersey Gazette.* IV: 208 (December 19, 1781) p.2. Baird, Charles W. *Chronicle of a Border Town: History of Rye, Westchester County, New York, 1660-1870, Including Harrison and the White Plains till 1788.* New York: Anson D.F. Randolph and Co., 1871. pp.257-258.

298. *Connecticut Courant.* 898 (April 9, 1782) p.2.

299. *Providence Gazette; and Country Journal.* 12:606 p.3. *The New-Hampshire Gazette and Historical Chronicle*: XIX:984 (Aug 11, 1775) p.1.

300. *Newport Gazette.* (Thursday, March 13, 1777). NDAR 8:100.

301. Diary of Christopher Vail [September 6–7] NDAR 6:733. Mackenzie, Frederick. *The Diary of Frederick Mackenzie.* Cambridge, MA: Harvard University Press, 1930. I:40 for September 7, 1776.

302. *Connecticut Journal.* (Wednesday, November 6, 1776); NDAR 7:63. *Connecticut Gazette.*(Friday, November 8, 1776). NDAR 7:86. Prison Diary Of Major Christopher French, US Revolution. NDAR 7:105–106.

303. Hall, Charles Samuel. *Life and letters of Samuel Holden Parsons: Major General in the Continental Army and Chief Judge of the Northwestern Territory, 1737–1789.* New York: From the archives of James Pugliese, 1968. pp.109–110, 134–137. *Long Island in the American Revolution.* Myron H. Luke and Robert W. Venables. Albany: New York State American Revolution Bicentennial Commission, 1976. pp.47–48. *The Independent Chronicle and the Universal Advertiser.* 10:473 (September 11, 1777) p.3.

304. *Long Island in the American Revolution.* Myron H. Luke and Robert W. Venables. Albany: New York State American Revolution Bicentennial Commission, 1976. p.48. Journal of HM Sloop *Falcon,* Commander Harry Harmood. British National Archives, Admiralty 51/336. NDAR 10:699. Continental Navy sloop *Schuyler,* Lieutenant John Kerr, owned by the Continental Congress, from Norwalk to Setauket, taken on 10 Dec. off Setauket, sent to Rhode Island as prize of the *Falcon.* Howe's Prize List, 30 Oct. 1778, British National Archives, Admiralty 1/488, 485. *Continental Journal.* LXXXIII (December 25, 1777) p 3. *Connecticut Gazette.* (December 19, 1777). Hall, Charles Samuel. *Life and letters of Samuel Holden Parsons: Major General in the Continental Army and Chief Judge of the Northwestern territory, 1737–1789.* New York: From the archives of James Pugliese, 1968. pp.134–137. Webb, Samuel Blachley. *Correspondence and Journals of Samuel Blachley Webb.* Ford, Worthington C. comp. & ed. New York: Wickersham Press, 1893 (Eyewitness accounts of the American Revolution). [New York]: New York Times; Arno Press, c1969. I:395-96. Colonel John Ely to Thomas Mumford and Nathaniel Shaw, Jr. *Jonathan Trumbull Papers.* VII:237. NDAR. 10:688, 699, 734, 739, 745, 756, 761–62, 823–24.

304a. *Royal Gazette.* 227 (December 2, 1778) p.3.

305. Onderdonk, Henry. *Revolutionary Incidents of Suffolk and Kings Counties, with an account of the Battle of Long Island and the British Prisons and Prison Ships at New York.* New York: Leavitt & Co., 1849. p.102.

306. *The New-York Gazette; and the Weekly Mercury* (July 2, 1781).

307. *The New-York Gazette; and the Weekly Mercury.* 1304 (October12, 1776) p.3. *Connecticut Gazette.* October 4, 1776. NDAR 6:1127.

308. Journal of HM Sloop *Senegal.* British National Archives, Admiralty 51/885. NDAR 7:127–128.

309. HMS *Halifax* Captain's log. British National Archives, Admiralty 51/771 part 10 p.373. Peckham, Howard Henry. *The Toll of Independence: Engagements & Battle Casualties of the American Revolution.* Chicago: University of Chicago Press, 1974. p.50.

310. Roberts, Robert B. *New York's Forts in the Revolution.* Rutherford: Fairleigh Dickinson University Press, 1980. p.255. *Long Island in the American Revolution.* Myron H. Luke and Robert W. Venables. Albany: New York State American Revolution Bicentennial Commission, 1976. p.44. Meyer, Lois J. *The Irony of Submission: The British Occupation of Huntington and Long Island 1776–1783.* [Huntington]: L. J. Meyer, 1992. pp.33–35.

311. *Royal Gazette.* 200 (August 29, 1778) p.3. *The Massachusetts Spy: or, American Oracle of Liberty.* IX:447 (November 25, 1779) p.2. *The Independent Chronicle and the Universal Advertiser.* XII:588 (December 2, 1779) p.2. *The New Jersey Gazette.* II:103 (December 15, 1779) p.3.

312. *Maryland Journal.* V:259 (October 13, 1778) p.4.

313. *The New-York Gazette; and the Weekly Mercury* (June 28, 1779). Platt, Henry C. *«Old times in Huntington»* An *Historical Address.* Huntington [N.Y.] Long Islander Print, 1876. pp.65–66.

314. Journal of HMS *Niger*. British National Archives Admiralty 51/637. NDAR 7:386.

315. Master's Log of HM Brig *Halifax*. British National Archives, Admiralty 52/1775. NDAR 8:997.

316. Master's Journal of HM Galley *Dependence*, Lt. James Clark. British National Archives, Admiralty 52/1964, fol. 86. NDAR 11:774.

317. Extract of another letter from Newport (RI) dated May 31, 1778. *Royal Gazette*. 177 (June 10, 1778) p.3.

318. *The New-York Gazette; and the Weekly Mercury* (June 28, 1779). Onderdonk, Henry. *Documents and Letters Intended to Illustrate the Revolutionary Incidents of Queens County: with Connecting Narratives, Explanatory Notes, and Additions*. New York: Leavitt, Trow, 1846. p.216.

319. *Rivington's New-York Gazetteer*. (July 31, 1779). Onderdonk, Henry. *Documents and Letters Intended to Illustrate the Revolutionary Incidents of Queens County: with Connecting Narratives, Explanatory Notes, and Additions*. New York: Leavitt, Trow, 1846. p.217.

320. Onderdonk, Henry. *Documents and Letters Intended to Illustrate the Revolutionary Incidents of Queens County: with Connecting Narratives, Explanatory Notes, and Additions*. New York: Leavitt, Trow, 1846. p.219. The New Jersey Gazette. II:103 (December 15, 1779) p.3. *The Independent Chronicle and the Universal Advertiser*. 12:588 (December 2, 1779) p.2.

321. Onderdonk, Henry. *Documents and Letters Intended to Illustrate the Revolutionary Incidents of Queens County: with Connecting Narratives, Explanatory Notes, and Additions*. New York: Leavitt, Trow, 1846. p219.

322. Peckham, Howard Henry. *The Toll of Independence: Engagements & Battle Casualties of the American Revolution*. Chicago: University of Chicago Press, 1974. p.66.

323. Ward, Christopher. *The War of the Revolution*. New York: Macmillan, 1952. 323–324. *Journals of the Continental Congress 1774–1789*. Washington, 1904–1937. 8:579–580. *Long Island in the American Revolution*. Myron H. Luke and Robert W. Venables. Albany: New York State American Revolution Bicentennial Commission, 1976. pp.45–47. Jones, Thomas. *History of New York During the Revolutionary War*. New York, 1879. I:180–181. Roberts, Robert B. *New York's Forts in the Revolution*. Rutherford: Fairleigh Dickinson University Press, 1980. pp.244–46.

324. Stuart, Isaac William. *Life of Jonathan Trumbull, sen., Governor of Connecticut*. Boston: Crocker and Brewster, 1859. pp.329–330.

325. *Long Island in the American Revolution*. Myron H. Luke and Robert W. Venables. Albany: New York State American Revolution Bicentennial Commission, 1976. p.49.

326. Jones, Thomas. *History of New York During The Revolutionary War*. Edited by Edward Floyd De Lancey. New York: New York Historical Society, 1879. pp.182–183.

327. *Journals of the Continental Congress 1774–1789*. Washington, 1904–1937. VI (December 4th and 6th, 1780).

328. *Rivington's Gazette*. (December 2, 1780). Moore, Frank. *Diary of the American Revolution: from Newspapers and Original Documents*. New York: Charles Scribner; London: Sampson Low, Son & Co., 1890. 2:347–348. *The Pennsylvania Packet*. (December 12, 1780). www.longwood.k12.ny.us/history/. Tallmadge, Benjamin. *Memoir Of Col. Benjamin Tallmadge*. New York: Thomas Holman, 1858. pp.40–42.

329. *The New-York Gazette; and the Weekly Mercury*. 1356 (October 20, 1777) p.2.

330. Peckham, Howard Henry. *The Toll of Independence: Engagements & Battle Casualties of the American Revolution*. Chicago: University of Chicago Press, 1974. p.43.

331. Master's Journal of HM Sloop *Haerlem*. British National Archives, Admiralty 52/1789. NDAR10:712. Journal of HM Sloop *Swan* British National Archives, Admiralty 51/960. NDAR10:713.

332. *Continental Journal*. LXXXIII (December 25, 1777) p 3.

333. *The New-York Packet, and the American Advertiser*. (Thursday, March 5, 1778). NDAR 11:496–497.

334. *The Royal American Gazette*. CCCXII (October 10, 1780) p.3.

335. *Rivington's Gazette*. (April 27, 1778). Onderdonk, Henry. *Documents and Letters Intended to Illustrate the Revolutionary Incidents of Queens County, N.Y. with Connecting Narratives, Explanatory Notes, and Additions*. Hempstead, L.I., L. Van de Water, 1884. p.206.

336. *The New-York Gazette; and the Weekly Mercury* (June 29, 1778). Onderdonk, Henry. *Documents and Letters Intended to Illustrate the Revolutionary Incidents of Queens County, N.Y. with Connecting Narratives, Explanatory Notes, and Additions*. Hempstead, L.I., L. Van de Water, 1884. p.208.

337. *Rivington's New-York Loyal Gazette*. (June 27, 1778). Onderdonk, Henry. *Documents and Letters Intended to Illustrate the Revolutionary Incidents of Queens County, N.Y. with Connecting Narratives, Explanatory Notes, and Additions*. New York: Leavitt, Trow, 1846. p.208. Barck, Oscar Theodore. *New York City During the War for Independence: with Special Reference to the Period of British Occupation*. New York: Columbia University Press, 1931. p.202.

338. *The New-York Gazette; and the Weekly Mercury* (Sept. 7, 1778). Onderdonk, Henry. *Documents and Letters Intended to Illustrate the Revolutionary Incidents of Queens County, N.Y. with Connecting Narratives, Explanatory Notes, and Additions*. Hempstead, L.I., L. Van de Water, 1884. p.208.

339. *Hartford Courant*. (Sept. 3. 1778). Onderdonk, Henry. *Documents and Letters Intended to Illustrate the Revolutionary Incidents of Queens County, N.Y. with Connecting Narratives, Explanatory Notes, and Additions*. Hempstead, L.I., L. Van de Water, 1884. p.208. Jones, Thomas. *History of New York During The Revolutionary War*. Edited by Edward Floyd De Lancey. New York: New York Historical Society, 1879. 1:267.

340. Tallmadge, Benjamin. *Memoir Of Col. Benjamin Tallmadge*. New York: Thomas Holman, 1858. pp.32–33. *Long Island in the American Revolution*. Myron H. Luke and Robert W. Venables. Albany: New York State American Revolution Bicentennial Commission, 1976. pp.48–49.

341. *The Pennsylvania Evening Post.* V:630 (September 29, 1779) p.233.

342. *Royal Gazette.* 470 (March 31, 1781) p.2. *The New-York Gazette; and the Weekly Mercury* (March 31, 1781). *The New-York Gazette; and the Weekly Mercury.* 1537 (April 2, 1781) p.2.

343. Tallmadge, Benjamin. *Memoir Of Col. Benjamin Tallmadge.* New York: Thomas Holman, 1858. pp.32–34.

344. Letter to Gov. Franklin, from Lt. Col. Upham of the Associated Loyalists, and commandant at Lloyd's Neck, dated Fort Franklin, July 13. *The Scots Magazine.* Vol. 43 MDCCLXXXI. p.469.

345. Metcalf, Reginald H. *The Order of the Ancient and Honorable Huntington Militia Presents the 200th Anniversary Reenactment of the Battle of Fort Franklin: July 12, 1781–July 12, 1981, Lloyd Neck, Huntington, N.Y.* [Huntington, N.Y.: The Order], 1981.

346. Extract of another letter from Newport (RI) dated May 31, 1778. *Royal Gazette.* 177 (June 10, 1778) p.3.

347. Journal of HMS *Niger*. British National Archives, Admiralty 51/637. NDAR 6:307.

348. Master's Log of HM Brig *Halifax*. British National Archives, Admiralty 52/1775. NDAR 7:324.

349. Master's Log of HM Brig *Halifax*. British National Archives, Admiralty 52/1775. NDAR 7:386.

350. Master's Log of HM Brig *Halifax*. British National Archives, Admiralty 52/1775. NDAR 7:528.

351. *The Pennsylvania Evening Post.* V:625 (August 30, 1779) p.216.

352. *Royal Gazette.* 483 (May 16, 1781) p.3.

353. *Royal Gazette.* 206 (September 19, 1778) p.3.

354. *The New-York Gazette; and the Weekly Mercury.* 1411 (November 2, 1778) p.3.

355. Mackenzie, Frederick. *The Diary of Frederick Mackenzie.* Cambridge, MA: Harvard University Press, 1930. 2:595–596.

356. Onderdonk, Henry. *Documents and Letters Intended to Illustrate the Revolutionary Incidents of Queens County: with Connecting Narratives, Explanatory Notes, and Additions.* New York: Leavitt, Trow, 1846. pp.216. *Royal Gazette.* 285 (June 23, 1779) p.3.

357. *The Freeman's Journal: or, the North-American Intelligencer.* Issue XXVI (October 17, 1781) p.3. Marhoefer, Barbara.; Guardineer, Fred. *Witches, Whales, Petticoats & Sails: Adventures and Misadventures from Three Centuries of Long Island History.* Port Washington, N.Y., I. J. Friedman Division of Kennikat Press, 1971, 1966. pp.37–39. Tallmadge, Benjamin. *Memoir Of Col. Benjamin Tallmadge.* New York: Thomas Holman, 1858. p.46. Onderdonk, Henry. *Documents and Letters Intended to Illustrate the Revolutionary Incidents of Queens County, N.Y. with Connecting Narratives, Explanatory Notes, and Additions.* New-York: Leavitt & Co., 1849. p.105. Leggett, Abraham. *The Narrative Of Major Abraham Leggett, Of the Army Of the Revolution With An Introduction And Notes By Charles I. Bushnell.* New York: Privately Printed, 1865. pp.70–71. *Long Island in the American Revolution.* Myron H. Luke and Robert W. Venables. Albany: New York State American Revolution Bicentennial Commission, 1976. pp.50–51.

358. *The George Washington Papers at the Library of Congress, 1741–1799. George Washington, April 27, 1783, General Orders (April 27, 1783).* (memory.loc.gov/cgi-bin/query/r?ammem/mgw:@field(DOCID+@lit(gw260410)).

359. *The George Washington Papers at the Library of Congress, 1741–1799. George Washington, June 8, 1783, General Orders (June 8, 1783).* (memory.loc.gov/cgi-bin/query/r?ammem/mgw: @field(DOCID+@lit(gw260530)).

360. *The New-York Gazette; and the Weekly Mercury.* 1446 (July 5, 1779) p.1.

361. *The Pennsylvania Packet or the General Advertiser.* (August 26, 1779) p.2.

362. *Rivington's New-York Gazetteer.* August 25, 1779. Onderdonk, Henry. *Documents and letters intended to illustrate the revolutionary incidents of Queens County; with connecting narratives, explanatory notes, and additions.* New York: Leavitt, Trow, 1846. p.171.

363. Flint, Martha Bockée. *Early Long Island, a Colonial Study.* New York: G. P. Putnam's sons, 1896. p.440. Onderdonk, Henry. *Documents and Letters Intended to Illustrate the Revolutionary Incidents of Queens County: with Connecting Narratives, Explantory Notes, and Additions.* New York: Leavitt, Trow, 1846. p.173.

364. *The New-York Gazette; and the Weekly Mercury.* 1616. (October 7, 1782) p.3. Onderdonk, Henry. *Documents and Letters Intended to Illustrate the Revolutionary Incidents of Queens County: with Connecting Narratives, Explanatory Notes, and Additions.* New York: Leavitt, Trow, 1846. pp.176–177.

365. Onderdonk, Henry. *Documents and Letters Intended to Illustrate the Revolutionary Incidents of Queens County: with Connecting Narratives, Explanatory Notes, and Additions.* New York: Leavitt, Trow, 1846. pp.177–178.

366. *New York Gazetteer.* I:30 (December 23, 1782) p.2.

367. Middlebrook, Louis F. (Louis Frank). *History of Maritime Connecticut during the American Revolution, 1775–1783.* Salem, Mass.: The Essex institute, 1925. II:233.

368. Some accounts list this event as happening on November 30. Captain Johann von Ewald's diary lists it as happening on November 15. Ewald, Johann von. *Diary of the American War: a Hessian Journal.* translated and edited by Joseph P. Tustin New Haven: Yale University Press, 1979. pp.251–252.

369. Letter of Major Charles Cochrane to Major-General Sir William Erskine dated 1st Feb. 1779. *Royal Gazette.* 246 (February 6, 1779) p.3. *The New-York Gazette; and the Weekly Mercury.* 1425 (February 8, 1779) p.3. *The Pennsylvania Evening Post.* V:576 (February 26,1779) p.48.

370. *The Norwich Packet and the Weekly Advertiser.* 398 (May 17, 1781) p.3.

371. *Connecticut Courant.* 774 (November 23, 1779) p.3.

372. *The New-York Gazette; and The Weekly Mercury.* 1446 (July 5, 1779) p.1.

373. Ibid.

374. Ibid.

375. *Annals of Staten Island, From Its Discovery to the Present Time.* J. J. Clute. New York: Press of C. Vogt, 1877. p.112.

376. *Documents Relating to the Revolutionary History, State Of New Jersey.* Edited by William S. Stryker. Trenton: The John L. Murphy Publishing Co., 1901. Series 2. 5:285. New York Historical Society.

377. *The New Jersey Gazette.* IV:177 (May 16, 178) p.2.

378. *The New-York Gazette; and the Weekly Mercury.* 1592 (April 22, 1782) p.3.

379. longislandgenealogy.com/bluepoint/1.htm.

380. *The Pennsylvania Packet or the General Advertiser.* X:789 (October 2, 1781) p.3.

381. Ibid.

382. Tallmadge to Heath, Nov. 12, 1781, Heath, "Letters and Papers," *Mass. Hist. Soc. Collections,* Seventh Series, Vol. V part III pp.309–313. Hall, Charles Swain. *Benjamin Tallmadge, Revolutionary Soldier and American Businessman.* New York: Columbia University Press, 1943. p.72.

383. Peckham, Howard Henry. *The Toll of Independence: Engagements & Battle Casualties of the American Revolution.* Chicago: University of Chicago Press, 1974. p.95. *The Boston Evening-Post and the General Advertiser.* 1:34 (June 8, 1782) p.2.

384. Journal of HMS *Phoenix* British National Archives, Admiralty 51/693. NDAR 4:739.

385. Bangs, Isaac. *Journal Of Lieutenant Isaac Bangs, April 1 To July 29, 1776.* Edited by Edward Bangs. Cambridge: John Wilson And Son. University Press, 1890. p.55. Journal of HM Sloop *Senegal,* Captain Roger Curtis, British National Archives, Admiralty 51/885. NDAR 5:896–897.

386. *New York Gazette.* (Monday, June 10, 1776). NDAR 5:452.

387. *Annals of Staten Island, from its Discovery to the Present Time.* J. J. Clute. New York: Press of C. Vogt, 1877. p.111.

388. Washington, George. *The Writings of George Washington,* ed. John C. Fitzpatrick. Washington, D.C., 1963 V:476–477. NDAR 6:284. *Continental Journal.* XV (September 5, 1776) p 3. Heath, William. *Memoirs of Major General William Heath.* [New York]: New York Times [1968, c1901] pp.47–49. *Diary of Captain William Yarrington (1738–1811).* Transcribed by Elizabeth Yarrington Russell and Clara Hoyt Russell (new transcript by Carol Russell Law, 1976). *Freeman's Journal.* (September 7, 1776). Moore, Frank. *Diary of the American Revolution: from Newspapers and Original Documents.* New York: Charles Scribner; London: Sampson Low, Son & Co., 1890. 1:295. *Essex Journal.* III:142 (September 20, 1776) p 4.

389. *The New-York Gazette; and the Weekly Mercury* (June 15, 1778). *Documents Relating to the Revolutionary History, State Of New Jersey.* Edited by William S. Stryker. Trenton: The John L. Murphy Publishing Co., 1901. Series 2. 2:253–255. *The New Jersey Gazette.* I:29 (1778–06–17) p 3. Kemble, Stephen. *Journals of Lieut.-Col. Stephen Kemble, 1773–1789; and British Army Orders: Gen. Sir William Howe, 1775–1778; Gen. Sir Henry Clinton, 1778; and Gen. Daniel Jones, 1778.* Prepared by new York Historical Society; Boston: Gregg Press, 1972. p.151.

390. *Annals of Staten Island, from its Discovery to the Present Time.* J. J. Clute. New York: Press of C. Vogt, 1877. p.112.

391. Gallagher, John. *The Battle of Brooklyn, 1776.* Edison, NJ: Castle Books, 2002 (c1995). pp.117–118.

392. Stiles, Henry Reed. *A History of the City of Brooklyn Including the Old Town and Village of Brooklyn, the Town of Bushwick, and the Village and City of Williamsburgh.* Brooklyn: Pub. by subscription, 1867–1870. 1:254–255. Gallagher, John. *The Battle of Brooklyn, 1776.* Edison, NJ: Castle Books, 2002 (c1995). p.101.

393. Gallagher, John. *The Battle of Brooklyn, 1776.* Edison, NJ: Castle Books, 2002 (c1995). pp.473–476.

394. Kemble, Stephen. *Journals of Lieut.-Col. Stephen Kemble, 1773–1789; and British Army Orders: Gen. Sir William Howe, 1775–1778; Gen. Sir Henry Clinton, 1778; and Gen. Daniel Jones, 1778.* Prepared by New York Historical Society; Boston: Gregg Press, 1972. Gallagher, John. *The Battle of Brooklyn, 1776.* Edison, NJ: Castle Books, 2002 (c1995). pp.101–107; 117–118. Stiles, Henry Reed. *A History of the City of Brooklyn Including the Old Town and Village of Brooklyn, the Town of Bushwick, and the Village and City of Williamsburgh.* Brooklyn: Pub. by subscription, 1867–1870. 1:74–275.

395. *Encyclopedia of the American Revolution.* Harold E. Selesky, editor in chief.—2nd Ed. Detroit: Charles Scribner's Sons, 2007. 1:646–655. *The Encyclopedia of the American Revolutionary War: a political, social, and military history.* Gregory Fremont-Barnes, Richard Alan Ryerson, editors. Santa Barbara, CA: ABC-CLIO, 2006. II:728–731. Billias, George A. ed. *George Washington's Generals and Opponents: Their Exploits and Leadership,* 1964. reprint, New York: Da Capo, 1994. Black, Jeremy. *War for America: the Fight for Independence.* Stroud, UK: Alan Sutton, 1991. Clinton, Henry. *The American Rebellion: Sir Henry Clinton's Narrative of His Campaigns, 1775–1782, with an appendix of original documents.* Edited by William B. Willcox. New Haven: Yale University Press, 1954. Conway, Stephen. *The War of American Independence, 1775–1783.* London: Arnold, 1995. Fleming, Thomas J. *1776: Year of Illusions.* New York: Norton, 1975. Gallagher, John. *The Battle of Brooklyn, 1776.* Edison, NJ: Castle Books, 2002 (c1995). Gruber, Ira D. *The Howe Brothers and the American Revolution.* New York: Norton, 1972. Higginbotham, Don. *The War of American Independence: Military Attitudes, Policies, and Practice, 1763–1789.* New York: Macmillan, 1971. Johnson, Henry P. *The Campaign of 1776 Around New York and Brooklyn.* 1878; Cranbury, NJ: Scholar's Bookshelf, 2005. Keegan, John. *Fields of Battle: The Wars for North America.* New York: Vintage, 1997. Makesy, Piers. *The War for America, 1775–1783.* Lincoln: University of Nebraska Press, 1993. Manders, Eric. *The Battle of Long Island.* Monmouth, NJ: Philip Freneau Press, 1978. McCullough, David. *1776: The Illustrated Edition,* excerpts from the acclaimed history, with letters, maps, and seminal artwork. New York: Simon & Schuster, 2007. pp.141–181. Onderdonk, Henry. *Revolutionary Incidents of Suffolk and Kings Counties: with an Account of the Battle of Long Island and the British Prisons and Prison-ships at New York.* New-York: Leavitt & Co., 1849. Schecter,

Barnet. *The Battle for New York: The City at the Heart of the American Revolution.* New York: Penguin, 2003. Scheer, George F. and Hugh F. Rankin. *Rebels and Redcoats.* Cleveland and New York: World Publishing Co., 1957. Serle, Ambrose. *The American Journal of Ambrose Serle.* [New York]: New York Times; Arno Press, c1969. Stevenson, Charles G. and Irene Wilson. *The Battle of Long Island ("the Battle of Brooklyn").* Brooklyn, NY: Brooklyn Bicentennial Commission, 1975. Ward, Christopher. *The War of the Revolution.* New York: Macmillan, 1952. 211–237. Wright, Esmond, ed. *The Fire of Liberty.* London: Hamish Hamilton, 1979.

396. *Encyclopedia of the American Revolution.* Harold E. Selesky, editor in chief.–2nd Ed. Detroit: Charles Scribner's Sons, 2007.I:655–656. Freeman, Douglas Southall. *George Washington, a Biography.* New York: Scribner, 1948–1957. McCullough, David. *1776: The Illustrated Edition,* excerpts from the acclaimed history, with letters, maps, and seminal artwork. New York: Simon & Schuster, 2007. Ward, Christopher. *The War of the Revolution.* New York: Macmillan, 1952. pp.231–237.

397. Heath, William. *Memoirs of Major-General Heath, Containing Anecdotes, Details of Skirmishes, Battles, and other Military Events, during the American War.* Written by Himself. Boston, 1898. (Edition edited by William Abbott, New York, 1901.) 47–49. NDAR 6:323. Bolton, Robert. *The History of the Several Towns, Manors, and Patents of the County of Westchester from its First Settlement to the Present Time.* New York: Chas. F. Roper, 1881 II:83–84.

398. Master's Log Of HMS Brig *Halifax,* British National Archives, Admiralty 52/1775. NDAR 6:355.

399. William Dansey to Mrs. Dansey Dansey Newport, Rhode Island January 10, 1777. Delaware Historical Society. Robertson, Archibald. *Archibald Robertson, Lieutenant-General Royal Engineers: his Diaries and Sketches in America, 1762–1780.* edited with and introduction by Harry Miller Lydenberg. New York: The New York Public Library, 1930; The New York Public Library and The New York Times & Arno Press, 1971. p.103.

400. Mackenzie, Frederick. *The Diary of Frederick Mackenzie.* Cambridge, MA: Harvard University Press, 1930. 1:77.

401. Jones, Thomas. *History of New York During The Revolutionary War.* Edited by Edward Floyd De Lancey. New York: New York Historical Society, 1879. pp.620–621. See also **Rhode Island: Fogland Ferry** in the volume on Canada and New England.

402. Peckham, Howard Henry. *The Toll of Independence: Engagements & Battle Casualties of the American Revolution.* Chicago: University of Chicago Press, 1974. p.84.

403. Mackenzie, Frederick. *The Diary of Frederick Mackenzie.* Cambridge, MA: Harvard University Press, 1930. 2:570–571.

404. *The Massachusetts Spy: or, American Oracle of Liberty.* XI:532 (July 19, 1781) p.3.

405. *Connecticut Journal.* Issue 718 (August 2, 1781) p.2.

406. *The Providence Gazette; and Country Journal.* 8:642 (April 20, 1776) p.2..

407. Jones, Thomas. *History of New York During The Revolutionary War.* Edited by Edward Floyd De Lancey. New York: New York Historical Society, 1879. pp.112–114.

408. Master's log of the HMS *Roebuck.* British National Archives Admiralty 52/1965. NDAR 6:377.

409. Master's log of the HMS *Roebuck.* British National Archives Admiralty 52/1965. NDAR 6:640. Narrative of Captain Andrew Snape Hamond. Hamond, No. 5. Charlottesville, VA. University of Virginia Library. NDAR 6:1063.

410. *Memoirs of Gen. William Heath.* Abbatt, ed. p.50. Journal of HMS *Rose* British National Archives Admiralty 51/805. NDAR, 6:655, 666.

411. Journal of HM fireship *Strombolo.* British National Archives, Admiralty 51/931. NDAR, 6:724–725.

412. Journal of HM Fireship *Strombolo,* Captain Charles Phipps. British National Archives, Admiralty 51/931. NDAR 6:724–725. Journal Of HMS *Carysfort,* Captain Robert Fanshaw, British National Archives, Admiralty 51/168. NDAR 6:805. Major General Joshua Babcock to Governor Nicholas Cooke. Westerly 21st Sept. 1776. Letters to the Governor, vol. 8. RI Arch. NDAR 6:924. Mackenzie, Frederick. *The Diary of Frederick Mackenzie.* Cambridge, MA: Harvard University Press, 1930 1:45. Serle, Ambrose. *The American Journal Of Ambrose Serle Secretary To Lord Howe 1776–1778.* Edited with an introduction by Edward H. Tatum, Jr. San Marino, CA: The Huntington Library, 1940. pp.99–103; NDAR 6:823. Heath, William. *Memoirs of Major-General William Heath.* Ed. by William Abbatt. New York: William Abbatt, 1901. p.51. NDAR 6:804. Journal Of HMS *Eagle,* Captain Henry Duncan, National Maritime Museum, London, Admiralty L/E/11. NDAR 6:805. *The Massachusetts Spy: or, American Oracle of Liberty.* VI:283 (October 2, 1776) p.3. *The Pennsylvania Evening Post.* 2:265 (October 1, 1776) p.488.

413. Serle, Ambrose. *The American Journal of Ambrose Serle, Secretary to Lord Howe, 1776–1778.* Edited by Edward H. Tatum, Jr., San Marino, California, 1940; Eyewitness accounts of the American Revolution). [New York]: New York Times; Arno Press, c1969. pp.101–103. NDAR, v6, p.823.

414. Major General Joshua Babcock to Governor Nicholas Cooke. Westerly 21st Sept. 1776. Letters to the Governor, vol. 8. RI Arch. NDAR 6:924.

415. Journal of HMS *Niger.* British National Archives Admiralty 51/637. NDAR 6:662.

416. Journal of HMS *Niger.* British National Archives Admiralty 51/637. NDAR 6:723.

417. *Annals of Staten Island, from its Discovery to the Present Time.* J. J. Clute. New York: Press of C. Vogt, 1877. 111–12.

418. Ibid.

419. Roberts, Robert B. *New York's Forts in the Revolution.* Rutherford: Fairleigh Dickinson University Press, 1980. pp.261–308. Besides describing the forts and their locations, Roberts briefly covers their history.

420. *New York Journal.* (Thursday, June 15, 1775). NDAR 1:688.

421. Joshua T. De St. Croix to Christopher Champlin. New York, Aug. 26, 1775. Ship Papers, Ship *Peggy*, NHS; NDAR 1:1240.

422. Nash, Solomon. *Journal of Solomon Nash, a Soldier of the Revolution, 1775–1777.* with an introduction and notes, by Charles I. Bushnell. New York: Privately printed, 1861. p.23. Peckham, Howard Henry. *The Toll of Independence: Engagements & Battle Casualties of the American Revolution.* Chicago: University of Chicago Press, 1974. p.19.

423. Mackenzie, Frederick. *The Diary of Frederick Mackenzie.* Cambridge, MA: Harvard University Press, 1930 1:p.38.

424. Journal of HMS *Rose*, Captain James Wallace. British National Archives, Admiralty 51/805. NDAR 6:709.

425. Peckham, Howard Henry. *The Toll of Independence: Engagements & Battle Casualties of the American Revolution.* Chicago: University of Chicago Press, 1974. p.43.

426. Serle, Ambrose. *The American Journal of Ambrose Serle, Secretary to Lord Howe, 1776–1778.* edited by Edward H. Tatum, Jr., San Marino, California, 1940; Eyewitness accounts of the American Revolution). [New York]: New York Times; Arno Press, c1969. p.133. NDAR 6:1445.

427. Brigadier General William Heath to John Hancock April 3, 1776. Papers CC (Letters from General Officers), 157, 5, NA; NDAR 4:646. *Constitutional Gazette.* (Wednesday, April 3, 1776). Journal of HMS *Asia*, Capt. George Vandeput. British National Archives, Admiralty 51/67; NDAR 4:647. Heath, William, *Memoirs of Major-General Heath, Containing Anecdotes, Details of Skirmishes, Battles, and other Military Events, during the American War.* Written by Himself. Boston, 1898. (Edition edited by William Abbott, New York, 1901.) p.37; NDAR 4:647.

428. Journal of HMS *Asia*. British National Archives Admiralty 51/67 NDAR 4:547.

429. *The American Gazette or the Constitutional Journal.* 1:6 (July 23, 1776) p.23.

430. Journal of the HMS *Eagle* National Maritime Museum (London), Admiralty L/E/11; NDAR, v6, p.724.

431. Mackenzie, Frederick. *The Diary of Frederick Mackenzie.* Cambridge, MA: Harvard University Press, 1930 1:37–38. Serle, Ambrose. *The American Journal of Ambrose Serle, Secretary to Lord Howe, 1776–1778.* edited by Edward H. Tatum, Jr., San Marino, California, 1940; Eyewitness accounts of the American Revolution). [New York]: New York Times; Arno Press, c1969, 89, 90–91. NDAR 6:666. Journal of HMS *Rose*. British National Archives, Admiralty 51/805. NDAR 6:666.

432. Master's log HM Brig *Halifax*. British National Archives, Admiralty 52/1775. NDAR 6:709.

433. Mackenzie, Frederick. *The Diary of Frederick Mackenzie.* Cambridge, MA: Harvard University Press, 1930. 1:82.

434. Journal of HMS *Niger*. British National Archives, Admiralty 51/637. NDAR 6:1337.

435. Mackenzie, Frederick. *The Diary of Frederick Mackenzie.* Cambridge, MA: Harvard University Press, 1930 1:p.43. "The Kemble Papers." *Collections of the New York Historical Society for the Year 1883.* New York, 1884. I, 87. NDAR 6:782. *The Massachusetts Spy: or, American Oracle of Liberty.* VI:283 (October 2, 1776) p 3. *The Pennsylvania Evening Post.* 2:265 (October 1, 1776) p.488. *Documents Relating to the Revolutionary History, State Of New Jersey.* Edited by William S. Stryker. Trenton: The John L. Murphy Publishing Co., 1901. Series 2. vol. I, 227. *Revolution in America: Confidential Letters and Journals 1776–1784 of Adjutant General Major Baurmeister of the Hessian Forces.* Translated and annotated by Berhard A. Uhlendorf. New Brunswick, NJ: Rutgers University Press, 1957. p.47.

436. Heath, William. *Memoirs of Major-General William Heath.* Ed. by William Abbatt. New York: William Abbatt, 1901. pp.56–57. NDAR 6:962–964. Mackenzie, Frederick. *The Diary of Frederick Mackenzie.* Cambridge, MA: Harvard University Press, 1930 1:62–63. *The Norwich Packet and the Connecticut, Massachusetts, New Hampshire and Rhode Island Weekly Advertiser.* IV:158 (Monday, September 30 to Monday October 7, 1776) p.3.

437. Extract of a Letter from New York, Oct. 10. *Whitehall Evening Post.* (November 16 to November 19, 1776). NDAR 6:1200.

438. Mackenzie, Frederick. *The Diary of Frederick Mackenzie.* Cambridge, MA: Harvard University Press, 1930 1:p.44. Serle, Ambrose. *The American Journal of Ambrose Serle, Secretary to Lord Howe, 1776–1778.* edited by Edward H. Tatum, Jr., San Marino, California, 1940; Eyewitness accounts of the American Revolution). [New York]: New York Times; Arno Press, c1969. p.98. NDAR 6:792. *The Massachusetts Spy: or, American Oracle of Liberty.* VI:283 (October 2, 1776) p 3. *The Pennsylvania Evening Post.* 2:265 (October 1, 1776) p.488. *Documents Relating to the Revolutionary History, State Of New Jersey.* Edited by William S. Stryker. Trenton: The John L. Murphy Publishing Co., 1901. Series 2. I: 227. Heath, William. *Memoirs of Major-General William Heath.* Ed. by William Abbatt. New York: William Abbatt, 1901 51. NDAR 6:804. Roberts, Robert B. *New York's Forts in the Revolution.* Rutherford: Fairleigh Dickinson University Press, 1980. pp.285–286.

438. Hibbert, Christopher. *Redcoats and Rebels: the American Revolution Through British Eyes.* New York: Norton, 1990. p.126.

439. McCullough, David G. *1776.* New York: Simon & Schuster, c2005. p.211.

440. *Encyclopedia of the American Revolution.* Harold E. Selesky, editor in chief.–2nd Ed. Detroit: Charles Scribner's Sons, 2007.I:589–590. *The Encyclopedia of the American Revolutionary War: a political, social, and military history.* Gregory Fremont-Barnes, Richard Alan Ryerson, editors. Santa Barbara, CA: ABC-CLIO, 2006. II:672–673. Bliven, Bruce, Jr. *Battle for Manhattan.* New York: Henry Holt, 1955. Fleming, Thomas J. *1776: Year of Illusions.* New York: Norton, 1975. Johnston, Henry P. *The Campaign of 1776 Around New York and Brooklyn.* [n.d.]; reprint, New York: Da Capo, 1971. Martin, Joseph Plumb. *Private Yankee Doodle; being a narrative of some of the adventures, dangers, and sufferings of a Revolutionary Soldier,* edited by George F. Scheer, originally published in Hallowell, Me., 1830, anonymously. (Republished, Boston, 1962.). *A Narrative of Some of the Adventures, Dangers and Sufferings of a Revolutionary Soldier.* (Eyewitness accounts of the American Revolution). [New York] New York Times [1968] pp.33–40. Stokes, I.N. Phelps, comp. *The Iconography of Manhattan Island, 1498–1909.* New York: R.H. Dodd, 1915–1928. Ward, Christopher. *The War of the Revolution.* New York: Macmillan, 1952.

441. *Encyclopedia of the American Revolution.* Harold E. Selesky, editor in chief.–2nd Ed. Detroit: Charles Scribner's Sons, 2007. I:490–492. *The Encyclopedia of the American Revolutionary War: a political, social, and military history.* Gregory Fremont-Barnes, Richard Alan Ryerson, editors. Santa Barbara, CA: ABC-CLIO, 2006. II:577–579. André, John. *Major André's Journal: Operations of the British Army under Lieutenant Generals Sir William Howe and Sir Henry Clinton June 1777 to November 1778.* Tarrytown, NY: William Abbatt, 1930; New York Times & Arno Press, 1968. Black, Jeremy. *War for America: the Fight for Independence.* Stroud, UK: Alan Sutton, 1991. Carrington, Henry B. *Battles of the American Revolution 1775–1781, including Battle Maps and Charts of the American Revolution.* New York: Promontory Press, (1974), originally published in 1877 and 1881. Conway, Stephen. *The War of American Independence, 1775–1783.* London: Arnold, 1995. Higginbotham, Don. *The War of American Independence: Military Attitudes, Policies, and Practice, 1763–1789.* New York: Macmillan, 1971. Johnston, Henry Phelps. *The Battle of Harlem Heights, September 16, 1776.* New York: AMS Press, (1880) 1970. Mackenzie, Frederick. *The Diary of Frederick Mackenzie.* Cambridge, MA: Harvard University Press, 1930. Mackesy, Piers. *The War for America, 1775–1783.* Lincoln: University of Nebraska Press, 1993. Ward, Christopher. *The War of the Revolution.* New York: Macmillan, 1952. 246–252.

442. Heath, William. *Memoirs of Major-General William Heath.* Ed. by William Abbatt. New York: William Abbatt, 1901. pp.52–53. Graydon, Alexander. *Memoirs of His Own Time with Reminiscences of the Men and Events of the Revolution.* edited by John Stockton Littell. Philadelphia: Lindsay & Blakiston, 1846;—Eyewitness Accounts of the American Revolution.—New York: The New York Times & Arno Press. p.198.

443. Heath, William. *Memoirs of Major-General William Heath.* Ed. by William Abbatt. New York: William Abbatt, 1901. pp.54–55.

444. Richards, Samuel. *Diary of Samuel Richards, Captain of Connecticut Line War of the Revolution, 1775–1781.* Philadelphia: Published by his great grandson, 1909. pp.40–41.

445. Ambrose Serle to Lord Dartmouth New York, 25th Sept. 1776, Stevens, ed., *Facsimiles,* No. 2043. NDAR 6:990.

446. Freeman, Douglas Southall. *George Washington: a Biography.* New York: Charles Scribner's Sons, 1951. 4:384.

447. Heath, William. *Memoirs of Major-General William Heath.* Ed. by William Abbatt. New York: William Abbatt, 1901. pp.99–104. www.ctssar.org/monthly_history/y1777january.htm. Bolton, Robert. *The History of the Several Towns, Manors, and Patents of the County of Westchester from its First Settlement to the Present Time.* New York: Chas. F. Roper, 1881. II:612.

448. *The Independent Chronicle and the Universal Advertiser.* 10:473 (September 11, 1777) p.3.

449. *The New-York Gazette; and the Weekly Mercury.* 1405 (September 21, 1778) p.2.

450. *Pennsylvania Packet* (December 31, 1777) p.3.

451. Major General Israel Putnam to General George Washington dated New Rochal 28th Nov. 1777. Washington, George. *The Papers of George Washington.* Revolutionary War series. Philander D. Chase, editor. Charlottesville: University Press of Virginia, 1985–<2008> 12:440–441. NDAR 10:623. *New-York Loyal Gazette.* 146 (December 6, 1777) p.3.

452. *Pennsylvania Evening Post.* III:437 (December 27,1777) p.601.

453. *The Boston Gazette, and Country Journal.* 1218 (January 5, 1778) p.2.

454. Simcoe, John Graves. *Simcoe's Military Journal. A History of the Operations of a Partisan Corps Called The Queen's Rangers, Commanded by Lieut. Col. J. G. Simcoe, During the War of the American Revolution.* New-York: Bartlett & Welford, 1844; [New York]: New York Times; Arno Press.–Eyewitness Accounts of the American Revolution. [1968]. pp.76–79. Hufeland, Otto. *Westchester County during the American Revolution, 1775–1783.* White Plains: Westchester County Historical Society, 1926; Harrison, New York: Harbor Hill Books, 1974. pp.254–258.

455. Simcoe, John Graves. *Simcoe's Military Journal. A History Of the Operations Of A Partisan Corps, Called The Queen's Rangers, Commanded By Lieut. Col. J. G. Simcoe.* New-York: Bartlett & Welford, 1844. pp.83–88. Ewald, Johann. *Diary of the American War: A Hessian Journal.* Translated and edited by Joseph P. Tustin. New Haven and London: Yale University Press, 1979. pp.144–145. Bolton, Robert. *The History of the Several Towns, Manors, and Patents of the County of Westchester from its First Settlement to the Present Time.* New York: Chas. F. Roper, 1881. II:651–.

456. Simcoe, John Graves. *Simcoe's Military Journal. A History Of the Operations Of A Partisan Corps, Called The Queen's Rangers, Commanded By Lieut. Col. J. G. Simcoe.* New York: Bartlett & Welford, 1844. pp.88–89. *Narratives Of the Revolution In New York: A Collection Of Articles From The New-York Historical Society Quarterly.* New-York: The New-York Historical Society, 1975. p.254. *Maryland Journal.* V:260 (October19,1778) p.1. Hufeland, Otto. *Westchester County during the American Revolution, 1775–1783.* White Plains: Westchester County Historical Society, 1926; Harrison, New York: Harbor Hill Books, 1974. pp.259–261. Bolton, Robert. *The History of the Several Towns, Manors, and Patents of the County of Westchester from its First Settlement to the Present Time.* New York: Chas. F. Roper, 1881. II:622–62.

457. *Maryland Journal.* V:260 (October19,1778) p.1.

458. Peckham, Howard Henry. *The Toll of Independence: Engagements & Battle Casualties of the American Revolution.* Chicago: University of Chicago Press, 1974. p.67.

459. Bolton, Robert. *The History of the Several Towns, Manors, and Patents of the County of Westchester from its First Settlement to the Present Time.* New York: Chas. F. Roper, 1881. II:525–526.

460. Ward, Christopher. *The War of the Revolution.* New York: Macmillan, 1952. *881–882.*

461. *The Independent Chronicle and the Universal Advertiser.* XIII:706 (July 26, 1781) p.2. Bolton, Robert. *The History of the Several Towns, Manors, and Patents of the County of Westchester from its First Settlement to the Present Time.* New York: Chas. F. Roper, 1881. II:621–622.

462. *The Freeman's Journal: or, The North-American Intelligencer.* II:LXIX (August 14, 1782) p.3.

463. Ward, Christopher. *The War of the Revolution.* New York: Macmillan, 1952. pp.258–259.

464. *Maryland Journal.* V:221 January 27, 1778. p.2.

465. Montresor, John. *The Montresor Journals*; ed. and annotated by G.D. (Gideon Delaplaine) Scull. Collections of the New York Historical Society for the year 1881. New York: Printed for the Society, 1882. p.506.

466. Heath, William, *Memoirs of Major-General Heath, Containing Anecdotes, Details of Skirmishes, Battles, and other Military Events, during the American War*. Written by Himself. Boston, 1898. (Edition edited by William Abbott, New York, 1901.) pp.227–228. Bolton, Robert. *A history of the County of Westchester, from its First Settlement to the Present Time*. New York: Printed by Alexander S. Gould, 1848. 2:318.

467. Mackenzie, Frederick. *The Diary of Frederick Mackenzie*. Cambridge, MA: Harvard University Press, 1930 1:101.

468. *Encyclopedia of the American Revolution*. Harold E. Selesky, editor in chief.–2nd Ed. Detroit: Charles Scribner's Sons, 2007.I:378–381. *The Encyclopedia of the American Revolutionary War: a political, social, and military history*. Gregory Fremont-Barnes, Richard Alan Ryerson, editors. Santa Barbara, CA: ABC-CLIO, 2006. II:444–445. McCullough, David. *1776: The Illustrated Edition*, excerpts from the acclaimed history, with letters, maps, and seminal artwork. New York: Simon & Schuster, 2007. pp.191–194. Scheer, George F. and Hugh F. Rankin. *Rebels and Redcoats*. Cleveland and New York: World Publishing Co., 1957. Stember, Sol. *The Bicentennial Guide to the American Revolution*. New York: Saturday Review Press, [distributed by] Dutton, 1974; [s.l.]: New York Times and Arno Press, 1969.II. Ward, Christopher. *The War of the Revolution*. New York: Macmillan, 1952. Washington, George. *Papers of George Washington*. Dorothy Twohig, ed.–Revolutionary War Series.–Charlottesville and London: University Press of Virginia.

469. Journal Of HM Galley *Dependence*, Lieutenant James Clark, British National Archives, Admiralty 51/4159. NDAR 9:744.

470. Peckham, Howard Henry. *The Toll of Independence: Engagements & Battle Casualties of the American Revolution*. Chicago: University of Chicago Press, 1974. p.53.

471. Hall, Charles Samuel. *Life and Letters of Samuel Holden Parsons: Major General in the Continental Army and Chief Judge of the Northwestern Territory, 1737–1789*. New York: From the archives of James Pugliese, 1968. pp.327–329.

472. Roberts, Robert B. *New York's Forts in the Revolution*. Rutherford: Fairleigh Dickinson University Press, 1980. pp.322–23.

473. *New England Chronicle*. 8:384 (November 30, 1775).

474. *Documents Relating to the Revolutionary History, State Of New Jersey*. Edited by William S. Stryker. Trenton: The John L. Murphy Publishing Co., 1901. Series 2. vol. I, 42–43.

475. *The Pennsylvania Evening Post*. 2:192 (April 13, 1776) p.186. Journal of HMS *Phoenix*, Captain Hyde Parker, Jr. British National Archives, Admiralty 51/693; NDAR 4:698–699. Heath, William. *Memoirs of Major-General William Heath*. Ed. by William Abbatt. New York: William Abbatt, 1901. p.37. *The Providence Gazette; and Country Journal*. 8:642 (April 20, 1776) p.2.

476. Journal of HMS *Asia*. British National Archives, Admiralty 51/67; NDAR 4:819.

477. Drake, J. Madison. *Historical Sketches of the Revolutionary and Civil Wars*. New York: Webster Press, 1908. p.10. Kemble, Stephen. *Journals of Lieut.-Col. Stephen Kemble, 1773–1789; and British Army Orders: Gen. Sir William Howe, 1775–1778; Gen. Sir Henry Clinton, 1778; and Gen. Daniel Jones, 1778*. Prepared by New York Historical Society; Boston: Gregg Press, 1972. p.79. Nash, Solomon. *Journal of Solomon Nash, a Soldier of the Revolution, 1775–1777*. with an introduction and notes, by Charles I. Bushnell. New York: Privately printed, 1861. p.23.

478. Journal of HMS *Asia*. British National Archives, Admiralty 51/67; NDAR 5:921. Journal Of HMS *Chatham*, Captain John Raynor, British National Archives, Admiralty 51/192. NDAR 5:897.

479. Peckham, Howard Henry. *The Toll of Independence: Engagements & Battle Casualties of the American Revolution*. Chicago: University of Chicago Press, 1974. p.20. *The New-York Gazette; and the Weekly Mercury* (August 5, 1776). *Documents Relating to the Revolutionary History, State Of New Jersey*. Edited by William S. Stryker. Trenton: The John L. Murphy Publishing Co., 1901. Series 2. I:159; Clayton, W. Woodford. *History of Union and Middlesex Counties*. Philadelphia: Everts and Peck, 1882. p.72.

480. Clayton, W. Woodford, ed. *History of Union and Middlesex Counties, New Jersey, with Biographical Sketches of Many of their Pioneers and Prominent Men*. Philadelphia: Everts & Peck, 1882. p.621.

481. *Documents Relating to the Revolutionary History, State Of New Jersey*. Edited by William S. Stryker. Trenton: The John L. Murphy Publishing Co., 1901. Series 2. I:220–221.

482. Journal of HMS *Perseus*. British National Archives, Admiralty 51/688. NDAR 6:1262.

483. Brigadier General Hugh Mercer to George Washington. Amboy. October 16, 1776. NDAR 6:1292. Washington, George. *The Papers of George Washington*. Revolutionary War series. Philander D. Chase, editor. Charlottesville: University Press of Virginia, 1985–<2008>. 6:577-578. Richardson, William H. "Washington and the New Jersey Campaign of 1776." *Proceedings Of the New Jersey Historical Society: A Magazine Of New Jersey History*. 50:2 (April, 1932) p.141–142. Whitehead, William A. *Contributions to the Early History of Perth Amboy and Adjoining Country*. New York: D. Appleton & Company, 1856. p.336.

484. *The New-York Gazette; and the Weekly Mercury* (March 17, 1777). *Documents Relating to the Revolutionary History, State Of New Jersey*. Edited by William S. Stryker. Trenton: The John L. Murphy Publishing Co., 1901. Series 2. 1:316.

485. *Annals of Staten Island, From Its Discovery to the Present Time*. J. J. Clute. New York: Press of C. Vogt, 1877. pp.96–97.

486. *The New-York Gazette; and the Weekly Mercury* (August 25, 1777). *Documents Relating to the Revolutionary History, State Of New Jersey*. Edited by William S. Stryker. Trenton: The John L. Murphy Publishing Co., 1901. Series 2. I:451–452. *The Independent Chronicle and the Universal Advertiser*. 10:473 (September 11, 1777) p.3.

487. John Sullivan to John Hancock Philadelphia, August 31, 1777. *The Providence Gazette; and Country Journal*. XIV:717 (September 27, 1777) p.1. Sullivan, John. *Letters and Papers of Major-General John Sullivan, Continental Army*.

Edited by Otis G. Hammond. Concord, N.H.: New Hampshire Historical Society, 1930–39. I:438–442. *The New-York Gazette; and the Weekly Mercury* (August 25, 1777). *The Independent Chronicle and the Universal Advertiser.* 10:473 (September 11, 1777) p.3. *Documents Relating to the Revolutionary History, State Of New Jersey.* Edited by William S. Stryker. Trenton: The John L. Murphy Publishing Co., 1901. Series 2. I:451–452. Baurmeister, Carl Leopold. *Revolution in America: Confidential Letters and Journals, 1776–1784.* trans. and annotated by Bernhard A. Uhlendorf. New Brunswick: Rutgers University Press, 1957. p.122. *The New York Gazette; and the Weekly Mercury.* 1349 (September 1, 1777) p.3.

488. *The New-York Gazette; and the Weekly Mercury* (December 1, 1777). *Documents Relating to the Revolutionary History, State Of New Jersey.* Edited by William S. Stryker. Trenton: The John L. Murphy Publishing Co., 1901. Series 2. 1: 487–489. Washington, George. *The Writings of George Washington From the Original Manuscript Sources, 1745–1799.* prepared under the direction of the United States George Washington Bicentennial Commission and published by authority of Congress; John C. Fitzpatrick, editor. Washington, DC: U.S. Govt. Print. Off. [1931–44]. 10:233.

489. Half-Pay to Hunterdon County Families of the Revolution–1780–1796. *Proceedings of the New Jersey Historical Society: A Quarterly Magazine.* NS, 13:2 (April, 1928) pp.196–197.

490. Adair, William. "The Revolutionary War Diary of William Adair." *Delaware History.* 13 (1968) p.162. Boatner, Mark Mayo. *Encyclopedia of the American Revolution* (New York, 1966) 1054. Sullivan Papers, New Hampshire Historical Society in Sullivan, John. *Letters and Papers of Major-General John Sullivan, Continental Army.* Edited by Otis G. Hammond. Concord, N.H.: New Hampshire Historical Society, 1930–39. I:446.

491. *The New-York Gazette; and the Weekly Mercury* (September 22, 1777). *Documents Relating to the Revolutionary History, State Of New Jersey.* Edited by William S. Stryker. Trenton: The John L. Murphy Publishing Co., 1901. Series 2. 1:473.

492. *New York Gazette and Weekly Mercury.* (November 24, 1777). *Documents Relating to the Revolutionary History, State Of New Jersey.* Edited by William S. Stryker. Trenton: The John L. Murphy Publishing Co., 1901. Series 2. I:485. Clayton, W. Woodford, ed. *History of Union and Middlesex Counties, New Jersey, with Biographical Sketches of Many of their Pioneers and Prominent Men.* Philadelphia: Everts & Peck, 1882. p.80.

493. *The New-York Gazette; and the Weekly Mercury.* (December 1, 1777). *Documents Relating to the Revolutionary History, State Of New Jersey.* Edited by William S. Stryker. Trenton: The John L. Murphy Publishing Co., 1901. Series 2. 1:487–489. Clayton, W. Woodford, ed. *History of Union and Middlesex Counties, New Jersey, with Biographical Sketches of Many of their Pioneers and Prominent Men.* Philadelphia: Everts & Peck, 1882. p.80.

494. Wickes, Stephen. *History of the Oranges, in Essex County, N.J.: from 1666 to 1806.* Newark, N.J.: Printed by Ward & Tichenor for the New England Society of Orange, 1892. p.185.

495. Papas, Phillip. *That Ever Loyal Island: Staten Island and the American Revolution.* New York, London: New York University Press, 2007. p.85. Simcoe, John Graves. *Simcoe's Military Journal. A History of the Operations of a Partisan Corps Called The Queen's Rangers, Commanded by Lieut. Col. J. G. Simcoe, During the War of the American Revolution.* New-York: Bartlett & Welford, 1844; [New York]: New York Times; Arno Press. – Eyewitness Accounts of the American Revolution. [1968]. pp.268–286.

496. *Documents Relating to the Revolutionary History, State Of New Jersey.* Edited by William S. Stryker. Trenton: The John L. Murphy Publishing Co., 1901. Series 2.. II:270.

497. *Rivington's Gazette.* no. 175. *The New-York Gazette; and the Weekly Mercury.* 1390 in Clayton, W. Woodford, ed. *History of Union and Middlesex Counties, New Jersey, with Biographical Sketches of Many of their Pioneers and Prominent Men.* Philadelphia: Everts & Peck, 1882. p.81.

498. Papas, Phillip. *That Ever Loyal Island: Staten Island and the American Revolution.* New York, London: New York University Press, 2007. p.85. Barefoot Daniel W. *Spirits of '76: Ghost Stories of the American Revolution.* Winston-Salem: John F. Blair, 2009. p.107. Simcoe, John Graves. *Simcoe's Military Journal. A History of the Operations of a Partisan Corps Called The Queen's Rangers, Commanded by Lieut. Col. J. G. Simcoe, During the War of the American Revolution.* New-York: Bartlett & Welford, 1844; [New York]: New York Times; Arno Press. – Eyewitness Accounts of the American Revolution. [1968]. pp.268–286.

499. Clayton, W. Woodford, ed. *History of Union and Middlesex Counties, New Jersey, with Biographical Sketches of Many of their Pioneers and Prominent Men.* Philadelphia: Everts & Peck, 1882. p.81; *New Jersey Journal.* no.155. *The New-York Gazette; and the Weekly Mercury.* 1392 (June 29, 1780).

500. *The New-York Gazette; and the Weekly Mercury* (November 9, 1778). *Documents Relating to the Revolutionary History, State Of New Jersey.* Edited by William S. Stryker. Trenton: The John L. Murphy Publishing Co., 1901. Series 2. II:523.

501. *New Jersey History.* 1st Series, 7, 93.

502. Extract of a letter from a Correspondent at Woodbridge, dated February 10, 1779. *The New Jersey Gazette.* 2:63 (February 17, 1779) p.2. *Documents Relating to the Revolutionary History, State Of New Jersey.* Edited by William S. Stryker. Trenton: The John L. Murphy Publishing Co., 1901. Series 2. III:65.

503. *The New-York Gazette; and the Weekly Mercury.* 1431 (March 22, 1779). *Documents Relating to the Revolutionary History, State Of New Jersey.* Edited by William S. Stryker. Trenton: The John L. Murphy Publishing Co., 1901. Series 2. III:163.

504. *Documents Relating to the Revolutionary History, State Of New Jersey.* Edited by William S. Stryker. Trenton: The John L. Murphy Publishing Co., 1901. Series 2. III:493.

505. *The Pennsylvania Journal.* (July 14, 1779). *Documents Relating to the Revolutionary History, State Of New Jersey.* Edited by William S. Stryker. Trenton: The John L. Murphy Publishing Co., 1901. Series 2. III:494.

506. *The Royal Gazette.* No. 290 (July 10, 1779). *Documents Relating to the Revolutionary History, State Of New Jersey.* Edited by William S. Stryker. Trenton: The John L. Murphy Publishing Co., 1901. Series 2. 3:463.

507. *Documents Relating to the Revolutionary History, State Of New Jersey.* Edited by William S. Stryker. Trenton: The John L. Murphy Publishing Co., 1901. Series 2. 3:555.

508. Ibid.

509. Morris, Ira K. *Morris's Memorial History of Staten Island, New York.* New York: Memorial Publishing Co., c1898–1900. I:301.

510. *Annals of Staten Island, from Its Discovery to the Present Time.* J. J. Clute. New York: Press of C. Vogt, 1877 102–104. *The Pennsylvania Evening Post.* 5:636 (November 6, 1779) p.246.

511. Wall, John P. T*he Chronicles of New Brunswick, New Jersey 1667-1931.* New Brunswick: Thatcher-Anderson Company, 1931. pp.232-235. *The Pennsylvania Evening Post.* V:636 (November 6, 1779) p.246. *Documents Relating to the Revolutionary History, State Of New Jersey.* Edited by William S. Stryker. Trenton: The John L. Murphy Publishing Co., 1901. Series 2. III, 719-720; NJDOD #2244. See also **Quibbletown/Van Veghten's bridge** in the subsequent volume on New Jersey.

512. *The Pennsylvania Packet or the General Advertiser.* (January 22, 1780) p.2. *The Royal Gazette.* No. 345 (January 19, 1780). *New Jersey Gazette.* (Jan. 19, 1780) p.3. *Documents Relating to the Revolutionary History, State Of New Jersey.* Edited by William S. Stryker. Trenton: The John L. Murphy Publishing Co., 1901. Series 2. IV:134–135, 137. Boatner, Mark M. *Encyclopedia of the American Revolution.* McKay: New York, 3d ed., 1980 16. *Maryland Journal.* (February 8, 1780). Moore, Frank. *Diary of the American Revolution: from Newspapers and Original Documents.* New York: Charles Scribner; London: Sampson Low, Son & Co., 1890. 2:254. Leiby, Adrian Coulter. *The Revolutionary War in the Hackensack Valley; the Jersey Dutch and the Neutral Ground, 1775–1783.* New Brunswick, N.J., Rutgers University Press, 1962. pp.226–227.

513. Extract of a letter from General Washington to his Excellency the President of Congress dated Morristown, January 18, 1780, including Lord Stirling's Report. *The Pennsylvania Gazette.* (January 26, 1780). *The Pennsylvania Packet or the General Advertiser.* (January 22, 1780) p.2.

514. Simcoe, John Graves. *Simcoe's Military Journal. A History of the Operations of a Partisan Corps Called The Queen's Rangers, Commanded by Lieut. Col. J. G. Simcoe, During the War of the American Revolution.* New-York: Bartlett & Welford, 1844; [New York]: New York Times; Arno Press.–Eyewitness Accounts of the American Revolution. [1968]. Pp.130–134.

515. *The Pennsylvania Packet, 1776–1783.* (Feb. 19, 1780) p.3. *Documents Relating to the Revolutionary History, State Of New Jersey.* Edited by William S. Stryker. Trenton: The John L. Murphy Publishing Co., 1901. Series 2. 4:190.

516. Papas, Phillip. *That Ever Loyal Island: Staten Island and the American Revolution.* New York, London: New York University Press, 2007. p.97. Michael S. Adelberg, «'A Combination to Trample All Law Underfoot': The Association for Retaliation and the American Revolution in Monmouth County,» *New Jersey History. 115* (1997):1–35.

517. *Documents Relating to the Revolutionary History, State Of New Jersey.* Edited by William S. Stryker. Trenton: The John L. Murphy Publishing Co., 1901. Series 2. IV:623.

518. Ibid.

519. Ibid. p.665.

520. Krafft, John Charles Philip von. *Journal of Lieutenant John Charles Philip von Krafft.* Collections of the New-York Historical Society for the year 1882. –Eyewitness Accounts of the American Revolution.—New York: The New York Historical Society; New York: The New York Times & Arno Press, 1968. pp.124–125.

521. *The New Jersey Gazette.* IV:158 (January 3, 1781) p.4.

522. *The New Jersey Gazette.* IV:172 (April 11,1781) p.3. *Connecticut Journal.* 705 (May 2, 1781) p.1. *Documents Relating to the Revolutionary History, State Of New Jersey.* Edited by William S. Stryker. Trenton: The John L. Murphy Publishing Co., 1901. Series 2. V:229.

523. *Documents Relating to the Revolutionary History, State Of New Jersey.* Edited by William S. Stryker. Trenton: The John L. Murphy Publishing Co., 1901. Series 2. V:239. *The Pennsylvania Gazette.* April 25, 1781. *Connecticut Journal.* Issue 705 (May 2, 1781) p.1. *New Jersey Gazette.* no. 234. *New Jersey Journal.* no. 111, no. 113. *The American Journal and General Advertiser.* III:126 (May, 12, 1781) p.2. Clayton, W. Woodford, ed. *History of Union and Middlesex Counties, New Jersey, with Biographical Sketches of Many of their Pioneers and Prominent Men.* Philadelphia: Everts & Peck, 1882. pp.92–3. *Documents Relating to the Revolutionary History, State Of New Jersey.* Edited by William S. Stryker. Trenton: The John L. Murphy Publishing Co., 1901. Series 2. V:239.

524. Yellow Hook was on the Brooklyn shore of Long Island. Robin's Reef must have been near the Staten Island shore near the Watering Place. *Annals of Staten Island, From Its Discovery to the Present Time.* J. J. Clute. New York: Press of C. Vogt, 1877 111–12.

525. Some accounts say this event occurred on Wednesday night, May, 9, 1781. *The New-York Gazette; and the Weekly Mercury.* 1543. *Rivington's Gazette.* no. 488. *Royal Gazette.* 483 (May 16,1781) p.3. Clayton, W. Woodford, ed. *History of Union and Middlesex Counties, New Jersey, with Biographical Sketches of Many of their Pioneers and Prominent Men.* Philadelphia: Everts & Peck, 1882. p.93.

526. *The New Jersey Gazette.* IV:188 (August 1,1781) p.3.

527. *Documents Relating to the Revolutionary History, State Of New Jersey.* Edited by William S. Stryker. Trenton: The John L. Murphy Publishing Co., 1901. Series 2. V:288.

528. *The New-York Gazette; and the Weekly Mercury.* 1558 (August 27, 1781) p.3.

529. Extract of a Letter from New-Brunswick, Dated October 15, 1781. *The New Jersey Gazette.* IV:199 (October 17, 1781) p.3. *The Pennsylvania Packet or the General Advertiser.* X:797 (October 23, 1781) p.3.

530. *The New-York Gazette; and the Weekly Mercury.* 1569. *Rivington's Gazette.* no 534. Clayton, W. Woodford, ed. *History of Union and Middlesex Counties, New Jersey, with Biographical Sketches of Many of their Pioneers and Prominent Men.* Philadelphia: Everts & Peck, 1882. pp.94–95.

531. Remainder of the Returns, Omitted the Two Last Weeks for Want of Room. *The New Jersey Gazette.* IV: 203 (November 14, 1781) p.3. *The New Jersey Gazette.* IV: 207 (December 12, 1781) p.4.

532. *The Freeman's Journal: or, The North-American Intelligencer.* XXXVI (December 26, 1781) p.3. *The Boston Gazette, and the Country Journal.* 1430 (January 21, 1782) p.3.

533. *Royal Gazette.* 555 (January 23, 1782) p.3. *The New-York Gazette; and the Weekly Mercury.* 1580 (January 28, 1782) p.2.

534. Extract of a Letter from Elizabeth-Town, Dated March 4, 1783. *New Jersey Gazette.* VI:273 (March 19, 1783) p.3. *New Jersey Gazette.* VI:272 (March 12, 1783) p.3.

535. Clayton, W. Woodford, ed. *History of Union and Middlesex Counties, New Jersey, with Biographical Sketches of Many of their Pioneers and Prominent Men.* Philadelphia: Everts & Peck, 1882. p.95.

536. Extract of a letter from Freehold. Monmouth County, dated April 15, 1782. *Documents Relating to the Revolutionary History, State Of New Jersey.* Edited by William S. Stryker. Trenton: The John L. Murphy Publishing Co., 1901. Series 2. V:425–426. *The New Jersey Gazette.* V: 226 (April 24, 1782) p.3.

537. *Connecticut Journal.* 764 (June 20, 1782) p.2.

538. Ibid.

539. *Documents Relating to the Revolutionary History, State Of New Jersey.* Edited by William S. Stryker. Trenton: The John L. Murphy Publishing Co., 1901. Series 2. V:464.

540. *The New-York Gazette; and the Weekly Mercury.* 1603 (July 8, 1782) p.3. *Annals of Staten Island, From Its Discovery to the Present Time.* J. J. Clute. New York: Press of C. Vogt, 1877. p.112.

541. *Annals of Staten Island, From Its Discovery to the Present Time.* J. J. Clute. New York: Press of C. Vogt, 1877. p.112.

542. *The New-York Gazetteer or Northern Intelligencer.* I:26 (November 25, 1782) p.2. *The Pennsylvania Evening Post, and Public Advertiser.* VIII: 877 (November 22, 1782) p.172. *The Independent Gazetteer.* 42 (November 19, 1782) p.3. *The New Jersey Gazette.* 255 (November 13, 1782). p.3. *Annals of Staten Island, From Its Discovery to the Present Time.* J. J. Clute. New York: Press of C. Vogt, 1877. p.112.

Glossary

1. *Oxford English Dictionary.*

Glossary

Abatis: Sharpened branches pointing out from a fortification at an angle toward the enemy to slow or disrupt an assault.

Accoutrement: Piece of military equipment carried by soldiers in addition to their standard uniform and weapons.

Bar shot: A double shot consisting of two half cannon balls joined by an iron bar, used in sea-warfare to damage masts and rigging (see Photos NY-3A and NY-3B).

Bastion: A fortification with a projecting part of a wall to protect the main walls of the fortification (see Photos NY-1 and NY-2).

Battalion: The basic organizational unit of a military force, generally 500 to 800 men. Most regiments consisted of a single battalion which was composed of ten companies.

Bateau: A light flat-bottomed riverboat with sharply tapering stern and bow (see Photo NY-7).

Battery: Two or more similar artillery pieces that function as a single tactical unit; a prepared position for artillery; an army artillery unit corresponding to a company in an infantry regiment.

Bayonet: A long, slender blade that can be attached to the end of a musket and used for stabbing.

Best bower: The large anchor (about 4,000 pounds) on the starboard side of the bow of a vessel. The other is called the small-bower. Also the cable attached to this anchor. (See Photo NY-33)

Blunderbuss: A short musket with a large bore and wide muzzle capable of holding a number of musket or pistol balls, used to fire shot with a scattering effect at close range. It is very effective for clearing a narrow passage, door of a house or staircase, or in boarding a ship (see Photo NY-5).

Bomb: An iron shell, or hollow ball, filled with gunpowder. It has a large touch-hole for a slow-burning fuse which is held in place by pieces of wood and fastened with a cement made of quicklime, ashes, brick dust, and steel filings worked together with glutinous water. A bomb is shot from a mortar mounted on a carriage. It is fired in a high arc over fortifications and often detonates in the air, raining metal fragments with high velocity on the fort's occupants. (See Photo NY-4.)

Bombproof: A structure built strong enough to protect the inhabitants from exploding bombs and shells.

Brig: A small two-masted sailing vessel with square-rigged sails on both masts.

Brigade: A military unit consisting of about 800 men.

Broadside: 1. The firing of all guns on one side of a vessel as nearly simultaneously as possible. 2. A large piece of paper printed on one side for advertisements or public notices.

Canister or **Cannister shot:** A kind of case-shot consisting of a number of small iron balls packed in sawdust in a cylindrical tin or canvas case. They were packed in four tiers between iron plates. (See Photos NY-3A and NY-3B.)

Carronade: A short, stubby piece of artillery, usually of large caliber, having a chamber for the powder like a mortar. It is chiefly used on shipboard.

Chain shot: A kind of shot formed of two balls, or half-balls, connected by a chain, chiefly used in naval warfare to destroy masts, rigging, and sails (see Photo NY-3A).

Chandeliers: Large and strong wooden frames used instead of a parapet. Fascines are piled on top of each other against it to cover workmen digging trenches. Sometimes they are only strong planks with two pieces of wood perpendicular to hold the fascines.

Chevaux-de-frise: Obstacles consisting of horizontal poles with projecting spikes to block a passageway. They were used on land and modified to block rivers to enemy ships.

Cohorn or **coehorn:** A short, small-barreled mortar for throwing grenades.

Company: The smallest military unit of the army consisting of about 45 to 110 men commanded by a captain, a lieutenant, and an ensign, and sometimes by a second lieutenant. A company usually has two sergeants, three or four corporals and two drums.

Crown forces: The allied forces supporting King George III. They consisted primarily of the British army, Hessian mercenaries, Loyalists, and Native Americans.

Cutter: 1. A single-masted sailing vessel similar to a sloop but having its mast positioned further aft. 2. A ship's boat, usually equipped with both sails and oars. In the eighteenth century, the terms sloop and cutter seem to have been used almost interchangeably.

Glossary

Demilune: Fortification similar to a bastion but shaped as a crescent or half-moon rather than as an arrow.
Dragoon: A soldier who rode on horseback like cavalry. Dragoons generally fought dismounted in the 17th and 18th centuries.
Earthworks: A fortification made of earth.
Embrasure: A slanted opening in the wall or parapet of a fortification designed for the defender to fire through it on attackers (see Photo NY-36).
Envelopment: An assault directed against an enemy's flank. An attack against two flanks is a double envelopment.
Espontoon: See **Spontoon.**
Fascine: A long bundle of sticks tied together, used in building earthworks and in strengthening ramparts (see Photo NY-37).
Fraise: Sharpened stakes built into the exterior wall of a fortification to deter attackers
Gabion: A cylindrical basket made of wicker and filled with earth for use in building fortifications (see Photo NY-37).
Galley: A long boat propelled by oars. These boats had a shallow draft and were particularly useful in rivers, lakes, and other shallow bodies of water.
General engagement: An encounter, conflict, or battle in which the majority of a force is involved.
Grape shot: A number of small iron balls tied together to resemble a cluster of grapes. When fired simultaneously from a cannon, the balls separate into multiple projectiles. The shot usually consisted of nine balls placed between two iron plates (see Photos NY-3A and NY-3B).
Grenadier: A soldier armed with grenades; a specially selected foot soldier in an elite unit selected on the basis of exceptional height and ability (see Photos NY-8 and NY-34)
Gun: A cannon. Guns were referred to by the size of the shot they fired. A 3-pounder fired a 3-pound ball, a 6-pounder fired a 6-pound ball. (See Photo NY-16.)
Gundalow: An open, flat bottomed vessel about 53 feet long, 15 feet wide, and almost four feet deep in the center. It is equipped with both sails and oars, designed to carry heavy loads, usually armed with one gun at the bow and two mid-ship (See Photo NY-10).
Hessian: A German mercenary soldier who fought with the British army. Most of the German soldiers came from the kingdom of Hesse-Cassel, hence the name. Other German states that sent soldiers include Brunswick, Hesse-Hanau, Waldeck, Ansbach-Bayreuth, and Anhalt-Zerbst. (See Photo NY-34.)
Howitzer: A cannon with a short barrel and a bore diameter greater than 30 mm and a maximum elevation of 60 degrees, used for firing shells at a high angle of elevation to reach a target behind cover or in a trench.
Hussars or **Huzzars:** Horse soldiers resembling Hungarian horsemen. They usually wore furred bonnets adorned with a cock's feather, a doublet with a pair of breeches, to which their stockings are fastened, and boots. They were armed with a saber, carbines, and pistols. (See Photo NY-27.)
Jaeger: A hunter and gamekeeper who fought with the Hessians for the British army. They wore green uniforms, carried rifles, and were expert marksmen.
Jollyboat: A sailing vessel's small boat, such as a dinghy, usually carried on the stern. "A clincher-built ship's boat, smaller than a cutter, with a bluff bow and very wide transom, usually hoisted at the stern of the vessel, and used chiefly as a hack-boat for small work."[1]
Langrage: A particular kind of shot, formed of bolts, nails, bars, or other pieces of iron tied together, and forming a sort of cylinder, which corresponds with the bore of the cannon.
Letter of marque: A license granted by a monarch authorizing a subject to take reprisals on the subjects of a hostile state for alleged injuries. Later: Legal authority to fit out an armed vessel and use it in the capture of enemy merchant shipping and to commit acts which would otherwise have constituted piracy. See also **Privateer.**
Light infantry: Foot soldiers who carried lightweight weapons and minimal field equipment.
Loophole: Aperture or slot in defenses through which the barrels of small arms or cannon can be directed at an outside enemy. (See Photo NY-17.)
Loyalist: An American who supported the British during the American Revolution; also called Tory.
Magazine: A structure to store weapons, ammunition, explosives, and other military equipment or supplies.
Man-of-war: A warship (see Photo NY-33).
Matross: A private in an artillery unit who needed no specialized skills. Matrosses usually hauled cannon and positioned them. They assisted in the loading, firing, and sponging the guns.

Militia: Civilians who are part-time soldiers who take military training and can serve full-time for short periods during emergencies.

Minuteman: Member of a special militia unit, called a Minute Company. A minuteman pledged to be ready to fight at a minute's notice.

Mortar: A cannon with a relatively short and wide barrel, used for firing shells in a high arc over a short distance, particularly behind enemy defenses. They were not mounted on wheeled carriages. (See Photo NY-6.)

Musket: A firearm with a long barrel, large caliber, and smooth bore. It was used between the 16th and 18th centuries, before rifling was invented.

Open order: A troop formation in which the distance between the individuals is greater than in close order (which is shoulder to shoulder). Also called extended order. (See Photos NY-35a and NY-35b.)

Parapet: Earthen or stone defensive platform on the wall of a fort.

Parley: A talk or negotiation, under a truce, between opposing military forces.

Parole: A promise given by a prisoner of war, either not to escape, or not to take up arms again as a condition of release. Individuals on parole can remain at home and conduct their normal occupations. Breaking parole makes one subject to immediate arrest and often execution. From the French *parole* which means one's word of honor.

Pettiauger or **pettyauger:** 1. A long, narrow canoe hollowed from the trunk of a single tree or from the trunks of two trees fastened together. 2. An open flat-bottomed schooner-rigged vessel or two-masted sailing barge, of a type used in North America and the Caribbean. (See Photo NY-21.)

Pinnace: 1. A small light vessel, usually having two schooner-rigged (originally square-rigged) masts, often in attendance on a larger vessel and used as a tender or scout, to carry messages, etc. 2. A small boat, originally rowed with eight oars, later with sixteen, forming part of the equipment of a warship or other large vessel. It could also be navigated with a sail. (See Photo NY-18.)

Polacre: A three-masted vessel with square-rigged sails and pole masts without tops and crosstrees.

Portage: An overland route used to transport a boat or its cargo from one waterway to another; the act of carrying a boat or its cargo from one waterway to another.

Privateer: An armed vessel owned and crewed by private individuals and holding a government commission known as a letter of marque authorizing the capture of merchant shipping belonging to an enemy nation. See **Letter of marque**.

Rampart: An earthen fortification made of an embankment and often topped by a low protective wall

Ravelin: A small outwork fortification shaped like an arrowhead or a V that points outward in front of a larger defense work to protect the sally port or entrance.

Redoubt: A temporary fortification built to defend a prominent position such as a hilltop.

Regiment: A permanent military unit usually consisting of two or three companies. British regiments generally consisted of ten companies, one of which was grenadiers. Some German regiments consisted of 2,000 men.

Regular: Belonging to or constituting a full-time professional military or police force as opposed to, for example, the reserves or militia.

Round shot: Spherical ball of cast-iron or steel for firing from smooth-bore cannon, a cannon ball. The shots were referred to by the weight of the ball: a 9-pound shot weighed 9 pounds; a 12-pound shot weighed 12 pounds. Round shot was used principally to batter fortifications. The balls could be heated ("hot shot") and fired at the hulls of ships or buildings to set them on fire. The largest balls (32- and 64-pounders) were sometimes called "big shot." (See Photo NY-3B.)

Sapper: A soldier who specializes in making entrenchments and tunnels for siege operations.

Schooner: A fast sailing ship with at least two masts and with fore and aft sails on all lower masts.

Scow: A flat-bottomed sailboat with a rectangular hull.

Shell: An explosive projectile fired from a large-bore gun such as a howitzer or mortar. See also **Bomb, Howitzer,** and **Mortar**. (See Photo NY-4.)

Ship of the line: A large warship with sufficient armament to enter combat with similar vessels in the line of battle. A ship of the line carried 60 to 100 guns. (See Photo NY-33.)

Shot: A bullet or projectile fired from a weapon. See also: **Bar shot, Canister shot, Chain shot, Grapeshot, Round shot, Sliding bar shot, Star shot**. (See Photos NY-3A and NY-3B.)

Sliding bar shot: A projectile similar to a bar shot. A sliding bar shot has two interlocked bars that extend almost double the length of a bar shot, thereby increasing the potential damage to a ship's rigging and sails. (See Photo NY-3A.)

Glossary

Sloop: A small single-masted sailing vessel with sails rigged fore-and-aft and guns on only one deck. In the 18th century, the terms sloop and cutter seem to have been used almost interchangeably.

Sloop of war: A three-masted, square-rigged naval vessel with all her guns mounted on a single uncovered main deck.

Snow: A small sailing-vessel resembling a brig, carrying a main and fore mast and a supplementary trysail mast close behind the mainmast; formerly employed as a warship.

Sons of Liberty: Patriots who belonged to secret organizations to oppose British attempts at taxation after 1765. They often resorted to violence and coercion to achieve their purposes.

Spike [a gun]: To destroy a cannon by hammering a long spike into the touch hole or vent, thereby rendering it useless.

Spontoon: A type of half-pike or halberd carried by infantry officers in the 18th century (from about 1740).

Stand of arms: A complete set of arms (musket, bayonet, cartridge box, and belt) for one soldier.

Star shot: A kind of chain-shot (see Photo NY-3B).

Tory: A Loyalist, also called refugee and Cow-Boy. The Whigs usually used the term in a derogatory manner.

Trunnions: Two pieces of metal sticking out of the sides of an artillery piece. They serve to hold the artillery piece on the carriage and allow it to be raised or lowered. The trunnions are generally as long as the diameter of the cannonball and have the same diameter. (See Photo NY-16.)

Whig: Somebody who supported independence from Great Britain during the American Revolution. The name comes from the British liberal political party that favored reforms and opposed many of the policies of the King and Parliament related to the American War for Independence.

Index

1st Battalion of Grenadiers, 91
1st Battalion, New York Continentals, 58
1st British Light Infantry Battalion, 93, 177
1st British Regiment of guards, 119
1st Connecticut Regiment, 44
2nd Battalion of Grenadiers, 91
2nd British light infantry, 91, 177, 181
2nd British Regiment of guards, 119
2nd Connecticut Regiment, 126, 151
2nd Continental Light Dragoons, 91, 104, 149
2nd New York, 24
3rd British light infantry, 181
3rd Massachusetts, 119
3rd New Jersey Regiment, 61
3rd Pennsylvania Regiment, 194
3rd Street, 166
4th Massachusetts, 97
4th Pennsylvania Regiment, 49
5th Connecticut Regiment, 125, 151
5th Massachusetts Regiment, 114
5th New York Regiment, 67
6th Connecticut Regiment, 144
6th Massachusetts, 125
7th Street, 161
8th Regiment, 61
8th Street, 161, 166
9th Massachusetts, 119
9th Regiment, 25
14th Continental Infantry, 97
14th Massachusetts, 97, 119
15th Massachusetts, 119
16th Massachusetts Continental Infantry, 177
16th Virginia Regiment, 90
20th Regiment, 25
21st Regiment, 25
22nd Regiment, 83
26th Continental Infantry, 97
27th Regiment, 202
31st Regiment, 58
32nd Street, 179
33rd Regiment of Foot, 168
34th Street, 179
35th Street, 179, 180
38th Street, 164, 179, 180
39th Street, 164
42nd Highland Regiment ("Black Watch"), 91, 165, 181, 194, 195
42nd Street, 180
46th Street, 179
47th Regiment, 43
47th Street, 175
53rd Regiment, 15, 43
55th Regiments, 202
71st Regiment (Fraser's Highlanders), 166, 178, 188
88th Street, 178
90th Street, 181
92nd Street, 178
97th Street, 181
105th Street, 181
106th Street, 181
110th Street, 182
119th Street, 181
120th Street, 180, 181
125th Street, 180
153rd Street, 180
159th Streets, 180
160th Street, 180, 193
183rd Street, 193
192nd Street, 174, 193, 196
207th Street, 174, 196
227th Street, 174
230th Street, 174
231st Street, 174
246th Street, 183

Abatis, 78, 111, 149, 174, 199
Abercromby or Abercrombie, Robert, 120
Adair, William, 204
Adams, John, 199
African American, 79, 99, 160
African Americans, 73, 94, 128, 134
Albany, 1, 2, 11, 17, 22, 25, 29, 31, 32, 37, 39, 47, 48, 51, 59, 65, 67, 81
Albany Guards, 67
Albany Post Road, 183
Albany road, 184
Alexander, William (Earl of Stirling), 163, 192, 208, 209
Allen, Ethan, 1, 3, 6, 9, 15
Allen, Isaac, 202
Althause, Captain, 119
Althouse, John, 213
Amboy, 158, 204, 210
Amboy Ferry Post, 199
Amboy, New Jersey, 100, 201, 202
Ambuscade, 65, 105, 126, 188, 191, 207, 210
Ambush, 35, 37, 41, 48, 50, 59, 71, 155, 207
American Independence Museum, 151
Amherst, Jeffrey, 9
Anderson, James, 116
Anderson, John, 116
André, John, 52, 104, 112, 113, 115, 116, 117
Andrustown, 48, 49
Angell, Israel, 99
Anspachers, 202, 203
Anthony's Nose, 102
Appletown, 62
Arlington Avenue, 174
Armonk, 129
Armstrong, Thomas, 104
Armstrong, Major, 207, 208, 209, 210
Arnold, Benedict, 9, 12, 15, 16, 18, 19, 20, 22, 23, 30, 32, 34, 80, 112, 113, 115, 116, 149, 151, 157
Arnold's Bay, Vermont, 20
Arsenal, 135
Arthur Kill, 205
Arthur Kill Road, 198
Artillery, 1, 5, 9, 10, 11, 12, 13, 15, 22, 25, 29, 32, 43, 44, 57, 61, 62, 78, 84, 85, 88, 92, 97, 98, 101, 102, 103, 110, 146, 147, 162, 163, 165, 166, 167, 170, 171, 175, 176, 177, 179, 180, 185, 186, 187, 190, 192, 198, 201, 202, 204
Asia, 74, 158, 170, 175, 176, 200
Aspinwall Cornell, 151
Associated Loyalists, 146
Association, 135, 147

Index 245

Association for Retaliation, 210
Associators, 135
Atayataroughta, Louis, 72, 73
Atlee, Samuel John, 164
Aubrey, Thomas, 43
Audubon Avenue, 174, 196
Auriesville, 44
Auriesville Shrine, 66
Austin, John Wilson, 85
Ayres, Major, 157
Ayscough, James, 134, 135, 143

Babcock's Hill, 90
Babcock's house, 188
Babcock's Heights, 187
Bache, Theophilus, 160
Badge of Military Merit, 150
Baily, Mr., 76
Bainbridge Avenue, 183
Baker's Tavern, 166
Balcarres redoubt, 34
Baldwin, Jeduthan, 13, 36
Baldwin, Loammi, 97
Ballston, 70
Barber farm, 33
Barber, Lieutenant, 107
Barbette battery, 84
Baremore, Mansfield, 105, 107, 119
Barns, Captain, 192
Barnet, William, 202
Barracks, 5, 13, 27, 69, 70, 71, 101, 102, 103, 125, 134, 137, 140, 193, 197
Barras, Admiral Louis, Comte de, 146
Barrick, Richard, 152
Barrymore *see* Baremore
Barton, Henry L., 211
Barton, Joseph, 202, 203, 204
Basic Creek, 67
Bastion, 5, 27, 64, 183
Bateaux, 14, 23, 24, 25
Battery, 13, 14, 74, 77, 78, 84, 89, 91, 92, 103, 104, 106, 147, 170, 174, 175, 176, 178, 196, 198, 201, 212, 213
Battery Hill, 174
Battery Park, 174
Battle at the Flockey, 37
Battle Avenue, 82
Battle of Bemis Heights, 34
Battle of Bennington, 39
Battle of Brooklyn Heights, 160, 167
Battle of Chemung, 60, 61
Battle of Freeman's Farm, 32, 33
Battle of Harlem Heights, 92, 180
Battle of Harlem Plains, 180
Battle of Johnstown, 55, 56, 71
Battle of Kip's Bay, 179
Battle of Long Island, 160, 162, 168, 170, 179
Battle of Newtown, 60, 61, 62
Battle of Pell's Point, 95
Battle of Saratoga, 41, 69, 81
Battle of White Plains, 193
Battle Pass, 164, 165
Battle Pass Marker, 160
Batty, John, 11
Baum, Friedrich, 38, 39, 40
Baxter, William, 196
Bayonet, 23, 40, 42, 62, 68, 88, 102, 111, 119, 127, 129, 130, 139, 140, 141, 147, 160, 165, 189, 191, 197, 203
Bayonet charge, 68, 86, 91, 141, 194, 203

Bayonne Neck, New Jersey, 199
Bayonne–Staten Island ferry, 199
Beacon, 79
Bear Mountain, 80, 100
Bear Mountain bridge, 110
Bear Mountain State Park, 80
Bearmore *see* Baremore
Becker, Joseph, 54
Beckwith, George, 209
Bedford, 119, 122, 127, 128, 151, 165, 197
Bedford Pass, 163, 164
Bedford Avenue, 163
Bedford Village, 164
Bedlock, James, 47
Bedloe's Island, 176
Beebe, Bezaleel, 128
Beeckman wood, 105
Bellinger, Peter, 49
Bellinger's militia, 49
Bemis Heights, 30, 31
Bennington Battle Monument, 39
Bennington Battlefield State Historic Site, 39
Bennington militia, 40
Bennington, Vermont, 29, 31, 38, 39, 40, 41
Benton, Selah, 124
Bergen County Volunteers, 201
Bergen County, New Jersey, 204
Bergen Neck, 199
Bergen Point ferry, 207
Billopp, Christopher, 199, 205, 206
Billop's Point, 100, 201, 206, 207
Bissell, Daniel, 151
Black Point, 158
Black Rock, Connecticut, 134
Blackwell's Island, 171, 176, 178
Blanchard, John, 199
Blauveldt, Abraham, 88
Blazing Star, 205, 208
Blazing Star Landing, 206
Blazing Star road, 208
Blockade, 146
Blockhouse, 26, 41, 52, 69, 63, 64, 66, 69, 71, 150
Bloody Pond, 27, 41
Bloomingdale, 90
Bloomingdale Road, 180
Blue Mountain Valley, 176
Blue Point, 156
Blunderbuss, 6, 135
Boar Hill, 90
Bogart, 160
Boland, William, 47
Bombardment, 43, 84, 104, 146, 195
Bonnel, James, 107
Bonnell, Isaac, 206
Bordentown, 20, 208
Borst, Jacob, 45, 46
Borst, Joseph, 45
Boston, 3, 10, 20, 96, 162, 200
Boston Post Road, 94, 97, 107, 123, 180, 183
Boston, Massachusetts, 1
Bouck's Island, 38
Boudinot, Elias, 205
Bouton, Noah, 98
Bowling Green, 174
Bowman's Creek, 68
Boyd, Thomas, 64
Brandon, John, 98
Brant, Joseph, 22, 23, 24, 36, 37, 45, 47, 49, 52, 54, 59, 61, 65, 72
Brant, Mary or Molly [Koñwatsiätsiaiéñni], 36

Breastwork, 13, 43, 61, 69, 70, 72, 73, 77, 80, 134, 179
Brewster, Caleb, 109, 142
Breymann redoubt, 34
Breymann, Heinrich Christoph von, 34, 40, 41
Bridge Street, 174
Bridgeport, Connecticut, 131
British dragoons, 208
British Grenadiers, 93
British Hussars, 184
British Infantry Corps, 151
British Legion, 86, 154
British light infantry, 182, 184
British Queen, 78
Broadside, 17, 20, 77, 143, 170
Broadsword, 41, 120, 122
Broadway, 164, 174, 180, 181, 183, 193, 196
Broadway, 163
Bronx, 92, 124, 154, 168, 171, 174, 183, 187, 192, 196
Bronx Park, 183, 186, 196
Bronx River, 83, 84, 98, 129, 183, 188, 192, 196, 197
Bronx River Parkway, 196
Brookhaven, 135, 140
Brookland, 170
Brooklyn, 74, 158, 167, 172, 198
Brooklyn Bridge, 162, 167
Brooklyn Heights, 161, 162, 170, 173
Brooklyn Museum of Art, 158
Brooks, Dr., 155
Brown, John (d. 1781), 43, 71, 72
Brown, John M. (1745-1803), 15, 45, 46
Brown, Nathan, 101
Brown, Prosper, 155, 156
Brown, William, 151
Brundage, Gilbert, 109
Brundage James, 109
Brune, 168, 175, 177, 178
Brunswick, 206, 208
Brunswick dragoons, 39
Brunswickers, 26
Brush, Jesse, 144, 149
Bryan, Captain, 186
Bryant or Briant, David, 184
Buchanan's Island, 177, 178
Bucks County Volunteers, 196
Bucks County, Pennsylvania, 196
Buckshot, 153
Bugler, 181
Bunker Hill, 163
Burdett's ferry, 83
Burgoyne, John, 3, 11, 14, 17, 22, 23, 24, 25, 28, 30, 31, 33, 34, 38, 39, 60, 81
Burgoyne Street, 30
Burlington County, New Jersey, 205
Burnt Island, 205
Burr, Aaron, 180
Burr James, 152
Burtis, John, 153
Burying Hill, 136
Bushnell, David, 88, 170
Bushwick, 176
Bushwick Creek, 171
Bushwick hills, 165
Buskirk, Jacob Van, 204
Butler, Richard, 86
Butler, Walter, 47, 51, 55, 56, 61, 67, 73
Butler, William, 49, 54
Butler's Creek, 152
Butler's Rangers, 50, 56, 66, 72

Butter Hill, 106
Butternuts, 37
Buttonmold Bay, 20
Byram Bridge, 94, 107, 110
Byram River, 106, 109, 143

Cadwalader, John, 194
Cakiatt, 87
Caldwell, William, 49, 50, 68
Cambridge, Massachusetts, 10, 152
Cambridge, New York, 38
Campbell, Archibald, 98
Campbell, Archibald (1739-1791), 188
Campbell, Archibald (d. 1777), 98
Campbell, John (d. 1806), 203, 204
Campbell, Stephen, 119
Canada, 1, 3, 11, 16, 17, 19, 21, 31, 35, 39, 46, 50, 51, 55, 60, 73, 114, 118
Canadians, 39, 40, 43
Canajoharie, 52, 64, 65, 66, 67
Canajoharie Creek, 64
Canal Place, 48
Canandaigua, 63
Canarsie, 172
Canister shot, 78, 89, 102, 103
Cannonade, 23, 83, 85, 88, 91, 101, 104, 106, 141, 146, 147, 170, 178, 179, 182, 184, 185, 200, 201, 205
Canoe-Place, 155
Carbine, 153
Carillon, 9
Carl Schurz Park, 178
Carleton, 19
Carleton Island, 50, 51
Carleton, Christopher, 26
Carleton, Guy, 5, 12, 16, 17, 19, 20, 71
Carmel, 87
Caroline Church, 131
Carpenter, Benjamin, 128
Carpenter, Thomas, 109
Carrying Place, 15
Carysfort, 171
Caselman, Mr., 45
Cashman, Captain, 213
Cashong, 63
Castleton, Vermont, 9, 24
Castletown road, 14
Catherine Street, 175
Catherine's Town, 62
Catholic, 115, 116
Catskill, 52
Caughnawaga, 44, 66, 71
Cayadutta, 66
Cayuga Lake, 63
Cayugas, 22, 50
Cedar Beach, 141
Central Park, 175, 180, 181
Chain, 2, 80, 81, 102, 113, 114, 115, 182
Chambers Street, 174
Chance, 213
Chandeliers, 185
Charles Redoubt, 174, 191
Charlotte River, 51
Charlotte River valley, 52
Chasseurs, 103, 128, 186, 187
Chatham, Lord, 34
Chatterton Hill, 82, 83, 84, 85
Chemung, 61
Chemung River, 61
Chemung Valley, 60

Index 247

Cherry Street, 175
Cherry Valley, 42, 47, 48, 49, 57, 65
Cherry Valley Museum, 47
Chesapeake Bay, 3
Chevaux-de-frise, 77, 82, 88, 115
Chief Nimham, 183
Chimney Point, 42
Chipman, John, 41, 42
Church, Captain, 146
Churchill, Elijah, 149, 150
Cilley's Regiment, 61
Citizens Redoubt, 174
City Island, 136, 146, 168, 169
City Orchard, 168, 169
Clap, Benjamin, 128
Clark, James, 44, 78, 89, 90, 103, 104, 105, 106, 138, 196
Clarke Avenue, Staten Island, 198
Clarke, Robert, 201
Claverack militia, 26
Clement, John, 50
Clinton County Historical Museum, 17
Clinton, George, 44, 45, 66, 67, 72, 80
Clinton, Henry, 3, 20, 33, 57, 60, 8, 810, 104, 107, 110, 115, 125, 145, 163, 164, 165
Clove, 82
Cobleskill, 45, 46, 54
Cobus Kill *see* Cobleskill
Cochecton, 54
Cochran, Major, 57
Cochrane, Charles, 154
Cock's or Cox Hill, 190, 196 *see also* Fort Cox Hill
Cocknewago Native Americans, 13
Coercive (Intolerable) Acts, 1
Cohorn, 54, 148, 149
Collingsworth, Joseph, 143
Columbia University, 180
Columbus Avenue, 96, 98
Commisary General of Prisoners, 205
Conesus, 63
Coney Island, 158
Conference (Billopp) House, 199, 205
Congress, 19, 20, 31, 162
Conklin, Cornelius, 144
Conklin, Jacob, 144
Connecticut, 1, 16, 98, 115, 118, 135, 136, 137, 138, 145, 148
Connecticut brigade, 180
Connecticut Continentals, 100
Connecticut levies, 108, 128
Connecticut Loyalists, 145, 152
Connecticut militiamen, 99, 100, 155, 181
Connecticut rangers, 181
Connecticut River, 1, 154
Connecticut state troops, 99, 190
Connecticut troops, 133, 170
Connor, Richard, 206
Constitution Island, 113
Continental Congress, 3, 9, 15, 16, 115, 169
Continental Navy, 76
Continental Village, 102, 103
Convention, 34
Convention army, 34
Coogle, Captain, 207
Cooper, James, 119
Coram, 135, 137, 141, 142
Corbin, Margaret Cochran (Molly), 113, 195
Cornwall on Hudson, 106
Cornwallis, Charles, 20, 56, 91, 163, 165, 166, 195, 212

Cortelyou House, 161, 166
Cortelyou, Colonel, 206
Cortland's Ridge, 188, 189
Cortlandt Nursing Home, 100
Cortlandt's bridge, 191
Cortlandt's Regiment, 61
Count Rumford, 136
County House Road, 118
Covenhoven, Abraham, 64
Cow Bay, 153
Cow Neck, 151, 152, 153
Cowboys, 93
Cox, F., 51
Crafts, Edward, 88
Crane, 81, 91, 100, 103, 105, 106, 196
Crane Neck, 135, 157
Crane Neck Bend, 134
Crane, John, 170
Crane, William, 212, 213
Crary, Archibald, 181
Crawford, Samuel, 86
Crickettown Road, 112
Crompond, 120, 121, 126
Crompond Presbyterian Church, 120
Cromwell, James, 64
Croton, 112, 113, 120
Croton Acqueduct, 105
Croton on Hudson, 79, 112
Croton Point
Croton River, 113, 119, 126, 127, 128, 192, 197
Crown Point, 10, 13, 15, 16, 17, 20, 66, 88, 104
Crum Elbow, 105
Crysler, Adam, 37, 54
Crysler, William, 54
Cuck, George, 64, 65
Cuckolds Town, 202
Culloden, 156
Cumberland Gounty, 1
Currytown, 50, 67, 68
Curtis Hook, 170
Curtis, Roger, 136
Cushing, Thomas, 189, 190
Cuyler, Abraham C., 72, 144

D.A.R. *see* Daughters of the American Revolution
Dansey, William, 168, 200
Dansey's Company, 200
Daughters of the American Revolution, 95, 174, 183, 195, 196
Davenport House, 126
Davenport, Richardson, 127
Davis, George, 143
Davis, Nathan, 58, 62
Davis's brook, 105
Dayton, Elias, 21, 202, 208
Dayton's Regiment, 61
De Boor, General, 202
De Hart, William, 176
De Hart's Point, 208, 209
De Lancey, James, 86, 93, 105, 106, 119, 124, 125, 126, 127, 128, 129, 157, 169, 187, 189, 190, 192, 197
De Lancey, James, Jr., 93
De Lancey, Jr., Oliver, 107, 125
De Lancey, Oliver, 79, 90, 113, 117, 129, 186
De Lancey, Stephen, 139
De Lancey's Brigade, 2nd Battalion
De Lancey's Brigade, 3rd Battalion
De Lancey's bridge, 94, 123, 124, 125, 197
De Lancey's horsemen, 107
De Lancey's mill, 123, 186, 192, 193

De Lancey's corps, 121, 139
Dean, John, 118, 119
Decker's Ferry, 199, 200, 202, 203, 207, 208
Declaration of Independence, 55, 169, 170
Deerfield, New Hampshire, 151
Delavan, Samuel, 98
Delaware, 3, 115, 213
Delaware Bay, 3
Delaware Avenue, 43
Delaware Regiment, 83, 166
Delaware River, 54, 59, 65, 66, 195
Demilunes, 5
Dennet, John, 124
Denyse Point, 163
Dependence, 44, 78, 79, 81, 89, 90, 91, 102, 103, 104, 105, 106, 138, 196
Detroit, 60
Diamond Island, 42
Dickie, Robert, 158, 213
Dickinson, Philemon, 187, 204
Dievendorff, Jacob, 68
Diligence, 106
Diligent, 44, 79, 81, 90, 102, 103, 105, 106
Dispatch, 149
Dix, John, 124
Dobbs Ferry, 85, 88, 89, 90, 91, 92, 96, 117, 186, 190, 193
Dorchester Heights, 10, 162, 167
Dorrance, David, 124
Douban's Mills, 208
Doxtader, John, 67, 68
Dragoons, 39, 84, 85, 86, 87, 91, 93, 94, 99, 101, 104, 105, 107, 108, 109, 110, 119, 122, 123, 126, 127, 128, 129, 130, 137, 139, 141, 142, 145, 146, 149, 163, 165, 169, 175, 186, 187, 188, 189, 190, 191, 193, 208, 209
Drake, Benjamin, 98
Drake, Samuel, 120
Drew Hills, 87
Drum Hill, 101
Drummond, Robert, 202
Drury,Captain, 200
DuBois, Lewis, 72
Duggeret, William, 49
Dungan, Colonel, 202
Dunham, Samuel, 35
Durkee (Durgee), Robert, 47
Dutch Church Fort, 199
Dutch Reformed, 198
Dutch Reformed Church, 48, 69, 161
Dutchess County, 74, 98, 154
Dutchess of Gordon, 176
Dyckman, Michael, 189
Dygert, William, 49

Eagle, 176, 212
Eagles, John, 108
Earthwork, 69, 71, 83, 91, 112, 137, 147, 17, 1764, 193
East 88th Street, 178
East 107th Street, 175
East 208th Street, 183
East 233rd St., 95
East Canada Creek, 45
East Chester, 94, 99, 110, 123, 124, 125, 184, 197
East Chester Bay, 100
East Chester Creek, 93
East Drive, 165
East End Avenue, 178
East Gun Hill Road, 183, 196

East Hampton, 135
East India Company, 1
East River, 83, 90, 92, 162, 167, 169, 171, 173, 175, 176, 177, 179
East River Drive, 178
Eastchester, 93, 94, 96, 98, 99, 123, 197
Eastchester Bay, 97
Eastchester Creek, 95
Eastchester Road, 126
Eastern Parkway, 163
Easton, John, 15
Easton, Pennsylvania, 61, 62, 63
Eastview, 118
Edgecombe Avenue, 181, 193
Edick, Christian, 51
Edmonds James, 143
Edwards, Evan, 208
Egg Harbor, New Jersey, 213
Elderkin, Elisha, 153
Elerson, David, 52
Elijah Miller House, 82
Elizabeth Ferry redoubts, 199
Elizabeth, New Jersey *see* Elizabethtown, New Jersey
Elizabethtown Point, 207
Elizabethtown, New Jersey, 200, 201, 202, 204, 205, 206, 209, 210, 211, 212, 213
Ellice, Alexander, 51
Ellis's (Ellice's) Mill, 48, 51
Elmsford Church, 118
Emmerich, Andreas, 85, 87, 90, 103, 104, 107, 119, 123, 151, 184, 186, 187, 188, 189, 190, 191
Enterprise, 19, 20
Ephrata, 45
Erskine, William, 86
Esopus, 43
Esopus Creek, 44, 105
Esopus Meadows, 106
Essex county light-horse, 199
Ewald, Johann von, 87, 120, 153
Exeter, New Hampshire, 151

Fagan, Christopher Tarleton, 122
Fairfield, Connecticut, 73, 136, 141, 142, 146, 157
Falcon, 134
Farley, Michael, 119
Farmers or Dyckman Bridge, 174
Farnham, Thomas, 79, 90, 105
fascines, 86, 185
Feake, John, 69
Ferris Bay, 20
Ferry Street, 30
Field of Grounded Arms, 30
Fieley, Lieutenant, 144
Fifth Avenue, 166, 175, 179, 180, 164
Fire Island, 148, 149
Fire Place, 149
fireships, 78
First Avenue, 179
First Presbyterian Church, 136
Fisher (Visscher), Frederick, 66
Fisher's Island, 131, 155, 156
Fishkill, 79, 102, 105
Fishkill Clove, 79
Fishkill Landing, 79
Fitch, Jabez, Jr, 169
Fitch, Major, 152
Fitz Randolph, Asher, 211
Fitz Randolph, Lewis, 210
Fitz Randolph, Nathaniel, 205, 206
Flag of truce, 89, 103, 117, 182

Index **249**

Flagg, Ebenezer, 126, 127
Flagstaff Fort, 199, 213
Flatbush, 158, 163, 165, 172
Flatbush Avenue, 162, 166
Flatbush Pass, 163, 165
Flatbush Road, 164
Flatlands, 161, 162
Flatlands Avenue, 161
Fleet, Arnold, 138
Fleury, François Louis Teissedre de, 112
Flockey, 37
Flockeys, 70
Floyd, Benjamin, 135
Flushing, 177
Fonda, 66
Forage, 35, 39, 54, 98, 103, 125, 139, 141, 197, 201
Foraging, 98, 99, 101, 107, 109, 131, 139, 164, 187, 190, 196, 211
Foraging party, 190
Ford, Jacob Jr, 47
Fordham, 174, 193
Fordham Heights, 124, 192
Fordham Road, 174
Forlorn hope, 111
Forman, David, 210
Fort Amsterdam, 174
Fort Anne, 12, 25, 26, 27, 29, 42, 43
Fort Anne Road, 26
Fort Arnold, 80, 113
Fort Caughnawaga, 66
Fort Clinton, 1, 33, 80, 81, 82, 113, 114
Fort Clyde, 64
Fort Cock Hill (Cock's Hill or Cox Hill), 174, 196
Fort Constitution (Lee), 1, 81, 88, 92, 93, 114
Fort Crown Point *see* Crown Point
Fort Dayton, 22, 24, 35, 48, 49, 50, 51, 73
Fort Defiance, 69
Fort Edward, New York, 12, 25, 26, 27, 29, 39, 41
Fort Franklin, 145, 146
Fort George, 1, 16, 26, 27, 30, 41, 42, 174
Fort George (Laurel Hill), 128, 174, 190, 196
Fort Golgotha, 136, 145
Fort Greene Park, 161
Fort Hamilton, 163
Fort Herkimer, 48, 49, 65, 73
Fort Herkimer Church, 48
Fort Hill, 135, 199
Fort Hunter, 41, 42, 55, 67
Fort Independence, 15, 101, 108, 175, 183, 184, 190, 191, 192, 197
Fort Independence Park, 183
Fort Johnstown, 56
Fort Keyser, 45, 71
Fort Klock, 72
Fort Knyphausen, 128, 190, 195, 196, 199
Fort La Présentation, 57
Fort Lafayette, 104, 112
Fort Lee, 78, 80, 83, 173, 181, 190, 195
Fort Lee, New Jersey, 194
Fort Lewis, 67
Fort Miller, 30
Fort Montgomery, 1, 33, 80, 81, 82, 102, 114
Fort Montgomery State Historic Site, 80
Fort Mount Hope, 8
Fort Niagara, 37, 60
Fort No. 1, 84, 174
Fort No. 2, 174
Fort No. 3, 174
Fort No. 4, 174
Fort No. 5, 174
Fort No. 6, 174
Fort No. 7, 174
Fort No. 8, 126, 174, 192, 193
Fort No. 9, 174
Fort Paris, 71
Fort Plain, 24, 45, 56, 64, 65, 67, 68, 72
Fort Plank, 64, 70
Fort Pond Bay, 156
Fort Prince Charles, 174
Fort Putnam, 113, 114, 116, 161
Fort Rensselaer, 64, 67, 68
Fort Richmond, 211
Fort Road, 52
Fort Salonga, 149
Fort Schuyler, 21, 23, 24, 56, 57, 59
Fort Slongo, 149
Fort St. George, 141, 142, 149, 156
Fort Stanwix, 10, 21, 22, 24, 31, 32, 35, 36, 115
Fort Stanwix National Monument, 21
Fort Ticonderoga, 5, 8, 9, 11, 12, 13, 14, 15, 16, 17, 20, 22, 24, 26, 29, 43 *see also* Ticonderoga
Fort Tryon, 128, 175, 190, 195
Fort Tryon Park, 175, 193
Fort Wadsworth, 199
Fort Washington, 78, 80, 83, 84, 85, 88, 92, 93, 101, 108, 109, 113, 173, 174, 175, 180, 181, 190, 193, 194, 195, 196, 197
Fort Washington Avenue, 193
Fort Washington Park, 193
Fort William Henry, 41
Fortification, 1, 92, 34, 104, 140, 169, 173, 196
Four Corners, 118, 119
Fowey, 78
Fox, Christopher P., 124
Fox, Elisha, 124
Fox Creek bridge, 52
Foxes Creek, 54
Framingham, 10
Frank Road, 112
Franklin, Benjamin, 199
Franklin, William, 145
Fraser Hill, 30
Fraser, Simon (1729–1777), 12, 14, 24, 32, 34, 39, 53, 69
Freeman's Farm, 32, 33, 34
Frelinghuysen, Frederick, 202
French, 1, 9, 17, 30, 43, 86, 91, 92, 105, 112, 122, 128, 129, 146, 147, 190, 191, 192, 207
French and Indian War, 11, 21 *see also* Seven Years War
French dragoons, 191
French grenadiers, 128
French hussars, 86
Fresh Kill, 198, 202
Freysbush, 64
Frog's Neck, or Point *see* Throgs Neck
Frog's Point *see also* Hunt's Point
Fugilman, 60
Fulton Avenue, 166
Fulton County Court House, 55
Fulton Street, 165
Fusiliers, 103

Gabions, 185
Gagsshongwa, 63
Gale, 74
Gallows Hill, 100, 101
Gallupville, 52
Gansevoort, Peter, 21, 22, 23, 35, 36
Garden Street, 139
Gardiner's Island, 131

Gardinier, Jacob, 64
Garlinghouse, Joseph, 60
Garoga Creek, 51
Gates, 19, 33
Gates, Horatio, 10, 16, 30, 31, 33, 34, 118, 195
General Monk, 92
General Wooster,, 135
Genesee, 63
Genesee River, 63
Geneseo, 63
Geneva, 63
George, 78, 200
George III, 134, 170
George Washington, 92
George Washington Bridge, 175, 193
George Washington High School, 196
Germain, George, 32
German Flats, 24, 48, 49, 50, 51, 67, 72, 73
German grenadiers, 163
German Regiment, 61
Germans, 11, 23, 34, 43, 97, 165, 166, 167, 194, 195
Getman, Frederick, 51
Giles Place, 175, 183
Gill, Erasmus, 99
Gist, Mordecai, 187, 188
Gist, Nathaniel, 90
Glenville, 106
Gloucester County, 1
Glover, John, 30, 85, 93, 94, 96, 97, 123, 167, 193
Glover, Mr., 146
Golden's Bridge, 197
Gondola, 76
Gordon Bennett Park, 193
Gordon, James, 71
Governor's Island, 74, 169, 170, 171, 174
Gowanus, 164, 172
Gowanus Bay, 162, 163, 165
Gowanus Creek, 166
Gracie Mansion, 178
Graham, John, 24
Graham, Morris, 168
Graham, Robert, 85
Grand Army Plaza, 160
Grand Battery, 174
Grant, Ensign, 42
Grant, James, 164, 165
Grant Memorial, 180
Grant's Tomb, 180, 181
Grape shot, 17, 78, 85, 89, 102, 103, 105, 106, 112, 138, 140, 147, 154, 195
Grasslands Hospital, 118
Graves, Thomas, 149
Gravesend Bay, 99, 158, 163, 172
Gray, James, 25
Gray, Neigal, 124
Great Bay, 168
Great Gull Island, 156
Great Lakes, 21
Great Neck, 153, 157
Great Peconic Bay, 143
Great South Bay, 156
Green Mountain Boys, 3, 9
Greenburg, 88
Greene, Christopher, 126, 127
Greene, Nathanael, 83, 93, 118, 161, 162, 181, 193, 195
Greenman, Jeremiah, 127
Greenville, 67
Greenwich Street, 175
Greenwich, Connecticut, 93, 106, 107, 110, 123, 148, 149, 152, 187, 197, 198

Gregg, William, 38
Grenadier's Battery, 43, 175
Grenadiers, 14, 39, 93, 120, 128, 163, 184, 194
Grey, Charles, 91
Grey, Major, 145
Greyhound, 201
Griffin, Samuel, 201
Gross, John, 67, 68
Groton, Connecticut, 107, 149, 157
Guard Hill Road, 129
Guards, 80, 86, 91, 119, 125, 127, 133, 140, 145, 146, 165, 177, 184, 185, 186, 197
Guilford, Connecticut, 139
Gull, Lieutenant, 94
Gunboats, 91, 92, 103

Hackensack, 195
Haerlem, 143
Haldimand, Frederick, 24, 117
Haggidorn, Derrick [Richard], 38
Haines, Alexander, 152
Hale, Nathan, 117, 179
Haley's Point, 202
Half Moon, 27, 42
Halifax, 136, 138, 148, 168, 177, 213
Hall Avenue, 55
Halsey's Point, 203
Halstead's Point, 204, 206, 208
Hamilton, James, 32
Hand, Edward, 61, 83, 163, 164
Hand's Brigade, 61
Hand's Cove, 9
Hand's New Jersey troops, 61
Hankins, John, 156
Hanover, 202
Harlem, 93, 134, 168, 186
Harlem Cove, 180, 181
Harlem Creek, 124, 125, 169, 181, 182, 183, 185, 194
Harlem Heights, 179, 180, 181, 182
Harlem Plain, 84, 182
Harlem Point, 169
Harlem River, 85, 119, 125, 128, 162, 174, 177, 178, 192, 194, 196, 197
Harles, David, 45
Harmood, Harry, 134
Harper, 66
Harper, Alexander, 60, 65
Harper, Colonel, 56
Harper, John, Jr., 37
Harpersfield, 59, 65
Harriman, General, 36
Harris, Robert, 199
Harrison, 129
Harrison Street, 175
Hart, Elisha, 134, 135, 143, 144, 156
Hart, Samuel, Sr., 143
Hart, William De, 176
Hartford, Connecticut, 10, 192
Haslet, John, 83, 108
Hatfield or Hetfield, Cornelius, Jr., 207
Hatfield or Hetfield, Job, 207
Hatfield or Hetfield, William, 212
Hatfield, Colonel, 123, 128
Hatfield, Isaac, 123
Hatfield Hill, 83
Havana, 62
Haverstraw, 79, 92, 112
Haverstraw Bay, 79, 111
Hawley, Thomas, 139, 154
Hazen, Moses, 197

Index

Hazen's Regiment, 198
Heath, William, 35, 88, 98, 100, 101, 122, 149, 167, 176, 177, 182, 184, 186, 193
Heathcote, Caleb, 168
Heely, Christopher, 81, 82
Heights of Guan, 162
Heister, Leopold von, 163, 164
Hellgate, 83, 171, 178
Helmer Adam F., 48, 49
Hempstead, 156
Hempstead Harbor, 134, 143, 151, 155
Hempstead Plains, 152
Hendricks, Baker, 211
Henley, Major, 178
Henry Clinton, 147
Henry Hudson Monument, 84, 174
Henry, John, 13
Herchheimer, Johan Jost, 48, 51
Herkimer, 36, 48
Herkimer village, 50
Herkimer, Nicholas, 22, 35, 36, 48, 51
Herringtown, 87
Hessian, 72, 80, 87
Hessian chasseurs, 194
Hessian dragoons, 39, 107
Hessian grenadiers, 93
Hessian jaegers, 72, 182, 186
Hessian riflemen, 168
Hessian troops, 98, 179, 201
Hessians, 38, 40, 41, 83, 84, 90, 95, 97, 98, 119, 151, 153, 163, 164, 170, 171, 174, 179, 181, 185, 186, 190, 192, 193, 196, 201, 211
Hetfield *see* Hatfield
Hewlets Island, 177
Hewlett, James, 152
Hewlett, John, 149
Hewlett, Richard, 134, 141
High Street, 201
Highland Avenue, 100, 101
Highland Falls, New York, 113
Highlanders, 178, 181, 182
Highlands, 100, 103, 183, 197
Hill, John, 25
Hinman, Benjamin, 16
Hoagland (or Hoogland), Oakley, 208
Hockaback, 134
Hog Island, 154
Hog Neck, 153
Holland's ferry, 192
Hollow Way, 180, 181
Holm, 81, 82
Honeoye, 63
Honeywell or Hunnewell, Israel, 125, 126
Hoosick Falls, New York, 39
Hoosick River, 38
Hopewell, 79
Hopkins, David, 104, 105, 119
Hopkins, David, 105
Hopkins, George, 43
Horn's Hook, 169, 174, 178, 181
Hornneck, Jacob, 78
Horseneck, 93, 94, 99, 106, 107, 110, 123, 148, 187, 198
Horton, Jotham, 88
Hospital Redoubt, 175
Hospital Rock, 59
House of Commons, 5, 29, 165
House of Lords, 34
Howe, 78
Howe, Richard, 162, 169, 173, 176, 179, 199

Howe, Robert, 91, 92, 151
Howe, William, 3, 5, 19, 22, 32, 83, 85, 92, 93, 97, 117, 135, 161, 162, 164, 165, 168, 173, 177, 179, 193, 200
Howell, James, 139
Howitzer, 10, 85, 88, 91, 92, 186, 208
Howorth, Captain, 104
Hubbardton, Vermont, 12, 14
Hubbell, Amos, 135
Hubley's Regiment, 61
Hudson, 7, 12, 30, 33, 89, 102, 104, 162
Hudson Highlands, 1, 81, 83
Hudson River, 1, 3, 27, 29, 30, 31, 43, 74, 76, 77, 78, 79, 80, 81, 82, 87, 88, 92, 100, 101, 103, 104, 105, 111, 112, 113, 114, 119, 167, 171, 175, 180, 193
Hudson Valley, 3, 20, 101, 102, 173
Huff, John, 54
Huggerford or Huggerssford, Major, 123, 128
Hull, William, 103, 124, 125, 197
Humphreys, David, 144, 187
Hunnewell *see* Honeywell
Hunt's Hill, 188
Hunt's Point, 177, 182 *see also* Throg's Point
Huntington Bay, 135, 136, 146, 147, 148
Huntington Harbor, 138, 146
Huntington, Jedediah, 129
Huntington, Long Island, 108, 134, 136, 137, 138, 145, 147, 148, 149
Hunt's or Frog's Point, 182
Hurlbut, George, 91
Hussars, 109, 121, 122, 129, 210
Hutchinson River Parkway, 94
Hutton, Lieutenant, 86
Hyatt's tavern, 185
Hylan Boulevard, Tottenville, 199
Hyler, Adam, 155, 156, 158, 172, 211, 212, 213

Icanderoga, 41
Inchenberg, 179, 180
Independence, 78
Indian Field, 183
Inflexible, 14, 19, 25
Inwood Hill, 174, 196
Iroquois, 1, 3, 22, 51, 60, 61, 66
Irvine, James, 209
Irvine, William, 208
Isle La Motte, 17
Islip, 154
Ives, David, 146

Jackson, Dan, 135
Jackson, Jacob S., 213
Jackson, Michael, 177
Jacob Purdy House, 82, 83
Jaeger Cavalry, 128
Jaegers, 50, 72, 87, 90, 97, 103, 105, 119, 120, 121, 123, 151, 163, 165, 182, 186, 188, 189, 190, 191
Jamaica, 134, 158
Jamaica Avenue, 163, 164
Jamaica Bay, 158
Jamaica Pass, 162, 163, 165
Jamaica Road, 164
Jamaica–Bedford road, 162, 163
James, 200
James, Nicholas, 43
Jameson, John, 116
Jeffery's Hook, 77
Jericho Turnpike, 144
Jerome Park Reservoir, 174, 183
Jersey, 161

Jersey Battery, 175
Jersey Militia, 208
Jervis, David, 153
Jockeytown, 101
Johnson Hall, 55, 56
Johnson Hall State Historic Site, 55
Johnson, Captain, 138
Johnson, Guy, 37, 45
Johnson, Henry, 111, 112
Johnson, John, 35, 50, 51, 52, 54, 55, 56, 63, 66, 71, 72
Johnson, Samuel, 43
Johnson, Walter, 73
Johnson, William, 36, 54, 55
Johnstown, 42, 44, 46, 50, 54, 56, 65
Johnstown Battlefield, 54
Jones Hill Fort, 175
Jones, Captain, 156
Jones, David, 29
Jones, Thomas, 154
Jones's farm, 181
Joseph, 78
Jumel mansion, 181

Kakeate, 87
Kakiat, 87, 88
Kanadesaga, 63
Kanagha, 63
Kanowalohale, 23
Katy, 212
Kayser *see* Keyser
Keeler, Samuel, Jr., 123
Keisar *see* Keyser
Keith, George Keith Elphinstone, viscount, 201
Kemble, Stephen, 165
Kentucky, 60
Keppel, 135
Kerr, John, 134
Ketcham, 155
Ketcham, Captain, 144
Ketchum, 156
Keyser (Kayser, Keisar), Johannes, 71
Kill van Kull, 199
Killing, Long Island, 148
Kimball Avenue, 184, 189
Kindaia', 62
King Street, 109, 110, 129
King's Bridge Avenue, 183
King's Ferry, 100, 103
King's American Dragoons, 136
Kings Highway, 161, 162, 164
Kingsbridge, 78, 83, 92, 93, 96, 98, 99, 103, 108, 123, 124, 125, 162, 171, 173, 183, 184, 185, 186, 187, 189, 190, 191, 192, 194, 197, 198, 204
Kingsbridge Redoubt, 175
Kingsbridge Road, 174
Kingsbury, 27
Kingston, 33, 43
Kingston Landing, 44
Kingston Point Park, 43
Kingstreet, 197
Kip's Bay, 83, 92, 179, 180, 181
Kipp, James, 107,128,129
Kissam, Benjamin T., 152
Kissam, Daniel, 152
Kissam, John, 153
Kittle, John, 69
Klock, Jacob, 50
Klock, Johann George, 72
Klock, Johannes, 72
Klock's Field, 71, 72

Knap, Mr., 106
Knight, John, 143
Knight, Lieutenant, 143
Knowlton, Thomas, 181
Knowlton's Rangers, 181
Knox, Henry, 10
Knox's artillery, 88
Knyphausen, Wilhelm von, 95, 97, 98, 169, 194, 209
Kosciusko, Thaddeus, 32, 113, 114
Kultonville, 64

Lackawaxen, Pennsylvania, 59
Ladies Delight, 213
Lady Gage, 176
Lady Washington, 76
Lake Champlain, 3, 8, 9, 11, 12, 13, 15, 17, 19, 20, 22, 24, 27, 29, 41, 42, 43, 66, 114
Lake George, 3, 5, 9, 12, 14, 16, 22, 29, 41, 42, 55
Lake George Battleground Park, 41
Lake Oneida, 21, 24, 42
Lake Ontario, 5, 22, 37
Lamb, Roger, 12
Lauzun, Armand Louis de Gontaut-Biron, Duc de, 122, 128, 190
Lauzun's Legion, 122, 129
Lawrence, Oliver, 124
Lawyer, Lawrence, 45, 46
Learned, Ebenezer, 32, 33
Leavenworth, David, 107
Lee, 19, 20
Lee, Charles, 83, 97, 169, 193, 195
Lee, Ezra, 170
Leitch, Andrew, 181
Lent's Cove, 101
Lent's Creek, 102, 103
Lesher, John, 205
Lewis, Morgan, 72
Lexington Avenue, 180
Liberty, 17, 19, 20
Liberty Bell, 95
Liberty Pole, 91
Light Dragoons, 116
Light infantry, 14, 39, 93, 108, 111, 120, 122, 146, 163, 164, 165, 177, 181, 184, 189, 190, 194
Lilly, Captain, 79
Lincoln, Benjamin, 12, 31, 43, 118, 128, 184, 186, 190
Line Kill, 37
Lispenard's Hill, 175
Lispenard's Redoubt, 175
Little Beard's town, 64
Little Falls, 45, 48, 51
Little Gull Island, 156
Little Peconic Bay, 143
Little White Creek, 40
Lively, 138
Livingston, Henry Beekman (1750-1831), 27
Livingston, Robert R., Sr., 44
Livingston, William, 199
Lloyd Harbor, 146, 147
Lloyd Harbor Rd., 145
Lloyd's beach, 138
Lloyd's Neck, 137, 145, 146
Lockwood, Daniel, 100, 123
Lockwood, Ebenezer, 121, 122
Lockwood, Samuel, 138
London, 5, 12, 29, 34, 118
Long Beach, 139, 211
Long Island, 3, 109, 127, 131, 135, 141, 148, 149, 153, 155, 156, 167, 171, 173, 178, 199, 200, 206, 207, 213

Index 253

Long Island Sound, 85, 107, 108, 128, 131, 133, 134, 135, 137, 139, 141, 143, 146, 147, 153, 169
Long Neck Point, 138
Long Wharf, 139, 154
Long, Edward, 52
Long, Pierse, 25
Lookout Hill, 161
loopholes, 71, 72, 199
Lord Chatham, 34
Lossburg, Friedrich Wilhelm von, 191
Lot, Jeromus, 156
Lott, Jerome, 155
Louis Atayataroughta, 72, 73
Lower Barracks, 174
Lower Fort, 52, 53, 65, 69
Loyal Convert, 19
Loyalist, 23, 26, 29, 36, 39, 43, 45, 47, 48, 49, 50, 51, 52, 56, 61, 64, 66, 67, 70, 71, 72, 78, 79, 80, 86, 110, 115, 119, 120, 123, 125, 126, 128, 129, 133, 134, 135, 136, 139, 141, 145, 146, 147, 149, 151, 154, 155, 156, 169, 175, 186, 189, 191, 199, 204, 205, 206, 207, 210, 211, 212
Loyalist artillery, 147
Loyalist dragoons, 86
Loyalist militia, 46, 147, 205, 206, 210, 211
Loyalist rangers, 47
Loyalists, 1, 5, 23, 24, 25, 26, 28, 30, 32, 36, 37, 38, 39, 40, 45, 46, 47, 49, 50, 51, 54, 55, 59, 60, 61, 65, 66, 67, 68, 70, 73, 78, 88, 93, 106, 107, 119, 120, 121, 128, 130, 138, 139, 191, 192, 193, 197, 200, 205
Ludlow, Cornelius, 151
Ludlow, George Duncan, 151
Luke, P., 144
Lutwidge, Skeffington, 24

Madison Avenue, 2
Madison Street, 174
Maffet, Captain, 211
Magaw, Robert, 83, 84, 193
Malaria, 162
Malcom or Malcolm, William, 24
Mamaroneck, 93, 107, 108, 123, 129, 138
Manhasset Valley, 152
Manhattan Avenue, 181
Manhattan Island, 74, 83, 92, 97, 120, 128, 140, 162, 167, 169, 170, 173, 174, 175, 179, 182, 183, 184, 190, 192, 193, 196, 198 *see also* York Island
Manheim, 45
Manor of St. George, 140, 141
Marblehead Regiment, 97, 167
Marenis, John, 45
Maria, 19
Marines, 74, 76, 79, 138, 143, 144, 166, 196, 199
Market Street, 174
Marks, Nehemiah, 157
Marriner, William, 160
Marsh, Christopher, 206
Martense Lane, 164
Martin, Sr. Silvanus., 152, 153
Martyrs' Monument, 161
Maryland, 108, 115
Maryland Monument, 161
Maryland Regiment, 166, 180, 181
Marylanders, 164
Massachusetts, 16, 115
Massachusetts Committee of Safety, 9, 15
Massachusetts militia, 84, 187
Massachusetts Provincial Congress, 16
Mastic, 141
Mastic Beach, 140

Mathew, Edward, 86, 194
Matrosses, 167
Matthews, David, 160
Mattituck, Long Island, 157
Maxwell, Hugh, 124, 197
Maxwell, William, 61
Maxwell's Brigade, 61
Mayfield Patent, 65
McClennan, Thomas, 58
McCrea, Jane "Jenny," 27, 29
McDonald, Donald, 50
McDonald, John, 37
McDonald, Lewis, 151
McDougall, Alexander, 83, 101, 102, 103, 199
McGinnie, Teddy, 49
McGowan's Pass Redoubt, 175
McGowan's Pass, 181
McGregor, Captain, 51
McGregor's Company, 51
McKean, Robert, 68, 72, 73
McKenzie, Kenneth, 143
McKoy, Captain or McCoy, 13
McLean Avenue, 189
Mead, John, 123
Mead's Regiment, 123
Medal of Honor, 151
Meeker, Samuel, 206
Meigs Monument, 139
Meigs, Return Jonathan, 134, 139, 144, 145, 187, 192
Mercer, Hugh, 194, 201
Mercereau or Mersereau, Jacob, 206
Mercury, 79, 81, 103, 106, 196
Merritt, Thomas , 107
Merritt's tavern, 129
Mersereau *see* Mercereau
Mianos Creek, 99
Middle Country Road, 144
Middle Fort, 53, 69, 70
Middle Fort Road, 69
Middle Patent, 127, 128
Middleburg, 37, 52, 53, 69
Middlesex, Connecticut, 147
Middleton, 153, 154
Middletown, 213
Middletown Point, 160
Mifflin, 134
Mile Square, 90, 97, 99, 124, 184, 188
Mile Square Road, 184, 189, 191
Miles, Samuel, 163
Militia, 1, 13, 14, 22, 26, 27, 32, 34, 35, 36, 38, 39, 40, 41, 42, 45, 46, 47, 49, 54, 59, 65, 66, 67, 68, 73, 84, 87, 88, 98, 99, 100, 106, 107, 110, 119, 120, 122, 123, 124, 130, 131, 133, 146, 147, 149, 152, 156, 162, 179, 186, 187, 193, 195, 200, 205, 206, 208, 210, 211
Militiamen, 2, 11, 12, 17, 21, 22, 25, 26, 35, 36, 37, 38, 46, 48, 49, 50, 51, 56, 59, 60, 63, 66, 67, 68, 69, 71, 72, 74, 82, 87, 89, 91, 94, 98, 99, 100, 102, 110, 116, 118, 119, 123, 124, 127, 128, 129, 131, 133, 143, 145, 147, 154, 155, 160, 162, 176, 181, 189, 195, 199, 202, 205, 206, 207, 211, 212
Mill Creek, 136
Mill Neck, 138
Mill Street, 48
Miller Hill, 82, 85
Miller, Dirck, 46
Miller, Mary, 68
Miller, Mr., 135
Miller, Richard, 135
Millville, 142

Milton, 110
Minden, 64
Minisink, 54, 59, 60, 66
Minisink Ford, 59
Minutemen, 52
Mitchell's Landing, 151
Mohawk, 2, 22, 49, 56, 64, 66, 72
Mohawk River, 21, 41, 42, 44, 45, 48, 54, 56, 64, 65, 72, 73
Mohawk Valley, 2, 3, 5, 10, 22, 35, 44, 46, 47, 50, 60, 61, 64, 66, 67, 72
Mohawks, 22, 24, 60, 65
Moncrieff, James, 160
Money, Captain, 25
Monmouth County, 206, 210
Montagu, James, 79, 81
Montauk, 131
Montcalm de Saint-Véran, Louis Joseph Marquis de, 9
Montgomery Street, 27
Montgomery, Samuel, 26
Montréal, 35, 66
Montresor, John, 177
Montresor's Island, 174, 177, 178, 183, 186
Monument Avenue, 39
Monument Circle, 39
Moody, James, 130
Morgan, Daniel, 12, 30, 32, 33, 49, 61, 64
Morgan's riflemen, 33, 49, 64
Morris house, 83
Morris Charles, 44
Morris, Robert, 118
Morrisania, 86, 98, 123, 124, 125, 126, 128, 129, 169, 182, 186, 190, 191, 192, 193, 197
Morrisania Point, 192
Morris–Jumel Mansion, 180, 193
Morris's house, 182
Morristown, New Jersey, 208
Mortars, 10, 72, 85
Moses Creek, 22
Mosher, William, 127, 129
Mosquito, 148
Mosquito Cove, 138, 155
Mott, Edward, 15
Mount Beacon, 79
Mount Defiance, 8, 11, 13, 15, 24
Mount Hope, 11, 14
Mount Independence, 8, 11, 13, 14, 26, 43
Mount Independence State Historic Site, 13
Mount Kisco, 100, 122, 127
Mount Pleasant, 118
Mount Vernon, 98, 187, 189
Mount Vernon Avenue, 184, 189
Moylan, Stephen, 93, 104, 193
Moylan's dragoons, 93, 104,193
Muirson, Heathcote, 146, 147
Muirson, Sylvester, 86
Munroe, John, 71
Murfree, Hardy, 111
Murphy Road, 52
Murphy, Timothy, 34, 52, 53, 69
Murray Hill, 180
Musquetoons, 134
Mutton Hollow, 137

Narrows, 163, 198, 199, 200, 206, 212, 213
Nassau Ferry, 199
Nassau Road, 145
National Museum of American History, 18
National Purple Heart Hall of Honor, 151

Native American, 3, 5, 9, 19, 25, 26, 27, 29, 30, 36, 37, 38, 46, 49, 50, 51, 52, 56, 59, 60, 61, 62, 63, 64, 70, 94, 189
Native Americans, 3, 5, 9, 11, 12, 16, 17, 19, 21, 22, 23, 24, 25, 26, 27, 28, 29, 30, 31, 32, 35, 36, 37, 38, 39, 40, 41, 42, 45, 46, 47, 48, 49, 50, 51, 54, 55, 56, 57, 58, 59, 60, 61, 62, 66, 67, 68, 71, 73, 134, 189
Negro Fort, 186
Neilson, John, 207
Neptune, 153, 207
Netherland Avenue, 174
New Battery, 174
New Blazing Star, 201, 202
New Bridge, 185
New Brunswick, New Jersey, 20, 156, 212, 207
New Canaan, 146
New City Island, 168
New Dorlach, 67
New England, 1, 12, 16, 31, 100, 111, 120, 135
New England militia, 29, 39
New England militiamen, 31, 74
New Englanders, 10, 16, 133, 135, 181
New Hampshire, 1, 115
New Hampshire Grants, 3
New Hampshire men, 40
New Haven, 20, 133, 155
New Haven, Connecticut, 131
New Hempstead, 87
New Jersey, 83, 115, 125, 172, 175, 190, 193, 195, 198, 202, 204
New Jersey militiamen, 60, 176, 206, 210, 211
New Jersey troops, 57
New Jersey Volunteers, 1st Battalion, 134, 211
New Jersey Volunteers, 3rd Battalion, 202
New levies, 74, 98
New London, Connecticut, 131, 131, 148, 149, 155, 156
New Paltz, 68
New Rochelle, 83, 93, 94, 97, 98, 107, 108, 110, 123, 169, 184, 197
New Rochelle Harbor, 168, 169
New Windsor Cantonment, 151
New Windsor, New York, 106, 151
New York, 1, 2, 3, 5, 9, 15, 16, 18, 20, 33, 34, 35, 39, 43, 54, 55, 57, 58, 60, 61, 67, 69, 73, 74, 77, 81, 82, 83, 86, 88, 89, 92, 96, 97, 98, 103, 106, 107, 110, 111, 115, 116, 122, 123, 130, 134, 138, 139, 144, 152, 154, 158, 162, 167, 168, 169, 170, 171, 173, 174, 175, 176, 179, 186, 190, 194, 195, 197, 199, 200, 202, 204, 208, 209, 211, 212, 213
New York City, 182, 183
New York Bay, 1, 3, 19, 39, 74, 80, 98, 149, 167, 170, 175, 176, 183, 186, 198, 204
New York harbor, 158, 176, 198
New York highlands, 12, 193, 195
New York levies, 69, 126, 128, 129
New York militia, 24, 25, 36, 43, 47, 124, 186
New York Provincial Congress, 16
New York Provincial Convention, 170
New York Public Library, 179
New York State Museum, 2
New York troops, 98
New York University's Hall of Chemistry, 174
New Yorkers, 16
Newark, New Jersey, 11, 135, 209
Newburgh, 79, 105, 106
Newport, Rhode Island, 20, 131, 134, 135, 146, 147, 156
Newtown Battlefield, 60

Index 255

Newtown Battlefield Reservation, 60
Niagara, 50, 52
Nicholas Schenck house, 158
Niger, 137, 148, 168, 171, 172, 177
Niles, Robert, 133
Nimham, Daniel, 183, 189
Nixon, John, 26, 30, 181
North River *see* Hudson River
North Carolina, 3
North Castle, 85, 99, 100, 104, 116, 122, 127, 128, 129, 186, 193
North Country Road, 131, 133
North Main Street, Schoharie, 52
North Market Street, 55
North River, 43, 74, 78, 82, 83, 84, 88, 108, 109, 191
North Stamford, Connecticut, 146
Norton, Chapel, 86, 119
Norton's Guards, 119
Norwalk Islands, 108, 148
Norwalk, Connecticut, 134 136, 138, 148
Nostrand Avenue, 165
Noyack Road, 139
Noyack–Long Beach Road, 139
Nutten Island, 169, 170
Nyack, 87

Oak Neck, 148
Oakley, Miles, 85
Oath of allegiance, 40, 201
Oblenus Ford, 126
Ocean Drive West, 145
Odgensburg, 57
Ogden, Matthias, 202, 203
Ogden's Regiment, 61
Ogilvie, Mr., 187
Old Blazing Star, 198, 203, 209
Old Cadet Chapel, 113
Old Fort House Museum, 27
Old Fort Street, 27
Old Man's (Mt. Sinai) Harbor, 134, 135, 141, 142
Old Star, 212
Old Stone Fort, 52
Old Stone Fort Museum Complex, 52
Old Storm King Highway, 113
Olney, Jeremiah, 127
Ommanney, Cornthwaite, 89
Onandago Castle, 59
Oneida, 22, 51, 73
Oneida Carry, 21
Oneida Creek, 42
Oneida Lake, 23, 42, 71
Oneidas, 22, 23, 42, 49, 50, 56, 72
Oneonta, 65
Onondagas, 22, 46, 50, 57
Onondago Creek, 58
Onondagos, 59
Oquaga Creek, 64
Orange County militia, 87
Oregon Road, 100
Oriskany, 22, 36, 48
Oriskany Battlefield, 35
Orpheus, 171, 179, 201
Orwell, 13
Ossernenon, 66
Ossining, 87 *see also* Singsing
Oswegatchie, 58
Oswegatchie River, 57
Oswego, 5, 22, 23, 37, 42, 56, 73
Oswegoche, 50

Otsego County, 47
Otsego Lake, 47
Owl Kill, 38
Oyster Bay, 136, 138, 139, 145, 146, 147, 152
Oyster Bay militiamen, 147

Palatine Bridge, 71
Palatine Church, 72
Palatine house, 52
Palatine villages, 48
Palisade, 41, 71, 174, 193
Palfrey, John, 207
Panther Mountain, 38
Panton, Vermont, 20
Parapet, 57, 114, 146, 147
Paris, Isaac, 71
Park Avenue, 135
Parker, Hyde, Jr., 77, 78, 79, 87
Parkway Drive, 139
Parley, 41
Parliament, 1, 165
Parrot, James, 143
Parsons, Samuel Holden, 125, 134, 139, 141, 146, 184, 187, 197, 198
Patchogue, 148
Patrick, William, 45, 46
Patterson, Alexander, 201
Paulus Hook, 74, 170
Pavillion Hill, 199
Pawling, Albert, 50, 69
Pearl, 78, 84, 194
Pearl Street, 174
Pearsall, Thomas, 152
Peconic Bay, 139
Peekskill, 74, 89, 100, 101, 102, 103, 120, 190, 193
Peekskill Bay, 101
Pelham Bay Park, 92, 154
Pelham Manor, 92, 93, 95
Pell, Stephen, 5
Pell, William Ferris, 5
Pell's Point, 83, 92, 97
Pembroke, 78
Pennsylvania, 54, 115, 195, 212
Pennsylvania Regiment, 164
Pennsylvania riflemen, 83, 163
Pennsylvanians, 164
Percy, Hugh, 83, 165, 167, 181, 194
Perseus, 201
Perth Amboy, New Jersey, 20, 205
Petri, Daniel, 51
Petri, John Joost, 51
Pettiauger, 81, 89, 105
Phelps, Noah, 15
Philadelphia, 18, 20, 22, 34, 95, 156, 195, 211
Philip's farm, 187
Phillip's bridge, 90, 188
Phillips Farm, 90
Phillips, Frederick, 89
Phillips, William, 8, 11, 14, 24
Phillips's house, 190, 191
Phillips's mills, 88
Phillipsburgh, 88, 89, 90, 129, 174, 187
Phipps, Charles, 171
Phoenix, 74, 76, 77, 78, 79, 87, 88, 158, 170, 171, 176, 179, 200
Phoenix Avenue, 100, 101
Pickering, Timothy, 118
Picket guard, 11
Pickford, Joseph, 143

Pierpoint, Joseph, 155
Pine Hills, 107
Pines Bridge, 120, 126, 127, 128, 197
Pines Bridge Road, 118
Pinnace, 74
Plank, Frederick, 64
Platt Carll, 137
Plum Island, 131, 156
Point au Fer, 15
Point Comfort, 213
Point Lookout, 156
Polhemus, John, 208
Pollepel's Island, 82
Pontoon bridge, 197
Poor, Enoch, 33, 61
Poor's Brigade, 61
Pope, Charles, 151
Popolopen Creek, 80
Port Chester, 106, 134
Port Jervis, 59
Port Richmond, 199, 207
Port Washington, 157
Portage, 9, 12, 21, 27, 29
Post, Nathan, 148
Post Road, 101, 109, 175, 183
Poughkeepsie, 43, 105, 106
Pound Ridge, 121, 122
Powell, Henry Watson, 43
Presbyterian church, 134
Prendergast, Matthew, 144
Preston, 81
Prime, Ebenezer, 137
Prince Frederick Regiment, 43
Prince's Bay, 206, 211, 213
Princeton, 20
Prisoners of war, 195, 203, 204
Pritchard, Thomas, 124, 125, 126
Privateer, 92, 136, 137, 138, 145, 146, 148, 149, 154, 156
Proctor's artillery, 61
Prospect Park, 160, 165
Provincial Congress of New York, 16
Pruschenk, Major, 90, 190
Purdy Hill, 83
Purple Heart, 150, 151
Putman, John, 44
Putnam County, 87
Putnam, Israel, 1, 44, 99, 103, 110, 162, 180, 181, 187, 194
Putnam, Rufus, 12, 102, 113, 114

Quackenboss, Abraham D., 64
Quaker, 121, 160
Quarme, William, 148, 168, 177
Quartermaster General, 118
Québec, 34, 41, 115, 118
Québeck, 15
Queen's American Rangers, 108
Queen's Rangers, 87, 93, 98, 107, 109, 110, 121, 123, 139, 186, 188, 189, 209, 210
Queens, 178
Queens County militia, 152
Quibbletown, 207
Quigley, Robert, 212, 213

Rahway, New Jersey, 206, 209, 210
Randall's Island *see* Montresor's Island
Randle, Captain, 206
Ranson, Samuel, 47
Raritan Landing, 207
Raritan River, 155

Rattlesnake Hill, 11, 13
Raven, 136, 145
Rawdon, Francis, 122, 179
Rawlings, Moses, 195
Reade Street, 175
Rechtmyer, George, 69
Red Hook, 74, 169, 170
Red Lion Inn, 164
Redoubt, 34, 74, 112, 124, 134, 146, 174, 185, 186, 191, 193, 195, 199
Redoubt No. 8, 124, 192
Redoubt No. 10, 151
Reed, Joseph, 97, 181
Reed's Regiment, 61
Reese, John, 45
Refugee, 50, 78, 145, 146
Renown, 78, 179
Repulse, 78, 84
Reservoir Avenue, 174
Restoration, 146, 156
Revenge, 19, 20, 148
Revere, Paul, 7
Rhinecliff, 106
Rhode Island, 20, 90, 115, 133
Rhode Island Regiment, 126
Rhode Islanders, 127
Rhynebeck, 43
Rhynebeck Flats, 44
Richards, Samuel, 74
Richland Road, 90
Richmond, 202, 207, 210
Richmond Town, 158, 198, 200, 201, 208
Ridgebury, 128
Ridgefield, 122
Ridgeway Ave., 133
Riedesel, Friedrich von, 12, 29, 32, 33, 39
Rifle companies, 181
Riflemen, 12, 30, 32, 59, 182, 187, 200, 201
Rising Sun Tavern, 164
Riverside Drive, 181, 193
Roberts, Captain, 92
Roberts, Moses, 119
Robin's Reef, 211
Robins, Captain, 212
Robinson, Beverley, 187
Rochambeau, Jean Baptiste Donatien de Vimeur Comte de, 116, 125
Rochester, 63
Rockaway Path, 165
Rodman's Point, 97
Rodney, George Brydges, 149
Roebuck, 88, 170, 171
Rogers, Captain, 144
Rogers, Robert, 108
Rogers Island, 27
Rogers Island Visitors Center, 27
Rogers Rangers, 27
Rome, New York, 21
Rondout Creek, 44
Roosevelt Island, 176
Rose, 74, 76, 77, 78, 79, 170, 171, 175, 176, 179
Rosebank, 199
Rose, Private, 37
Ross, John, 42, 50, 55, 56, 67, 73, 188
Rossville Avenue, 198
Round Hill, 86
Round shot, 23, 78, 89, 90, 102, 103, 104, 105, 106, 140, 171, 186
Rowe, John, 135
Roxbury, Massachusetts, 101

Index 257

Royal Artillery, 171
Royal George, 14, 25
Royal Greens, 37, 56, 66
Royal Greens, 2nd battalion, 50
Royal Highland Regiment (Black Watch), 196
Royal Navy, 3
Royal Provincials, 205
Royal Refugees, 144
Royal Savage, 19, 20
Ruckstull, Frederic Wellington, 160
Rue, Benjamin, 18
Rumford, Count, 136
Rutgers Hill, 174
Rutledge, Edward, 199
Rye, 99, 109
Rye Neck, 110
Rye Woods, 109
Rye-Pond, 110
Ryerson's Ferry, 208
Ryker, John, 208

Sabbath Day Point, 13
Sabre, 123
Sacanda, 46
Sacandaga, 65
Sacandaga Lake, 65
Sacandaga River, 66
Sachem's Head, 139
Sackett, Richard, 126, 127, 128, 129
Sackintago, 44
Sacondaga, 55
Sag Harbor, 131, 139, 153
Saint Coick's Mill *see* Sancoick's Mill
Salisbury, 45, 73
Sally, 186
Salsberry, Herman, 45
Salt Lake, 58
Salt works, 110
Salter, Mr., 211
Sammons, Jacob, 50, 68, 72
San Coick's Mill *see* Sancoick's Mill
Sancoick's Mill , 38, 40
Sand Flats, 66
Sandy Hook, 1, 100, 176, 201
Sandy Hook lighthouse, 199, 211
Sanford, Peter, 207
Saratoga, 12, 22, 30, 31, 32, 33, 34, 35, 81, 115
Saratoga National Historical Park, 30
Saratoga Victory Monument, 30
Sargent, Paul Dudley, 85, 88
Sargent's Regiment, 85
Savage, 92, 200
Saw Log Swamp, 134
Saw Mill Creek, 87
Saw Mill River Road, 118, 119
Saw Mill Road, 188
Saw Mill Valley, 90, 190
Saw Pits *see* Sawpits
Sawmill River, 127, 128
Sawpits or Saw Pits, 106, 110, 134
Saybrook, Connecticut, 156, 157
Scalp, 5, 11, 21, 23, 24, 26, 28, 30, 37, 50, 51, 56, 59, 60, 61, 62, 65, 66, 68, 73
Scammel, Alexander, 129, 197
Scammel's Regiment, 61
Schank, John, 160
Schenectady, 24, 36, 55
Schenck, Nicholas, 160
Schoharie, 37, 42, 45, 46, 49, 51, 54, 55, 59, 65, 66, 67, 69

Schoharie County Historical Society, 52
Schoharie Creek, 41, 56, 69
Schoharie Native Americans, 45, 46
Schoharie River, 37
Schoharie Valley, 2, 24, 37, 46, 50, 51, 54, 65
Schoyere, 63
Schuyler, 134
Schuyler, Philip, 10, 12, 16, 21, 25, 29, 30, 31
Schuylerville, 30, 32
Scotch Cove, 138
Scots, 164
Scott, Charles, 90, 184
Scovel or Scovil, Daniel, 154
Seaman, Uriah, 156
Searl, William, 143
Second Avenue, 164, 179
Secretary at War, 118
Sedgwick Avenue, 174, 175, 183
Seneca Castle, 63
Seneca Falls, 63
Seneca Lake, 62, 63
Senecas, 3, 22, 46, 54, 63
Senegal, 136
Sentinel Rock, 59
Serle, Ambrose, 179
Service, Joseph Brant, 46, 52
Setauket, 131, 133, 134, 135, 145, 157
Setauket Presbyterian Church, 133
Seven Mile Island, 59
Seven Years, 1
Seven Years War, 27, 48 *see also* French and Indian War
Shank, David, 210
Sharon Springs, 67
Sharon Springs Swamp, 68
Sheldon 's dragoons, 87, 91, 94, 104, 123, 169, 193
Sheldon, Elisha, 87, 91, 93, 104, 109, 121, 122, 123, 141, 169, 190, 193
Shell's Bush, 48, 50
Shelter Island, 143
Shepard, William, 74, 97
Sherburne's Redoubt, 113
Sherman, Peleg, 197
Sherrard's Bridge, 106
Sherwood, Seth, 26, 27
Sherwood's Bridge, 106
Shew, Godfrey, 45
Shew, Jacob, 45
Shew, Stephen, 45
Shippan Point, 108, 109, 145
Shippen, Margaret, 115
Shipyard Battery, 175
Shoemaker Lane, 137
Shoreham, Vermont, 9, 137
Short's Corps, 61
Shrewsbury Point, 211
Shrewsbury, New Jersey, 212
Shrive's Regiment, 61
Shuldham, 77
Shutter Corners, 52
Sidman's Clove, 130
Siege, 9, 20, 22, 23, 35, 36, 141, 161, 173, 193, 200
Signal Hill, 199
Sill, Thomas, 42
Silliman, Gold Sellick, 146
Simcoe, John Graves, 85, 87, 90, 93, 109, 121, 123, 139, 186, 187, 188, 205, 207, 208, 209
Simmons, Morris, 125, 154
Singsing, 87, 105, 190, 191
Sir H. Clinton, 135
Sir John's regiment, 72

Six Nations, 1, 3, 16, 22, 62
Skaigus, 63
Skene, Philip, 15, 24, 25, 40
Skenesborough Falls, 25
Skenesborough, Vermont, 14, 24, 25, 26, 43
Skinner, Cortlandt, 203, 204, 208
Skinner, Gershom, 51
Skinner, Richard, 206
Skinner's Corps, 204
Slapshine (Sleepshine) Island, 44
Sleight, Mr., 206
Slough, Matthias, 201, 203
Smallwood, William, 180, 202
Smith Tavern, 144
Smith, Captain, 52, 133
Smith, Jacob, 133
Smith, Samuel, 201, 203
Smith, William (1728-1793), 206
Smith's Point, 140, 141
Smithsonian Institution, 18
Smithtown, Long Island, 144, 149
Snowshoes, 73
Snyders Bush, 45
Soissonais Regiment, 91
Soldier's Spring, 100
Somerset County, 60
South Amboy, New Jersey, 176, 207, 213
South Bay, 14, 25, 26, 148, 213
South Bronx, 123, 177
South Carolina, 3
South Columbus Avenue, 94
South Ferry, 175
South Oyster Bay, 139
South River, 207, 208
South Woodhull Road, 135
Southold, 131, 134, 139, 143, 153, 155, 157
Spalding's Company, 61
Spanktown, 202
Spencer, Joseph, 181, 192
Spencer's Regiment, 61
Spitfire, 20, 76, 81, 90, 103, 105, 106
Split Rock, 20, 94
Split Rock Road, 94, 97
Spoor, John, 21
Springfield, 47
Spuyten Duyvil, 184, 186, 190, 191
Spuyten Duyvil Creek, 78, 128, 174, 175, 183, 185, 191, 196
Spuyten Duyvil Hill, 174
Spy/Spies, 7, 115, 116, 117, 122, 125, 151, 179
Spy, 133, 134
St. Andrew's Church, 201
St. Clair, Arthur, 11, 24, 25
St. John's, Canada, 20, 35, 66
St. John's Episcopal Church, 55
St. Johnsville, 72
St. Lawrence River, 5, 57
St. Leger, Barry, 5, 22, 32, 35, 36, 42
St. Paul's Episcopal Church, 94, 98
St. Stephen's Church, 183
Stamford (Connecticut) Yacht Club, 145
Stamford harbor, 138
Stamford, Connecticut, 99, 108, 110, 135, 138, 145, 146, 153
Stamp Act, 1
Stamp Act Congress, 1
Stanhope, Captain, 136
Stanwix, John, 21
Staring, Adam, 49
Stark, John, 35, 38, 40, 41

Stark's militia, 38
State Street, 174
Staten Island, 78, 86, 158, 162, 163, 173, 176, 187, 198, 200, 201, 202, 204, 205, 206, 208, 210, 211, 213
Stedman, Charles, 102
Stephens, Shore, 212
Stephenson *see* Stevenson
Sterling Iron Works, 114
Sterling, General, 194
Stevenson, Hugh, 200
Stevenson's riflemen, 200
Stewart, John (d. 1782), 111, 112
Stillwater, New York, 29, 30, 39
Stockade, 14, 26, 52, 63, 69, 134, 141, 145, 149, 150
Stockbridge Indians, 183, 189
Stone Arabia, 54, 71
Stone House, 70
Stony Brook, 157
Stony Point, 79, 80, 103, 104, 112
Stony Point Battlefield State Historic Site, 110
Storer, John, 211, 213
Storm, Garret, 79, 80
Storm King, 106
Storm King State Park, 106
Storm's Bridge, 87
Storms's wood, 105
Stratford Connecticut, 154
Strombolo, 171
Strong, Mr., 154
Stuyvesant, Mr., 74
Submarine, 88
Suffern, 130
Suffolk County, 108, 154
Sugar Act, 1
Sugar Loaf, 11
Sugar Loaf Hill, 13, 14, 15
Sukey, 158
Sullivan Co., 54
Sullivan Hill, 60
Sullivan, John, 49, 60, 61, 62, 63, 64, 160, 162, 163, 202, 203, 204
Sullivan's artillery, 62
Superintendent of Finance, 118
Susannah, 211
Susquehanna, 51
Susquehannah River, 59
Sutton, William, 138
Swallow, 149
Swan, 134, 135, 143
Switz, Abraham, 36
Swivel gun, 15, 17, 18, 19, 134, 135, 138, 146, 148, 213
Sycamore Avenue, 84, 174
Sylvester, Muirson, 107
Syracuse, 57

Talbert, Captain, 78
Talbot, George, 137, 148, 172, 177
Tallmadge, Benjamin, 108, 116, 122, 141, 145, 146, 147, 149, 157
Tappan, 88, 91, 190
Tappan Bay, 74
Tappan Meadows, 87
Tappan Zee, 74, 77
Tappan, New York, 117
Tappen, Ashar, 206
Tarleton, Banastre, 85, 86, 120, 121, 122, 186, 187, 188, 189
Tarleton's Legion, 120, 122, 187, 189

Index

Tarrytown, 52, 74, 79, 81, 87, 90, 91, 101, 104, 105, 116, 118, 184, 192
Tarrytown road, 105
Tartar, 79, 88, 89, 91, 104, 196
Teller's Point, 88, 89, 90, 92, 104
Terrat, Peter, 212
Terry Point, 131, 143
Thacher, James, 120
The Father's Desire, 100
Third Avenue, 161
Thomas, Captain, 146
Thomas, John, Jr. (1751-1819), 109, 110
Thomas, John, Sr. (1720-1811), 109
Thompson, Benjamin, 136
Thompson, John, 125
Thompson, Joseph, 119
Thorne, Edward, 151
Thorne, Stephen, 151
Throckmorton's or Throgmorton's Neck, 168
Throg's Neck, 83, 92, 124, 125, 157, 168, 169, 197
Throg's Point, 92, 97, 168, 177
Thunderer, 19
Tibbett's Hill, 185
Ticonderoga, 5, 10, 11, 20, 26, 42, 43, 66
Tienonderoga, 41
Timpany, Robert, 201
Tioga, 61
Toepath Mountain, 53
Tomahawk, 21, 36, 56
Tompkinsville, 199
Tompkinville, 199
Topsand Bay, 74
Totten, Gilbert, 125, 191
Townsend, John, 138
Townsend, Robert, 116
Trading post, 71
Travis Hil, 85
Treadwell's Farm, 149
Treadwell's Neck, 149
Tredwell, Dr. Benjamin, 152
Tredwell's Farm, 149
Trenton, New Jersey, 20, 137
Trescott Lemuel, 120, 125, 149
Tribes Hill, 44
Trinity Lutheran Church., 71
Trophy Point, 113, 114, 115
Trumback Regiment, 103
Trumbull, 19, 20
Trumbull, Jonathan, 139, 152, 153, 154
Tryal, 74, 77, 78, 79, 88
Tryon County militiamen, 51
Tryon, William, 99, 103, 110, 176, 200
Tupper, Benjamin, 77
Turkehoe, 98
Turkey Mountain, 127
Turncoat, 36
Turtle, 88, 170
Turtle Bay, 175
Turtle Bay Depot, 175
Tuscaroras, 3, 22, 49
Tusten, Benjamin, 59
Twin Hills, 101
Two Brothers, 153
Tye, Colonel, 210
Tyler, Captain, 54

U.S. Military Academy, 113, 114
U.S. Veterans Hospital, 174
Unadilla, 49, 52
Unadilla River, 48

Union Street, 139
Unionville, 118
Unionville Road, 118
United Nations Building, 175, 179
United States Custom House, 174
United States Military Academy, 113, 114
University Avenue, 174
University Heights, 174
Upper Barracks, 174
Upper Barracks Guard, 175
Upper Fort, 52, 59, 69
Upper Van Cortlandt Manor House, 100
Upstate New York, 44
Utica, 73
Utman, Peter, 46

Valcour Island, 16, 19, 115
Valentine's Hill, 183, 187, 188, 190
Valentine's house, 184, 185, 186
Valentine–Varian house, 183
Van Burrens Mills, 105
Van Buskirk, Abraham, 202, 204, 208
Van Buskirk, Jacob, 204
Van Cortlandt House Museum, 183
Van Cortlandt mansion, 183
Van Cortlandt Park, 183, 189
Van Cortlandt, Philip, 24, 184, 187
Van Cortlandt's house, 186
Van Cortlandtville, 100, 101
Van Den Burgh Road, 65
Van Rensselaer, Henry B., 25, 26
Van Rensselaer, Philip, 26
Van Rensselaer, Robert, 63, 71, 72, 73
Van Schaick, Goose, 46, 57, 58, 59
Van Schaick's Mill *see* Sancoick's Mill
Van Schaick's troops, 58
Van Tassel, Cornelius, 90
Van Wart, Isaac, 113
Van Zuyler, John, 64, 65
Van Zuyler's house, 64
Vandeput, George, 175, 176, 200
Varnum, James Mitchell, 99
Vaughan *see* Vaughn
Vaughn, John, 44, 86, 103, 104
Veeder, Volkert, 68
Venus, 149
Vermont, 3, 20, 39, 115, 118
Vermont militia, 38, 41
Vermont rangers, 40
Verplanck's Point, 89, 100, 103, 104, 110, 112
Verrazano–Narrows Bridge, 163, 199
Victory, 213
Vincent, Jeremiah, 86
Virginia, 3, 34, 108, 118
Virginia riflemen, 61, 186
Visscher *see* Fisher
Von Donop, Count Karl Emil Kurt, 163
Von Rau, Carl, 128
Von Wreden, Carl August, 90, 188
Von Wurmb, Ludwig Johann Adolph, 87, 105, 153, 187, 188, 191, 199
Voorhees, Peter, 208
Vroman, Ephraim, 66
Vrooman, Isaac, 37
Vrooman, Peter, 37, 65
Vrooman, Walter, 63
Vrooman's, 37, 38
Vulture, 112, 116

Wading River, 137, 157

Wakefield, Charles, 143
Waldeckers, 97, 202
Wall Street, 173
Wallabout Bay, 161
Wallace, James, 74, 77, 79, 175, 176
Walloomsac River, 40
Walton, Abraham, 155
Wappingers Creek, 105
Ward, Andrew, 99
Ward, Samuel, Jr., 126
Ward, Stephen, 96, 98
Ward's house, 98, 99, 110
Wards Island, 177
Warner, George, 46
Warner, George, Sr., 54
Warner, Jonathan, 187
Warner, Seth, 15, 41, 42
Warren Street, 174
Warrensbush, 42, 55, 56, 67
Washington, 19, 20, 85
Washington Heights, 193
Washington Park, 161
Washington Street, 101, 175
Washington, George, 1, 3, 10, 12, 16, 19, 20, 27, 31, 34, 45, 57, 60, 83, 92, 93, 100, 108, 110, 112, 116, 125, 126, 129, 130, 141, 142, 146, 149, 151, 161, 162, 167, 168, 169, 170, 171, 173, 177, 179, 180, 181, 190, 192, 193, 197, 204, 207, 209
Waterbury, David, 169, 190
Waterbury's Battery, 175
Watering party, 89
Watering Place, 74, 199, 200, 201, 202, 208, 209, 213
Watson, Abraham, 119
Watson, Titus, 99
Watsonville, 52
Wawarsing, 68
Wayne,'Mad Anthony", 111
Wayne Avenue, 112
Webb, Samuel Blachley, 93, 134
Webb's Regiment, 93
Welcher Avenue, 101
Wells 3rd, Thomas, 149
West 106th Street, 181
West 125th Street, 180, 181
West 147th, 180
West 161st Street, 181
West 230th Street, 84, 174, 183
West Broadway, 175
West Canada Creek, 48, 50, 51, 56, 73
West Chester, 93, 125, 183, 192
West Farm Point, 177
West Farms, 124, 183, 186, 189
West Indies, 139
West Neck Rd, 145
West New Brighton, 201
West Point, 1, 80, 106, 116, 120, 195
West Point Museum, 113
Westbrook, Dirck, 60
Westchester, 92, 99, 126, 192
Westchester County, 74, 118, 129, 151, 168, 189
Westchester County volunteers, 125
Westchester court house, 193
Westchester Loyalists, 122
Westchester militia, 98
Westchester Refugees, 93
Wethersfield, 152
Whaleboat, 78, 102, 103, 133, 134, 135, 137, 138, 143, 146, 148, 149, 150, 151, 152, 153, 154, 156, 157, 158, 211, 213

Wheeler, Thomas, 11
Wicks, Ezekiel, 137
Whigs, 1
Whitcomb, Benjamin, 13
White, Captain, 125
White, Stanford, 161
White Plains, 82, 83, 85, 86, 87, 93, 99, 104, 108, 119, 121, 122, 123, 126, 127, 129, 184, 192, 197
White Plains National Battlefield Site, 82
White Plains Road, 96, 98
White, Henry, 86, 87, 93
Whitehall Battery, 175
Whitehall Dock, 175
Whitehall, New York, 12, 14, 24, 26
Whitehall Street, 174
Whitestone, 169, 171, 177
Whitestone Bay, 171
Whiting, John, 11
Wiccopee Pass, 79
Wild Cat, 138, 145
Wilkinson, Thomas, 78
Willett, Marinus, 24, 42, 51, 56, 57, 65, 67, 68, 71, 73, 101, 102, 208, 209
Willett's Pont, Long Island, 168
William Floyd Parkway, 140
William H. Morris's house, 192
William, Captain, 49, 189
Williams, Benjamin, 205
Williams, Daniel, 189
Williams, David, 52, 126
Williams, J., 124
Williams, Mr., 86
Williams, Samuel William, 124
Williams's Bridge, 98, 123, 125, 129, 183, 184, 186, 190, 191, 196,197
Williamsbridge Park, 183
Williamsburg Bridge, 175
Williamsburg, Virginia, 5
Williamson, Matthias, Sr., 201
Wills, Solomon, 163
Winant, Jacob, 212
Wind Mill Point, 17
Wirt, David, 37
Wolfe, James, 41
Wood Creek, 21, 24, 25
Wood Creek Landing, 21
Woodbridge Creek, 210
Woodbridge, Benjamin Ruggles, 43, 126
Woodbridge, New Jersey, 205, 206, 209, 210, 211, 212
Woodhull, Nathan, 135
Woodlawn Heights, 184, 189
Woodworth, Solomon, 50, 65
Woolsey, Melancthon Lloyd, 53
Wooster, David, 93, 98, 99, 131, 184
Worth Street, 175
Wright, Anthony, 210
Wright, Sergeant, 210
Wyandot Panther, 29
Wyoming, 57
Wyoming Valley, 57
Wyoming Valley, 60

Yaphank, 142
Yellow Hook, 211
Yonkers, 88, 98, 174, 190
York Island, 78, 84, 90, 171, 174, 175, 177, 182, 186 *see also* Manhattan Island
Yorktown Heights, 126
Yorktown Presbyterian Church, 126, 127

Yorktown, New York, 126
Yorktown, Virginia, 56, 91, 149, 151
Young *see also* Youngs
Young Cromwell, 156
Young, Captain, 149
Young's house, 86
Youngs, Jonas, 138
Youngs or Young, Joseph, 118, 119
Youngs, Samuel, 118
Youngs's House, 118, 119

Zenger, John Peter, 95
Zimmer, Jacob, Jr., 54
Zimmer, Peter, 54

www.ingramcontent.com/pod-product-compliance
Lightning Source LLC
Chambersburg PA
CBHW030309080526
44584CB00012B/497